THE MESSAGES AND PAPERS OF
JEFFERSON DAVIS
AND THE **CONFEDERACY**

CONFEDERATE CAPITOL AT MONTGOMERY.

THE MESSAGES AND PAPERS OF
JEFFERSON DAVIS
AND THE CONFEDERACY

Including Diplomatic Correspondence

1861–1865

A New Edition with a Comprehensive Introduction by
ALLAN NEVINS

Edited and Compiled by James D. Richardson

VOLUME

I

New York
Chelsea House–Robert Hector
Publishers
In Association With
R. R. Bowker
1966

Copyright © 1966
by Harold Steinberg and Robert Hector

Originally published by Resolution of Congress

Library of Congress Catalogue Card Number : 66–29296
Published by Chelsea House–Robert Hector Publishers
Printed in the United States of America
Chelsea House–Hector
485 Fifth Avenue
New York, N. Y. 10017

TO THE SOLDIERS ON BOTH SIDES WHO LAID DOWN
THEIR LIVES IN THE FOUR YEARS' WAR, 1861–1865,
EACH FIGHTING FOR WHAT HE THOUGHT WAS
RIGHT, AND ALSO TO THOSE WHO, AFTER HOSTILI-
TIES CEASED, GAVE THEIR BEST ENDEAVORS TO
PROMOTE PEACE AND HARMONY BETWEEN THE
SECTIONS LATELY IN ARMS, THIS WORK IS RE-
SPECTFULLY DEDICATED, NOT TO PERPETUATE THE
RECORD OF THE STRIFE, BUT IN TOKEN OF THOSE
BETTER FEELINGS WHICH HAVE SINCE REUNITED
THE PEOPLE OF ALL SECTIONS UNDER ONE FLAG,
WITH ONE HOPE AND ONE DESTINY, IN A UNION
OF STATES THAT IS INDISSOLUBLE.

Resolution Permitting the Compilation.

Be it enacted by the Senate and House of Representatives of the United States of America in Congress assembled,

. . . .

SEC. 5. That permission is hereby granted to James D. Richardson to compile, edit, and publish, without expense to the Government, the State papers and diplomatic correspondence of the late Confederate States, and access to said papers and correspondence shall be given him for that purpose by the heads of the Executive Departments having such papers in charge, under such regulations as may be respectively prescribed by them.

. . . .

Approved April 17, 1900.

Prefatory Note.

THE official papers of all the Presidents of the United States from Washington to McKinley were compiled by me a few years ago. That compilation is entitled "Messages and Papers of the Presidents," is in ten volumes, and was published by the authority of Congress. I have now, by permission of Congress, compiled and edited all the messages, proclamations, and inaugural addresses of Jefferson Davis, President of the Confederate States, together with the important and interesting diplomatic correspondence of the Confederacy. This compilation is a fitting companion piece to the former work. Biographical sketches of President Davis, Vice President Stephens, General Robert E. Lee, and the three Secretaries of State, Robert Toombs, Robert M. T. Hunter, and Judah P. Benjamin, have been prepared and are included. There will be two volumes of this work, the first containing the official papers of the President, the second comprising the diplomatic correspondence. The only omission of any message has been in the case where it contained simply a formal nomination without comment. Neither the State papers of Mr. Davis nor the diplomatic correspondence of the Confederacy have ever before been compiled.

The "Messages and Papers of the Presidents" contains their official papers without any political coloring by the editor and compiler, and so the papers herein published are given to the public entirely without any sectional or political bias. The object in view in making this publication is to place all the messages and papers of the Confederacy and the diplomatic correspondence before the public at large of all sections of our country in a convenient and enduring form. As stated, these are given without comment, and the reader is left to draw his own conclusions.

It will be conceded that no man more fully appreciated and understood the motives and principles which actuated the Southern States and their people in their conduct in withdrawing from the Union than the man they chose to be their President, and it

vii

is equally true that but few men ever lived in our land who were so happy in finding language to give adequate and forcible expression to these motives and principles.

These volumes contain the sentiments and opinions entertained by Mr. Davis as he gave utterance to them during that stormy and perilous period of war, and those who agreed and acted with him then, and who now think as he did, should find ample and complete satisfaction for themselves as they peruse the pages of this work; while those who did not then and who do not now so agree with him and his associates should not only be willing to have what he said in behalf of the Confederacy brought to light, but, on the other hand, should be desirous of having this done, so that from every standpoint publicity may be given to what they consider to have been his and their errors and mistakes.

There will be found in the Index of Volume I a number of encyclopedic articles which are intended to furnish the reader definitions of politico-historical words and phrases, some of which occur in the papers of the Chief Magistrate, or to develop more fully questions or subjects to which only indirect reference is made, or which are but briefly discussed by him. There will also be found brief accounts of more than a hundred battles in which the armies of the Confederate States were engaged. I have earnestly endeavored to make these articles historically correct, and to this end have carefully compared them with the best authorities. There has been no effort or inclination on my part to inject partisan or political opinions of any nature into these articles. On the other hand, I have sought only to furnish reliable historical data and well-authenticated definitions, and to avoid the expression of my own opinion.

The great wonder is that those who delight in hunting up and publishing interesting history, which was so thrilling when the events that made it were being enacted, have not heretofore dug up these papers from their hidden repositories in the archives of the Government at Washington, and given them to the public. This is true especially of the diplomatic correspondence. The addresses, messages, and proclamations of Mr. Davis were all read during the war with the keenest interest as they were published, although they have been buried out of sight since its close. They relate to the establishment of the provisional, and later to the permanent, Government of the Confederacy, its rise, progress, and fall, and contain a frequent statement of the fundamental grounds on which the rights of the Southern people to set up a Government for themselves rested, and tell vividly of the successes and defeats of the Confederate Army on many bloody fields. Much of the history and many events shown by them have been overlooked, or linger only in the minds of many persons in a half-forgotten way. But this is not true of the diplomatic correspondence, for it has never heretofore been published. It was all, or nearly all, profoundly secret and confidential at the time the communications were passed between the Confederate Commissioners and the State Department of the Confederacy. It will be remembered that the Commissioners to the leading nations of Europe were William L. Yancey, of Alabama, Pierre A. Rost, of Louisiana, and A. Dudley Mann, of Virginia. Later there were sent abroad James M. Mason, of Virginia, John Slidell, of Louisiana, and L. Q. C. Lamar, of Mississippi. Messrs. Yancey and Mason spent much of their time at the Court of St. James, Mr. Slidell, at Paris, Mr. Rost, at Madrid, Mr. Lamar, at St. Petersburg, and Mr. Mann, at Brussels, although each made visits to other capitals. John T. Pickett was the Commissioner to Mexico. The foreign correspondence, therefore, was written and signed in the most part by these gentlemen, or some one of them. The letters to them emanated from the State Department, and were signed by the Secretary for the time being. The Secretaries of State were Robert Toombs, of Georgia, Robert M. T. Hunter, of Virginia, and Judah P. Benjamin, of Louisiana, in the order named, all scholarly men of the highest culture, and all of them prior to the war had been members of the United States Senate. Mr. Mason and Mr. Slidell had also been members of that body, and Mr. Yancey had been a member of the House of Representatives. All of them had also held other high positions in their respective States. Some of the papers are signed by William M. Browne, of Mississippi, who occasionally acted as Secretary of State.

When the war closed, the soldiers of both sides of the four years' desperate conflict returned to their peaceful pursuits, and were soon busy in their efforts to recover lost fortunes and to gain the mastery over new and complicated questions arising out of changed conditions. For these and other reasons, they did not bestow attention upon this correspondence, and it has never been unearthed and given to the public in either the Southern or Northern States. It will, therefore, be new in both sections, and the people of each must alike find enjoyment and pleasure in reading it. Interest in it will begin with the first notes given the Commissioners by the Government, and their departure for Europe. The story of their efforts to evade the blockade of the Southern ports, the successful passage of Mason and Slidell from their own shores to Cuba, and their embarkment for Europe on an English vessel, from which they were captured on the high seas, and brought to the United States as prisoners, the peremptory demand by Great Britain upon the United States for their restoration to her ships, the compliance with this demand, and their safe arrival and reception in Europe are all of thrilling interest, even at this remote day.

If the United States Government had persisted in holding these gentlemen, it would in all probability have become embroiled in war with Great Britain, the results of which no one could have foretold; nor is it possible to conceive what might have been the effect of such a war upon the fate and fortunes of the Confederacy.

When divested of the sad memories of that dark and gloomy period, this correspondence reads almost like romance.

From Mexico there will be found valuable and important correspondence. These communications are mainly to and from Mr. Pickett, and in them, among other things of interest, will be found something of the story of the installation by France of Maximilian, the unfortunate young Austrian archduke, upon the throne as Emperor of Mexico, which he subsequently lost, and which cost him his life.

The reader will find a carefully prepared Index in each volume, which will materially assist in the investigation of the subjects therein discussed. These Indices are largely the labor of my son, James D. Richardson, Jr., who has also aided me in the entire work.   JAMES D. RICHARDSON.

January 1, 1905.

Contents of Volume I.

Illustrations.

The Embattled Confederacy:
Its Tasks and Its Leadership

by Allan Nevins

Professor Emeritus of American History
Columbia University

The most remarkable fact about the Civil War is not that it ended as it did, but that it lasted so long before the end came. That statement partially sums up both the poignant tragedy and the unforgettable heroism of the conflict. For the hard-beset Southern people the exertions, the losses, and the anguish were incalculable; their struggle presented the first spectacle in modern history of a *levée en masse,* the mobilization of an entire nation. To the imaginative eye the official papers of their civil helmsmen evoke a picture of a battered ship staggering through murk and storm, lurid lightning and crashing wave, to a dim and unattainable goal.*

The South, in fighting its war to Appomattox, was in most respects dismally unmatched with the North. The weight of population, with about nineteen million white people in the freesoil States

---

* When James D. Richardson published his *Compilation of the Messages and Papers of the Confederacy, Including the Diplomatic Correspondence, 1861–1865,* in Nashvile in 1905, he performed a valuable public service. Both volumes were at once used by all students of the war; both are still constantly employed and footnoted by scholars; and the more than 700 pages of diplomatic reports and correspondence especially contain many documents not conveniently and accurately accessible elsewhere. *The Official Records of the Union and Confederate Armies* had been completed in 128 volumes (1880–1901), but the *Official Records* for the two navies were just well under way, and their 30 volumes would not be finished until 1927. The *Journal of the Congress of the Confederate States,* in 7 volumes, was issued in Washington in 1904–05. The invaluable *Calendar of Confederate Papers,* edited by Douglas S. Freeman, would be published by the Confederate Museum in 1908, and Dunbar Rowland's ten-volume edition of the *Letters, Papers, and Speeches of Jefferson Davis* would appear in Jackson, Miss., in 1923. But the compilation by Richardson still holds its valuable place.

and eight millions in the slave States, overwhelmingly favored the Union. As the people of the border slave States, Missouri, Kentucky, and Maryland, divided themselves between the two causes, the disparity became even greater. To be sure, the Confederacy could use its three and a half million slaves to grow food, perform hard work on roads, railways, and bridges, and serve as army laborers, but this did little to redress the balance. In its factories, railroads, canals, and shipping the North held a superiority not only immense but growing. While the blockaded South was more and more completely cut off from the outer world, Northern ports remained open to European markets, and a stream of immigration flowed in to swell the labor force and augment the armies.

Financial strength, a swelling population, large and efficient transport facilities, open ports, and a supply of European manpower, enabled the North to face the Confederacy with confidence. The South fought from interior lines, an apparent advantage—and one often real. But the extensive and flexible supply system of the Union enabled it, using ocean, rails, and rivers, to shift bases and field depots in such a way that it had a choice of lines of movement. For example, Stonewall Jackson could outflank Pope in 1862, but could not prevent him from taking refuge in Alexandria; Grant could swiftly change his thrust in 1863 from Cold Harbor to the James and Petersburg. The Federal Quartermaster Department had the use of hundreds of ocean and lake vessels in the East, and owned more than 200 others, while it counted its steamers, barges, and coal boats on the Mississippi at above 500.

A fundamental difference in strategic aims existed, however, and here the South held a distinct advantage. The North had to fight for a decisive victory in the field; for a knockout blow in the destruction or hopeless crippling of the main Confederate armies. The South could pursue a less difficult objective. If it fought the war to a seemingly hopeless deadlock, that would suffice. European Powers, suffering harsh economic losses and sickened by the slaughter, might intervene; or Northern war weariness and Copperhead sedition might compel Washington to acquiesce in Confederate independence. While plenty of Yankees were as determined as Lincoln to crush the rebellion, plenty were also willing to let the erring sisters go in peace; by 1864 not only the Peace Democrats but Greeley talked of negotiation. With the North requiring total armed victory, and the South merely a paralysis of the will to fight, the odds did not seem so uneven.

The Confederacy plunged into the war with high hope that it could use its martial skill, its ardor for freedom, and its command of King Cotton to bring Britain and France to its side. Or, fighting on the defensive, it could hold back the Union onslaught until its Northern sympathizers, led by men like Senator Jesse D. Bright of Indiana, Clement L. Vallandigham of Indiana, Senator James A. Bayard of Delaware, and Fernando Wood of New York, joined hands with pacifists in demanding peace by conciliation. It could appeal to propertied Yankees anxious about their moneybags, conservatives afraid that Lincoln would convert a government of limited powers into a centralized despotism, and grumblers about civil rights. Many Southerners realized that in defending the expansion of slavery their moral position before the world was bad. They believed, however, that as champions of self-determination they held impregnable ground. As Jefferson Davis put it, the South stood for the same rights as those for which American patriots had fought in 1776.

The government, delegated from six cotton States created in Montgomery, Alabama, early in 1861, under a Constitution copied in the main from that of the United States, was destined to remain a crisis government until its extinguishment by the surrender of Lee in April, 1865. The copying was deliberate. Southerners wished to emphasize their contention that they were not seceding from the old Constitution, which they had helped frame, but from the abuses of that instrument. Their government was still being organized when the first shell burst over Sumter on April 14, 1861, and Lincoln next day called for 75,000 men to overthrow it. Month by month the crisis deepened and the pressures upon the Confederacy grew fiercer. Not a week, not a day of serenity did President Davis, his Cabinet, and Congress have to make normal use of their powers. The abnormalities and the resulting improvisation increased.

"The new government sprang forth as if by magic," later wrote an Alabamian, J. L. M. Curry. Some of the best minds of the Lower South contributed both to the Provisional Constitution written in February, 1861, and the Permanent Constitution which almost immediately (March 11) followed it. The text of the latter document was singularly interesting and is worth study for its divergences from and additions to the Federal instrument. State Rights principles underlaid most of the changes. In these tenets alone it clung to the old Jeffersonian doctrines, discarding nearly everything else, in spirit if not in letter, that reminded men of Jeffersonian democracy. The ideal, asserted a Richmond editor, was a system of government "encouraging the virtues which make the gentleman," and discouraging rough plebeian traits. Had the Confederacy been allowed time and ease, it would have moved toward an aristocratic conservatism strange in the modern world; but it had neither.

Nor did it have an opportunity to test some governmental innovations that might have repaid trial. Nobody liked the old Federal method of choosing a President, but nobody had time to think of a better, so the electoral college was kept. A single six-year term, however, was prescribed. The President was charged with the presentation of an executive budget, and any appropriation made outside it, with few exceptions, required a two-thirds vote of Congress. In the final budget the President might veto particular items. He was given full powers of removal only with respect to Cabinet members and diplomatic officials, all other removals requiring justification to the Senate. One important new feature embodied an effort to use supposed advantages of the British ministerial system. The head of each executive department was given seats on the floor of the two houses, with the privilege of discussing any matter pertaining to his department. Though legislation to lend full effect to this privilege was never passed, Cabinet members did make occasional appearances in Congress with happy effect. The smelly Congressional pork barrel in Washington having attracted Southern condemnation, the new Constitution forbade any internal improvements except a few elementary aids to navigation. Duties were restricted to the raising of revenue, protective tariffs being sternly forbidden. Bounties were interdicted, and the post office was required after a brief interval to pay its way from its own revenues.

"In short," as J. L. M. Curry writes, "stubborn and corrupting controversies about tariffs, post offices, improvements of rivers and harbors, subsidies, and extra pay were avoided. . . . Money in the treasury was protected against purchasable majorities and wicked combinations." In the North, these evils were to grow more and more pernicious.

The Presidential leadership of the Confederacy, the toils of a half-dozen really able and devoted departmental chieftains, the counsel of the finer spirits in a generally mediocre Congress, the efforts of a full score of bureau managers who varied from the competent to the brilliant, and the attempt of several diplomats to conquer unconquerable obstacles, must all be judged in the light of the fact that they served a crisis government. They rose from one desperate emergency only to meet another more exigent. This government, despite some remarkable exhibitions of courage and resourcefulness in civil affairs, grew inexorably weaker. It was never able to think of long-range plans because short-range necessities hammered at the door. All wartime governments can of course be called crisis governments. A vast difference nevertheless exists between one that is newly formed, freshly manned, and thrown upon angry problems with little machinery and no precedents to help it, and a government like that in Washington, panoplied with old customs, outlooks, and personnel. The North could go on with a thousand tasks in building the nation—planning a Pacific railroad, looking after freedmen, passing homestead legislation, encouraging immigration—while it fought the war; the South had to concentrate upon battle, devastation, and growing debility, never letting them daunt it.

"While we weep with the friends of our gallant dead," wrote General James Longstreet, "we must confess that a soldier's grave, is so holy and just a cause, is the highest honor that a man can attain." This was the spirit that nerved the South throughout the struggle. Every true Confederate occupying a civil post felt that *he* was a soldier too, and tried to share Jefferson Davis's confidence even in November, 1864, in an "assured result."

The head of the Confederate Bureau of War, Robert G. H. Kean, gave in his wartime diary seven reasons for the failure of the Confederacy. Some, inherent in the situation, were traceable to no fault of government. When Kean mentioned the want of men as one reason he meant primarily the lack of a proper reservoir of manpower, although desertions attributable to insufficient supplies were a contributory factor. When he listed the incompetence of military leaders as a cause, he pointed to a defect hardly remediable on either Northern or Southern side; officers like Lee and Jackson, Grant and Sherman, are rare in all wars. A better system of promotion fixed by law might have helped the Confederacy, but this is not certain. When Kean spoke of slavery as a cause of failure in that countless Negroes joined the Northern armies as laborers or recruits, he touched upon a flaw built into the fabric of Southern society, beyond the reach of government.

But Kean did identify certain weaknesses that he thought a wiser, more farsighted administration could have prevented or remedied. One was the bankruptcy of the Treasury, a prolific source of breakdown along all lines. One was the failure to get and keep sufficient horses for transport and artillery. Another was the difficulty of recruiting under the conscription laws, and of getting supplies under the impressment acts, when jealous and selfish State leaders created discontent and interposed obstacles. Again and again Kean pointed also to the failures arising from the bad military organization of the Confederacy. Each Department was too nearly autonomous; Richmond refused to compel any cooperation or coordination of forces; no general achieved the comprehensive authority given to Grant early in 1864. Lee might have gone to the assistance of the hardpressed West in the summer of 1864, instead of invading Pennsylvania; the trans-Mississippi armies might have sent help to Vicksburg instead of sitting inert—so Kean thought, and so have others.

Above all, Kean gave emphasis to a cardinal Southern failure: "the absence of a Representative Man, a leader in the council as well as in the field, who should comprehend and express the movement." It is assuredly true that while much can be said in praise of Lee and Jefferson Davis, the South in this life-and-death crisis failed to produce a Pericles or Winston Churchill—not to mention another name that springs to every mind. But to ask for this, as human history goes, is to ask for a great deal.

I

The chosen leader of the Confederacy, Jefferson Davis, to whom the entire first volume in this collection is devoted, was unquestionably the best leader available for the Presidency, a man whose resolution, industry, and gentlemanly dignity never wavered. Abandoning a military career early in life for study and politics, he had made a brilliant success as State Rights leader and Senator. In 1850 he had dreamed of a new slaveholding republic that should expand into Mexico, Yucatán, and Cuba, but the Compromise of that year had thrown his energies back into national channels. When Calhoun died, Davis had swiftly taken his place as the strongest champion of the South. Under Pierce he had been an able and very pro-Southern Secretary of War, still supporting Cuban annexation, helping engineer the Gadsden Purchase to protect a Southern railroad to the Pacific, and casting covetous eyes toward Kansas. He was elected President over the popular Howell Cobb, the ambitious William L. Yancey, and the impetuous elbow-bending Robert Toombs by as close an approach to general acclamation as was possible. As he was ushered into office, Toombs proclaimed: "The hour and the man have met!"

For a time he seemed likely to be a great President—but not for long. His principal deficiencies were not of intellectual power, character, or will, but of temper and vision. He lacked the fire and eloquence, the elevation and magnanimity, the spiritual depth, that the finest national leader must possess. Proud as John Adams and unbendable as Andrew Johnson, he could not adjust himself to the swift changes of the time. He chose an acceptable Cabinet, but failed to treat members tactfully, to give it coherence, and to defend it against waspish newspapers and Congressmen. The result was instability; in four tempestuous years fourteen men occupied the six offices. Secretary of War Seddon's remark that Davis was the most difficult man he had ever known to get along with offers much of the explanation. Moreover, he lacked the sense of proportion a statesman ought to have. Highly sensitive to criticism, he gave way to fits of temperament. "Oh for a . . . William of Orange, a man of calm steadfast temper," wrote Kean in 1863. When not a moment of time or ounce of strength could well be spared, Davis would halt his work and the machinery of government to write a quarrelsome letter or deliver an impatient speech.

As the war dragged on, internal dissension increased. "Davis is inveterately obstinate," wrote one friendly observer: "between neuralgia and dyspepsia his health is so bad that only patriotism and obstinacy combined could keep him at his desk; but his death would be one of the direst of Southern misfortunes." It was not mere obstinacy, however, that lamed Davis as a statesman. It was obstinacy in clinging to fixed ideas and prejudices that were quite erroneous. He had an intense dislike of P. G. T. Beauregard and Joseph E. Johnston that did these generals wrong; he indulged a predilection for Braxton Bragg and John C. Pemberton that sound observers could not comprehend. He believed that the Negro was helpless without white guidance, and so made inadequate use of his services; he thought that Northerners were mainly mean-spirited money-grubbers, and so underrated their patriotic constancy. "A great general is so rare that their names mark the eras of history," Davis wrote in 1862, never dreaming that his era would get its name from a civilian railsplitter of Illinois.

A thickening cloud of Southern opponents accused Davis of tyrannous acts, and of becoming more and more dictatorial. Seeing that a great war cannot be waged without some use of arbitrary authority, Davis was rightly no more afraid than Lincoln of being termed a despot. Vice-President Alexander H. Stephens applied that name to him just as Ben Wade applied it to the occupant of the White House. "His whole policy on the discipline and organization of the Army is perfectly consistent with the hypothesis that he is aiming at absolute power," wrote Stephens in the spring of 1864. Sheer wartime necessities did impel Davis to take rigorous measures, and to pardon the issuance of orders by Earl Van Dorn, Bragg, and other commanders for the application of martial law to wide districts.

The historical fact, however, is that the Confederacy would have profited from a greater centralization of authority and from more drastic measures than Davis found feasible. If the Richmond government could have taken over all the Southern railroads in 1862, placing under one head all the locomotives, cars, shops, rails, ties, and miscellaneous ironware of the section, the South would have fought much more efficiently in 1863 and 1864. To most of the many railroad companies the director of railroad transportation seemed at times a very czar, but actually successive holders of that office were too feeble for the vast emergency. Again, conscription seemed to many Southerners a ruthless exercise of despotism. Applied in three laws, one in the spring of 1862, one (the most important) that autumn, and a third at the beginning of 1864, it began by laying hands on all white males of 18 to 35, and ended by grasping all of them between 17 and 50. From the cradle to the grave, wrote General Grant! But the Bureau of Conscription should really have been more powerful. Theoretically, its authority was broad enough, in enrolling and assigning men, to enable it to act as a priorities board, sending skilled mechanics to factories, engineers to railroads, and experienced clerks to government departments as well as fighters to regiments.

Actually, however, the Bureau never assumed such wide authority. Interpreting its powers narrowly, it starved vital services of the experts they needed simply to add more privates to the army rolls. Altogether, Davis cannot justly be reproached for dictatorial tendencies. A bit more of dictatorship, had it been possible, would have helped the South.

As President, Davis did not lack foresight. He saw at the outset that peaceful secession was almost impossible, and predicted a sanguinary combat. The long duration of the war did no more astonish him than it astonished Lincoln and nearly everybody else. He saw far more clearly than most prominent Confederates that if the South won it would have to be as a unitary nation, not a loose bundle of States. Lee's loyalty was primarily to Virginia, and Joseph E. Brown's was primarily to Georgia, but Davis's was to the South as a whole. His message to Congress in 1864 urging that the government buy 40,000 slaves for war service, and free them at the end, was as farsighted a step as public sentiment would tolerate. Moreover, it was meant to explore public opinion upon the arming of slaves.

Like nearly everybody else, he failed to realize in time that the war would be as much an economic struggle as a military contest. He ignored the fact, plain as the Census of 1860 could make it, that the free North and Northwest was a far richer agricultural domain than the slaveholding South. Its wheat, hay, oats, corn, rye, potatoes, and livestock had much greater value than the cotton, tobacco, and rice of the Confederacy. Like a host of other Southerners, he placed a faith in King Cotton, never bluntly stated but quite clearly felt, that events failed to justify. He was abused by his critics for not doing more with cotton to support the credit of the Confederacy as it issued floods of paper money, and for not using it to induce Britain and France to break the blockade. These attacks, however, were unfounded. He mistakenly thought that King Cotton would be a potent ally, but found that the two vital problems, collection of the staple and its immediate transportation overseas, were practically insoluble.

Just why did cotton not prove the all-conquering potentate that many Southerners fancied it? Why did the South not obtain a great fleet of merchantmen early in 1861, load them with the fleecy bales, and hurry the cotton abroad? Critics said later that four million bales could have been warehoused in Britain, France, and Belgium to pay for arms and shells. Only if four thousand ships had been at hand! A succinct statement of the reasons for the weakness of King

Cotton was made after the war by the last Confederate Secretary of the Treasury, G. A. Trenholm. The Confederate Government was born in February, 1861. Up to the end of that month about three million bales of the large 1860–61 crop had been received at Southern ports and shipped to New England, Britain, and the Continent. By the end of May nearly six hundred thousand additional bales had been shipped. Thus, before the new government was fully organized, nearly the whole crop was beyond its reach. When the ensuing crop was ready, the exportation of any considerable part of it was forbidden by the blockade. Normal commerce was at a standstill. The blockade runners that crept hesitantly and singly into Wilmington, Charleston, and Mobile, laden with costly munitions and luxuries, could carry but small amounts of cotton overseas.

Mrs. Davis tells us in her *Memoirs* that the President and his advisers thought cotton so irresistible that they anticipated Anglo-French recognition as "almost an assumed fact." One adviser thought it certain that King Cotton would "command the guns of European fleets." That Davis was deeply grieved by the refusal of the British Government to break the blockade is certain, but he was helpless.

An equal error on the part of Davis and his helpers lay in their underestimation of the force of European, and especially British, antipathy to slavery. No evidence of a desire to placate the British sensitivity on the subject appears in Davis's state papers. How could he express such a feeling when he and his brother Joseph had ranked among the large slaveowners of Mississippi, and he had long advocated a separate slaveholding republic extending its dominion to wide lands bordering the Caribbean? But when his envoys Yancey, P. A. Rost, and A. D. Mann addressed Lord Russell in 1861, they had to acknowledge that "the antislavery sentiment so universally prevalent in England had shrunk from the idea of forming friendly public relations with a Government recognizing the slavery of a part of the human race." And at a critical moment later Lord John Russell asserted that "in my opinion the men of England would have been forever infamous if, for the sake of their own interest, they had violated the law of nations, and made war, *in conjunction with these slaveholding States of America,* against the Federal States." To say that Lancashire stood firmly with the

North because it had read *Uncle Tom's Cabin* is an oversimplification, but the statement has some truth.

Davis strove hard to meet the demands of his people. In every year of his Presidency, despite harassing duties, frail health, and nervous tension, he made a tour of some kind into the interior of the Confederacy. The most important was the long trip beginning in December, 1862, which carried him at a critical moment as far as Jackson and Vicksburg. He delivered speeches, wrote public letters, and made assiduous use of other instruments of publicity. His proclamations of days of prayer impressed a highly religious folk. Now and then his addresses had a touch of the defiant eloquence that had stamped his speeches in the United States Senate. In Augusta, during a tour in October, 1864, he called upon the Southern States to trust each other for support, for they were "distinct as the billows, yet one as the sea." In communicating with the governors he made frequent use of circular letters, trying to be reasonable and cordial. To loyal friends like Pettus of Alabama and T. O. Moore of Louisiana, he was kindly and grateful; to gadflies like Zebulon M. Vance of North Carolina he sometimes showed more courtesy than they had earned.

He wrote a telling letter of condolence to Mrs. Mary Wilkinson of Vicksburg in 1862 after the death of her husband in battle; he frowned upon the enlistment of volunteers of sixteen or seventeen; and he did as much to look after the welfare of soldiers in the field as circumstances permitted. In the last year of the war he made an effort to examine the cases of all the men sentenced to death in Lee's army. Nearly all his public papers expressed confidence and hope. Complaints that the struggle had class aspects and was "a rich man's war but a poor man's fight" aroused him deeply. Never, he asserted, would a law bearing unfairly upon the poor, even to a feather's weight, receive his signature. "The poor have fought our battles," asserted, "and so have the rich." The fact that owners of twenty slaves could claim exemption from military service to oversee the labor force did seem to many a discrimination in favor of the wealthy. The novelist Augusta J. Evans wrote that, when overseers and masters escaped service, the resultant ill-feeling was alarming. It means "the creation of an antislavery element among our soldiers who openly complain that others are torn from their homes, and their families, consigned to starvation, solely in order that they may protect the property of slaveholders . . . in luxuriant ease." But again Davis was helpless in the grip of circumstance.

One unhappy aspect of Davis's war years was the increasing intemperance and abusiveness of his references to the North. He asserted that the issue before Southerners was whether they should be free, or be slaves of "the most depraved and intolerant and tyrannical and hated people upon earth." In a reply to a serenade in Richmond early in 1863 he declared : "Our foes come as savages to murder, rob, and desecrate, and we must treat them as such." In a message to Congress at the end of that year he said that the malignant rage of the Yankees "aims at nothing less than the extermination of yourselves, your wives, and children. They seek to destroy what they cannot plunder. . . . They design to excite servile insurrection and light the fires of incendiarism wherever they can reach your homes, and they debauch the inferior race, hitherto docile and contented, by promising indulgence of the vilest passions as the price of treachery." Other outbusts of the same sort could be quoted.

The provocation was unquestionably great. Thaddeus Stevens did speak late in the war of "extermination" as a necessity with stubborn Southern rebels. That egregious blunderer, John Pope, just before he met his well-merited defeat at Second Manassas, had issued orders which stained the Northern war effort and unfortunately exercised a wide influence. One of them, directing the Army of the Potomac to subsist on the country so far as possible, inspired a taste for looting that officers found hard to check. Another decreed that any person detected in firing on Federal troops from a house should be shot without trial. A third and still harsher order required officers to arrest all disloyal Virginians within reach, to give them a choice between taking the oath of allegiance and accepting deportation to the South, and to put to death those who returned or who violated their oaths. General W. T. Sherman countenanced a wanton destruction of property in Mississippi, Alabama, Georgia, and the Carolinas, and ordered excessively harsh reprisals on civilians for guerrilla attacks. Sheridan reported to Grant in the autumn of 1864 that in moving down the Shenandoah Valley he had burned more than two thousand barns filled with wheat, hay, and farming implements, and more than seventy mills filled with flour.

It was Sheridan who used the phrase about leaving Southerners only their eyes to weep with, a phrase long afterward quoted by

Germans with unction. In the papers of Governor John A. Andrew of Massachusetts is a letter from C. C. Coffin, correspondent of the Boston *Journal,* dated Hilton Head, S. C., February 17, 1863, and marked "private and confidential." "I am sorry to say," wrote Coffin "that the Mass. 24th has been acting outrageously here, robbing, burning houses, killing cattle, etc.—ravishing negro women— beating their husbands who attempted protection." All war is savagery. Tennessee and Missouri guerrillas under the Confederate flag were especially vicious, their crimes chilling the blood. Recognizing that war is essentially loathsome, and that outrages took place on both sides (though Lee's army showed exemplary discipline), President Davis should have curbed his tongue. Some of his angry words did not befit the chief of a proud nation, and they stand in sorry contrast with Lincoln's abstention from reproach or anger, and general magnanimity of tone.

Still, after all deductions are made, the volume on Davis in this collection is creditable to a leader of eminent if not transcendent virtues and talents. He, more than anybody else, including Lee, thought of the South as a separate and unified entity, with the potentialities of a grand future. He did his best to awaken in the hearts of eight million people a strong sentiment of patriotism. We may agree with William E. Gladstone's indiscreet remark—an indiscretion because it violated official neutrality—that by Antietam and Fredericksburg he and like-minded men had created a nation.

II

As it was admitted even by patriotic Southerners that the Confederate Congress was a weak and inadequate body, Richardson would have felt no regret that he was unable to collect papers reflecting its activities. That large and complex task had to wait long for even a scrappy and unsatisfactory fulfillment.

In a crisis government the executive is everything. The debates of the Richmond Congress lacked the weight, vigor, and elevation that had often marked the Washington debates in the spacious days when Calhoun, Clay, Benton, and Webster had dominated the Senate, and John Quincy Adams, David Wilmot, and Howell Cobb had enlivened the House. The rebel Congress had difficulty in maintaining a decent attendance. It displayed a peevish, fault-finding temper, wrangled incessantly, and wasted time interminably over

petty questions. It was too timid to touch pocket nerves by levying
proper taxes, and to write courageously fair laws upon the conscription of men and impressment of supplies. It continually failed
to look ahead. Kean in the War Bureau bewailed its "smallness,"
and generals in the field, including Lee, thought it weak. Some able
men strove hard to keep out of it, and when Robert B. Rhett, who
had been ignored in Cabinet making, sought election to the House
to "invigorate" it, he was defeated.

The reasons for the low estate of Congress were numerous.
Southerners had always regarded military service as more dignified
than any but the highest political service, and when the cannon
boomed ambitious men felt an imperative call to the field. Davis's
wartime powers as commander-in-chief made him and his principal
Secretaries overshadow the best figures in the two houses; they
and the generals held the imagination of the country. Men who
should have set an example, Alexander H. Stephens and Howell
Cobb among them, refused to play a part in Congress even when
duty called most plainly.

As 1863 closed Herschel V. Johnson of Georgia reproached the
Vice-President bitterly for not occupying his seat as presiding
officer of the Senate. "I sincerely believe there has never been a
time during this revolution when the opportunity for usefulness was
as great as it is now," he wrote from his Senate desk. "The currency question is engaging all minds and hearts. I assure you all is
confusion. Nobody has a definite plan of relief. . . . Your views
would be received with great respect." But Stephens sat inert on his
Georgia plantation, nursing his enmity for Davis, trying to clog
conscription, and acrid in denunciation of half the other legislation
passed.

Another reason for the want of energy and nerve in Congress
was indicated by Senator Johnson's comment that "nobody has a
definite plan." By the end of 1863, after Vicksburg and Gettysburg, many problems of the Confederacy—problems of finance, of
recruiting, of supply, of foreign relations—were plainly becoming
insoluble. They daunted men who would have given the debates
strength if they had known anything useful to say. Meanwhile, the
everlasting quarrel between supporters of Davis and his determined
opponents, far outrunning the quarrel in Washington between supporters and enemies of Lincoln, paralyzed parliamentary discussion
or tempted men to talk for the acrimonious newspapers. Congress

ultimately became a noisy bear pit. Too many members felt like C. C. Clay, Jr., an Alabama Senator of ability. He wrote in the late summer of 1863 that he did not wish to serve any longer. "I am sick of the selfishness, corruption, demagogism, and bigotry which characterize so large a portion of those in office," he wrote his friend Louis T. Wigfall. When he saw how many skulked from army duty, how many cheated their way to riches in commissary and quartermaster offices, and how many abused high trusts for personal applause or special favors, he added, he felt that private life was his only refuge.

The internal problems of the South which Congress neglected or treated inadequately, leaving them in large part to the executive, the governors, or private effort, constantly thickened. One problem was posed by the vast displacements of population. As the Union armies advanced, and State after State became a battleground, refugees fled to the interior. Some went to escape hateful Northern controls, some to get their slaves into temporary security, and some to save cherished personal possessions. Country folk fled to the towns; Richmond, Mobile, Atlanta, Columbia, and Charleston filled up with strangers who were first welcomed with compassion, then coldly tolerated, and finally frowned upon as an intolerable burden. A quarter of the South seemed in time to be on the run or in refugee centers. The plight of tens of thousands, the old people exhausted, the children without education, was pitiable.

John W. Burgess, later one of the makers of Columbia University, tells us that his Tennessee parents had their fortunes wrecked beyond recovery. He was stationed as a Union soldier in Nashville, his office overlooking the railway station. Often he saw wives and daughters of once wealthy planters clamber out of boxcars, clad in tatters, carrying a few blankets, and looking about vacantly for food and shelter. "Some of them were already stricken with famine and disease, and would sink down exhausted in the streets and alleyways, often to die." For multitudes the dread moment came when, as Union garrisons appeared, rations were offered to hungry families with an oath of allegiance attached, and they had to yield or die. Yet local and regional charity was seldom stinted.

Another insoluble problem was the growing insubordination of the slaves. Romantic Southern images of slave devotion to masters and mistresses had some truth, but more falsity. That a great majority of the slaves desired liberation, and that large numbers resented their maltreatment in bondage, is unquestionable. "The negroes are worse than free," Mrs. C. C. Clay, Sr., wrote her son from Huntsville, Alabama, in the summer of 1863. "They say they *are* free. We cannot exert any authority. I beg ours to do what little is to be done. . . . I have to work harder than I ever did, but am patient, silent, and prayerful. . . . The negroes are so bold that Alfred told me this morning that if your father . . . lets the overseer punish him for disobedience, then someone would kill the overseer." Insoluble, too, was the problem of inflation, a natural result of the slender financial resources of the Confederacy, the failure of the government to impose stern taxation, and the torrents of paper currency flooding the land. When Augusta J. Evans denounced "the shameless tribe of speculators and extortioners who swarm in every nook and cranny of the Confederacy," she pointed to one clear result of inflation—and little could be done about it.

Class feeling, and resentment against unscrupulous moneymakers, was aroused by every discussion of revenue measures. They were mainly futile discussions. Herschel V. Johnson, demanding taxes to raise a hundred million dollars, wished them laid almost entirely on gross income, not property. This was an agrarian voice. Yet when the House Finance Committee proposed a tax in kind of one tenth in agricultural production, he supported it as the only feasible means of furnishing supplies to the armies, and enabling penniless soldiers to meet the government levies. The $13 a month that the privates received, equaling in 1863 perhaps a dollar in gold, was desperately needed by their families. The Confederate Treasury ran a steadily losing race with bankruptcy. It was so hard pressed that even the puny receipts from the Erlanger loan floated in Paris and London by the envoy John Slidell, amounting in the end to only about $2,500,000 in gold, were most welcome. To the very close of the war Confederate leadership could be criticized for neglect of taxation. The sacrifices of the Southern people far exceeded the sacrifices of American patriots in the Revolution, for multitudes lost all they had, but governmental measures were weak. Truth supported the caustic comment: "The Confederacy was more prodigal of its blood than of its money."

Among the Cabinet officers of the Confederacy, places of special distinction may be assigned to Judah P. Benjamin of the State Department, the man most valued by Jefferson Davis; to James A. Seddon, the tireless Secretary of War during the most grueling years; to Stephen R. Mallory, the resourceful head of the Navy Department; and to the rough-hewn John A. Reagan, who for four years kept an apparently hopeless postal system operating. They were all interesting men, as indeed was Memminger at the Treasury, struggling with the impossible. Jefferson Davis was properly deferential to his department heads. Not one of them complained that the Cabinet councils lacked efficiency and system, and that important members were ignored, as Salmon P. Chase complained of Lincoln's conduct. The Confederate President discussed policies with the Cabinet, sometimes took its advice, and let Reagan in particular disagree with him sharply. He tended to be his own Secretary of State, as most American Presidents have been, but he allowed Judah P. Benjamin to give him constant advice. A believer in his own military talent, he tended also to be his own Secretary of War, so that Seddon was far more deferential to him than Stanton was to Lincoln. However, he recognized Seddon's genius for detail and administrative capacity.

With the backing of Davis, Secretary Seddon did give hard battle to the Southern governors who disputed the essential measures of conscription and impressment. He made the Confederacy shake in his contests with Joseph E. Brown of Georgia, a tough plebeian like Andrew Johnson with a sharp poor-white intelligence, a fanatic upon State rights; and with Zebulon B. Vance of North Carolina, a much abler man, who could be called the most eloquent Southerner of his day. The Southern diarist, J. B. Jones, has often been quoted on the stricken appearance of Seddon, gaunt, emaciated, his hair half gray and half black, his face lined with neuralgia. "He looks like a dead man galvanized into muscular animation. His eyes are shrunken and his features have the hue of a man who has been in his grave a full month." But he stuck valiantly to his post until early in 1865, when Virginia members of Congress demanded a reorganization of the government to face the last fatal crisis. He never ceased to favor the offensive; he had urged Johnston to attack the Union lines before Vicksburg, and thought when that city was lost that Richard Taylor ought to have crossed the Mississippi in an attempt to relieve it. He applauded Lee's decision to invade Pennsylvania in 1863, and agreed to the removal of Johnston at Atlanta in the hope that Hood would give successful battle to Sherman. This seeming Lazarus lived into 1880.

Of Mallory, who like Benjamin was born in the West Indies, we see little in these volumes. They treat of other subjects than the navy. For his correspondence we have to go to the *Official Records of the Union and Confederate Navies.* The Confederacy had no warships, no yards, few sailors, and still fewer naval officers, Franklin Buchanan and Raphael Semmes offering the best talent at hand. Mallory failed to build ironclads. He succeeded, however, in making some Southern rivers impregnable, in fortifying Charleston, and in one still greater aim. He could not break the blockade, but he could send out cruisers like the *Alabama* and *Florida,* both obtained in Britain, to destroy Northern commerce. Bringing James D. Bulloch to Montgomery at the beginning of the war, he appointed this Georgian navy agent to purchase or build warships in Europe. The harm the cruisers did to the Northern merchant marine was less important than their diversion of naval effort from maintenance of the blockade. Meanwhile, the ingenious Mallory played a notable part in the development of torpedoes and submarines by the Confederates.

The Confederate Government had to create a bureaucracy, and although it was built with haste and economy, some parts of it possessed merit. The Commissary Department, supplying the soldiers with food, had one staff of officers; the Quartermaster Department, furnishing them with clothing, shoes, blankets, tents and hospital requirements (except medicines) had quite another. Both, but especially the second, did reasonably good work against appalling difficulties. Inevitably, both became highly unpopular, for they had to take from the civil population goods and provisions spared with hardship, and they used more and more compulsion in taking them. The officer charged with commissary work, however, Lucius B. Northrop, a West Pointer from South Carolina, plumbed depths of general opprobrium that the heads of the quartermaster service, Abraham C. Myers and Alexander R. Lawton, were spared. Even Myers nevertheless met vitriolic attacks.

The troubles all three men encountered were gigantic. The loss of Tennessee with its grain, meats, iron, and factories was a heavy blow. Importation provided almost nothing for commissary work. The archangel Michael would have been staggered, and mere routine efficiency (for none of the three men was a miracle worker) did not suffice. Richardson did not deal with these departments, which are well documented in the *Official Records.* Had he touched Northrop's work he could only have repeated the words of a lesser

Confederate commissary officer in 1863: "Our battle against want and starvation is greater than against our enemies."

But Jefferson Davis braved a storm of criticism to give Northrop his firm support. "To direct the production, collection, preservation, and transportation of food for the army required a man of rare capacity," Davis wrote later. He paid tribute also to Lawton, who was outspoken in condemning the State selfishness that in 1864 kept supplies spoiling at home that the armies piteously needed. These were men not only of industry and practical sense, but (unlike some of the subordinates) incorruptible integrity.

The most conspicuously gifted and enterprising bureau officer was Josiah Gorgas, head of the Ordnance Department in Richmond. His was the task, as his biographer Frank E. Vandiver writes, of supplying an agrarian nation, its workshops few and small, its mechanics a mere corporal's guard, and its traditions those of the farm and plantation, with enough arms and ammunition to resist the crushing industrial power of the North. He quickly ascertained what muskets, rifles, pistols, and sabres the South held in its armories; he found that the Confederacy had 358 pieces of artillery of all sizes and shapes; he spurred the arsenals in Charleston, Baton Rouge, Augusta, and other centers into feverish exertion; and he made strenuous efforts to bring weapons in through the blockade. He sent the resourceful Caleb Huse, some of whose papers are printed here, abroad to buy arms for a long war—for Gorgas saw that it would be long. This agent did well. As Gorgas astutely remarked, "capacity for running in debt is the best evidence of the ability of Major Huse." And Gorgas made arrangements which converted Bermuda, the Bahamas, and Matamoras into lively centers of transshipment.

Problem upon problem, like Pelion on Ossa! The ordnance chief, the commissary officers, and the quartermasters were all given acute pain by the growing shortages of transportation; the want of trackage at vital points, the paucity of locomotives, and the tendency of rolling stock and roundhouse equipment to wear out. Food enough was grown in the Confederacy to satisfy all needs, and cloth enough was spun. But to coax both out of the hands of the holders, along with other supplies, was one difficulty, and to distribute all the needed commodities was another and greater. The forced seizure of provisions, draft animals, wagons, harness, clothing, and utensils began in the first year of the war. The rigorous measures adopted provoked such an uproar of anguish and indignation that by 1863 frantic efforts were undertaken to systematize the collections and make certain of the payment of fair prices. But then, as trains crept along the rails at ten miles an hour, as bridges were destroyed, and as mutually jealous railroads still hoarded their facilities, more and more goods were lost in transit, or were immobilized and rotted away untouched.

III

Perhaps the sorest disappointment of Jefferson Davis and his associates lay in the failure of the Confederacy to obtain the intervention of Great Britain and France in the war. This is a story documented at length in the second volume of this collection. Among the documents are some of the most vehement letters Davis ever wrote, full of chagrin and vexation. He had expected that economic forces would bring the British into the conflict. Instead, economic pressures helped keep them cautiously neutral—and France followed in Britain's wake, for she dared not act independently. President Davis had also hoped that sentiment would lead the British people to align themselves with the Confederacy. One sentimental consideration was the sympathy the British had long felt for small peoples battling for freedom. Another was the dislike of conservative and aristocratic Britons for the bumptious democracy of the North, which had so often scolded and even threatened the mother country. But, alas for the South, sentiment proved to be one of the main forces that kept Britain coldly aloof.

Davis was quite correct in his supposition that the halting of cotton shipments by the blockade would strike the rich British textile industry a fearful blow. The mills, after working a time on accumulated stocks, shut down. The streets of Manchester and Preston were filled with unemployed hands; pauperism hid itself in the bare tenements of Ashton, Stockport, and a hundred other towns; troops of thin ragged workers wandered the squares of London and Liverpool, singing hymns to collect pennies, the women hiding in the rear, and the discouraged men sometimes walking backward in their shame to be seen begging. Soup kitchens had to be opened and public relief granted on an unprecedented scale. The spectacle touched the heart of the world; for a brief time it seemed to show that Cotton *was* King.

But did the brave and intelligent folk of Lancashire demand intervention? On the contrary, they gave mankind a moving exhibition of moral staunchness. Sharply as they felt the tooth of want, they remembered how sternly they detested slavery, and how deeply they were attached to the cause of democracy. As they stood firm, assistance poured in from all over the globe. The Mansion House Relief Committee in Manchester received subscriptions from every British colony, every large city in the empire, and every nation outside, even Haiti and Japan. Schools were opened, and long lines of women, under the supervision of tailors and seamstresses, began plying the needle to make clothing and bedding. Work was found for the men. The number of persons needing relief fell in December, 1863, to 180,000, and in December, 1864, to 130,000, a manageable figure. The economic pressures were not so great, after all.

And as economic pressures favorable to intervention lost force, those opposing it grew stronger. By 1863 commercial observers in America saw that powerful new forces were making themselves felt in Britain. The East India shippers, merchants, and capitalists knew well that the blockade of the South was equivalent to a protective tariff on Indian cotton, and a bounty on Indian trade and shipping. Let it continue five years longer, they predicted, and Englishmen could snap their fingers at American cotton. Cotton was coming forward from Egypt, Brazil, and the West Indies. Meanwhile, the munitions makers of Great Britain and France, the steel and iron interests, the general hardware dealers, and the woolen and linen manufacturers, were making large fortunes from their wartime trade with America. More and more of the shipping business of the world was passing under the British flag. Blockade running was for a time one of the most profitable businesses in the world, cargoes sent into the Confederacy frequently returning a profit of 500 percent. First and last, more than a million bales of cotton were brought out through the blockade. In his estimate of economic forces Jefferson Davis had plainly miscalculated.

Still greater was his miscalculation of moral forces. Despite unfair suffrage restrictions, the power of the middle classes was steadily increasing in England, and that of the upper classes declining. The middle classes, led by Richard Cobden and John Bright, hesitated until after Lincoln's emancipation proclamation in September, 1862. Thereafter they were immovably on the side of the North, and the government of Palmerston and John Russell dared take no step that would defy them. A great meeting in Exeter Hall in London just after the proclamation resounded like a thunderclap throughout the kingdom, and was echoed by meetings in a score of other cities, pouring their resolutions into Parliament. Nor did England, which yet vividly remembered the slaughter of the Crimean War, wish to lose young men in battle, or sacrifice Canada, or see her merchant marine driven from the seas. If war began, as John Bright said, England would be the most vulnerable nation in the world. Pacifism was far stronger in the island than any military impulses.

In France, too, the disapproval of the French people, as distinguished from Napoleon III and his minister, for any warlike step, was strong and clear. Like the British, the French sympathized with the North because it stood for freedom and the South for slavery; and because, too, of the traditional ties of the French with the American republic. Napoleon III was an unpopular monarch, and his subjects took comfort in every victory that democracy won in America. Nor did the French, in their jealousy of England, fail to see that a strong and united American republic would be the best counterweight to the British Empire. Here, too, Davis, with Judah P. Benjamin as his Secretary of State and John Slidell as his strongest diplomat, had miscalculated.

The story of the Confederate efforts to gain recognition as an independent nation, and not merely as a belligerent force, is nevertheless of compelling interest. The hopes and despairs of that story, the small brief gains and the big enduring reverses, the parts played by the shrewd Slidell, the stupid James Mason, and their subordinates, the resourceful Caleb Huse and indefatigably alert Henry Hotze, are all fascinating. The student of history who has not read these important documents is to be pitied, for he has missed much. Those who attentively examine these papers, from Robert Toombs's first hopeful dispatch in 1861, to Lord John Russell's decisive delivery of the final *coup de grâce* in 1865, will find a memorable drama unrolled before them; a drama that is an essential part of the great heroic effort made by the Confederacy and its chieftains.

San Marino, California
August, 1966

Constitution for the Provisional Government.

Constitution for the Provisional Government.

We, the deputies of the sovereign and independent States of South Carolina, Georgia, Florida, Alabama, Mississippi, and Louisiana, invoking the favor of Almighty God, do hereby, in behalf of these States, ordain and establish this Constitution for the Provisional Government of the same: to continue one year from the inauguration of the President, or until a permanent constitution or confederation between the said States shall be put in operation, whichsoever shall first occur.

ARTICLE I.

Section 1. All legislative powers herein delegated shall be vested in this Congress now assembled until otherwise ordained.

Sec. 2. When vacancies happen in the representation from any State, the same shall be filled in such manner as the proper authorities of the State shall direct.

Sec. 3. (1) The Congress shall be the judge of the elections, returns, and qualifications of its members; any number of deputies from a majority of the States, being present, shall constitute a quorum to do business; but a smaller number may adjourn from day to day, and may be authorized to compel the attendance of absent members; upon all questions before the Congress, each State shall be entitled to one vote, and shall be represented by any one or more of its deputies who may be present.

(2) The Congress may determine the rules of its proceedings, punish its members for disorderly behavior, and, with the concurrence of two-thirds, expel a member.

(3) The Congress shall keep a journal of its proceedings, and from time to time publish the same, excepting such parts as may in their judgment require secrecy; and the yeas and nays of the members on any question shall, at the desire of one-fifth of those

3

present, or at the instance of any one State, be entered on the journal.

Sec. 4. The members of Congress shall receive a compensation for their services, to be ascertained by law, and paid out of the Treasury of the Confederacy. They shall in all cases, except treason, felony, and breach of the peace, be privileged from arrest during their attendance at the session of the Congress, and in going to and returning from the same; and for any speech or debate they shall not be questioned in any other place.

Sec. 5. (1) Every bill which shall have passed the Congress shall, before it becomes a law, be presented to the President of the Confederacy; if he approve, he shall sign it; but if not, he shall return it with his objections to the Congress, who shall enter the objections at large on their journal, and proceed to reconsider it. If, after such reconsideration, two-thirds of the Congress shall agree to pass the bill, it shall become a law. But in all such cases the vote shall be determined by yeas and nays; and the names of the persons voting for and against the bill shall be entered on the journal. If any bill shall not be returned by the President within ten days (Sundays excepted) after it shall have been presented to him, the same shall be a law, in like manner as if he had signed it, unless the Congress, by their adjournment, prevent its return; in which case it shall not be a law. The President may veto any appropriation or appropriations and approve any other appropriation or appropriations in the same bill.

(2) Every order, resolution, or vote intended to have the force and effect of a law, shall be presented to the President, and before the same shall take effect, shall be approved by him, or, being disapproved by him, shall be repassed by two-thirds of the Congress, according to the rules and limitations prescribed in the case of a bill.

(3). Until the inauguration of the President, all bills, orders, resolutions, and votes adopted by the Congress shall be of full force without approval by him.

Sec. 6. (1) The Congress shall have power to lay and collect taxes, duties, imposts, and excises for the revenue necessary to pay the debts and carry on the Government of the Confederacy; and all duties, imposts, and excises shall be uniform throughout the States of the Confederacy.

(2) To borrow money on the credit of the Confederacy.

(3) To regulate commerce with foreign nations, and among the several States, and with the Indian tribes.

(4) To establish a uniform rule of naturalization, and uniform laws on the subject of bankruptcies throughout the Confederacy.

(5) To coin money, regulate the value thereof, and of foreign coin, and fix the standard of weights and measures.

(6) To provide for the punishment of counterfeiting the securities and current coin of the Confederacy.

(7) To establish post offices and post roads.

(8) To promote the progress of science and useful arts by securing, for limited times, to authors and inventors the exclusive right to their respective writings and discoveries.

(9) To constitute tribunals inferior to the Supreme Court.

(10) To define and punish piracies and felonies committed on the high seas, and offenses against the law of nations.

(11) To declare war, grant letters of marque and reprisal, and make rules concerning captures on land and water.

(12) To raise and support armies; but no appropriation of money to that use shall be for a longer term than two years.

(13) To provide and maintain a navy.

(14) To make rules for the government and regulation of the land and naval forces.

(15) To provide for calling forth the militia to execute the laws of the Confederacy, suppress insurrections, and repel invasions.

(16) To provide for organizing, arming, and disciplining the militia, and for governing such part of them as may be employed in the service of the Confederacy, reserving to the States respectively the appointment of the officers, and the authority of training the militia according to the discipline prescribed by Congress.

(17) To make all laws that shall be necessary and proper for carrying into execution the foregoing powers and all other powers expressly delegated by this Constitution to this Provisional Government.

(18) The Congress shall have power to admit other States.

(19) This Congress shall also exercise executive powers, until the President is inaugurated.

Sec. 7. (1) The importation of African negroes from any foreign country other than the slave-holding States of the United

States, is hereby forbidden; and Congress are required to pass such laws as shall effectually prevent the same.

(2) The Congress shall also have power to prohibit the introduction of slaves from any State not a member of this Confederacy.

(3) The privilege of the writ of *habeas corpus* shall not be suspended unless, when in cases of rebellion or invasion, the public safety may require it.

(4) No bill of attainder or *ex post facto* law shall be passed.

(5) No preference shall be given, by any regulation of commerce or revenue, to the ports of one State over those of another; nor shall vessels bound to or from one State be obliged to enter, clear, or pay duties in another.

(6) No money shall be drawn from the treasury, but in consequence of appropriations made by law; and a regular statement and account of the receipts and expenditures of all public money shall be published from time to time.

(7) Congress shall appropriate no money from the treasury, unless it be asked and estimated for by the President or some one of the heads of departments, except for the purpose of paying its own expenses and contingencies.

(8) No title of nobility shall be granted by the Confederacy; and no person holding any office of profit or trust under it shall, without the consent of the Congress, accept of any present, emolument, office, or title of any kind whatever, from any king, prince, or foreign state.

(9) Congress shall make no law respecting an establishment of religion, or prohibiting the free exercise thereof, or abridging the freedom of speech, or of the press; or the right of the people peaceably to assemble, and to petition the Government for a redress of such grievances as the delegated powers of this Government may warrant it to consider and redress.

(10) A well-regulated militia being necessary to the security of a free state, the right of the people to keep and bear arms shall not be infringed.

(11) No soldier shall, in time of peace, be quartered in any house without the consent of the owner; nor in time of war, but in a manner to be prescribed by law.

(12) The right of the people to be secure in their persons, houses,

papers, and effects against unreasonable searches and seizures shall not be violated; and no warrants shall issue but upon probable cause, supported by oath or affirmation, and particularly describing the place to be searched, and the persons or things to be seized.

(13) No person shall be held to answer for a capital or otherwise infamous crime unless on a presentment or indictment of a grand jury, except in cases arising in the land or naval forces, or in the militia, when in actual service in time of war or public danger; nor shall any person be subject for the same offense to be twice put in jeopardy of life or limb; nor shall be compelled in any criminal case to be a witness against himself; nor be deprived of life, liberty, or property without due process of law; nor shall private property be taken for public use without just compensation.

(14) In all criminal prosecutions the accused shall enjoy the right to a speedy and public trial, by an impartial jury of the State and district wherein the crime shall have been committed, which district shall have been previously ascertained by law, and to be informed of the nature and cause of the accusation; to be confronted with the witnesses against him; to have compulsory process for obtaining witnesses in his favor; and to have the assistance of counsel for his defense.

(15) In suits at common law, where the value in controversy shall exceed twenty dollars, the right of trial by jury shall be preserved; and no fact tried by a jury shall be otherwise reëxamined in any court of the Confederacy than according to the rules of the common law.

(16) Excessive bail shall not be required, nor excessive fines imposed, nor cruel and unusual punishments inflicted.

(17) The enumeration, in the Constitution, of certain rights shall not be construed to deny or disparage others retained by the people.

(18) The powers not delegated to the Confederacy by the Constitution, nor prohibited by it to the States, are reserved to the States respectively, or to the people.

(19) The judicial power of the Confederacy shall not be construed to extend to any suit in law or equity, commenced or prosecuted against one of the States of the Confederacy, by citizens of another State, or by citizens or subjects of any foreign state.

Sec. 8. (1) No State shall enter into any treaty, alliance, or confederation; grant letters of marque and reprisal; coin money; emit bills of credit; make anything but gold and silver coin a tender in payment of debts; pass any bill of attainder, *ex post facto* law, or law impairing the obligation of contracts; or grant any title of nobility.

(2) No State shall, without the consent of the Congress, lay any imposts or duties on imports or exports, except what may be absolutely necessary for executing its inspection laws; and the net produce of all duties and imposts, laid by any State on imports or exports, shall be for the use of the Treasury of the Confederacy, and all such laws shall be subject to the revision and control of the Congress. No State shall, without the consent of Congress, lay any duty of tonnage, enter into any agreement or compact with another State, or with a foreign power, or engage in war, unless actually invaded, or in such imminent danger as will not admit of delay.

Article II.

Section 1. (1) The executive power shall be vested in a President of the Confederate States of America. He, together with the Vice President, shall hold his office for one year, or until this Provisional Government shall be superseded by a permanent government, whichsoever shall first occur.

(2) The President and Vice President shall be elected by ballot by the States represented in this Congress, each State casting one vote, and a majority of the whole being requisite to elect.

(3) No person, except a natural born citizen, or a citizen of one of the States of this Confederacy at the time of the adoption of this Constitution, shall be eligible to the office of President; neither shall any person be eligible to that office who shall not have attained the age of thirty-five years, and been fourteen years a resident of one of the States of this Confederacy.

(4) In case of the removal of the President from office, or of his death, resignation, or inability to discharge the powers and duties of the said office (which inability shall be determined by a vote of two-thirds of the Congress), the same shall devolve on the Vice President; and the Congress may by law provide for the case of removal, death, resignation, or inability, both of the President and

Vice President, declaring what officer shall then act as President; and such officer shall act accordingly until the disability be removed or a President shall be elected.

(5) The President shall at stated times receive for his services, during the period of the Provisional Government, a compensation at the rate of $25,000 per annum; and he shall not receive during that period any other emolument from this Confederacy, or any of the States thereof.

(6) Before he enter on the execution of his office he shall take the following oath or affirmation:

I do solemnly swear (or affirm) that I will faithfully execute the office of President of the Confederate States of America, and will, to the best of my ability, preserve, protect, and defend the Constitution thereof.

Sec. 2. (1) The President shall be Commander-in-Chief of the Army and Navy of the Confederacy, and of the militia of the several States, when called into the actual service of the Confederacy; he may require the opinion, in writing, of the principal officer in each of the executive departments, upon any subject relating to the duties of their respective offices; and he shall have power to grant reprieves and pardons for offenses against the Confederacy, except in cases of impeachment.

(2) He shall have power, by and with the advice and consent of the Congress, to make treaties; provided two-thirds of the Congress concur; and he shall nominate, and, by and with the advice and consent of the Congress, shall appoint ambassadors, other public ministers, and consuls, judges of the courts, and all other officers of the Confederacy whose appointments are not herein otherwise provided for, and which shall be established by law. But the Congress may, by law, vest the appointment of such inferior officers as they think proper in the President alone, in the courts of law, or in the heads of departments.

(3) The President shall have power to fill up all vacancies that may happen during the recess of the Congress, by granting commissions, which shall expire at the end of their next session.

Sec. 3. (1) He shall, from time to time, give to the Congress informatic of the state of the Confederacy, and recommend to their consideration such measures as he shall judge necessary and expedient; he may, on extraordinary occasions, convene the Congress at such times as he shall think proper; he shall receive ambassadors and other public ministers; he shall take care that the laws be faithfully executed; and shall commission all the officers of the Confederacy.

(2) The President, Vice President, and all civil officers of the Confederacy shall be removed from office on conviction by the Congress of treason, bribery, or other high crimes and misdemeanors: a vote of two-thirds shall be necessary for such conviction.

ARTICLE III.

Section 1. (1) The judicial power of the Confederacy shall be vested in one Supreme Court, and in such inferior courts as are herein directed, or as the Congress may from time to time ordain and establish.

(2) Each State shall constitute a district, in which there shall be a court called a district court, which, until otherwise provided by the Congress, shall have the jurisdiction vested by the laws of the United States, as far as applicable, in both the district and circuit courts of the United States, for that State; the judge whereof shall be appointed by the President, by and with the advice and consent of the Congress, and shall, until otherwise provided by the Congress, exercise the power and authority vested by the laws of the United States in the judges of the district and circuit courts of the United States, for that State, and shall appoint the times and places at which the courts shall be held. Appeals may be taken directly from the district courts to the Supreme Court, under similar regulations to those which are provided in cases of appeal to the Supreme Court of the United States, or under such regulations as may be provided by the Congress. The commissions of all the judges shall expire with this Provisional Government.*

---

*This paragraph was amended as follows:

Be it ordained by the Congress of the Confederate States of America, That the second paragraph of the first section of the third article of the Constitution of the Confederate States of America be so amended in the first line of said paragraph as to read, "Each State shall, until otherwise enacted by law, constitute a district;" and in tne sixth line, after the word "judge," add "or judges."

Approved May 21, 1861.

(3) The Supreme Court shall be constituted of all the district judges, a majority of whom shall be a quorum, and shall sit at such times and places as the Congress shall appoint.

(4) The Congress shall have power to make laws for the transfer of any causes which were pending in the courts of the United States, to the courts of the Confederacy, and for the execution of the orders, decrees, and judgments heretofore rendered by the said courts of the United States; and also all laws which may be requisite to protect the parties to all such suits, orders, judgments, or decrees, their heirs, personal representatives, or assignees.

Sec. 2. (1) The judicial power shall extend to all cases of law and equity, arising under this Constitution, the laws of the United States, and of this Confederacy, and treaties made, or which shall be made, under its authority; to all cases affecting ambassadors, other public ministers, and consuls; to all cases of admiralty and maritime jurisdiction; to controversies to which the Confederacy shall be a party; controversies between two or more States; between citizens of different States; between citizens of the same State claiming lands under grants of different States.

(2) In all cases affecting ambassadors, other public ministers, and consuls, and those in which a State shall be a party, the Supreme Court shall have original jurisdiction. In all the other cases before mentioned, the Supreme Court shall have appellate jurisdiction, both as to law and fact, with such exceptions and under such regulations as the Congress shall make.

(3) The trial of all crimes, except in cases of impeachment, shall be by jury, and such trial shall be held in the State where the said crimes shall have been committed; but when not committed within any State, the trial shall be at such place or places as the Congress may by law have directed.

Sec. 3. (1) Treason against this Confederacy shall consist only in levying war against it, or in adhering to its enemies, giving them aid and comfort. No person shall be convicted of treason unless on the testimony of two witnesses to the same overt act, or on confession in open court.

(2) The Congress shall have power to declare the punishment of treason; but no attainder of treason shall work corruption of blood, or forfeiture, except during the life of the person attainted.

ARTICLE IV.

Section 1. (1) Full faith and credit shall be given in each State to the public acts, records, and judicial proceedings of every other State. And the Congress may, by general laws, prescribe the manner in which such acts, records, and proceedings shall be proved and the effect of such proof.

Sec. 2. (1) The citizens of each State shall be entitled to all privileges and immunities of citizens in the several States.

(2) A person charged in any State with treason, felony, or other crime, who shall flee from justice, and be found in another State, shall, on demand of the executive authority of the State from which he fled, be delivered up, to be removed to the State having jurisdiction of the crime.

(3) A slave in one State, escaping to another, shall be delivered up on claim of the party to whom said slave may belong by the executive authority of the State in which such slave shall be found, and in case of any abduction or forcible rescue, full compensation, including the value of the slave and all costs and expenses, shall be made to the party, by the State in which such abduction or rescue shall take place.

Sec. 3. (1) The Confederacy shall guarantee to every State in this Union a republican form of government, and shall protect each of them against invasion; and, on application of the Legislature, or of the Executive (when the Legislature cannot be convened), against domestic violence.

ARTICLE V.

1. The Congress, by a vote of two-thirds, may, at any time, alter or amend this Constitution.

ARTICLE VI.

1. This Constitution, and the laws of the Confederacy which shall be made in pursuance thereof, and all treaties made, or which shall be made, under the authority of the Confederacy, shall be the supreme law of the land; and the judges in every State shall be bound thereby, anything in the constitution or laws of any State to the contrary notwithstanding.

2. The Government hereby instituted shall take immediate steps

for the settlement of all matters between the States forming it, and their other late confederates of the United States in relation to the public property and public debt at the time of their withdrawal from them; these States hereby declaring it to be their wish and earnest desire to adjust everything pertaining to the common property, common liability, and common obligations of that Union, upon the principles of right, justice, equity, and good faith.

3. Until otherwise provided by the Congress, the city of Montgomery, in the State of Alabama, shall be the seat of government.

4. The members of the Congress and all executive and judicial officers of the Confederacy shall be bound by oath or affirmation to support this Constitution; but no religious test shall be required as a qualification to any office or public trust under this Confederacy.

Done in the Congress, by the unanimous consent of all the said States, the eighth day of February, in the year of our Lord one thousand eight hundred and sixty-one, and of the Confederate States of America the first.

In witness whereof we have hereunto subscribed our names.

HOWELL COBB, *President of the Congress.*

South Carolina: R. Barnwell Rhett, R. W. Barnwell, James Chesnut, Jr., C. G. Memminger, William Porcher Miles, Lawrence M. Keitt, William W. Boyce, Thomas J. Withers.

Georgia: R. Toombs, Francis S. Bartow, Martin J. Crawford, E. A. Nisbet, Benjamin H. Hill, Augustus R. Wright, Thomas R. R. Cobb, A. H. Kenan, Alexander H. Stephens.

Florida: Jackson Morton, James B. Owens, J. Patton Anderson.

Alabama: Richard W. Walker, Robert H. Smith, Colin J. McRae, John Gill Shorter, William Parish Chilton, Stephen F. Hale, David P. Lewis, Thomas Fearn, J. L. M. Curry.

Mississippi: W. P. Harris, Alex. M. Clayton, W. S. Wilson, James T. Harrison, Walker Brooke, William S. Barry, J. A. P. Campbell.

Louisiana: John Perkins, Jr., Alex. de Clouet, C. M. Conrad, Duncan F. Kenner, Edward Sparrow, Henry Marshall.

By a vote of the Congress, on the 2d day of March, in the year 1861, the deputies from the State of Texas were authorized to sign the Provisional Constitution above written.

Attest.   J. J. HOOPER, *Secretary.*

Texas: Thomas N. Waul, Williamson S. Oldham, John Gregg, John H. Reagan, W. B. Ochiltree, John Hemphill, Louis T. Wigfall.

Jefferson Davis.

Jefferson Davis

Jefferson Davis.

Jefferson Davis was born in that part of Christian County, Ky., which now forms Todd County on June 3, 1808. His grandfather was a colonist from Wales, and lived in Virginia and Maryland, and rendered important public service to both while they were colonies. His father, Samuel Emory Davis, was a Revolutionary soldier, as were also his brothers. During the Revolution his father served for a time with Georgia cavalry, and was an officer in the infantry in the siege of Savannah. Three of the brothers of Jefferson Davis, all older than himself, participated in the war of 1812; two of them were with Andrew Jackson, and were specially mentioned by him for gallantry at New Orleans. After the Revolution Samuel Davis removed to Kentucky, where he resided for a time, and, when Jefferson Davis was an infant, removed with his family to a place near Woodville, Wilkinson County, Miss. Jefferson Davis received his academic education in early life near his home, and then entered Transylvania College, Kentucky, but in 1824 left there to enter the United States Military Academy at West Point, having been appointed as a cadet by President Monroe; graduated in 1828, and was assigned to the First Infantry as second lieutenant; was engaged with his regiment in several battles in the Black Hawk War of 1831-32; was transferred to a new command called the First Dragoons, and on March 4, 1833, was promoted to be first lieutenant, and was appointed adjutant; was actively in the service, fighting the Pawnees, Comanches, and other Indians during the next two years; but on June 30, 1835, suddenly resigned and entered upon the duties of civil life. It is said that he was persuaded to this course by his uncle and other relatives who considered him unusually qualified to win distinction in a civil career. He married Miss Sallie Knox Taylor, the daughter of Zachary Taylor, then colonel of the First Infantry, and became a cotton planter near Vicksburg, Miss., being about twenty-seven years of age. His wife lived only a few months. In 1845, in the month of February, he married

Miss Varina Howell, a daughter of William B. Howell, of Natchez, Miss. She still survives. On his farm he pursued a course of close study, preparing himself for a public life. In 1843 he entered politics in an exciting gubernatorial campaign, and acquired reputation as a popular speaker. In 1844 he was an elector for Polk and Dallas, and in 1845 was sent to Congress, taking his seat in December of that year. The Tariff, the Oregon question, the Annexation of Texas were live issues, and he took an active part at once in their discussion, giving especial attention to the preparations for war with Mexico. In a speech on the Oregon question, February 6, 1846, he spoke of the "love of the Union in our hearts;" and, referring to the battles of the Revolution, said: "They form a monument to the common glory of our common country." He advocated converting certain forts into schools of instruction for the military of the States. War having begun with Mexico, he determined to reënter military life, and promptly resigned from Congress in June, 1846, and accepted the position of colonel of the First Mississippi Volunteer Rifles, to which he had been unanimously elected. He joined his regiment at New Orleans, and proceeded with it to the Rio Grande to reënforce the army under Gen. Taylor. On September 21, 1846, he led his disciplined command in the battle of Monterey, and won a brilliant victory in the assault, without bayonets, on Fort Teneria, advancing through the streets nearly to the Grand Plaza through a storm of shot and shell, and served later on the commission for the surrender of the place. At Buena Vista his command was charged by a Mexican brigade of lancers, greatly its superior in numbers, in full gallop, in a desperate effort to break the American lines, but Colonel Davis formed his men in the shape of the letter V, the flanks resting in the ravines, exposing the enemy to a converging fire, utterly routing them. During the day he charged up and broke the Mexican lines on their right, and was seriously wounded, remaining on the field, however, until the victory was won. Later he was complimented for coolness and gallantry under fire, by General Taylor in a special dispatch. On the expiration of its term of enlistment, his regiment was ordered home. Colonel Davis was then appointed brigadier general by President Polk, but he declined the commission, on the ground that a militia appointment by the Federal Executive was not constitutional. In August, 1847, he was appointed by the Governor of Mississippi to the vacancy in the United States Senate caused by the death of Senator Spight, and took his seat December 6, 1847; was unanimously elected by the Legislature in January, 1848, for the remainder of the term, and in 1850 was re-elected for a full term. He was made Chairman of the Senate Committee on Military Affairs, and here, as in the House, he was active in the discussions of the slavery question in its various phases, the Compromise Measures of 1850, and all other important issues. He said he saw very little in the compromise legislation favorable to the Southern States, and declared that to his view of it, "it bore the impress of that sectional spirit so widely at variance with the general purposes of the Union and destructive of the harmony and mutual benefit which the Constitution was intended to secure." He favored the extension of the Missouri compromise line to the Pacific Ocean, and was at all times an earnest and ardent advocate of the rights of the States. Although just fairly entering upon a full term of six years in the Senate, with almost a certainty of continued service in that distinguished body, he resigned his seat therein after a brief service, and accepted the nomination for governor of his State. His party at the preceding election had been defeated by over seven thousand majority, and while he was defeated at the election in 1851, he reduced the majority to nine hundred and ninety-nine. After a year's retirement he was appointed Secretary of War in the Cabinet of Mr. Pierce, whom he had warmly supported for the presidency, and administered the office with great ability. He made important and valuable reforms in the military service while filling the office of Secretary of War. Among them were the introduction of an improved system of infantry tactics, iron gun carriages, rifled muskets and pistols, and the use of the Minie ball. Four regiments were added to the army, the defenses on the seacoast and frontier were strengthened, and, as a result of experiments, heavy guns were cast hollow, and a larger grain of powder was adopted. He promoted surveys of the Western Territories with a view to the construction of a railroad to the Pacific, which he had favored as a Senator, and was deeply interested in the extension of the Capitol at Washington City. At the close of Mr. Pierce's term he left the Cabinet, and in the same year (1857) again entered the Senate. He opposed the bill to pay French spoliation claims, advocated the southern route for the Pacific railroad, and opposed Mr. Douglas's doctrine of "popular sovereignty." On January 9, 1861, Mississippi seceded, and on January 24—having been officially informed of the fact—he delivered a farewell address, and withdrew from the Senate and went to his home. Before reaching his home he had been appointed by the convention of his State commander in chief of the Army of Mississippi, with the rank of major general. On February 9 he was elected President of the Provisional Government of the Confederate States, at Montgomery, Ala., and on the 18th day of the same month he was inaugurated as such President. He delivered an inaugural address that day, which he said was deliberately prepared and uttered as written, and, in connection with his farewell speech to the Senate, presented a clear and authentic statement of the principles and purposes which actuated him in assuming the duties of the high office to which he had been called. In this inaugural address, among other things, he said: "Our present political position has been achieved in a manner unprecedented in the history of nations. It illustrates the American idea that governments rest on the consent of the governed, and that it is the right of the people to alter or abolish them at will whenever they become destructive of the ends for which they were established. The declared purpose of the compact of the Union from which we have withdrawn was to 'establish justice, insure domestic tranquillity, provide for the common defense, promote the general welfare, and secure the blessings of liberty to ourselves and our posterity;' and when, in the judgment of the sovereign States composing this Confederacy, it has been perverted from the purposes for which it was ordained, and ceased to answer the ends for which it was established, a peaceful appeal to the ballot box declared that, so far as they are concerned, the government created by that compact should cease to exist. In this they merely asserted the right which the Declaration of Independence of July 4, 1776, defined to be 'inalienable.' Of the time and occasion of its exercise they as sovereigns were the final judges, each for itself. The impartial and enlightened verdict of mankind will vindicate the rectitude of our conduct; and He who knows the hearts of men will judge of the sincerity with which we have labored to preserve the government of our fathers in its spirit. The right solemnly proclaimed at the birth of the United States, and which has been solemnly affirmed and reaffirmed in the Bills of Rights of the States subsequently admitted into the Union of 1789, undeniably recognizes in the people the power to resume the authority delegated for the purposes of government. Thus the sovereign States here represented have proceeded to form this Confederacy; and it is by abuse of language that their act has been denominated a revolution. They formed a new alliance, but within each State its government has remained; so that the rights of person and property have not been disturbed. The agent through which they communicated with foreign nations is changed, but this does not necessarily interrupt their international relations. Sustained by the consciousness that the transition from the former Union to the present Confederacy has not proceeded from a disregard on our part of just obligations, or any failure to perform every constitutional duty, moved by no interest or passion to invade the rights of others, anxious to cultivate peace and commerce with all nations, if we may not hope to avoid war, we may at least expect that posterity will acquit us of having needlessly engaged in it." Again, he said: "We have entered upon the career of independence, and it must be inflexibly pursued. Through many years of controversy with our late associates of the Northern States we have vainly endeavored to secure tranquillity and obtain respect for the rights to which we were entitled. As a necessity, not a choice, we have resorted to the remedy of separation, and henceforth our energies must be directed to the conduct of our own affairs, and the perpetuity of the Confederacy which we have formed. If a just perception of mutual interest shall permit us peaceably to pursue our separate political career, my most earnest desire will have been fulfilled. But if this be denied to us, and the integrity of our territory and jurisdiction be assailed, it will but remain for us with firm resolve to appeal to arms and invoke the blessing of Providence on a just cause." Continuing, he said: "With a Constitution differing only from that of our fathers in so far as it is explanatory of their well-known intent, freed from sectional conflicts, which have interfered with the pursuit of the general welfare, it is not unreasonable to expect that States from which we have recently parted may seek to unite their fortunes to ours under the government which we have instituted."

He insisted that he and those associated with him were "actuated solely by the desire to preserve our own rights and to promote our own welfare," and that "the separation by the Confederate States has been marked by no aggression upon others, and followed by no domestic convulsion." He said: "Should reason guide the action of the government from which we have separated, a policy so detrimental to the civilized world, the Northern States included, could not be dictated by even the strongest desire to inflict injury upon us; but, if the contrary should prove true, a terrible responsibility will rest upon it, and the suffering of millions will bear testimony to the folly and wickedness of our aggressors." Near the close of his inaugural he used these words: "We have changed the constituent parts, but not the system of government. The Constitution framed by our fathers is that of these Confederate States. In their exposition of it, and in the judicial construction it has received, we have a light which reveals its true meaning. Thus instructed as to the true meaning and just interpretation of that instrument, and ever remembering that all offices are but trusts held for the people, and that powers delegated are to be strictly construed, I will hope by due diligence in the performance of my duties, though I may disappoint your expectations, yet to retain, when retiring, something of the good will and confidence which welcome my entrance into office." In his message to Congress of April 29, 1861, shortly after the opening of the war at Fort Sumter, he made official announcement of the purpose and policy of the government at Montgomery in regard to the war. He said: "We feel that our cause is just and holy; we protest solemnly in the face of mankind that we desire peace at any sacrifice save that of honor and independence; we seek no conquest, no aggrandizement, no concession of any kind from the States with which we were lately confederated; all we ask is to be let alone; that those who never held power over us shall not now attempt our subjugation by arms. This we will, this we must, resist to the direst extremity. The moment that this pretension is abandoned the sword will drop from our grasp, and we shall be ready to enter into treaties of amity and commerce that cannot but be mutually beneficial. So long as this pretension is maintained, with a firm reliance on that divine power which covers with its protection the just cause, we will continue to struggle for our inherent right to freedom, independence, and self-government."

War followed, and was prolonged for four years, during which time Mr. Davis was continued as President. In November, 1861, an election was held under the permanent Constitution, and he was chosen President, without opposition, for six years. The first Congress under the permanent government met in Richmond on February 18, 1862, and he was inaugurated on the 22d of that month. The Confederate army in Virginia under General Lee surrendered April 9, 1865, and soon after the war ended. Mr. Davis left Richmond on Sunday night, April 2, and went to Danville, Va., and from there to Charlotte, N. C., where he remained until the 26th of April, when he left with a small force of cavalry as an escort. He reached the Savannah River and crossed it May 4, and went to Washington, Ga., where he remained a few days. In his work, the "Rise and Fall of the Confederate Government," Mr. Davis says: "When I left Washington, Ga., with the small party which has been enumerated, my object was to go to the south far enough to pass below the points reported to be occupied by Federal troops, and then turn to the west, cross the Chattahoochie, and then go on to meet the forces still supposed to be in the field in Alabama. If, as now seemed probable, there should be no prospect of a successful resistance east of the Mississippi, I intended then to cross to the Trans-Mississippi Department, where I believed Gens. E. K. Smith and Magruder would continue to uphold our cause." On May 10 he was captured by Federal cavalry, and, with members of his family, his wife and several small children, one an infant, who were traveling with him, was carried to Macon, Ga., and from there to Hampton Roads. He was then removed to Fortress Monroe, and incarcerated in a cell, his wife and family being returned to Savannah, Ga. In mentioning his imprisonment at Fortress Monroe, in his work to which reference has just been made, he says: "Bitter tears have been shed by the gentle, and stern reproaches have been made by the magnanimous, on account of the needless torture to which I was subjected, and the heavy fetters riveted upon me, while in a stone casemate and surrounded by a strong guard; but all these were less excruciating than the mental agony my captors were able to inflict. It was long before I was permitted to hear from my wife and children, and this and things like this was the power which education added to cruelty; but I do not propose now and here to enter upon the story of my imprisonment, or more than merely to refer to other matters which concern me personally, as distinct from my connection with the Confederacy." He was kept in prison about two years, and on May 6, 1866, was indicted for treason in the United States Court for the District of Virginia. With his counsel he insisted on a prompt and speedy trial, but the government postponed the trial and held him without bail until May, 1867, when upon a writ of *habeas corpus* he was brought before the court at Richmond and admitted to bail, the bond being fixed at $100,000. The bond was promptly given, and he was released. After an enthusiastic reception at Richmond, he went to New York, then to Canada, and in the summer of 1868 visited England and France. While in England he declined an offer to enter upon business with a Liverpool firm. In December, 1868, a *nolle prosequi* was entered by the government in his case, and he was therefore never brought to trial; and in the general amnesty of that month he was included. He subsequently removed to Memphis, Tenn., and became the president of a life insurance company. In 1879 he was bequeathed an estate by a lady admirer, Mrs. Dorsey, of Beauvoir, Miss., where he went to reside and where, living a life of seclusion, he gave himself up largely to literary pursuits. Occasional public demonstrations in the South revealed the attachment of the people there for him. This was notably the case when he attended the unveiling of the statue of Benjamin Hill, in Atlanta, the dedication of a monument to Confederate soldiers at Montgomery in 1886, and when he at another time visited the Georgia State Fair, at Macon. He avoided ostentatious display of himself; but when opportunity offered, the Southern people, by imposing popular demonstrations, gave evidence of their undiminished attachment to his personal character, and their sympathy for him in his misfortunes. They believed him to be a man of the highest personal integrity, a sincere Christian, a gentleman of refined and elevated character, and one thoroughly impressed with the correctness of the political and constitutional views he held, and the rightfulness and righteousness of the cause he espoused. He devoted much time of the last years of his life to the writing of his history of the war, the "Rise and Fall of the Confederate Government," published in 1881. The purpose he had in view in preparing and publishing this work he set forth briefly but succinctly in his preface thereto in these words: "The object of this work has been from historical data to show that the Southern States had rightfully the power to withdraw from a Union into which they had, as sovereign communities, voluntarily entered; that the denial of that right was a violation of the letter and spirit of the compact between the States; and that the war waged by the Federàl Government against the seceding States was in disregard of the limitations of the Constitution, and destructive of the principles of the Declaration of Independence." He closed the second and last volume of this work with the following words: "In asserting the right of secession, it has not been my wish to incite to its exercise: I recognize the fact that the war showed it to be impracticable, but this did not prove it to be wrong; and now that it may not again be attempted, and that the Union may promote the general welfare, it is needful that the truth, the whole truth, should be known, so that crimination and recrimination may forever cease; and then, on the basis of fraternity and faithful regard for the rights of the States, there may be written on the arch of the Union 'Esto perpetua.' "

The death of Mr. Davis occurred at New Orleans about one o'clock A.M., December 6, 1889. His funeral ceremonies were worthy of the illustrious character of the deceased statesman. Public meetings were held in many cities and towns of the South to give expression to the common sorrow, and the flags of the State Capitols were placed at half-mast. His character was eulogized, and the newspapers generally, North as well as South, printed complimentary and laudatory notices of him. He was buried temporarily in New Orleans, and later his remains were removed to Richmond, the capital of the Confederacy, where there were erected for them a tomb and monument. A special funeral train conveyed them from New Orleans to Richmond, passing through several States. At many places convenient stops were made, that the assembled people might make respectful and affectionate tributes to his memory. The train moved day and night almost literally in review before the line of people who thronged the route and stood with uncovered heads to see it pass. It was appropriate that his remains should rest at last in Richmond, the city which was the immediate scene of his labors as the Confederacy under his guidance for four years maintained an unequal struggle for a permanent place among the nations of the earth, and which, so long defended by the immortal Lee and his heroic battalions, successfully withstood the fierce and terrible assaults of the great armies of the Union, led by brave and renowned soldiers.

Provisional Congress.

Provisional Congress.

FIRST SESSION.

ASSEMBLED AT MONTGOMERY, ALA., FEBRUARY 4, 1861. ADJOURNED MARCH 16, 1861, TO MEET SECOND MONDAY IN MAY.

ELECTION OF PRESIDENT AND VICE PRESIDENT FOR PROVISIONAL GOVERNMENT.

Saturday, February 9, 1861.

OPEN SESSION.

Congress met pursuant to adjournment.

An appropriate prayer was offered up by the Rev. Dr. Basil Manly.

The Chair announced that the first business in order was the administration of the oath to the deputies to support the Constitution of the Provisional Government.

Whereupon Judge Richard W. Walker, of the supreme court of the State of Alabama, administered the oath to the President, and the President administered the oath to the members of Congress.

The oath thus taken was as follows:

You do solemnly swear that you will support the Constitution for the Provisional Government of the Confederate States of America, so help you God.

At the suggestion of Mr. Memminger, while the oath was being administered all the members stood upon their feet.

*　　*　　*　　*　　*　　*　　*

The Congress then proceeded to the election of a President and a Vice President for the Provisional Government.

Mr. Curry moved that two tellers be appointed to conduct said election, which was agreed to.

29

Whereupon the President appointed Mr. Curry and Mr. Miles as tellers.

The vote being taken by States for President, the Hon. Jefferson Davis, of Mississippi, received all the votes cast, being six, and was duly declared unanimously elected President of the Provisional Government.

On motion of Mr. Toombs, a committee of three was appointed to inform Mr. Davis of his election.

Whereupon the President appointed Mr. Toombs, Mr. Rhett, and Mr. Morton.

The vote was then taken by States for Vice President, and the Hon. Alexander Hamilton Stephens, of Georgia, received all the votes cast, being six, and he was duly declared unanimously elected Vice President of the Provisional Government.

Mr. Perkins moved that a committee of three be appointed to inform Mr. Stephens of his election, which was agreed to.

And the President appointed Mr. Perkins, Mr. Harris, and Mr. Shorter.

Congress then adjourned till Monday next at 11 o'clock.

NOTIFICATION OF ELECTION TO PRESIDENT AND VICE PRESIDENT.

MONTGOMERY, ALA., February 9, 1861.

Hon. Jefferson Davis, Jackson.

Sir: We are directed to inform you that you were this day unanimously elected President of the Provisional Government of the Confederate States of America, and to request you to come to Montgomery immediately.   We send also a special messenger. Do not wait for him.   R. TOOMBS,

R. BARNWELL RHETT,

JACKSON MORTON.

MONTGOMERY, ALA., February 9, 1861.

Hon. Alexander H. Stephens.

Sir: The Congress for the Provisional Government for the Confederate States of America have this day unanimously elected you to the office of Vice President of the Confederate States, and we have been appointed to communicate the fact, and to respectfully invite your acceptance. In performing this pleasing duty, allow us to express the hope that you will accept, and we beg to suggest that it would be most agreeable to the body we represent, as you are a member of the Congress, that you should signify to it in person your consent to serve the country in the high position to which you have been called.

We have the honor to be, very respectfully, yours,

JOHN PERKINS, JR.,
W. P. HARRIS,
JNO. GILL SHORTER.

INAUGURATION OF PRESIDENT.

Monday, February 18, 1861.

SECRET SESSION.

*   *   *   *   *   *   *

At 1 P.M. the President elect of the Confederate States of America, escorted by the Vice President and the Committee of Arrangements, appeared within the hall of Congress, and was escorted to the chair, supported on his right by the Vice President and on his left by the President of Congress.

On motion of Mr. Chilton, the Congress then repaired, in company with the President elect, to the front of the Capitol for the purpose of inaugurating the President.

The President of the Congress presented the President elect to the Congress.

The Rev. Dr. Basil Manly, as chaplain of the day, offered prayer.

The President elect then delivered his inaugural address, after which the oath of office was administered to him by the President of the Congress.

On motion of Mr. Chilton, the Congress returned to its hall, accompanied by the President of the Confederate States.

On motion of Mr. Chilton, it was ordered that the inaugural address of the President be spread upon the journal of this body, and that five thousand copies thereof be printed for the use of the Congress.

And then the Congress adjourned.

INAUGURAL ADDRESS OF THE PRESIDENT OF THE PROVISIONAL GOVERNMENT.

February 18, 1861.

Gentlemen of the Congress of the Confederate States of America, Friends, and Fellow-citizens: Called to the difficult and responsible station of Chief Magistrate of the Provisional Government which you have instituted, I approach the discharge of the duties assigned to me with humble distrust of my abilities, but with a sustaining confidence in the wisdom of those who are to guide and aid me in the administration of public affairs, and an abiding faith in the virtue and patriotism of the people. Looking forward to the speedy establishment of a permanent government to take the place of this, which by its greater moral and physical power will be better able to combat with many difficulties that arise from the conflicting interests of separate nations, I enter upon the duties of the office to which I have been chosen with the hope that the beginning of our career, as a Confederacy, may not be obstructed by hostile opposition to our enjoyment of the separate existence and independence we have asserted, and which, with the blessing of Providence, we intend to maintain.

Our present political position has been achieved in a manner unprecedented in the history of nations. It illustrates the American idea that governments rest on the consent of the governed, and that it is the right of the people to alter or abolish them at will whenever they become destructive of the ends for which they were established. The declared purpose of the compact of the Union from which we have withdrawn was to "establish justice, insure domestic tranquillity, provide for the common defense, promote the general welfare, and secure the blessings of liberty to ourselves and our posterity;" and when, in the judgment of the sovereign States composing this Confederacy, it has been perverted from the purposes for which it was ordained, and ceased to answer the ends for which it was established, a peaceful appeal to the ballot box declared that, so far as they are concerned, the Government created by that compact should cease to exist. In this they merely asserted the right which the Declaration of Independence of July 4, 1776, defined to be "inalienable." Of the time and occasion of its exercise they as sovereigns were the final judges, each for itself. The impartial and enlightened verdict of mankind will vindicate the rectitude of our conduct; and He who knows the hearts of men will judge of the sincerity with which we have labored to preserve the Government of our fathers in its spirit.

The right solemnly proclaimed at the birth of the United States, and which has been solemnly affirmed and reaffirmed in the Bills of Rights of the States subsequently admitted into the Union of 1789, undeniably recognizes in the people the power to resume the authority delegated for the purposes of government. Thus the sovereign States here represented have proceeded to form this Confederacy; and it is by abuse of language that their act has been denominated a revolution. They formed a new alliance, but within each State its government has remained; so that the rights of person and property have not been disturbed. The agent through which they communicated with foreign nations is changed, but this does not necessarily interrupt their international relations. Sustained by the consciousness that the transition from the former Union to the present Confederacy has not proceeded from a disregard on our part of just obligations, or any failure to perform every constitutional duty, moved by no interest or passion to invade the rights of others, anxious to cultivate peace and commerce with all nations, if we may not hope to avoid war, we may at least expect that posterity will acquit us of having needlessly engaged in it. Doubly justified by the absence of wrong on our part, and by wanton aggression on the part of others, there can be no cause to doubt that the courage and patriotism of the people of the Confederate States will be found equal to any measure of defense which their honor and security may require.

An agricultural people, whose chief interest is the export of commodities required in every manufacturing country, our true policy is peace, and the freest trade which our necessities will permit. It is alike our interest and that of all those to whom we would sell, and from whom we would buy, that there should be the fewest practicable restrictions upon the interchange of these commodities. There can, however, be but little rivalry between ours and any manufacturing or navigating community, such as the Northeastern States of the American Union. It must follow, therefore, that mutual interest will invite to good will and kind offices on both parts. If, however, passion or lust of dominion should cloud the judgment or inflame the ambition of those States, we must prepare to meet the emergency and maintain, by the final arbitrament of the sword, the position which we have assumed among the nations of the earth.

We have entered upon the career of independence, and it must be inflexibly pursued. Through many years of controversy with our late associates of the Northern States, we have vainly endeavored to secure tranquillity and obtain respect for the rights to which we were entitled. As a necessity, not a choice, we have resorted to the remedy of separation, and henceforth our energies must be directed to the conduct of our own affairs, and the perpetuity of the Confederacy which we have formed. If a just perception of mutual interest shall permit us peaceably to pursue our separate political career, my most earnest desire will have been fulfilled. But if this be denied to us, and the integrity of our territory and jurisdiction be assailed, it will but remain for us with firm resolve to appeal to arms and invoke the blessing of Providence on a just cause.

As a consequence of our new condition and relations, and with a view to meet anticipated wants, it will be necessary to provide for the speedy and efficient organization of branches of the Executive department having special charge of foreign intercourse, finance, military affairs, and the postal service. For purposes of defense, the Confederate States may, under ordinary circumstances, rely mainly upon the militia; but it is deemed advisable, in the present condition of affairs, that there should be a well-instructed and disciplined army, more numerous than would usually be required on a peace establishment. I also suggest that, for the protection of our harbors and commerce on the high seas, a navy adapted to those objects will be required. But this, as well as other subjects appropriate to our necessities, have doubtless engaged the attention of Congress.

With a Constitution differing only from that of our fathers in so far as it is explanatory of their well-known intent, freed from sectional conflicts, which have interfered with the pursuit of the general welfare, it is not unreasonable to expect that States from which we have recently parted may seek to unite their fortunes to ours under the Government which we have instituted. For this your Constitution makes adequate provision; but beyond this, if I mistake not the judgment and will of the people, a re-union with the States from which we have separated is neither practicable nor desirable. To increase the power, develop the resources, and promote the happiness of the Confederacy, it is requisite that there should be so much of homogeneity that the welfare of every portion shall be the aim of the whole. When this does not exist, antagonisms are engendered which must and should result in separation.

Actuated solely by the desire to preserve our own rights, and promote our own welfare, the separation by the Confederate States has been marked by no aggression upon others, and followed by no domestic convulsion. Our industrial pursuits have received no check, the cultivation of our fields has progressed as heretofore, and, even should we be involved in war, there would be no considerable diminution in the production of the staples which have constituted our exports, and in which the commercial world has an interest scarcely less than our own. This common interest of the producer and consumer can only be interrupted by exterior force which would obstruct the transmission of our staples to foreign markets—a course of conduct which would be as unjust, as it would be detrimental, to manufacturing and commercial interests abroad.

Should reason guide the action of the Government from which we have separated, a policy so detrimental to the civilized world, the Northern States included, could not be dictated by even the strongest desire to inflict injury upon us; but, if the contrary should prove true, a terrible responsibility will rest upon it, and the suffering of millions will bear testimony to the folly and wickedness of our aggressors. In the meantime there will remain to us, besides the ordinary means before suggested, the well-known resources for retaliation upon the commerce of an enemy.

Experience in public stations, of subordinate grade to this

which your kindness has conferred, has taught me that toil and care and disappointment are the price of official elevation. You will see many errors to forgive, many deficiencies to tolerate; but you shall not find in me either want of zeal or fidelity to the cause that is to me the highest in hope, and of most enduring affection. Your generosity has bestowed upon me an undeserved distinction, one which I neither sought nor desired. Upon the continuance of that sentiment, and upon your wisdom and patriotism, I rely to direct and support me in the performance of the duties required at my hands.

We have changed the constituent parts, but not the system ot government. The Constitution framed by our fathers is that of these Confederate States. In their exposition of it, and in the judicial construction it has received, we have a light which reveals its true meaning.

Thus instructed as to the true meaning and just interpretation of that instrument, and ever remembering that all offices are but trusts held for the people, and that powers delegated are to be strictly construed, I will hope by due diligence in the performance of my duties, though I may disappoint your expectations, yet to retain, when retiring, something of the good will and confidence which welcome my entrance into office.

It is joyous in the midst of perilous times to look around upon a people united in heart, where one purpose of high resolve animates and actuates the whole; where the sacrifices to be made are not weighed in the balance against honor and right and liberty and equality. Obstacles may retard, but they cannot long prevent, the progress of a movement sanctified by its justice and sustained by a virtuous people. Reverently let us invoke the God of our fathers to guide and protect us in our efforts to perpetuate the principles which by his blessing they were able to vindicate, establish, and transmit to their posterity. With the continuance of his favor ever gratefully acknowledged, we may hopefully look forward to success, to peace, and to prosperity.

Constitution of the Confederate States.

We, the people of the Confederate States, each State acting in its sovereign and independent character, in order to form a permanent federal government, establish justice, insure domestic tranquillity, and secure the blessings of liberty to ourselves and our posterity—invoking the favor and guidance of Almighty God—do ordain and establish this Constitution for the Confederate States of America.

ARTICLE I.

Section 1. All legislative powers herein delegated shall be vested in a Congress of the Confederate States, which shall consist of a Senate and House of Representatives.

Sec. 2. (1) The House of Representatives shall be composed of members chosen every second year by the people of the several States; and the electors in each State shall be citizens of the Confederate States, and have the qualifications requisite for electors of the most numerous branch of the State Legislature; but no person of foreign birth, not a citizen of the Confederate States, shall be allowed to vote for any officer, civil or political, State or Federal.

(2) No person shall be a Representative who shall not have attained the age of twenty-five years, and be a citizen of the Confederate States, and who shall not, when elected, be an inhabitant of that State in which he shall be chosen.

(3) Representatives and direct taxes shall be apportioned among the several States, which may be included within this Confederacy, according to their respective numbers, which shall be determined by adding to the whole number of free persons, including those bound to service for a term of years, and excluding Indians not taxed, three-fifths of all slaves. The actual enumera-

37

tion shall be made within three years after the first meeting of the Congress of the Confederate States, and within every subsequent term of ten years, in such manner as they shall by law direct. The number of Representatives shall not exceed one for every fifty thousand, but each State shall have at least one Representative; and until such enumeration shall be made, the State of South Carolina shall be entitled to choose six; the State of Georgia ten; the State of Alabama nine; the State of Florida two; the State of Mississippi seven; the State of Louisiana six; and the State of Texas six.

(4) When vacancies happen in the representation from any State the executive authority thereof shall issue writs of election to fill such vacancies.

(5) The House of Representatives shall choose their Speaker and other officers; and shall have the sole power of impeachment; except that any judicial or other Federal officer, resident and acting solely within the limits of any State, may be impeached by a vote of two-thirds of both branches of the Legislature thereof.

Sec. 3. (1) The Senate of the Confederate States shall be composed of two Senators from each State, chosen for six years by the Legislature thereof, at the regular session next immediately preceding the commencement of the term of service; and each Senator shall have one vote.

(2) Immediately after they shall be assembled, in consequence of the first election, they shall be divided as equally as may be into three classes. The seats of the Senators of the first class shall be vacated at the expiration of the second year; of the second class at the expiration of the fourth year; and of the third class at the expiration of the sixth year; so that one-third may be chosen every second year; and if vacancies happen by resignation, or otherwise, during the recess of the Legislature of any State, the Executive thereof may make temporary appointments until the next meeting of the Legislature, which shall then fill such vacancies.

(3) No person shall be a Senator who shall not have attained the age of thirty years, and be a citizen of the Confederate States; and who shall not, when elected, be an inhabitant of the State for which he shall be chosen.

(4) The Vice President of the Confederate States shall be president of the Senate, but shall have no vote unless they be equally divided.

(5) The Senate shall choose their other officers; and also a president *pro tempore* in the absence of the Vice President, or when he shall exercise the office of President of the Confederate States.

(6) The Senate shall have the sole power to try all impeachments. When sitting for that purpose, they shall be on oath or affirmation. When the President of the Confederate States is tried, the Chief Justice shall preside; and no person shall be convicted without the concurrence of two-thirds of the members present.

(7) Judgment in cases of impeachment shall not extend further than to removal from office, and disqualification to hold and enjoy any office of honor, trust, or profit under the Confederate States; but the party convicted shall, nevertheless, be liable and subject to indictment, trial, judgment, and punishment according to law.

Sec. 4. (1) The times, places, and manner of holding elections for Senators and Representatives shall be prescribed in each State by the Legislature thereof, subject to the provisions of this Constitution; but the Congress may, at any time, by law, make or alter such regulations, except as to the times and places of choosing Senators.

(2) The Congress shall assemble at least once in every year; and such meeting shall be on the first Monday in December, unless they shall, by law, appoint a different day.

Sec. 5. (1) Each House shall be the judge of the elections, returns, and qualifications of its own members, and a majority of each shall constitute a quorum to do business; but a smaller number may adjourn from day to day, and may be authorized to compel the attendance of absent members, in such manner and under such penalties as each House may provide.

(2) Each House may determine the rules of its proceedings, punish its members for disorderly behavior, and, with the concurrence of two-thirds of the whole number, expel a member.

(3) Each House shall keep a journal of its proceedings, and

from time to time publish the same, excepting such parts as may in their judgment require secrecy; and the yeas and nays of the members of either House, on any question, shall, at the desire of one-fifth of those present, be entered on the journal.

(4) Neither House, during the session of Congress, shall, without the consent of the other, adjourn for more than three days, nor to any other place than that in which the two Houses shall be sitting.

Sec. 6. (1) The Senators and Representatives shall receive a compensation for their services, to be ascertained by law, and paid out of the Treasury of the Confederate States. They shall, in all cases, except treason, felony, and breach of the peace, be privileged from arrest during their attendance at the session of their respective Houses, and in going to and returning from the same; and for any speech or debate in either House, they shall not be questioned in any other place.

(2) No Senator or Representative shall, during the time for which he was elected, be appointed to any civil office under the authority of the Confederate States, which shall have been created, or the emoluments whereof shall have been increased during such time; and no person holding any office under the Confederate States shall be a member of either House during his continuance in office. But Congress may, by law, grant to the principal officer in each of the Executive Departments a seat upon the floor of either House, with the privilege of discussing any measures appertaining to his department.

Sec. 7. (1) All bills for raising revenue shall originate in the House of Representatives; but the Senate may propose or concur with amendments, as on other bills.

(2) Every bill which shall have passed both Houses, shall, before it becomes a law, be presented to the President of the Confederate States; if he approve, he shall sign it; but if not, he shall return it, with his objections, to that House in which it shall have originated, who shall enter the objections at large on their journal, and proceed to reconsider it. If, after such reconsideration, two-thirds of that House shall agree to pass the bill, it shall be sent, together with the objections, to the other House, by which it shall likewise be reconsidered, and if approved by two-thirds of that

House, it shall become a law. But in all such cases, the votes of both Houses shall be determined by yeas and nays, and the names of the persons voting for and against the bill shall be entered on the journal of each House respectively. If any bill shall not be returned by the President within ten days (Sundays excepted) after it shall have been presented to him, the same shall be a law, in like manner as if he had signed it, unless the Congress, by their adjournment, prevent its return; in which case it shall not be a law. The President may approve any appropriation and disapprove any other appropriation in the same bill. In such case he shall, in signing the bill, designate the appropriations disapproved; and shall return a copy of such appropriations, with his objections, to the House in which the bill shall have originated; and the same proceedings shall then be had as in case of other bills disapproved by the President.

(3) Every order, resolution, or vote, to which the concurrence of both Houses may be necessary (except on a question of adjournment) shall be presented to the President of the Confederate States; and before the same shall take effect, shall be approved by him; or, being disapproved by him, shall be repassed by two-thirds of both Houses, according to the rules and limitations prescribed in case of a bill.

Sec. 8. The Congress shall have power—

(1) To lay and collect taxes, duties, imposts, and excises for revenue, necessary to pay the debts, provide for the common defense, and carry on the Government of the Confederate States; but no bounties shall be granted from the Treasury; nor shall any duties or taxes on importations from foreign nations be laid to promote or foster any branch of industry; and all duties, imposts, and excises shall be uniform throughout the Confederate States.

(2) To borrow money on the credit of the Confederate States.

(3) To regulate commerce with foreign nations, and among the several States, and with the Indian tribes; but neither this, nor any other clause contained in the Constitution, shall ever be construed to delegate the power to Congress to appropriate money for any internal improvement intended to facilitate commerce; except for the purpose of furnishing lights, beacons, and buoys, and other aids to navigation upon the coasts, and the improvement of harbors

and the removing of obstructions in river navigation; in all which cases such duties shall be laid on the navigation facilitated thereby as may be necessary to pay the costs and expenses thereof.

(4) To establish uniform laws of naturalization, and uniform laws on the subject of bankruptcies, throughout the Confederate States; but no law of Congress shall discharge any debt contracted before the passage of the same.

(5) To coin money, regulate the value thereof, and of foreign coin, and fix the standard of weights and measures.

(6) To provide for the punishment of counterfeiting the securities and current coin of the Confederate States.

(7) To establish post offices and post routes; but the expenses of the Post Office Department, after the 1st day of March in the year of our Lord eighteen hundred and sixty-three, shall be paid out of its own revenues.

(8) To promote the progress of science and useful arts, by securing for limited times to authors and inventors the exclusive right to their respective writings and discoveries.

(9) To constitute tribunals inferior to the Supreme Court.

(10) To define and punish piracies and felonies committed on the high seas, and offenses against the law of nations.

(11) To declare war, grant letters of marque and reprisal, and make rules concerning captures on land and water.

(12) To raise and support armies; but no appropriation of money to that use shall be for a longer term than two years.

(13) To provide and maintain a navy.

(14) To make rules for the government and regulation of the land and naval forces.

(15) To provide for calling forth the militia to execute the laws of the Confederate States, suppress insurrections, and repel invasions.

(16) To provide for organizing, arming, and disciplining the militia, and for governing such part of them as may be employed in the service of the Confederate States; reserving to the States, respectively, the appointment of the officers, and the authority of training the militia according to the discipline prescribed by Congress.

(17) To exercise exclusive legislation, in all cases whatsoever,

over such district (not exceeding ten miles square) as may, by cession of one or more States and the acceptance of Congress, become the seat of the Government of the Confederate States; and to exercise like authority over all places purchased by the consent of the Legislature of the State in which the same shall be, for the erection of forts, magazines, arsenals, dockyards, and other needful buildings; and

(18) To make all laws which shall be necessary and proper for carrying into execution the foregoing powers, and all other powers vested by this Constitution in the Government of the Confederate States, or in any department or officer thereof.

Sec. 9. (1) The importation of negroes of the African race from any foreign country other than the slaveholding States or Territories of the United States of America, is hereby forbidden; and Congress is required to pass such laws as shall effectually prevent the same.

(2) Congress shall also have power to prohibit the introduction of slaves from any State not a member of, or Territory not belonging to, this Confederacy.

(3) The privilege of the writ of *habeas corpus* shall not be suspended, unless when in cases of rebellion or invasion the public safety may require it.

(4) No bill of attainder, *ex post facto* law, or law denying or impairing the right of property in negro slaves shall be passed.

(5) No capitation or other direct tax shall be laid, unless in proportion to the census or enumeration hereinbefore directed to be taken.

(6) No tax or duty shall be laid on articles exported from any State, except by a vote of two-thirds of both Houses.

(7) No preference shall be given by any regulation of commerce or revenue to the ports of one State over those of another.

(8) No money shall be drawn from the Treasury, but in consequence of appropriations made by law; and a regular statement and account of the receipts and expenditures of all public money shall be published from time to time.

(9) Congress shall appropriate no money from the Treasury except by a vote of two-thirds of both Houses, taken by yeas and nays, unless it be asked and estimated for by some one of the heads

of departments and submitted to Congress by the President; or for the purpose of paying its own expenses and contingencies; or for the payment of claims against the Confederate States, the justice of which shall have been judicially declared by a tribunal for the investigation of claims against the Government, which it is hereby made the duty of Congress to establish.

(10) All bills appropriating money shall specify in Federal currency the exact amount of each appropriation and the purposes for which it is made; and Congress shall grant no extra compensation to any public contractor, officer, agent, or servant, after such contract shall have been made or such service rendered.

(11) No title of nobility shall be granted by the Confederate States; and no person holding any office of profit or trust under them shall, without the consent of the Congress, accept of any present, emolument, office, or title of any kind whatever, from any king, prince, or foreign state.

(12) Congress shall make no law respecting an establishment of religion, or prohibiting the free exercise thereof; or abridging the freedom of speech, or of the press; or the right of the people peaceably to assemble and petition the Government for a redress of grievances.

(13) A well-regulated militia being necessary to the security of a free State, the right of the people to keep and bear arms shall not be infringed.

(14) No soldier shall, in time of peace, be quartered in any house without the consent of the owner; nor in time of war, but in a manner to be prescribed by law.

(15) The right of the people to be secure in their persons, houses, papers, and effects, against unreasonable searches and seizures, shall not be violated; and no warrants shall issue but upon probable cause, supported by oath or affirmation, and particularly describing the place to be searched and the persons or things to be seized.

(16) No person shall be held to answer for a capital or otherwise infamous crime, unless on a presentment or indictment of a grand jury, except in cases arising in the land or naval forces. or in the militia, when in actual service in time of war or public danger; nor shall any person be subject for the same offense to

be twice put in jeopardy of life or limb; nor be compelled, in any criminal case, to be a witness against himself; nor be deprived of life, liberty, or property without due process of law; nor shall private property be taken for public use, without just compensation.

(17) In all criminal prosecutions the accused shall enjoy the right to a speedy and public trial, by an impartial jury of the State and district wherein the crime shall have been committed, which district shall have been previously ascertained by law, and to be informed of the nature and cause of the accusation; to be confronted with the witnesses against him; to have compulsory process for obtaining witnesses in his favor; and to have the assistance of counsel for his defense.

(18) In suits at common law, where the value in controversy shall exceed twenty dollars, the right of trial by jury shall be preserved; and no fact so tried by a jury shall be otherwise reëxamined in any court of the Confederacy, than according to the rules of common law.

(19) Excessive bail shall not be required, nor excessive fines imposed, nor cruel and unusual punishments inflicted.

(20) Every law, or resolution having the force of law, shall relate to but one subject, and that shall be expressed in the title.

Sec. 10. (1) No State shall enter into any treaty, alliance, or confederation; grant letters of marque and reprisal; coin money; make anything but gold and silver coin a tender in payment of debts; pass any bill of attainder, or *ex post facto* law, or law impairing the obligation of contracts; or grant any title of nobility.

(2) No State shall, without the consent of the Congress, lay any imposts or duties on imports or exports, except what may be absolutely necessary for executing its inspection laws; and the net produce of all duties and imposts, laid by any State on imports or exports, shall be for the use of the Treasury of the Confederate States; and all such laws shall be subject to the revision and control of Congress.

(3) No State shall, without the consent of Congress, lay any duty on tonnage, except on seagoing vessels, for the improvement of its rivers and harbors navigated by the said vessels; but such duties shall not conflict with any treaties of the Confederate States

with foreign nations; and any surplus revenue thus derived shall, after making such improvement, be paid into the common treasury. Nor shall any State keep troops or ships of war in time of peace, enter into any agreement or compact with another State, or with a foreign power, or engage in war, unless actually invaded, or in such imminent danger as will not admit of delay. But when any river divides or flows through two or more States they may enter into compacts with each other to improve the navigation thereof.

ARTICLE II.

Section 1. (1) The executive power shall be vested in a President of the Confederate States of America. He and the Vice President shall hold their offices for the term of six years; but the President shall not be reëligible. The President and Vice President shall be elected as follows:

(2) Each State shall appoint, in such manner as the Legislature thereof may direct, a number of electors equal to the whole number of Senators and Representatives to which the State may be entitled in the Congress; but no Senator or Representative or person holding an office of trust or profit under the Confederate States shall be appointed an elector.

(3) The electors shall meet in their respective States and vote by ballot for President and Vice President, one of whom, at least, shall not be an inhabitant of the same State with themselves; they shall name in their ballots the person voted for as President, and in distinct ballots the person voted for as Vice President, and they shall make distinct lists of all persons voted for as President, and of all persons voted for as Vice President, and of the number of votes for each, which lists they shall sign and certify, and transmit, sealed, to the seat of the Government of the Confederate States, directed to the President of the Senate; the President of the Senate shall, in the presence of the Senate and House of Representatives, open all the certificates, and the votes shall then be counted; the person having the greatest number of votes for President shall be the President, if such number be a majority of the whole number of electors appointed; and if no person have such majority, then from the persons having the highest numbers, not ex-

ceeding three, on the list of those voted for as President, the House of Representatives shall choose immediately, by ballot, the President. But in choosing the President the votes shall be taken by States—the representation from each State having one vote; a quorum for this purpose shall consist of a member or members from two-thirds of the States, and a majority of all the States shall be necessary to a choice. And if the House of Representatives shall not choose a President, whenever the right of choice shall devolve upon them, before the 4th day of March next following, then the Vice President shall act as President, as in case of the death, or other constitutional disability of the President.

(4) The person having the greatest number of votes as Vice President shall be the Vice President, if such number be a majority of the whole number of electors appointed; and if no person have a majority, then, from the two highest numbers on the list, the Senate shall choose the Vice President; a quorum for the purpose shall consist of two-thirds of the whole number of Senators, and a majority of the whole number shall be necessary to a choice.

(5) But no person constitutionally ineligible to the office of President shall be eligible to that of Vice President of the Confederate States.

(6) The Congress may determine the time of choosing the electors, and the day on which they shall give their votes; which day shall be the same throughout the Confederate States.

(7) No person except a natural-born citizen of the Confederate States, or a citizen thereof at the time of the adoption of this Constitution, or a citizen thereof born in the United States prior to the 20th of December, 1860, shall be eligible to the office of President; neither shall any person be eligible to that office who shall not have attained the age of thirty-five years, and been fourteen years a resident within the limits of the Confederate States, as they may exist at the time of his election.

(8) In case of the removal of the President from office, or of his death, resignation, or inability to discharge the powers and duties of said office, the same shall devolve on the Vice President; and the Congress may, by law, provide for the case of removal, death, resignation, or inability, both of the President and

Vice President, declaring what officer shall then act as President; and such officer shall act accordingly until the disability be removed or a President shall be elected.

(9) The President shall, at stated times, receive for his services a compensation, which shall neither be increased nor diminished during the period for which he shall have been elected; and he shall not receive within that period any other emolument from the Confederate States, or any of them.

(10) Before he enters on the execution of his office he shall take the following oath or affirmation:

"I do solemnly swear (or affirm) that I will faithfully execute the office of President of the Confederate States, and will, to the best of my ability, preserve, protect, and defend the Constitution thereof."

Sec. 2. (1) The President shall be Commander-in-Chief of the Army and Navy of the Confederate States, and of the militia of the several States, when called into the actual service of the Confederate States; he may require the opinion, in writing, of the principal officer in each of the Executive Departments, upon any subject relating to the duties of their respective offices; and he shall have power to grant reprieves and pardons for offenses against the Confederate States, except in cases of impeachment.

(2) He shall have power, by and with the advice and consent of the Senate, to make treaties; provided two-thirds of the Senators present concur; and he shall nominate, and by and with the advice and consent of the Senate shall appoint, ambassadors, other public ministers and consuls, judges of the Supreme Court, and all other officers of the Confederate States whose appointments are not herein otherwise provided for, and which shall be established by law; but the Congress may, by law, vest the appointment of such inferior officers, as they think proper, in the President alone, in the courts of law, or in the heads of departments.

(3) The principal officer in each of the Executive Departments, and all persons connected with the diplomatic service, may be removed from office at the pleasure of the President. All other civil officers of the Executive Departments may be removed at any time by the President, or other appointing power, when their services are unnecessary, or for dishonesty, incapacity, inefficiency,

misconduct, or neglect of duty; and when so removed, the removal shall be reported to the Senate, together with the reasons therefor.

(4) The President shall have power to fill all vacancies that may happen during the recess of the Senate, by granting commissions which shall expire at the end of their next session; but no person rejected by the Senate shall be reappointed to the same office during their ensuing recess.

Sec. 3. (1) The President shall, from time to time, give to the Congress information of the state of the Confederacy, and recommend to their consideration such measures as he shall judge necessary and expedient; he may, on extraordinary occasions, convene both Houses, or either of them; and in case of disagreement between them, with respect to the time of adjournment, he may adjourn them to such time as he shall think proper; he shall receive ambassadors and other public ministers; he shall take care that the laws be faithfully executed, and shall commission all the officers of the Confederate States.

Sec. 4. (1) The President, Vice President, and all civil officers of the Confederate States, shall be removed from office on impeachment for and conviction of treason, bribery, or other high crimes and misdemeanors.

ARTICLE III.

Section 1. (1) The judicial power of the Confederate States shall be vested in one Supreme Court, and in such inferior courts as the Congress may, from time to time, ordain and establish. The judges, both of the Supreme and inferior courts, shall hold their offices during good behavior, and shall, at stated times, receive for their services a compensation which shall not be diminished during their continuance in office.

Sec. 2. (1) The judicial power shall extend to all cases arising under this Constitution, the laws of the Confederate States, and treaties made, or which shall be made, under their authority; to all cases affecting ambassadors, other public ministers and consuls; to all cases of admiralty and maritime jurisdiction; to controversies to which the Confederate States shall be a party; to controversies between two or more States; between a State and citizens of another State, where the State is plaintiff; between citizens claiming lands under grants of different States; and between a State or the citizens thereof, and foreign states, citizens, or subjects; but no State shall be sued by a citizen or subject of any foreign state.

(2) In all cases affecting ambassadors, other public ministers and consuls, and those in which a State shall be a party, the Supreme Court shall have original jurisdiction. In all the other cases before mentioned, the Supreme Court shall have appellate jurisdiction both as to law and fact, with such exceptions and under such regulations as the Congress shall make.

(3) The trial of all crimes, except in cases of impeachment, shall be by jury, and such trial shall be held in the State where the said crimes shall have been committed; but when not committed within any State, the trial shall be at such place or places as the Congress may by law have directed.

Sec. 3. (1) Treason against the Confederate States shall consist only in levying war against them, or in adhering to their enemies, giving them aid and comfort. No person shall be convicted of treason unless on the testimony of two witnesses to the same overt act, or on confession in open court.

(2) The Congress shall have power to declare the punishment of treason; but no attainder of treason shall work corruption of blood, or forfeiture, except during the life of the person attainted.

ARTICLE IV.

Section 1. (1) Full faith and credit shall be given in each State to the public acts, records, and judicial proceedings of every other State; and the Congress may, by general laws, prescribe the manner in which such acts, records, and proceedings shall be proved, and the effect thereof.

Sec. 2. (1) The citizens of each State shall be entitled to all the privileges and immunities of citizens in the several States; and shall have the right of transit and sojourn in any State of this Confederacy, with their slaves and other property; and the right of property in said slaves shall not be thereby impaired.

(2) A person charged in any State with treason, felony, or other crime against the laws of such State, who shall flee from justice,

and be found in another State, shall, on demand of the executive authority of the State from which he fled, be delivered up, to be removed to the State having jurisdiction of the crime.

(3) No slave or other person held to service or labor in any State or Territory of the Confederate States, under the laws thereof, escaping or lawfully carried into another, shall, in consequence of any law or regulation therein, be discharged from such service or labor; but shall be delivered up on claim of the party to whom such slave belongs, or to whom such service or labor may be due.

Sec. 3. (1) Other States may be admitted into this Confederacy by a vote of two-thirds of the whole House of Representatives and two-thirds of the Senate, the Senate voting by States; but no new State shall be formed or erected within the jurisdiction of any other State, nor any State be formed by the junction of two or more States, or parts of States, without the consent of the Legislatures of the States concerned, as well as of the Congress.

(2) The Congress shall have power to dispose of and make all needful rules and regulations concerning the property of the Confederate States, including the lands thereof.

(3) The Confederate States may acquire new territory; and Congress shall have power to legislate and provide governments for the inhabitants of all territory belonging to the Confederate States, lying without the limits of the several Sates; and may permit them, at such times, and in such manner as it may by law provide, to form States to be admitted into the Confederacy. In all such territory the institution of negro slavery, as it now exists in the Confederate States, shall be recognized and protected by Congress and by the Territorial government; and the inhabitants of the several Confederate States and Territories shall have the right to take to such Territory any slaves lawfully held by them in any of the States or Territories of the Confederate States.

(4) The Confederate States shall guarantee to every State that now is, or hereafter may become, a member of this Confederacy, a republican form of government; and shall protect each of them against invasion; and on application of the Legislature (or of the Executive when the Legislature is not in session) against domestic violence.

ARTICLE V.

Section 1. (1) Upon the demand of any three States, legally assembled in their several conventions, the Congress shall summon a convention of all the States, to take into consideration such amendments to the Constitution as the said States shall concur in suggesting at the time when the said demand is made; and should any of the proposed amendments to the Constitution be agreed on by the said convention—voting by States—and the same be ratified by the Legislatures of two-thirds of the several States, or by conventions in two-thirds thereof—as the one or the other mode of ratification may be proposed by the general convention—they shall thenceforward form a part of this Constitution. But no State shall, without its consent, be deprived of its equal representation in the Senate.

ARTICLE VI.

1. The Government established by this Constitution is the successor of the Provisional Government of the Confederate States of America, and all the laws passed by the latter shall continue in force until the same shall be repealed or modified; and all the officers appointed by the same shall remain in office until their successors are appointed and qualified, or the offices abolished.

2. All debts contracted and engagements entered into before the adoption of this Constitution shall be as valid against the Confederate States under this Constitution, as under the Provisional Government.

3. This Constitution, and the laws of the Confederate States made in pursuance thereof, and all treaties made, or which shall be made, under the authority of the Confederate States, shall be the supreme law of the land; and the judges in every State shall be bound thereby, anything in the constitution or laws of any State to the contrary notwithstanding.

4. The Senators and Representatives before mentioned, and the members of the several State Legislatures, and all executive and judicial officers, both of the Confederate States and of the several States, shall be bound by oath or affirmation to support this Constitution; but no religious test shall ever be required as a qualification to any office or public trust under the Confederate States.

5. The enumeration, in the Constitution, of certain rights shall not be construed to deny or disparage others retained by the people of the several States.

6. The powers not delegated to the Confederate States by the Constitution, nor prohibited by it to the States, are reserved to the States, respectively, or to the people thereof.

Article VII.

1. The ratification of the conventions of five States shall be sufficient for the establishment of this Constitution between the States so ratifying the same.

2. When five States shall have ratified this Constitution, in the manner before specified, the Congress under the Provisional Constitution shall prescribe the time for holding the election of President and Vice President; and for the meeting of the Electoral College; and for counting the votes, and inagurating the President. They shall, also, prescribe the time for holding the first election of members of Congress under this Constitution, and the time for assembling the same. Until the assembling of such Congress, the Congress under the Provisional Constitution shall continue to exercise the legislative powers granted them; not extending beyond the time limited by the Constitution of the Provisional Government.

Adopted unanimously by the Congress of the Confederate States of South Carolina, Georgia, Florida, Alabama, Mississippi, Louisiana, and Texas, sitting in convention at the capitol, in the city of Montgomery, Ala., on the eleventh day of March, in the year eighteen hundred and sixty-one.

Howell Cobb,
President of the Congress.

South Carolina: R. Barnwell Rhett, C. G. Memminger, Wm. Porcher Miles, James Chesnut, Jr., R. W. Barnwell, William W. Boyce, Lawrence M. Keitt, T. J. Withers.

Georgia: Francis S. Bartow, Martin J. Crawford, Benjamin H. Hill, Thos. R. R. Cobb.

Florida: Jackson Morton, J. Patton Anderson, Jas. B. Owens.

Alabama: Richard W. Walker, Robt. H. Smith, Colin J. McRae, William P. Chilton, Stephen F. Hale, David P. Lewis, Tho. Fearn, Jno. Gill Shorter, J. L. M. Curry.

Mississippi: Alex. M. Clayton, James T. Harrison, William S. Barry, W. S. Wilson, Walker Brooke, W. P. Harris, J. A. P. Campbell.

Louisiana: Alex. de Clouet, C. M. Conrad, Duncan F. Kenner, Henry Marshall.

Texas: John Hemphill, Thomas N. Waul, John H. Reagan, Williamson S. Oldham, Louis T. Wigfall, John Gregg, William Beck Ochiltree.

MESSAGES.

EXECUTIVE DEPARTMENT,
MONTGOMERY, ALA., February 25, 1861.

Hon. Howell Cobb, President of the Congress.

Sir: I hereby transmit for the advice of the Congress the following nominations of Commissioners to the Government of the United States of America in accordance with the resolution* of Congress providing for such commission, and declaratory of the purposes thereof: A. B. Roman, of Louisiana; M. J. Crawford, of Georgia; John Forsyth, of Alabama.

JEFF'N DAVIS.

LETTER OF PRESIDENT DAVIS TO PRESIDENT LINCOLN.

MONTGOMERY, February 27, 1861.

The President of the United States: Being animated by an earnest desire to unite and bind together our respective countries by friendly ties, I have appointed M. J. Crawford, one of our most settled and trustworthy citizens, as special commissioner of the Confederate States of America to the Government of the United States; and I have now the honor to introduce him to you, and to ask for him a reception and treatment corresponding to his station and to the purpose for which he is sent. Those purposes he will more particularly explain to you. Hoping that through his agency, &c. [*sic.*] JEFF'N DAVIS.

---

*The resolution is as follows:

"A RESOLUTION FOR THE APPOINTMENT OF COMMISSIONERS TO THE GOVERNMENT OF THE UNITED STATES OF AMERICA.

"*Resolved by the Confederate States of America in Congress Assembled,* That it is the sense of this Congress that a commission of three persons be appointed by the President elect, as early as may be convenient after his inauguration, and sent to the government of the United States of America, for the purpose of negotiating friendly relations between that government and the Confederate States of America, and for the settlement of all questions of disagreement between the two governments upon principles of right, justice, equity, and good faith."

Adopted February 15, 1861.

For the purpose of establishing friendly relations between the Confederate States and the United States, and reposing special trust, &c., Martin J. Crawford, John Forsyth, and A. B. Roman are appointed special commissioners of the Confederate States to the United States. I have invested them with full and all manner of power and authority for and in the name of the Confederate States to meet and confer with any person or persons duly authorized by the Government of the United States being furnished with like powers and authority, and with them to agree, treat, consult, and negotiate of and concerning all matters and subjects interesting to both nations, and to conclude and sign a treaty or treaties, convention or conventions, touching the premises, transmitting the same to the President of the Confederate States for his final ratification by and with the consent of the Congress of the Confederate States.

Given under my hand at the city of Montgomery this 27th day of February, A.D. 1861, and of the Independence of the Confederate States the eighty-fifth.

JEFF'N DAVIS.

ROBERT TOOMBS, *Secretary of State.*

EXECUTIVE OFFICE, February 26, 1861.

Gentlemen of the Congress: Though the General Government of the Confederate States is specially charged with the questions arising from the present condition of Forts Sumter and Pickens, and the Executive is required by negotiation or other means to obtain possession of those works, and though the common defense and the issues of peace or war of the Confederate States must necessarily be conducted by their general agents, the only material of war which we possess is held by the authorities of the several States. To distribute the arms and munitions so as best to provide for the defense of the country, it is needful that they be placed under the control of the General Government. We have now but little information as to the quantity and quality of the military supplies on hand, and have no authority to call for returns from the officers of the States. The courtesy and patriotism of the respective Governors would no doubt willingly meet such inquiry, and would probably induce them to transfer either armament or stores in compliance with a requisition from this Government, but efficiency requires the exclusive control as well of the means as of the works of defense. The General Government being also charged with foreign intercourse, may have in the course of negotiation to account for the property of the United States which, as a consequence of secession, passed under the authority of the several States anterior to the formation of this Government. For these considerations I respectfully suggest that the proper legislation be adopted to secure the transfer of all arms and munitions now in the forts, arsenals, and navy yards to the custody of the Government of the Confederate States, and that full returns be made of all arms and munitions which have been distributed from the public stores to the troops of the several States, with authority to this Government to take charge of the accountability for them, and also to receive, to be accounted for to the several States, such arms and munitions as have been purchased by them, and which they are willing to devote to the common service of the Confederacy. The difficulty of supplying our wants in that regard by purchases abroad or by manufacture at home is well known to the Congress, and will render unnecessary an argument to enforce the general policy herein presented, and I have only respectfully to commend the subject to your consideration.   JEFF'N DAVIS.

EXECUTIVE DEPARTMENT,
MONTGOMERY, ALA., February 26, 1861.

Hon. Howell Cobb, President of the Congress.

Sir: I hereby transmit for the advice of the Congress the following nominations, in accordance with a resolution passed February 13, 1861, to provide for a commission to proceed to Europe under instructions to be given: W. L. Yancey, of Alabama; P. A. Rost, of Louisiana; A. Dudley Mann, of Confederate States.
                                        JEFF'N DAVIS.

MONTGOMERY, ALA.,
EXECUTIVE OFFICE, March 5, 1861.

Hon. Howell Cobb, President of the Congress.

Sir: Herewith I have the honor to transmit the estimate of the

Secretary of War of the amount required for the support of the Army of the Confederate States, also, of that requisite for the support of a portion of the provisional army, authorized to be raised.

The estimate, it will be observed, is for the authorized strength of the army, and as a large portion of that force will probably not be enlisted or commissioned, there will be a balance of appropriation which, if permitted, might be used to support additional troops of a provisional army, a character of force which may be more speedily raised, and on which we must, in any early necessity, expect mainly to rely.   JEFFERSON DAVIS.

EXECUTIVE DEPARTMENT, March 12, 1861.

Hon. Howell Cobb, President of the Congress.

Sir. To enable the Secretary of War most advantageously to perform the duties devolved upon him in relation to the Indian tribes by the second section of the Act to establish the War Department of February 21, 1861, it is deemed desirable that there should be established a Bureau of Indian Affairs, and, if the Congress concur in this view, I have the honor respectfully to recommend that provision be made for the appointment of a Commissioner of Indian Affairs, and for one clerk to aid him in the discharge of his official duties.   JEFFERSON DAVIS.

EXECUTIVE DEPARTMENT, March 15, 1861.

Hon. Howell Cobb, President of the Congress.

Sir: I hereby transmit a communication from the Secretary of War, suggesting for the consideration of Congress an additional appropriation of one hundred and ten thousand dollars for the purchase of cannon powder and musket powder. Concurring in his belief that his former estimate was insufficient, the additional appropriation asked for is commended to the favorable consideration of the Congress.   JEFFERSON DAVIS.

EXECUTIVE DEPARTMENT, March 16, 1861.

Hon. Howell Cobb, President of the Congress.

Sir: I hereby transmit a communication from the Secretary of

War, suggesting an appropriation of five thousand dollars to meet the salaries and incidental expenses of the Bureau of Indian Affairs. JEFFERSON DAVIS.

VETO MESSAGE.

EXECUTIVE DEPARTMENT, February 28, 1861.

Gentlemen of Congress: With sincere deference to the judgment of Congress, I have carefully considered the bill in relation to the slave trade, and to punish persons offending therein, but have not been able to approve it, and therefore do return it with a statement of my objections. The Constitution (section 7, article I.) provides that the importation of African negroes from any foreign country other than slave-holding States of the United States is hereby forbidden, and Congress is required to pass such laws as shall effectually prevent the same. The rule herein given is emphatic, and distinctly directs the legislation which shall effectually prevent the importation of African negroes. The bill before me denounces as high misdemeanor the importation of African negroes or other persons of color, either to be sold as slaves or to be held to service or labor, affixing heavy, degrading penalties on the act, if done with such intent. To that extent it accords with the requirements of the Constitution, but in the sixth section of the bill provision is made for the transfer of persons who may have been illegally imported into the Confederate States to the custody of foreign States or societies, upon condition of deportation and future freedom, and if the proposition thus to surrender them shall not be accepted, it is then made the duty of the President to cause said negroes to be sold at public outcry to the highest bidder in any one of the States where such sale shall not be inconsistent with the laws thereof. This provision seems to me to be in opposition to the policy declared in the Constitution—the prohibition of the importation of African negroes—and in derogation of its mandate to legislate for the effectuation of that object. Wherefore the bill is returned to you for your further consideration, and, together with the objections, most respectfully submitted. JEFF'N DAVIS.

PROCLAMATIONS.

BY THE PRESIDENT OF THE CONFEDERATE STATES.

A PROCLAMATION.

Whereas, an extraordinary occasion has occurred, rendering it necessary and proper that the Congress of the Confederate States shall convene to receive and act upon such communications as may be made to it on the part of the Executive;

Now, therefore, I, Jefferson Davis, President of the Confederate States, do issue this my proclamation, convoking the Congress of the Confederate States for the transaction of business at the capitol, in the city of Montgomery, on the 29th day of April, at twelve o'clock noon of that day, of which all who shall at that time be entitled to act as members of that body are hereby required to take notice.

Given under my hand and the seal of the Confederate States, at Montgomery, this 12th day of April, A.D. 1861.

[L. S.]   JEFFERSON DAVIS.

By the President: R. TOOMBS, *Secretary of State.*

BY THE PRESIDENT OF THE CONFEDERATE STATES.

A PROCLAMATION.

Whereas, Abraham Lincoln, the President of the United States, has, by proclamation, announced the intention of invading this Confederacy with an armed force for the purpose of capturing its fortresses, and thereby subverting its independence and subjecting the free people thereof to the dominion of a foreign power; and, whereas, it has thus become the duty of this government to repel the threatened invasion, and to defend the rights and liberties of the people by all the means which the laws of nations and the usages of civilized warfare place at its disposal;

Now, therefore, I, Jefferson Davis, President of the Confederate States of America, do issue this my proclamation, inviting all those who may desire, by service in private armed vessels on the high seas, to aid this government in resisting so wanton and wicked an aggression, to make application for commissions or letters of marque and reprisal to be issued under the seal of these Confederate States.

And I do further notify all persons applying for letters of marque to make a statement in writing, giving the name and a suitable description of the character, tonnage, and force of the vessel, and the name and place of residence of each owner concerning therein, and the intended number of the crew, and to sign said statement and deliver the same to the Secretary of State, or to the collector of any port of entry of these Confederate States, to be by him transmitted to the Secretary of State.

And I do further notify all applicants aforesaid that before any commission or letter of marque is issued to any vessel, the owner or owners thereof, and the commander for the time being, will be required to give bond to the Confederate States, with at least two responsible sureties, not interested in such vessel, in the penal sum of five thousand dollars; or if such vessel be provided with more than one hundred and fifty men, then in the penal sum of ten thousand dollars, with condition that the owners, officers, and crew who shall be employed on board such commissioned vessel shall observe the laws of these Confederate States and the instructions given to them for the regulation of their conduct. That they shall satisfy all damages done contrary to the tenor thereof by such vessel during her commission, and deliver up the same when revoked by the President of the Confederate States.

And I do further specially enjoin on all persons holding offices, civil and military, under the authority of the Confederate States, that they be vigilant and zealous in discharging the duties incident thereto; and I do, moreover, solemnly exhort the good people of these Confederate States, as they love their country, as they prize the blessings of free governmnt, as they feel the wrongs of the past and these now threatened in aggravated form by those whose enmity is more implacable because unprovoked, that they exert themselves in preserving order, in promoting concord, in maintaining the authority and efficacy of the laws, and in supporting and invigorating all the measures which may be adopted for the common defense, and by which, under the blessings of Divine Providence, we may hope for a speedy, just, and honorable peace.

In testimony whereof I have hereunto set my hand, and caused the seal of the Confederate States to be affixed, this seventeenth day of April, 1861.

[Signed]   JEFFERSON DAVIS.

By the President: R. TOOMBS, *Secretary of State.*

JEFFERSON DAVIS, PRESIDENT OF THE CONFEDERATE STATES OF AMERICA, TO ALL WHOM THESE PRESENTS SHALL CONCERN, GREETING:

Know ye, that for the purpose of establishing friendly relations between the Confederate States of America and the Commonwealth of Virginia, and reposing special trust and confidence in the integrity, prudence, and ability of Alexander .H. Stephens, Vice President of the Confederate States of America, appointed special commissioner of the Confederate States to the Commonwealth of Virginia, I have invested him with full and all manner of power and authority, for and in the name of the Confederate States, to meet and confer with any person or persons authorized by the Government of Virginia, being furnished with like power and authority, and with him or them to agree, treat, consult, and negotiate of and concerning all matters and subjects interesting to both Republics; and to conclude and sign a treaty or treaties, convention or conventions, touching the premises, transmitting the same to the President of the Confederate States for his final ratification, by and with the advice and consent of the Congress of the Confederate States.

In testimony whereof I have caused the seal of the Confederate States to be hereunto affixed.

Given under my hand at the city of Montgomery this 19th day of April, A.D. 1861.   JEFF'N DAVIS.

By the President: ROBERT TOOMBS, *Secretary of State.*

SECOND SESSION (CALLED).

MET AT MONTGOMERY, ALA., APRIL 29, 1861. ADJOURNED
MAY 21, 1861.

MESSAGES.

MONTGOMERY, April 29, 1861.

Gentlemen of the Congress: It is my pleasing duty to announce
to you that the Constitution framed for the establishment of a
permanent Government for the Confederate States has been ratified by conventions in each of those States to which it was referred. To inaugurate the Government in its full proportions
and upon its own substantial basis of the popular will, it only
remains that elections should be held for the designation of the
officers to administer it. There is every reason to believe that at
no distant day other States, identified in political principles and
community of interests with those which you represent, will join
this Confederacy, giving to its typical constellation increased
splendor, to its Government of free, equal, and sovereign States
a wider sphere of usefulness, and to the friends of constitutional
liberty a greater security for its harmonious and perpetual existence. It was not, however, for the purpose of making this announcement that I have deemed it my duty to convoke you at an
earlier day than that fixed by yourselves for your meeting. The
declaration of war made against this Confederacy by Abraham
Lincoln, the President of the United States, in his proclamation
issued on the 15th day of the present month, rendered it necessary, in my judgment, that you should convene at the earliest
practicable moment to devise the measures necessary for the defense of the country. The occasion is indeed an extraordinary
one. It justifies me in a brief review of the relations heretofore
existing between us and the States which now unite in warfare
against us and in a succinct statement of the events which have
resulted in this warfare, to the end that mankind may pass intelligent and impartial judgment on its motives and objects. During
the war waged against Great Britain by her colonies on this continent a common danger impelled them to a close alliance and to
the formation of a Confederation, by the terms of which the col-

onies, styling themselves States, entered *"severally* into a firm league of friendship with each other for their common defense, the security of their liberties, and their mutual and general welfare, binding themselves to assist each other against all force offered to or attacks made upon them, or any of them, on account of religion, sovereignty, trade, or any other pretense whatever." In order to guard against any misconstruction of their compact, the several States made explicit declaration in a distinct article—that *"each* State *retains its* sovereignty, freedom, and independence, and every power, jurisdiction, and right which is not by this Confederation *expressly delegated* to the United States in Congress assembled."

Under this contract of alliance, the war of the Revolution was successfully waged, and resulted in the treaty of peace with Great Britain in 1783, by the terms of which the several States were *each by name* recognized to be independent. The Articles of Confederation contained a clause whereby all alterations were prohibited unless confirmed by the Legislatures of *every State* after being agreed to by the Congress; and in obedience to this provision, under the resolution of Congress of the 21st of February, 1787, the several States appointed delegates who attended a convention "for the *sole and express purpose* of revising the Articles of Confederation and reporting to Congress and the several Legislatures such alterations and provisions therein as shall, when agreed to in Congress *and confirmed by the States,* render the Federal Constitution adequate to the exigencies of Government and the preservation of the Union." It was by the delegates chosen by the *several States* under the resolution just quoted that the Constitution of the United States was framed in 1787 and submitted to the *several States* for ratification, as shown by the seventh article, which is in these words: "The ratification of the *conventions of nine States* shall be sufficient for the establishment of this Constitution *between the States* so ratifying the same." I have italicized certain words in the quotations just made for the purpose of attracting attention to the singular and marked caution with which the States endeavored in every possible form to exclude the idea that the separate and independent sovereignty of each State was merged into one common government and nation, and the earnest desire they evinced to impress on the Constitution its true character—that of a *compact between* independent States. The Constitution of 1787, having, however, omitted the clause already recited from the Articles of Confederation, which provided in explicit terms that each State *retained* its sovereignty and independence, some alarm was felt in the States, when invited to ratify the Constitution, lest this omission should be construed into an abandonment of their cherished principle, and they refused to be satisfied until amendments were added to the Constitution placing beyond any pretense of doubt the reservation by the States of all their sovereign rights and powers not expressly delegated to the United States by the Constitution.

Strange, indeed, must it appear to the impartial observer, but it is none the less true that all these carefully worded clauses proved unavailing to prevent the rise and growth in the Northern States of a political school which has persistently claimed that the government thus formed was not a compact *between* States, but was in effect a national government, set up *above* and *over* the States. An organization created by the States to secure the blessings of liberty and independence against *foreign* aggression, has been gradually perverted into a machine for their control in their *domestic* affairs. The *creature* has been exalted above its *creators;* the *principals* have been made subordinate to the *agent* appointed by themselves. The people of the Southern States, whose almost exclusive occupation was agriculture, early perceived a tendency in the Northern States to render the common government subservient to their own purposes by imposing burdens on commerce as a protection to their manufacturing and shipping interests. Long and angry controversies grew out of these attempts, often successful, to benefit one section of the country at the expense of the other. And the danger of disruption arising from this cause was enhanced by the fact that the Northern population was increasing, by immigration and other causes, in a greater ratio than the population of the South. By degrees, as the Northern States gained preponderance in the National Congress, self-interest taught their people to yield ready assent to any plausible advocacy of their right as a majority to govern the minority without control. They learned to listen with impatience to the suggestion of any constitutional impediment to the exercise of their will, and so utterly have the principles of the Constitution been corrupted in the Northern mind that, in the inaugural address delivered by President Lincoln in March last, he asserts as an axiom, which he plainly deems to be undeniable, that the theory of the Constitution requires that in all cases the majority shall govern; and in another memorable instance the same Chief Magistrate did not hesitate to liken the relations between a State and the United States to those which exist between a county and the State in which it is situated and by which it was created. This is the lamentable and fundamental error on which rests the policy that has culminated in his declaration of war against these Confederate States. In addition to the long-continued and deep-seated resentment felt by the Southern States at the persistent abuse of the powers they had delegated to the Congress, for the purpose of enriching the manufacturing and shipping classes of the North at the expense of the South, there has existed for nearly half a century another subject of discord, involving interests of such transcendent magnitude as at all times to create the apprehension in the minds of many devoted lovers of the Union that its permanence was impossible. When the several States delegated certain powers to the United States Congress, a large portion of the laboring population consisted of African slaves imported into the colonies by the mother country. In twelve out of the thirteen States negro slavery existed, and the right of property in slaves was protected by law. This property was recognized in the Constitution, and provision was made against its loss by the escape of the slave. The increase in the number of slaves by further importation from Africa was also secured by a clause forbidding Congress to prohibit the slave trade anterior to a certain date, and in no clause can there be found any delegation of power to the Congress authorizing it in any manner to legislate to the prejudice, detriment, or discouragement of the owners of that species of property, or excluding it from the protection of the Government.

The climate and soil of the Northern States soon proved unpropitious to the continuance of slave labor, whilst the converse was the case at the South. Under the unrestricted free intercourse between the two sections, the Northern States consulted their own interests by selling their slaves to the South and prohibiting slavery within their limits. The South were willing purchasers of a property suitable to their wants, and paid the price of the acquisition without harboring a suspicion that their quiet possession was to be disturbed by those who were inhibited not only by want of constitutional authority, but by good faith as vendors, from disquieting a title emanating from themselves. As soon, however, as the Northern States that prohibited African slavery within their limits had reached a number sufficient to give their representation a controlling voice in the Congress, a persistent and organized system of hostile measures against the rights of the owners of slaves in the Southern States was inaugurated and gradually extended. A continuous series of measures was devised and prosecuted for the purpose of rendering insecure the tenure of property in slaves. Fanatical organizations, supplied with money by voluntary subscriptions, were assiduously engaged in exciting amongst the slaves a spirit of discontent and revolt; means were furnished for their escape from their owners, and agents secretly employed to entice them to abscond; the constitutional provision for their rendition to their owners was first evaded, then openly denounced as a violation of conscientious obligation and religious duty; men were taught that it was a merit to elude, disobey, and violently oppose the execution of the laws enacted to secure the performance of the promise contained in the constitutional compact; owners of slaves were mobbed and even murdered in open day solely for applying to a magistrate for the arrest of a fugitive slave; the dogmas of these voluntary organizations soon obtained control of the Legislatures of many of the Northern States, and laws were passed providing for the punishment, by ruinous fines and long-continued imprisonment in jails and penitentiaries, of citizens of the Southern States who should dare to ask aid of the officers of the law for the recovery of their property. Emboldened by success, the theater of agitation and aggression against the clearly expressed constitutional rights of the Southern States was transferred to the Congress; Senators and Representatives were sent to the common councils of the nation, whose chief title to this distinction consisted in the display of a spirit of ultra fanaticism, and whose business was not "to promote the general welfare or insure domestic tranquillity," but to awaken the bitterest hatred against the citizens of sister States by violent denunciation of their institutions; the transaction of public affairs was impeded by repeated efforts to usurp powers not delegated by the Constitution, for the purpose of impairing the security of property in slaves, and reducing those States which held slaves to a condition of inferiority. Finally a great party was organized for the purpose of obtaining the administration of the Government, with the avowed object of using its power for the total exclusion of the slave States from all participation in the benefits of the public domain acquired by all the States in common, whether by conquest or purchase; of surrounding them entirely by States in which slavery should be prohibited; of thus rendering the property in slaves so insecure as to be comparatively worthless, and thereby annihilating in effect property worth thousands of millions of dollars. This party, thus organized, succeeded in the month of November last in the election of its candidate for the Presidency of the United States.

In the meantime, under the mild and genial climate of the Southern States and the increasing care and attention for the well-being and comfort of the laboring class, dictated alike by interest and humanity, the African slaves had augmented in number from about 600,000, at the date of the adoption of the constitutional compact, to upward of 4,000,000. In moral and social condition they had been elevated from brutal savages into docile, intelligent, and civilized agricultural laborers, and supplied not only with bodily comforts but with careful religious instruction. Under the supervision of a superior race their labor had been so directed as not only to allow a gradual and marked amelioration of their own condition, but to convert hundreds of thousands of square miles of the wilderness into cultivated lands covered with a prosperous people; towns and cities had sprung into existence, and had rapidly increased in wealth and population under the social system of the South; the white population of the Southern slaveholding States had augmented from about 1,250,000 at the date of the adoption of the Constitution to more than 8,500,000 in 1860; and the productions of the South in cotton, rice, sugar, and tobacco, for the full development and continuance of which the labor of African slaves was and is indispensable, had swollen to an amount which formed nearly three-fourths of the exports of the whole United States and had become absolutely necessary to the wants of civilized man. With interests of such overwhelming magnitude imperiled, the people of the Southern States were driven by the conduct of the North to the adoption of some course of action to avert the danger with which they were openly menaced. With this view the Legislatures of the several States invited the people to select delegates to conventions to be held for the purpose of determining for themselves what measures were best adapted to meet so alarming a crisis in their history. Here it may be proper to observe that from a period as early as 1798 there had existed in *all* of the States of the Union a party almost uninterruptedly in the majority based upon the creed that each State was, in the last resort, the sole judge as well of its wrongs as of the mode and measure of redress. Indeed, it is obvious that under the law of nations this principle is an axiom as applied to the relations of independent sovereign States, such as those which had united themselves under the constitutional compact. The Democratic party of the United States repeated, in its successful canvass in 1856, the declaration made in numerous previous political contests, that it would "faithfully abide by and uphold the principles laid down in the Kentucky and Virginia resolutions of 1798, and in the report of Mr. Madison to the Virginia Legislature in 1799; and that it adopts those principles as constituting one of the main foundations of its political creed." The principles thus emphatically announced embrace that to which I have already adverted—the right of each State to judge of and redress the wrongs of which it complains. These principles were maintained by overwhelming majorities of the people of all the States of the Union at different elections, especially in the elections of Mr. Jefferson in 1805, Mr. Madison in 1809, and Mr. Pierce in 1852. In the exercise of a right so ancient, so well-established, and so necessary for self-preservation, the people of the Confederate States, in their conventions, determined that the wrongs which they had suffered and the evils with which they were menaced required that they should revoke the delegation of powers to the Federal Government which they had ratified in their several conventions. They consequently passed ordinances resuming all their rights as sovereign and independent States and dissolved their connection with the other States of the Union.

Having done this, they proceeded to form a new compact amongst themselves by new articles of confederation, which have been also ratified by the conventions of the several States with an approach to unanimity far exceeding that of the conventions which adopted the Constitution of 1787. They have organized their new Government in all its departments; the functions of the executive, legislative, and judicial magistrates are performed in accordance with the will of the people, as displayed not merely in a cheerful acquiescence, but in the enthusiastic support of the Government thus established by themselves; and but for the interference of the Government of the United States in this legitimate exercise of the right of a people to self-government, peace, happiness, and prosperity would now smile on our land. That peace is ardently desired by this Government and people has been manifested in every possible form. Scarce had you assembled in February last when, prior even to the inauguration of the Chief Magistrate you had elected, you passed a resolution expressive of your desire for the appointment of commissioners to be sent to the Government of the United States "for the purpose of negotiating friendly relations between that Government and the Confederate States of America, and for the settlement of all questions of disagreement between the two Governments upon principles of right, justice, equity, and good faith." It was my pleasure as well as my duty to coöperate with you in this work of peace. Indeed, in my address to you on taking the oath of office, and before receiving from you the communication of this resolution, I had said "as a necessity, not a choice, we have resorted to the remedy of separation, and henceforth our energies must be directed to the conduct of our own affairs and the perpetuity of the Confederacy which we have formed. If a just perception of mutual interests shall permit us peaceably to pursue our separate political career, my most earnest desire will have been fulfilled." It was in furtherance of these accordant views of the Congress and the Executive that I made choice of three discreet, able, and distinguished citizens, who repaired to Washington. Aided by their cordial coöperation and that of the Secretary of State, every effort compatible with self-respect and the dignity of the Confederacy was exhausted before I allowed myself to yield to the conviction that the Government of the United States was determined to attempt the conquest of this people and that our cherished hopes of peace were unattainable.

On the arrival of our commissioners in Washington on the 5th of March they postponed, at the suggestion of a friendly intermediary, doing more than giving informal notice of their arrival. This was done with a view to afford time to the President, who had just been inaugurated, for the discharge of other pressing official duties in the organization of his Administration before engaging his attention in the object of their mission. It was not until the 12th of the month that they officially addressed the Secretary of State, informing him of the purpose of their arrival, and stating, in the language of their instructions, their wish "to .make to the Government of the United States overtures for the opening of negotiations, assuring the Government of the United States that the President, Congress, and people of the Confederate States earnestly desire a peaceful solution of these great questions; that it is neither their interest nor their wish to make any demand which is not founded on strictest justice, nor do any act to injure their late confederates."

To this communication no formal reply was received until the 8th of April. During the interval the commissioners had consented to waive all questions of form. With the firm resolve to avoid war if possible, they went so far even as to hold during that long period unofficial intercourse through an intermediary, whose high position and character inspired the hope of success, and through whom constant assurances were received from the Government of the United States of peaceful intentions; of the determination to evacuate Fort Sumter; and further, that no measure changing the existing status prejudicially to the Confederate States, especially at Fort Pickens, was in contemplation, but that in the event of any change of intention on the subject, notice would be given to the commissioners. The crooked paths of diplomacy can scarcely furnish an example so wanting in courtesy, in candor, and directness as was the course of the United States Government toward our commissioners in Washington. For proof of this I refer to the annexed documents marked ——,* taken in connection with further facts, which I now proceed to relate.

Early in April the attention of the whole country, as well as that of our commissioners, was attracted to extraordinary preparations for an extensive military and naval expedition in New York and other Northern ports. These preparations commenced in secrecy, for an expedition whose destination was concealed,

---

*Not found herewith, but see message of President Davis, May 8, 1861, page 82.

only became known when nearly completed, and on the 5th, 6th, and 7th of April transports and vessels of war with troops, munitions, and military supplies sailed from Northern ports bound southward. Alarmed by so extraordinary a demonstration, the commissioners requested the delivery of an answer to their official communication of the 12th of March, and thereupon received on the 8th of April a reply, dated on the 15th of the previous month, from which it appears that during the whole interval, whilst the commissioners were receiving assurances calculated to inspire hope of the success of their mission, the Secretary of State and the President of the United States had already determined to hold no intercourse with them whatever; to refuse even to listen to any proposals they had to make, and had profited by the delay created by their own assurances in order to prepare secretly the means for effective hostile operations. That these assurances were given has been virtually confessed by the Government of the United States by its sending a messenger to Charleston to give notice of its purpose to use force if opposed in its intention of supplying Fort Sumter. No more striking proof of the absence of good faith in the conduct of the Government of the United States toward this Confederacy can be required than is contained in the circumstances which accompanied this notice. According to the usual course of navigation the vessels composing the expedition designed for the relief of Fort Sumter might be expected to reach Charleston Harbor on the 9th of April. Yet, with our commissioners actually in Washington, detained under assurances that notice should be given of any military movement, the notice was not addressed to *them,* but a messenger was sent to Charleston to give the notice to the Governor of South Carolina, and the notice was so given at a late hour on the 8th of April, the eve of the very day on which the fleet might be expected to arrive.

That this maneuver failed in its purpose was not the fault of those who contrived it. A heavy tempest delayed the arrival of the expedition and gave time to the commander of our forces at Charleston to ask and receive the instructions of this Government. Even then, under all the provocation incident to the contemptuous refusal to listen to our commissioners, and the tortuous course of the Government of the United States, I was sincerely anxious to avoid the effusion of blood, and directed a proposal to be made to the commander of Fort Sumter, who had avowed himself to be nearly out of provisions, that we would abstain from directing our fire on Fort Sumter if he would promise not to open fire on our forces unless first attacked. This proposal was refused and the conclusion was reached that the design of the United States was to place the besieging force at Charleston between the simultaneous fire of the fleet and the fort. There remained, therefore, no alternative but to direct that the fort should at once be reduced. This order was executed by General Beauregard with the skill and success which were naturally to be expected from the well-known character of that gallant officer; and although the bombardment lasted but thirty-three hours our flag did not wave over its battered walls until after the appearance of the hostile fleet off Charleston. Fortunately, not a life was lost on our side, and we were gratified in being spared the necessity of a useless effusion of blood, by the prudent caution of the officers who commanded the fleet in abstaining from the evidently futile effort to enter the harbor for the relief of Major Anderson.

I refer to the report of the Secretary of War, and the papers which accompany it, for further details of this brilliant affair. In this connection I cannot refrain from a well-deserved tribute to the noble State, the eminent soldierly qualities of whose people were so conspicuously displayed in the port of Charleston. For months they had been irritated by the spectacle of a fortress held within their principal harbor as a standing menace against their peace and independence. Built in part with their own money, its custody confided with their own consent to an agent who held no power over them other than such as they had themselves delegated for their own benefit, intended to be used by that agent for their own protection against foreign attack, they saw it held with persistent tenacity as a means of offense against them by the very Government which they had established for their protection. They had beleaguered it for months, felt entire confidence in their power to capture it, yet yielded to the requirements of discipline, curbed their impatience, submitted without complaint to the unaccustomed hardships, labors, and privations of a protracted siege; and when at length their patience was rewarded by the signal for attack, and success had crowned their steady and gallant conduct, even in the very moment of triumph they evinced a chivalrous regard for the feelings of the brave but unfortunate officer who had been compelled to lower his flag. All manifestations of exultation were checked in his presence. Their commanding general, with their cordial approval and the consent of his Government, refrained from imposing any terms that could wound the sensibilities of the commander of the fort. He was permitted to retire with the honors of war, to salute his flag, to depart freely with all his command, and was escorted to the vessel in which he embarked with the highest marks of respect from those against whom his guns had been so recently directed.

Not only does every event connected with the siege reflect the highest honor on South Carolina, but the forbearance of her people and of this Government from making any harsh use of a victory obtained under circumstances of such peculiar provocation attest to the fullest extent the absence of any purpose beyond securing their own tranquillity and the sincere desire to avoid the calamities of war. Scarcely had the President of the United States received intelligence of the failure of the scheme which he had devised for the reënforcement of Fort Sumter, when he issued the declaration of war against this Confederacy which has prompted me to convoke you. In this extraordinary production that high functionary affects total ignorance of the existence of an independent Government, which, possessing the entire and enthusiastic devotion of its people, is exercising its functions without question over seven sovereign States, over more than 5,000,000 of people, and over a territory whose area exceeds half a million of square miles. He terms sovereign States "combinations too powerful to be suppressed by the ordinary course of judicial proceedings or by the powers vested in the marshals by law." He calls for an army of 75,000 men to act as a *posse comitatus* in aid of the process of the courts of justice in States where no courts exist whose mandates and decrees are not cheerfully obeyed and respected by a willing people. He avows that "the *first* service to be assigned to the forces called out" will be not to execute the process of courts, but to capture forts and strongholds situated within the admitted limits of this Confederacy and garrisoned by its troops; and declares that "this effort" is intended "to maintain the perpetuity of popular government." He concludes by commanding "the persons composing the combinations

aforesaid"—to wit, the 5,000,000 of inhabitants of these States—
"to retire peaceably to their respective abodes within twenty
days." Apparently contradictory as are the terms of this singular
document, one point is unmistakably evident. The President of
the United States called for an army of 75,000 men, whose *first*
service was to be to capture our forts. It was a plain declaration
of war which I was not at liberty to disregard because of my
knowledge that under the Constitution of the United States the
President was usurping a power granted exclusively to the Congress. He is the sole organ of communication between that country and foreign powers. The law of nations did not permit me to
question the authority of the Executive of a foreign nation to declare war against this Confederacy. Although I might have refrained from taking active measures for our defense, if the States
of the Union had all imitated the action of Virginia, North Carolina, Arkansas, Kentucky, Tennessee, and Missouri, by denoun-
cing the call for troops as an unconstitutional usurpation of power
to which they refused to respond, I was not at liberty to disregard
the fact that many of the States seemed quite content to submit
to the exercise of the power assumed by the President of the
United States, and were actively engaged in levying troops to be
used for the purpose indicated in the proclamation. Deprived of
the aid of Congress at the moment, I was under the necessity of
confining my action to a call on the States for volunteers for the
common defense, in accordance with the authority you had confided to me before your adjournment. I deemed it proper, further,
to issue proclamation* inviting application from persons disposed
to aid our defense in private armed vessels on the high seas, to
the end that preparations might be made for the immediate issue
of letters of marque and reprisal which you alone, under the Constitution, have power to grant. I entertain no doubt you will concur with me in the opinion that in the absence of a fleet of public
vessels it will be eminently expedient to supply their place by private armed vessels, so happily styled by the publicists of the United
States "the militia of the sea," and so often and justly relied on
by them as an efficient and admirable instrument of defensive
warfare. I earnestly recommend the immediate passage of a law
authorizing me to accept the numerous proposals already received.

* See page 60.

I cannot close this review of the acts of the Government of the United States without referring to a proclamation issued by their President, under date of the 19th instant, in which, after declaring that an insurrection has broken out in this Confederacy against the Government of the United States, he announces a blockade of all the ports of these States, and threatens to punish as pirates all persons who shall molest any vessel of the United States under letters of marque issued by this Government. Notwithstanding the authenticity of this proclamation you will concur with me that it is hard to believe it could have emanated from a President of the United States. Its announcement of a mere paper blockade is so manifestly a violation of the law of nations that it would seem incredible that it could have been issued by authority; but conceding this to be the case so far as the Executive is concerned, it will be difficult to satisfy the people of these States that their late confederates will sanction its declarations—will determine to ignore the usages of civilized nations, and will inaugurate a war of extermination on both sides by treating as pirates open enemies acting under the authority of commissions issued by an organized government. If such proclamation was issued, it could only have been published under the sudden influence of passion, and we may rest assured mankind will be spared the horrors of the conflict it seems to invite.

For the details of the administration of the different Departments I refer to the reports of the Secretaries, which accompany this message.

The State Department has furnished the necessary instructions for three commissioners who have been sent to England, France, Russia, and Belgium since your adjournment to ask our recognition as a member of the family of nations, and to make with each of those powers treaties of amity and commerce. Further steps will be taken to enter into like negotiations with the other European powers, in pursuance of your resolutions passed at the last session. Sufficient time has not yet elapsed since the departure of these commissioners for the receipt of any intelligence from them. As I deem it desirable that commissioners or other diplomatic agents should also be sent at an early period to the independent American powers south of our Confederacy, with all of whom it is our interest and earnest wish to maintain the most cordial and friendly relations, I suggest the expediency of making the necessary appropriations for that purpose. Having been officially notified by the public authorities of the State of Virginia that she had withdrawn from the Union and desired to maintain the closest political relations with us which it was possible at this time to establish, I commissioned the Hon. Alexander H. Stephens, Vice President of the Confederate States, to represent this Government at Richmond.* I am happy to inform you that he has concluded a convention with the State of Virginia by which that honored Commonwealth, so long and justly distinguished among her sister States, and so dear to the hearts of thousands of her children in the Confederate States, has united her power and her fortunes with ours and become one of us. This convention, together with the ordinance of Virginia adopting the Provisional Constitution of the Confederacy, will be laid before you for your constitutional action. I have satisfactory assurances from other of our late confederates that they are on the point of adopting similar measures, and I cannot doubt that ere you shall have been many weeks in session the whole of the slaveholding States of the late Union will respond to the call of honor and affection, and by uniting their fortunes with ours promote our common interests and secure our common safety.

In the Treasury Department regulations have been devised and put into execution for carrying out the policy indicated in your legislation on the subject of the navigation of the Mississippi River, as well as for the collection of revenue on the frontier. Free transit has been secured for vessels and merchandise passing through the Confederate States; and delay and inconvenience have been avoided as far as possible, in organizing the revenue service for the various railways entering our territory. As fast as experience shall indicate the possibility of improvement in these regulations no effort will be spared to free commerce from all unnecessary embarrassments and obstructions. Under your act authorizing a loan, proposals were issued inviting subscriptions for $5,000,000, and the call was answered by the prompt subscription of more than $8,000,000 by our own citizens, and not a single bid was made under par. The rapid development of the purpose of the President of the United States to invade our soil, capture our

_____

*See page 62.

forts, blockade our ports, and wage war against us induced me
to direct that the entire subscription should be accepted. It will
now become necessary to raise means to a much larger amount to
defray the expenses of maintaining our independence and repelling
invasion. I invite your special attention to this subject, and the
financial condition of the Government, with the suggestion of
ways and means for the supply of the Treasury, will be presented
to you in a separate communication.

To the Department of Justice you have confided not only the
organization and supervision of all matters connected with the
courts of justice, but also those. connected with patents and with
the bureau of public printing. Since your adjournment all the
courts, with the exception of those of Mississippi and Texas, have
been organized by the appointment of marshals and district attorneys and are now prepared for the exercise of their functions.
In the two States just named the gentlemen confirmed as judges
declined to accept the appointment, and no nominations have yet
been made to fill the vacancies. I refer you to the report of the
Attorney-General and concur in his recommendation for immediate legislation, especially on the subject of patent rights. Early
provision should be made to secure to the subjects of foreign nations the full enjoyment of their property in valuable inventions,
and to extend to our own citizens protection, not only for their
own inventions, but for such as may have been assigned to them
or may hereafter be assigned by persons not alien enemies. The
Patent Office business is much more extensive and important than
had been anticipated. The applications for patents, although confined under the law exclusively to citizens of our Confederacy, already average seventy per month, showing the necessity for the
prompt organization of a bureau of patents.

The Secretary of War in his report and accompanying documents conveys full information concerning the forces—regular,
volunteer, and provisional—raised and called for under the several acts of Congress—their organization and distribution; also
an account of the expenditures already made, and the further estimates for the fiscal year ending the 18th of February, 1862, rendered necessary by recent events. I refer to his report also for a
full history of the occurrences in Charleston Harbor prior to and
including the bombardment and reduction of Fort Sumter, and

of the measures subsequently taken for the common defense on receiving the intelligence of the declaration of war against us, made by the President of the United States. There are now in the field at Charleston, Pensacola, Forts Morgan, Jackson, Saint Philip, and Pulaski 19,000 men, and 16,000 are now *en route* for Virginia. It is proposed to organize and hold in readiness for instant action, in view of the present exigencies of the country, an army of 100,000 men. If further force should be needed, the wisdom and patriotism of Congress will be confidently appealed to for authority to call into the field additional numbers of our noble-spirited volunteers who are constantly tendering service far in excess of our wants.

The operations of the Navy Department have been necessarily restricted by the fact that sufficient time has not yet elapsed for the purchase or construction of more than a limited number of vessels adapted to the public service. Two vessels purchased have been named the Sumter and McRae, and are now being prepared for sea at New Orleans with all possible dispatch. Contracts have also been made at that city with two different establishments for the casting of ordnance—cannon shot and shell—with the view to encourage the manufacture of these articles, so indispensable for our defense, at as many points within our territory as possible. I call your attention to the recommendation of the Secretary for the establishment of a magazine and laboratory for preparation of ordnance stores and the necessary appropriation for that purpose. Hitherto such stores have usually been prepared at the navy yards, and no appropriation was made at your last session for this object. The Secretary also calls attention to the fact that no provision has been made for the payment of invalid pensions to our own citizens. Many of these persons are advanced in life; they have no means of support, and by the secession of these States have been deprived of their claim against the Government of the United States. I recommend the appropriation of the sum necessary to pay these pensioners, as well as those of the Army, whose claims can scarcely exceed $70,000 per annum.

The Postmaster General has already succeeded in organizing his Department to such an extent as to be in readiness to assume the direction of our postal affairs on the occurrence of the contingency contemplated by the act of March 15, 1861, or even sooner if desired by Congress. The various books and circulars have been prepared and measures taken to secure supplies of blanks, postage stamps, stamped envelopes, mail bags, locks, keys, etc. He presents a detailed classification and arrangement of his clerical force, and asks for its increase. An auditor of the Treasury for this Department is necessary, and a plan is submitted for the organization of his bureau. The great number and magnitude of the accounts of this Department require an increase of the clerical force in the accounting branch in the Treasury. The revenues of this Department are collected and disbursed in modes peculiar to itself, and require a special bureau to secure a proper accountability in the administration of its finances. I call your attention to the additional legislation required for this Department; to the recommendation for changes in the law fixing the rates of postage on newspapers, periodicals, and sealed packages of certain kinds, and specially to the recommendation of the Secretary, in which I concur, that you provide at once for the assumption by him of the control of our entire postal service.

In the military organization of the States provision is made for brigadier and major generals, but in the Army of the Confederate States the highest grade is that of brigadier general. Hence it will no doubt sometimes occur that where troops of the Confederacy do duty with the militia, the general selected for the command and possessed of the views and purposes of this Government will be superseded by an officer of the militia not having the same advantages. To avoid this contingency in the least objectionable manner I recommend that additional rank be given to the general of the Confederate Army, and concurring in the policy of having but one grade of generals in the Army of the Confederacy, I recommend that the law of its organization be amended so that the grade be that of general. To secure a thorough military education it is deemed essential that officers should enter upon the study of their profession at an early period of life and have elementary instruction in a military school. Until such school shall be established it is recommended that cadets be appointed and attached to companies until they shall have attained the age and have acquired the knowledge to fit them for the duties of lieutenants. I also call

your attention to an omission in the law organizing the Army, in relation to military chaplains, and recommend that provision be made for their appointment.

In conclusion, I congratulate you on the fact that in every portion of our country there has been exhibited the most patriotic devotion to our common cause. Transportation companies have freely tendered the use of their lines for troops and supplies. The presidents of the railroads of the Confederacy, in company with others who control lines of communication with States that we hope soon to greet as sisters, assembled in convention in this city, and not only reduced largely the rates heretofore demanded for mail service and conveyance of troops and munitions, but voluntarily proffered to receive their compensation, at these reduced rates, in the bonds of the Confederacy, for the purpose of leaving all the resources of the Government at its disposal for the common defense. Requisitions for troops have been met with such alacrity that the numbers tendering their services have in every instance greatly exceeded the demand. Men of the highest official and social position are serving as volunteers in the ranks. The gravity of age and the zeal of youth rival each other in the desire to be foremost for the public defense; and though at no other point than the one heretofore noticed have they been stimulated by the excitement incident to actual engagement and the hope of distinction for individual achievement, they have borne what for new troops is the most severe ordeal—patient toil and constant vigil, and all the exposure and discomfort of active service, with a resolution and fortitude such as to command approbation and justify the highest expectation of their conduct when active valor shall be required in place of steady endurance. A people thus united and resolved cannot shrink from any sacrifice which they may be called on to make, nor can there be a reasonable doubt of their final success, however long and severe may be the test of their determination to maintain their birthright of freedom and equality as a trust which it is their first duty to transmit undiminished to their posterity. A bounteous Providence cheers us with the promise of abundant crops. The fields of grain which will within a few weeks be ready for the sickle give assurance of the amplest supply of food for man; whilst the corn, cotton, and other staple productions of our soil afford abundant proof that up to this period the season has been propitious. We feel that our cause is just and holy; we protest solemnly in the face of mankind that we desire peace at any sacrifice save that of honor and independence; we seek no conquest, no aggrandizement, no concession of any kind from the States with which we were lately confederated; all we ask is to be let alone; that those who never held power over us shall not now attempt our subjugation by arms. This we will, this we must, resist to the direst extremity. The moment that this pretension is abandoned the sword will drop from our grasp, and we shall be ready to enter into treaties of amity and commerce that cannot but be mutually beneficial. So long as this pretension is maintained, with a firm reliance on that Divine Power which covers with its protection the just cause, we will continue to struggle for our inherent right to freedom, independence, and self-government.   JEFFERSON DAVIS.

To the Congress of the Confederate States.

I lay before the Congress, for their consideration and advice as to its ratification, a copy of the convention between the Confederate States and the Commonwealth of Virginia, which was signed at the city of Richmond on the twenty-fourth day of April, 1861, by the Hon. Alexander H. Stephens on the part of the Confederate States, and by commissioners appointed for that purpose on the part of the State of Virginia.

While performing this act, I congratulate the Congress and the people of the Confederate States upon the conclusion of this alliance by which the great and powerful State of Virginia has made common cause with us and joined her energies and resources to ours for our common defense against the unprovoked war of aggression which the Chief Magistrate of the United States has declared against us.   JEFFERSON DAVIS.

Montgomery, May 6, 1861.

MONTGOMERY, Wednesday, May 8, 1861.

Gentlemen of the Congress: In the message addressed to you on the 29th ultimo,* I referred to the course of conduct of the Gov-

---

*See page 63.

ernment of the United States toward the commissioners of this
Government sent to Washington for the purpose of effecting, if
possible, a peaceful adjustment of the pending difficulties between
the two Governments.* I also made allusion to "an intermediary,
whose high position and character inspired the hope of success;"
but I was not then at liberty to make any communication on the
subject as specific as was desirable for a full comprehension of the
whole subject. It is now, however, in my power to place before
you other papers, which I herewith address to you from them.
You will perceive that the intermediary referred to was Hon. John
A. Campbell, a judge of the Supreme Court of the United States,
who made earnest efforts to promote the successful issue of the
mission intrusted to our commissioners, and by whom I was kept
advised, in confidential communication, of the measures taken by
him to secure so desirable a result. It is due to you, to him, and to
history that a narration of the occurrences with which he was connected should be made known, the more especially as it will be
seen by the letters hereto appended that the correctness and accuracy of the recital have not been questioned by the Secretary of
State of the United States, to whom it was addressed. I avail myself of this opportunity to correct an error in one of the statements
made in my message of the 29th of April. It is there recited† that
I was prompted to call you together in extraordinary session by
reason of the declarations contained in the proclamation of President Lincoln of the 15th of April. My proclamation, convoking
you, was issued on the 12th of April,‡ and was prompted by the
declaration of hostile purposes contained in the message sent by
the President to the Governor of South Carolina on the 8th of
April. As the proclamation of President Lincoln of the 15th of
April repeated the same hostile intention in more specific terms
and on a much more extensive scale, it created a stronger impression on my mind, and led to the error above alluded to, and which,
however unimportant, I desire to correct.   JEFF'N DAVIS.

---

*See page 70.   †See page 63.   ‡See page 60.

CORRESPONDENCE BETWEEN THE CONFEDERATE COMMISSIONERS, MR. SECRETARY SEWARD AND JUDGE CAMPBELL.

The Commissioners to Mr. Seward.

WASHINGTON CITY, March 12, 1861.

Hon. William H. Seward, Secretary of State of the United States.

Sir: The undersigned have been duly accredited by the Government of the Confederate States of America as commissioners to the Government of the United States, and, in pursuance of their instructions, have now the honor to acquaint you with that fact, and to make known, through you to the President of the United States, the objects of their presence in this capital.

Seven States of the late Federal Union, having in the exercise of the inherent right of every free people to change or reform their political institutions, and through conventions of their people, withdrawn from the United States and reassumed the attributes of sovereign power delegated to it, have formed a government of their own. The Confederate States constitute an independent nation, *de facto* and *de jure,* and possess a government perfect in all its parts, and endowed with all the means of self-support.

With a view to a speedy adjustment of all questions growing out of this political separation, upon such terms of amity and good will as the respective interests, geographical contiguity, and future welfare of the two nations may render necessary, the undersigned are instructed to make to the Government of the United States overtures for the opening of negotiations, assuring the Government of the United States that the President, Congress, and people of the Confederate States earnestly desire a peaceful solution of these great questions; that it is neither their interest nor their wish to make any demand which is not founded in strictest justice, nor do any act to injure their late confederates.

The undersigned have now the honor, in obedience to the instructions of their Government, to request you to appoint as early a day as possible, in order that they may present to the President of the United States the credentials which they bear and the objects of the mission with which they are charged.

We are, very respectfully, your obedient servants,

[Signed]   JOHN FORSYTH,
[Signed]   MARTIN J. CRAWFORD.

Memorandum.

DEPARTMENT OF STATE, WASHINGTON, March 15, 1861.

Mr. John Forsyth, of the State of Alabama, and Mr. Martin J. Crawford, of the State of Georgia, on the 11th inst., through the kind offices of a distinguished Senator, submitted to the Secretary of State their desire for an unofficial interview. This request was, on the 12th inst., upon exclusively public considerations, respectfully declined.

On the 13th inst., while the Secretary was preoccupied, Mr. A. D. Banks, of Virginia, called at this Department, and was received by the Assistant Secretary, to whom he delivered a sealed communication, which he had been charged by Messrs. Forsyth and Crawford to present to the Secretary in person.

In that communication Messrs. Forsyth and Crawford inform the Secretary of State that they have been duly accredited by the Government of the Confederate States of America as commissioners to the Government of the United States, and they set forth the objects of their attendance at Washington. They observe that seven States of the American Union, in the exercise of a right inherent in every free people, have withdrawn, through conventions of their people, from the United States, reassumed the attributes of sovereign power, and formed a government of their own, and that those Confederate States now constitute an independent nation, *de facto* and *de jure,* and possess a government perfect in all its parts, and fully endowed with all the means of self-support.

Messrs. Forsyth and Crawford, in their aforesaid communication, thereupon proceeded to inform the Secretary that, with a view to a speedy adjustment of all questions growing out of the political separation thus assumed, upon such terms of amity and good will as the respective interests, geographical contiguity, and the future welfare of the supposed two nations might render necessary, they are instructed to make to the Government of the United States overtures for the opening of negotiations, assuring this Government that the President, Congress, and the people of the Confederate States earnestly desire a peaceful solution of these great questions, and that it is neither their interest nor their wish to make any demand which is not founded in the strictest justice, nor do any act to injure their late confederates.

After making these statements, Messrs. Forsyth and Crawford close their communication, as they say, in obedience to the instructions of their Government, by requesting the Secretary of State to appoint as early a day as possible, in order that they may present to the President of the United States the credentials which they bear and the objects of the mission with which they are charged.

The Secretary of State frankly confesses that he understands the events which have recently occurred, and the condition of political affairs which actually exists in the part of the Union to which his attention has thus been directed, very differently from the aspect in which they are presented by Messrs. Forsyth and Crawford. He sees in them, not a rightful and accomplished revolution and an independent nation, with an established Government, but rather a perversion of a temporary and partisan excitement to the inconsiderate purposes of an unjustifiable and unconstitutional aggression upon the rights and the authority vested in the Federal Government, and hitherto benignly exercised, as from their very nature they always must so be exercised, for the maintenance of the Union, the preservation of liberty, and the security, peace, welfare, happiness, and aggrandizement of the American people. The Secretary of State, therefore, avows to Messrs. Forsyth and Crawford that he looks patiently, but confidently, for the cure of evils which have resulted from proceedings so unnecessary, so unwise, so unusual, and so unnatural, not to irregular negotiations, having in view new and untried relations with agencies unknown to and acting in derogation of the Constitution and laws, but to regular and considerate action of the people of those States, in coöperation with their brethren in the other States, through the Congress of the United States, and such extraordinary conventions, if there shall be need thereof, as the Federal Constitution contemplates and authorizes to be assembled.

It is, however, the purpose of the Secretary of State, on this occasion, not to invite or engage in any discussion of these subjects, but simply to set forth his reasons for declining to comply with the request of Messrs. Forsyth and Crawford.

On the 4th of March instant, the then newly elected President of the United States, in view of all the facts bearing on the present question, assumed the Executive Administration of the Government, first delivering, in accordance with an early, honored custom, an inaugural address to the people of the United States. The Secretary of State respectfully submits a copy of this address to Messrs. Forsyth and Crawford.

A simple reference to it will be sufficient to satisfy these gentlemen that the Secretary of State, guided by the principles therein announced, is prevented altogether from admitting or assuming that the States referred to by them have, in law or in fact, withdrawn from the Federal Union, or that they could do so in the manner described by Messrs. Forsyth and Crawford, or in any other manner than with the consent and concert of the people of the United States, to be given through a National Convention, to be assembled in conformity with the provisions of the Constitution of the United States. Of course, the Secretary of State cannot act upon the assumption, or in any way admit that the so-called Confederate States constitute a foreign power, with whom diplomatic relations ought to be established.

Under these circumstances, the Secretary of State, whose official duties are confined, subject to the direction of the President, to the conducting of the foreign relations of the country, and do not at all embrace domestic questions, or questions arising between the several States and the Federal Government, is unable to comply with the request of Messrs. Forsyth and Crawford, to appoint a day on which they may present the evidences of their authority and the objects of their visit to the President of the United States. On the contrary, he is obliged to state to Messrs. Forsyth and Crawford that he has no authority, nor is he at liberty, to recognize them as diplomatic agents, or hold correspondence or other communication with them.

Finally, the Secretary of State would observe that, although he has supposed that he might safely and with propriety have adopted these conclusions, without making any reference of the subject to the Executive, yet, so strong has been his desire to practice entire directness, and to act in a spirit of perfect respect and candor toward Messrs. Forsyth and Crawford, and that portion of the people of the Union in whose name they present themselves before him, that he has cheerfully submitted this paper to the President, who coincides generally in the views it expresses, and sanctions the Secretary's decision declining official intercourse with Messrs. Forsyth and Crawford.

April 8, 1861.

The foregoing memorandum was filed in this Department on the 15th of March last. A delivery of the same to Messrs. Forsyth and Crawford was delayed, as was understood, with their consent. They have now, through their secretary, communicated their desire for a definite disposition of the subject. The Secretary of State therefore directs that a duly verified copy of the paper be now delivered.

The Commissioners in Reply to Mr. Seward.

WASHINGTON, April 9, 1861.

Hon. William H. Seward, Secretary of State for the United States, Washington.

The "memorandum" dated Department of State, Washington, March 15, 1861, with postscript under date of 8th instant, has been received through the hands of Mr. J. T. Pickett, secretary of this commission, who, by the instructions of the undersigned, called for it on yesterday at the Department.

In that memorandum you correctly state the purport of the official note addressed to you by the undersigned on the 12th ultimo. Without repeating the contents of that note in full, it is enough to say here that its object was to invite the Government of the United States to a friendly consideration of the relations between the United States and the seven States lately the Federal Union, but now separated from it by the sovereign will of their people, growing out of the pregnant and undeniable fact that those people have rejected the authority of the United States, and established a government of their own. Those relations had to be friendly or hostile. The people of the old and new Governments, occupying contiguous territories, had to stand to each other in the relation of good neighbors, each seeking their happiness and pursuing their national destinies in their own way, without interference with the other; or they had to be rival and hostile nations. The Government of the Confederate States had no hesitation in electing its choice in this alternative. Frankly and unreservedly, seeking the good of the people who had intrusted them with power, in the spirit of humanity, of the Christian civilization of the age, and of that Americanism which **regards** the true welfare and happiness of the people, the Government of the Confederate States, among its first acts, commissioned the undersigned to approach the Government of the United States with the olive branch of peace, and to offer to adjust the great questions pending between them in the only way to be justified by the consciences and common sense of good men who had nothing but the welfare of the people of the two confederacies at heart.

Your Government has not chosen to meet the undersigned in the conciliatory and peaceful spirit in which they are commissioned. Persistently wedded to those fatal theories of construction of the Federal Constitution always rejected by the statesmen of the South, and adhered to by those of the Administration school, until they have produced their natural and often predicted result of the destruction of the Union, under which we might have continued to live happily and gloriously together, had the spirit of the ancestry who framed the common Constitution animated the hearts of all their sons, you now, with a persistence untaught and uncured by the ruin which has been wrought, refuse to recognize the great fact presented to you of a completed and successful revolution; you close your eyes to the existence of the Government founded upon it, and ignore the high duties of moderation and humanity which attach to you in dealing with this great fact. Had you met these issues with the frankness and manliness with which the undersigned were instructed to present them to you and treat them, the undersigned had not now the melancholy duty to return home and tell their Government and their countrymen that their earnest and ceaseless efforts in behalf of peace had been futile, and that the Government of the United States meant to subjugate them by force of arms. Whatever may be the result, impartial history will record the innocence of the Government of the Confederate States, and place the responsibility of the blood and mourning that may ensue upon those who have denied the great fundamental doctrine of American liberty, that "governments derive their just powers from the consent of the governed," and who have set naval and land armaments in motion to subject the people of one portion of this land to the will of another portion. That that can never be done, while a freeman survives in the Confederate States to wield a weapon, the undersigned appeal to past history to prove. These military demonstrations against the people of the seceded States are certainly far from being in keeping and consistency with the theory of the Secretary of State, maintained in his memorandum, that these States are still component parts of the late American Union, as the undersigned are not aware of any constitutional power in the President of the United States to levy war, without the consent of Congress, upon a foreign people, much less upon any portion of the people of the United States.

The undersigned, like the Secretary of State, have no purpose to "invite or engage in discussion" of the subject on which their two Governments are so irreconcilably at variance. It is this variance that has broken up the old Union, the disintegration of which has only begun. It is proper, however, to advise you that it were well to dismiss the hopes you seem to entertain that, by any of the modes indicated, the people of the Confederate States will ever be brought to submit to the authority of the Government of the United States. You are dealing with delusions, too, when you seek to separate our people from our Government, and to characterize the deliberate sovereign act of that people as a "perversion of a temporary and partisan excitement." If you cherish these dreams, you will be awakened from them and find them as unreal and unsubstantial as others in which you have recently indulged. The undersigned would omit the performance of an obvious duty, were they to fail to make known to the Government of the United States that the people of the Confederate States have declared their independence with a full knowledge of all the responsibilities of that act, and with as firm a determination to maintain it by all the means with which nature has endowed them as that which sustained their fathers when they threw off the authority of the British Crown.

The undersigned clearly understand that you have declined to appoint a day to enable them to lay the objects of the mission with which they are charged before the President of the United States, because so to do would be to recognize the independence and separate nationality of the Confederate States. This is the

vein of thought that pervades the memorandum before us. The
truth of history requires that it should distinctly appear upon the
record that the undersigned did not ask the Government of the
United States to recognize the independence of the Confederate
States. They only asked audience to adjust, in a spirit of amity
and peace, the new relations springing from a manifest and accomplished revolution in the Government of the late Federal
Union. Your refusal to entertain these overtures for a peaceful
solution, the active naval and military preparations of this Government, and a formal notice to the commanding General of the
Confederate forces in the harbor of Charleston that the President intends to provision Fort Sumter by forcible means, if necessary, are viewed by the undersigned, and can only be received
by the world, as a declaration of war against the Confederate
States; for the President of the United States knows that Fort
Sumter cannot be provisioned without the effusion of blood. The
undersigned, in behalf of their Government and people, accept
the gage of battle thus thrown down to them; and, appealing to
God and the judgment of mankind for the righteousness of their
cause, the people of the Confederate States will defend their liberties to the last, against this flagrant and open attempt at their
subjugation to sectional power.

This communication cannot be properly closed without adverting to the date of your memorandum. The official note of the
undersigned, of the 12th of March, was delivered to the Assistant
Secretary of State on the 13th of that month, the gentleman who
delivered it informing him that the secretary of this commission
would call at twelve o'clock, noon, on the next day, for an answer.
At the appointed hour Mr. Pickett did call, and was informed by
the Assistant Secretary of State that the engagements of the Secretary of State had prevented him from giving the note his attention. The Assistant Secretary of State then asked for the address of Messrs. Crawford and Forsyth, the members of the
commission then present in this city, took note of the address on
a card, and engaged to send whatever reply might be made to
their lodgings. Why this was not done, it is proper should be
here explained. The memorandum is dated March 15, and was
not delivered until April 8. Why was it withheld during the
intervening twenty-three days? In the postscript to your mem-

orandum you say it "was delayed, as was understood, with their [Messrs. Forsyth and Crawford's] consent." This is true; but it is also true that, on the 15th of March, Messrs. Forsyth and Crawford were assured by a person occupying a high official position in the Government, and who, as they believed, was speaking by authority, that Fort Sumter would be evacuated in a very few days, and that no measure changing the existing *status* prejudicially to the Confederate States, as respects Fort Pickens, was then contemplated, and these assurances were subsequently repeated, with the addition that any contemplated change as respects Pickens would be notified to us. On the 1st of April we were again informed that there might be an attempt to supply Fort Sumter with provisions, but that Governor Pickens should have previous notice of this attempt. There was no suggestion of any reënforcement. The undersigned did not hesitate to believe that these assurances expressed the intentions of the Administration at the time, or at all events of prominent members of that Administration. This delay was assented to for the express purpose of attaining the great end of the mission of the undersigned—to wit, a pacific solution of existing complications. The inference deducible from the date of your memorandum, that the undersigned had, of their own volition and without cause, consented to this long *hiatus* in the grave duties with which they were charged, is therefore not consistent with a just exposition of the facts of the case. The intervening twenty-three days were employed in active unofficial efforts, the object of which was to smooth the path to a pacific solution, the distinguished personage alluded to coöperating with the undersigned; and every step of that effort is recorded in writing and now in the possession of the undersigned and of their Government. It was only when all those anxious efforts for peace had been exhausted, and it became clear that Mr. Lincoln had determined to appeal to the sword to reduce the people of the Confederate States to the will of the section or party whose President he is, that the undersigned resumed the official negotiation temporarily suspended, and sent their secretary for a reply to their official note of March 12.

It is proper to add that, during these twenty-three days, two gentlemen, of official distinction as high as that of the personage hitherto alluded to, aided the undersigned as intermediaries in these unofficial negotiations for peace.

The undersigned, commissioners of the Confederate States of America, having thus made answer to all they deem material in the memorandum filed in the Department on the 15th of March last, have the honor to be

JOHN FORSYTH,
MARTIN J. CRAWFORD,
A. B. ROMAN.

Mr. Seward in Reply to the Commissioners.

DEPARTMENT OF STATE, WASHINGTON, April 10, 1861.

Messrs. Forsyth, Crawford, and Roman, having been apprised by a memorandum, which has been delivered to them, that the Secretary of State is not at liberty to hold official intercourse with them, will, it is presumed, expect no notice from him of the new communication which they have-addressed to him under date of the 9th inst., beyond the simple acknowledgment of the receipt thereof, which he hereby very cheerfully gives.

Judge Campbell to Mr. Seward.

WASHINGTON CITY, April 13, 1861.

Sir: On the 15th of March ult., I left with Judge Crawford, one of the commissioners of the Confederate States, a note in writing to the effect following:

"I feel entire confidence that Fort Sumter will be evacuated in the next five days. And this measure is felt as imposing great responsibility on the Administration.

"I feel entire confidence that no measure changing the existing *status,* prejudicially to the Southern Confederate States, is at present contemplated.

"I feel an entire confidence that an immediate demand for an answer to the communication of the commissioners will be productive of evil and not of good. I do not believe that it ought, at this time, to be pressed."

The substance of this statement I communicated to you the same evening by letter. Five days elapsed, and I called with a telegram from General Beauregard to the effect that Sumter was not evacuated, but that Major Anderson was at work making repairs.

The next day, after conversing with you, I communicated to Judge Crawford, in writing, that the failure to evacuate Sumter was not the result of bad faith, but was attributable to causes consistent with the intention to fulfill the engagement, and that as regarded Pickens, I should have notice of any design to alter the existing *status* there. Mr. Justice Nelson was present at these conversations, three in number, and I submitted to him each of my written communications to Judge Crawford, and informed Judge C. that they had his (Judge Nelson's) sanction. I gave you, on the 22d of March, a substantial copy of the statement I had made on the 15th.

The 30th of March arrived, and at that time a telegram came from Governor Pickens, inquiring concerning Colonel Lamon, whose visit to Charleston he supposed had a connection with the proposed evacuation of Fort Sumter.

I left that with you, and was to have an answer the following Monday (1st of April). On the 1st of April I received from you the statement in writing: "(I am satisfied) the Government will not undertake to supply Fort Sumter without giving notice to Governor P." The words "I am satisfied" were for me to use as expressive of confidence in the remainder of the declaration.

The proposition as originally prepared was, "the President *may desire* to supply Sumter, but will not do so," etc., and your verbal explanation was that you did not believe any such attempt would be made, and that there was no design to reënforce Sumter.

There was a departure here from the pledges of the previous month, but with the verbal explanation, I did not consider it a matter then to complain of. I simply stated to you that I had that assurance previously.

On the 7th day of April I addressed you a letter on the subject of the alarm that the preparations by the Government had created, and asked you if the assurances I had given were well or illfounded. In respect to Sumter your reply was, "Faith as to Sumter fully kept—wait and see." In the morning's paper I read, "An authorized messenger from President Lincoln informed

Governor Pickens and General Beauregard that provisions will be sent to Fort Sumter—peaceably, *or otherwise by force."* This was the 8th of April, at Charleston, the day following your last assurance, and is the last evidence of the full faith I was invited to *wait for* and *see.* In the same paper, I read that intercepted dispatches disclosed the fact that Mr. Fox, who had been allowed to visit Major Anderson, on the pledge that his purpose was pacific, employed his opportunity to devise a plan for supplying the Fort by force, and that this plan had been adopted by the Washington Government, and was in process of execution. My recollection of the date of Mr. Fox's visit carries it to a day in March. I learn he is a near connection of a member of the Cabinet. My connection with the commissioners and yourself was superinduced by a conversation with Justice Nelson. He informed me of your strong disposition in favor of peace, and that you were oppressed with a demand of the commissioners of the Confederate States for a reply to their first letter, and that you desired to avoid it if possible at that time.

I told him I might perhaps be of some service in arranging the difficulty. I came to your office entirely at his request and without the knowledge of either of the commissioners. Your depression was obvious to both Judge Nelson and myself. I was gratified at the character of the counsels you were desirous of pursuing and much impressed with your observation that a civil war might be prevented by the success of my mediation. You read a letter of Mr. Weed to show how irksome and responsible the withdrawal of troops from Sumter was. A portion of my communication to Judge Crawford on the 15th of March was founded upon these remarks, and the pledge to evacuate Sumter is less forcible than the words you employed. These words were: "Before this letter reaches you [a proposed letter by me to President Davis], Sumter will have been evacuated."

The commissioners who received those communications conclude they have been abused and overreached. The Montgomery Government hold the same opinion. The commissioners have supposed that my communications were with you, and upon the [that] hypothesis were prepared to arraign you before the country in connection with the President. I placed a peremptory prohibition upon this as being contrary to the terms of my communications with them. I pledged myself to them to communicate information upon what I considered as the best authority, and they were to confide in the ability of myself, aided by Judge Nelson, to determine upon the credibility of my informant.

I think no candid man who will read over what I have written, and consider for a moment what is going on at Sumter, but will agree that the equivocating conduct of the Administration, as measured and interpreted in connection with these promises, is the proximate cause of the great calamity.

I have a profound conviction that the telegrams of the 8th of April of General Beauregard, and of the 10th of April of General Walker, the Secretary of War, can be referred to nothing else than their belief that there has been systematic duplicity practiced on them through me. It is under an oppressive sense of the weight of this responsibility that I submit to you these things for your explanation. Very respectfully,

[Signed]   JOHN A. CAMPBELL,
            Associate Justice of the Supreme Court, U. S.
HON. WILLIAM H. SEWARD, *Secretary of State.*

DISPATCHES.

To L. P. Walker, Secretary of War.

An authorized message from President Lincoln just informed Governor Pickens and myself that provisions will be sent to Fort Sumter peaceably, or otherwise by force.

Gen. P. G. T. Beauregard.

If you have no doubt as to the authorized character of the agent who communicated to you the intention of the Washington Government to supply Fort Sumter by force, you will at once demand its evacuation, and, if this is refused, proceed in such manner as you may determine to reduce it.

Judge Campbell to Mr. Seward.

WASHINGTON CITY, April 20, 1861.

Sir: I enclose you a letter, corresponding very nearly with one I addressed to you a week ago (13th April), to which I have **not** had any repiy. The letter is simply one of inquiry in reference to facts concerning which, I think, I am entitled to an explanation. I have not adopted any opinion in reference to them which may not be modified by explanation, nor have I affirmed in that letter, nor do I in this, any conclusion of my own unfavorable to your integrity in the whole transaction.

All that I have said and mean to say is, that an explanation is due from you to myself. I will not say what I shall do in case this request is not complied with, but I am justified in saying that I shall feel at liberty to place these letters before any person who is entitled to ask an explanation of myself. Very respectfully,

JOHN A. CAMPBELL,
Associate Justice of the Supreme Court, U. S.
HON. WILLIAM H. SEWARD, *Secretary of State.*

No reply has been made to this letter, April 24, 1861.

Judge Campbell to the President of the Confederate States.

MONTGOMERY, ALA., May 7, 1861.

Sir: I submit to you two letters that were addressed by me to the Hon. W. H. Seward, Secretary of State of the United States, that contain an explanation of the nature and result of an intervention by me in the intercourse of the commissioners of the Confederate States with that officer. I considered that I could perform no duty in which the entire American people, whether of the Federal Union or of the Confederate States, were more interested than that of promoting the counsels and the policy that had for their object the preservation of peace. This motive dictated my intervention. Besides the interview referred to in these letters, I informed the Assistant Secretary of State of the United States (not being able to see the Secretary) on the 11th April, ult., of the existence of a telegram of that date, from General Beauregard to the commissioners, in which he informed the commissioners that he had demanded the evacuation of Sumter, and if refused he would proceed to reduce it. On the same day, I had been told that President Lincoln had said that none of the vessels sent to Charleston were war vessels, and that force was not to be used in the attempt to supply the Fort. I had no means of testing the accuracy of this information; but offered that if the information was accurate I would send a telegram to the authorities at Charleston, and it might prevent the disastrous consequences of a collision at that fort between the opposing forces. It was the last effort that I would make to avert the calamities of war. The Assistant Secretary promised to give the matter attention, but I had no other intercourse with him or any other person on the subject, nor have I had any reply to the letters submitted to you.

Very respectfully,   JOHN A. CAMPBELL.
GENERAL DAVIS, *President of the Confederate States.*

EXECUTIVE DEPARTMENT, MONTGOMERY, May 9, 1861.
Hon. Howell Cobb, President of the Congress.

Sir: I herewith transmit to the Congress a communication from the Secretary of War, covering the report of operations in the reduction of Fort Sumter, together with the flag used on that occasion.   JEFFERSON DAVIS.

MONTGOMERY, May 10, 1861.
The Congress of the Confederate States of America.

It is with sincere pleasure that I inform you that the government of North Carolina has accredited the Hon. Thomas L. Clingman as commissioner to represent that Commonwealth near the Government of the Confederate States. Mr. Clingman presented to me this day his letters of credence, and I received him in a manner corresponding to his station and the high purpose of his mission. It afforded me much gratification to receive from Mr. Clingman the assurance which he was instructed by his government to convey to me of the determination of his State "to link her fortunes with those of the Confederate States, and to draw the sword in the common defense of our liberties." This proof of North Carolina's sympathy, and this promise of her early union with the Confederate States, are the more signal because conveyed by one of such high station and reputation as Mr. Clingman.   JEFF'N DAVIS.

MONTGOMERY, May 13, 1861.

The Congress of the Confederate States of America.

I lay before Congress, for their consideration and action in relation thereto, copies of a convention between the Confederate States and the State of Tennessee, which was concluded and signed by the commissioners of both parties at the city of Nashville on the 7th day of May, A.D. 1861, and of the ratification and confirmation of the same by the General Assembly of the State of Tennessee. JEFF'N DAVIS.

EXECUTIVE DEPARTMENT,
MONTGOMERY, ALA., May 14, 1861.

Hon. Howell Cobb, President of the Congress.

Sir: I herewith transmit to the Congress the several estimates of the Secretary of War for the fiscal year, ending the 18th of February, 1862. JEFFERSON DAVIS.

EXECUTIVE DEPARTMENT, May 16, 1861.

Hon. Howell Cobb, President of the Congress.

Sir: I herewith transmit to the Congress additional estimates of the Secretary of War. JEFFERSON DAVIS.

EXECUTIVE DEPARTMENT, May 17, 1861.

Hon. Howell Cobb, President of the Congress.

I herewith transmit to the Congress a communication from the Postmaster General, covering additional estimates for the service of his Department for the year ending February 4, 1862.
JEFFERSON DAVIS.

MONTGOMERY, ALA., May 18, 1861.

Hon. Howell Cobb, President of the Congress.

I herewith transmit to the Congress the estimate of the Secretary of War for incidental expenses of officers of the Confederate Army assigned to duty among the Indian tribes, for the fiscal year ending February 18, 1862. The functions which said officers will be required to perform are generally those of agents of Indian Affairs.   JEFF'N DAVIS.

EXECUTIVE DEPARTMENT, May 20, 1861.
Hon. Howell Cobb, President of the Congress.

I herewith transmit to the Congress certain estimates of the Secretary of the Navy for the year ending February 18, 1862.
JEFFERSON DAVIS.

EXECUTIVE DEPARTMENT, May 20, 1861.
Hon. Howell Cobb, President of the Congress.

I herewith transmit to the Congress certain resolutions* of the Board of Mayor and Aldermen of the city of Memphis.
JEFFERSON DAVIS.

VETO MESSAGES.

MONTGOMERY, ALA., May 17, 1861.
To the Congress of the Confederate States.

I have this day received your resolution providing for the adjournment of Congress "to meet again at Richmond on the twentieth day of July next," etc., and have the honor to return it to you with a statement of my objections.

By the third clause of the sixth article of the Constitution of the Provisional Government of the Confederate States of America, it was enacted that "until otherwise provided by the Congress the city of Montgomery, in the State of Alabama, shall be the seat of government."

There is no provision in the resolution before me to remove the seat of government, and it hence follows that the office of the Executive and those of the Executive Departments of the Government must remain at the city of Montgomery.

---

*Inviting the Congress to hold its next session in the city of Memphis, Tenn.

Though there is no specified requirement that the Congress should assemble at the seat of government, the obvious necessity for its doing so will require extraordinary circumstances to justify the holding of a session of Congress at a place remote from that where the Executive Departments are located. Great embarrassment and probable detriment to the public service must result from a want of co-intelligence between the coördinate branches of the Government incident to such separation. The estimates on which appropriations can alone be made not infrequently require explanation, which, under such circumstances, could not well be made.

Members of the Cabinet who are also members of the Congress must of necessity be prevented from performing one duty or the other.

With these views deferentially and most respectfully submitted, I have the honor to return the resolution for such further action as the Congress may in its wisdom deem it proper to adopt.

JEFFERSON DAVIS.

To the Congress.

Gentlemen: I have the honor to return to you without my approval the act entitled "An act to establish a court of admiralty and maritime jurisdiction in the State of Mississippi for the counties lying on the Mississippi River in said State."

Although I am unable to perceive the advantage of an additional court in Mississippi, as provided (by) the bill, this would not constitute a sufficient reason for withholding my approval. But the bill goes farther. It creates a jurisdiction for a certain portion of the bank of the Mississippi River, entirely different from that which exists above, below, and on the opposite bank of the river. This cannot but lead to conflict of jurisdiction, embarrassment, and confusion, and I cannot perceive the necessity for so exceptional a measure.

I therefore return it to the Congress with my objections.

[Received May 21, 1861.]   JEFFERSON DAVIS.

PROCLAMATIONS.

By the President of the Confederate States.

A PROCLAMATION.

Whereas, a treaty or convention of alliance, offensive and defensive, between the Confederate States of America and the Commonwealth of Virginia, was concluded and signed at the ·city of Richmond on the 24th day of April, A.D. 1861, which treaty or convention of alliance is, word for word, as follows:*

And whereas, the said treaty or convention of alliance has been duly ratified on both parts:

Now, therefore, be it known that I, Jefferson Davis, President of the Confederate States of America, have caused the said treaty or convention of alliance to be made public, to the end that the same, and every clause and article thereof, may be observed and fulfilled with good faith by the Confederate States and the citizens thereof.

In witness whereof I have hereunto set my hand and caused the seal of the Confederate States to be affixed at the city of Montgomery this 8th day of May, A.D. 1861.   JEFF'N DAVIS.

By the President:

R. TOOMBS, *Secretary of State.*

By the President of the Confederate States.

A PROCLAMATION.

To All Who Shall See These Presents, Greeting.

Know ye, that by virtue of the power vested in me by law I have commissioned and do hereby commission, have authorized and do hereby authorize, the schooner or vessel called the Savannah (more particularly described in the schedule hereunto annexed†), whereof T. Harrison Baker is commander, to act as

---

*Omitted.

†Schedule of description of the vessel: Name, Schooner Savannah; tonnage, fifty-three and forty-one ninety-fifth tons; armament, one large pivot gun and small arms; number of crew, thirty.

a private armed vessel in the service of the Confederate States on the high seas against the United States of America, their ships, vessels, goods, and effects, and those of their citizens during the pendency of the war now existing between the said Confederate States and the said United States.

This commission to continue in force until revoked by the President of the Confederate States for the time being.

Given under my hand and seal of the Confederate States at Montgomery this 18th day of May, A.D. 1861.   JEFF'N DAVIS.

By the President:

R. TOOMBS, *Secretary of State.*

BY THE PRESIDENT OF THE CONFEDERATE STATES.

A PROCLAMATION.

To the People of the Confederate States.

When a people who recognize their dependence upon God, feel themselves surrounded by peril and difficulty, it becomes them to humble themselves under the dispensation of Divine Providence, to recognize his righteous government, to acknowledge his goodness in times past, and supplicate his merciful protection for the future.

The manifest proofs of the Divine blessing hitherto extended to the efforts of the people of the Confederate States of America, to maintain and perpetuate public liberty, individual rights, and national independence, demand their devout and heartfelt gratitude. It becomes them to give public manifestation of this gratitude, and of their dependence upon the Judge of all the earth, and to invoke the continuance of his favor.   Knowing that none but a just and righteous cause can gain the Divine favor, we would implore the Lord of hosts to guide and direct our policy in the paths of right, duty, justice, and mercy, to unite our hearts and our efforts for the defense of our dearest rights; to strengthen our weakness, crown our arms with success, and enable us to secure a speedy, just, and honorable peace.

To these ends, and in conformity with the request of Congress, I invite the people of the Confederate States to the observance of a day of fasting and prayer by such religious services as may be suitable for the occasion, and I recommend Thursday, the 13th day of June next, for that purpose, and that we may all, on that day, with one accord, join in humble and reverential approach to him in whose hands we are, invoking him to inspire us with a proper spirit and temper of heart and mind to bear our evils, to bless us with his favor and protection, and to bestow his gracious benediction upon our Government and country.

JEFFERSON DAVIS.

By the President:

R. TOOMBS, *Secretary of State.*

[May 28, 1861.]

AN ACT

RECOGNIZING THE EXISTENCE OF WAR BETWEEN THE UNITED STATES AND THE CONFEDERATE STATES, AND CONCERNING LETTERS OF MARQUE, PRIZES, AND PRIZE GOODS.

Whereas, the earnest efforts made by this Government to establish friendly relations between the Government of the United States and the Confederate States, and to settle all questions of disagreement between the two Governments upon principles of right, justice, equity, and good faith, have proved unavailing by reason of the refusal of the Government of the United States to hold any intercourse with the commissioners appointed by this Government for the purposes aforesaid, or to listen to any proposal they had to make for the peaceful solution of all causes of difficulty between the two Governments; and

Whereas, the President of the United States of America has issued his proclamation making requisition upon the States of the American Union for 75,000 men for the purpose, as therein indicated, of capturing forts and other strongholds within the jurisdiction of, and belonging to, the Confederate States of America, and has detailed naval armaments upon the coasts of the Confederate States of America, and raised, organized, and equipped a large military force to execute the purpose aforesaid, and has issued his other proclamation announcing his purpose to set on foot a blockade of the ports of the Confederate States; and

Whereas, the State of Virginia has seceded from the Federal Union and entered into a convention of alliance offensive and defensive with the Confederate States, and has adopted the Provisional Constitution of the said States; and the States of Maryland, North Carolina, Tennessee, Kentucky, Arkansas, and Missouri have refused, and it is believed that the State of Delaware and the inhabitants of the Territories of Arizona and New Mexico, and the Indian Territory south of Kansas, will refuse to cooperate with the Government of the United States in these acts of hostility and wanton aggression, which are plainly intended to overawe, oppress, and finally subjugate the people of the Confederate States; and

Whereas, by the acts and means aforesaid, war exists between the Confederate States and the Government of the United States and the States and Territories thereof, except the States of Maryland, North Carolina, Tennessee, Kentucky, Arkansas, Missouri, and Delaware, and the Territories of Arizona and New Mexico, and the Indian Territory south of Kansas: Therefore,

Section 1. *The Congress of the Confederate States of America do enact,* That the President of the Confederate States is hereby authorized to use the whole land and naval force of the Confederate States to meet the war thus commenced, and to issue to private armed vessels commissions or letters of marque and general reprisal in such form as he shall think proper, under the seal of the Confederate States, against the vessels, goods, and effects of the Government of the United States, and of the citizens or inhabitants of the States and Territories thereof, except the States and Territories hereinbefore named: *Provided, however,* That property of the enemy (unless it be contraband of war) laden on board a neutral vessel shall not be subject to seizure under this act: *And provided further,* That vessels of the citizens or inhabitants of the United States now in the ports of the Confederate States, except such as have been since the 5th of April last, or may hereafter be, in the service of the Government of the United States, shall be allowed thirty days after the publication of this act to leave said ports and reach their destination; and such vessels and their cargoes, excepting articles contraband of war, shall not be subject to capture under this act during said period unless they shall have previously reached the destination for which they were bound on leaving said ports.

Sec. 2. That the President of the Confederate States shall be, and he is hereby, authorized and empowered to revoke and annul at pleasure all letters of marque and reprisal which he may at any time grant pursuant to this act.

Sec. 3. That all persons applying for letters of marque and reprisal, pursuant to this act, shall state in writing the name and a suitable description of the tonnage and force of the vessel, and the name and place of residence of each owner concerned therein and the intended number of the crew, which statement shall be signed by the person or persons making such application and filed with the Secretary of State, or shall be delivered to any other officer or person who shall be employed to deliver out such commissions, to be by him transmitted to the Secretary of State.

Sec. 4. That before any commission or letters of marque and reprisal shall be issued as aforesaid, the owner or owners of the ship or vessel for which the same shall be requested, and the commander thereof for the time being, shall give bond to the Confederate States, with at least two responsible sureties not interested in such vessel, in the penal sum of $5,000, or if such vessel be provided with more than 150 men, then in the penal sum of $10,000, with condition that the owners, officers, and crew who shall be employed on board such commissioned vessel shall and will observe the laws of the Confederate States and the instructions which shall be given them according to law for the regulation of their conduct, and will satisfy all damages and injuries which shall be done or committed contrary to the tenor thereof by such vessel during her commission, and to deliver up the same when revoked by the President of the Confederate States.

Sec. 5. That all captures and prizes of vessels and property shall be forfeited and shall accrue to the owners, officers, and crews of the vessels by whom such captures and prizes shall be made, and on due condemnation had shall be distributed according to any written agreement which shall be made between them; and if there be no such written agreement, then one moiety to the owners and the other moiety to the officers and crew, as nearly as may be, according to the rules prescribed for the distribution of prize money by the laws of the Confederate States.

Sec. 6. That all vessels, goods, and effects, the property of any citizen of the Confederate States, or of persons resident within and under the protection of the Confederate States, or of persons permanently within the territories and under the protection of any foreign prince, government, or State in amity with the Confederate States, which shall have been captured by the United States, and which shall be recaptured by vessels commissioned as aforesaid, shall be restored to the lawful owners upon payment by them of a just and reasonable salvage, to be determined by the mutual agreement of the parties concerned, or by the decree of any court having jurisdiction, according to the nature of each case, agreeably to the provisions established by law. And such salvage shall be distributed among the owners, officers, and crews of the vessels commissioned as aforesaid and making such captures, according to any written agreement which shall be made between them; and in case of no such agreement, then in the same manner and upon the principles hereinbefore provided in cases of capture.

Sec. 7. That before breaking bulk of any vessel which shall be captured as aforesaid, or other disposal or conversion thereof, or of any articles which shall be found on board the same, such captured vessel, goods, or effects shall be brought into some port of the Confederate States or of a nation or State in amity with the Confederate States, and shall be proceeded against before a competent tribunal; and after condemnation and forfeiture thereof shall belong to the owners, officers, and crew of the vessel capturing the same, and be distributed as before provided; and in the case of all captured vessels, goods, and effects which shall be brought within the jurisdiction of the Confederate States, the district courts of the Confederate States shall have exclusive original cognizance thereof, as in civil causes of admiralty and maritime jurisdiction; and the said courts, or the courts, being courts of the Confederate States, into which such cases shall be removed and in which they shall be finally decided, shall and may decree restitution in whole or in part when the capture shall have been made without just cause; and if made without probable cause, may order and decree damages and costs to the party injured, for which the owners and commanders of the vessels making such captures, and also the vessels, shall be liable.

Sec. 8. That all persons found on board any captured vessels, or on board any recaptured vessel, shall be reported to the collector of the port in the Confederate States in which they shall first arrive, and shall be delivered into the custody of the marshal of the district or some court or military officer of the Confederate States, or of any State in or near such port, who shall take charge of their safe-keeping and support, at the expense of the Confederate States.

Sec. 9. That the President of the Confederate States is hereby authorized to establish and order suitable instructions for the better governing and directing the conduct of the vessels so commissioned, their officers and crews, copies of which shall be delivered by the collector of the customs to the commanders, when they shall give bond as before provided.

Sec. 10. That a bounty shall be paid by the Confederate States of $20 for each person on board any armed ship or vessel belonging to the United States at the commencement of an engagement, which shall be burnt, sunk, or destroyed by any vessel commissioned as aforesaid, which shall be of equal or inferior force, the same to be divided as in other cases of prize money; and a bounty of $25 shall be paid to the owners, officers, and crews of the private armed vessels commissioned as aforesaid for each and every prisoner by them captured and brought into port and delivered to an agent authorized to receive them in any port of the Confederate States; and the Secretary of the Treasury is hereby authorized to pay or cause to be paid to the owners, officers, and crews of such private armed vessels commissioned as aforesaid, or their agent, the bounties herein provided.

Sec. 11. That the commanding officer of every vessel having a commission or letters of marque and reprisal, during the present hostilities between the Confederate States and the United States, shall keep a regular journal, containing a true and exact account of his daily proceedings and transactions with such vessel and the crew thereof; the ports and places he shall put into or cast anchor in; the time of his stay there and the cause thereof; the prizes he shall take and the nature and probable value thereof;

the times and places when and where taken, and in what manner
he shall dispose of the same; the ships or vessels he shall fall in
with; the times and places when and where he shall meet with
them, and his observations and remarks thereon; also of whatever else shall occur to him or any of his officers or marines, or
be discovered by examination or conference with any marines
or passengers of or in any other ships or vessels, or by any other
means touching the fleets, vessels, and forces of the United
States, their ports and places of station and destination, strength,
numbers, intents, and designs; and such commanding officer
shall, immediately on his arrival in any port of the Confederate
States, from or during the continuance of any voyage or cruise,
produce his commission for such vessel, and deliver up such
journal so kept as aforesaid, signed with his proper name and
handwriting, to the collector or other chief officer of the customs
at or nearest to such port; the truth of which journal shall be
verified by the oath of the commanding officer for the time being. And such collector or other chief officer of the customs
shall, immediately on the arrival of such vessel, order the proper
officer of the customs to go on board and take an account of the
officers and men, the number and nature of the guns, and whatever else shall occur to him on examination material to be known;
and no such vessel shall be permitted to sail out of port again
until such journal shall have been delivered up, and a certificate
obtained under the hand of such collector or other chief officer
of the customs that she is manned and armed according to her
commission; and upon delivery of such certificate any former
certificate of a like nature which shall have been obtained by the
commander of such vessel shall be delivered up.

Sec. 12. That the commanders of vessels having letters of
marque and reprisal as aforesaid, neglecting to keep a journal
as aforesaid, or willfully making fraudulent entries therein, or
obliterating the record of any material transactions contained
therein, where the interest of the Confederate States is concerned, or refusing to produce and deliver such journal, commission, or certificate, pursuant to the preceding section of this
act, then, and in such cases, the commissions or letters of marque
and reprisal of such vessels shall be liable to be revoked; and such
commanders, respectively, shall forfeit for every such offense

the sum of $1,000, one moiety thereof to the use of the Confederate States, and the other to the informer.

Sec. 13. That the owners or commanders of vessels having letters of marque and reprisal as aforesaid, who shall violate any of the acts of Congress for the collection of the revenue of the Confederate States, and for the prevention of smuggling, shall forfeit the commission or letters of marque and reprisal, and they and the vessels owned or commanded by them shall be liable to all the penalties and forfeitures attaching to merchant vessels in like cases.

Sec. 14. That on all goods, wares, and merchandise captured and made good and lawful prizes of war by any private armed ship having commission or letters of marque and reprisal under this act, and brought into the Confederate States, there shall be allowed a deduction of 33 1-3 per cent on the amount of duties imposed by law.

Sec. 15. That 5 per centum on the net amount (after deducting all charges and expenditures) of the prize money arising from captured vessels and cargoes, and on the net amount of the salvage of vessels and cargoes recaptured by the private armed vessels of the Confederate States, shall be secured and paid over to the collector or other chief officer of the customs, at the port or place in the Confederate States at which such captured or recaptured vessels may arrive, or to the consul or other public agent of the Confederate States residing at the port or place not within the Confederate States at which such captured or recaptured vessel may arrive. And the moneys arising therefrom shall be held, and are hereby pledged by the Government of the Confederate States as a fund for the support and maintenance of the widows and orphans of such persons as may be slain, and for the support and maintenance of such persons as may be wounded and disabled on board of the private armed vessels commissioned as aforesaid, in any engagement with the enemy, to be assigned and distributed in such manner as shall hereafter be provided by law.   HOWELL COBB,
                                    President of the Congress.

Approved May 6, 1861.

                                    JEFF'N DAVIS.

President's Instructions to Private Armed Vessels.

1. The tenor of your commission, under the act of Congress entitled "An Act recognizing the existence of war between the United States and the Confederate States, and concerning letters of marque, prizes, and prize goods," a copy of which is hereto annexed, will be kept constantly in your view. The high seas, referred to in your commissions, you will understand generally to refer to low water mark, but with the exception of the space within one league or three miles from the shore of countries at peace both with the United States and the Confederate States. You may, nevertheless, execute your commission within that distance of the shore of a nation at war with the United States, and even on the waters within the jurisdiction of such nation, if permitted to do so.

2. You are to pay the strictest regard to the rights of neutral powers and the usages of civilized nations; and in all your proceedings toward neutral vessels you are to give them as little molestation or interruption as will consist with the right of ascertaining their neutral character and of detaining and bringing them in for regular adjudication in the proper cases. You are particularly to avoid even the appearance of using force or seduction with a view to deprive such vessels of their crews or of their passengers other than persons in the military service of the enemy.

3. Toward enemy vessels and their crews you are to proceed, in exercising the rights of war, with all the justice and humanity which characterize this Government and its citizens.

4. The master and one or more of the principal persons belonging to the captured vessels are to be sent, as soon after the capture as may be, to the judge or judges of the proper court in the Confederate States, to be examined upon oath touching the interest or property of the captured vessel and her lading, and at the same time are to be delivered to the judge or judges all papers, charter-parties, bills of lading, letters, and other documents and writings found on board, the said papers to be proved by affidavit of the commander of the capturing vessel or some other person present at the capture, to be produced as they were received, without fraud, addition, subduction, or embezzlement.

5. Property even of the enemy is exempt from seizure on neutral vessels, unless it be contraband of war. If goods contraband of war are found on any neutral vessel, and the commander thereof shall offer to deliver them up, the offer shall be accepted and the vessel left at liberty to pursue its voyage, unless the quantity of contraband goods be greater than can be conveniently received on board your vessel, in which case the neutral vessel may be carried into port for the delivery of the contraband goods. The following articles are deemed by this Government contraband of war as well as all others that are so declared by the law of nations, viz.: All arms and implements serving for the purposes of war by land or sea, such as cannons, mortars, guns, muskets, rifles, pistols, petards, bombs, grenades, ball, shot, shell, fuses, pikes, swords, bayonets, javelins, lances, horse furniture, holsters, belts, and generally all other implements of war. Also, timber for shipbuilding, pitch, tar, rosin, copper in sheets, sails, hemp, cordage, and generally whatever may serve directly to the equipment of vessels, unwrought iron and planks only excepted. Neutral vessels conveying enemy's dispatches or military persons in the service of the enemy forfeit their neutral character, and are liable to capture and condemnation. But this rule does not apply to neutral vessels bearing dispatches from the public ministers or ambassadors of the enemy residing in neutral countries.

By command of the President of the Confederate States:

ROBERT TOOMBS, *Secretary of State.*

FORM OF BOND.

Know all men by these presents:

That we (*Note 1*), ——— ———, are bound to the Confederate States of America in the full sum of (*Note 2*) ——— thousand dollars, to the payment whereof, well and truly to be made,

---

NOTE 1.—This blank must be filled with the name of the commander for the time being and the owner or owners, and at least two responsible sureties, not interested in the vessel.

NOTE 2.—This blank must be filled with a "five" if the vessel be provided only with 150 men or a less number; if with more than that number, the blank must be filled with a "ten."

we bind ourselves, our heirs, executors, and administrators, jointly and severally, by these presents.

The condition of this obligation is such that whereas application has been made to the said Confederate States of America for the grant of a commission or letter of marque and general reprisals, authorizing the (*Note 3*) ———— or vessel, called the ————, to act as a private armed vessel in the service of the Confederate States on the high seas against the United States of America, its ships and vessels, and those of its citizens, during the pendency of the war now existing between the said Confederate States and the said United States.

Now, if the owners, officers, and crew who shall be employed on board of said vessel when commissioned shall observe the laws of the Confederate States and the instructions which shall be given them according to law for the regulation of their conduct, and shall satisfy all damages and injuries which shall be done or committed contrary to the tenor thereof by such vessel during her commission, and shall deliver up said commission when revoked by the President of the Confederate States, then this obligation shall be void, but otherwise shall remain in full force and effect.

Signed, sealed, and delivered in the presence of ———— ————, on this —— day of ————, ————.

A. B.,

C. D.,

    Witnesses.

[SEAL.]

[SEAL.]

[SEAL.]

[SEAL.]

AN ACT

TO AMEND AN ACT ENTITLED "AN ACT RECOGNIZING THE
EXISTENCE OF WAR BETWEEN THE UNITED STATES AND
THE CONFEDERATE STATES AND CONCERNING LET-
TERS OF MARQUE, PRIZES, AND PRIZE GOODS,
APPROVED MAY 6, 1861."

The Congress of the Confederate States [of America] do enact, That the tenth section of the above entitled act be so amend-

---

NOTE 3.—This blank must be filled with the character of the vessel— "ship," "brig," "schooner," "steamer," etc.

ed that, in addition to the bounty therein mentioned, the Government of the Confederate States will pay to the cruiser or cruisers of any private armed vessel commissioned under said act 20 per centum on the value of each and every vessel of war belonging to the enemy that may be sunk or destroyed by such private armed vessel or vessels, the value of the armament to be included in the estimate; the valuation to be made by a board of naval officers appointed and their award to be approved by the President, and the amount found to be due to be payable in 8 per cent bonds of the Confederate States.

Sec. 2. That if any person who may have invented or may hereafter invent any new kind of armed vessel, or floating battery, or defense, shall deposit a plan of the same, accompanied by suitable explanations or specifications, in the Navy Department, together with an affidavit setting forth that he is the inventor thereof, such deposit and affidavit (unless the facts set forth therein shall be disproved) shall entitle such inventor or his assigns to the sole and exclusive enjoyment of the rights and privileges conferred by this act, reserving, however, to the Government, in all cases, the right of using such invention.

Approved May 21, 1861.

RESOLUTION OF THANKS.

Be it unanimously resolved by the Congress of the Confederate States of America, That the thanks of the people of the Confederate States are due, and through this Congress are hereby tendered, to Brigadier General P. G. T. Beauregard and the officers, military and naval, under his command, and to the gallant troops of the State of South Carolina for the skill, fortitude, and courage by which they reduced and caused the surrender of Fort Sumter, in the harbor of Charleston, on the twelfth and thirteenth days of April, eighteen hundred and sixty-one. And the commendation of Congress is also hereby declared of the generosity manifested by their conduct toward a brave and vanquished foe.

Be it further resolved, That a copy of this resolution be communicated by the President to General Beauregard, and through him to the army then under his command.

Approved May 4, 1861.

LETTER OF PRESIDENT DAVIS TO PRESIDENT LINCOLN.

RICHMOND, July 6, 1861.

To Abraham Lincoln, President and Commander in Chief of the Army and Navy of the United States.

Sir: Having learned that the schooner Savannah, a private armed vessel in the service, and sailing under a commission issued by authority of the Confederate States of America, had been captured by one of the vessels forming the blockading squadron off Charleston harbor, I directed a proposition to be made to the officer commanding that squadron for an exchange of the officers and crew of the Savannah for prisoners of war held by this Government "according to number and rank." To this proposition, made on the 19th ult., Captain Mercer, the officer in command of the blockading squadron, made answer on the same day that "the prisoners (referred to) are not on board of any of the vessels under my command."

It now appears by statements made without contradiction in newspapers published in New York, that the prisoners above mentioned were conveyed to that city, and have there been treated not as prisoners of war, but as criminals; that they have been put in irons, confined in jail, brought before the courts of justice on charges of piracy and treason, and it is even rumored that they have been actually convicted of the offenses charged, for no other reason than that they bore arms in defense of the rights of this Government and under the authority of its commission.

I could not, without grave discourtesy, have made the newspaper statements above referred to the subject of this communication, if the threat of treating as pirates the citizens of this Confederacy, armed for service on the high seas, had not been contained in your proclamation of the —— April last. That proclamation, however, seems to afford a sufficient justification for considering these published statements as not devoid of probability.

It is the desire of this Government so to conduct the war now existing as to mitigate its horrors as far as may be possible; and, with this intent, its treatment of the prisoners captured by its forces has been marked by the greatest humanity and leniency consistent with public obligations; some have been permitted to return home on parole, others to remain at large under similar conditions within this Confederacy, and all have been furnished with rations for their subsistence, such as are allowed to our own troops. It is only since the news has been received of the treatment of the prisoners taken on the Savannah that I have been compelled to withdraw these indulgencies, and to hold the prisoners taken by us in strict confinement.

A just regard to humanity and to the honor of this Government now requires me to state explicitly that, painful as will be the necessity, this Government will deal out to the prisoners held by it the same treatment and the same fate as shall be experienced by those captured on the Savannah, and if driven to the terrible necessity of retaliation by your execution of any of the officers or the crew of the Savannah, that retaliation will be extended so far as shall be requisite to secure the abandonment of a practice unknown to the warfare of civilized man, and so barbarous as to disgrace the nation which shall be guilty of inaugurating it.

With this view, and because it may not have reached you, I now renew the proposition made to the commander of the blockading squadron to exchange for the prisoners taken on the Savannah, an equal number of those now held by us, according to rank. I am yours, etc.,   JEFFERSON DAVIS,

President and Commander in Chief of the Army and Navy of the Confederate States.

THIRD SESSION.

MESSAGES.

To the Congress of the Confederate States of America.

Gentlemen: My message,* addressed to you at the commencement of the session, contained such full information of the state of the Confederacy as to render it unnecessary that I should now do more than call your attention to such important facts as have occurred during the recess, and to matters connected with the public defense.

I have again to congratulate you on the accession of new members to our confederation of free, equal, and sovereign States. Our loved and honored brethren of North Carolina and Tennessee have consummated the action, foreseen and provided for at your last session, and I have had the gratification of announcing, by proclamation, in conformity with law, that those States were admitted into the Confederacy.

The people of Virginia also, by a majority previously unknown in her history, have ratified the action of her Convention, uniting her fortunes with ours. The States of Arkansas, North Carolina, and Virginia have likewise adopted the permanent Constitution of the Confederate States, and no doubt is entertained of its adoption by Tennessee at the election to be held early next month.

I deemed it advisable to direct the removal of the several Executive Departments, with their archives, to this city, to which you had removed the seat of government, immediately after your adjournment. The aggressive movements of the enemy required prompt and energetic action. The accumulation of his forces on the Potomac sufficiently demonstrated that his efforts were to be directed against Virginia; and from no point could the necessary measures for her defense and protection be so efficiently protected as from her own capital.

The rapid progress of events for the last few weeks has fully sufficed to strip the veil behind which the true policy and pur-

---

*Page 63.

poses of the Government of the United States had been previously concealed; their odious features now stand fully revealed; the message of their President and the action of their Congress during the present month confess the intention of subjugating these States by war, whose folly is equaled by its wickedness; a war by which it is impossible to attain the proposed result, whilst its dire calamities, not to be avoided by us, will fall with double severity on themselves.

Commencing in March last, with an affectation of ignoring the secession of the seven States which first organized this Government; persisting in April in the idle and absurd assumption of the existence of a riot which was to be dispersed by a *posse comitatus;* continuing in successive months the false representation that these States intended offensive war, in spite of the conclusive evidence to the contrary, furnished as well by official action as by the very basis on which this Government is constituted, the President of the United States and his advisers succeeded in deceiving the people of those States into the belief that the purpose of this Government was not peace at home, but conquest abroad; not the defense of its own liberties, but the subversion of those of the people of the United States.

The series of maneuvers by which this impression was created: the art with which they were devised, and the perfidy with which they were executed, were already known to you; but you could scarcely have supposed that they would be openly avowed, and their success made the subject of boast and self-laudation in an executive message. Fortunately for the truth of history, however, the President of the United States details with minuteness the attempt to reënforce Fort Pickens, in violation of an armistice of which he confesses to have been informed, but "only by rumors too vague and uncertain to fix attention;" the hostile expedition dispatched to supply Fort Sumter, admitted to have been undertaken with a knowledge that its success was impossible; the sending of notice to the Governor of South Carolina of his intention to use force to accomplish his object; and then, quoting from his inaugural address the assurance that there could be no conflict unless these States were the aggressors, he proceeds to declare that his conduct, as just related by himself, was a performance of this promise, "so free from the power of ingenious sophistry as that the world should not be able to misunderstand it;" and in defiance of his own statement that he gave notice of the approach of a hostile fleet, he charges these States with becoming the assailants of the United States, "without a gun in sight or in expectancy to return their fire, save only the few in the fort." He is indeed fully justified in saying that the case "is so free from the power of ingenious sophistry that the world will not be able to misunderstand it."

Under cover of this unfounded pretense that the Confederate States are the assailants, that high functionary, after expressing his concern that some foreign nations "had so shaped their action as if they supposed the early destruction of our National Union was probable," abandons all further disguise, and proposes "to make this contest a short and decisive one," by placing at the control of the Government for the work at least 400,000 men and $400,000,000. The Congress, concurring in the doubt thus intimated as to the sufficiency of the force demanded, has increased it to half a million of men. These enormous preparations in men and money, for the conduct of a war on a scale more gigantic than any which the new world has ever witnessed, is a distinct avowal, in the eyes of civilized man, that the United States are engaged in a conflict with a great and powerful nation; they are at last compelled to abandon the pretense of being engaged in dispersing rioters and suppressing insurrections; and are driven to the acknowledgment that the ancient Union has been dissolved. They recognize the separate existence of these Confederate States, by the interdiction, embargo, and blockade of all commerce between them and the United States, not only by sea, but by land; not only in ships, but in rail cars; not only with those who bear arms, but with the entire population of the Confederate States. Finally, they have repudiated the foolish conceit that the inhabitants of this Confederacy are still citizens of the United States, for they are waging an indiscriminate war upon them all, with a savage ferocity unknown to modern civilization. In this war, rapine is the rule; private residences, in peaceful rural retreats, are bombarded and burnt; grain crops in the field are consumed by the torch; and when the torch is not convenient, careful labor is bestowed to render complete the destruction of every article of use or ornament remaining in private dwellings, after their inhabitants have fled from the outrages of a brutal soldiery.

In 1781 Great Britain, when invading her revolted colonies, took possession of the very district of country near Fortress Monroe, now occupied by troops of the United States. The houses then inhabited by the people, after being respected and protected by avowed invaders, are now pillaged and destroyed by men who pretend that the victims are their fellow-citizens.

Mankind will shudder to hear the tales of outrages committed on defenseless females by soldiers of the United States now invading our homes; yet these outrages are prompted by inflamed passions and the madness of intoxication. But who shall depict the horror with which they will regard the cool and deliberate malignity which, under pretext of suppressing an insurrection, said by themselves to be upheld by a minority only of our people, makes special war on the sick, including the women and the children, by carefully devised measures to prevent their obtaining the medicines necessary for their cure. The sacred claims of humanity, respected even during the fury of actual battle, by careful diversion of attack from the hospitals containing wounded enemies, are outraged in cold blood by a government and people that pretend to desire a continuance of fraternal connections.

All these outrages must remain unavenged, save by the universal reprobation of mankind, in all cases where the actual perpetrators of the wrongs escape capture. They admit of no retaliation. The humanity of our people would shrink instinctively from the bare idea of waging a like war upon the sick, the women, and the children of the enemy.

But there are other savage practices which have been resorted to by the Government of the United States, which do admit of repression by retaliation. I have been driven to the necessity of enforcing this repression. The prisoners of war taken by the enemy on board the armed schooner Savannah, sailing under our commission, were, as I was credibly advised, treated like common felons; put in irons; confined in a jail usually appropriated to criminals of the worst dye, and threatened with punishment as such. I had made an application for the exchange of these prisoners, to the commanding officer of the enemy's squadron off Charleston harbor, but that officer had already sent the prisoners to New York when the application was made. I, therefore, deemed it my duty to renew the proposal for the exchange, to the constitutional Commander in Chief of the Army and Navy of the United States, the only officer having control of the prisoners. To this end I dispatched an officer to him, under a flag of truce; and, in making the proposal, I informed President Lincoln of my resolute purpose to check all barbarities on prisoners of war, by such severity of retaliation on the prisoners held by us as should secure the abandonment of the practice.

This communication was received and read by the officer in command of the Army of the United States, and a message was brought from him, by the bearer of my communication, that a reply would be returned by President Lincoln as soon as possible. I earnestly hope that this promised reply, which has not yet been received, will convey the assurance that prisoners of war will be treated, in this unhappy contest, with that regard to humanity which has made such conspicuous progress in the conduct of modern warfare. As a measure of precaution, however, and until the promised reply is received, I still retain in close custody some officers captured from the enemy, whom it had been my pleasure previously to enlarge on parole, and whose fate must necessarily depend on that of the prisoners held by the enemy.

I append a copy of my communication* to the President and Commander in Chief of the Army and Navy of the United States, and of the report of the officer charged to deliver it, marked Doc. A.

There are some other passages in the remarkable paper to which I have directed your attention, having reference to the peculiar relations which exist between this Government and the States usually termed the border slave States, which cannot properly be withheld from notice.

The hearts of our people are animated by sentiments toward the inhabitants of these States, which found expression in your enactment refusing to consider them as enemies, or to authorize hostilities against them. That a very large portion of the people of those States regard us as brethren; that if unrestrained by the actual presence of large armies, the subversion of civil authority

*See page 115.

and the declaration of martial law, some of them at least would joyfully unite with us; that they are with almost entire unanimity opposed to the prosecution of the war waged against us, are facts of which daily recurring events fully warrant the assertion.

The President of the United States refuses to recognize in these, our late sister States, the right of refraining from attack on us; and justifies his refusal by the assertion that the States have no other power "than that reserved to them in the Union by the Constitution, no one of them having ever been a State out of the Union."

This view of the constitutional relations between the States and the General Government is a fitting introduction to another assertion of the message, that the Executive possesses the power of suspending the writ of *habeas corpus,* and of delegating that power to military commanders, at his discretion; and both these propositions claim a respect equal to that which is felt for the additional statement of opinion in the same paper, that it is proper, in order to execute the laws, that "some single law, made in such extreme tenderness of the citizen's liberty, that practically it relieves more of the guilty than the innocent, should, to a very limited extent, be violated."

We may well rejoice that we have forever severed our connection with a government that thus tramples on all the principles of constitutional liberty, and with a people in whose presence such avowals could be hazarded.

The operations in the field will be greatly extended by reason of the policy which, heretofore secretly entertained, is now avowed and acted on by the United States. The forces hitherto raised proved ample for the defense of the seven States which originally organized the Confederacy, as is evinced by the fact that, with the exception of three fortified islands, whose defense is efficiently aided by a preponderating naval force, the enemy has been driven completely out of those States; and now, at the expiration of five months from the formation of the Government, not a single hostile foot presses their soil. These forces, however, must necessarily prove inadequate to repel the invasion by half a million of men, now proposed by the enemy; and a corresponding increase in our forces will become necessary. The recommendations for the raising and efficient equipment of this additional force will be contained in the communication of the Secretary of War, to which I need scarcely invite your earnest attention.

In my message delivered in April last, I referred to the promise of abundant crops, with which we were cheered.* The grain crops, generally, have since been harvested, and the yield has proven to be the most abundant known in our history. Many believe the supply adequate to two years' consumption of our population. Cotton, sugar, and tobacco, forming the surplus production of our agriculture, and furnishing the basis of our commercial interchanges, present the most cheering promise; and a kind Providence has smiled on the labor which extracts the teeming wealth of our soil in all portions of our Confederacy.

It is the more gratifying to be able to give you this assurance, because of the need of a large and increased expenditure in the support of our Army. Elevated and purified by the sacred cause they maintain, our fellow-citizens of every condition of life exhibit the most self-sacrificing devotion. They manifest a laudable pride in upholding their independence, unaided by any resources other than their own; and the immense wealth which a fertile soil and genial climate have accumulated in this Confederacy of agriculturists could not be more strikingly displayed than in the large revenues which, with eager zeal, they have contributed at the call of their country. In the single article of cotton the subscriptions to the loan proposed by the Government cannot fall short of fifty millions of dollars, and will probably largely exceed that amount; and scarcely an article required for the consumption of the Army is provided otherwise than by subscription to the produce loan, so happily devised by your wisdom. The Secretary of the Treasury, in the report submitted to you by him, will give you the amplest details connected with that branch of the public service.

But it is not alone in their prompt pecuniary contributions that the noble race of freemen who inhabit these States evince how worthy they are of the liberties which they so well know how to defend. In numbers far exceeding those authorized by your laws they have pressed the tender of their services against the enemy. Their attitude of calm and sublime devotion to their country; the cool and confident courage with which they are already preparing

---

*See page 81.

to meet the threatened invasion in whatever proportions it may assume; the assurance that their sacrifices and their services will be renewed from year to year with unfaltering purpose, until they have made good to the uttermost their right to self-government; the generous and almost unquestioning confidence which they display in their Government during the pending struggle—all combine to present a spectacle such as the world has rarely, if ever, seen.

To speak of subjugating such a people, so united and determined, is to speak a language incomprehensible to them. To resist attacks on their rights or their liberties is with them an instinct. Whether this war shall last one, or three, or five years, is a problem they leave to be solved by the enemy alone; it will last till the enemy shall have withdrawn from their borders—till their political rights, their altars, and their homes are freed from invasion. Then, and then only, will they rest from this struggle to enjoy in peace the blessings which with the favor of Providence they have secured by the aid of their own strong hearts and sturdy arms.   JEFFERSON DAVIS.

Richmond, July 20, 1861.

DISPATCH OF PRESIDENT DAVIS TO THE CONGRESS.

Soon after prayer in the Confederate Congress, on the morning of the 22d,* the following dispatch was read to that body:

MANASSAS JUNCTION, Sunday night [July 21, 1861].

Night has closed upon a hard-fought field. Our forces were victorious. The enemy was routed, and fled precipitately, abandoning a large amount of arms, ammunition, knapsacks, and baggage. The ground was strewed for miles with those killed, and the farmhouses and the ground around were filled with wounded.

Pursuit was continued along several routes toward Leesburg and Centerville until darkness covered the fugitives. We have captured several field batteries, stands of arms, and Union and State flags. Many prisoners have been taken. Too high praise

---

*July, 1861.

cannot be bestowed, whether for the skill of the principal officers or for the gallantry of all of our troops. The battle was mainly fought on our left. Our force was 15,000; that of the enemy estimated at 35,000. JEFFERSON DAVIS.

RICHMOND, July 30, 1861.

Hon. Howell Cobb, President of the Congress, C. S. A.

Sir: I have the honor to acknowledge the resolution of inquiry of this date in relation to hostile preparations for the descent of the river Mississippi, and whether preparations for defense against such threatened attack have been made, with advice as to the mode of adopting a plan for that purpose, and in reply have to state that the only information I have in relation to the described preparations for descent is derived from public newspapers and rumors; they had, however, such stamp of credibility as to induce to measures to repel the attack if attempted. Estimates have been prepared by the Secretary of the Navy for means described in the accompanying report, and which, in conjunction with the land batteries constructed and others devised, will, it is hoped, be adequate for the need. JEFFERSON DAVIS.

EXECUTIVE DEPARTMENT,
RICHMOND, July 31, 1861.

Hon. Howell Cobb, President of the Congress.

Sir: In accordance with a resolution of the Congress adopted on the 29th inst., I herewith transmit a copy of the report* of Lieut. Col. James H. Burton, in charge of Va. Ord. to Maj. J. Gorgas, Chief of Ordnance. JEFFERSON DAVIS.

RICHMOND, August 1, 1861.

Hon. Howell Cobb, President of Congress of Confederate States.

Sir: I have the honor to acknowledge the resolution of inquiry of this date in relation to the commissariat of the Confederate States, and to reply that its condition is, in my judgment, quite

---

*Relating to the use of the machinery for the manufacture of muskets, removed from Harpers Ferry.

as good as was reasonable to expect. The occupation of the railroads in the transportation of troops and munitions of war has interfered with the collection of the desired supply of bacon, but no complaint of insufficiency of rations has reached me until within a few days past. I have been informed of a failure of issues to troops at Manassas; the chief commissary there has communicated to me that the failure was restricted to the articles of hard bread and bacon. As this, however, was not consistent with the complaint made, inquiries have been instituted as well to remedy any existing irregularities as to prevent such occurrence in future.

                                                   JEFF'N DAVIS.

RICHMOND, August 3, 1861.

To the President of Congress of Confederate States.

Sir: I have reliable information that a considerable force of Missourians now coöperating with our troops near the northern frontier of Arkansas are destitute of the supplies necessary to their efficiency, and that the enemy have such power within the limits of the State as to deprive its Government of the capacity to give to said force the necessary relief. Under these circumstances I recommend the enactment of a law appropriating, say one million of dollars, to supply the Missourians who are or may be coöperating with us with such clothing, subsistence, arms, and ammunition as may be necessary for them, and which it may be practicable to furnish. The same to be supplied under such regulations as Congress may determine.   JEFF'N DAVIS.

EXECUTIVE DEPARTMENT,
RICHMOND, August 8, 1861.

Hon. Howell Cobb, President of the Congress.

Sir: I herewith transmit to the Congress the inclosed communication from the Hon. Secretary of War, recommending certain appropriations therein mentioned.   JEFFERSON DAVIS.

EXECUTIVE DEPARTMENT,
RICHMOND, August 10, 1861.

Hon. Howell Cobb, President of the Congress.

Sir: I herewith transmit to the Congress a communication from the Hon. Secretary of War, asking for an appropriation, herein named, for the support of the military hospitals.

JEFFERSON DAVIS.

EXECUTIVE DEPARTMENT,
RICHMOND, August 15, 1861.

Hon. Howell Cobb, President of the Congress.

Sir: I herewith transmit to the Congress a communication from the Hon. Secretary of War, asking for an appropriation of one hundred and thirty thousand dollars to provide for cooks and nurses to minister to the sick and wounded of the Army.

JEFFERSON DAVIS.

EXECUTIVE DEPARTMENT,
CONFEDERATE STATES OF AMERICA,
RICHMOND, August 17, 1861.

The Hon. Howell Cobb, President of the Congress.

Sir: In reply to the resolution of Congress of the 15th inst., calling upon me to furnish that body with the official reports of the various battles fought by our armies since its last adjournment, I have the honor herewith to submit the report of the Secretary of War concerning your resolution.

JEFFERSON DAVIS.

EXECUTIVE DEPARTMENT,
RICHMOND, August 21, 1861.

Hon. Howell Cobb, President of the Congress.*

Sir: In response to the resolution of the Congress of August 17, 1861, I herewith transmit all the official information † which I have in relation to the subject of inquiry. Letters of an un-

---

*See also message of August 23, 1861, page 128.

†Relative to the hanging of two sentinels of the South Carolina troops by Federal forces, and treatment of Confederate prisoners by Federal authorities.

official character have been received, and though not entirely accordant in their statements, the general tenor has shown that the treatment received by our fellow-citizens, whether prisoners of war or captives taken from their homes, has not been such as the usage of the most civilized nations prescribes.

JEFFERSON DAVIS.

EXECUTIVE DEPARTMENT,
RICHMOND, August 22, 1861.

Hon. Howell Cobb, President of the Congress.

Sir: I herewith transmit to the Congress the inclosed estimate of the Hon. Postmaster General for the service of his Department for the year ending February 18, 1862, with an accompanying explanation.   JEFFERSON DAVIS.

EXECUTIVE DEPARTMENT, August 23, 1861.

Hon. Howell Cobb, President of the Congress.*

Sir: In response to the resolution of the Congress of the 22d inst., I herewith transmit the inclosed communication† from the Hon. Secretary of War.   JEFFERSON DAVIS.

EXECUTIVE DEPARTMENT, August 28, 1861.

Hon. Howell Cobb, President of the Congress.

Sir: I hereby nominate, for the advice and consent of the Congress, the Hon. James M. Mason, of Virginia, to be Commissioner to England, and the Hon. John Slidell, of Louisiana, to be Commissioner to France.   JEFFERSON DAVIS.

EXECUTIVE DEPARTMENT,
RICHMOND, August 30, 1861.

Hon. Howell Cobb, President of the Congress.

Sir: The Congress having passed an act to aid the people of Kentucky in repelling an invasion or occupation of their soil by

---

*See also message of August 21, 1861, page 127.
†Relative to the hanging of two sentinels of the South Carolina troops by Federal forces.

the armed forces of the United States I would recommend that an appropriation of one million of dollars be made for the purpose of carrying into effect the object of said act.

JEFFERSON DAVIS.

RICHMOND, August 31, 1861.

Hon. Howell Cobb, President of the Congress.

Sir: The resolution of the Congress of this date, calling for all the information in my possession in relation to the landing of the Federal troops upon the coast of North Carolina, and inquiring what steps, if any, have been taken to repel the invasion, and to put the coast in a state of defense, has just been received; and I have to reply that no official report of the occurrence has been received. I transmit copies of the telegrams* which contain all the information which has been received by the Executive Department.

Preparations to put the coast of the State of North Carolina in a proper condition for defense are still in progress, and will receive such additional attention as this occasion indicates to be necessary. It is not deemed consistent with the public interest further to state the movements of troops which, in this connection, have been ordered and are in contemplation.

JEFFERSON DAVIS.

RICHMOND, August 31, 1861.

Hon. Howell Cobb, President of the Congress.

I nominate the officers on the accompanying list to be Generals in the Army of the Confederate States, to take rank according to the dates set opposite to their names, respectively, agreeably to the recommendation of the Secretary of War.

JEFFERSON DAVIS.

Sam'l Cooper, to date from 16th May, 1861.
Albert S. Johnston,† to date from 30th May, 1861.
Robt. E. Lee, to date from 14th June, 1861.
Joseph E. Johnston, to date from 4th July, 1861.
G. T. Beauregard, to date from 21st July, 1861.

---

*Relative to the capture of Hatteras Inlet.
†Killed in battle of Shiloh, April 6, 1862.

VETO MESSAGE.

To the Congress.

Gentlemen: I have had under consideration the bill entitled "An Act to authorize the appointment of an additional Assistant Surgeon to each regiment in the Army of the Confederate States," and feel so well convinced that the expenditure which it requires is unnecessary, and that the means can ill be spared in the present condition of the Treasury, that I am reluctantly compelled to return it for your reconsideration.

The medical and surgical force already provided by law, including the provision recently made for surgeons for hospitals, will require an expenditure of about two millions and a half of dollars. Power is already vested in me to employ temporarily the aid of physicians in hospitals, and you have appropriated $50,000 for that purpose. Discretion is also given to the Secretary of War, by the act of 26th February, 1861, to appoint as many assistant surgeons as the service may require; and the legislation on the entire subject is on the most liberal scale.

Yet the act now presented leaves me no discretion to limit the number of the additional assistant surgeons to be appointed. It orders an additional officer to the medical staff of each regiment, whether wanted or not; and thus requires an additional annual expenditure of seven hundred and thirty-two thousand dollars ($732,000).

I am aware that there have been causes of complaint in relation to neglect of our sick and wounded soldiers; but this, it is believed, arises not so much from an insufficiency in the number of the surgeons and assistant surgeons as from inattention or want of qualification, and I am endeavoring to apply the proper remedy by organizing a board of examiners, so as to ascertain who are the officers really to blame, and replace them by others more competent and efficient. I feel confident that, by this course, ample medical assistance would be secured for the troops without further expenditure. The surgeons and assistant surgeons, heretofore appointed, have in most instances received their commissions in consequence of the recommendations of the officers of the regiments to which they are attached. This was almost the only means of making selections in the sudden emergencies of the war, and experience has suggested that many of the officers so appointed are unequal to the duties of their stations.

For these reasons, I hope that when you take the subject into reconsideration, you will be able to concur with me in the opinion that this additional expenditure can be avoided, and that there is no necessity for the passage of the bill.   JEFFERSON DAVIS.

[Received August 22, 1861.]

PROCLAMATIONS.

BY THE PRESIDENT OF THE CONFEDERATE STATES.

A PROCLAMATION.

Whereas, the Congress of the Confederate States of America did by an act approved on the 8th day of August, 1861, entitled "An Act respecting alien enemies," make provision that proclamation should be issued by the President in relation to alien enemies, and in conformity with the provision of said act:

Now, therefore, I, Jefferson Davis, President of the Confederate States of America, do issue this my proclamation; and I do hereby warn and require every male citizen of the United States of the age of fourteen years and upward now within the Confederate States and adhering to the Government of the United States and acknowledging the authority of the same, and not being a citizen of the Confederate States, to depart from the Confederate States within forty days from the date of this proclamation. And I do warn all persons above described who shall remain within the Confederate States after the expiration of said period of forty days that they will be treated as alien enemies.

Provided, however, That this proclamation shall not be considered as applicable during the existing war to citizens of the United States residing within the Confederate States with intent to become citizens thereof, and who shall make a declaration of such intention in due form, acknowledging the authority of this Government; nor shall this proclamation be considered as extending to the States of Delaware, Maryland, Kentucky, Missouri, the District of Columbia, the Territories of Arizona and New

Mexico, and the Indian Territory south of Kansas, who shall not be chargeable with actual hostility or other crime against the public safety, and who shall acknowledge the authority of the Government of the Confederate States.

And I do further proclaim and make known that I have established the rules and regulations hereto annexed in accordance with the provisions of said law.

Given under my hand and the seal of the Confederate States of America at the city of Richmond on this 14th day of August, A.D. 1861.   JEFFERSON DAVIS.

By the President:

R. M. T. HUNTER, *Secretary of State.*

REGULATIONS RESPECTING ALIEN ENEMIES.

The following regulations are hereby established respecting alien enemies, under the provisions of an act approved 8th of August, 1861, entitled "An Act Respecting Alien Enemies:"

1. Immediately after the expiration of the term of forty days from the date of the foregoing proclamation, it shall be the duty of the several district attorneys, marshals, and other officers of the Confederate States to make complaint against aliens or alien enemies coming within the purview of the act aforesaid, to the end that the several courts of the Confederate States and of each State having jurisdiction may order the removal of such aliens or alien enemies beyond the territory of the Confederate States or their restraint and confinement, according to the terms of said law.

2. The marshals of the Confederate States are hereby directed to apprehend all aliens against whom complaints may be made under said law and to hold them in strict custody until the final order of the court, taking special care that such aliens obtain no information that could possibly be made useful to the enemy.

3. Whenever the removal of any alien beyond the limits of the Confederate States is ordered by any competent authority under the provisions of said law the marshal shall proceed to execute the order in person or by deputy or other discreet person in such manner as to prevent the alien so removed from obtaining any information that could be used to the prejudice of the Confederate States.

4. Any alien who shall return to these States during the war after having been removed therefrom under the provisions of said law shall be regarded and treated as an alien enemy, and if made prisoner shall be at once delivered over to the nearest military authority to be dealt with as a spy or as a prisoner of war, as the case may require.

BY THE PRESIDENT OF THE CONFEDERATE STATES.

A PROCLAMATION.

Whereas, through accident a bill to authorize the President to continue the appointments made by him in the military and naval service during the recess of Congress or the present session, and to submit them to Congress at its next session, failed to be delivered to the President for his signature prior to the adjournment of Congress; and

Whereas, the failure of said bill to become a law would cause serious inconvenience to the public service:

Now, therefore, I, Jefferson Davis, President of the Confederate States, do issue this my proclamation, convoking the Congress of the Confederate States for the transaction of business, at the Capitol, in the city of Richmond, on the 3d day of September, at 12 o'clock noon of that day, of which all who shall at that time be entitled to act as members of that body are hereby required to take notice.

Given under my hand and the seal of the Confederate States, at Richmond, this 2d day of September, A.D. 1861.

[SEAL.]   JEFFERSON DAVIS.

By the President:

R. M. T. HUNTER, *Secretary of State.*

RESOLUTIONS OF THANKS.

Resolved by the Congress of the Confederate States of America, That the thanks of Congress are eminently due, and are hereby cordially given, to General Joseph E. Johnston and General Gustave T. Beauregard, and to the officers and troops under their command, for the great and signal victory obtained by them over forces of the United States far exceeding them in number, in the battle of the twenty-first of July, at Manassas; and for the gallantry, courage, and endurance evinced by them, in a protracted and continuous struggle of more than ten hours; a victory, the great results of which will be realized in the future successes of the war, and which, in the judgment of Congress, entitles all who contributed to it to the gratitude of their country.

Resolved, further, That the foregoing resolution be made known in appropriate general orders, by the Generals in command, to the officers and troops to whom they are addressed.

Approved August 6, 1861.

Whereas, it has pleased Almighty God to vouchsafe to the arms of the Confederate States another glorious and important victory in a portion of the country where a reverse would have been disastrous by exposing the families of the good people of the State of Missouri to the unbridled license of the brutal soldiery of an unscrupulous enemy: Therefore be it

Resolved by the Congress of the Confederate States, That the thanks of Congress are cordially tendered to Brig. Gen. Ben McCulloch and the officers and soldiers of his brave command for their gallant conduct in defeating, after a battle of six hours and a half, a force of the enemy equal in numbers and greatly superior in all their appointments, thus proving that a right cause nerves the hearts and strengthens the arms of the Southern people, fighting, as they are, for their liberty, their homes, and firesides, against an unholy despotism.

Resolved further, That in the opinion of Congress General McCulloch and his gallant troops are entitled to and will receive the grateful thanks of our people.

Resolved further, That the foregoing resolutions be communicated to that command by the proper Department.

Approved August 22, 1861.

FOURTH SESSION (CALLED).

MET AT RICHMOND, VA., SEPTEMBER 3, 1861. ADJOURNED SAME DAY.

MESSAGE.

Gentlemen of the Congress.

The bill important to the public service, being one to continue in office persons who have been appointed and nominated, and whose nominations had not been acted upon, was, I learned after your adjournment on the 31st ultimo, enrolled for my signature, but by some accident was not delivered to me, and thus failed to become a law; wherefore it has become necessary to convene you.

You may either make the provisions contemplated, or by acting upon the nominations, or otherwise as in your judgment may seem best relieve the Government of the embarrassment to which otherwise it must be subjected.   JEFFERSON DAVIS.

September 3, 1861.

PROCLAMATION.

BY THE PRESIDENT OF THE CONFEDERATE STATES.

A PROCLAMATION.

Whereas it hath pleased Almighty God, the Sovereign Disposer of events, to protect and defend the Confederate States hitherto in their conflict with their enemies, and to be unto them a shield: and

Whereas, with grateful thanks we recognize his hand, and acknowledge that not unto us, but unto him, belongeth the victory; and in humble dependence upon his almighty strength, and trusting in the justness of our cause, we appeal to him, that he may set at naught the efforts of our enemies, and put them to confusion and shame;

Now, therefore, I, Jefferson Davis, President of the Confederate States, in view of the impending conflict, do hereby set apart Friday, the 15th day of November, as a day of fasting, humiliation, and prayer; and I do hereby invite the reverend clergy and people of these Confederate States to repair on that day to their usual places of public worship, and to implore the blessings of Almighty God upon our arms, that he may give us victory over our enemies, preserve our homes and altars from pollution, and secure to us the restoration of peace and prosperity.

[SEAL.] Given under my hand and the seal of the Confederate States, at Richmond, this thirty-first day of October, in the year of our Lord one thousand eight hundred and sixty-one.   JEFFERSON DAVIS.

By the President:

R. M. T. HUNTER, *Secretary of State.*

FIFTH SESSION.

MET AT RICHMOND, VA., NOVEMBER 18, 1861.   ADJOURNED FEBRU-
ARY 17, 1862.

MESSAGES.

RICHMOND, November 18, 1861.

The Congress of the Confederate States.

The few weeks which have elapsed since your adjournment have brought us so near the close of the year that we are now able to sum up its general results. The retrospect is such as should fill the hearts of our people with gratitude to Providence for his kind interposition in their behalf. Abundant yields have rewarded the labor of the agriculturist, whilst the manufacturing industry of the Confederate States was never so prosperous as now. The necessities of the times have called into existence new branches of manufactures and given a fresh impulse to the activity of those heretofore in operation. The means of the Confederate States for manufacturing the necessaries and comforts of life within themselves increase as the conflict continues, and we are gradually becoming independent of the rest of the world for the supply of such military stores and munitions as are indispensable for war.

The operations of the Army, soon to be partially interrupted by the approaching winter, have afforded a protection to the country and shed a luster upon its arms through the trying vicissitudes of more than one arduous campaign which entitle our brave volunteers to our praise and our gratitude. From its commencement to the present period the war has been enlarging its proportions and expanding its boundaries so as to include new fields. The conflict now extends from the shores of the Chesapeake to the confines of Missouri and Arizona; yet sudden calls from the remotest points for military aid have been met with promptness enough not only to avert disaster in the face of superior numbers, but also to roll back the tide of invasion from the border.

When the war commenced the enemy were possessed of certain strategic points and strong places within the Confederate States. They greatly exceeded us in numbers, in available resources, and in the supplies necessary for war. Military establishments had been long organized and were complete; the Navy, and for the most part the Army, once common to both, were in their possession. To meet all this we had to create not only an Army in the face of war itself, but also the military establishments necessary to equip and place it in the field. It ought indeed to be a subject of gratulation that the spirit of the volunteers and the patriotism of the people have enabled us, under Providence, to grapple successfully with these difficulties. A succession of glorious victories at Bethel, Bull Run, Manassas, Springfield, Lexington, Leesburg, and Belmont has checked the wicked invasion which greed of gain and the unhallowed lust of power brought upon our soil, and has proved that numbers cease to avail when directed against a people fighting for the sacred right of self-government and the privileges of freemen. After more than seven months of war the enemy have not only failed to extend their occupancy of our soil, but new States and Territories have been added to our Confederacy, while, instead of their threatened march of unchecked conquest, they have been driven, at more than one point, to assume the defensive, and, upon a fair comparison between the two belligerents as to men, military means, and financial condition, the Confederate States are relatively much stronger now than when the struggle commenced.

Since your adjournment the people of Missouri have conducted the war in the face of almost unparalleled difficulties with a spirit and success alike worthy of themselves and of the great cause in which they are struggling. Since that time Kentucky, too, has become the theater of active hostilities. The Federal forces have not only refused to acknowledge her right to be neutral, and have insisted upon making her a party to the war, but have invaded her for the purpose of attacking the Confederate States. Outrages of the most despotic character have been perpetrated upon her people; some of her most eminent citizens have been seized and borne away to languish in foreign prisons, without knowing who were their accusers or the specific charges made against them, while others have been forced to abandon their homes, families, and property, and seek a refuge in distant lands.

Finding that the Confederate States were about to be invaded through Kentucky, and that her people, after being deceived into a mistaken security, were unarmed and in danger of being sub-jugated by the Federal forces, our armies were marched into that State to repel the enemy and prevent their occupation of certain strategic points which would have given them great advantages in the contest—a step which was justified not only by the neces-sities of self-defense on the part of the Confederate States, but also by a desire to aid the people of Kentucky. It was never in-tended by the Confederate Government to conquer or coerce the people of that State; but, on the contrary, it was declared by our generals that they would withdraw their troops if the Federal Government would do likewise. Proclamation was also made of the desire to respect the neutrality of Kentucky and the inten-tion to abide by the wishes of her people as soon as they were free to express their opinions. These declarations were approved by me, and I should regard it as one of the best effects of the march of our troops into Kentucky if it should end in giving to her people liberty of choice and a free opportunity to decide their own destiny according to their own will.

The Army has been chiefly instrumental in prosecuting the great contest in which we are engaged, but the Navy has also been effective in full proportion to its means. The naval officers, deprived to a great extent of an opportunity to make their pro-fessional skill available at sea, have served with commendable zeal and gallantry on shore and upon inland waters, further de-tail of which will be found in the reports of the Secretaries of the Navy and War. In the transportation of the mails many diffi-culties have arisen, which will be found fully developed in the report of the Postmaster General. The absorption of the ordi-nary means of transportation for the movements of troops and military supplies; the insufficiency of the rolling stock of rail-roads for the accumulation of business resulting both from mil-itary operations and the obstruction of water communication by the presence of the enemy's fleet; the failure, and even refusal, of contractors to comply with the terms of their agreements; the difficulties inherent in inaugurating so vast and complicated a system as that which requires postal facilities for every town and village in a territory so extended as ours, have all combined to impede the best-directed efforts of the Postmaster General, whose zeal, industry, and ability have been taxed to the utmost extent.

Some of these difficulties can only be overcome by time and an improved condition of the country upon the restoration of peace, but others may be remedied by legislation, and your attention is invited to the recommendations contained in the report of the head of that Department.

The condition of the Treasury will doubtless be a subject of anxious inquiry on your part. I am happy to say that the financial system already adopted has worked well so far, and promises good results for the future. To the extent that Treasury notes may be issued the Government is enabled to borrow money without interest, and thus facilitate the conduct of the war. This extent is measured by the portion of the field of circulation which these notes can be made to occupy. The proportion of the field thus occupied depends again upon the amount of the debts for which they are receivable; and when dues, not only to the Confederate and State governments, but also to corporations and individuals, are payable in this medium, a large amount of it may be circulated at par. There is every reason to believe that the Confederate Treasury note is fast becoming such a medium. The provision that these notes shall be convertible into Confederate stock bearing 8 per cent interest, at the pleasure of the holder, insures them against a depreciation below the value of that stock, and no considerable fall in that value need be feared so long as the interest shall be punctually paid. The punctual payment of this interest has been secured by the act passed by you at the last session, imposing such a rate of taxation as must provide sufficient means for that purpose.

For the successful prosecution of this war it is indispensable that the means of transporting troops and military supplies be furnished, as far as possible, in such manner as not to interrupt the commercial intercourse between our people nor place a check on their productive energies. To this end the means of transportation from one section of our country to the other must be carefully guarded and improved. And this should be the object of anxious care on the part of State and Confederate governments, so far as they may have power over the subject.

We have already two main systems of through transportation from the north to the south—one from Richmond along the seaboard; the other through Western Virginia to New Orleans. A third might be secured by completing a link of about forty miles between Danville, in Virginia, and Greensboro, in North Carolina. The construction of this comparatively short line would give us a through route from north to south in the interior of the Confederate States and give us access to a population and to military resources from which we are now in great measure debarred. We should increase greatly the safety and capacity of our means for transporting men and military supplies. If the construction of this road should, in the judgment of Congress as it is in mine, be indispensable for the most successful prosecution of the war, the action of the Government will not be restrained by the constitutional objection which would attach to a work for commercial purposes, and attention is invited to the practicability of securing its early completion by giving the needful aid to the company organized for its construction and administration.

If we husband our means and make a judicious use of our resources, it would be difficult to fix a limit to the period during which we could conduct a war against the adversary whom we now encounter. The very efforts which he makes to isolate and invade us must exhaust his means, whilst they serve to complete the circle and diversify the productions of our industrial system. The reconstruction which he seeks to effect by arms becomes daily more and more palpably impossible. Not only do the causes which induced us to separate still exist in full force, but they have been strengthened, and whatever doubt may have lingered in the minds of any must have been completely dispelled by subsequent events. If instead of being a dissolution of a league it were indeed a rebellion in which we are engaged, we might find ample vindication for the course we have adopted in the scenes which are now being enacted in the United States. Our people now look with contemptuous astonishment on those with whom they had been so recently associated. They shrink with aversion from the bare idea of renewing such a connection. When they see a President making war without the assent of Congress; when they behold judges threatened because they maintain the writ of *habeas corpus* so sacred to freemen; when they see justice and law trampled under the armed heel of military authority, and upright men and innocent women dragged to distant dungeons upon the mere edict of a despot; when they find all this tolerated and applauded by a people who had been in the full enjoyment of freedom but a few months ago—they believe that there must be some radical incompatibility between such a people and themselves. With such a people we may be content to live at peace, but the separation is final, and for the independence we have asserted we will accept no alternative.

The nature of the hostilities which they have waged against us must be characterized as barbarous wherever it is understood. They have bombarded undefended villages without giving notice to women and children to enable them to escape, and in one instance selected the night as the period when they might surprise them most effectually whilst asleep and unsuspicious of danger. Arson and rapine, the destruction of private houses and property, and injuries of the most wanton character, even upon noncombatants, have marked their forays along our borders and upon our territory. Although we ought to have been admonished by these things that they were disposed to make war upon us in the most cruel and relentless spirit, yet we were not prepared to see them fit out a large naval expedition, with the confessed purpose not only to pillage, but to incite a servile insurrection in our midst. If they convert their soldiers into incendiaries and robbers, and involve us in a species of war which claims noncombatants, women, and children as its victims, they must expect to be treated as outlaws and enemies of mankind. There are certain rights of humanity which are entitled to respect even in war, and he who refuses to regard them forfeits his claims, if captured, to be considered as a prisoner of war, but must expect to be dealt with as an offender against all law, human and divine.

But not content with violating our rights under the law of nations at home, they have extended these injuries to us within other jurisdictions. The distinguished gentlemen whom, with your approval at the last session, I commissioned to represent the Confederacy at certain foreign courts, have been recently seized by the captain of a U. S. ship of war on board a British steamer on their voyage from the neutral Spanish port of Havana to England. The United States have thus claimed a general jurisdiction over the high seas, and entering a British ship, sailing under its country's flag, violated the rights of embassy, for the most part held sacred even amongst barbarians, by seizing our ministers whilst under the protection and within the dominions of a neutral nation. These gentlemen were as much under the jurisdiction of the British Government upon that ship and beneath its flag as if they had been on its soil, and a claim on the part of the United States to seize them in the streets of London would have been as well founded as that to apprehend them where they were taken. Had they been malefactors and citizens even of the United States they could not have been arrested on a British ship or on British soil, unless under the express provisions of a treaty and according to the forms therein provided for the extradition of criminals.

But rights the most sacred seem to have lost all respect in their eyes. When Mr. Faulkner, a former minister of the United States to France, commissioned before the secession of Virginia, his native State, returned in good faith to Washington to settle his accounts and fulfill all the obligations into which he had entered, he was perfidiously arrested and imprisoned in New York, where he now is. The unsuspecting confidence with which he reported to his Government was abused, and his desire to fulfill his trust to them was used to his injury. In conducting this war we have sought no aid and proposed no alliances offensive and defensive abroad. We have asked for a recognized place in the great family of nations, but in doing so we have demanded nothing for which we did not offer a fair equivalent. The advantages of intercourse are mutual amongst nations, and in seeking to establish diplomatic relations we were only endeavoring to place that intercourse under the regulation of public law. Perhaps we had the right, if we had chosen to exercise it, to ask to know whether the principle that "blockades to be binding must be effectual," so solemnly announced by the great powers of Europe at Paris, is to be generally enforced or applied only to particular parties. When the Confederate States, at your last session, became a party to the declaration reaffirming this principle of international law, which has been recognized so long by publicists and governments, we certainly supposed that it was to be universally enforced. The customary law of nations is made up of their practice rather than their declarations; and if such declarations are only to be enforced in particular instances at the pleasure of those who make them, then the commerce of the world, so far from being placed under the regulation of a general law, will become subject to the caprice of those who execute or suspend it at will. If such is to be the course of nations in regard to this law, it is plain that it will thus become a rule for the weak and not for the strong.

Feeling that such views must be taken by the neutral nations of the earth, I have caused the evidence to be collected which proves completely the utter inefficiency of the proclaimed blockade of our coast, and shall direct it to be laid before such governments as shall afford us the means of being heard. But, although we should be benefited by the enforcement of this law so solemnly declared by the great powers of Europe, we are not dependent on that enforcement for the successful prosecution of the war. As long as hostilities continue the Confederate States will exhibit a steadily increasing capacity to furnish their troops with food, clothing, and arms. If they should be forced to forego many of the luxuries and some of the comforts of life, they will at least have the consolation of knowing that they are thus daily becoming more and more independent of the rest of the world. If in this process labor in the Confederate States should be gradually diverted from those great Southern staples which have given life to so much of the commerce of mankind into other channels, so as to make them rival producers instead of profitable customers, they will not be the only or even the chief losers by this change in the direction of their industry. Although it is true that the cotton supply from the Southern States could only be totally cut off by the subversion of our social system, yet it is plain that a long continuance of this blockade might, by a diversion of labor and an investment of capital in other employments, so diminish the supply as to bring ruin upon all those interests of foreign countries which are dependent on that staple. For every laborer who is diverted from the culture of cotton in the South, perhaps four times as many elsewhere, who have found subsistence in the various employments growing out of its use, will be forced also to change their occupation.

While the war which is waged to take from us the right of self-government can never attain that end, it remains to be seen how far it may work a revolution in the industrial system of the world, which may carry suffering to other lands as well as to our own.

In the meantime we shall continue this struggle in humble dependence upon Providence, from whose searching scrutiny we cannot conceal the secrets of our hearts, and to whose rule we confidently submit our destinies. For the rest we shall depend upon ourselves. Liberty is always won where there exists the unconquerable will to be free, and we have reason to know the strength that is given by a conscious sense not only of the magnitude but of the righteousness of our cause.   JEFF'N DAVIS.

RICHMOND, November 25, 1861.

To the Congress of the Confederate States.

I transmit to you for your consideration two acts passed by the General Assembly of Missouri on the 31st of last October, the one entitled "An Act declaring the political ties heretofore existing between the State of Missouri and the United States of America dissolved;" the other entitled "An Act ratifying the Constitution of the Provisional Government of the Confederate States of America." Together with these I send a letter from Governor C. F. Jackson, of Missouri, addressed to myself and dated November 5, 1861.

An act of the Confederate Congress, approved August 20, 1861, in reference to Missouri, provided that when the "Constitution for the Provisional Government of the Confederate States shall be adopted and ratified by the properly and legally constituted authorities of said State, and the Governor of said State shall transmit to the President of the Confederate States an authentic copy of the proceedings touching said adoption and ratification by said State of said Provisional Constitution, upon the receipt thereof the President, by proclamation, shall announce the fact." It was also declared by this act that upon a proclamation thus made the admission of the said State into this Confederacy shall be complete "without any further proceedings on the part of Congress." I am thus empowered to judge as to the authorities in the State of Missouri which are properly and legally constituted to adopt and ratify the Constitution for the Provisional Government of the Confederate States. I am also authorized without further consultation with Congress to proclaim the admission of the State. Had the case been thus presented to me

during the recess of Congress, I should have deemed it my duty.
to issue the proclamation under this power; but as these acts are
transmitted during the session of Congress, I feel it to be due to
you, in a matter of so much importance as the admission of a
new State into the Confederacy, to lay before you the acts to
which I have referred, that you may take such action upon them
as in your judgment may be necessary and proper. I also submit
to you, for your consideration and action in relation thereto, a
copy of a convention between the Confederate States and the
State of Missouri which was concluded and signed by the commissioners of both parties at the city of Richmond, on the 31st day
of October, 1861. JEFF'N DAVIS.

November 25, 1861.
Hon. Howell Cobb, President of the Congress.

I have the honor herewith to transmit a communication from
the Provisional Governor of Kentucky informing me of the appointment of commissioners on the part of that State to treat
with the Government of the Confederate States of America for
the recognition of said State and its admission into the Confederacy. Also a communication from the president and members
of the convention which declared the separation of Kentucky from
the United States and adopted the provisional government as
therein recited. Two of the three commissioners thus appointed
have presented their credentials and submitted a proposition to
enter upon negotiations for the admission of the State of Kentucky into the Confederacy. Before entering upon such negotiation I have deemed it proper to lay the case before Congress and
ask its advice. The history of this controversy involving the
State of Kentucky is so well known to the Congress that it is
deemed unnecessary to enter here into a statement of the various
stages through which it has passed. It may, however, be proper
to advert to the fact that in every form in which the question has
been presented to the people of Kentucky we have sufficient evidence to assure us that by a large majority their will has been
manifested to unite their destinies with the Southern States whenever, despairing of the preservation of the Union, they should be
required to choose between association with the North or the

South. In both the communications presented will be found a powerful exposition of the misrepresentation of the people by the government of Kentucky, and it has led me to the conclusion that the revolution in which they are engaged offered the only remedy within their reach against usurpation and oppression, to which it would be a reflection upon that gallant people to suppose that they would tamely submit. That this proceeding for the admission of Kentucky into the Confederacy is wanting in the formality which characterized that of the States which seceded by the action of their organized government is manifested—indeed, admitted—by terming it revolutionary. This imposes the necessity for examining the evidence to establish the fact that the popular will is in favor of admission of the State into the Confederacy. To this end I refer the Congress to the commissioners who have presented to me many facts which (if opportunity be afforded them) they will no doubt as freely communicate to the Congress, The conclusion at which I have arrived is that there is enough of merit in the application to warrant a disregard of its irregularity; that it is the people—that is to say, the State—who seek to confederate with us; that though embarrassed they cannot rightfully be controlled by a Government which violates its obligations and usurps powers in derogation of the liberty which it was instituted to preserve; and that, therefore, we may rightfully recognize the provisional government of Kentucky and under its auspices admit the State into the Confederacy. In reaching this conclusion I have endeavored to divest myself of the sentiments which strongly attract me toward that State, and to regard considerations, military and political, subordinate to propriety and justice in the determination of the question. I now invite the early attention of Congress that I may be guided by its advice in my action.   JEFF'N DAVIS.

EXECUTIVE DEPARTMENT,
RICHMOND, November 27, 1861.

To the Hon. President of the Congress.

Sir: I herewith transmit to the Congress a communication from the Hon. Attorney-General, with the report of the Superintendent of Public Printing, asking for certain appropriations therein mentioned.   JEFFERSON DAVIS.

RICHMOND, VA., November 27, 1861.

To the President of the Congress, Hon. Howell Cobb.

Sir: I have the honor to acknowledge the receipt of the resolution requesting me "to communicate to Congress the reports
of all battles not heretofore communicated to Congress or published in full to the country," and to reply that copies of all such
reports have been prepared to accompany the report of the Secretary of War, to which it was supposed proper to append them
as documents. I hope very soon to be able to transmit the report of the Secretary of War with all the documents which
usually and properly attend it, those specially called for, included.

JEFFERSON DAVIS.

EXECUTIVE DEPARTMENT,
RICHMOND, November 30, 1861.

To the Hon. President of the Congress.

I herewith transmit a communication from the Hon. Secretary
of War, and recommend it to the favorable consideration of the
Congress. JEFFERSON DAVIS.

EXECUTIVE DEPARTMENT,
RICHMOND, December 3, 1861.

To the Hon. President of the Congress.

Sir: In response to the resolution of the Congress of the 28th
Nov. ulto., inquiring "whether any restrictions (and if so,
what) have been placed upon vessels leaving the ports of the
Confederate States other than those imposed by law, and if any
such have been imposed, by what authority," I herewith transmit copies of letters* furnished by the War Department, marked
"A, B, C, and D,"† which will show all the action taken on the
subject of inquiry and that no restrictions have been imposed
other than those incident to a state of war and which the public
defense, as it was believed, not only justified but demanded. It
will be noted that the instructions were given to an officer commanding the defensive line of a port threatened by the enemy's

---

*From Judah P. Benjamin, Acting Secretary of War, and A. T. Bledsoe,
to Brig. Gen. Joseph R. Anderson.

†Omitted.

fleet and related to articles usually recognized as contraband of war.　　　　　　　　　　　　　　　　　JEFFERSON DAVIS.

RICHMOND, December 4, 1861.

To the Congress of the Confederate States.

The nominations sent to the Congress at the last session not having been acted on, I respectfully request that they be returned, that they may be replaced by fuller and more perfect lists prepared for submission to your action at the present session.

JEFFERSON DAVIS.

To the Congress of the Confederate States.

I herewith communicate to Congress an act of the provisional government of Kentucky to appoint a commissioner to the Confederate States of America on the subject of banks; and also the commission of John D. Morris, Esq., who has been duly accredited to me as the commissioner appointed under said act.

It appears from the terms of said act that various banks in Kentucky have, in violation of .the State Constitution, at the dictation of foreign military power, contributed large sums of money to assist in the subjugation of the people of Kentucky. That the State of Kentucky is a stockholder in said banks, the stock having been purchased with the funds raised by taxation of all the people, and is entitled to control the said funds, and to prevent their being used for the subjugation of her people.

To prevent such injustice the act authorizes the Governor to appoint a commissioner to proceed to the Capital of the Confederate States to confer with the proper authorities as to the most practicable manner of securing all moneys and other assets of said banks; and the Confederate States are requested to cooperate with said commissioner in securing said moneys and assets.

In pursuance with the request of the provisional government of Kentucky I submit the matter to your consideration and invite such coöperation as you may deem it advisable to afford.

JEFFERSON DAVIS.

Richmond, Va., December 11, 1861.

EXECUTIVE DEPARTMENT,
RICHMOND, December 12, 1861.

To the Congress of the Confederate States.

I submit for your constitutional action treaties recently made with the Chickasaw and Choctaw, Creek, Seminole, and Cherokee tribes of Indians. In pursuance of a resolution passed by Congress the 5th day of March, 1861, I appointed Albert Pike, a citizen of Arkansas, commissioner of this Government to all the Indian tribes west of Arkansas and south of Kansas. His powers and duties were not defined in that resolution, but on the 21st of May, 1861, Congress passed "An Act for the protection of certain Indian tribes," by which the general policy of Congress in reference to those tribes was more fully declared. Considering this act as a declaration by Congress of our future policy in relation to those Indians, a copy of that act was transmitted to the commissioner and he was directed to consider it as his instructions in the contemplated negotiation.

The general policy of that act is the basis of the treaties herewith submitted; but in relation to pecuniary obligations there is a material departure, which will be more fully referred to in its appropriate connection. The general provisions of all the treaties are similar, and in each the Confederate States assume the guardianship over the tribe and become responsible for all the obligations to the Indians imposed by former treaties on the Government of the United States. Important modifications are proposed in favor of the respective local governments of these Indians, to which your special attention is invited. That their advancement in civilization justified an enlargement of their power in that regard will scarcely admit of a doubt; but whether the proposed concessions in favor of their local governments are within the bounds of a wise policy may well claim your serious consideration. In this connection your attention is specially invited to the clauses giving to certain tribes the unqualified right of admission as a State into the compact of the Confederacy, and in the meantime allowing each of these tribes to have a delegate in Congress. These provisions are regarded not only as impolitic but unconstitutional, it not being within the limits of the treaty-making power to admit a State or to control the House of Representatives in the matter of admission to its privileges. I rec-

ommend that the former provision be rejected, and that the latter
be so modified as to leave the question to the future action of
Congress; and also do recommend the rejection of those articles
in the treaties which confer upon Indians the right to testify in
the State courts, believing that the States have the power to decide that question, each for itself, independently of any action of
the Confederate Government.

The pecuniary obligations of these treaties are of great importance. Apart from the annuities secured to them by former
treaties, and which we are to assume by those now submitted,
these tribes have large permanent funds in the hands of the Government of the United States as their trustee. These funds may
be divided into three classes: First. Money which the Government of the United States stipulated to invest in its own stocks
or stocks of the States, and which has been partly invested in its
own stocks and partly uninvested, remains in its Treasury, but
upon which it is bound to pay interest. Second. Funds invested
in the stocks of States not members of this Confederacy. Third.
Money invested in stocks of States now members of this Confederacy. These three classes include all the important pecuniary obligations involved in these treaties, except interest collected by the Federal Government and not paid over to the Indians and arrearage of annual payments due under existing
treaties; to which exceptions a further notice will be given. By
the treaties now submitted to you the first and second classes are
absolutely assumed by this Government; but this Government
only undertakes as trustee to collect the third class from the
States which owe the money and pay over the amounts to the
Indians when collected. It is fortunate for the Indians and ourselves that the amounts embraced in classes one and two are
relatively small, and the obligations incurred by their assumption
cannot be onerous, as the amount due by States of the Confederacy on account of investments in the funds of Northern Indians considerably exceeds the amount to be assumed under this
provision of the treaties. We thereby have the means to compel
the Government of the United States to do justice to the Indians
within the jurisdiction of the Confederate States, or to indemnify
ourselves for its breach of faith.

By the treaty with the Cherokees we undertake to advance

$150,000, and the interest of $50,000 for educational purposes on what are known as the Cherokee neutral lands, lying between the State of Kansas and the Cherokee Territory, for which the Indians paid the United States Government $500,000, and which lands we guarantee to the Indians against the hazard of being lost by the fortune of war or ceded by treaty of peace. I herewith submit to you estimates of the entire pecuniary obligations assumed by these treaties, in tabular exhibits A and B. They are generally stated with great minuteness in the treaties, but I have caused them to be abstracted and put in tabular form for more convenient reference. I also submit to you the report of Albert Pike, the commissioner, which contains a history of his negotiations and submits his reasons for a departure from his instructions in relation to the pecuniary obligations to be incurred. In view of the circumstances by which we are surrounded, the great importance of preserving peace with the Indians on the frontier of Texas, Arkansas, and Missouri, and, not least, because of the spirit these tribes have manifested in making common cause with us in the war now existing, I recommend the assumption of the stipulated pecuniary obligations, and, with the modifications herein suggested, that the treaties submitted be ratified.

JEFFERSON DAVIS.

EXECUTIVE DEPARTMENT,
RICHMOND, December 16, 1861.

To the Hon. President of the Congress.

Sir: I herewith transmit to the Congress the report of the Hon. Secretary of War, with accompanying papers.

JEFFERSON DAVIS.

To the Provisional Congress of the Confederate States.

I herewith transmit a copy of a communication from Mr. William S. Ashe urging the completion of certain railroads as necessary for the proper transportation of troops and military stores in the exigencies of the present war. I also transmit a copy of a communication from Mr. E. Fontaine, President of the Central Railroad of Virginia, urging the completion of twenty miles of the Covington and Ohio Railroad upon consideration of military necessity.

I communicate to you with these letters a series of resolutions adopted at a convention of railroad presidents, held in Richmond on the 6th of December, asking for the assistance of the Confederate Government in procuring certain supplies, which are indispensable to the railroad system of the country.

That certain appropriations which otherwise could not be constitutionally made by the Confederate Government come within the range of its power, when absolutely necessary for the prosecution of a war, there is no doubt. It is equally clear that when this military necessity ceases, the right to make such appropriations no longer exists.

To exercise this power, when it exists, and to confine it within the proper limits, is a matter for the just discretion of Congress, and to enable it to act upon the interesting subjects to which they relate, I transmit the communications and resolutions which accompany this message.

I have already recommended that the Confederate Government should assist in making a railroad from Danville, Va., to Greensboro, N. C.,* upon the ground of a strong military necessity for completing an interior through line from Virginia to the Southern Atlantic States. I deem this to be necessary, not only on account of the superior safety of such a line from hostile inroads and invasions, but because of the great additional facilities which its completion would afford for the transportation of troops and military supplies.

The road from Selma, Ala., to Meridian, Miss., is a link that has claims similar to the road already recommended to your assistance in a previous message.* Whilst the completion of the twenty miles of the Covington and Ohio Railroad, as proposed by Mr. Fontaine, might be eminently useful for military purposes, I cannot, in the present condition of the Treasury, recommend that you should contribute by direct appropriation.

The resolutions of the convention of the railroad presidents and superintendents relate to a most important subject.

If the railroads should be generally disabled from transporting

---

*See page 139.

troops and military supplies for the prosecution of the war, the result would be most disastrous. It is urged that the capital necessary to construct the establishments required for re-rolling rails and the manufacture of locomotives cannot well be had unless the Confederate Government would make some advance for the purpose. With the machinery proper for rolling the rails, there might be connected that which is necessary for rolling plates which are wanted in the naval service. How far it would be proper for Congress to authorize advances to be made on contracts to furnish these plates or engines it would be for that body to consider and determine. Some such advance might facilitate and secure the establishment of works which would at the same time furnish what is required by the Government, re-rolling the railroad iron and constructing locomotives for the use of the railroads. The exigency is believed to be such as to require the aid of the Government, and is commended to your favorable consideration. JEFFERSON DAVIS.

Richmond, December 17, 1861.

EXECUTIVE DEPARTMENT,
RICHMOND, December 18, 1861.

To the Hon. President of the Congress.

Sir: Herewith I transmit a letter of the Attorney General, covering a communication on the subject of taxes due upon property sequestered by the Government of the Confederate States, and for which it is liable to be sold on account of the several States.

The attention of Congress is called to the necessity of providing for the payment of sums now due as well as those which will become due on account of the property referred to, and which, it is believed, must remain subject to taxation by the several States. JEFFERSON DAVIS.

EXECUTIVE DEPARTMENT,
RICHMOND, December 18, 1861.

To the President of the Congress.

Sir: I herewith transmit to the Congress a copy of a joint resolution of the State of Tennessee, in accordance with the request of that body. JEFFERSON DAVIS.

EXECUTIVE DEPARTMENT,
RICHMOND, December 23, 1861.

To the President of the Congress.

Sir: I herewith transmit a communication from the Secretary of War, inclosing an estimate of appropriations, rendered necessary by the ratification of the treaties with certain Indian tribes.

JEFFERSON DAVIS.

EXECUTIVE DEPARTMENT,
RICHMOND, December 30, 1861.

To the President of the Confederate Congress.

Sir: I herewith transmit to the Congress a communication from the Secretary of War, with the estimate of certain additional appropriations therein mentioned. JEFFERSON DAVIS.

EXECUTIVE DEPARTMENT,
RICHMOND, January 6, 1862.

To the Confederate Congress.

I herewith transmit from the War Department a copy of the official report of the battle on Alleghany Mountain on the 13th December.

I would invite special attention to the suggestions of the Secretary of War in his communication accompanying the report, with which I fully concur. JEFFERSON DAVIS.

EXECUTIVE DEPARTMENT,
RICHMOND, January 11, 1862.

President of the Congress.

I herewith transmit to the Congress a communication from the Secretary of War recommending a certain appropriation* therein mentioned. JEFFERSON DAVIS.

---

*To pay interest on money borrowed from certain banks in Tennessee.

RICHMOND, January 13, 1862.

To the Provisional Congress of the Confederate States.

I transmit herewith a report and accompanying papers from the Secretary of State in answer to a resolution* of the Congress of the Confederate States of the 10th instant.

JEFFERSON DAVIS.

EXECUTIVE OFFICE,
RICHMOND, January 23, 1862.

Hon. Howell Cobb, President of the Provisional Congress.

Sir: I return to you an act entitled "An Act to provide for raising and organizing, in the State of Missouri, additional troops for the Provisional Army of the Confederate States," indorsed "Passed January 9, 1861 [1862]," and delivered to me probably on the 10th day of January, 1862. After its delivery I was informed by the clerk that it had been reconsidered and substituted by an act entitled "An Act to provide for raising and organizing, in the State of Missouri, additional forces for the Provisional Army of the Confederate States," which was in many respects similar in its provisions and which was this day returned with my objections.† Regarding the first act as having been abrogated by Congress, I took no action upon it. But to-day I am informed by the Secretary of Congress that the record of the reconsideration is not to be found on the Journal. Ten days having now elapsed since the act was sent to me, I am precluded from doing anything with it except to transmit it to you with a statement of the circumstances which caused me to regard the paper as invalid and not requiring consideration or action on my part.

JEFFERSON DAVIS.

EXECUTIVE DEPARTMENT,
RICHMOND, January 25, 1862.

To the Hon. President of the Congress.

In response to the resolution of the Congress of the 11th inst.

---

*Requesting the President to communicate to Congress copies of all correspondence with Confederate commissioners abroad.

†See page 160.

I herewith transmit a communication from the Secretary of War with the report of the Chief of the Commissariat of the Army.

JEFFERSON DAVIS.

EXECUTIVE DEPARTMENT,
RICHMOND, February 15, 1862.

To the Honorable President of the Congress.

In response to the resolution of the Congress adopted on the 10th instant, I herewith transmit communications from all the respective Departments, except the War Department.

I am informed by the Secretary of War that so great is the press of important business on his Department, that he has not had time, as yet, to prepare the list of officers as desired, but will do so at his earliest opportunity.   JEFFERSON DAVIS.

VETO MESSAGES.

To the Congress of the Confederate States.

Gentlemen: I deem it my duty to return for your reconsideration, with my objections, "An Act regulating furloughs and discharges in certain cases." I am unable to sign this act, as my judgment does not approve it, and I respectfully submit to you my reasons for withholding my signature.

By the terms of the act any sick or invalid soldier now out of camp, whether in hospital or not, shall be entitled to furlough or discharge on the ground of bodily disability, upon the certificate of any surgeon of the Confederate States, or of any surgeon of a hospital where the soldier is treated, whether such surgeon be in the Army or not. My objections to both as to the principles of this act and the practical difficulties which will embarrass its execution:

1st. I cannot but regard it as extremely unwise to grant control over any soldier, to the extent of discharging him from service, to any body of men not employed in the service of the Government, over whom it exercises no control, and who present to it no guarantee whatever for the faithful discharge of the duties imposed on them. In the medical, as in all other professions, there are incompetent as well as unworthy men. This bill proposes to place the power of discharging from the public service the whole body of absent soldiers, now amounting to probably not less than thirty thousand men, at the mercy of any physician who may call his office a hospital. The absent soldiers, out of camp, scattered over the entire Confederacy, are to be allowed to leave the service at pleasure on producing the certificate of some man who signs himself a physician in charge of a hospital. No means are provided by the bill, and in the nature of things no means can well be devised, by which it can be ascertained at the office of the Adjutant General whether the signature to the certificate is genuine or not; whether, if genuine, the signature is that of a physician, nor whether the signer, if he be a physician, have really a hospital in which the sick soldier is treated. I venture to say that there is not a man now out of camp, whether sick or well, who could not readily find means for securing such a certificate as this bill contemplates at the most trifling cost.

2d. Again, the bill applies to those only who are now out of camp. But if the principle of the bill is right, its application should be continuous and permanent, and I cannot discover any reason why it should be confined to those not in camp. If a man out of camp is to have his discharge on a certificate of a surgeon and when far removed from the supervision of commanders, why not give the same right to the soldier in camp, where the presence of the commander would at least check the issue of fraudulent certificates. And if it be right to adopt this rule at all, why is it not as well applicable to men who will be absent from camp next week as to those now absent? The special limitations of the bill to soldiers out of camp, and to those only now out of camp, indicate an intention to provide for some present exceptional emergency not defined with sufficient accuracy to prevent great mischief in the practical working of the law. If there be such emergency, to what class of cases does it extend? Does it exist everywhere, or only at one or more determinate points? The language of the bill requires to be better guarded to meet what I infer from its phraseology to be an exceptional case; and if there be such a case, I respectfully submit to Congress that it might be remedied in a less objectionable manner than is provided for in the bill.

3d. It is obvious that the intent and purpose of this bill was humane, and directed to ameliorating the condition of the sick soldier, but in very many cases the opposite effect will be produced. The sick soldier, entitled to either furlough or discharge, now obtains it through the regularly appointed officers of the Government, provided with blank forms to be properly filled up, by means of which the rights of the soldier to his transportation and allowances can be readily liquidated. But by the provisions of the bill it will very frequently occur that owing to irregularities in his papers it will be impossible that his account can be settled at the office of the paymaster; still worse, he may be exposed to the loss of his cherished honor, to be branded as a deserter by his failure to secure the proper evidence of his honorable discharge.

I do not think that Congress can have been aware that some weeks prior to the passage of this bill the War Department had issued regulations, relaxing the former rules, dispensing with many of the formalities, and simplifying the means of obtaining furloughs and discharges for the sick. I annex a copy of these regulations, which go as far as, in my opinion, compatible with the necessities of the service, and which seem to me to render the legislation now proposed unnecessary.   JEFFERSON DAVIS.

[Received December 14, 1861.]

EXECUTIVE OFFICE, January 22, 1862.

To the Congress of the Confederate States.

After mature consideration of the bill to encourage the manufacture of small arms, saltpeter, and of gunpowder within the Confederate States, I felt constrained to return it with the following statement of objections: By its provisions the bill deprives the Executive of the discretionary power to protect the Government against unnecessary or improvident contracts, and confers upon individuals who may propose to furnish to the Government any of the supplies enumerated the right to demand that their proposition shall be accepted, and that 50 per cent of the amount proposed to be invested shall be paid from the public Treasury without any other condition than that the person making such proposition shall have actually expended in the prosecution of the proposed work one-fourth of the capital to be invested in it, and that his undertaking shall not be, in the opinion of the Secretary of War, visionary or impracticable, or at points too remote for the advantage of the Confederacy. As an example of the disadvantageous operation of the bill herewith returned, the attention of Congress is called to the contemplated case of the manufacture of gunpowder. Our present necessity is not for an increase of powder mills, but for a supply of the material for the manufacture of gunpowder. The mills now in existence, and which could be readily put to work, far exceed in their capacity to manufacture our ability to supply the requisite material. Yet under the operation of this bill it would follow that any one who should propose to establish a powder mill upon unobjectionable locality, and that he had invested one-fourth the capital to be employed, would be entitled to claim an advance equal to 50 per cent of that amount for a work which the Government did not require, and which, as there is no limitation of time for the fulfillment of his contract, could not be pronounced visionary or impracticable. The power already exists to make advances equal to 33 1-3 per cent on contracts for arms or munitions of war, and experience has not shown that any larger advance is necessary to stimulate the undertaking of such contracts; on the contrary, it has not yet been found necessary in a single instance to make advances to the full amount now permitted by law. The requirement of the bill that liberal profits shall be granted and an extraordinary advance be made, coupled with the absence of any Executive discretion to refuse any contract proposed for the supplies mentioned in the bill, would inevitably expose the Treasury to heavy drafts from the class of speculating contractors.

I regret that these features of the bill compel its return, as some of its provisions would be valuable adjuncts to existing legislation in enabling the Government to aid in the establishment of manufactures of arms and the creation of artificial saltpeter beds.

JEFFERSON DAVIS.

EXECUTIVE OFFICE, RICHMOND, January 22, 1862.

To the Congress of the Confederate States.

I have considered a bill to authorize the Secretary of War to receive into the service of the Confederate States a regiment of volunteers for the protection of the frontier of Texas, and herewith return it to the Congress with a statement of my objections, which are respectfully submitted for consideration.

The bill provides that a regiment of volunteers is to be raised by the State of Texas, under the provisions of an act of the Legislature of said State, and directs that the Secretary of War shall receive the regiment to be so raised and incorporate it into the Provisional Army of the Confederate States.

By reference to the act of the Legislature of Texas, a copy of which accompanied the bill, it appears that all that discretion and control, which of necessity is vested in the Executive of the Confederate States over all troops employed in their service, are withheld by the act, the provisions of which are adopted in your bill, the posting and movement of the troops being therein confided to the Governor of the State under the plan of the Legislature.

There are other objections which are mainly important because they disturb the uniformity and complicate the system of military administration prescribed by the laws of the Confederate States.

Unity and coöperation by the troops of all the States are indispensable to success, and I must view with regret this as all other indications of a purpose to divide the power of the States by dividing the means to be employed in efforts to carry on separate operations; but, if in any case it be advisable that such separate action should be taken, it seems to me palpably clear that it should be a charge against the individual State, rather than upon the common treasury of the Confederate States.   JEFFERSON DAVIS.

EXECUTIVE OFFICE, January 22, 1862.

To the Congress of the Confederate States.

After mature deliberation I have not been able to approve the bill herewith returned, entitled "An Act to provide for raising and organizing, in the State of Missouri, additional forces for the Provisional Army of the Confederate States."

In a message just submitted to the Congress in relation to cer-

tain forces to be raised in the State of Texas,* I have stated the
objections entertained to any legislative discrimination for or
against a particular State, thereby disturbing the harmony of the
system adopted for the common defense. In a bill very recently
passed by the Congress a new plan has been established for raising
and organizing troops for the Confederate service. By the provisions of this last-mentioned law you have given me authority to
raise and organize troops in all the States by granting commissions
in advance of the actual enlistment of the troops to officers below
the grade of general officers and above that of subalterns. To the
officers thus commissioned you do not give any pay or allowances
until the actual organization of the companies, battalions, or regiments that the officers so commissioned were empowered to raise,
and you do not allow pay, but have even prohibited the allowance
of subsistence or transportation to the men enrolled in order to
enable them to reach the rendezvous of their companies. By the
terms of the bill now returned an exception is made in favor of
the State of Missouri alone. By the provisions of the bill it is contemplated that advance commissions shall be granted to officers of
all grades from the highest general officer of the Provisional Army
to the lowest subaltern of a company, and that the officers, whether
of the staff or the line, thus appointed shall receive pay from the
date of their respective appointments without any condition rendering this pay dependent on their success in raising the troops.
The general bill which has now become a law applicable to Missouri as to all the other States fixes a reasonable term within which
officers commissioned in advance must succeed in raising troops,
under penalty of forfeiting their commissions. The present bill
removes this salutary restriction and vests in the Executive the
dangerous power not only of appointing at his discretion an unlimited number of military officers irrespective of any troops to
be commanded by them, but allows him to retain the officers so
appointed in the public service at the public expense during the
Executive pleasure.

I am not able to perceive in the present condition of public affairs in the State of Missouri the necessity which would form the
only possible excuse for a grant of such power to a constitutional

---

*See page 160.

Executive. I receive assurances from those whose sources of information are entirely reliable that the raising and organization of troops in Missouri for service in the Confederate Army are successfully progressing, and that within a very few days the muster rolls will be received, thus placing it in my power to organize the Army in that State on precisely the same footing as in all the others, and thus avoid any need for exceptional legislation.

In addition to these objections founded on principle there would be a practical difficulty in the operation of the bill, which appears insurmountable. All the troops now in service in the State of Missouri are State troops, commanded by State officers, which have never been tendered or received in the Confederate service. In exercising the power of appointment proposed to be vested in me by the bill the best hope for success in its purpose would be founded on selecting those officers who had distinguished themselves in command and had become endeared to the troops. But this would be to deprive the State troops of their commanding officers during the whole period necessary for the enrollment and organization of the troops under Confederate laws. Missouri would thus be left comparatively defenseless whilst the reorganization was progressing. Therefore regarding this bill as impolitic and unnecessary, it is submitted for your reconsideration.

JEFFERSON DAVIS.

EXECUTIVE DEPARTMENT, February 1, 1862.

To the Confederate Congress.

I return with my objections the bill passed by you entitled "An Act to provide for granting furloughs in certain cases."

Before proceeding to lay before you the special objections entertained to the provisions of this bill it is proper that I should express the firm conviction that it is, from the nature of things, impracticable to administer an army in the field by statute. The Constitution vests in the Congress the power "to make rules for the government and regulation of the land and naval forces." None can deny the wisdom of this provision, nor the propriety of the exercise of this power by the Congress in its full extent; but there is an obvious distinction between making rules for the gov-

ernment of the Army and undertaking to administer the Army by
statute. When rules are established for the regulation of such
matters as are in their nature susceptible of fixed and unvarying
application, there can be no impolicy in providing them by statute.
Thus we have by law fixed guides for organization, for the composition of the different corps, for the number of officers and their
grades, for the respective duties assigned to the staff in its several branches, and numerous like provisions that remain in force
in all localities, in the presence as well as the absence of the enemy,
and uninfluenced by the exigencies of any particular occasion.
But there are other matters which are essentially administrative
in their character, and are not susceptible of being determined by
the rigid prescriptions of statutes which executive officers are
bound to obey under all circumstances and without the exercise of
any discretion. Suppose Congress should attempt to fix by law
of what camp equipage should always consist, or the precise kind
and quality of clothing to be furnished, or the exact amount and
kind of transportation to be allowed for each regiment, is it not
obvious that these details depend so entirely on time, place, and
circumstances, and are so essentially variable in their character,
that the uniform compliance with such laws would be practically
impossible? Suppose Congress should establish by law the precise proportion of infantry, cavalry, and artillery to be attached
to each body of troops in service. This would not be a rule for
the government of the Army, but an attempt at a statutory administration of it which could not but be found impolitic, even if it
were practicable.

Now, the act in question presents precisely the same objectionable features. It establishes a rule over which there is no discretionary power under any circumstances whatsoever by which
a commanding general, in the face of superior numbers and with
his capacity for defense taxed to the utmost, may find his forces
still further reduced by the action of his subordinates, not only
against his consent, but without his knowledge, and in ignorance
of his necessities and the purposes of their Government. No more
striking example could be afforded of the impolicy of such a law
than is presented by our condition at this time. Our armies are in
force inferior to the enemy at the two points most vital to the defense of the country. The enlistment of the twelve-months' men

is soon to expire, and in order to secure their entry for a further term into service you have directed that furloughs be granted to them as far as compatible with the safety of the respective commands. If the bill in question becomes a law, it will at once be necessary to diminish the number of furloughs, which might otherwise be granted as inducement to reënlistments, and to that extent the attainment of this most desirable object must be obstructed. From the West and from the South, from many and important points urgent calls for reënforcement are received by the Department of War which it is not possible to satisfy. At this crisis, without any check or control by commanding generals, 5 per cent of their effective forces would be withdrawn under the provisions of this bill. With conflicts impending against an enemy greatly our superior in numbers, our safety is dependent on keeping in the field every effective man that can be furnished with a weapon; this bill, therefore, it seems to me, is most inopportunely presented.

If from these general objections we turn to the details of the bill, other considerations are presented which would alone prevent my giving it approval. This may be stated briefly as follows, viz.:

First. The furlough for disability is to be granted upon the surgeon's certificate, not of the vital necessity for leave of absence, but of the surgeon's opinion that the patient's "health would be improved by a temporary sojourn at home." It is plain that every man in the Army, to whose health camp life was thus believed to be detrimental, could at once demand a furlough under this provision.

Second. The colonel's power to grant a furlough on such a certificate as is above mentioned is without the check or control of higher authority, and is unlimited as to time and to number of cases.

Third. Any soldier that can get the certificate of any hospital surgeon can be sent home on furlough or discharged without the knowledge or consent of any of his officers, either company or regimental. The surgeon has only to certify that the soldier "is too remote from his commanding officer to procure his certificate for a furlough or discharge without inconvenience and delay."

When troops are in the field, it is *always* true of a soldier in hospital, that the commanding officer's certificate cannot be obtained "without inconvenience and delay," so that the soldier, absent from camp, can *always* get a furlough or discharge without the knowledge of his commander.

Fourth. The large number of soldiers, that will be constantly traveling on the railroads on the proposed system of a ten days' furlough for five per cent of all the effective men, together with the sick leaves provided for, will form an average of probably not less than fifteen or twenty thousand men in constant movement. This would occupy the transportation facilities, already much too limited, to such an extent as seriously to impair the movement of troops and supplies.

In whatever aspect the proposed legislation is contemplated, I cannot view it otherwise than as dangerous to the public safety, and I most earnestly recommend that, in taking it again into consideration, Congress will weigh any possible advantage that can result from this measure against the disasters, that are not only the possible, but, as it appears to me, the probable results of its adoption.   JEFFERSON DAVIS.

EXECUTIVE DEPARTMENT, February 4, 1862.

To the Congress of the Confederate States.

Gentlemen: I return, with my objections, the bill entitled "An Act to repeal so much of the laws of the United States adopted by the Congress of the Confederate States as authorizes the naturalization of aliens." My objections are the following, viz.:

First. The bill does not save the rights of aliens who were domiciled in the Confederate States at the beginning of this revolution, and had already commenced the proceedings necessary to their naturalization. It would be manifest injustice to such aliens as have remained among us and have sympathized with and aided us in our struggle to cut them off from these rights, at least inchoate, and deprive them of the boon held out to them by laws to which we were assenting parties at the time they emigrated to the Confederacy.

Second. While there is perhaps no direct prescription of the Constitution making it the duty of Congress to establish a rule of naturalization, I submit that in addition to the grant of that power made to Congress the States in the permanent Constitution have surrendered the power formerly exercised by some of them of permitting aliens to vote even in State elections until naturalized as citizens of the Confederate States—Article I, Section 2. A comparison of these provisions leads to the conclusion that it was in contemplation of the States that Congress should exercise the power vested in it, and it does not appear to me to be a fair compliance with the just expectations of the States to repeal in mass all laws providing for the naturalization of aliens without substituting some other system that may commend itself to the wisdom of Congress.

These are my special objections to the act as passed, but I beg permission to say that the general policy indicated by its provisions appears to be at least questionable. That there is no present necessity for such legislation is obvious, for there has not been, and we cannot expect there will be, immigration, except on the part of such as are disposed to aid us in our struggle. To the future, which may well be left to take care of itself on this subject, it is submitted whether legislation intended to effect entire exclusion from citizenship of all who are not born on the soil will be deemed in accordance with the civilization of the age.

In conclusion, it can scarcely be necessary to point out the evil effects that may be produced on aliens now serving in our Army and on those of our fellow-citizens who are of foreign birth, by what will be considered as a legislative stigma cast on them as a class.   JEFFERSON DAVIS.

PROCLAMATIONS.

BY THE PRESIDENT OF THE CONFEDERATE STATES.

A ·PROCLAMATION.

Whereas, an act of the Congress of the Confederate States of America, approved this, the 28th day of November, 1861, provides that, "the State of Missouri be, and is hereby admitted, as a member of the Confederate States of America, upon an equal footing with the other States of this Confederacy, under the Constitution for the Provisional Government of the same:"

Now, therefore, I, Jefferson Davis, President of the Confederate States of America, do issue this, my proclamation, making known to all whom it may concern that the admission of the said State of Missouri into the Confederacy is complete, and that the laws of the Confederacy are extended over said State as fully and completely as over the other States composing the same.

       In testimony whereof, I have hereunto signed my name and caused the seal of the Confederate States to [SEAL.] be affixed, at Richmond, this 28th day of November, A.D. 1861.   JEFFERSON DAVIS.

By the President:

       R. M. T. HUNTER, *Secretary of State.*

BY THE PRESIDENT OF THE CONFEDERATE STATES.

A PROCLAMATION.

Whereas, an act of the Congress of the Confederate States of America entitled "An Act to organize the Territory of Arizona," was approved by me on the 18th day of January, 1862; and whereas, it is therein declared that the provisions of the act are suspended until the President of the Confederate States shall issue his proclamation declaring the act to be in full force and operation, and shall proceed to appoint the officers therein provided to be appointed in and for said Territory:

Now, therefore, I, Jefferson Davis, President of the Confederate States of America, do issue this my proclamation declaring said "Act to organize the Territory of Arizona" to be in full force and operation, and that I have proceeded to appoint the officers therein provided to be appointed in and for said Territory.

Given under my hand and the seal of the Confederate States of America at Richmond, this fourteenth day of February, A.D. 1862.

    [SEAL.]   JEFFERSON DAVIS.

By the President:

       R. M. T. HUNTER, *Secretary of State.*

RESOLUTIONS OF THANKS.

Be it resolved by the Congress of the Confederate States of America, That the thanks of the people of the Confederate States are eminently due, and are hereby tendered, to Major General Sterling Price, and the Missouri Army under his command, for the gallant conduct they have displayed throughout their service in the present war, and especially for the skill, fortitude, and courage by which they gained the brilliant achievement at Lexington, Mo., resulting, on the twentieth day of September last, in the reduction of that town and the surrender of the entire Federal Army there employed.

Be it resolved further, That a copy of this resolution be communicated by the President to General Price, and, through him to the army then under his command.

Approved December 3, 1861.

Whereas, under the providence of God, the valor of the soldiers of the Confederate States has added another glorious victory, achieved at Belmont, in the State of Missouri, on the seventh day of November last, to those which had been so graciously vouchsafed to our arms, whereby the reduction of Columbus, in the State of Kentucky, has been prevented, and the contemplated descent of the enemy down the Mississippi River effectually stayed; therefore,

Be it resolved by the Congress of the Confederate States of America, That the thanks of Congress are most heartily tendered to Major General Leonidas Polk, Brigadier General Gideon J. Pillow, Brigadier General Benjamin F. Cheatham, and the officers and soldiers of their gallant commands for the desperate courage they exhibited in sustaining for several hours, and under most disadvantageous circumstances, an attack by a force of the enemy greatly superior to their own, both in numbers and appointments; and for the skill and gallantry by which they converted what at first threatened so much disaster, into a triumphant victory.

Resolved further, That these resolutions are intended to express what is believed to be the grateful and admiring sentiment of the whole people of the Confederacy.

Resolved further, That they be communicated to the commands

of Major General Polk, Brigadier General Pillow, and Brigadier General Cheatham by the proper Department of the Government.

Approved December 6, 1861.

Be it resolved by the Congress of the Confederate States of America, That the thanks of Congress are due, and are hereby tendered, to Brigadier General N. G. Evans, and the officers and soldiers under his command, for the brilliant victory achieved by them over largely superior forces of the enemy in the battle of Leesburg.

Approved December 18, 1861.

First. *Resolved by the Congress of the Confederate States of America,* That the thanks of Congress are due, and are hereby tendered, to Colonel Edward Johnson, and to the officers and men under his command, for gallant and meritorious services at the summit of Alleghany Mountain, in Virginia, on the thirteenth day of December, eighteen hundred and sixty-one, when for more than six hours they, with remarkable courage and constancy, sustained an assault made upon their position by fourfold their number, and finally drove the enemy in disorder, and with heavy loss, from the field.

Second. That the foregoing resolution be communicated to said command, by the Secretary of War, and be made known in general orders.

Approved January 10, 1862.

Alexander H. Stephens.

Alexander H. Stephens

Alexander H. Stephens.

ALEXANDER HAMILTON STEPHENS was born near Crawfords-
ville, Ga., on February 11, 1812. His grandfather, Alexander
Stephens, was an Englishman and an adherent of Prince Charles
Edward, and came to this country in 1746. He settled in the
Penn colony, was in several conflicts with the Indians, and
was a captain in the Revolutionary War. After the war was over
he removed to Georgia. At the age of fifteen Alexander Hamilton
became an orphan and was given a place in the school in Washington, Ga., that was being taught by Rev. Alexander Hamilton
Webster, a Presbyterian minister, from whom he took his middle
name. With the intention of becoming a Presbyterian minister
himself, he accepted the offer of their educational society to attend college. He entered Franklin College (afterwards the State
University) in 1828, and graduated therefrom in 1832 with the
first honors. Having determined not to become a minister, he
subsequently taught school, earned the money, and repaid the in-
debtedness for his education. On July 22, 1834, he was admitted
to the bar. In 1836 was elected to the State Legislature, after
bitter opposition because of his fight against nullification. This
opposition was repeated until 1841, when he declined reëlection.
As a member, he favored liberal appropriations for railroads in
his State, and, by his advocacy, a charter for the female college
at Macon, Ga., was secured, the first in the world for the regular
graduation of young women in the classics and sciences; was
a delegate to the Charleston Commercial Convention of 1839;
was elected to Congress in 1843, on a general State ticket, but
supported an act requiring the States to be divided into Congressional districts. He remained in Congress for sixteen years. In
1838-39 he favored the annexation of Texas by resolution of Congress, but opposed President Tyler's treaty of 1844, and also opposed Mr. Polk's Mexican War policy. In 1848, in a personal
difficulty with Judge Cone, in Atlanta, growing out of a political

173

dispute, he was severely cut in the right hand. He supported General Taylor for President in 1848. In 1850, he opposed secession, and wrote what was called the "Georgia Platform," which declared "the American Union secondary in importance only to the rights and principles it was designed to perpetuate." He declined to support General Scott for President in 1852, but, with a few other prominent Whigs, voted for Mr. Webster after he was dead. In 1854, he defended "Popular Sovereignty," as formulated by Mr. Douglas in the Kansas-Nebraska Act. He aided in electing President Buchanan in 1856, although he had formerly opposed him, and during his term of office he placed himself in antagonism to his administration. He resigned his seat in Congress in 1859, and in 1860 supported Mr. Douglas for President. He did not regard the election of Mr. Lincoln of itself a justification for secession, and on November 14, 1860, made a Union speech which attracted attention throughout the country. He was elected a member of the Georgia Convention of 1861, and sought to delay the passage of the Secession Ordinance. His objections were to the expediency of immediate secession and not at all to the right of his State to withdraw from the Union. When the State Convention of Georgia adopted the Ordinance of Secession, however, he at once yielded obedience and was chosen a delegate to the Provisional Congress which had been appointed to assemble at Montgomery, Ala., by which he was chosen Vice President of the Provisional Government of the Confederate States. He was sent as a commissioner on behalf of the Confederacy to treat with Virginia on the subject of her union with the Confederacy and to negotiate and advise with her. He assisted earnestly in framing the Constitution for the new Government, and believed it was a great improvement on the Constitution of the United States. He said of it that "the whole document utterly negatives the idea which so many have been active in endeavoring to put in the enduring form of history, that the convention at Montgomery was nothing but a set of 'conspirators' whose object was the overthrow of the principles of the Constitution of the United States and the erection of a great 'Slave Oligarchy' instead of the free institutions thereby secured and guaranteed. This work of the Montgomery Convention, with that of the Constitution for a Provisional Government, will ever remain not only as a monument of the wisdom, foresight, and statesmanship of the men who constituted it, but an everlasting refutation of the charges which have been brought against them. These works together show clearly that their only leading object was to sustain, uphold, and perpetuate the fundamental principles of the Constitution of the United States." He favored the "peace policy" which was manifested by the sending of commissioners by the Confederacy to Washington in 1861, and said he was astonished at the treatment they received there, and charged Mr. Seward with duplicity in dealing with them.

At the election in November, 1861, he was chosen by a unanimous vote Vice President of the Confederate States, on the ticket with President Davis; was inaugurated on February 22, 1862, and filled this position throughout the life of the Confederacy. He was called upon and made numerous addresses to the people at critical periods during the war, in all of which he characterized the invasion of the South as an unjust war for conquest and subjugation.

In a speech delivered during the second year of the war, he said: "The States south had done nothing but what was their right— their inalienable right to do, the same as their ancestors did, in common with the North, when they severed their connection with the British Government. This war was waged by the North in denial of this right, and for the purpose of conquest and subjugation. It was, therefore, aggressive, wanton, and unjust. Such must be the judgment of mankind, let its results be what they may. The responsibility, therefore, for all its sacrifices of treasure and blood, heretofore or hereafter to be made in its prosecution, rests not upon us. What is all this for? Why this array of armies? Why this fierce meeting in mortal combat? What is all this carnage and slaughter for? Why the prolongation of this conflict? Why this lamentation and mourning going up from almost every house and family from Maine to the Rio Grande, and from the Atlantic and Gulf to the Lakes, for friends and dear ones who have fallen by disease and violence in this unparalleled struggle? The question, if replied to by the North, can have but one true answer. What is all this for, on their part, but to overturn the principle upon which their own Government, as well as ours, is based— to reverse the doctrine that governments derive 'their just powers from the consent of the governed?' What is it for but to overturn the principles and practice of their own Government from the beginning? That Government was founded and based upon the political axiom that all States and peoples have the inalienable right to change their forms of government at will. This principle was acted on in the recognition by the United States of the South American republics. It was the principle acted on in the recognition of Mexico. It was acted on in the struggle of Greece to overthrow the Ottoman rule. On that question, the great constitutional expounder of the North, Mr. Webster, gained his first laurels as an American statesman. This principle was acted on in the recognition of the Government of Louis Philippe, on the overthrow of Charles X. of France; and again in the recognition of the Lamartine Government, on the overthrow of Louis Philippe in 1848. The same principle was again acted upon without dissent in 1852, in the recognition of the Government of Louis Napoleon; and in the recognition of Texas, when she seceded, or withdrew, from the Government of Mexico. Well may any and every one, North or South, exclaim, What is all this for? What have we done to the North? When have we ever wronged them? We quit them, it is true, as our ancestors and their ancestors quit the British Government. We quit as they quit—upon a question of constitutional right. That question they determined for themselves, and we have but done the same. What, therefore, is all this for? Why this war on their part against the uniform principles and practice of their own Government? It is a war, in short, on their part against right, against reason, against justice, against nature. If asked on our side what is all this for, the reply from every honest breast is that it is for home, for firesides, for our altars, for our birthrights, for property, for honor, for life—in a word, for everything for which freemen should live, and for which all deserving to be freemen should be willing, if need be, to die."

He opposed earnestly some of the financial measures of the administration of Mr. Davis during the war, as he also did the Conscription Act and the suspension of the writ of *habeas corpus*, but his friendly intercourse with President Davis and Cabinet was not broken. He said "these differences, however wide and thorough as they were, caused no personal break between us," a statement concurred in by Mr. Davis. When Mr. Davis was charged with being guilty of cruel treatment of Northern prisoners of war, Mr. Stephens vigorously defended him and characterized all such charges as one of "the boldest and baldest attempted outrages upon the truths of history which has ever been essayed; not less so than the infamous attempt to fix upon him and other high officials on the Confederate side the guilt of Mr. Lincoln's assassination." A final effort was made to secure peace by means of a Commission, in February, 1865, of which Mr. Stephens was the head, his associates being John A. Campbell and R. M. T. Hunter. This Commission met Mr. Lincoln and Mr. Seward in Hampton Roads, on February 3, and Mr. Stephens was the chief spokesman. The effort failed, and with the other Confederate commissioners he returned to Richmond, and subsequently gave a full statement of his recollections of all that occurred in the Conference. Soon after returning to Richmond, he left for his home, where he remained in retirement until his arrest, on May 11, 1865. He was sent as a prisoner to Fort Warren, Boston Harbor, where he was kept in confinement for five months. In October, he was released on his own parole. In February, 1866, he was elected to the Senate of the United States by the Legislature of Georgia, but was refused his seat by the Senate. In 1867, he published the first volume of his "War between the States." He was chosen Professor of Political Science and History in the University of Georgia in December, 1868; but declined to accept, on account of failing health. He published the second volume of his "War between the States" in 1870, and later published "A School History of the United States." In 1871, he taught a law class and became the editor and part proprietor of a newspaper in Atlanta. He was a candidate, in November, 1871, for the United States Senate, but failed of election. In 1874, he was elected to the House of Representatives, and remained in Congress until 1882, when he resigned. The same year, he was elected Governor of his State, by a majority of more than 60,000 over Gen. L. J. Gartrell, a lawyer and an ex-Confederate officer. His last speech was made at the Georgia Sesquicentennial Celebration, in Savannah, on February 12, 1883. In personal appearance Mr. Stephens was slender and boyish-looking, and his voice was weak and piping. He was a chronic sufferer from illness, and weighed less than one hundred pounds. During his last years of service in Congress he was crippled by a fall and by rheumatism, was compelled to use crutches, and was moved from place to place in a wheel chair.   Notwithstanding his infirmity and great physical weakness, his mind and intellect were perfectly clear and keen, and he was still a vigorous thinker, participating quite prominently in the debates.   He enjoyed in an unusual degree the confidence of both sides of the House, and always when he spoke, as he was compelled to do from his invalid chair, the members of either side clustered about him in order that they might catch every word which fell from his lips.   A tribute such as this from his political opponents on the floor of the House of Representatives was the more marked and noticeable when bestowed upon Mr. Stephens, because he had been, next to Mr. Davis, the most conspicuous officeholder in the Confederacy, and at that time the bitterness engendered by the Civil War was still very pronounced in that body.   He died while still in the office of Governor, on March 4, 1883, and was buried at Atlanta.

First Congress.

First Congress.

FIRST SESSION.

MET AT RICHMOND, VA., FEBRUARY 18, 1862. ADJOURNED
APRIL 21, 1862.

INAUGURATION OF JEFFERSON DAVIS

AT

RICHMOND, VA., FEBRUARY 22, 1862.

PROGRAMME.

I. Col. Charles Dimmock to be Chief Marshal, assisted by four aids.

II. The Senate and House of Representatives will meet in their respective halls at half-past eleven o'clock A.M., and then, with their respective officers, repair to the hall of the House of Delegates of Virginia, which has been kindly tendered by the House of Delegates.

III. The President and Vice President-elect will be conducted to the hall by the Joint Committee of Arrangements at a quarter to twelve o'clock, and be received by the assembly standing.

IV. The President of the Senate will occupy the seat on the right of the President-elect; the Vice President-elect that on the left of the President, and the Speaker of the House that on the left of the Vice President.

V. Invitations are extended to the following persons and bodies, to wit: Members of the Cabinet, who will be seated on the right and left of the President of the Senate and Speaker of the House; the Governor of Virginia and his staff, the Governors of any other of the Confederate States who may be in Richmond, and ex-Gov. Lowe, of Maryland; the Senate and House of Delegates of Virginia, with their respective officers; the Judges of the Supreme Court of Virginia, and of the Supreme Court of any other of the Confederate States who may be in Richmond; the Judge of the

Confederate District Court at Richmond, and any other Judge of a Confederate Court who may be in Richmond; the members of the late Provisional Congress, the officers of the Army and Navy of the Confederate States who may be in Richmond; the Mayor and corporate authorities of the city of Richmond; the reverend clergy and Masonic and other benevolent societies, and the members of the Press.

VI. At half-past twelve o'clock the procession will move from the hall by the eastern door of the Capitol to the statue of Washington, on the public square, by such route as the Chief Marshal may direct, in the following order, to wit:

1. The Chief Marshal.

2. The band.

3. Six members of the Committee of Arrangements, including their respective Chairmen.

4. The President elect, attended by the President of the Senate.

5. The Vice President elect, attended by the Speaker of the House of Representatives.

6. The members of the Cabinet.

7. The officiating clergyman and the Judge of the Confederate Court at Richmond.

8. The Senate of the Confederate States, with its officers, in columns of fours.

9. The House of Representatives, with its officers, in columns of fours.

10. The Governors of Virginia and other States, and staffs.

11. The members of the Senate and House of Delegates of Virginia and their officers.

12. The Judges of the Supreme Court of Virginia and other States, who may be in the city of Richmond.

13. The officers of the Army and Navy.

14. The reverend clergy.

15. The Mayor and corporate authorities of the city of Richmond.

16. The Masons and other benevolent societies.

17. Members of the Press.

18. Citizens generally.

Seats will be provided by the Chief Marshal for the Governors of States, the Judges, and, as far as practicable, for the other guests.

The invited guests are requested to present themselves at the door of the hall in the order above indicated.

At the statue of Washington the President elect, the Vice President elect, the President of the Senate, the Speaker of the House of Representatives, the officiating clergyman, Confederate Judge, Governors of States, Judges of the Supreme Courts of States, the Chief Marshal and his aids, and six of the Committee of Arrangements will take position on the platform. Prayer will then be offered by the Right Rev. Bishop Johns.

The inaugural address will then be delivered, after which the oath will be administered to the President by the Confederate Judge, in Richmond, the Hon. J. D. Halyburton, and the result will be announced by the President of the Senate.

The oath will then be administered to the Vice President by the President of the Senate, who will also announce the result.

The several legislative bodies will then return to their respective halls, and the President and Vice President will then be escorted to their respective homes by the Committee of Arrangements.

INAUGURAL ADDRESS.

February 22, 1862.

Fellow-Citizens: On this the birthday of the man most identified with the establishment of American independence, and beneath the monument erected to commemorate his heroic virtues and those of his compatriots, we have assembled to usher into existence the Permanent Government of the Confederate States. Through this instrumentality, under the favor of Divine Providence, we hope to perpetuate the principles of our revolutionary fathers. The day, the memory, and the purpose seem fitly associated.

It is with mingled feelings of humility and pride that I appear to take, in the presence of the people and before high Heaven, the oath prescribed as a qualification for the exalted station to which the unanimous voice of the people has called me. Deeply sensible of all that is implied by this manifestation of the people's confidence, I am yet more profoundly impressed by the vast responsibility of the office, and humbly feel my own unworthiness.

In return for their kindness I can offer assurances of the gratitude with which it is received; and can but pledge a zealous devotion of every faculty to the service of those who have chosen me as their Chief Magistrate.

When a long course of class legislation, directed not to the general welfare, but to the aggrandizement of the Northern section of the Union, culminated in a warfare on the domestic institutions of the Southern States—when the dogmas of a sectional party, substituted for the provisions of the constitutional compact, threatened to destroy the sovereign rights of the States, six of those States, withdrawing from the Union, confederated together to exercise the right and perform the duty of instituting a Government which would better secure the liberties for the preservation of which that Union was established.

Whatever of hope some may have entertained that a returning sense of justice would remove the danger with which our rights were threatened, and render it possible to preserve the Union of the Constitution, must have been dispelled by the malignity and barbarity of the Northern States in the prosecution of the existing war. The confidence of the most hopeful among us must have been destroyed by the disregard they have recently exhibited for all the time-honored bulwarks of civil and religious liberty. Bastiles filled with prisoners, arrested without civil process or indictment duly found; the writ of *habeas corpus* suspended by Executive mandate; a State Legislature controlled by the imprisonment of members whose avowed principles suggested to the Federal Executive that there might be another added to the list of seceded States; elections held under threats of a military power; civil officers, peaceful citizens, and gentlewomen incarcerated for opinion's sake—proclaimed the incapacity of our late associates to administer a Government as free, liberal, and humane as that established for our common use.

For proof of the sincerity of our purpose to maintain our ancient institutions, we may point to the Constitution of the Confederacy and the laws enacted under it, as well as to the fact that through all the necessities of an unequal struggle there has been no act on our part to impair personal liberty or the freedom of speech, of thought, or of the press. The courts have been open, the judicial functions fully executed, and every right of the peaceful citizen maintained as securely as if a war of invasion had not disturbed the land.

The people of the States now confederated became convinced that the Government of the United States had fallen into the hands of a sectional majority, who would pervert that most sacred of all trusts to the destruction of the rights which it was pledged to protect. They believed that to remain longer in the Union would subject them to a continuance of a disparaging discrimination, submission to which would be inconsistent with their welfare, and intolerable to a proud people. They therefore determined to sever its bonds and establish a new Confederacy for themselves.

The experiment instituted by our revolutionary fathers, of a voluntary Union of sovereign States for purposes specified in a solemn compact, had been perverted by those who, feeling power and forgetting right, were determined to respect no law but their own will. The Government had ceased to answer the ends for which it was ordained and established. To save ourselves from a revolution which, in its silent but rapid progress, was about to place us under the despotism of numbers, and to preserve in spirit, as well as in form, a system of government we believed to be peculiarly fitted to our condition, and full of promise for mankind, we determined to make a new association, composed of States homogeneous in interest, in policy, and in feeling.

True to our traditions of peace and our love of justice, we sent commissioners to the United States to propose a fair and amicable settlement of all questions of public debt or property which might be in dispute. But the Government at Washington, denying our right to self-government, refused even to listen to any proposals for a peaceful separation. Nothing was then left to do but to prepare for war.

The first year in our history has been the most eventful in the annals of this continent. A new Government has been established, and its machinery put in operation over an area exceeding seven hundred thousand square miles. The great principles upon which we have been willing to hazard everything that is dear to man have made conquests for us which could never have been achieved by the sword. Our Confederacy has grown from six to thirteen States; and Maryland, already united to us by hallowed memories and material interests, will, I believe, when able to speak with unstifled voice, connect her destiny with the South. Our people have rallied with unexampled unanimity to the support of the great principles of constitutional government, with firm resolve to perpetuate by arms the right which they could not peacefully secure. A million of men, it is estimated, are now standing in hostile array, and waging war along a frontier of thousands of miles. Battles have been fought, sieges have been conducted, and, although the contest is not ended, and the tide for the moment is against us, the final result in our favor is not doubtful.

The period is near at hand when our foes must sink under the immense load of debt which they have incurred, a debt which in their effort to subjugate us has already attained such fearful dimensions as will subject them to burdens which must continue to oppress them for generations to come.

We too have had our trials and difficulties. That we are to escape them in future is not to be hoped. It was to be expected when we entered upon this war that it would expose our people to sacrifices and cost them much, both of money and blood. But we knew the value of the object for which we struggled, and understood the nature of the war in which we were engaged. Nothing could be so bad as failure, and any sacrifice would be cheap as the price of success in such a contest.

But the picture has its lights as well as its shadows. This great strife has awakened in the people the highest emotions and qualities of the human soul. It is cultivating feelings of patriotism, virtue, and courage. Instances of self-sacrifice and of generous devotion to the noble cause for which we are contending are rife throughout the land. Never has a people evinced a more determined spirit than that now animating men, women, and children in every part of our country. Upon the first call the men flew to arms, and wives and mothers send their husbands and sons to battle without a murmur of regret.

It was, perhaps, in the ordination of Providence that we were to be taught the value of our liberties by the price which we pay for them.

The recollections of this great contest, with all its common traditions of glory, of sacrifice and blood, will be the bond of harmony and enduring affection amongst the people, producing unity in policy, fraternity in sentiment, and just effort in war.

Nor have the material sacrifices of the past year been made without some corresponding benefits. If the acquiescence of foreign nations in a pretended blockade has deprived us of our commerce with them, it is fast making us a self-supporting and an independent people. The blockade, if effectual and permanent, could only serve to divert our industry from the production of articles for export and employ it in supplying commodities for domestic use.

It is a satisfaction that we have maintained the war by our unaided exertions. We have neither asked nor received assistance from any quarter. Yet the interest involved is not wholly our own. The world at large is concerned in opening our markets to its commerce. When the independence of the Confederate States is recognized by the nations of the earth, and we are free to follow our interests and inclinations by cultivating foreign trade, the Southern States will offer to manufacturing nations the most favorable markets which ever invited their commerce. Cotton, sugar, rice, tobacco, provisions, timber, and naval stores will furnish attractive exchanges. Nor would the constancy of these supplies be likely to be disturbed by war. Our confederate strength will be too great to tempt aggression; and never was there a people whose interests and principles committed them so fully to a peaceful policy as those of the Confederate States. By the character of their productions they are too deeply interested in foreign commerce wantonly to disturb it. War of conquest they cannot wage, because the Constitution of their Confederacy admits of no coerced association. Civil war there cannot be between States held together by their volition only. The rule of voluntary association, which cannot fail to be conservative, by securing just and impartial government at home, does not diminish the security of the obligations by which the Confederate States may be bound to foreign nations. In proof of this, it is to be remembered that, at the first moment of asserting their right to secession, these States proposed a settlement on the basis of the common liability for the obligations of the General Government.

Fellow-citizens, after the struggle of ages had consecrated the right of the Englishman to constitutional representative government, our colonial ancestors were forced to vindicate that birthright by an appeal to arms. Success crowned their efforts, and they provided for their posterity a peaceful remedy against future aggression.

The tyranny of an unbridled majority, the most odious and least responsible form of despotism, has denied us both the right and the remedy. Therefore we are in arms to renew such sacrifices as our fathers made to the holy cause of constitutional liberty. At the darkest hour of our struggle the Provisional gives place to the Permanent Government. After a series of successes and victories, which covered our arms with glory, we have recently met with serious disasters. But in the heart of a people resolved to be free these disasters tend but to stimulate to increased resistance.

To show ourselves worthy of the inheritance bequeathed to us by the patriots of the Revolution, we must emulate that heroic devotion which made reverse to them but the crucible in which their patriotism was refined.

With confidence in the wisdom and virtue of those who will share with me the responsibility and aid me in the conduct of public affairs; securely relying on the patriotism and courage of the people, of which the present war has furnished so many examples, I deeply feel the weight of the responsibilities I now, with unaffected diffidence, am about to assume; and, fully realizing the inequality of human power to guide and to sustain, my hope is reverently fixed on Him whose favor is ever vouchsafed to the cause which is just. With humble gratitude and adoration, acknowledging the Providence which has so visibly protected the Confederacy during its brief but eventful career, to thee, O God, I trustingly commit myself, and prayerfully invoke thy blessing on my country and its cause.

MESSAGES.

February 25, 1862.

To the Senate and House of Representatives of the Confederate States.

In obedience to the constitutional provision requiring the President from time to time to give to the Congress information of the state of the Confederacy and recommend to their consideration such measures as he shall judge necessary and expedient, I have to communicate that since my message at the last session of the Provisional Congress events have demonstrated that the Government had attempted more than it had power successfully to achieve. Hence, in the effort to protect by our arms the whole of the territory of the Confederate States, seaboard and inland, we have been so exposed as recently to encounter serious disasters. When the Confederacy was formed the States composing it were, by the peculiar character of their pursuits and a misplaced confidence in their former associates, to a great extent destitute of the means for the prosecution of the war on so gigantic a scale as that which it has attained. The workshops and artisans were mainly to be found in the Northern States, and one of the first duties which devolved upon this Government was to establish the necessary manufactories, and in the meantime to obtain by purchase from abroad, as far as practicable, whatever was required for the public defense. No effort has been spared to effect both these ends; and though the results have not equaled our hopes, it is believed that an impartial judgment will, upon full investigation, award to the various Departments of the Government credit for having done all which human power and foresight enabled them to accomplish. The valor and devotion of the people have not only sustained the efforts of the Government but have gone far to supply its deficiencies.

The active state of military preparation among the nations of Europe in April last, the date when our agents first went abroad, interposed unavoidable delays in the procurement of arms, and the want of a navy has greatly impeded our efforts to import military supplies of all sorts. I have hoped for several days to receive official reports in relation to our discomfiture at Roanoke Island and the fall of Fort Donelson. They have not yet reached me, and I am therefore unable to communicate to you such information of those events and the consequences resulting from them as would enable me to make recommendations founded upon the changed conditions which they have produced. Enough is known of the surrender at Roanoke Island to make us feel that it was deeply humiliating, however imperfect may have been the preparations for defense. The hope is still entertained that our reported losses at Fort Donelson have been greatly exaggerated, inasmuch as I am not only unwilling but unable to believe that a large army of our people have surrendered without a desperate effort to cut their way through investing forces, whatever may have been their numbers, and to endeavor to make a junction with other divisions of the army. But in the absence of that exact information which can only be afforded by official reports it would be premature to pass judgment, and my own is reserved, as I trust yours will be, until that information is received. In the meantime strenuous efforts have been made to throw forward re-enforcements to the armies at the positions threatened, and I cannot doubt that the bitter disappointments we have borne, by nerving the people to still greater exertions, will speedily secure results more accordant with our just expectation and as favorable to our cause as those which marked the earlier periods of the war. The reports of the Secretaries of War and the Navy will exhibit the mass of resources for the conduct of the war which we have been enabled to accumulate notwithstanding the very serious difficulties against which we have contended. They afford the cheering hope that our resources, limited as they were at the beginning of the contest, will during its progress become developed to such an extent as fully to meet our future wants.

The policy of enlistment for short terms, against which I have steadily contended from the commencement of the war, has, in my judgment, contributed in no immaterial degree to the recent reverses which we have suffered, and even now renders it difficult to furnish you an accurate statement of the Army. When the war first broke out many of our people could with difficulty be persuaded that it would be long or serious. It was not deemed possible that anything so insane as a persistent attempt to subjugate these States could be made, still less that the delusion would so far prevail as to give to the war the vast proportions which it has assumed. The people, incredulous of a long war, were naturally averse to long enlistments, and the early legislation of Congress rendered it impracticable to obtain volunteers for a greater period than twelve months. Now that it has become probable that the war will be continued through a series of years, our high-spirited and gallant soldiers, while generally reënlisting, are, from the fact of having entered the service for a short term, compelled in many instances to go home to make the necessary arrangements for their families during their prolonged absence. The quotas of new regiments for the war, called for from the different States, are in rapid progress of organization. The whole body of new levies and reënlisted men will probably be ready in the ranks within the next thirty days, but in the meantime it is exceedingly difficult to give an accurate statement of the number of our forces in the field. They may, in general terms, be stated at 400 regiments of infantry, with a proportionate force of cavalry and artillery, the details of which will be shown by the report of the Secretary of War. I deem it proper to advert to the fact that the process of furloughs and reënlistment in progress for the last month had so far disorganized and weakened our forces as to impair our ability for successful defense, but I heartily congratulate you that this evil, which I had foreseen and was powerless to prevent, may now be said to be substantially at an end, and that we shall not again during the war be exposed to seeing our strength diminished by this fruitful cause of disaster—short enlistments.

The people of the Confederate States, being principally engaged in agricultural pursuits, were unprovided at the commencement of hostilities with ships, shipyards, materials for ship-building, or skilled mechanics and seamen in sufficient numbers to make the prompt creation of a navy a practicable task, even if the required appropriations had been made for the purpose. Notwithstanding our very limited resources, however, the report of the Secretary will exhibit to you a satisfactory progress in preparation, and a certainty of early completion of vessels of a number and class on which we may confidently rely for contesting the vaunted control of the enemy over our waters.

The financial system devised by the wisdom of your predecessors has proved adequate to supplying all the wants of the Government, notwithstanding the unexpected and very large increase of expenditures resulting from the great augmentation in the necessary means of defense. The report of the Secretary of the Treasury will exhibit the gratifying fact that we have no floating debt; that the credit of the Government is unimpaired, and that the total expenditure of the Government for the year has been in round numbers $170,000,000—less than one-third of the sum wasted by the enemy in his vain effort to conquer us; less than the value of a single article of export, the cotton crop, of the year.

The report of the Postmaster General will show the condition of that Department to be steadily improving, its revenues increasing, and already affording the assurance that it will be self-sustaining at the date required by the Constitution, while affording ample mail facilities for the people.

In the Department of Justice, which includes the Patent Office and public printing, some legislative provisions will be required, which will be specifically stated in the report of the head of that Department. I invite the attention of Congress to the duty of organizing a Supreme Court of the Confederate States, in accordance with the mandate of the Constitution.

I refer you to my message* communicated to the Provisional Congress in November last for such further information touching the condition of public affairs as it might be useful to lay before you, the short interval which has since elapsed not having produced any material changes in that condition other than those to which reference has already been made.

In conclusion I cordially welcome Representatives wno, recently chosen by the people, are fully imbued with their views and feelings, and can so ably advise me as to the needful provisions for the public service. I assure you of my hearty coöperation in all your efforts for the common welfare of the country.

JEFFERSON DAVIS.

To the Speaker of the House of Representatives.

In response to the resolution of the House of Representatives, requesting the President to furnish the report of Col. Walter H. Jenifer of the battle of Leesburg, I have to state that a copy of General Evans's report of that battle, with all the accompanying

*Page 136.

papers, including the report of Col. Walter H. Jenifer, was sent with the report of the Secretary of War in December last to the Congress, and it is supposed that the notice of this fact will be accepted by you as a satisfactory compliance with the resolution above described. JEFFERSON DAVIS.

[Received March 1, 1862.]

To the Speaker of the House of Representatives.

In response to the resolution of the House of Representatives of the 19th inst., asking for "the report of Major General Thomas J. Jackson respecting the recent operations of the division under his command in the Valley District of Va.:"

Also, "the report of Col. George Lay, Inspector General of the Department of Northern Virginia, as to the condition of the command in the Valley District:"

I have to state that upon an examination of the files of the War Department, it appears that no such report from Major General Jackson as that called for has reached that Department, and that the report of Col. Lay was made without actual inspection on his part of the army at Romney, then under the immediate command of General Loring, and only gives, in relation to it, such information as he received from officers at Winchester.

The usual and generally necessary practice is to consider inspection reports as confidential. It would frequently happen that the publication of such reports would needlessly wound the feelings of officers and would promote discord and heartburnings among the troops.

The present instance forms no exception to the general rule, and it is believed that the public interest would receive detriment from the communication of the report which is called for. Justice to the parties concerned would require that much more should be communicated than the report, if it were submitted.

JEFFERSON DAVIS.

[Received March 1, 1862.]

To the Senate of the Confederate States.

I herewith transmit the report of the Secretary of the Navy, which I recommend be considered in secret session.

JEFFERSON DAVIS.

[Received March 1, 1862.]

EXECUTIVE DEPARTMENT, March 3, 1862.

To the Senate and House of Representatives.

I herewith transmit the report of the Department of Justice.

JEFFERSON DAVIS.

To the Senate and House of Representatives.

I herewith transmit the report of the Secretary of War, with accompanying documents, inviting attention to the facts therein presented, and commending the recommendation to your favorable consideration.   JEFFERSON DAVIS.

[Received March 4, 1862.]

RICHMOND, March 4, 1862.

To the Speaker of the House of Representatives.

In response to the resolution of the House of yesterday, calling on the President to communicate "what additional means in money, men, arms, and munitions of war are in his judgment necessary, or may be within the present year, for the public service, including operations on land and water," I have to reply that the military forces, whether land or naval, which will be required must depend upon the operations of the enemy and upon contingencies which cannot be foreseen. Taking our present condition as the basis of the calculation, it may be stated in general terms that our land forces should be increased by the addition of, say, 300,000 men in the field and those for whom call has already been made; that the Navy should be increased by a number of vessels suited to river and harbor defense, say, fifty iron-clad propellers, and a fleet of, say, ten of the most formidable war vessels to protect our commerce upon the high seas, with the requisite armaments and crews. For this additional force, land and naval, there would be required, say, 750,000 small arms of all kinds, and of siege, and field, and seacoast artillery, say, 5,000 guns; of powder, say, 5,000 tons in addition to that which can be made within the limits of the Confederacy. The manufacture of projectiles could, it is believed, be carried to the requisite extent in our own foundries, at a cost which must be measured by the number of guns actively employed. For further details I refer to the accompanying reports of the Secretaries of War and Navy. The amount of money which will be required will depend upon the extent to which the articles needed may be obtained, and as I cannot hope to get more than a small part of that which a reply to the resolution required me to enumerate, I have not attempted to convert the articles into their probable money value. Estimates have been prepared and will be laid before the Congress showing the appropriations which it is deemed proper to ask, in view of the public wants and the possibility to supply them, as well as of the condition of the finances of the Confederate States.

JEFFERSON DAVIS.

To the Senate and House of Representatives.

I herewith transmit to Congress the report of the Postmaster General, and invite attention to the recommendation contained therein. JEFFERSON DAVIS.

March 5, 1862.

EXECUTIVE DEPARTMENT, March 6, 1862.

To the Speaker of the House of Representatives.

I herewith transmit a report from the Secretary of War, in answer to a resolution of the House of Representatives of the 4th inst., which I referred to the Department for the information therein contained, or for copies of the reports called for if they had been received. JEFFERSON DAVIS.

EXECUTIVE DEPARTMENT, RICHMOND, March 7, 1862.

To the Speaker of the House of Representatives.

I transmit herewith a report* from the Secretary of the Navy, *ad interim,* in answer to a resolution of the House of Representatives of the 6th instant. JEFFERSON DAVIS.

EXECUTIVE DEPARTMENT, RICHMOND, March 7, 1862.

To the Speaker of the House of Representatives.

I transmit herewith a report from the Secretary of State, *ad interim,* in answer to a resolution of the House of Representatives of the 6th inst. JEFFERSON DAVIS.

---

*Relating to certain foreign (French) vessels in Chesapeake Bay, and whether these vessels are probably here for the purpose of exporting cotton or tobacco from the Confederate States.

EXECUTIVE DEPARTMENT, RICHMOND, March 8, 1862.
To the Senate of the Confederate States.

I transmit herewith a report and accompanying papers from the Secretary of State, *ad interim,* in answer to a resolution* of the Senate of the 3d instant.   JEFFERSON DAVIS.

RICHMOND, March 10, 1862.
To the Speaker of the House of Representatives.

Sir: Annexed I submit a letter from the Secretary of the Navy indicating a plan for the further defense of the Bay of Mobile and the Alabama River, asking for an appropriation to carry it into execution.

The general purpose and means proposed are similar to those authorized by an act of the Provisional Congress for the better defense of the Mississippi River.

I commend the proposition to the favorable consideration of Congress and would suggest, if it be adopted, that the disbursement of the money be made in the manner provided for appropriations for the Navy.   JEFFERSON DAVIS.

EXECUTIVE DEPARTMENT, March 11, 1862.
To the Speaker of the House of Representatives.

I transmit herewith copies of such official reports as have been received at the War Department of the defense and fall of Fort Donelson. They will be found incomplete and unsatisfactory. Instructions have been given to furnish further information upon the several points not made intelligible by the reports. It is not stated that reënforcements were at any time asked for; nor is it demonstrated to have been impossible to have saved the army by evacuating the position; nor is it known by what means it was found practicable to withdraw a part of the garrison, leaving the remainder to surrender; nor upon what authority or principle of action the senior Generals abandoned responsibility, by transferring the command to a junior officer.

In a former communication to Congress I presented the propriety of a suspension of judgment in relation to the disaster at

---

*Requesting the President to communicate to Congress copies of all correspondence with Confederate commissioners abroad.

Fort Donelson, until official reports could be received. I regret that the information now furnished is so defective. In the meantime, hopeful that satisfactory explanation may be made, I have directed, upon the exhibition of the case as presented by the two senior Generals,* that they should be relieved from command to await further orders whenever a reliable judgment can be rendered on the merits of the case. JEFFERSON DAVIS.

To the Senate and House of Representatives of the Confederate States.

I herewith transmit a letter† of the Secretary of the Navy, of this date, covering the official report of the naval engagement between the James River squadron and the enemy's fleet, in Hampton Roads, on the 8th instant.

The officers and men of our Navy, engaged in this brilliant affair, deserve well of their country, and are commended to the consideration of the Congress.

The disparity of the forces engaged did not justify the anticipation of so great a victory; and it is doubly gratifying that it has been won upon an element where we were supposed to be least able to compete with our enemy.

Special attention is called to the perfidious conduct of the enemy in hoisting on the frigate Congress a white flag, and renewing fire, from that vessel, under the impunity thus obtained.

JEFFERSON DAVIS.

March 11, 1862.

RICHMOND, March 11, 1862.

To the President.

Sir: I have the honor to lay before you the official report of the naval engagement between the James River squadron, under the command of Flag Officer Franklin Buchanan, and the enemy's fleet, in Hampton Roads, on the 8th instant.

Flag Officer Buchanan, in the immediate command of the steam sloop Virginia, was disabled near the close of the engagement by a painful though not dangerous wound, and the report is made by the Executive Officer, upon whom the command devolved, Lieutenant Jones.

The steam sloop Virginia, of ten guns, the Patrick Henry, Commander Tucker, of six guns, the Jamestown, Lieutenant Commanding Barney, of two guns, the Raleigh, Lieutenant Commanding Alexander, the Beaufort,

---

* Floyd and Pillow. † See also page 210.

Lieutenant Commanding Parker, and the Teaser, Lieutenant Commanding Webb, each of one gun, composed our squadron. With this force of twenty-one guns, Flag Officer Buchanan engaged the enemy's fleet, consisting of the frigate Cumberland of twenty-four guns, the Congress of fifty guns, 'the St. Lawrence of fifty guns, and the steam frigates Minnesota and Roanoke each of forty guns, the enemy's batteries at Newport News, and several small steamers armed with heavy rifled guns.

The engagement commenced at 3:30 P.M., and at 6 o'clock P.M. he had sunk the Cumberland, captured and burnt the Congress, disabled and driven the Minnesota ashore, and defeated the St. Lawrence and the Roanoke, which sought shelter under the guns of Fortress Monroe. Two of the enemy's small steamers were blown up, and two transport schooners were captured.

The Cumberland went down with all on board, her tops only remaining above water; but many of her people were saved by boats from the shore.

The loss of the enemy has not been ascertained. Our loss is very small but has not been officially communicated.

The flag of the Congress and the sword of the officer commanding at the time of her surrender are at this Department, together with the flag and sword of the gunboat Fanny, captured by Flag Officer Lynch, in October last; and I submit for your consideration the propriety of providing for the safe-keeping of these and similar trophies.

To the dashing courage, the patriotism and eminent ability of Flag Officer Buchanan and the officers and men of his squadron our country is indebted for this brilliant achievement, which will hold a conspicuous place among the heroic contests of naval history.

With much respect, your obedient servant,

S. R. MALLORY,
Secretary of the Navy.

EXECUTIVE DEPARTMENT, March 12, 1862.

To the Senate and House of Representatives.

I transmit herewith to the Congress the official report of Col. William B. Taliaferro, of the action at Carrick's Ford, July 13, 1861.   JEFFERSON DAVIS.

EXECUTIVE DEPARTMENT, March 13, 1862.

To the Senate and House of Representatives.

I herewith transmit to the Congress the report* of the Acting Commissioner of Indian Affairs.   JEFFERSON DAVIS.

---

*Relating to treaties with Indians.

RICHMOND, March 13, 1862.

To the House of Representatives.

In response to the resolution of the 26th ultimo calling for a statement as to the establishments under contract for the supply of small arms and of powder, and what means are employed in furnishing percussion caps, and whether the various manufacturing establishments now employed by the Government will be able to furnish an ample supply of arms, powder, and percussion caps for the use of our Army, I herewith transmit a report to the Secretary of War, which gives such information in relation to the ability of the establishments employed as, it is hoped, will be satisfactory to the Congress. The Government has secured a supply of sulphur sufficient for any proximate want; proper charcoal can be obtained in any requisite quantity, and it only requires an adequate supply of saltpeter to insure the manufacture of more powder than can be profitably used. In addition to the mills now in active operation a very extensive one has been constructed in Georgia, which we have not started because the supply of saltpeter did not justify it. Establishments for the manufacture of small arms are being constructed and developed, but, as was to have been anticipated, the progress has been slow and the want of mechanics does not permit us to hope for such extensive results as would satisfy existing necessities. The attention of Congress is called to the remarks of the Secretary on the subject of iron, and a method of increasing its production. For further information reference is made to the tabular statement of the Chief of Ordnance, which is annexed to the letter of the Secretary of War.   JEFF'N DAVIS.

EXECUTIVE DEPARTMENT, March 14, 1862.

To the House of Representatives.

I transmit herewith a communication from the Secretary of the Treasury with estimates of appropriations required for the support of the Government from April 1 to November 30, 1862. The estimates of the various Executive Departments are inclosed, and it will be seen by the letter of the Secretary of the Treasury that no estimates for the expenses of the Congress have been received.   JEFFERSON DAVIS.

EXECUTIVE DEPARTMENT, March 15, 1862.

To the Speaker of the House of Representatives.

I transmit herewith an official report of the engagement at Coosaw River,* January 1, 1862.   JEFFERSON DAVIS.

EXECUTIVE DEPARTMENT, March 17, 1862.

To the President of the Senate.

I have appointed Burton N. Harrison, of Mississippi, my Private Secretary in the place of Robert Josselyn, resigned.

JEFFERSON DAVIS.

EXECUTIVE DEPARTMENT, March 18, 1862.

To the Honorable the Speaker of the House of Representatives.

Sir: I herewith transmit a communication from the Secretary of War, relative to a resolution of the 14th inst., requesting a copy of General George B. Crittenden's report of the battle of Fishing Creek.   JEFFERSON DAVIS.

EXECUTIVE DEPARTMENT, March 18, 1862.

To the Honorable the Speaker of the House of Representatives.

I herewith transmit a communication from the Secretary of War, relative to a resolution of the House of Representatives of the 12th inst., requesting a copy of the report of Major General Braxton Bragg, of the bombardment of Pensacola on the 22d and 23d of November last.   JEFFERSON DAVIS.

EXECUTIVE DEPARTMENT, March 18, 1862.

To the Honorable the Speaker of the House of Representatives.

I herewith inclose a report of the Secretary of War, supplementary to a report heretofore made by him to the House of Representatives, and referred to in that document.

JEFFERSON DAVIS.

---

*Port Royal Ferry, S. C.

Executive Department, March 19, 1862.

To the Senate and House of Representatives.

I herewith transmit a report of the Secretary of War, supplementary to a report heretofore submitted by him, and referred to in that document. JEFFERSON DAVIS.

Executive Department,
Richmond, Va., March 20, 1862.

To the Speaker of the House of Representatives.

Herewith I submit a letter from the Secretary of the Navy, with an estimate for an appropriation to enable him to purchase or construct ironclad vessels.

Though it is certainly doubtful whether a change in the present condition of affairs in Europe will occur which would render it practicable to effect the object in the manner proposed, it may be proper to put the Department in a position which will enable it to take advantage of any opportunity which may be presented for the rapid increase of that class of vessels which are believed to be the best suited to coast and harbor defense.

I recommend, therefore, that the appropriation asked for be granted. JEFFERSON DAVIS.

Richmond, Va., March 20, 1862.

To the House of Representatives, Confederate States of America.

In reply to the resolution of the House of Representatives of the 24th ultimo, requesting the President to furnish certain information in reference to the James River defenses and the defenses of the city of Richmond, with his own opinion thereon, and to cause a survey to be made of the Chickahominy and its branches, with reference to its being occupied as a defensive line, I transmit herewith a communication from the Secretary of War, submitting a report of Capt. Alfred L. Rives, in charge of the Engineer Bureau, on the subjects referred to, so far as the information obtained will admit.

The report of Captain Rives states the facts in regard to the state of the defenses of the James River and the city of Richmond; and in the views presented by him I generally concur. It may be proper, however, to add something in explanation of the facts presented, and my own impressions derived from various sources from time to time. The work at Day's Point possesses but little value for the defense proper of the James River. It was located with regard to the protection of Burwell's Bay and the country above from foraging excursions of the enemy by water, and as a protection to our own boats in the river. A site somewhat lower down would have been preferable, according to information obtained since the location of the work, but it has thus far fulfilled its object; and as it has been well constructed, with much labor and expense, it is probably best not to disturb it except by the addition of a small outwork to command the approaches in its rear, which, I am told, is being done.

The next position above, defended by the works at Hardy's Bluff and Mulberry Island, possesses great importance from being the right flank of General Magruder's chosen defensive line on the Peninsula, and the lowest point which gives the hope of a successful protection of the river against the wooden fleets of the enemy. Ironclad vessels, of which we have not had sufficient experience to form a correct judgment, can pass these works, as the channel is too wide and deep for obstructions, unless wrought-iron bolts, now being prepared for trial against the Ericsson battery (Monitor) and others of the same class, prove more effective than can be reasonably hoped for; but still the transports necessary for a formidable expedition ought to be kept back by the batteries so long as they are held; and it is thought that they should not be silenced by a few ironclad vessels operating with a small number of guns at long range, especially as the battery at Hardy's Bluff has considerable elevation. Both works are strong against a land attack. The guns at Jamestown Island will probably be removed to the position just referred to, as soon as it is fully prepared for them.

The position at Drewry's Bluff, seven or eight miles below Richmond, which has intimate relations with the defenses proper of the city, was chosen to obstruct the river against such vessels as the Monitor. The work is being rapidly completed. Either Fort Powhatan or Kennon's Marshes, if found to be the proper positions, will be fortified and obstructed as at Drewry's Bluff to prevent the ascent of the river by ironclad vessels. Blocking the channel, where sufficiently narrow, by strong lines of obstructions, filling it with submarine batteries, and flanking the obstructions by well-protected batteries of the heaviest guns, seem to offer the best and speediest chances of protection, with the means at our disposal, against ironclad floating batteries. The field works for the defense of Richmond, which are arranged upon the plan of the detached system, conceded by most military men to be the best, are completed, with the exception of two on the side of the city, and one main and two accessory works on the Manchester side. The unfinished works will be completed as soon as more important ones farther from the city are in a more efficient condition. The line occupied by these works was chosen to make it as short as possible, partly from the difficulty of defending a longer line, and partly from the time, labor, and expense necessary to construct such a one. It is rather nearer the city than desirable, but the enemy must remain out of reach of our guns, at least as heavy as his, until the line is carried, and then the city must fall, whether the line be near or removed within the limits of a few miles. I see no advantage in constructing a new line more removed from the city, unless the Chickahominy be found suited to the system of dams and overflow, which, I think, from the information in my possession, is problematical. Should the enemy get near enough to lay siege to this city, additional works can be thrown up as he develops his plans and means; and these, with those already constructed, can be armed with the guns which would necessarily be brought back with the troops to defend them. The want of heavy guns and the requisite carriages has prevented the fortifications here from being armed with them to any extent, and I do not think it wise to take them for this purpose from other points where, in my opinion, they are more needed. Any system of fortification which could be constructed during the war for the defense of this city would only serve to gain time. An army which allows itself to be shut up in a fortified city must finally yield to an enemy superior in numbers and munitions of war.   JEFFERSON DAVIS.

EXECUTIVE DEPARTMENT, March 24, 1862.

To the Honorable the Speaker of the House of Representatives.

Sir: Inclosed I send for the consideration and action of the House of Representatives a communication from the Acting Secretary of War, explaining the appropriations already made of one million dollars, for the floating defenses of the western waters, and asking a further appropriation of half a million dollars, to be used for the same purposes.

I recommend that the money be appropriated as requested.

JEFFERSON DAVIS.

EXECUTIVE DEPARTMENT, March 24, 1862.

To the Speaker of the House of Representatives.

Sir: I herewith transmit for the consideration of the House of Representatives a communication from the Secretary of the Navy, with accompanying papers* which afford the information sought by the resolution of the House of Representatives on the 17th inst.

I also suggest that these papers be regarded confidential and be considered in secret session.   JEFFERSON DAVIS.

EXECUTIVE DEPARTMENT,
RICHMOND, VA., March 25, 1862.

To the House of Representatives of the Confederate States.

In answer to your resolution of the 21st instant, calling upon the President for information in regard to the protection of our principal cities from iron-plated vessels by means of obstructions and submarine batteries, and whether any additional appropriations are needed for these objects, I have to state generally that the channels of approach to our principal cities have been and are being obstructed according to the means at hand; that submarine batteries have been and are being prepared, and that no additional appropriations for these objects are considered to be needed. Until recently the character of the enemy's iron-plated vessels was not well enough known to arrange obstructions specially for them, but the same principle obtains and the obstructions already prepared can be strengthened when necessary. For the want of insulated wire we are deprived of that class of submarine batteries exploded at will by electricity, which promises the best results.

*Relating to purchase and construction of ships and munitions of war, and purchase of vessels abroad.

Experiments upon several kinds of such as are exploded by impact have been in progress since an early period of the war. These torpedoes can be rendered harmless by the enemy in most cases by setting adrift floating bodies to explode them, as is said to have been done on the Mississippi River, and as they cannot be put in place so long as all the channels are required for use by our own boats no great degree of importance is attached to them. They may serve, however, to gain time by making the enemy more cautious; and most of our seacoast defenses have already received, or will as soon as practicable receive, a certain supply of them.

JEFF'N DAVIS.

EXECUTIVE DEPARTMENT, March 25, 1862.

To the Hon. the Speaker of the House of Representatives.

Sir: I herewith transmit for the consideration and action of the House of Representatives a communication from the Secretary of the Navy covering "an estimate of an additional appropriation required for the service of the Navy Department from April 1 to November 30, 1862."

I recommend that an appropriation be made of the sum and for the purpose specified.   JEFFERSON DAVIS.

EXECUTIVE DEPARTMENT, March 28, 1862.

To the Senate and House of Representatives of the Confederate States.

The operation of the various laws now in force for raising armies has exhibited the necessity for reform. The frequent changes and amendments which have been made have rendered the system so complicated as to make it often quite difficult to determine what the law really is, and to what extent prior enactments are modified by more recent legislation. There is also embarrassment from conflict between State and Confederate legislation. I am happy to assure you of the entire harmony of purpose and cordiality of feeling which have continued to exist between myself and the Executives of the several States; and it is to this cause that our success in keeping adequate forces in the field is to be attributed. These reasons would suffice for inviting your earnest attention to the necessity of some simple and general system for exercising the power of raising armies, which is vested in the Congress by the Constitution. But there is another and more important consideration. The vast preparations made by the enemy for a combined assault at numerous points on our frontier and seacoast have produced the result that might have been expected. They have animated the people with a spirit of resistance so general, so resolute, and so self-sacrificing that it requires rather to be regulated than to be stimulated. The right of the State to demand, and the duty of each citizen to render, military service, need only to be stated to be admitted. It is not, however, wise or judicious policy to place in active service that portion of the force of a people which experience has shown to be necessary as a reserve. Youths under the age of eighteen years require further instruction; men of matured experience are needed for maintaining order and good government at home and in supervising preparations for rendering efficient the armies in the field. These two classes constitute the proper reserve for home defense, ready to be called out in case of emergency, and to be kept in the field only while the emergency exists. But in order to maintain this reserve intact it is necessary that in a great war like that in which we are now engaged all persons of intermediate age not legally exempt for good cause should pay their debt of military service to the country, that the burdens should not fall exclusively on the most ardent and patriotic. I therefore recommend the passage of a law declaring that all persons residing within the Confederate States, between the ages of eighteen and thirty-five years, and rightfully subject to military duty, shall be held to be in the military service of the Confederate States, and that some plain and simple method be adopted for their prompt enrollment and organization, repealing all the legislation heretofore enacted which would conflict with the system proposed.   JEFFERSON DAVIS.

EXECUTIVE OFFICE, RICHMOND, March 29, 1862.

To the Speaker of the House of Representatives.

I herewith transmit a report and accompanying tabular statement from the Secretary of State, in answer to a resolution of the House of Representatives of the 26th inst.

JEFFERSON DAVIS.

EXECUTIVE DEPARTMENT, April 1, 1862.

To the Senate and House of Representatives of the Confederate States.

I herewith transmit the report* of the Secretary of the Navy, which I recommend be considered in secret session.

JEFFERSON DAVIS.

EXECUTIVE DEPARTMENT, April 1, 1862.

To the Hon. Speaker of the House of Representatives.

Sir: I herewith transmit to the House of Representatives a communication from the Secretary of War, affording, as far as practicable, the information sought by the "resolution of inquiry adopted by the House of Representatives in regard to the disasters at Forts Henry and Donelson," &c., and replying to the "additional resolution of the House of Representatives," adopted March 31, 1862, calling for the official response of General A. S. Johnston to the interrogatories propounded to him in regard to those subjects; and also for a copy of the supplementary report of General Pillow in regard to the affair at Fort Donelson, &c.

JEFFERSON DAVIS.

To the Hon. the Speaker of the House of Representatives.

Sir: I herewith transmit to the House of Representatives a communication from the Secretary of the Treasury, covering additional estimates for clerks to be employed in the offices of the Treasurer, Assistant Treasurer, and Depositaries of the Confederate States, and I recommend that the appropriation be made of the sums and for the purposes specified.   JEFFERSON DAVIS.

[Received April 1, 1862.]

To the Hon. the Speaker of the House of Representatives.

Sir: I herewith transmit to the House of Representatives a communication from the Secretary of War, in reference to a "resolution of the House," requesting the President to furnish to the

---

*In compliance with a resolution of the House of Representatives requesting a report on the plan and construction of the Virginia, the reasons for applying the plan to the Merrimac, and what persons rendered especial aid in designing and building the ship.

House "a copy of the report of Gen. H. A. Wise, touching the fall of Roanoke Island, which was made by him to the Secretary of War, under date of the 21st February, 1862, if not inconsistent with the public interest."   JEFFERSON DAVIS.

[Received April 1, 1862.]

EXECUTIVE DEPARTMENT, April 1, 1862.

To the Hon. the Speaker of the House of Representatives.

Sir: I herewith transmit to the House of Representatives a communication of the Secretary of the Navy, covering information sought by a resolution of the House requesting the President to communicate to the House what additional sums of money, if any, are in his judgment necessary to the Departments of War and Navy, in order to secure a successful prosecution of the war and effective defense of the Confederate States during the time for which Congress at its present session should make provision.

JEFFERSON DAVIS.

To the Senate and House of Representatives of the Confederate States of America.

The great importance of the news first received from Tennessee induces me to depart from established usage, and to make to you this communication in advance of official reports.

From telegraphic dispatches received from official sources, I am able to announce to you with entire confidence that it has pleased Almighty God to crown the Confederate arms with a glorious and decisive victory over our invaders.

On the morning of the 6th inst., the converging columns of our army were combined by its commander in chief, Gen. A. S. Johnston, in an assault on the Federal army, then encamped near Pittsburg, on the Tennessee River. After a hard-fought battle of ten hours, the enemy was driven in disorder from his position and pursued to the Tennessee River, where, under cover of his gunboats, he was, at the last accounts, endeavoring to effect his retreat by aid of his transports.

The details of this great battle are yet too few and incomplete to enable me to distinguish with merited praise all of those who may have conspicuously earned the right to such distinction; and

I prefer to delay my own gratification in recommending them to your special notice, rather than incur the risk of wounding the feelings of any by failing to include them in the list. Where such a victory has been won over troops as numerous, as well disciplined, armed, and appointed as those which have just been so signally routed, we may well conclude that one common spirit of unflinching bravery and devotion to our country's cause must have animated every breast, from that of the Commanding General to that of the humblest patriot who served in the ranks.

There is enough in the continued presence of invaders on our soil to chasten our exultation over this brilliant success, and to remind us of the grave duty of continued exertion until we shall extort from a proud and vainglorious enemy the reluctant acknowledgment of our right to self-government. But an all-wise Creator has been pleased, while vouchsafing to us his countenance in battle, to afflict us with a severe dispensation, to which we must bow in humble submission. The last lingering hope has disappeared, and it is but too true that General Albert Sidney Johnston is no more. The tale of his death is simply narrated in a dispatch first received from Col. William Preston in the following words: "General Johnston fell yesterday at half-past two o'clock, while leading a successful charge, turning the enemy's right and gaining a brilliant victory. A Minie ball cut the artery of his leg, but he rode on till, from loss of blood, he fell exhausted, and died without pain in a few minutes. His body has been intrusted to me by Gen. Beauregard, to be taken to New Orleans, and remain until directions are received from his family."

My long and close friendship with this departed chieftain and patriot forbids me to trust myself in giving vent to the feelings which this sad intelligence has evoked. Without doing injustice to the living, it may safely be asserted that our loss is irreparable; and that among the shining hosts of the great and the good who now cluster around the banner of our country, there exists no purer spirit, no more heroic soul than that of the illustrious man whose death I join you in lamenting.

In his death he has illustrated the character for which, through life, he was conspicuous, that of singleness of purpose and devotion to duty. With his whole energies bent on attaining the victory which he deemed essential to his country's cause, he rode on to the accomplishment of his object, forgetful of self, while his very lifeblood was fast ebbing away. His last breath cheered his comrades to victory. The last sound he heard was their shout of triumph. His last thought was his country's, and long and deeply will his country mourn his loss.   JEFFERSON DAVIS.

April 8, 1862.

EXECUTIVE DEPARTMENT, April 10, 1862.

To the Senate and House of Representatives of the Confederate States.

I herewith transmit to Congress a communication* from the Secretary of the Navy, covering a "detailed report of Flag Officer Buchanan, of the brilliant triumph of his squadron over the vastly superior forces of the enemy, in Hampton Roads, on the 8th and 9th of March last."   JEFFERSON DAVIS.

CONFEDERATE STATES OF AMERICA, NAVY DEPARTMENT,
RICHMOND, April 7, 1862.

To the President.

Sir: I have the honor to submit herewith copy of the detailed report† of Flag Officer Buchanan, of the brilliant triumph of his squadron over the vastly superior forces of the enemy, in Hampton Roads, on the 8th and 9th of March last, a brief report, by Lieut. Jones, of the battle of the 8th, having been previously made.

The conduct of the officers and men of the squadron, in this contest, reflects unfading honor upon themselves and upon the navy. The report will be read with deep interest, and its details will not fail to rouse the ardor and nerve the arms of our gallant seamen.

It will be remembered that the Virginia was a novelty in naval architecture, wholly unlike any ship that ever floated; that her heaviest guns were equal novelties in ordnance; that her motive power and obedience to her helm were untried, and her officers and crew strangers, comparatively, to the ship and to each other; and yet, under all these disadvantages, the dashing courage and consummate professional ability of Flag Officer Buchanan and his associates achieved the most remarkable victory which naval annals record.

When the Flag Officer was disabled, the command of the Virginia devolved upon her Executive and Ordnance Officer, Lieut. Catesby Ap R. Jones, and the cool and masterly manner in which he fought the ship in her encounter with the ironclad Monitor justified the high estimate which the country places upon his professional merit.

---

* See also message of March 11, 1862, page 197.   † Omitted.

To his experience, skill, and untiring industry as her Ordnance and Executive Officer the terrible effect of her fire was greatly due. Her battery was determined in accordance with his suggestions, and in all investigations and tests, which resulted in its thorough efficiency, he was zealously engaged.

The terms of commendation used by the Flag Officer in characterizing the conduct of his officers and men meet the cordial indorsement of the Department, and the concurrent testimony of thousands who witnessed the engagement places his own conduct above all praise.

With much respect, your obedient servant,

S. R. MALLORY, *Secretary of the Navy.*

To the Senate of the Confederate States.

I transmit herewith a letter from the Secretary of the Navy, submitting a proposition for the construction of ironclad vessels in Europe, and commend it to the attention of Congress.

JEFFERSON DAVIS.

Richmond, Va., April 10, 1862.

[The same message was sent to the House of Representatives.]

EXECUTIVE DEPARTMENT, April 11, 1862.

To the Senate of the Confederate States.

I herewith transmit to Congress a report of the Postmaster General, supplementary to a report previously submitted, and covering certain documents relative to "frauds perpetrated on the revenues of the Post Office Department by the Southern Express Company."

I recommend that the suggested alteration of the existing laws receive the careful attention of Congress.   JEFFERSON DAVIS

EXECUTIVE DEPARTMENT, RICHMOND, April 12, 1862.

To the Senate of the Confederate States.

I nominate Braxton Bragg, of Louisiana, to the rank of General in the Army of the Confederate States, agreeably to the recommendation of the Secretary of War, to take rank from the 6th day of April, 1862.   JEFFERSON DAVIS.

To the House of Representatives.

I herewith transmit a communication from the Secretary of War, conveying information, so far as practicable, in response to a resolution of the House of Representatives, requesting the President to communicate what steps have been taken to carry out the act for connecting the Richmond and Danville and the North Carolina railroads, and for the connection of the railroad from Selma, in Alabama, to Meridian, in Mississippi.

JEFFERSON DAVIS.

[Received April 14, 1862.]

EXECUTIVE DEPARTMENT, April 16, 1862.

To the Senate of the Confederate States.

In compliance with your request for information, expressed in a resolution of the 14th inst., I herewith transmit a communication from the Secretary of War, covering a copy of the report of General Branch of the battle of Newbern, North Carolina.

JEFFERSON DAVIS.

April 17, 1862.

To the Senate and House of Representatives of the Confederate States.

I deem it my duty to call your attention to some practical difficulties which will occur in the execution of the law just passed for the conscription of all persons subject to military duty between the ages of eighteen and thirty-five years, and to point out some omissions that it seems wise to supply. First. There are a number of troops in the service of the several States for which no provision is made. They have been organized for State defense, which is necessarily the public defense, but are not a part of the armies of the Confederacy. It would not be politic to break up these organizations for the purpose of taking out of them such of the men as are subject to conscription for distribution among other troops. I suggest that power be granted to the Executive to accept a transfer of such regiments, battalions, squadrons, or companies now in the service of the respective States as may be tendered by the States, according to any organization consistent with the Confederate laws. Second. In the tenth section of the bill there is a seeming conflict between two clauses, one of which requires that in all cases elections shall be held to fill the lowest grade, while another gives power to promote from the ranks to any vacant office a private who may have distinguished himself conspicuously. I would be glad to have the intent of Congress on this point stated in an amendment to the bill. Third. Under the fourth section of the act of the 11th of December, 1861, it was declared that all troops revolunteering or reënlisting shall, at the expiration of their present term of service, have the power to reorganize themselves into companies and elect their company officers, and that said companies should have the right to reorganize themselves into battalions or regiments, and elect their field officers, &c. By the second section of the act just passed, 16th of April, 1862, it is prohibited to include in the organization of such new companies and regiments as may be completed within thirty days "any persons now in the service." It is submitted whether bare justice to the men who first entered the military service, and who have again voluntarily enrolled themselves to serve for the war, does not require that the Government should carry out the understanding under which they reënlisted, by permitting them to serve in organizations more acceptable to them than those in which they are now embraced. I should regret to see men now for the first time brought into the service under the stringency of the law vested with the right of choosing their association, while the same privilege is denied to those who have distinguished themselves by the alacrity with which they have volunteered. JEFFERSON DAVIS.

EXECUTIVE DEPARTMENT, April 17, 1862.

To the Senate and House of Representatives.

I herewith transmit for the information of Congress a communication from the Secretary of the Navy, covering estimates for the amount required by the Navy Department for specified purposes.

I recommend that an appropriation be made of the sums and for the objects mentioned. JEFFERSON DAVIS.

EXECUTIVE DEPARTMENT, April 17, 1862.

To the House of Representatives.

I herewith transmit a communication from the Secretary of

War, containing an estimate of additional funds required for the Ordnance Bureau for the period ending December 1, 1862.

I recommend that an appropriation be made of the sums and for the purposes specified.   JEFFERSON DAVIS.

EXECUTIVE DEPARTMENT, April 18, 1862.

Hon. Thos. S. Bocock, Speaker of the House of Representatives.

Sir: I transmit herewith Lieut. Commanding Robert B. Pegram's report of the cruise of the Nashville, and certain official correspondence called for by the resolution of the House of Representatives of the 15th inst.   JEFFERSON DAVIS.

EXECUTIVE DEPARTMENT, April 18, 1862.

To the Senate and House of Representatives.

I herewith transmit for the information of Congress a communication from the Secretary of War, covering "a copy of the official report of Major General Earl Van Dorn of the battle between his forces and those of Generals Sigel and Curtis in Arkansas."

JEFFERSON DAVIS.

EXECUTIVE DEPARTMENT, April 21, 1862.

To the Honorable the House of Representatives.

I herewith transmit a communication from the Secretary of the Treasury, covering an estimate of an appropriation required to carry into effect an act therein mentioned.

I recommend that an appropriation be made of the sum and for the purposes specified.   JEFFERSON DAVIS.

April 21, 1862.

To the Senate and House of Representatives of the Confederate States.

I deem it proper to inform you that a number of acts passed by the Congress were presented to me at a very late hour on Saturday night. I have examined them as carefully as the limited time at my disposal has permitted, and have returned nearly all of them with my approval. There are, however, three of them to which I have objections, which it is impossible to communicate to you in writing within the few remaining hours of the session, and which will therefore fail to become laws. Happily the acts in question are not of great public importance. Recognizing, as I do, the right of Congress to receive the fullest information from the Executive on all matters of legislation on which his concurrence is required by the Constitution, I have considered it more respectful to Congress to make this statement of the cause which has prevented my action on these bills than to retain them without assigning my reason for so doing. JEFFERSON DAVIS.

VETO MESSAGES.

EXECUTIVE DEPARTMENT, March 14, 1862.

To the Speaker of the House of Representatives.

Not being able to approve, I return with my objections, in accordance with the duty imposed by the Constitution, an act entitled "An Act to create the office of commanding general of the armies of the Confederate States." The act creates an office which is to continue during the pleasure of the President, but the tenure of office of the general to be appointed is without any other limitation than that of the office itself. The purpose of the act, so far as it creates a military bureau, the head of which, at the seat of government, under direction of the President, shall be charged with the movement of troops, the supply and discipline of the Army, I fully approve; but, by what I cannot regard otherwise than as an inadvertence on the part of Congress, the officer so appointed is authorized to take the field at his own discretion and command any army or armies he may choose, not only without the direction but even against the will of the President, who could not consistently with this act prevent such conduct of the general otherwise than by abolishing his office. To show that the effect of this act would be highly detrimental to the Army, it might be enough to say that no general would be content to prepare troops for battle, conduct their movements, and share their privations during a whole campaign if he expected to find himself superseded at the very moment of action. But there is another ground which to my mind is conclusive. The Constitution vests in the Executive the command in chief of the armies of the Confederacy; that command is totally inconsistent with the existence of an officer authorized, at his own discretion, to take command of armies assigned by the President to other generals. The Executive could in no just sense be said to be Commander in Chief if without the power to control the discretion of the general created by this act. As it cannot have been the intention of Congress to create the office of a general not bound to obey orders of the Chief Magistrate, and as this seems to be the effect of the act, I can but anticipate the concurrence of the Congress in my opinion that it should not become a law.   JEFFERSON DAVIS.

CONFEDERATE STATES OF AMERICA,
EXECUTIVE DEPARTMENT, April 19, 1862.

To the Senate of the Confederate States.

I herewith return, without my approval, to the Senate, the "joint resolution directing how prize money shall be paid in certain cases."

This resolution declares that the share of prize money awarded, or which may be awarded, to any seaman or marine who is or may be a prisoner in the hands of the enemy, shall, under the direction of the Secretary of the Navy, be paid to the wife of such seaman or marine during his captivity.

However praiseworthy the motive which prompts to provide for the wives of our seamen or marines now held in captivity by the enemy, I do not believe that Congress can, constitutionally, without the consent of the husband, direct the payment to his wife of any money now due him. The husband's right to the control and disposition of prize money already awarded him is as absolute as that to any other property owned by him. Congress has no greater power over the prize money due him than over any other property which he owns. Vested rights cannot be disturbed or impaired by legislative authority, except in the very special cases named in the Constitution.   JEFFERSON DAVIS.

CONFEDERATE STATES OF AMERICA,
EXECUTIVE DEPARTMENT,
RICHMOND, VA., April 19, 1862.

To the Senate of the Confederate States.

I am constrained by the view which I take of the constitutional powers of Congress, to return, without my approval, a bill to be entitled "An Act relative to the pay and allowances of deceased soldiers," originating in the Senate.

The bill in express terms declares and enacts that the pay and allowances now due to any deceased officer, non-commissioned officer, musician, private, or other person, for services in the Army of the Confederate States, shall be paid to the widow of the deceased, if living, or to others who may be his heirs, if she be not living. In other words, Congress, by this act, is making a distribution law to affect a portion of the estates of persons already deceased. To the several States composing the Confederacy properly belongs the power to pass laws for the administration and distribution of the estates of deceased persons. I doubt very much the constitutional power of Congress to pass any law on this subject, even of a prospective character. But this bill operates on the past as well as the future. Rights already vested and governed by the law of the State in which the deceased soldier had his domicile are attempted to be disturbed by the provisions of this bill. In my judgment, Congress has no such power. The laws of the United States, which the Confederate States adopted, were in force here when our soldiers enlisted. These laws in reference to payment of arrears and effects of deceased soldiers may be regarded as a part of the contract of such deceased soldier. An examination of these laws will show that such arrears and effects were to be held and paid to the legal representatives of the deceased soldier. JEFFERSON DAVIS.

PROCLAMATIONS.

BY THE PRESIDENT OF THE CONFEDERATE STATES.

A PROCLAMATION.

To the People of the Confederate States.

The termination of the Provisional Government offers a fitting occasion again to present ourselves in humiliation, prayer, and thanksgiving before that God who has safely conducted us through our first year of national existence. We have been enabled to lay anew the foundations of free government and to repel the efforts of our enemies to destroy us. Law has everywhere reigned supreme, and throughout our widespread limits personal liberty and private right have been duly honored. A tone of earnest piety has pervaded our people, and the victories which we have obtained over our enemies have been justly ascribed to Him who ruleth the universe.

We had hoped that the year would close upon a scene of continued prosperity, but it has pleased the Supreme Disposer of events to order it otherwise. We are not permitted to furnish an exception to the rule of Divine government, which has prescribed affliction as the discipline of nations as well as of individuals. Our faith and perseverance must be tested, and the chastening which seemeth grievous will, if rightly received, bring forth its appropriate fruit.

It is meet and right, therefore, that we should repair to the only Giver of all victory, and, humbling ourselves before him, should pray that he may strengthen our confidence in his mighty power and righteous judgment. Then may we surely trust in him that he will perform his promise and encompass us as with a shield.

In this trust, and to this end, I, Jefferson Davis, President of the Confederate States, do hereby set apart Friday, the 28th day of February, instant, as a day of fasting, humiliation, and prayer; and I do hereby invite the reverend clergy and people of the Confederate States to repair to their respective places of public worship to humble themselves before Almighty God, and pray for his protection and favor to our beloved country, and that we may be saved from our enemies, and from the hand of all that hate us.

Given under my hand and seal of the Confederate [L. S.] States at Richmond, this 20th day of February, A.D. 1862.   JEFFERSON DAVIS.

By the President:

WILLIAM M. BROWNE, *Secretary of State, ad in.*

By the President of the Confederate States.

A PROCLAMATION.

Whereas the Congress of the Confederate States has by law vested in the President the power to suspend the writ of *habeas corpus* in cities in danger of attack by the enemy:

Now, therefore, I, Jefferson Davis, President of the Confederate States of America, do hereby proclaim that martial law is extended over the cities of Norfolk and Portsmouth and the surrounding country to the distance of 10 miles from said cities, and all civil jurisdiction and the privilege of the writ of *habeas corpus* are hereby declared to be suspended within the limits aforesaid.

This proclamation will remain in force until otherwise ordered.

In faith whereof I have hereunto set my hand and seal, at the city of Richmond, on this twenty-seventh day of February, in the year of our Lord, one thousand eight hundred and sixty-two.

JEFFERSON DAVIS.

War Department, Richmond, Va., March 5, 1862.

Maj. Gen. B. Huger, Norfolk, Va.

Sir: Martial law having been declared in Norfolk under the President's proclamation, he desires me to call your attention to the various measures which he hopes will at once be vigorously executed:

First. Some leading and reliable citizen to be appointed provost marshal in Norfolk and another in Portsmouth. In the former city he suggests the mayor, said to be a zealous friend of our cause.

Second. All arms to be required to be given up by the citizens; private arms to be paid for.

Third. The whole male population to be enrolled for military service; all stores and shops to be closed at 12 or 1 o'clock and the whole of the citizens forced to drill and undergo instructions.

Fourth. The citizens so enrolled to be armed with the arms given up and with those of infantry now in service at batteries.

Fifth. Send away as rapidly as can be done, without exciting panic, all women and children and reduce your population to such as can aid in defense.

Sixth. Give notice that all merchandise, cotton, tobacco, etc., not wanted for military use be sent away within the given time, or it will be destroyed.

Seventh. Imprison all persons against whom there is well-grounded suspicion of disloyalty.

Eighth. Purchase all supplies in the district that can be made useful for your army, allowing none to be carried away that you might want in the event that the city is beleaguered.

In executing these orders you will of course use your own discretion so to act as to avoid creating panic as far as possible.

Your obedient servant,

J. P. BENJAMIN, *Secretary of War.*

General Orders No. 8.

ADJUTANT AND INSPECTOR GENERAL'S OFFICE,
RICHMOND, March 1, 1862.

I. The following proclamation of the President is published for the information of all concerned:

A PROCLAMATION.

By virtue of the power vested in me by law to declare the suspension of the privilege of the writ of *habeas corpus* in cities threatened with invasion:

I, Jefferson Davis, President of the Confederate States of America, do proclaim that martial law is hereby extended over the city of Richmond and the adjoining and surrounding country to the distance of ten miles; and I do proclaim the suspension of all civil jurisdiction, with the exception of that of the Mayor of the city, and the suspension of the privilege of the writ of *habeas corpus* within the said city and surrounding country to the distance aforesaid.

[L. S.] In faith whereof, I have hereunto signed my name and set my seal at the city of Richmond, on this first day of March, in the year one thousand eight hundred and sixty-two. JEFFERSON DAVIS.

II. Brigadier General J. H. Winder, commanding Department of Henrico, is charged with the due execution of the foregoing proclamation. He will forthwith establish an efficient military police, and will enforce the following orders:

All distillation of spirituous liquors is positively prohibited, and the distilleries will forthwith be closed. The sale of spirituous liquors of any kind is also prohibited, and the establishments for the sale thereof will be closed.

III. All persons infringing the above prohibition will suffer such punishment as shall be ordered by the sentence of a court-martial, *provided* that no sentence to hard labor for more than one month shall be inflicted by the sentence of a regimental court-martial, as directed in the 67th Article of War.

By command of the Secretary of War.

S. Cooper, *Adjutant and Inspector General.*

General Orders No. 1.

HEADQUARTERS DEPARTMENT OF HENRICO,
RICHMOND, VA., March 2d, 1862.

I. By virtue of the authority conferred by General Orders No. 8, Adjutant and Inspector General's Office, March 1, 1862, Captain A. C. Godwin is appointed Provost Marshal of the city of Richmond and the adjoining and surrounding country for the distance of ten miles.

II. All distillation and distribution of spirituous liquors is prohibited by the proclamation of the President. The Provost Marshal will take immediate and effective steps to enforce this order, and all persons found transgressing, either by the distillation, sale, giving away, or in any manner disposing of spirituous liquors, will be prosecuted to the fullest extent of the law.

III. All persons of every degree, except those in the service of the State or Confederate States, having arms in their possession, will deliver the same to the Ordnance Department on or before the 5th of March, 1862, otherwise they will be seized and taken possession of by the Provost Marshal. All public arms not in the public service will be receipted for, and all private arms will be paid for.

By order of Brigadier General John H. Winder, Commanding, etc.

L. R. PAGE, *Assistant Adjutant General.*

General Orders No. 11.

WAR DEPARTMENT,
ADJUTANT AND INSPECTOR GENERAL'S OFFICE,
RICHMOND, March 8, 1862.

I. The following proclamation is published for the information of all concerned:

A PROCLAMATION.

By virtue of the power vested in me by law to declare the suspension of the privilege of the writ of *habeas corpus* in cities threatened with invasion:

I, Jefferson Davis, President of the Confederate States of America, do proclaim that martial law is hereby extended over the city of Petersburg and the adjoining and surrounding country to the distance of ten miles; and I do proclaim the suspension of all civil jurisdiction (with the exception of that of the Mayor of the city, and that enabling the courts to take cognizance of the probate of wills, the administration of the estates of deceased persons, the qualifications of guardians, to enter decrees and orders for the partitioning and sale of property, to make orders concerning roads and bridges, to assess county levies, and to order the payment of county dues), and the suspension of the privilege of the writ of *habeas corpus* within the said city and surrounding country to the distance aforesaid.

In faith whereof, I have hereunto signed my name and [L. S.]   set my seal on the 8th day of March, in the year one thousand eight hundred and sixty-two.   JEFFERSON DAVIS.

II. William Pannill is appointed Provost Marshal, and is charged with the due execution of the foregoing proclamation. He will forthwith establish an efficient military police, and will enforce the following orders:

All distillation of spirituous liquors is positively prohibited, and the distilleries will forthwith be closed. The sale of spirituous liquor of any kind is also prohibited, and the establishments for the sale thereof will be closed.

III. All persons infringing the above prohibition will suffer such punishment as shall be ordered by the sentence of a court-martial, provided that no sentence to hard labor for more than one month shall be inflicted by the sentence of a regimental court-martial, as directed in the 67th Article of War.

By command of the Secretary of War.

S. COOPER, *Adjutant and Inspector General.*

General Orders No. 15.

WAR DEPARTMENT,
ADJUTANT AND INSPECTOR GENERAL'S OFFICE,
RICHMOND, March 14, 1862.

I. The following proclamation is published for the information of all concerned:

A PROCLAMATION.

By virtue of the power vested in me by law to declare the suspension of the privilege of the writ of *habeas corpus:*

I, Jefferson Davis, President of the Confederate States of America, do proclaim that martial law is hereby extended over the counties of Elizabeth City, York, Warwick, Gloucester, and Mathews (in Virginia), and I do proclaim the suspension of all civil jurisdiction (with the exception of that enabling the courts to take cognizance of the probate of wills, the administration of the estates of deceased persons, the qualification of guardians, to enter decrees and orders for the partition and sale of property, to make orders concerning roads and bridges, to assess county levies, and to order the payment of county dues), and the suspension of the privilege of the writ of *habeas corpus* in the counties aforesaid.

In faith whereof I have hereunto signed my name and set my seal this 14th day of March, in the year 1862.

JEFFERSON DAVIS.

II. Major General Magruder, commanding the Army of the Peninsula, is charged with the due execution of the foregoing proclamation. He will forthwith establish an efficient military police and will enforce the following orders:

III. All distillation of spirituous liquors is positively prohibited, and the distilleries will forthwith be closed. The sale of spirituous liquors of any kind is also prohibited, and establishments for the sale thereof will be closed.

IV. All persons infringing the above prohibition will suffer such punishment as shall be ordered by the sentence of a court-martial, provided that no sentence to hard labor for more than one month shall be inflicted by the sentence of a regimental court-martial, as directed by the 67th Article of War.

By command of the Secretary of War.

S. COOPER, *Adjutant and Inspector General.*

General Orders No. 18.

WAR DEPARTMENT,
ADJUTANT AND INSPECTOR GENERAL'S OFFICE,
RICHMOND, March 29, 1862.

I. The following proclamation is published for the information of all concerned:

A PROCLAMATION.

By virtue of the power vested in me by law to declare the suspension of the privilege of the writ of *habeas corpus:*

I, Jefferson Davis, President of the Confederate States of America, do proclaim that martial law is hereby extended over the counties of Greenbrier, Pocahontas, Bath, Alleghany, Monroe, Mercer, Raleigh, Fayette, Nicholas, and Randolph (in Virginia), and I do proclaim the suspension of all civil jurisdiction (with the exception of that enabling the courts to take cognizance of the probate of wills, the administration of the estates of deceased persons, the qualifications of guardians, to enter decrees and orders for the partition and sale of property, to make orders concerning roads and bridges, to assess county levies, and to order the payment of county dues), and the suspension of the privilege of the writ of *habeas corpus* in the counties aforesaid.

In faith whereof I have hereunto signed my name and [L. S.] set my seal this 29th day of March, in the year one thousand eight hundred and sixty-two.

JEFFERSON DAVIS.

II. Brigadier General Henry Heth is charged with the due execution of the foregoing proclamation. He will forthwith establish an efficient military police, and will enforce the following orders:

All distillation of spirituous liquors is positively prohibited, and the distilleries will forthwith be closed. The sale of spirituous liquors of any kind is also prohibited, and establishments for the sale thereof will be closed.

III. All persons infringing the above prohibition will suffer such punishment as shall be ordered by the sentence of a court-martial, provided that no sentence to hard labor for more than one month shall be inflicted by the sentence of a regimental court-martial, as directed by the 67th Article of War.

By command of the Secretary of War.

S. COOPER, *Adjutant and Inspector General.*

General Orders No. 21.

WAR DEPARTMENT,
ADJUTANT AND INSPECTOR GENERAL'S OFFICE,
RICHMOND, April 8, 1862.

I. The following proclamation is published for the information of all concerned:

A PROCLAMATION.

By virtue of the power vested in me by law to declare the suspension of the privilege of the writ of *habeas corpus:*

I, Jefferson Davis, President of the Confederate States of America, do proclaim that martial law is hereby extended over the Department of East Tennessee, under command of Maj. Gen. E. K. Smith; and I do proclaim the suspension of all civil jurisdiction (with the exception of that enabling the courts to take cognizance of the probate of wills, the administration of the estates of deceased persons, the qualification of guardians, to enter decrees and orders for the partition and sale of property, to make orders concerning roads and bridges, to assess county levies, and to order the payment of county dues), and the suspension of the writ of *habeas corpus* in the department aforesaid.

      In faith whereof, I have hereunto signed my name and [L. S.] set my seal this eighth day of April, in the year one thousand eight hundred and sixty-two.   JEFFERSON DAVIS.

II. Maj. Gen. E. K. Smith, commanding the Department of East Tennessee, is charged with the due execution of the foregoing proclamation. He will forthwith establish an efficient military police, and will enforce the following orders:

All distillation of spirituous liquors is positively prohibited, and the distilleries will forthwith be closed. The sale of spirituous liquors of any kind is also prohibited, and establishments for the sale thereof will be closed.

III. All persons infringing the above prohibition will suffer such punishment as shall be ordered by the sentence of a court-martial, provided that no sentence to hard labor for more than one month shall be inflicted by the sentence of a regimental court-martial, as directed by the 67th Article of War.

By command of the Secretary of War.

      S. COOPER. *Adjutant and Inspector General.*

General Orders No. 33.

WAR DEPARTMENT,
ADJUTANT AND INSPECTOR GENERAL'S OFFICE,
RICHMOND, VA., May 1, 1862.

I. The following proclamation is published for the information of all concerned:

A PROCLAMATION.

By virtue of the power vested in me to declare the suspension of the privilege of the writ of *habeas corpus:*

I, Jefferson Davis, President of the Confederate States of America, do proclaim that martial law is hereby extended over that part of the State of South Carolina from the Santee River to the South Edisto River in that State, under the command of Major General Pemberton; and I do proclaim the suspension of all civil jurisdiction (with the exception of that enabling the courts to take cognizance of the probate of wills, the administration of the estates of deceased persons, the qualification of guardians, to enter decrees and orders for the partition and sale of property, to make orders concerning roads and bridges, to assess county levies, and to order the payment of county dues), and the suspension of the writ of *habeas corpus* in the country aforesaid.

In faith whereof I have hereunto signed my name and set my seal this first day of May, in the year one thousand eight hundred and sixty-two.   JEFFERSON DAVIS.

II. Maj. Gen. J. C. Pemberton, commanding the Department of South Carolina and Georgia, is charged with the due execution of the foregoing proclamation. He will forthwith establish an efficient military police, and will enforce the following orders:

All distillation of spirituous liquors is positively prohibited, and the distilleries will forthwith be closed. The sale of spirituous liquors of any kind is also prohibited, and establishments for the sale thereof will be closed.

III. All persons infringing the above prohibition will suffer such punishment as shall be ordered by the sentence of a court-martial, provided that no sentence to hard labor for more than one month shall be inflicted by the sentence of a regimental court-martial, as directed by the 67th Article of War.

By command of the Secretary of War.

S. COOPER, *Adjutant and Inspector General.*

General Orders No. 19.

WAR DEPARTMENT,
ADJUTANT AND INSPECTOR GENERAL'S OFFICE,
RICHMOND, VA., May 3, 1862.

I. The following proclamation is published for the information of all concerned:

A PROCLAMATION.

By virtue of the power vested in me by law to declare the suspension of the privilege of the writ of *habeas corpus:*

I, Jefferson Davis, President of the Confederate States of America, do proclaim that martial law is hereby extended over the counties of Lee, Wise, Buchanan, McDowell, and Wyoming (in Virginia), under the command of Brig. Gen. Humphrey Marshall; and I do proclaim the suspension of all civil jurisdiction (with the exception of that enabling the courts to take cognizance of the probate of wills, the administration of estates of deceased persons, the qualification of guardians, to enter decrees and orders for the partition and sale of property, to make orders concerning roads and bridges, to assess county levies, and to order the payment of county dues), and the suspension of the writ of *habeas corpus* in the counties aforesaid.

In faith whereof I have hereunto signed my name and [L. S.] set my seal this third day of May, in the year one thousand eight hundred and sixty-two.   JEFFERSON DAVIS.

II. Brig. Gen. Humphrey Marshall is charged with the due execution of the foregoing proclamation. He will forthwith establish an efficient police, and will enforce the following orders:

All distillation of spirituous liquors is positively prohibited, and the distilleries will forthwith be closed. The sale of spirituous liquors of any kind is also prohibited, and establishments for the sale thereof will be closed.

III. All persons infringing the above prohibition will suffer such punishment as shall be ordered by the sentence of a court-martial, provided that no sentence to hard labor for more than one month shall be inflicted by the sentence of a regimental court-martial, as directed by the 67th Article of War.

By command of the Secretary of War.

S. COOPER, *Adjutant and Inspector General.*

BY THE PRESIDENT OF THE CONFEDERATE STATES.

A PROCLAMATION.

To the People of the Confederate States of America.

An enemy, waging war in a manner violative of the usage of civilized nations, has invaded our country. With presumptuous reliance on superior numbers, he has declared his purpose to reduce us to submission. We struggle to preserve our birthright of constitutional freedom. Our trust is in the justice of our cause and the protection of our God.

Recent disaster has spread gloom over the land, and sorrow sits at the hearthstones of our countrymen; but a people conscious of rectitude and faithfully relying on their Father in Heaven may be cast down, but cannot be dismayed. They may mourn the loss of the martyrs whose lives have been sacrificed in their defense, but they receive this dispensation of Divine Providence with humble submission and reverend faith. And now that our hosts are again going forth to battle, and loving hearts at home are filled with anxious solicitude for their safety, it is meet that the whole people should turn imploringly to their Almighty Father and beseech his all-powerful protection.

To this end, therefore, I, Jefferson Davis, President of the Confederate States of America, do issue my proclamation, inviting all the people to unite at their several places of worship, on Friday, the sixteenth day of the present month of May, in humble supplication to Almighty God that he will vouchsafe his blessings on our beloved country; that he will strengthen and protect our armies; that he will watch over and protect our people from the machinations of their enemies; and that he will, in his own good time, restore to us the blessing of peace and security under his sheltering care.

Given under my hand and the seal of the Confederate States, at Richmond, on the third day of May, A.D. 1862.

JEFFERSON DAVIS.

ADDRESSES.

ADDRESS.

EXECUTIVE OFFICE, June 2, 1862.

To the Army of Richmond.

I render to you my grateful acknowledgments for the gallantry and good conduct you displayed in the battles of the 31st of May and 1st instant, and with pride and pleasure recognize the steadiness and intrepidity with which you attacked the enemy in position, captured his advanced intrenchments, several batteries of artillery, and many standards, and everywhere drove him from the open field. At a part of your operations it was my fortune to be present. On no other occasion have I witnessed more of calmness and good order than you exhibited while advancing into the very jaws of death, and nothing could exceed the prowess with which you closed upon the enemy when a sheet of fire was blazing in your faces. In the renewed struggle in which you are on the eve of engaging I ask, and can desire, but a continuance of the same conduct which now attracts the admiration and pride of the loved ones you have left at home. You are fighting for all that is dearest to men; and, though opposed to a foe who disregards many of the usages of civilized war, your humanity to the wounded and the prisoners was the fit and crowning glory to your valor. Defenders of a just cause, may God have you in his holy keeping!

JEFFERSON DAVIS.

The general will cause the above to be read to the troops under his command.

ADDRESS.

RICHMOND, July 5, 1862.

To the Army of Eastern Virginia.

Soldiers: I congratulate you on the series of brilliant victories which, under the favor of Divine Providence, you have lately won, and, as the President of the Confederate States, do heartily tender to you the thanks of the country whose just cause you have so skillfully and heroically served. Ten days ago an invading army, vastly superior to you in numbers and in the material of war, closely beleaguered your capital, and vauntingly proclaimed its speedy conquest. You marched to attack the enemy in his intrenchments with well-directed movements and death-defying valor. You charged upon him in his strong positions, drove him from field to field over a distance of more than 35 miles, and, despite his reënforcements, compelled him to seek safety under cover of his gunboats, where he now lies cowering before the army so lately derided and threatened with entire subjugation. The fortitude with which you have borne toil and privation, the gallantry with which you have entered into each successive battle, must have been witnessed to be fully appreciated, but a grateful people will not fail to recognize your deeds and to bear you in loved remembrance. Well may it be said of you that you have "done enough for glory," but duty to a suffering country and to the cause of constitutional liberty claims from you yet further effort. Let it be your pride to relax in nothing which can promote your future efficiency, your one great object being to drive the invader from your soil and carry your standards beyond the outer boundaries of the Confederacy, to wring from an unscrupulous foe the recognition of your birthright, community independence.

JEFFERSON DAVIS.

RESOLUTIONS OF THANKS.

Resolved by the Congress of the Confederate States of America, That the thanks of Congress are due, and are hereby cordially tendered, to Captain Buchanan and all under his command for their unsurpassed gallantry, as displayed in the recent successful attack upon the naval forces of the enemy in Hampton Roads.

Approved March 12, 1862.

Resolved by the Congress of the Confederate States of America, That the thanks of Congress are due, and are hereby tendered, to Major General Thomas J. Jackson and the officers and men under his command for gallant and meritorious services in a successful engagement with a greatly superior force of the enemy near Kernstown, Frederick County, Virginia, on the twenty-third day of March, eighteen hundred and sixty-two.

Resolved, That these resolutions be communicated by the Secretary of War to Major General Jackson, and by him to his command.

Approved April 9, 1862.

Resolved by the Congress of the Confederate States of America, That the thanks of the Congress of the Confederate States are eminently due, and are hereby tendered, to the patriotic women of the Confederacy for the energy, zeal, and untiring devotion which they have manifested in furnishing voluntary contributions to our soldiers in the field, and in the various military hospitals throughout the country.

Approved April 11, 1862.

Resolved by the Congress of the Confederate States of America, That Congress has learned with gratitude to the Divine Ruler of nations the intelligence of the recent complete and brilliant victory which has been gained by the Army of the Confederate States under the command of Gen. A. S. Johnston over the Federal forces in Tennessee, on the battlefield of Shiloh.

Resolved, That the thanks of Congress are hereby tendered to Gen. G. T. Beauregard and the other surviving officers and privates of that Army for the signal exhibition of skill and gallantry displayed by them on that memorable occasion; and all who contributed to that signal triumph, in the judgment of Congress, are entitled to the gratitude of their country.

Resolved, That the intelligence of the death of General Albert Sidney Johnston, Commander in Chief, when leading the Confederate forces to victory on the sixth of April, in Tennessee, while it affects Congress with profound sorrow, at the same time obscures our joy with a shade of sadness at the loss of an officer so able, skillful, and gallant.

Resolved, That the foregoing resolutions be made known, by appropriate general orders by the Generals in command, to the officers and troops to whom they are addressed, and that they also be communicated to the family of General Johnston.

Approved April 15, 1862.

Resolved by the Congress of the Confederate States of America, That the thanks of Congress are hereby tendered to Brig. Gen. H. H. Sibley, and to the officers and men under his command, for the complete and brilliant victories achieved over our enemies in New Mexico.

Approved April 16, 1862.

Resolved by the Congress of the Confederate States of America, That the thanks of Congress are due, and are hereby tendered, to the officers and crews of the *Patrick Henry, Jamestown,*

Teaser, and other vessels engaged, for their gallant conduct and bearing in the naval combat and brilliant victory on the waters of James River, on the 8th and 9th of March, 1862.

Approved April 16, 1862.

Resolved by the Congress of the Confederate States of America, That the thanks of Congress be, and they are hereby, given to Major Generals Van Dorn and Price, and the officers and soldiers under their command, for their valor, skill, and good conduct in the battle of Elkhorn, in the State of Arkansas.

Resolved, further, That the Congress has heard with profound grief of the deaths of Generals McCulloch and McIntosh, who fell in the midst of the battle, gloriously leading their commands against the enemy.

Approved April 21, 1862.

SECOND SESSION.

MET AT RICHMOND, VA., AUGUST 18, 1862.   ADJOURNED OCTOBER 13, 1862.

MESSAGES.

RICHMOND, August 18, 1862.

To the Senate and House of Representatives of the Confederate States.

It is again our fortune to meet for devising measures necessary to the public welfare whilst our country is involved in a desolating war. The sufferings endured by some portions of the people excite the deep solicitude of the Government, and the sympathy thus evoked has been heightened by the patriotic devotion with which these sufferings have been borne. The gallantry and good conduct of our troops, always claiming the gratitude of the country, have been further illustrated on hard-fought fields, marked by exhibitions of individual prowess which can find but few parallels in ancient or modern history. Our Army has not faltered in any of the various trials to which it has been subjected, and the great body of the people has continued to manifest a zeal and unanimity which not only cheer the battle-stained soldier, but give assurance to the friends of constitutional liberty of our final triumph in the pending struggle against despotic usurpation.

The vast army which threatened the capital of the Confederacy has been defeated and driven from the lines of investment, and the enemy, repeatedly foiled in his efforts for its capture, is now seeking to raise new armies on a scale such as modern history does not record, to effect that subjugation of the South so often proclaimed as on the eve of accomplishment.

The perfidy which disregarded rights secured by compact, the madness which trampled on obligations made sacred by every consideration of honor, have been intensified by the malignity engendered by defeat. These passions have changed the character of the hostilities waged by our enemies, who are becoming daily less regardful of the usages of civilized war and the dictates of humanity. Rapine and wanton destruction of private property, war upon noncombatants, murder of captives, bloody threats to avenge the death of an invading soldiery by the slaughter of unarmed citizens, orders of banishment against peaceful farmers engaged in the cultivation of the soil, are some of the means used by our ruthless invaders to enforce the submission of a free people to foreign sway. Confiscation bills of a character so atrocious as to insure, if executed, the utter ruin of the entire population of these States, are passed by their Congress and approved by their Executive. The moneyed obligations of the Confederate Government are forged by citizens of the United States, and publicly advertised for sale in their cities with a notoriety that sufficiently attests the knowledge of their Government, and its complicity in the crime is further evinced by the fact that the soldiers of the invading armies are found supplied with large quantities of these forged notes as a means of despoiling the country people, by fraud, out of such portions of their property as armed violence may fail to reach. Two at least of the generals of the United States are engaged, unchecked by their Government, in exciting servile insurrection, and in arming and training slaves for warfare against their masters, citizens of the Confederacy. Another has been found of instincts so brutal as to invite the violence of his soldiery against the women of a captured city. Yet the rebuke of civilized man has failed to evoke from the authorities of the United States one mark of disapprobation of his acts, nor is there any reason to suppose that the conduct of Benjamin F. Butler has failed to secure from his Government the sanction and applause with which it is known to have been greeted by public meetings and portions of the press of the United States. To inquiries made of the Commander in Chief of the armies of the United States whether the atrocious conduct of some of their military commanders met the sanction of that Government, answer has been evaded on the pretext that the inquiry was insulting, and no method remains for the repression of these enormities but such retributive justice as it may be found possible to execute. Retaliation in kind for many of them is impracticable, for I have had occasion to remark in a former message that under no excess of provocation could our noble-hearted defenders be driven to wreak vengeance on unarmed men, on women, or on children. But stern and exemplary punishment can and must be meted out to the murderers and felons who, disgracing the profession of arms, seek to make of public war the occasion for the commission of the most monstrous crimes. Deeply as we may regret the character of the contest into which we are about to be forced, we must accept it as an alternative which recent manifestations give us little reason to hope can be avoided. The exasperation of failure has aroused the worst passions of our enemies. A large portion of their people, even of their clergymen, now engage in urging an excited populace to the extreme of ferocity, and nothing remains but to vindicate our rights and to maintain our existence by employing against our foe every energy and every resource at our disposal.

I append for your information a copy of the papers exhibiting the action of the Government up to the present time for the repression of the outrages committed on our people. Other measures now in progress will be submitted hereafter.

In inviting your attention to the legislation which the necessities of our condition require, those connected with the prosecution of the war command almost undivided attention. The acts passed at your last session intended to secure the public defense by general enrollment, and to render uniform the rules governing troops in the service, have led to some unexpected criticism that is much to be regretted. The efficiency of the law has been thus somewhat impaired, though it is not believed that in any of the States the popular mind has withheld its sanction from either the necessity or propriety of your legislation. It is only by harmonious as well as zealous action that a government as new as ours, ushered into existence on the very eve of a great war, and unprovided with the material for conducting hostilities on so vast a scale, can fulfill its duties. Upon you who are fully informed of the acts and purposes of the Government, and thoroughly imbued with the feelings and sentiments of the people, must reliance be placed to secure this great object. You can best devise the means for establishing that entire coöperation of the State and Confederate governments which is essential to the well-being of both at all times, but which is now indispensable to their very existence. And if any legislation shall seem to you appropriate for adjusting differences of opinion, it will be my pleasure as well as duty to coöperate in any measure that may be devised for reconciling a just care for the public defense with a proper deference for the most scrupulous susceptibilities of the State authorities.

The report of the Secretary of the Treasury will exhibit in detail the operations of that Department. It will be seen with satisfaction that the credit of the Government securities remains unimpaired, and that this credit is fully justified by the comparatively small amount of accumulated debt, notwithstanding the magnitude of our military operations. The legislation of the last session provided for the purchase of supplies with the bonds of the Government, but the preference of the people for Treasury notes has been so marked that legislation is recommended to authorize an increase in the issue of Treasury notes, which the public service seems to require. No grave inconvenience need be apprehended from this increased issue, as the provision of law by which these notes are convertible into 8 per cent bonds forms an efficient and permanent safeguard against any serious depreciation of the currency. Your attention is invited also to the means proposed by the Secretary for facilitating the preparation of these notes and for guarding them against forgery. It is due to our people to state that no manufacture of counterfeit notes exists within our limits, and that they are all imported from the Northern States.

The report of the Secretary of War, which is submitted, contains numerous suggestions for the legislation deemed desirable in order to add to the efficiency of the service. I invite your favorable consideration especially to those recommendations which are intended to secure the proper execution of the conscript law, and the consolidation of companies, battalions, and regiments when so reduced in strength as to impair that uniformity of organization which is necessary in the Army, while an undue burden is imposed on the Treasury. The necessity for some legislation for controlling military transportation on the railroads and improving their present defective condition forces itself upon the attention of the Government, and I trust you will be able to devise satisfactory measures for attaining this purpose. The legislation on the subject of general officers involves the service in some difficulties, which are pointed out by the Secretary, and for which the remedy suggested by him seems appropriate.

In connection with this subject, I am of opinion that prudence dictates some provision for the increase of the Army in the event of emergencies not now anticipated. The very large increase of forces recently called into the field by the President of the United States may render it necessary hereafter to extend the provisions of the conscript law so as to embrace persons between the ages of thirty-five and forty-five years. The vigor and efficiency of our present forces, their condition, and the skill and ability which distinguish their leaders inspire the belief that no further enrollment will be necessary, but a wise foresight requires that if a necessity should be suddenly developed during the recess of Congress requiring increased forces for our defense, means should exist for calling such forces into the field without awaiting the reassembling of the legislative department of the Government.

In the election and appointment of officers for the Provisional Army it was to be anticipated that mistakes would be made and incompetent officers of all grades introduced into the service. In the absence of experience, and with no reliable guide for selection, executive appointments as well as elections have been sometimes unfortunate. The good of the service, the interests of our country, require that some means be devised for withdrawing the commissions of officers who are incompetent for the duties required by their position, and I trust you will find means for relieving the Army of such officers by some mode more prompt and less wounding to their sensibility than the judgment of a court-martial.

Within a recent period we have effected the object so long desired of an arrangement for the exchange of prisoners, which is now being executed by delivery at the points agreed upon, and which will, it is hoped, speedily restore our brave and unfortunate countrymen to their places in the ranks of the Army, from which by the fortune of war they have for a time been separated. The details of this arrangement will be communicated to you in a special report when further progress has been made in their execution.

Of other particulars concerning the operations of the War Department you will be informed by the Secretary in his report and the accompanying documents.

The report of the Secretary of the Navy embraces a statement of the operations and present condition of this branch of the public service, both afloat and ashore; the construction and equipment of armed vessels both at home and abroad; the manufacture of ordnance and ordnance stores; and the establishment of workshops and the development of our resources of coal and iron. Some legislation seems essential for securing crews for vessels. The difficulties now experienced on this point are fully stated in the Secretary's report, and I invite your attention to providing a remedy.

The report of the Postmaster General discloses the embarrassments which resulted in the postal service from the occupation by the enemy of the Mississippi River and portions of the territory of the different States. The measures taken by the Department for relieving these embarrassments as far as practicable are detailed in the report. It is a subject of congratulation that during the ten months which ended on the 31st March last the expenses of the Department were largely decreased, whilst its revenue was augmented, as compared with a corresponding period ending on the 30th June, 1860, when the postal service for these States was conducted under the authority delegated to the United States. Sufficient time has not yet elapsed to determine whether the measures heretofore devised by Congress will accomplish the end of bringing the expenditures of the Department within the limit of its own revenues by the 1st of March next, as required by the Constitution.

I am happy to inform you that in spite of both blandishments and threats, used in profusion by the agents of the Government of the United States, the Indian nations within the Confederacy have remained firm in their loyalty and steadfast in the observance of their treaty engagements with this Government. Nor has their fidelity been shaken by the fact that, owing to the vacancies in some of the offices of agents and superintendents, delay has occurred in the payments of the annuities and allowances to which they are entitled. I would advise some provision authorizing payments to be made by other officers, in the absence of those specially charged by law with this duty.

We have never-ceasing cause to be grateful for the favor with which God has protected our infant Confederacy. And it becomes us reverently to return our thanks and humbly to ask of his bounteousness that wisdom which is needful for the performance of the high trusts with which we are charged.

JEFFERSON DAVIS.

RICHMOND, VA., August 19, 1862.

To the Senate and House of Representatives of the Confederate States.

I herewith transmit for your information the report of the Secretary of the Treasury and accompanying estimates, to which reference was made in my message* of yesterday, and invite your careful attention to the statements and recommendations contained in them.   JEFFERSON DAVIS.

RICHMOND, VA., Aug. 22, 1862.

To the Senate and House of Representatives of the Confederate States.

I herewith transmit for your information a communication from the Secretary of the Navy, supplementary to his report appended to my message to Congress of the 18th inst., and covering the report of Lieutenant John W. Dunnington, C. S. Navy, of the engagement at St. Charles, on the White River, in the State of Arkansas.   JEFFERSON DAVIS.

---

*See page 235.

RICHMOND, VA., August 22, 1862.

To the Senate and House of Representatives of the Confederate States.

I herewith transmit a communication from the Secretary of the Navy, covering estimates of the amount required to meet a certain contract, to which I invite your careful consideration.

JEFFERSON DAVIS.

RICHMOND, VA., Aug. 26, 1862.

To the Senate and House of Representatives.

I herewith transmit a communication from the Secretary of the Treasury, submitting an estimate of the amount required for a purpose specified, and covering a copy of a letter from the Hon. Howell Cobb in reference to the matter.

I recommend an appropriation of the sum, and for the object mentioned.

JEFFERSON DAVIS.

RICHMOND, VA., Aug. 27, 1862.

To the Senate and House of Representatives.

I herewith transmit a communication from the Secretary of the Treasury, submitting estimates "of the amount required to defray expenses incurred in detecting forgers of Treasury notes of the Confederate States, and bringing them to justice."

I recommend that an appropriation be made of the sum and for the purpose specified.

JEFFERSON DAVIS.

RICHMOND, VA., Aug. 28, 1862.

To the Senate of the Confederate States.

I herewith transmit a communication from the Secretary of the Treasury, submitting an estimate of the "amount required to refund to the State of North Carolina the excess over her quota paid into the Treasury on account of the war tax of the Confederate States." I recommend that an appropriation be made of the sum and for the purpose specified.

JEFFERSON DAVIS.

RICHMOND, VA., Aug. 29, 1862.

To the Senate of the Confederate States.

I herewith transmit a communication from the Surgeon General, containing the information sought by your resolution of the 25th inst., in reference to the Medical Board of Examiners for granting furloughs, its organization and duties.

JEFFERSON DAVIS.

RICHMOND, VA., Sept. 1, 1862.

To the Senate of the Confederate States.

I herewith transmit a communication from the Secretary of the Navy, containing the information sought by your resolution of the 26th ult., asking for a statement of the number of commissioned officers of every grade now in the naval service of the Confederate States; also the number of those appointed from civil life, and those who were heretofore in the naval service of the United States; also the number of such officers now on leave of absence or furlough; and the number now actually engaged in the naval service of the Confederate States.

JEFFERSON DAVIS.

To the House of Representatives.

I herewith transmit a communication from the Secretary of the Navy, containing the information sought by your resolutions of the 25th and 26th ult., asking respectively for "copies of the instructions given to naval officers in reference to the evacuation of Norfolk and New Orleans," and for information upon certain matters pertaining to the construction of the war steamers "Louisiana" and "Mississippi."   JEFFERSON DAVIS.

[Received September 1, 1862.]

EXECUTIVE OFFICE,
RICHMOND, VA., Sept. 2, 1862.

To the Senate and House of Representatives of the Confederate States.

I have the gratification of presenting to Congress two dispatches from General Robert E. Lee, commanding the Army of Northern Virginia, communicating the result of the operations north of the Rappahannock. From these dispatches it will be seen that God has again extended his shield over our patriotic Army, and has blessed the cause of the Confederacy with a second signal victory on the field already memorable by the gallant achievements of our troops.

Too much praise cannot be bestowed upon the skill and daring of the commanding General who conceived, or the valor and hardihood of the troops who executed, the brilliant movement, whose result is now communicated. After having driven from their intrenchments an enemy superior in numbers, and relieved from siege the city of Richmond, as·heretofore communicated,* our toil-worn troops advanced to meet another invading army, reënforced not only by the defeated army of General McClellan, but by the fresh corps of Generals Burnside and Hunter. After forced marches, with inadequate transportation, and across streams swollen to unusual height, by repeated combats they turned the position of the enemy, and, forming a junction of their columns, in the face of greatly superior forces, they fought the decisive battle† of the 30th, the crowning triumph of their toil and valor.

JEFFERSON DAVIS.

RICHMOND, VA., Sept. 2, 1862.

To the Senate of the Confederate States.

I have the honor to request you to return to me the nominations for appointment in the Army of the Confederate States, submitted on the 25th ult. JEFFERSON DAVIS.

To the House of Representatives.

I herewith transmit communications from the Secretary of War, in response to your resolutions of the 21st and 29th ult., asking, the one, for a copy of the cartel for the exchange of prisoners recently agreed upon with the enemy, and for information as to the manner in which the enemy has observed it. The other, for copies of the official reports of all the battles and engagements with the enemy which have occurred since the adjournment of Congress. JEFFERSON DAVIS.

[Received September 3, 1862.]

---

*See page 233. †Second battle of Manassas.

EXECUTIVE DEPARTMENT,
September 4, 1862.

To the House of Representatives.

I herewith transmit to your honorable body an estimate of appropriation* called for by the Secretary of War.

EXECUTIVE OFFICE,
RICHMOND, September 4, 1862.

To the Speaker of the House of Representatives.

Sir: I have the honor to transmit a communication from the Secretary of the Treasury, inclosing two statements, marked A and B, in reply to a resolution of the House of Representatives, requesting information concerning the amount of funds sent abroad to officers or agents of the Government for military and naval purposes, with certain particulars regarding the same.

Very respectfully your obt. servant,   JEFFERSON DAVIS.

EXECUTIVE OFFICE,
RICHMOND, Sept. 4, 1862.

To the President of the Senate.

I have the honor to transmit the accompanying communication from the Secretary of War in reply to a resolution of the Senate requesting certain information concerning the appointment and pay of provost marshals.   JEFFERSON DAVIS.

EXECUTIVE OFFICE,
RICHMOND, September 6, 1862.

To the House of Representatives.

I herewith transmit a communication from the Secretary of War in response to resolutions of your body requesting information concerning the prosecution of the work on the railroad for connecting the Richmond and Danville with the North Carolina railroad, and also concerning certain orders said to have been issued by Major General Thomas C. Hindman in the trans-Mississippi Department.   JEFFERSON DAVIS.

---

*For Indian affairs.

EXECUTIVE OFFICE,
RICHMOND, September 6, 1862.

To the House of Representatives.

I herewith transmit a letter from the Secretary of War, in response to a resolution of the House of Representatives, requesting information relative to arrests, by military authority, of citizens of the Confederate States. JEFFERSON DAVIS.

EXECUTIVE OFFICE,
RICHMOND, September 6, 1862.

To the House of Representatives.

I herewith transmit a letter from the Secretary of War, inclosing a communication from the Quartermaster General in response to a resolution of the House of Representatives requesting information relative to the payment of troops. The organization of the Army of the Confederate States gives a paymaster to each regiment, by devolving the payment of troops on the regimental quartermasters, a system by which we avoid at the same time all danger from delay in payment by the absence of the proper officer, as well as the hazard of transporting large sums of money from camp to camp, as would be the case if a corps of officers were employed for the sole purpose of paying the troops. The failures to pay regularly, as required by Regulations, should disappear with the prompt and regular supply of funds to the quartermasters of the different regiments. The ability of the Government to do this it is hoped will increase with the further development of the means of the Treasury Department.

JEFFERSON DAVIS.

To the House of Representatives.

I herewith transmit to your honorable body an estimate of appropriation called for by the Secretary of War.

JEFFERSON DAVIS.

[Received September 6, 1862,

EXECUTIVE OFFICE,
RICHMOND, Sept. 9, 1862.

To the Speaker of the House of Representatives.

I herewith transmit to your honorable body letters from the Secretary of War and Secretary of the Navy in response to the resolution requesting information as to whether the requisitions of the Heads of Bureaus on the Treasury have been promptly met, and if not, the reasons for the delay.   JEFFERSON DAVIS.

RICHMOND, VA., September 11, 1862.

To the Senate and House of Representatives.

The circumstances necessarily surrounding an army operating in the presence of an enemy render it inexpedient—next to impossible—to assemble frequent courts-martial, and to detail for them the best officers of the Army. The ordinary attendant of the circumstances referred to is frequent offenses against military discipline and trespass upon the property of individuals inhabiting the country.

To correct these evils, it is believed to be desirable that Congress should give authority to institute a commission to attend each army in the field, to be composed of men whose character and knowledge of the modes of administering justice would give the best assurance for the punishment of crime, the protection of private rights, and the security of the citizens of the country occupied by the enemy. Could courts-martial be assembled as frequently as occasion required, their functions under existing laws being limited to the consideration of offenses defined by the Rules and Articles of War, it will be perceived that a great variety of outrages against private rights might be committed of which a court-martial could not directly take cognizance. Under ordinary circumstances offenders in such cases would be turned over to the civil courts for trial. In a foreign country; or where the courts cannot hold their sessions, this is impossible, and in the case of a marching army would, for obvious reasons, be ineffectual. The witnesses whose testimony is indispensable to conviction would generally follow the march of the army and be out of the reach of the courts.

The powers delegated by the Constitution "to make rules for

the government and regulation of the land and naval forces," and "to ordain and establish from time to time inferior courts," would seem ample to justify such legislation as is herein recommended, especially as the necessity for the ordinary forms of indictment and trial "for capital and otherwise infamous crimes" is expressly dispensable with by the Constitution "in cases arising in the land or naval forces or in the militia when in actual service in time of war." JEFFERSON DAVIS.

EXECUTIVE OFFICE,
RICHMOND, September 11, 1862.

To the House of Representatives.

In compliance with the resolutions of your honorable body of the 20th ult., requesting me to transmit the official reports of all the battles and engagements which have occurred since the adjournment of Congress, including the reports of major generals and brigadier generals engaged, I herewith transmit the report of General Braxton Bragg, of the battle of Shiloh, accompanied by the reports of Generals Withers and Ruggles, and the report of Colonel J. W. Head, commanding a brigade at Fort Donelson; also the report of Brigadier General H. Marshall, of the attack upon the command of General Cox; the report of Major General Huger, of the affair at South Mills; the report of General Ledbetter, of operations on Tennessee River, and at Bridgeport; the report of Brigadier General T. M. Jones, of the evacuation of Pensacola Navy Yard, forts, etc.; the report of Colonel N. B. Forrest, of the evacuation and removal of public property from Nashville; and the report of Major General J. C. Pemberton, of the engagements on James Island. JEFFERSON DAVIS.

EXECUTIVE OFFICE,
RICHMOND, Sept. 11, 1862.

To the Senate of the Confederate States.

In reply to the resolution of your honorable body of the 8th instant, requesting information concerning the detention at certain points of the great Southwestern Mail, I herewith transmit a communication from the Postmaster General.

JEFFERSON DAVIS.

EXECUTIVE OFFICE,
RICHMOND, September 12, 1862.

To the Senate of the Confederate States.

Under the first clause of the sixth article of the Constitution, I entertain doubt whether it is intended that the officers either of the Regular or Provisional Army or of the Navy, appointed during the existence of the Provisional Government and confirmed by the Congress, require to be renominated and confirmed by the Senate, and I respectfully request your advice on this point.

JEFFERSON DAVIS.

EXECUTIVE OFFICE,
RICHMOND, September 15, 1862.

To the Senate of the Confederate States.

In reply to the inquiry of the Senate, presented in the following resolution of the 13th instant—

"Resolved, That the President be requested to communicate to the Senate whether any soldiers in the Army of the Confederate States have been shot by order of any general officer without trial, according to the rules and regulations for the government of the land forces, and if so, that he will lay before the Senate all the information he has upon the subject, and whether any steps have been taken by the Executive in the matter"—

I have to say that I have received no authentic information in relation to any such transaction as is therein described, and upon inquiry have learned that if any such fact exists it has not been communicated either to the Adjutant General or to the Secretary of War.

JEFFERSON DAVIS.

RICHMOND, VA., September 15, 1862.

To the Senate of the Confederate States.

In compliance with the request expressed in your resolution of the 12th inst., I herewith return your resolution of the 8th inst., asking information as to the number of troops furnished by each State to the Confederate Army since the commencement of the war.

JEFFERSON DAVIS.

EXECUTIVE CHAMBER,
RICHMOND, September 16th, 1862.

To the House of Representatives of the Confederate States.

I transmit herewith for the information of the House, in secret session, the report prepared by the Secretary of State, in response to the resolution of the House, adopted on the 1st inst.

JEFFERSON DAVIS.

RICHMOND, VA., September 19th, 1862.

To the House of Representatives.

I herewith transmit for your information several communications from the Secretary of War, in answer to your resolution of the 21st August, asking copies of the official reports of all the battles fought since the adjournment of Congress.

JEFFERSON DAVIS.

[To the House of Representatives.]

I herewith transmit for your information a communication from the Postmaster General in answer to your resolution of the 13th inst., asking "the reasons which have thus far prevented the carrying of the mails from the States east of the Mississippi to the State of Louisiana, west of that river." JEFFERSON DAVIS.

[Received September 20, 1862.]

[To the House of Representatives.]

I herewith transmit for your information a communication from the Commissary General in answer to your resolution of the 6th inst., relative to the supply of provisions furnished to the Army of the Peninsula, from the 4th of April to the 3d of May, 1862.

JEFFERSON DAVIS.

[Received September 20, 1862.]

[To the House of Representatives.]

I herewith transmit for your information a communication from the Secretary of the Navy, in response to your resolution of the 16th inst., asking the amount required to meet claims upon the Government for vessels and other property seized by the naval and military authorities for the use of the Government. I recommend an appropriation of the amount and for the purpose specified.

JEFFERSON DAVIS.

[Received September 22, 1862.]

RICHMOND, VIRGINIA, Sept. 22, 1862.

To the Senate and House of Representatives.

I herewith transmit for your consideration a communication from the Secretary of the Treasury, covering certain estimates.

I recommend an appropriation of the amounts, and for the purposes specified.

JEFFERSON DAVIS.

RICHMOND, VIRGINIA, Sept. 23, 1862.

To the Senate and House of Representatives.

I herewith transmit for your consideration a communication from the Secretary of War, covering an estimate "to supply the deficiencies in the Engineer appropriations for engineering purposes."

I recommend an appropriation of the amount, and for the purposes specified.

JEFFERSON DAVIS.

RICHMOND, VA., Sept. 23, 1862.

To the House of Representatives.

I herewith transmit for your information a communication from the Secretary of War in answer to your resolution of the 17th inst., asking what disposition is made of negroes captured by the enemy.

JEFFERSON DAVIS.

RICHMOND, VIRGINIA, September 23d, 1862.

To the House of Representatives.

I herewith transmit for your information a communication from the Secretary of War, in further answer to your resolution of the 21st August, requesting copies of all the reports of engagements with the enemy received since the adjournment of Congress.

JEFFERSON DAVIS.

EXECUTIVE OFFICE,
RICHMOND, September 24, 1862.

To the Speaker of the House of Representatives.

I herewith transmit for your consideration a communication from the Secretary of War, covering an estimate for a deficiency in the appropriation for ordnance.

I recommend an appropriation of the amount, and for the purpose specified. JEFFERSON DAVIS.

RICHMOND, VA., September 24, 1862.

To the Senate and House of Representatives.

I herewith transmit for your consideration a communication from the Secretary of War, covering an estimate "of the Commissary General of the sum necessary to purchase the supply of flour for the Army for the ensuing season."

I recommend an appropriation of the amount, and for the purpose specified. JEFFERSON DAVIS.

RICHMOND, VA., Sept. 24, 1862.

To the Senate and House of Representatives.

I herewith transmit for your consideration a communication from the Secretary of the Navy, covering an estimate for "an additional appropriation for the construction and equipment of ironclad, and other vessels abroad."

I recommend an appropriation of the amount, and for the purpose specified. JEFFERSON DAVIS.

RICHMOND, VA., Sept. 24, 1862.

To the Senate and House of Representatives.

I herewith transmit for your information a communication from the Secretary of War, in response to your resolution of the 22d August, in reference to regiments disbanded and consolidated. JEFFERSON DAVIS.

RICHMOND, VA., September 24th, 1862.

[To the House of Representatives.]

I herewith transmit for your consideration a communication from the Secretary of War, in reference to the proposed railroad from Blue Mountain, Alabama, to Rome, Ga., and to which I invite your special attention, because of the importance of this link in our system of railroads in the transportation needful for the public defense.   JEFFERSON DAVIS.

RICHMOND, VA., September 25th, 1862.

To the House of Representatives.

I herewith transmit for your information a communication from the Secretary of War, in further answer to your resolution of the 21st August, asking copies of all reports of all battles received since the adjournment of Congress. JEFFERSON DAVIS.

RICHMOND, VA., Sept. 25th, 1862.

To the Senate and House of Representatives.

I herewith transmit for your consideration a communication from the Secretary of War, submitting "estimates to supply deficiencies in the appropriation for the Medical Department of the Army."

I recommend an appropriation of the amount for the purpose specified.   JEFFERSON DAVIS.

RICHMOND, VA., Sept. 26, 1862.

To the Senate of the Confederate States.

I herewith transmit a communication from the Secretary of War, replying to your resolution of the 16th instant, in reference to the enforcement of the conscript act in the State of Georgia, and stating the action of the Department with regard to the command of the conscript camp in that State.   JEFFERSON DAVIS.

RICHMOND, VA., September 26, 1862.

To the Senate and House of Representatives.

I herewith transmit for your information a communication from the Secretary of War in reference to the defense of western and southern rivers, to which I invite your attention.

JEFFERSON DAVIS.

[To the House of Representatives.]

I herewith transmit for your information a communication from the Secretary of War, in further response to your resolution of the 21st August, asking for copies of the official reports of all engagements with the enemy received since the adjournment of Congress.   JEFFERSON DAVIS.

[Received September 26, 1862.]

RICHMOND, VA., September 27, 1862.

To the Senate of the Confederate States.

I herewith transmit for your information a communication from the Secretary of War, in response to your resolution of the 10th of April, requesting "a list of the commissioned officers in the Regular and Provisional Armies." This reply is communicated to you as an Executive document, it being deemed imprudent at this time to make it public, because of the information it would give to the enemy if it should chance to reach them.

JEFFERSON DAVIS.

RICHMOND, VA., September 27, 1862.

To the House of Representatives.

I herewith transmit for your information a report from the Secretary of War, upon the case of Charles K. Hyde, in response to your resolution of the 20th inst.   JEFFERSON DAVIS.

RICHMOND, VA., Sept. 29, 1862.

To the House of Representatives.

I herewith transmit for your consideration a communication from the Secretary of State, in response to your resolution of the 22d inst., submitting "estimates for the necessary expenses of the Department of State for the month of January, 1863."

I recommend an appropriation of the amount for the purpose specified.   JEFFERSON DAVIS.

To the House of Representatives.

I herewith transmit for your consideration communications from the Secretary of the Navy, submitting estimates in response to your resolutions of the 22d and 23d inst. I recommend appropriations of the sums for the purposes specified.

JEFFERSON DAVIS.

[Received September 29, 1862.

EXECUTIVE OFFICE,
RICHMOND, VA., September 30, 1862.

To the Senate and House of Representatives.

I herewith transmit a communication from the Postmaster General, to which I respectfully call your attention.

The seventh clause of the eighth section of the Constitution directs that after the first of March, 1863, the expenses of the postal service shall be paid out of its revenues.

The interruption of commerce and communication, resulting from the war and the occupation of a portion of our territory by the enemy, have necessarily curtailed, to a considerable extent, the revenues of the Department, and rendered it impossible, while the war continues and these causes exist, to make its revenues cover its expenses without such a reduction of the service as would seriously affect the interests of the people of the Confederate States.

If, in your opinion, the clause of the Constitution above referred to merely directs that Congress shall pass such laws as may be best calculated to make the postal service self-sustaining, and does not prohibit the appropriation of money to meet deficiencies, the question is one of easy solution. But if, on the contrary, you should consider that the constitutional provision is a positive and unqualified prohibition against any appropriation from the Treasury to aid the operations of the Post Office Department, it is for you to determine whether the difficulty can be overcome by a further increase of the rates of postage or by other constitutional means.

Doubtful as to the true intent of the Constitution, I submit the question to the Congress, and ask for it the deliberation which its importance may claim.

JEFFERSON DAVIS.

RICHMOND, VA., Sept. 30, 1862.

To the Senate and House of Representatives.

I herewith transmit for your consideration a communication from the Secretary of War, submitting estimates of the Quartermaster General.

I recommend that an appropriation be made of the amount for the purpose specified.　　　　　　　　JEFFERSON DAVIS.

RICHMOND, VA., Sept. 30, 1862.

To the Senate and House of Representatives.

I herewith transmit a communication from the Secretary of the Treasury, relative to the war tax of the State of Louisiana.

I recommend an appropriation of the amount for the purpose specified.　　　　　　　　JEFFERSON DAVIS.

To the House of Representatives of the Confederate States.

The resolution passed by the House in secret session on the 30th of last month has been communicated to me by the clerk of the House, and it is in the following words:

"Resolved, That the President be requested to cause the Department of State to ask for and transmit to this House estimates of the expenses incident to the sending of a diplomatic agent (supplied with such instructions as he shall deem most wise and proper) to the Court of His Majesty the Emperor of Brazil and such other South American States as he shall suppose to be judicious to open diplomatic intercourse with."

I deeply regret that, according to my views of constitutional duty, it is not in my power to comply with the request of the House. The Constitution expressly vests in the Executive Department the discretion of asking for such supplies as are deemed necessary to carry on the Government, and this discretion cannot, with a due regard to the provisions of that instrument, be controlled by the request of the Congress, still less by that of one branch of the Legislative Department.

The 9th paragraph of section 9, article one, of the Constitution, declares that "Congress shall appropriate no money from the Treasury, except by a vote of two-thirds of both Houses, taken by yeas and nays, unless it be asked and estimated for by some one of the Heads of Departments, and submitted to Congress by the President."

It seems too clear for argument that this clause of the Constitution would be completely without effect if the Executive should yield to the request of either House or of both Houses combined, "to cause a Department to ask for and transmit" an estimate for any purpose whatever. The design of the framers of the Constitution in inserting this new clause (not to be found in the Constitution under which the Confederate States were formerly united) is well known. It was determined that on the Executive Department of the Government should rest the responsibility of unwise and extravagant expenditures, while the Legislative Department not only retained the control over the grant of the appropriation, but was vested with power to compel the expenditure of money for purposes not recommended by the Executive, provided a vote of the two Houses, equal to that which is necessary for overruling an Executive veto, could be obtained.

If I should yield my consent to the request of the House now under consideration, the plain effect would be to concur in the establishment of a precedent by which the House might require the expenditure of a sum not asked for by the Head of a Department nor submitted by the President, by a vote of a bare majority instead of the vote of two-thirds by yeas and nays.

While thus unable to comply with the request of the House, so far as to cause the Department of State to ask for and transmit the estimate desired, a statement is submitted herewith for your information of the annual cost of each diplomatic mission sent abroad. It is also proper to add that the number of commissioners already authorized by law, and the amount of appropriations asked for by the Department of State, are sufficient for all the purposes suggested in the resolution without any further legislation on the subject.   JEFFERSON DAVIS.

October 1st, 1862. Richmond, Va.

RICHMOND, VA., Oct. 1, 1862.

To the Senate and House of Representatives.

I herewith transmit for your consideration several communications from the Secretary of War, submitting estimates for the month of January, 1863.

I recommend appropriation of the sums for the purposes specified. JEFFERSON DAVIS.

RICHMOND, VA., Oct. 1, 1862.

To the Senate and House of Representatives.

I herewith transmit for your consideration a communication from the Secretary of War, in reference to a loan by the Branch Bank of Tennessee to Genl. Hindman.

I recommend an appropriation of the amount for the purpose specified. JEFFERSON DAVIS.

EXECUTIVE OFFICE,
RICHMOND, October 2, 1862.

To the Senate and House of Representatives.

I herewith transmit for your information a communication from the Secretary of War, submitting "the report of the Adjutant General of the proceedings of courts-martial, in cases of drunkenness." JEFFERSON DAVIS.

RICHMOND, Oct. 2, 1862.

To the Senate and House of Representatives.

I herewith transmit for your information a communication from the Secretary of War, submitting a report of the Commissary General, to which I invite your attention.

JEFFERSON DAVIS.

RICHMOND, VA., October 2d, 1862.

To the House of Representatives.

I herewith transmit for your information a communication from the Secretary of War, in further answer to your resolution of the 21st August, requesting copies of reports of engagements with the enemy received since the adjournment of Congress.

JEFFERSON DAVIS.

RICHMOND, VA., Oct. 2, 1862.

To the Senate and House of Representatives.

I herewith transmit a communication from the Postmaster General, submitting estimates to which I invite your attention.

JEFFERSON DAVIS.

RICHMOND, VA., Oct. 3, 1862.

To the Senate and House of Representatives.

I herewith transmit a communication from the Attorney General, submitting certain estimates.

I recommend an appropriation of the amount for the purpose specified.   JEFFERSON DAVIS.

RICHMOND, VA., Oct. 3, 1862.

To the Senate and House of Representatives.

I herewith transmit a communication from the Secretary of War, submitting the estimates of the Commissary General for the month of January, 1863.

I recommend an appropriation of the amount for the purpose specified.   JEFFERSON DAVIS.

RICHMOND, VA., October 3, 1862.

To the Senate.

I herewith transmit for your information a communication from the Secretary of War in response to your resolution of the 26th ultimo, in reference to "the construction of a certain line of railroad in the States of Louisiana and Texas."

JEFFERSON DAVIS.

RICHMOND, VA., Oct. 4, 1862.

To the House of Representatives.

I herewith transmit for your information a communication from the Secretary of War, in response to your resolution of the 9th ult., in reference to the enrollment of persons as conscripts who are physically disabled from discharging the duties of soldiers.

JEFFERSON DAVIS.

RICHMOND, VA., Oct. 4, 1862.

To the Senate and House of Representatives.

I herewith transmit a communication from the Secretary of the Treasury, submitting estimates of the appropriations required for the service of the Treasury Department, and for miscellaneous objects for the month of January, 1863.

I recommend an appropriation of the amount for the purpose specified. JEFFERSON DAVIS.

RICHMOND, VA., Oct. 6, 1862.

To the Senate and House of Representatives.

I herewith transmit for your consideration a communication from the Postmaster General, submitting certain estimates.

I recommend an appropriation of the amount for the purposes specified. JEFFERSON DAVIS.

EXECUTIVE OFFICE,
RICHMOND, October 8, 1862.

The Senate and House of Representatives of the Confederate States of America.

The near approach of the day fixed for your adjournment induces me to renew certain recommendations made at the commencement of the session, and for which legislation has not yet provided. The subject of the efficiency of the Army is one of paramount importance, and the letter of the Secretary of War herewith submitted has been elicited by correspondence with the generals of our armies in the field, whose practical experience of the evils resulting from the defects in our present system entitles their opinion to great weight.

An army without discipline and instruction cannot be relied on for purposes of defense, still less for operations in an enemy's country. It is in vain to add men and munitions, unless we can at the same time give to the aggregated mass the character and capacity of soldiers. The discipline and instruction required for its efficiency cannot be imparted without competent officers. No power now exists by law for securing such officers to fill vacancies when elections and promotions fail to accomplish the object.

Extreme cases ought not to furnish a rule, yet some provision should be made to meet evils, even exceptional, in a matter so vitally affecting the safety of our troops.   Tender consideration for worthless and incompetent officers is but another name for cruelty toward the brave men who fall sacrifices to these defects of their leaders.   It is not difficult to devise a proper mode of obviating this evil.   The law authorizes the refusal to promote officers who are found incompetent to fill vacancies, and the promotion of their juniors in their stead; but instances occur in which no officer remaining in a regiment is fit to be promoted to the grade of colonel, and no officer remaining in a company is competent to command it as captain.   Legislation providing for the selection in such cases of competent officers from other regiments of the same State affords a ready remedy for this evil, as well as for the case when officers elected are found unfit for the positions to which they may be chosen.   This selection can be made in such manner as may seem to Congress most advisable; but this or some other remedy is indispensable for filling numerous vacancies now existing.

While this deficiency of competent officers exists in some cases, there is a large excess in others.   Numerous regiments and companies have been so reduced by the casualties of war, by sickness, and other causes as to be comparatively useless under the present organization.   There are companies in the Army in which the number of officers exceeds that of privates present for duty, and regiments in which the number of such privates does not exceed that which is required for a single effective company.   The cost of supporting the Army, already a very heavy burden on the resources of the country, is thus increased to an extravagant extent.   But this is of secondary importance compared with the inefficiency which results from this condition of things.   Some legislation which shall provide for the consolidation of companies and regiments when thus reduced in numbers, and where conscripts cannot be obtained from a State in sufficient numbers for filling the ranks, is of pressing necessity, and a deep sense of duty impels me to repeat that no consideration for the officers who may be unfortunately deprived of commands ought or can safely be permitted to obstruct this salutary reform.

It may be proper to remark that the necessity for this consolidation, and the consequent discharging of tried and meritorious officers, will obviously be increased by all legislative action permitting new organizations to be formed of men who, by the provisions of the conscript law, were directed to be incorporated into existing companies and regiments.   JEFFERSON DAVIS.

To the Senate and House of Representatives of the Confederate States.

I herewith transmit a letter from the Secretary of the Treasury in relation to the fiscal affairs of our Government, and invite for its statements your attention.

The propriety of providing for the payment of every loan or use of Government credit by an adequate tax is too obvious to require argument.

Though the day of payment may be postponed, as, to some extent, in the conduct of great wars, it must, still there must be such assurance of future payment as to maintain the credit of the Government or there will be a consequent depreciation of its currency and a proportionate increase of the burthen which the people must have hereafter to bear.

I trust it will be possible for the wisdom of Congress in some manner to secure the result sought for in the propositions submitted by the Secretary of the Treasury.   JEFFERSON DAVIS.

Executive Office, Richmond, October 8th, 1862.

RICHMOND, VA., October 8, 1862.

To the Senate.

I herewith transmit a communication from the Secretary of War, correcting mistakes in certain nominations recently sent in, to which I invite your special attention.   JEFFERSON DAVIS.

RICHMOND, VA., Oct. 8, 1862.

To the Senate.

I herewith transmit a communication from the Secretary of War, in response to your resolution of the 1st instant, submitting copies of all orders which have been issued from the War Department suspending the writ of *habeas corpus*.

It will be observed that in some cases, in addition to the suspension of the writ of *habeas corpus*, all civil jurisdiction (with the exceptions specified) was also suspended.

But the criminal jurisdiction of the ordinary courts has been in no instance interfered with; their action in all such cases being regarded as an assistance, and not an obstacle, to the military authorities in accomplishing the purposes of the proclamations.

The authority to suspend the writ of *habeas corpus* having expired by the limitation set in the act approved April 19, 1862, I have only to add that the writ is now nowhere suspended by action of the Executive   JEFFERSON DAVIS.

RICHMOND, VA., Oct. 10, 1862.

To the Senate and House of Representatives.

I herewith transmit a communication from the Secretary of War, relative to offices created and vacancies occurring during the session of Congress.

It is probable that some of the offices mentioned will be filled before the Congress adjourns. With regard to others, the alternative presented is an executive session of the Senate after the time now fixed for the adjournment of Congress, or the passage of an act such as that suggested by the Secretary of War.

I invite your special attention to the subject.

JEFFERSON DAVIS.

EXECUTIVE OFFICE,
RICHMOND, October 10, 1862.

To the Senate and House of Representatives of the Confederate States of America.

The importance, it might properly be said necessity, of a measure which has heretofore been recommended induces me at this time to renew the request for your attention to the want of some provision by which brigadier and major generals may be appointed when, by the casualties of service, commanders of brigades and divisions have become temporarily disabled.

Under the law as it now stands, if a brigadier be wounded the command of a brigade devolves upon the senior colonel, who may or may not be competent for such command, but whose presence is required with his regiment, and most of all under the circumstances usually existing where casualties like that referred to occur.

To illustrate this necessity I will cite an instance of an army corps from which seven brigadiers are now absent, six of whom have been recently wounded. There is an obvious objection to multiplying the number of general officers, but it may be readily removed by providing for the subsequent reduction whenever there are supernumeraries present for duty; and I would suggest that the determination as to who should be discharged might be made to depend upon the inquiry and report of an Army Board, to be organized according to established law and usage.

JEFFERSON DAVIS.

RICHMOND, VA., October 11, 1862.

To the House of Representatives.

I herewith transmit for your information communications from the Heads of the several Departments, submitting lists of their clerks and employees, in response to your resolution of the 5th April, asking for the same.　　　　JEFFERSON DAVIS.

RICHMOND, VA., October 11, 1862.

To the House of Representatives.

I herewith transmit a communication from the Sec. of War, in response to your resolution of the 9th inst., in reference to the disbanding of Wheat's Battalion of Louisiana.

JEFFERSON DAVIS.

RICHMOND, Oct. 11, 1862.

To the House of Representatives.

I herewith transmit for your information a communication from the Heads of the several Departments, in response to your resolution of the 21st April, asking the amount of funds which has been sent abroad, to officers or agents of the Government, for military or naval purposes.　　　　JEFFERSON DAVIS.

RICHMOND, VA., Oct. 13, 1862.

To the Senate and House of Representatives.

I herewith transmit for your consideration communications from the Heads of the several Departments, submitting certain estimates.

I recommend appropriations of the sums for the purposes specified.   JEFFERSON DAVIS.

To the Senate of the Confederate States of America.

I herewith transmit a communication from the Secretary of War in response to a resolution of your honorable body inquiring by what authority military officers along the several railroad lines are seizing produce and provisions, the property of private individuals, and prohibiting the transportation of produce and provisions from one State to another.   JEFFERSON DAVIS.

Executive Office, Richmond, Va., Oct. 13, 1862.

RICHMOND, VA., Oct. 13, 1862.

To the Senate and House of Representatives.

I herewith transmit for your consideration a communication from the Secretary of the Treasury, submitting certain estimates.

I recommend an appropriation for the purposes of the amount designated.   JEFFERSON DAVIS.

VETO MESSAGES.

EXECUTIVE OFFICE,
RICHMOND, October 6, 1862.

To the Senate of the Confederate States of America.

I return, without my approval, the bill which originated in your body, entitled "An Act to amend an act for the establishment and organization of a general staff for the Army of the Confederate States of America," approved February 26th, 1861.

By this act it is provided that "hereafter, the Quartermaster General shall have the rank, pay, and allowances of a brigadier general."

As Congress has passed another act (since the one now under

consideration was submitted to me), whereby the increased rank assigned to the Quartermaster General is restricted to the Provisional Army only, I infer that the act, now returned to you, no longer expresses the legislative will, and that it is, therefore, unnecessary to specify the objections which it would, otherwise, have been my duty to submit as the reasons which prevented my approval of the bill. JEFFERSON DAVIS.

To the House of Representatives of the Confederate States of America.

I return herewith, without my approval, an act which originated in your body, entitled "An Act to amend an act for the establishment and organization of the Provisional Army of the Confederate States of America," approved March 6th, 1861.

The act requires revision, as an error exists in the title, there being no such act on the statute book as that recited in the title. There is also an inconsistency between the first and second sections, which is probably the result of inadvertence or haste. The first section seems to refer to the Permanent Army, and the second to the Provisional Army.

I therefore return the act for such action as you may deem proper to take in relation to the errors above mentioned.

JEFFERSON DAVIS.

Executive Office, Richmond, Oct. 6th, 1862.

October 13, 1862.

To the House of Representatives of the Confederate States of America.

I regret to find myself compelled to return, without my signature, an act which originated in your body entitled "An Act to reorganize and promote the efficiency of the Medical Department of the Provisional Army." I entirely concur in the desire to accomplish the objects contemplated in the act, and have delayed its return in the hope that some additional legislation might obviate the difficulties that would embarrass the operation of the act in its present form.

The act seems to be based on the assumption that there exists a "Medical Department of the Provisional Army," and this fact is not only set forth in the title, but some of the provisions are so worded as to be inoperative by reason of this assumption. Thus the first section provides "that the rank, pay, and allowances of a brigadier general in the Provisional Army of the Confederate States be, and the same are hereby, conferred on the Surgeon General of the same." There exists no such officer as the Surgeon General of the Provisional Army. The plain intent, therefore, of Congress to confer the rank of brigadier general in the Provisional Army on the Surgeon General of the Permanent Army would be defeated unless the language of this section be changed.

According to the provisions of the law as it now stands there is a Medical Department organized for the Permanent Army under the act of the 26th of February, 1861, entitled "An Act for the establishment and organization of a general staff for the Army of the Confederate States of America," the chief of which is styled the Surgeon General. The only legislation providing for medical officers for provisional troops is the ninth section of the act of the 6th of March, 1861, which enacts that when volunteers or militia are called into service of the Confederate States in such numbers that the "officers of the Medical Department, which may be authorized by law for the regular service, are not sufficient for . . . furnishing them with the requisite medical attendance, it shall be lawful for the President to appoint, with the advice and consent of the Congress, as many additional officers of the said Department as the service may require, not exceeding . . . one surgeon and one assistant surgeon for each regiment, . . . to continue in service only so long as their services may be required in connection with the militia or volunteers."

There is an act of 14th of August, 1861, on the same subject, but it confines the appointments authorized by it to such surgeons and assistant surgeons as may be necessary for the various hospitals.

The third and fourth sections of the act now returned to you permit and require the assignment of a number of surgeons and assistant surgeons to military departments, to divisions, to brigades, and to infantry and cavalry regiments largely in excess of the number allowed by the law just quoted, but no authority is given for the appointment of the increased number of medical officers, and it would be impracticable to execute the law unless by adopting the inadmissible construction that an authority to assign officers to duty implies an authority to appoint new officers. Such construction would be the less justifiable in the present instance, because in the second section, in which new officers are authorized, the language of the act directs appointments to be made, but in the third and fourth sections the language is changed and assignments only are permitted.

There is another omission in the act which may give rise to pretension prejudicial to the service. In declaring the rank to which the several medical officers shall be entitled in the Provisional Army, including those of brigadier general, colonels, and lieutenant colonels, no express exclusion is made of their right to command troops, as has wisely been done in the law which regulates their rank in the Regular or Permanent Army. The officers of the medical corps have long evinced the desire to have some right of command of troops in certain contingencies, and this command ought either to be expressly forbidden or the cases in which it may be exercised ought to be distinctly defined.

The chief objection to the bill, however, remains to be stated. The fifth section is designed to effect a most humane and desirable object, but its provisions are inadequate to the end proposed. The purpose of Congress is evidently to provide some additional means for the care of the sick and wounded of armies in the field. At present after each battle the wounded are necessarily left in such temporary quarters as can be procured in the vicinity, but on the movement of the army most of the medical officers attached to it are compelled to follow, and the wounded are thus left with medical aid and attendance entirely insufficient for their relief.

The fifth section of the act provides for an infirmary corps of fifty men for each brigade, officered with one first and one second lieutenant, two sergeants, and two corporals, but no provision whatever is made for any additional medical officers, nor does the act provide for any control by medical officers over these infirmary corps, nor assign to these corps any fixed duties. Unless some provision be made on these points, the present deficiency of surgical aid will continue to exist, and the infirmary corps will necessarily follow the army to which they are attached when it moves after a battle, or, if left behind, will be subject to the orders only of their own officers, who are not medical men—or conflicts will arise between these officers and the medical officers.

Entertaining the conviction, therefore, that this act in its present form, while entailing heavy expense, will fail in the beneficial effects contemplated by Congress, I deem it my duty to return it, without my approval, but with the hope that some additional legislation may be devised to accomplish the purpose contemplated by its passage.   JEFFERSON DAVIS.

To the House of Representatives of the Confederate States.

I return herewith, unsigned, an act for the building of a vessel of war, which originated in your body.

This act authorizes the Secretary of the Navy to build, arm, and equip, with the least possible delay, if practicable, by contract with the inventor, otherwise directly by the Government, one vessel of war, on the plan of Robert Cruizebearr, for ocèan and river service, drawings of which, with suitable explanations, are deposited in said Department.

On a fair construction of the terms of this act, no discretion is allowed the Secretary to decline building the vessel described, and it will be his duty, if the act becomes a law, to proceed in the construction. The plan proposed by the inventor has been three times examined by different officers of the Navy Department, deemed fully competent to decide on such subjects, none of whom have recommended the construction, but have reported "that it is inexpedient to build such vessels at the present time, when the whole available force and materials at the command of the Department should be applied to the construction of vessels of acknowledged efficiency."

In a report by a number of eminent naval officers, it is further stated "that nothing has been done to prove the alleged claim to the speed, invulnerability, and efficiency of the vessel, in either or all of which we have no confidence."

As it is not probable that Congress was aware of the facts above stated, I deem it my duty to return the bill, in order that you may take such further action on the subject as is deemed by you advisable, and with a full knowledge that the plan proposed is not approved by the Executive Department, charged with the supervision of such subjects.   JEFFERSON DAVIS.

[Received October 13, 1862.]

To the Senate of the Confederate States.

I return herewith, without approval, an act which originated in your body entitled "An Act for the relief of the Bible Society of the Confederate States of America."

My objections to this act are of a grave character, and I regret that the very short time allowed to me for its consideration deprives me of any opportunity of stating them as fully as is desirable. The act was presented to me only yesterday. I confine myself, therefore, to a simple enumeration of the objections without attempting to enforce them by argument.

1st. If the sequestration fund is the property of the Government, Congress has no power under the Constitution to bestow it, or any part of it, as a gift.

2nd. If the fund be not the property of the Government, but is held merely as a trust fund, Congress has not the power to divert it from the beneficiaries and grant it to others.

3d. The faith of the Government is expressly and solemnly pledged by the 2nd section of the act of the 15th of February, 1862, that the fund, after being placed in the Treasury, "shall be refunded as required for the purposes aforesaid;" these purposes being the "equal indemnity of all persons loyal citizens of the Confederate States, or persons aiding the same in the present war who have suffered or may hereafter suffer loss or damage by confiscation by the Government of the United States, or by any State Government or pretended Government acknowledging and aiding the Government of the United States in this war, or by such acts of the enemy or other causes incident to the war, as by further act of Congress may be described or defined as affording under the circumstances proper cases for indemnity," etc.

4th. By the act of the 17th of March, 1862, Congress has conferred a title to indemnity out of the sequestration fund of all persons who may voluntarily destroy their property, or whose property may be destroyed by the military authorities to prevent the same from falling into the hands of the enemy; and it is not in the power of Congress to divert or impair this vested right.

5th. The act provides for the carrying out, by the Confederate Bible Society, of the purposes of any bequest that may have been made to the American Bible Society. These purposes are unknown, and may be of a character hostile to the interests and reprobated by the policy of our Government.

JEFFERSON DAVIS.

October 13, 1862.

PROCLAMATIONS.

BY THE PRESIDENT OF THE CONFEDERATE STATES.

A PROCLAMATION.

To the People of the Confederate States.

Once more upon the plains of Manassas have our armies been blessed by the Lord of Hosts with a triumph over our enemies. It is my privilege to invite you once more to his footstool, not now in the garb of fasting and sorrow, but with joy and gladness, to render thanks for the great mercies received at his hand. A few months since, and our enemies poured forth their invading legions upon our soil. They laid waste our fields, polluted our altars, and violated the sanctity of our homes. Around our capital they gathered their forces, and, with boastful threats, claimed it as already their prize. The brave troops which rallied to its defense have extinguished these vain hopes, and, under the guidance of the same Almighty hand, have scattered our enemies and driven them back in dismay. Uniting these defeated forces and the various armies which had been ravaging our coasts with the army of invasion in Northern Virginia, our enemies have renewed their attempt to subjugate us at the very place where their first effort was defeated, and the vengeance of retributive justice has overtaken the entire host in a second and complete overthrow.

To this signal success accorded to our arms in the East has been graciously added another equally brilliant in the West. On the very day on which our forces were led to victory on the plains of Manassas, in Virginia, the same Almighty arm assisted us to overcome our enemies at Richmond, in Kentucky. Thus, at one and the same time, have the two great hostile armies been stricken down and the wicked designs of our enemies set at naught.

In such circumstances it is meet and right that as a people we should bow down in adoring thankfulness to that gracious God who has been our bulwark and defense, and to offer unto him the tribute of thanksgiving and praise. In his hand is the issue of all events, and to him should we in an especial manner ascribe the honor of this great deliverance.

Now, therefore, I, Jefferson Davis, President of the Confederate States, do issue this my proclamation setting apart Thursday, the 18th day of September instant, as a day of prayer and thanksgiving to Almighty God, for the great mercies vouchsafed to our people, and more especially for the triumph of our arms at Richmond and Manassas, in Virginia, and at Richmond, in Kentucky; and I do hereby invite the people of the Confederate States to meet on that day at their respective places of public worship, and to unite in rendering thanks and praise to God for these great mercies, and to implore him to conduct our country safely through the perils which surround us, to the final attainment of the blessings of peace and security.

Given under my hand and the seal of the Confederate [SEAL.] States, at Richmond, this fourth day of September, A.D. 1862. JEFFERSON DAVIS.

By the President:

J. P. BENJAMIN, *Secretary of State.*

General Orders No. 111.

ADJUTANT AND INSPECTOR GENERAL'S OFFICE,
RICHMOND, December 24, 1862.

I. The following proclamation of the President is published for the information and guidance of all concerned therein:

BY THE PRESIDENT OF THE CONFEDERATE STATES.

A PROCLAMATION.

Whereas a communication was addressed on the 6th day of July last (1862) by General Robert E. Lee, acting under the instructions of the Secretary of War of the Confederate States of America, to Gen. H. W. Halleck, General in Chief of the United States Army, informing the latter that a report had reached this

Government that William B. Mumford, a citizen of the Confederate States, had been executed by the United States authorities at New Orleans for having pulled down the United States flag in that city before its occupation by the forces of the United States, and calling for a statement of the facts with a view to retaliation if such an outrage had really been committed under sanction of the authorities of the United States;

And whereas (no answer having been received to said letter), another letter was, on the 2d of August last (1862), addressed by Gen. Lee under my instructions to Gen. Halleck, renewing the inquiry in relation to the said execution of said Mumford, with the information that in the event of not receiving a reply within fifteen days it would be assumed that the fact alleged was true and was sanctioned by the Government of the United States;

And whereas, an answer, dated on the 7th August last (1862), was addressed to General Lee by General H. W. Halleck, the said General in Chief of the Armies of the United States, alleging sufficient cause for failure to make early reply to said letter of 6th of July, asserting that "no authentic information has been received in relation to the execution of Mumford, but measures will be immediately taken to ascertain the facts of the alleged execution," and promising that General Lee should be duly informed thereof;

And whereas, on the 29th of November last (1862) another letter was addressed under my instructions by Robert Ould, Confederate agent for the exchange of prisoners under the cartel between the two Governments, to Lieut. Col. W. H. Ludlow, agent of the United States under said cartel, informing him that the explanations promised in the said letter of General Halleck of 7th of August last had not yet been received, and that if no answer was sent to the Government within fifteen days from the delivery of this last communication it would be considered that an answer is declined;

And whereas, by letter dated on the 3d day of the present month of December the said Lieutenant Colonel Ludlow apprised the said Robert Ould that the above-recited communication of 29th of November had been received and forwarded to the Secretary of War of the United States;

And whereas, this last delay of fifteen days allowed for answer has elapsed and no answer has been received;

And whereas, in addition to the tacit admission resulting from the above refusal to answer I have received evidence fully establishing the truth of the fact that the said William B. Mumford, a citizen of this Confederacy, was actually and publicly executed in cold blood by hanging, after the occupation of the city of New Orleans by the forces under the command of General Benjamin F. Butler, when said Mumford was an unresisting and noncombatant captive, and for no offense even alleged to have been committed by him subsequent to the date of the capture of the said city;

And whereas, the silence of the Government of the United States and its maintaining of said Butler in high office under its authority for many months after his commission of an act that can be viewed in no other light than as a deliberate murder, as well as of numerous other outrages and atrocities hereafter to be mentioned, afford evidence only too conclusive that the said Government sanctions the conduct of said Butler and is determined that he shall remain unpunished for his crimes:

Now, therefore, I, Jefferson Davis, President of the Confederate States of America, and in their name, do pronounce and declare the said Benjamin F. Butler to be a felon deserving of capital punishment. I do order that he be no longer considered or treated simply as a public enemy of the Confederate States of America, but as an outlaw and common enemy of mankind, and that in the event of his capture the officer in command of the capturing force do cause him to be immediately executed by hanging; and I do further order that no commissioned officer of the United States taken captive shall be released on parole before exchange until the said Butler shall have met with due punishment for his crimes.

And whereas, the hostilities waged against this Confederacy by the forces of the United States under the command of said Benjamin F. Butler have borne no resemblance to such warfare as is alone permissible by the rules of international law or the usages of civilization, but have been characterized by repeated atrocities and outrages, among the large number of which the following may be cited as examples:

Peaceful and aged citizens, unresisting captives and noncombatants, have been confined at hard labor with balls and chains attached to their limbs, and are still so held in dungeons and fortresses. Others have been subjected to a like degrading punishment for selling medicines to the sick soldiers of the Confederacy.

The soldiers of the United States have been invited and encouraged by general orders to insult and outrage the wives, the mothers, and the sisters of our citizens.

Helpless women have been torn from their homes and subjected to solitary confinement, some in fortresses and prisons and one especially on an island of barren sand under a tropical sun; have been fed with loathsome rations that had been condemned as unfit for soldiers, and have been exposed to the vilest insults.

Prisoners of war who surrendered to the naval forces of the United States on agreement that they should be released on parole have been seized and kept in close confinement.

Repeated pretexts have been sought or invented for plundering the inhabitants of the captured city by fines levied and exacted under threat of imprisoning recusants at hard labor with ball and chain.

The entire population of the city of New Orleans have been forced to elect between starvation, by the confiscation of all their property, and taking an oath against conscience to bear allegiance to the invaders of their country.

Egress from the city has been refused to those whose fortitude withstood the test, even to lone and aged women and to helpless children; and, after being ejected from their homes and robbed of their property, they have been left to starve in the streets or subsist on charity.

The slaves have been driven from the plantations in the neighborhood of New Orleans till their owners would consent to share the crops with the commanding general, his brother Andrew J. Butler, and other officers; and when such consent had been extorted the slaves have been restored to the plantations and there compelled to work under the bayonets of guards of U. S. soldiers.

Where this partnership was refused armed expeditions have been sent to the plantations to rob them of everything that was susceptible of removal, and even slaves too aged or infirm for work have in spite of their entreaties been forced from the homes provided by the owners and driven to wander helplessly on the highway.

By a recent general order (No. 91) the entire property in that part of Louisiana lying west of the Mississippi River has been sequestrated for confiscation, and officers have been assigned to duty with orders to "gather up and collect the personal property and turn over to the proper officers upon their receipts such of said property as may be required for the use of the U. S. Army; to collect together all the other personal property and bring the same to New Orleans and cause it to be sold at public auction to the highest bidders"—an order which if executed condemns to punishment by starvation at least a quarter of a million human beings of all ages, sexes, and conditions; and of which the execution, although forbidden to military officers by the orders of President Lincoln, is in accordance with the confiscation law of our enemies which he has directed to be enforced through the agency of civil officials. And finally the African slaves have not only been excited to insurrection by every license and encouragement, but numbers of them have actually been armed for a servile war—a war in its nature far exceeding in horrors the most merciless atrocities of the savages.

And whereas, the officers under the command of the said Butler have been in many instances active and zealous agents in the commission of these crimes, and no instance is known of the refusal of any one of them to participate in the outrages above narrated;

And whereas, the President of the United States has by public and official declaration signified not only his approval of the effort to excite servile war within the Confederacy, but his intention to give aid and encouragement thereto if these independent States shall continue to refuse submission to a foreign power after the 1st day of January next, and has thus made known that all appeals to the laws of nations, the dictates of reason, and the instincts of humanity would be addressed in vain to our enemies, and that they can be deterred from the commission of these crimes only by the terms of just retribution:

Now, therefore, I, Jefferson Davis, President of the Confederate States of America, and acting by their authority, appealing to the Divine Judge in attestation that their conduct is not guided by the passion of revenge, but that they reluctantly yield to the solemn duty of repressing by necessary severity crimes of which their citizens are the victims, do issue this my proclamation, and by virtue of my authority as Commander in Chief of the Armies of the Confederate States do order—

1. That all commissioned officers in the command of said Benjamin F. Butler be declared not entitled to be considered as soldiers engaged in honorable warfare, but as robbers and criminals deserving death, and that they and each of them be, whenever captured, reserved for execution.

2. That the private soldiers and noncommissioned officers in the army of said Butler be considered as only the instruments used for the commission of the crimes perpetrated by his orders and not as free agents; that they therefore be treated, when captured, as prisoners of war with kindness and humanity and be sent home on the usual parole that they will in no manner aid or serve the United States in any capacity during the continuance of this war unless duly exchanged.

3. That all negro slaves captured in arms be at once delivered over to the executive authorities of the respective States to which they belong, to be dealt with according to the laws of said States.

4. That the like orders be executed in all cases with respect to all commissioned officers of the United States when found serving in company with armed slaves in insurrection against the authorities of the different States of this Confederacy.

In testimony whereof I have signed these presents and caused the seal of the Confederate States of America to be affixed thereto at the city of Richmond on this 23d day of December, in the year of our Lord one thousand eight hundred and sixty-two.   JEFF'N DAVIS.

[L. S.]

By the President:

J. P. BENJAMIN, *Secretary of State.*

II. Officers of the Army are charged with the observance and enforcement of the foregoing orders of the President. Where the evidence is not full or the case is for any reason of a doubtful character it will be referred through this office for the decision of the War Department.

By order: S. COOPER, *Adjutant and Inspector General.*

RESOLUTIONS OF THANKS.

Resolved by the Congress of the Confederate States of America, That the thanks of Congress are due, and are hereby presented, to Captain Raphael Semmes, and the officers and crew of the steamer Sumter, under his command, for gallant and meritorious services rendered by them in seriously injuring the enemy's commerce upon the high seas, thereby setting an example reflecting honor upon our infant Navy which cannot be too highly appreciated by Congress and the people of the Confederate States.

Approved September 9, 1862.

Resolved by the Congress of the Confederate States of America, That the thanks of Congress are eminently due, and are hereby most cordially tendered, to Commander E. Farrand, senior officer in command of the combined naval and military forces engaged, and Captain A. Drewry, senior military officer, and the officers and men under their command, for the great and signal victory achieved over the naval forces of the United States in the engagement on the fifteenth day of May, eighteen hundred and sixty-two, at Drewry's Bluff; and the gallantry, courage, and endurance in that protracted fight, which achieved a victory over the fleet of iron-clad gunboats of the enemy, entitle all who contributed thereto to the gratitude of the country.

Resolved further, That the President be requested, in appropriate general orders, to communicate the foregoing resolution to the officers and men to whom it is addressed.

Approved Sept. 16, 1862.

Resolved by the Congress of the Confederate States of America, That the thanks of Congress are hereby cordially tendered to Lieutenant Isaac N. Brown, and all under his command, for their signal exhibition of skill and gallantry on the fourteenth day of July last, on the Mississippi River, near Vicksburg, in the brilliant and successful engagement of the sloop of war Arkansas with the enemy's fleet.

Approved Oct. 2, 1862.

THIRD SESSION.

MET AT RICHMOND, VA., JANUARY 12, 1863. ADJOURNED MAY
1, 1863.

MESSAGES.

RICHMOND, January 12, 1863.

To the Senate and House of Representatives of the Confederate States.

At the date of your last adjournment the preparations of the enemy for further hostilities had assumed so menacing an aspect as to excite in some minds apprehension of our ability to meet them with sufficient promptness to avoid serious reverses. These preparations were completed shortly after your departure from the seat of government, and the armies of the United States made simultaneous advance on our frontiers on the western rivers, and on the Atlantic Coast, in masses so great as to evince their hope of overbearing all resistance by mere weight of numbers. This hope, however, like those previously entertained by our foes, has vanished. In Virginia their fourth attempt at invasion by armies whose assured success was confidently predicted has met with decisive repulse. Our noble defenders, under the consummate leadership of their general, have again, at Fredericksburg, inflicted on the forces under General Burnside the like disastrous overthrow as had been previously suffered by the successive invading armies commanded by Generals McDowell, McClellan, and Pope.

In the West obstinate battles have been fought with varying fortunes, marked by frightful carnage on both sides; but the enemy's hopes of decisive results have again been baffled, while at Vicksburg another formidable expedition has been repulsed with considerable loss on our side and severe damage to the assailing forces. On the Atlantic Coast the enemy has been unable to gain a footing beyond the protecting shelter of his fleets, and the city of Galveston has just been recovered by our forces, which succeeded not only in the capture of the garrison, but of one of the enemy's vessels of war, which was carried by boarding parties from merchant river steamers. Our fortified positions have everywhere been much strengthened and improved, affording assurance of our ability to meet with success the utmost efforts of our enemies, in spite of the magnitude of their preparations for attack.

A review of our history during the two years of our national existence affords ample cause for congratulation and demands the most fervent expression of our thankfulness to the Almighty Father, who has blessed our cause. We are justified in asserting, with a pride surely not unbecoming, that these Confederate States have added another to the lessons taught by history for the instruction of man; that they have afforded another example of the impossibility of subjugating a people determined to be free; and have demonstrated that no superiority of numbers or available resources can overcome the resistance offered by such valor in combat, such constancy under suffering, and such cheerful endurance of privation as have been conspicuously displayed by this people in the defense of their rights and liberties. The anticipations with which we entered into the contest have now ripened into a conviction which is not only shared with us by the common opinion of neutral nations, but is evidently forcing itself upon our enemies themselves. If we but mark the history of the present year, by resolute perseverance in the path we have hitherto pursued, by vigorous effort in the development of all our resources for defense, and by the continued exhibition of the same unfaltering courage in our soldiers and able conduct in their leaders as have distinguished the past, we have every reason to expect that this will be the closing year of the war. The war, which in its inception was waged for forcing us back into the Union, having failed to accomplish that purpose, passed into a second stage, in which it was attempted to conquer and rule these States as dependent provinces. Defeated in this second design, our enemies have evidently entered upon another, which can have no other purpose than revenge and thirst for blood and plunder of private property. But, however implacable they may be, they can have neither the spirit nor the resources required for a fourth year of a struggle uncheered by any hope of success, kept alive solely for the indulgence of mercenary and wicked passions, and demanding so exhaustive an expenditure of blood and money as has hitherto been imposed on their people. The advent of peace will be hailed with joy. Our desire for it has never been concealed. Our efforts to avoid the war, forced on us as it was by the lust of conquest and the insane passions of our foes, are known to mankind. But, earnest as has been our wish for peace and great as have been our sacrifices and sufferings during the war, the determination of this people has with each succeeding month become more unalterably fixed to endure any sufferings and continue any sacrifices, however prolonged, until their right to self-government and the sovereignty and independence of these States shall have been triumphantly vindicated and firmly established.

In this connection the occasion seems not unsuitable for some reference to the relations between the Confederacy and the neutral powers of Europe since the separation of these States from the former Union. Four of the States now members of the Confederacy were recognized by name as independent sovereignties in a treaty of peace concluded in the year 1783 with one of the two great maritime powers of Western Europe, and had been, prior to that period, allies in war of one another. In the year 1778 they formed a Union with nine other States under Articles of Confederation. Dissatisfied with that Union, three of them, Virginia, South Carolina, and Georgia, together with eight of the States now members of the United States, seceded from it in 1789, and these eleven seceding States formed a second Union, although by the terms of the Articles of Confederation express provision was made that the first Union should be perpetual. Their right to secede, notwithstanding this provision, was neither contested by the States from which they separated nor made the subject of discussion with any third power. When at a later period North Carolina acceded to that second Union, and when, still later, the other sovereign* States, now members of this Confederacy, became also members of the same Union, it was upon the recognized footing of equal and independent sovereignties; nor had it then entered into the minds of men that sovereign States could be compelled by force to remain members of a confederation into which they had entered of their own free will, if at a subsequent period the defense of their safety and honor should, in their judgment, justify withdrawal. The experience of the past had evinced the futility of any renunciation of such

*Originally written "seven;" see page 299.

inherent rights, and accordingly the provision for perpetuity contained in the Articles of Confederation of 1778 was omitted in the Constitution of 1789. When, therefore, in 1861, eleven of the States again thought proper, for reasons satisfactory to themselves, to secede from the second Union and to form a third one under an amended constitution, they exercised a right which, being inherent, required no justification to foreign nations, and which international law did not permit them to question. The usages of intercourse between nations do, however, require that official communication be made to friendly powers of all organic changes in the constitution of States, and there was obvious propriety in giving prompt assurance of our desire to continue amicable relations with all mankind. It was under the influence of these considerations that your predecessors, the Provisional Government, took early measures for sending to Europe commissioners charged with the duty of visiting the capitals of the different powers and making arrangements for the opening of more formal diplomatic intercourse. Prior, however, to the arrival abroad of those commissioners the United States had commenced hostilities against the Confederacy by dispatching a secret expedition for the reënforcement of Fort Sumter, after an express promise to the contrary, and with a duplicity which has been fully unveiled in a former message.* They had also addressed communications to the different Cabinets of Europe in which they assumed the attitude of being sovereign over this Confederacy, alleging that these independent States were in rebellion against the remaining States of the Union, and threatening Europe with manifestations of their displeasure if it should treat the Confederate States as having an independent existence. It soon became known that these pretensions were not considered abroad to be as absurd as they were known to be at home, nor had Europe yet learned what reliance was to be placed on the official statements of the Cabinet at Washington.

The delegation of power granted by these States to the Federal Government to represent them in foreign intercourse had led Europe into the grave error of supposing that their separate sovereignty and independence had been merged into one common sovereignty, and had ceased to have a distinct existence. Under

*See page 71.

the influence of this error, which all appeals to reason and historical fact were vainly used to dispel, our commissioners were met by the declaration that foreign governments could not assume to judge between the conflicting representations of the two parties as to the true nature of their previous mutual relations. The Governments of Great Britain and France accordingly signified their determination to confine themselves to recognizing the self-evident fact of the existence of a war, and to maintaining a strict neutrality during its progress. Some of the other powers of Europe pursued the same course of policy, and it became apparent that by some understanding, express or tacit, Europe had decided to leave the initiative in all action touching the contest on this continent to the two powers just named, who were recognized to have the largest interests involved, both by reason of proximity and of the extent and intimacy of their commercial relations with the States engaged in war. It is manifest that the course of action adopted by Europe, while based on an apparent refusal to determine the question, or to side with either party, was in point of fact an actual decision against our rights and in favor of the groundless pretensions of the United States. It was a refusal to treat us as an independent Government. If we were independent States, the refusal to entertain with us the same international intercourse as was maintained with our enemy was unjust, and was injurious in its effects, whatever may have been the motive which prompted it. Neither was it in accordance with the high moral obligations of that international code whose chief sanction is the conscience of sovereigns and the public opinion of mankind, that those eminent powers should decline the performance of a duty peculiarly incumbent on them from any apprehension of the consequences to themselves. One immediate and necessary result of their declining the responsibility of a decision which must have been adverse to the extravagant pretensions of the United States was the prolongation of hostilities to which our enemies were thereby encouraged, and which have resulted in nothing but scenes of carnage and devastation on this continent, and of misery and suffering on the other, such as have scarcely a parallel in history. Had those powers promptly admitted our right to be treated as all other independent nations, none can doubt that the moral effect of such action would have been to dispel the delusion under which the United States have persisted in their efforts to accomplish our subjugation. To the continued hesitation of the same powers in rendering this act of simple justice toward this Confederacy is still due the continuance of the calamities which mankind suffers from the interruption of its peaceful pursuits, both in the Old and the New World.

There are other matters in which less than justice has been rendered to this people by neutral Europe, and undue advantage conferred on the aggressors in a wicked war. At the inception of hostilities the inhabitants of the Confederacy were almost exclusively agriculturists; those of the United States, to a great extent, mechanics and merchants. We had no commercial marine, while their merchant vessels covered the ocean. We were without a navy, while they had powerful fleets. The advantage which they possessed for inflicting injury on our coasts and harbors was thus counterbalanced in some measure by the exposure of their commerce to attack by private armed vessels. It was known to Europe that within a very few years past the United States had peremptorily refused to accede to proposals for abolishing privateering, on the ground, as alleged by them, that nations owning powerful fleets would thereby obtain undue advantage over those possessing inferior naval forces. Yet no sooner was war flagrant between the Confederacy and the United States than the maritime powers of Europe issued orders prohibiting either party from bringing prizes into their ports. This prohibition, directed with apparent impartiality against both belligerents, was in reality effective against the Confederate States alone, for they alone could find a hostile commerce on the ocean. Merely nominal against the United States, the prohibition operated with intense severity on the Confederacy, by depriving it of the only means of maintaining with some approach to equality its struggle on the ocean against the crushing superiority of naval force possessed by its enemies. The value and efficiency of the weapon which was thus wrested from our grasp by the combined action of neutral European powers in favor of a nation which professes openly its intention of ravaging their commerce by privateers in any future war is strikingly illustrated by the terror inspired among the commercial classes of the United States by a single cruiser of the Confederacy. One national steamer, commanded by officers and manned by a crew who are debarred, by the closure of neutral ports, from the opportunity of causing captured vessels to be condemned in their favor as prizes, has sufficed to double the rates of marine insurance in Northern ports and consign to forced inaction numbers of Northern vessels, in addition to the direct damage inflicted by captures at sea. How difficult, then, to overestimate the effects that must have been produced by the hundreds of private armed vessels that would have swept the seas in pursuit of the commerce of our enemy if the means of disposing of their prizes had not been withheld by the action of neutral Europe.

But it is especially in relation to the so-called blockade of our coast that the policy of European powers has been so shaped as to cause the greatest injury to the Confederacy and to confer signal advantages on the United States. The importance of this subject requires some development. Prior to the year 1856 the principles regulating this subject were to be gathered from the writings of eminent publicists, the decisions of admiralty courts, international treaties, and the usages of nations. The uncertainty and doubt which prevailed in reference to the true rules of maritime law in time of war, resulting from the discordant and often conflicting principles announced from such varied and independent sources, had become a grievous evil to mankind. Whether a blockade was allowable against a port not invested by land as well as by sea; whether a blockade was valid by sea if the investing fleet was merely sufficient to render ingress to ' the blockaded port "evidently dangerous," or whether it was further required for its legality that it should be sufficient "really to prevent access," and numerous other similar questions had remained doubtful and undecided.

Animated by the highly honorable desire to put an end "to differences of opinion between neutrals and belligerents, which may occasion serious difficulties and even conflicts" (I quote the official language), the five great powers of Europe, together with Sardinia and Turkey, adopted in 1856 the following "solemn declaration" of principles:

1. Privateering is, and remains, abolished.

2. The neutral flag covers enemy's goods with the exception of contraband of war.

3. Neutral goods, with the exception of contraband of war, are not liable to capture under enemy's flag.

4. Blockades, in order to be binding, must be effective; that is to say, maintained by a force sufficient really to prevent access to the coast of the enemy.

Not only did this solemn declaration announce to the world the principles to which the signing powers agreed to conform in future wars, but it contained a clause to which those powers gave immediate effect, and which provided that the States not parties to the Congress of Paris should be invited to accede to the declaration. Under this invitation every independent State in Europe yielded its assent—at least, no instance is known to me of refusal; and the United States, while declining to assent to the proposition which prohibited privateering, declared that the three remaining principles were in entire accordance with their own views of international law. No instance is known in history of the adoption of rules of public law under circumstances of like solemnity, with like unanimity, and pledging the faith of nations with a sanctity so peculiar.

When, therefore, this Confederacy was formed, and when neutral powers, while deferring action on its demand for admission into the family of nations, recognized it as a belligerent power, Great Britain and France made informal proposals about the same time that their own rights as neutrals should be guaranteed by our acceding as belligerents to the declaration of principles made by the Congress of Paris. The request was addressed to our sense of justice, and therefore met immediate favorable response in the resolutions of the Provisional Congress of the 13th of August, 1861, by which all the principles announced by the Congress of Paris were adopted as the guide of our conduct during the war, with the sole exception of that relative to privateering. As the right to make use of privateers was one in which neutral nations had, as to the present war, no interest; as it was a right which the United States had refused to abandon, and which they remained at liberty to employ against us; as it was a right of which we were already in actual enjoyment, and which we could not be expected to renounce *flagrante bello* against an adversary possessing an overwhelming superiority of naval forces, it was reserved with entire confidence that neutral nations could not fail to perceive that just reason existed for the reservation. Nor was this confidence misplaced, for the official documents published by the British Government, usually called "Blue Books," contained the expression of the satisfaction of that Government with the conduct of the officials who conducted successfully the delicate business confided to their charge.

These solemn declarations of principle—this implied agreement between the Confederacy and the two powers just named—have been suffered to remain inoperative against the menaces and outrages on neutral rights committed by the United States with unceasing and progressive arrogance during the whole period of the war. Neutral Europe remained passive when the United States, with a naval force insufficient to blockade effectively the coast of a single State, proclaimed a paper blockade of thousands of miles of coast, extending from the capes of the Chesapeake to those of Florida, and encircling the Gulf of Mexico from Key West to the mouth of the Rio Grande. Compared with this monstrous pretension of the United States, the blockades known in history under the names of the Berlin and Milan decrees and the British orders in council, in the years 1806 and 1807, sink into insignificance. Yet those blockades were justified by the powers that declared them on the sole ground that they were retaliatory; yet those blockades have since been condemned by the publicists of those very powers as violations of international law; yet those blockades evoked angry remonstrances from neutral powers, among which the United States were the most conspicuous; yet those blockades became the chief cause of the war between Great Britain and the United States in 1812; yet those blockades were one of the principal motives that led to the declaration of the Congress of Paris, in 1856, in the fond hope of imposing an enduring check on the very abuse of maritime power which is now renewed by the United States in 1861 and 1862, under circumstances and with features of aggravated wrong without precedent in history.

The records of our State Department contain the evidence of the repeated and formal remonstrances made by this Government to neutral powers against the recognition of this blockade. It has been shown by evidence not capable of contradiction, and which has been furnished in part by the officials of neutral nations, that the few ports of this Confederacy, before which any naval forces at all have been stationed, have been invested so inefficiently that hundreds of entries have been effected into them since the declaration of the blockade; that our enemies have themselves admitted the inefficiency of their blockade in the most forcible manner by repeated official complaints of the sale to us of goods contraband of war, a sale which could not possibly affect their interests if their pretended blockade was sufficient "really to prevent access to our coast;" that they have gone farther and have alleged their inability to render their paper blockade effective as the excuse for the odious barbarity of destroying the entrance to one of our harbors by sinking vessels loaded with stone in the channel; that our commerce with foreign nations has been intercepted, not by effective investment of our ports, nor by the seizure of ships in the attempt to enter them, but by the capture on the high seas of neutral vessels by the cruisers of our enemies whenever supposed to be bound to any point on our extensive coast, without inquiry whether a single blockading vessel was to be found at such point; that blockading vessels have left the ports at which they were stationed for distant expeditions, have been absent for many days, and have returned without notice either of the cessation or renewal of the blockade; in a word, that every prescription of maritime law and every right of neutral nations to trade with a belligerent, under the sanction of principles heretofore universally respected, have been systematically and persistently violated by the United States. Neutral Europe has received our remonstrances and has submitted in almost unbroken silence to all the wrongs that the United States have chosen to inflict on its commerce. The Cabinet of Great Britain, however, has not confined itself to such implied acquiescence in these breaches of international law as results from simple inaction, but has, in a published dispatch of the Secretary of State for Foreign Affairs, assumed to make a change in the principle enunciated by the Congress of Paris, to which the faith of the British Government was considered to be pledged; a change too important and too prejudicial to the interests of the Confederacy to be overlooked, and against which I have directed solemn protest to be made, after a vain attempt to obtain satisfactory explanations from the British Government. In a published dispatch from Her Majesty's Foreign Office to her Minister at Washington, under the date of 11th of February, 1862, occurs the following passage:

Her Majesty's Government, however, are of opinion that, assuming that the blockade was duly notified, and also that a number of ships are stationed and remain at the entrance of a port sufficient really to prevent access to it, *or to create an evident danger on entering it or leaving it,* and that these ships do not voluntarily permit ingress or egress, the fact that various ships may have successfully escaped through it (as in the particular instance here referred to) will not of itself prevent the blockade from being an effectual one by international law.

The words which I have italicized are an addition made by the British Government of its own authority to a principle the exact terms of which were settled with deliberation by the common consent of civilized nations and by implied convention with this Government, as already explained, and their effect is clearly to reopen to the prejudice of the Confederacy one of the very disputed questions on the law of blockade which the Congress of Paris professed to settle. The importance of this change is readily illustrated by taking one of our ports as an example. There is "evident danger" in entering the port of Wilmington from the presence of a blockading force, and by this test the blockade is effective. "Access is not really prevented" by the blockading fleet to the same port,' for steamers are continually arriving and departing, so that tried by this test the blockade is ineffective and invalid. The justice of our complaint on this point is so manifest as to leave little room for doubt that further reflection will induce the British Government to give us such assurances as will efface the painful impressions that would result from its language if left unexplained.

From the foregoing remarks you will perceive that during nearly two years of struggle, in which every energy of our country has been evoked for maintaining its very existence, the neutral nations of Europe have pursued a policy which, nominally impartial, has been practically most favorable to our enemies and most detrimental to us. The exercise of the neutral right of refusing entry into their ports to prizes taken by both belligerents was eminently hurtful to the Confederacy. It was sternly asserted and maintained. The exercise of the neutral right of commerce with a belligerent whose ports are not blockaded by fleets sufficient really to prevent access to them would have been eminently hurtful to the United States. It was complacently abandoned. The duty of neutral States to receive with cordiality and recognize with respect any new confederation that independent States may think proper to form was too clear to admit of denial, but its postponement was eminently beneficial to the United States and detrimental to the Confederacy. It was postponed.

In this review of our relations with the neutral nations of Europe it has been my purpose to point out distinctly that this Government has no complaint to make that those nations declared their neutrality. It could neither expect nor desire more. The complaint is that the neutrality has been rather nominal than real, and that recognized neutral rights have been alternately asserted and waived in such manner as to bear with great severity on us, and to confer signal advantages on our enemy.

I have hitherto refrained from calling to your attention this condition of our relations with foreign powers for various reasons. The chief of these was the fear that a statement of our just grounds of complaint against a course of policy so injurious to our interests might be misconstrued into an appeal for aid. Unequal as we were in mere numbers and available resources to our enemies, we were conscious of powers of resistance, in relation to which Europe was incredulous, and our remonstrances were therefore peculiarly liable to be misunderstood. Proudly self-reliant, the Confederacy, knowing full well the character of the contest into which it was forced, with full trust in the superior qualities of its population, the superior valor of its soldiers, the superior skill of its generals, and above all in the justice of its cause, felt no need to appeal for the maintenance of its rights to other earthly aids, and it began and has continued this struggle with the calm confidence ever inspired in those who, with consciousness of right, can invoke the Divine blessing on their cause. This confidence has been so assured that we have never yielded to despondency under defeat, nor do we feel undue elation at the present brighter prospect of successful issue to our contest. It is, therefore, because our just grounds of complaint can no longer be misinterpreted that I lay them clearly before you. It seems to me now proper to give you the information, and, although no immediate results may be attained, it is well that truth should be preserved and recorded. It is well that those who are to follow us should understand the full nature and character of the tremendous conflict in which the blood of our people has been poured out like water, and in which they have resisted, unaided, the shock of hosts which would have sufficed to overthrow many of the powers which, by their hesitation in according our rights as an independent nation, imply doubt of our ability to maintain our national existence. It may be, too, that if in future times unfriendly discussions not now anticipated shall unfortunately arise between this Confederacy and some European power, the recollection of our forbearance under the grievances which I have enumerated may be evoked with happy influence in preventing any serious disturbance of peaceful relations.

It would not be proper to close my remarks on the subject of our foreign relations without adverting to the fact that the correspondence between the Cabinets of France, Great Britain, and Russia, recently published, indicate a gratifying advance in the appreciation by those Governments of the true interest of mankind as involved in the war on this continent. It is to the enlightened ruler of the French nation that the public feeling of Europe is indebted for the first official exhibition of its sympathy for the sufferings endured by this people with so much heroism, of its horror at the awful carnage with which the progress of the war has been marked, and of its desire for a speedy peace. The clear and direct intimation contained in the language of the French note, that our ability to maintain our independence has been fully established, was not controverted by the answer of either of the Cabinets to which it was addressed. It is indeed difficult to conceive a just ground for a longer delay on this subject after reading the following statement of facts contained in the letter emanating from the Minister of His Imperial Majesty:

There has been established, from the very beginning of this war, an equilibrium of forces between the belligerents, which has since been almost constantly maintained, and after the spilling of so much blood they are to-day in this respect in a situation which has not sensibly changed. Nothing authorizes the prevision that more decisive military operations will shortly occur. According to the last advices received in Europe, the two armies were, on the contrary, in a condition which permitted neither to hope within a short delay advantages sufficiently marked to turn the balance definitely and to accelerate the conclusion of peace.

As this Government has never professed the intention of conquering the United States, but has simply asserted its ability to defend itself against being conquered by that power, we may safely conclude that the claims of this Confederacy to its just place in the family of nations cannot long be withheld, after so frank and formal an admission of its capacity to cope on equal terms with its aggressive foes, and to maintain itself against their attempts to obtain decisive results by arms.

It is my painful duty again to inform you of the renewed examples of every conceivable atrocity committed by the armed forces of the United States at different points within the Confederacy, and which must stamp indelible infamy not only on the perpetrators but on their superiors, who, having the power to check these outrages on humanity, numerous and well-authenticated as they have been, have not yet in a single instance of which I am aware inflicted punishment on the wrongdoers. Since my last communication to you one General McNeil murdered seven prisoners of war in cold blood, and the demand for his punishment has remained unsatisfied. The Government of the United States, after promising examination and explanation in relation to the charges made against General Benjamin F. Butler, has by its subsequent silence, after repeated efforts on my part to obtain some answer on the subject, not only admitted his guilt but sanctioned it by acquiescence, and I have accordingly branded this criminal as an outlaw,* and directed his execution in expiation of his crimes if he should fall into the hands of any of our forces. Recently I have received apparently authentic intelligence of another general by the name of Milroy who has issued orders in Western Virginia for the payment of money to him by the inhabitants, accompanied by the most savage threats of shooting every recusant, besides burning his house, and threat-

---

*See page 269.

ening similar atrocities against any of our citizens who shall fail to betray their country by giving him prompt notice of the approach of any of our forces, and this subject has also been submitted to the superior military authorities of the United States with but faint hope that they will evince any disapprobation of the act. Humanity shudders at the appalling atrocities which are being daily multiplied under the sanction of those who have obtained temporary possession of power in the United States, and who are fast making its once fair name a byword of reproach among civilized men. Not even the natural indignation inspired by this conduct should make us, however, so unjust as to attribute to the whole mass of the people who are subjected to the despotism that now reigns with unbridled license in the city of Washington a willing acquiescence in its conduct of the war. There must necessarily exist among our enemies very many, perhaps a majority, whose humanity recoils from all participation in such atrocities, but who cannot be held wholly guiltless while permitting their continuance without an effort at repression.

The public journals of the North have been received, containing a proclamation, dated on the 1st day of the present month, signed by the President of the United States, in which he orders and declares all slaves within ten of the States of the Confederacy to be free, except such as are found within certain districts now occupied in part by the armed forces of the enemy. We may well leave it to the instincts of that common humanity which a beneficent Creator has implanted in the breasts of our fellowmen of all countries to pass judgment on a measure by which several millions of human beings of an inferior race, peaceful and contented laborers in their sphere, are doomed to extermination, while at the same time they are encouraged to a general assassination of their masters by the insidious recommendation "to abstain from violence unless in necessary self-defense." Our own detestation of those who have attempted the most execrable measure recorded in the history of guilty man is tempered by profound contempt for the impotent rage which it discloses. So far as regards the action of this Government on such criminals as may attempt its execution, I confine myself to informing you that I shall, unless in your wisdom you deem some other course more expedient, deliver to the several State authorities all commissioned officers of the United States that may hereafter be captured by our forces in any of the States embraced in the proclamation, that they may be dealt with in accordance with the laws of those States providing for the punishment of criminals engaged in exciting servile insurrection. The enlisted soldiers I shall continue to treat as unwilling instruments in the commission of these crimes, and shall direct their discharge and return to their homes on the proper and usual parole.

In its political aspect this measure possesses great significance, and to it in this light I invite your attention. It affords to our whole people the complete and crowning proof of the true nature of the designs of the party which elevated to power the present occupant of the Presidential chair at Washington and which sought to conceal its purpose by every variety of artful device and by the perfidious use of the most solemn and repeated pledges on every possible occasion. I extract in this connection as a single example the following declaration, made by President Lincoln under the solemnity of his oath as Chief Magistrate of the United States, on the 4th of March, 1861:

Apprehension seems to exist among the people of the Southern States that by the accession of a Republican Administration their property and their peace and personal security are to be endangered. There has never been any reasonable cause for such apprehension. Indeed, the most ample evidence to the contrary has all the while existed and been open to their inspection. It is found in nearly all the published speeches of him who now addresses you. I do but quote from one of those speeches when I declare that I have no purpose, directly or indirectly, to interfere with the institution of slavery in the States where it exists. I believe I have no lawful right to do so; and I have no inclination to do so. Those who nominated and elected me did so with full knowledge that I had made this and many similar declarations and had never recanted them; and more than this, they placed in the platform for my acceptance and as a law to themselves and to me the clear and emphatic resolution which I now read:

"*Resolved*, That the maintenance inviolate of the rights of the States, and especially the right of each State to order and control its own domestic institutions according to its own judgment exclusively, is essential to that balance of power on which the perfection and endurance of our political fabric depend; and we denounce the lawless invasion by armed force of the soil of any State or Territory, no matter under what pretext, as among the gravest of crimes."

Nor was this declaration of the want of power or disposition to interfere with our social system confined to a state of peace. Both before and after the actual commencement of hostilities the President of the United States repeated in formal official communication to the Cabinets of Great Britain and France that he was utterly without constitutional power to do the act which he has just committed, and that in no possible event, whether the secession of these States resulted in the establishment of a separate Confederacy or in the restoration of the Union, was there any authority by virtue of which he could either restore a disaffected State to the Union by force of arms or make any change in any of its institutions. I refer especially for verification of this assertion to the dispatches addressed by the Secretary of State of the United States, under direction of the President, to the Ministers of the United States at London and Paris, under date of 10th and 22d of April, 1861.

The people of this Confederacy, then, cannot fail to receive this proclamation as the fullest vindication of their own sagacity in foreseeing the uses to which the dominant party in the United States intended from the beginning to apply their power, nor can they cease to remember with devout thankfulness that it is to their own vigilance in resisting the first stealthy progress of approaching despotism that they owe their escape from consequences now apparent to the most skeptical. This proclamation will have another salutary effect in calming the fears of those who have constantly evinced the apprehension that this war might end by some reconstruction of the old Union or some renewal of close political relations with the United States. These fears have never been shared by me, nor have I ever been able to perceive on what basis they could rest. But the proclamation affords the fullest guarantee of the impossibility of such a result; it has established a state of things which can lead to but one of three possible consequences—the extermination of the slaves, the exile of the whole white population from the Confederacy, or absolute and total separation of these States from the United States.

This proclamation is also an authentic statement by the Government of the United States of its inability to subjugate the South by force of arms, and as such must be accepted by neutral nations, which can no longer find any justification in withholding our just claims to formal recognition. It is also in effect an intimation to the people of the North that they must prepare to submit to a separation, now become inevitable, for that people are too acute not to understand a restoration of the Union has been rendered forever impossible by the adoption of a measure which from its very nature neither admits of retraction nor can coexist with union.

Among the subjects to which your attention will be specially devoted during the present session you will no doubt deem the adoption of some comprehensive system of finance as being of paramount importance. The increasing public debt, the great augmentation in the volume of the currency, with its necessary concomitant of extravagant prices for all articles of consumption, the want of revenue from a taxation adequate to support the public credit, all unite in admonishing us that energetic and wise legislation alone can prevent serious embarrassment in our monetary affairs. It is my conviction that the people of the Confederacy will freely meet taxation on a scale adequate to the maintenance of the public credit and the support of their Government. When each family is sending forth its most precious ones to meet exposure in camp and death in battle, what ground can there be to doubt the disposition to devote a tithe of its income, and more, if more be necessary, to provide the Government with means for insuring the comfort of its defenders? If our enemies submit to an excise on every commodity they produce and to the daily presence of the taxgatherer, with no higher motive than the hope of success in their wicked designs against us, the suggestion of an unwillingness on the part of this people to submit to the taxation necessary for the success of their defense is an imputation on their patriotism that few will be disposed to make and that none can justify.

The legislation of your last session, intended to hasten the funding of outstanding Treasury notes, has proved beneficial, as shown by the returns annexed to the report of the Secretary of the Treasury. But it was neither sufficiently prompt nor far-reaching to meet the full extent of the evil. The passage of some enactment carrying still further the policy of that law by fixing a limitation not later than the 1st of July next to the delay allowed for funding the notes issued prior to the 1st of December, 1862, will, in the opinion of the Secretary, have the effect to withdraw from circulation nearly the entire sum issued previous to the last-named date. If to this be added a revenue from adequate taxation, and a negotiation of bonds guaranteed proportionately by the several States, as has already been generally proposed by some of them in enactments spontaneously adopted, there is little doubt that we shall see our finances restored to a sound and satisfactory condition, our circulation relieved of the redundancy now productive of so many mischiefs, and our credit placed on such a basis as to relieve us from further anxiety relative to our resources for the prosecution of the war.

It is true that at its close our debt will be large; but it will be due to our own people, and neither the interest nor the capital will be exported to distant countries, impoverishing ours for their benefit. On the return of peace the untold wealth which will spring from our soil will render the burden of taxation far less onerous than is now supposed, especially if we take into consideration that we shall then be free from the large and steady drain of our substance to which we were subjected in the late Union through the instrumentality of sectional legislation and protective tariffs.

I recommend to your earnest attention the whole report of the Secretary of the Treasury on this important subject, and trust that your legislation on it will be delayed no longer than may be required to enable your wisdom to devise the proper measures for insuring the accomplishment of the objects proposed.

The operations of the War Department have been in the main satisfactory. In the report of the Secretary, herewith submitted, will be found a summary of many memorable successes. They are with justice ascribed in large measure to the reorganization and reënforcement of our armies under the operation of the enactments for conscription. The wisdom and efficacy of these acts have been approved by results, and the like spirit of unity, endurance, and self-devotion in the people, which has hitherto sustained their action, must be relied on to assure their enforcement under the continuing necessities of our situation. The recommendations of the Secretary to this effect are tempered by suggestions for their amelioration, and the subject deserves the consideration of Congress. For the perfection of our military organization no appropriate means should be rejected, and on this subject the opinions of the Secretary merit early attention. It is gratifying to perceive that under all the efforts and sacrifices of war the power, means, and resources of the Confederacy for its successful prosecution are increasing. Dependence on foreign supplies is to be deplored, and should, as far as practicable, be obviated by the development and employment of internal resources. The peculiar circumstances of the country, however, render this difficult and require extraordinary encouragements and facilities to be granted by the Government. The embarrassments resulting from the limited capacity of the railroads to afford transportation and the impossibility of otherwise commanding and distributing the necessary supplies for the armies render the control of the roads under some general supervision and resort to the power of impressment military exigencies. While such powers have to be exercised, they should be guarded by judicious provisions against perversion or abuse and be, as recommended by the Secretary, under due regulation of law.

I specially recommend in this connection some revision of the exemption law of last session. Serious complaints have reached me of the inequality of its operation from eminent and patriotic citizens whose opinions merit great consideration, and I trust that some means will be devised for leaving at home a sufficient local police without making discriminations, always to be deprecated, between different classes of our citizens.

Our relations with the Indians generally continue to be friendly. A portion of the Cherokee people have assumed an attitude hostile to the Confederate Government, but it is gratifying to be able to state that the mass of intelligence and worth in that nation have remained true and loyal to their treaty engagements. With this exception there have been no important instances of disaffection among any of the friendly nations and tribes. Dissatisfaction recently manifested itself among certain portions of them, but this resulted from a misapprehension of the intentions of the Government in their behalf. This has been removed, and no further difficulty is anticipated.

The report of the Secretary of the Navy, herewith transmitted, exhibits the progress made in this branch of the public service since your adjournment, as well as its present condition. The details embraced in it are of such a nature as to render it, in my opinion, incompatible with the public interests that they should be published with this message. I therefore confine myself to inviting your attention to the information therein contained.

The report of the Postmaster General shows that during the first postal year under our Government, terminating on the 30th of June last, our revenues were in excess of those received by the former Government in its last postal year, while the expenses were greatly decreased. There is still, however, a considerable deficit in the revenues of the Department as compared with its expenses, and although the grants already made from the general Treasury will suffice to cover all liabilities to the close of the fiscal year ending on the 30th of June next, I recommend some legislation, if any can be constitutionally devised, for aiding the revenues of that Department during the ensuing fiscal year, in order to avoid too great a reduction of postal facilities. Your attention is also invited to numerous other improvements in the service recommended in the report, and for which legislation is required.

I recommend to the Congress to devise a proper mode of relief to those of our citizens whose property has been destroyed by order of the Government, in pursuance of a policy adopted as a means of national defense. It is true that full indemnity cannot now be made, but some measure of relief is due to those patriotic citizens who have borne private loss for the public good, whose property in effect has been taken for public use, though not directly appropriated. Our Government, born of the spirit of freedom and of the equality and independence of the States, could not have survived a selfish or jealous disposition, making each only careful of its own interest or safety. The fate of the Confederacy, under the blessing of Divine Providence, depends upon the harmony, energy, and unity of the States. It especially devolves on you, their representatives, as far as practicable, to reform abuses, to correct errors, to cultivate fraternity, and to sustain in the people a just confidence in the Government of their choice. To that confidence and to the unity and self-sacrificing patriotism hitherto displayed is due the success which has marked the unequal contest, and has brought our country into a condition at the present time such as the most sanguine would not have ventured to predict at the commencement of our struggle. Our armies are larger, better disciplined, and more thoroughly armed and equipped than at any previous period of the war. The energies of a whole nation devoted to the single object of success in this war have accomplished marvels, and many of our trials have, by a beneficent Providence, been converted into blessings. The magnitude of the perils which we encountered has developed the true qualities and illustrated the heroic character of our people, thus gaining for the Confederacy from its birth a just appreciation from the other nations of the earth. The injuries resulting from the interruption of foreign commerce have received compensation by the development of our internal resources. Cannon crown our fortresses that were cast from the products of mines opened and furnaces built during the war. Our mountain caves yield much of the niter for the manufacture of powder, and promise increase of product. From our own foundries and laboratories, from our own armories and workshops, we derive in a great measure the warlike material, the ordnance and ordnance stores which are expended so profusely in the numerous and desperate engagements that rapidly succeed each other. Cotton and woolen fabrics, shoes and harness, wagons and gun carriages are produced in daily increasing quantities by the factories springing into existence. Our fields, no longer whitened by cotton that cannot be exported, are devoted to the production of cereals and the growth of stock formerly purchased with the proceeds of cotton. In the homes of our noble and devoted women, without whose sublime sacrifices our success would have been impossible, the noise of the loom and of the spinning wheel may be heard throughout the land. With hearts swelling with gratitude let us, then, join in returning thanks to God, and in beseeching the continuance of his protecting care over our cause and the restoration of peace with its manifold blessings to our beloved country.

JEFFERSON DAVIS.

RICHMOND, VA., January 15, 1863.

To the Senate and House of Representatives.

I herewith transmit a communication from the Secretary of the Treasury, covering certain estimates.*

I recommend that an appropriation be made of the amount and for the purpose specified.   JEFFERSON DAVIS.

RICHMOND, VA., Jany. 15, 1863.

To the Senate and House of Representatives.

I herewith transmit a communication from the Secretary of the Treasury in reference to a matter which I commend to your special attention and early decision, in secret session.

JEFFERSON DAVIS.

RICHMOND, VA., January 17, 1863.

To the House of Representatives.

I herewith transmit a communication from the Secretary of War, covering a copy of an official report† recently made by Colonel Imboden, asked for in a resolution of the House of Representatives, on the 15th instant.   JEFFERSON DAVIS.

RICHMOND, VA., Jany. 19, 1863.

To the Senate of the Confederate States.

I herewith transmit a communication from the Secretary of War, covering copies of the reports of Major General G. W. Smith and his subordinates, of recent military operations in North Carolina, in response to a resolution of the Senate of the 14th instant.   JEFFERSON DAVIS.

---

*Of amount required for telegraphic service for six months ending June 30, 1863.

†Relating to outrages perpetrated by General Milroy upon people in Northwestern and Valley districts of Virginia; see also page 289.

EXECUTIVE OFFICE,
RICHMOND, January 20, 1863.

To the Senate of the Confederate States.

I have the honor to request that my message* sent to the Senate at the opening of the session may be returned to me, to change a word which is an error. JEFFERSON DAVIS.

[The same message was sent to the House of Representatives.]

RICHMOND, VA., Jan. 21, 1863.

To the Senate and House of Representatives.

I herewith return my message* sent to you on the 14th [12th] instant, calling your attention to the 12th line on the 7th page, where I have substituted the word "sovereign"† for "seven," as it previously stood, incorrectly written. JEFFERSON DAVIS.

RICHMOND, VA., January 24th, 1863.

To the House of Representatives.

I herewith transmit a communication from the Secretary of War, forwarding for your information copies of certain reports of military operations, being a response in part to your resolution of the 22d inst. JEFFERSON DAVIS.

RICHMOND, VA., January 27, 1863.

To the Senate and House of Representatives.

I herewith transmit a communication from the Secretary of War, covering an estimate of funds required by the Ordnance Bureau.

I recommend an appropriation of the amount specified for the purpose indicated. JEFFERSON DAVIS.

RICHMOND, VA., Jan. 30, 1863.

To the House of Representatives.

I herewith transmit, for your information, a communication from the Secretary of War, forwarding copies of "orders of impressment," in reply to your resolution of the 15th inst.

JEFFERSON DAVIS.

---

*Page 276. †See page 278.

RICHMOND, VA., February 3d, 1863.

To the House of Representatives.

I herewith transmit for your information a communication*
from the Secretary of War, in response to your resolution of the
27th ult.   JEFFERSON DAVIS.

RICHMOND, VA., February 3d, 1863.

To the House of Representatives.

I herewith transmit a communication from the Secretary of
War, in reference to the examination and appointment of ordnance officers, being a response to your resolution asking for information on the subject.   JEFFERSON DAVIS.

RICHMOND, VA., Feb. 3, 1863.

To the House of Representatives.

I herewith transmit for your information a communication†
from the Secretary of War, in response to your resolution of the
27th ult.   JEFFERSON DAVIS.

RICHMOND, VA., Feb. 4, 1863.

To the Senate of the Confederate States.

I herewith transmit for your information a communication
from the Secretary of War, covering a report of the Quartermaster General, in response to your resolution relative to communication, etc., of officers serving in cities.

JEFFERSON DAVIS.

RICHMOND, VA., February 4, 1863.

To the Senate and House of Representatives.

I herewith transmit a communication from the Secretary of
War, submitting estimates for the Indian Service to June 30, 1863.

---

*Relating to the enforcement of the conscript law, etc.

†Relating to findings of general court-martial held at Richmond for
month of January; and which of the rules and regulations for the government of the Army of the Confederate States, private L. B. Seymour,
Company E, 50th N. C. Regiment, was sentenced for desertion to receive
thirty-nine lashes on bare back.

I recommend an appropriation of the amount and for the purpose indicated. JEFFERSON DAVIS.

RICHMOND, VA., Feb. 4, 1863.
To the House of Representatives.

I herewith transmit for your information a communication from the Secretary of War, covering reports from the Surgeon General and the Chief of Engineers, in response to your resolution of the 22d ultimo. JEFFERSON DAVIS.

RICHMOND, VA., Feb. 4th, 1863.
To the House of Representatives.

I herewith transmit a communication from the Secretary of War, forwarding the report of the Chief of Ordnance, in partial response to your resolution of the 10th of September, 1862.
JEFFERSON DAVIS.

EXECUTIVE OFFICE,
RICHMOND, February 7, 1863.
To the House of Representatives of the Confederate States.

I have this day received the following resolution—

Resolved, That the President be requested to inform this House whether private property of citizens not in the Army has been seized and confiscated by his order or not; and if it has been, for what offense and under what law such seizure and confiscation have been ordered—

and reply that no private property of citizens, either in or not in the Army, has been seized and confiscated by my order.
JEFFERSON DAVIS.

RICHMOND, VA., Feb. 7, 1863.
To the Senate and House of Representatives.

I herewith transmit for your consideration, in secret session, a communication from the Secretary of the Treasury, submitting an estimate of the amount required to carry into effect the act entitled "An Act to authorize a foreign loan."

I recommend an appropriation of the amount and for the purpose specified. JEFFERSON DAVIS.

To the House of Representatives of the Confederate States.

In reply to your resolution of the 28th ult., I herewith transmit a letter from the Secretary of the Navy, in which will be found a partial answer to the inquiries submitted. It contains full information in relation to the number of vessels, their cost, and mode of payment, with a reference to laws conferring authority for what has been done.

I have not deemed it proper to communicate the names of officers employed abroad, and still less the names of contractors in foreign countries, for the obvious reason that to do so would endanger the execution of the work undertaken and for the paramount consideration that to reveal the names of parties who have contracted abroad with us would subject them to the penalties imposed by the laws of their own country, and to violate the faith at least impliedly given to them when they entered into contracts with the officers of our Government.

From such considerations, while the reports of the Secretary of the Navy made to this and previous sessions of Congress endeavored to give the fullest information in relation to the operations of the Department, executed or to be executed within the limits of our country, those in foreign countries were stated, with the reservation that whatever might be injurious to the public interest, or to persons who encountered hazards to render us service, should be considered in secret session.

The laws and resolutions to which reference is made as giving authority for the construction of vessels abroad, of necessity contemplated their execution in places where the laws would forbid any subject or citizen being a party to the transaction, and therefore implied so much of secrecy as would be inconsistent with the exhibition of contracts and the exposure of the names of contractors, at least until time should have removed them from the danger of prosecution or damages.

Although these considerations do not apply so strongly to a communication made in secret session, the objections still remain that the danger of the parties is increased by the multiplication of authentic papers, any one of which would furnish conclusive proof against them, a hazard which it is fair to presume they would be unwilling to incur, and which if known to them might have prevented their consent to the contract.

I trust that the House will find in the above stated reasons a justification for withholding fuller information than is contained in the message and the accompanying letter of the Secretary of the Navy.   JEFFERSON DAVIS.

[Received February 7, 1863.]

RICHMOND, VA., February 7, 1863.

To the Senate and House of Representatives.

I herewith transmit a communication from the Secretary of War, covering an estimate of the amount required for the remuneration of additional clerks in the War Department.

I recommend an appropriation of the amount, and for the purpose specified.   JEFFERSON DAVIS.

RICHMOND, VA., February 11, 1863.

To the House of Representatives.

I herewith transmit for your information a communication from the Secretary of War, in reference to the case of Colonel Richard Thomas, in response to your resolution of the 24th inst.

JEFFERSON DAVIS.

RICHMOND, VA., Feb. 11, 1863.

To the House of Representatives.

I herewith transmit a communication from the Secretary of War, inclosing copies of the findings of a general court-martial, in the cases of persons charged with desertion and absence without leave, being a response to your resolution of the 27th ult.

JEFFERSON DAVIS.

RICHMOND, VA., February 13, 1863.

To the Senate and House of Representatives.

I herewith transmit for your consideration a communication from the Secretary of War, covering an estimate for the incidental and contingent expenses of the Army, and of the Department of War, until the 30th of June next.

I recommend an appropriation of the amount, and for the purpose specified.   JEFFERSON DAVIS.

RICHMOND, VA., Feb. 16, 1863.

To the House of Representatives.

I herewith transmit a communication from the Secretary of War, covering a list of all the civilians now in custody, under authority of the War Department, in the city of Richmond, being a response in part to your resolution of the 5th instant.

JEFFERSON DAVIS.

RICHMOND, VA., Feb. 16, 1863.

To the Senate of the Confederate States.

I herewith transmit a communication from the Secretary of War, in response to your resolution of the 19th ult., in reference to impressments of flour, &c., in Petersburg and Lynchburg.

JEFFERSON DAVIS.

RICHMOND, VA., Feb. 17, 1863.

To the Senate and House of Representatives.

I herewith transmit a report of the Postmaster General, supplemental to his report submitted to Congress at the opening of the present session, to which I invite your special attention.

JEFFERSON DAVIS.

RICHMOND, VA., February 17, 1863.

To the House of Representatives.

I herewith transmit for your information a communication from the Secretary of War, in response to your resolution of the 30th ult., with regard to Lieut. Colonel Broadwell.

JEFFERSON DAVIS.

RICHMOND, VA., Feb. 17, 1863.

To the Senate and House of Representatives.

I herewith transmit a communication from the Secretary of War, asking for an appropriation to meet a claim of the State of North Carolina for reimbursement of sums expended upon clothing, etc., for troops of that State in the Confederate service.

I recommend an appropriation of the amount for the purpose specified.   JEFFERSON DAVIS.

RICHMOND, VA., Feb. 19, 1863.

To the House of Representatives.

I herewith transmit a communication from the Secretary of the Treasury, in reference to the settlement of the claims of deceased soldiers, in response to your resolution of the 12th inst.

JEFFERSON DAVIS.

RICHMOND, VA., Feb. 19, 1863.

To the House of Representatives.

I herewith transmit a communication from the Secretary of War, in response to your resolution of the 18th instant, in regard to the number of quartermasters on duty in the city of Richmond.

JEFFERSON DAVIS.

RICHMOND, VA., February 19th, 1863.

To the House of Representatives.

I herewith transmit a communication from the Secretary of the Navy, in response to your resolution of the 10th inst., asking for information "in regard to the quality and abundance of iron and coal to be obtained in the place in Alabama at which it is contemplated to establish a cannon foundry, &c."

JEFFERSON DAVIS.

RICHMOND, VA., February 19th, 1863.

To the Senate and House of Representatives.

I herewith transmit a communication from the Secretary of the Navy in regard to the destruction of the enemy's sloop "Hatteras," by the Confederate States steam sloop "Alabama," to which I invite your attention.

The conduct of the commander, officers, and crew is commended to your favorable notice. JEFFERSON DAVIS.

RICHMOND, VA., February 20th, 1863.

To the House of Representatives.

I herewith transmit for your information a communication from the Secretary of War, covering a report from the Commissioner of Indian Affairs, in response to your resolution of the 6th inst., in regard to sums invested or funded for the Cherokee Indians, under the treaty of New Echota.   JEFFERSON DAVIS.

RICHMOND, VA., Feb. 20, 1863.

To the Senate and House of Representatives.

I herewith transmit a communication from the Secretary of War, submitting an estimate for an additional appropriation required by the Engineer Bureau for the period ending June 30, 1863.

I recommend an appropriation for the purpose specified.

JEFFERSON DAVIS.

RICHMOND, VA., Feb. 20, 1863.

To the Senate and House of Representatives.

I herewith transmit a communication from the Postmaster General, submitting an estimate of the sum required for the compensation of certain officers and employees of the Post Office Department, from July 1st to October 12th, 1863.

I recommend an appropriation of the amount for the purpose specified.   JEFFERSON DAVIS.

RICHMOND, VA., February 20, 1863.

To the Senate and House of Representatives.

I herewith transmit a communication from the Secretary of War, submitting an estimate for the contingent expenses of the Adjutant and Inspector General's office for the period ending June 30, 1863.

I recommend an appropriation of the amount for the purpose specified.   JEFFERSON DAVIS.

EXECUTIVE DEPARTMENT,
RICHMOND, Feb. 21, 1863.

To the Senate of the Confederate States.

Agreeably to the recommendation of the Secretary of War, I nominate the officers on the accompanying list to the rank affixed to their names respectively.   JEFFERSON DAVIS.

Generals—

Samuel Cooper, Virginia, to take rank May 16, '61.

Robert E. Lee, Virginia, to take rank June 14, '61.

Joseph E. Johnston, Virginia, to take rank July 4, '61.

P. G. T. Beauregard, Louisiana, to take rank July 21, '61.

NOTE.—The fifth General* has been nominated and confirmed by the Senate, to rank from the date affixed, being that of the happening of the vacancy to which he succeeded.   J. D.

EXECUTIVE OFFICE,
RICHMOND, VA., Feb. 23, 1863.

To the House of Representatives.

I herewith transmit a communication from the Postmaster General, with accompanying papers, in reply .to the resolution of your body, of October 13th, 1862, asking information relative to the telegraphic companies in the Confederate States; the expenditures of the Government in that connection, and "such other information as may be deemed useful in determining the policy and practicability of merging the telegraph in the postal system of the Confederate States."

The documents presented contain all the information that it is practicable at present to furnish. As to the propriety of merging the telegraph in the postal system, it may well be doubted whether the development of the art of telegraphing would be better promoted by withdrawing the management of the lines from private companies, and placing it in the hands of the Government, and it is also doubted whether the present is an opportune time so largely to increase the administrative labors of the Executive Departments.

The extension of Executive patronage involving the political effect of giving the Government control of the transmission of the first intelligence, as well as the question of constitutional power, were, it is to be supposed, considered by the House before transmitting the resolution, and are therefore not regarded as proper subjects for remark on this occasion.   JEFFERSON DAVIS.

---

*Braxton Bragg; see page 211.

RICHMOND, VA., February 24th, 1863.

To the Senate.

I herewith transmit a communication from the Attorney General, in reference to the shares held by alien enemies in the Washington and New Orleans Telegraph Company, in response to your resolution of the 10th inst.   JEFFERSON DAVIS.

RICHMOND, VA., Feb. 25, 1863.

To the House of Representatives.

I herewith transmit for your information communications from the Secretary of the Treasury and the Attorney General, in regard to the sequestration of real estate belonging to alien enemies, in response to your resolution of the 12th inst.

JEFFERSON DAVIS.

RICHMOND, VA., February 25th, 1863.

To the House of Representatives.

I herewith transmit for your information a communication from the Secretary of the Treasury, in reference to the amount of funds paid into the Treasury under the operation of the sequestration act, in response to your resolution of the 21st inst.

JEFFERSON DAVIS.

RICHMOND, VA., February 27, 1863.

To the House of Representatives.

I herewith transmit a communication from the Secretary of War, covering a list of the civilian prisoners now in custody at the military prison at Salisbury, N. C., in further response to your resolution of the 5th instant, and invite attention to the recommendation in regard to a class of officers to be charged with the special duty of inquiring into the cases of prisoners arrested by military authority. I think such officers would be useful, they being selected for special qualifications, and invested with specific powers.   JEFFERSON DAVIS.

RICHMOND, VA., Feb. 27, 1863.

To the Senate of the Confederate States.

I herewith transmit for your information communications

from the Secretaries of the Treasury, of War, and of the Navy, in reference to claims for vessels seized for public use, in response to your resolution of the 5th inst.   JEFFERSON DAVIS.

RICHMOND, VA., Feb. 27, 1863.

To the Senate of the Confederate States.

I herewith transmit for your information a communication from the Attorney General in relation to the marshalship of Louisiana, in response to your resolution of the 19th inst.
JEFFERSON DAVIS.

RICHMOND, VA., February 27th, 1863.

To the Senate of the Confederate States.

In further response to your resolution of the 10th inst., in reference to the shares held by alien enemies in the Washington and New Orleans Telegraph Company, I herewith transmit a communication from the Postmaster General.
JEFFERSON DAVIS.

RICHMOND, VA., March 3rd, 1863.

To the Senate and House of Representatives.

I herewith transmit a communication from the Secretary of War, covering copies of the reports of Generals Polk, Hardee, and Cheatham of the part borne by their commands in the battle of Shiloh, April 6th and 7th, 1862.   JEFFERSON DAVIS.

RICHMOND, VA., March 4, 1863.

To the Senate and House of Representatives.

I herewith transmit a communication from the Secretary of War, covering an estimate of additional funds required for the service of the Ordnance Bureau, for the period ending June 30, 1863.

I recommend an appropriation of the amount for the purpose specified.   JEFFERSON DAVIS.

RICHMOND, VA., March 5, 1863.

To the Senate and House of Representatives.

I herewith inclose for your information a copy of an act of

the Legislature of South Carolina, offering a guaranty by that State of the bonds of the Confederate States, to which I invite your special attention.   JEFFERSON DAVIS.

RICHMOND, VA., March 10, 1863.

To the House of Representatives.

I herewith transmit a communication from the Secretary of the Navy, in further response to your resolution of the 5th ult., in regard to the number and amount of claims for vessels seized for public use.   JEFFERSON DAVIS.

RICHMOND, VA., March 10, 1863.

To the Senate and House of Representatives.

I herewith transmit a communication from the Secretary of War, covering an estimate of additional funds required for the subsistence of the Army for the period ending June 30, 1863.

I recommend that an appropriation be made of the amount, for the purpose indicated.   JEFFERSON DAVIS.

RICHMOND, VA., March 10, 1863.

To the Senate and House of Representatives.

I herewith transmit a communication from the Secretary of War, submitting an estimate of the amount required for the fulfillment of contracts made by the Medical Purveyors.

I recommend that an appropriation be made of the amount for the purpose indicated.   JEFFERSON DAVIS.

RICHMOND, VA., March 11, 1863.

To the House of Representatives.

In response to your resolution of the 3d ultimo, I herewith transmit for your information a copy of my correspondence, together with that of the Secretaries of War and of the Navy, with the Governor of Louisiana and Major General Lovell, during the period beginning October 25, 1861, and ending with the date of the capture of the city of New Orleans, in reference to the defenses of that city.   JEFFERSON DAVIS.

RICHMOND, VA., March 11, 1863.

To the Senate and House of Representatives.

I herewith transmit for your information a communication from the Secretary of War, covering several reports of engagements with the enemy. JEFFERSON DAVIS.

RICHMOND, VA., March 12, 1863.

To the House of Representatives.

I herewith transmit a communication from the Secretary of War, in further response to your resolution of the 5th instant, in reference to claims for vessels seized for public use.

JEFFERSON DAVIS.

RICHMOND, VA., March 12, 1863.

To the House of Representatives.

In response to your resolution of the 28th ultimo, I herewith transmit a communication from the Secretary of the Treasury, relative to cotton purchased for the Government in the State of Louisiana. JEFFERSON DAVIS.

RICHMOND, VA., March 16, 1863.

To the Senate of the Confederate States.

Agreeably to the recommendation of the Secretary of State, I hereby nominate Lucius Q. C. Lamar to be Commissioner to Russia, and Walker Fearn to be Secretary of the Commission.

JEFFERSON DAVIS.

Executive Session.
To the Senate of the Confederate States.

I deem it proper to inform the Senate that I have given commissions to James M. Mason, John Slidell, and Lucius Q. C. Lamar, investing them with the powers of Envoys Extraordinary and Ministers Plenipotentiary of this Government near the respective courts of London, Paris, and St. Petersburg.

As these commissions were to take effect only upon the contingency of the recognition of the Confederacy by those courts respectively, and are held in abeyance till that event, I considered that it would not be proper to submit the nominations for these appointments to the Senate for its advice and consent until the time arrived when the commissions are to take effect.

It has occurred to me, however, that the Senate may be of opinion that these nominations should be submitted to it at the present session. If such should be the judgment of the Senate, the nominations will be submitted before its adjournment.

JEFFERSON DAVIS.

Richmond, Va., March 17, 1863.

RICHMOND, VA., March 18, 1863.

To the Senate and House of Representatives.

Herewith is transmitted a communication from the Postmaster General, calling attention to the serious embarrassments in which the postal service is becoming involved under the operation of the act of 11th of October last, which rendered all postmasters, except those appointed by the President and confirmed by the Senate, and all contractors for carrying the mails, their riders and drivers, between the ages of 18 and 45, liable to military duty. In the opinion of the Postmaster General, it will be impracticable to continue the postal service in large districts of our country, without some modification of this legislation.

Under present military necessities, I am very reluctant to increase the list of exemptions, and, were this a case which did not involve a great public interest, would decline to communicate the recommendation to you. In view of the vital importance of maintaining mail communications throughout our country, and the small number of persons who appear to be necessary to the continuance of the postal service, I present the communication of the Postmaster General, and commend it to your attention.

Should you concur with me in the propriety of allowing some exemptions for the purpose proposed, I would suggest that it be confined to contractors, to the exclusion of subcontractors, and that the number of drivers be limited so as not to exceed one for, say, every 25 miles of service in coaches, and that the whole number of exemptions shall not exceed, say, 1,500.

With these or similar restrictions, I am of the opinion that the rule of subjecting all citizens alike to the performance of their duty in defense of the country might be relaxed in the present case as being for the interest both of the people at large and their defenders in the field. JEFFERSON DAVIS.

RICHMOND, VA., March 25, 1863.

To the House of Representatives.

I herewith transmit a communication from the Secretary of War, in response to your resolution of the 21st ult., inquiring whether official notice has been given to the proper officers of the provisions of "An Act to protect the rights of owners of slaves taken by or employed in the Army." JEFFERSON DAVIS.

RICHMOND, VA., April 2d, 1863.

To the House of Representatives.

I herewith transmit a communication from the Secretary of State, to be read in secret session, in partial response to your resolution of February 28th, asking for copies of such portions of the correspondence between the State Department and our commissioners abroad as can be communicated without detriment to the public interest. JEFFERSON DAVIS.

RICHMOND, VA., April 6, 1863.

To the Senate and House of Representatives.

I herewith transmit a communication from the Secretary of the Navy, to be read in secret session.

I invite your especial attention to the subject he presents.

JEFFERSON DAVIS.

RICHMOND, VA., April 10th, 1863.

To the Senate and House of Representatives.

I herewith transmit for your information a communication from the Secretary of War, covering copies of General Braxton Bragg's reports of several battles. JEFFERSON DAVIS.

RICHMOND, VA., April 11, 1863.

To the Senate and House of Representatives.

I herewith transmit a communication from the Secretary of

the Treasury, covering estimates for the support of the Government from July 1st to December 31st, 1863, in compliance with resolutions adopted respectively by the Senate and House of Representatives.

I recommend that appropriation be made of the amounts for the purposes specified.   JEFFERSON DAVIS.

RICHMOND, VA., April 16, 1863.

To the House of Representatives.

Having approved and signed a bill, which originated in your body, entitled, "An Act to allow minors to hold commissions in the Army," I deem it due to many meritorious officers in the service to make a short explanation.

The bill, in my opinion, is only declaratory of the preëxisting law. No prohibition existed, prior to its passage, against the issue of commissions either in the Permanent or Provisional Army to persons under twenty-one years of age. Many of the commissioned officers of the Provisional Army have attained high rank by election and promotion before attaining the age of twenty-one years. The only objection, therefore, that I could entertain to signing the bill in question, was based on the apprehension that the approval of an act allowing commissions to be issued to minors "from and after the passage of the act," might imply that the commissions heretofore issued to minors are invalid.

It seemed, however, more proper to sign the act which in itself was unobjectionable, and to address to you this explanation, which will obviate, it is believed, the only ill consequence that could flow from the passage of the law.   JEFFERSON DAVIS.

RICHMOND, VA., April 18, 1863.

To the Senate and House of Representatives.

I herewith transmit a communication from the Secretary of War, covering an estimate of the amount required to liquidate claims to be paid for river defense service.

I recommend an appropriation of the amount for the purpose specified.   JEFFERSON DAVIS.

RICHMOND, VA., April 18, 1863.

To the Senate of the Confederate States.

I hereby transmit for your information, in executive session, a communication from the Secretary of State, in response to your resolution of the 13th inst., and setting forth generally the reasons upon which I have deemed it expedient to send a commissioner to Russia. JEFFERSON DAVIS.

RICHMOND, Va., April 18, 1863.

To the Senate and House of Representatives.

I herewith transmit a communication from the Secretary of War, covering an estimate of the amount required for the use of the Surgeon General before the close of the current fiscal year.

I recommend an appropriation of the amount for the purpose specified. JEFFERSON DAVIS.

RICHMOND, Va., April 18th, 1863.

To the House of Representatives.

I herewith transmit a communication from the Secretary of War, in response to your resolution of the 4th inst., relative to the case of Surgeon J. E. Dixon, a prisoner of Johnson's Island.

JEFFERSON DAVIS.

RICHMOND, VA., April 18, 1863.

To the House of Representatives.

I herewith transmit for your information, in secret session, a communication from the Secretary of State, in further response to your resolution of February 28th, asking for copies of such portions of the correspondence between the State Department and our commissioners abroad as can be communicated without detriment to the public service. JEFFERSON DAVIS.

RICHMOND, VA., April 18, 1863.

To the Senate of the Confederate States.

I herewith transmit for your information a communication from the Secretary of War, in response to your resolution of the 2d instant, and stating that no orders have been issued for the arrest and confinement of soldiers in Richmond whose furloughs have not expired.   JEFFERSON DAVIS.

RICHMOND, VA., April 20, 1863.

To the Senate and House of Representatives.

I herewith transmit for your information a communication from the Secretary of War, covering copies of the official reports of several engagements with the enemy.   JEFFERSON DAVIS.

RICHMOND, VA., April 20th, 1863.

To the House of Representatives.

I herewith transmit a communication from the Secretary of War, in response to your resolution of the first and fourth inst., calling for copies of the official reports of certain battles.

JEFFERSON DAVIS.

RICHMOND, VA., April 20, 1863.

To the House of Representatives.

I herewith transmit for your information a communication from the Secretary of War, in response to your resolution of January 24th, in reference to the exchange or release "of persons who, taken from civil life, have been transported and confined beyond the limits of the Confederacy."   JEFFERSON DAVIS.

RICHMOND, VA., April 21, 1863.

To the House of Representatives.

I herewith transmit for your information communications from the Secretary of War and the Attorney General, in response to your resolution of February 21st, inquiring "whether the Government holds, or has at any time held, itself liable for the value of slaves impressed by its authority and escaping to the enemy while so impressed, and whether the owners of such slaves have been paid."

Whether the liability of the Government shall be extended to such cases is a question to be determined, not by the Executive, but by Congress.   JEFFERSON DAVIS.

RICHMOND, VA., April 21, 1863.

To the Senate of the Confederate States.

I herewith transmit for your information, in secret session, a communication from the Secretary of the Treasury, in response to your resolution of the 11th instant, inquiring as to the terms on which cotton has been sold in foreign markets under cover of certificates referred to in his report dated January 10th, 1862. From the report it appears that cotton has not been thus sold.

JEFFERSON DAVIS.

RICHMOND, VA., April 21, 1863.

To the Senate of the Confederate States.

I herewith transmit for your information, in secret session, a communication from the Secretary of War, in response to your resolution of the 11th instant, in reference to the revocation of restrictions upon commerce across the Rio Grande.

JEFFERSON DAVIS.

RICHMOND, VA., April 23, 1863.

To the Senate and House of Representatives.

I herewith transmit for your information a communication from the Secretary of War, covering copies of certain reports of the battle of Murfreesboro. JEFFERSON DAVIS.

RICHMOND, VA., April 23, 1863.

To the Senate and House of Representatives.

I herewith transmit for your consideration, in secret session, a communication from the Secretary of the Navy, submitting an estimate of the amount required to meet the charges upon exchange for the sum recently appropriated for the use of the Navy Department abroad.

I recommend an additional appropriation of the amount for the purpose specified, or such provision as will secure to the Department the use of the appropriation in funds current at the place where required. JEFFERSON DAVIS.

RICHMOND, VA., April 24, 1863.

To the Senate and House of Representatives.

I herewith transmit for your consideration a communication

from the Secretary of the Treasury, covering additional estimates of the sum required for the support of the Government from July 1st to December 31st, 1863.   JEFFERSON DAVIS.

RICHMOND, VIRGINIA, April 24th, 1863.

To the House of Representatives.

I herewith transmit a communication from the Secretary of War, in response to your resolution of the 2d inst., asking for certain information relative to hospitals, and the provision for the sick and wounded of the Army in them.

JEFFERSON DAVIS.

RICHMOND, VIRGINIA, April 25th, 1863.

To the Senate and House of Representatives.

I herewith transmit for your consideration a communication from the Secretary of War, covering an estimate for the contingent expenses of the Adjutant and Inspector General's office, for the six months ending December 31st, 1863. I recommend an appropriation of the amount for the purpose specified.

JEFFERSON DAVIS.

RICHMOND, VIRGINIA, April 25th, 1863.

To the Senate and House of Representatives.

I herewith transmit for your consideration a communication from the Postmaster General, submitting an estimate of the amount required to prepare a building for the post office for the city of Richmond. I recommend an appropriation of the sum for the purpose specified.   JEFFERSON DAVIS.

RICHMOND, VA., April 25, 1863.

To the Senate of the Confederate States.

I herewith transmit for your information a communication from the Postmaster General, relative to the removal of certain postmasters from office.   JEFFERSON DAVIS.

RICHMOND, VA., April 29th, 1863.

To the House of Representatives.

I herewith transmit for your information a communication from the Secretary of the Navy, in reference to your resolution of the 25th instant, asking for a copy of the finding of the court of inquiry in the case of John H. Mitchell, C. S. N.

° JEFFERSON DAVIS.

RICHMOND, VA., April 30, 1863.

To the Senate of the Confederate States.

I herewith transmit for your information, in secret session, communications from the Secretaries of the Treasury and of War, in response to your resolution of the 7th inst., of inquiry relative "to the sale or hypothecation of cotton, or cotton certificates or bonds, in Europe." JEFFERSON DAVIS.

RICHMOND, VA., April 30, 1863.

To the Senate and House of Representatives.

I herewith transmit a communication from the Secretary of the Navy in reference to a recent act of Congress establishing a "Volunteer Navy."

I concur with him in the opinion that the injunction of secrecy should be removed from the law. JEFFERSON DAVIS.

RICHMOND, VA., April 30th, 1863.

To the Senate and House of Representatives.

I herewith transmit for, your consideration a communication from the Secretary of War, submitting an estimate of the sum needed to pay for a submarine telegraph cable at Charleston, S. C.

I recommend an appropriation of the amount for the purpose specified. JEFFERSON DAVIS.

RICHMOND, VA., May 1st, 1863.

To the House of Representatives.

In response to your resolution of the 29th January and the

28th February, I herewith transmit a communication from the Secretary of War, covering a report of the Commissary General and copies of other papers relative to Lt. Col. W. A. Broadwell.

In addition to the information furnished by the Secretary of War, I may state that, before his appointment to his present commission, Mr. Broadwell was an agent of the Government to pay and purchase certain supplies for the troops of the State of Missouri in the year 1861. His accounts were adjusted to the satisfaction of the accounting officers of the Government.

JEFFERSON DAVIS.

RICHMOND, VA., May 1st, 1863.

To the House of Representatives.

I herewith transmit for your information a communication from the Secretary of War, covering copies of the reports of the battle of McDowell, in response to your resolution of the 25th ult.

JEFFERSON DAVIS.

VETO MESSAGES.

To the Senate of the Confederate States.

I regret that a sense of duty compels me to return to you, with my objections, an act which originated in the Senate, entitled "An Act to increase the strength and efficiency of heavy artillery for seacoast defense."

This act selects from the Provisional Army a particular regiment, known as the First Regiment of South Carolina Infantry, and directs that it shall hereafter be known as the Second Regiment of South Carolina Artillery, and shall have the same organization as is now allowed by law to the First Regiment of South Carolina Artillery.

It next directs that the First and Second Regiments of South Carolina Artillery shall be increased to twelve companies each, and that the complement of a company shall be one hundred and twenty-five enlisted men.

The objections entertained to these provisions are grave, and I submit them as succinctly as possible.

1. The organization of artillery into regiments is subject to great inconvenience and impairs the efficiency of that important arm of the service.

Both in the Regular and in the Provisional Army, the organization of the artillery is a corps composed of batteries, the commander of a battery being a captain, and the men being formed into companies. This organization applies to both heavy or siege and field artillery, and experience has shown it to be more efficient than the organization into regiments.

Under the law, as it now exists, the exact number of batteries required at any point can be ordered there, and an officer of such rank as is appropriate to the number of guns is assigned to their command. It is thus in the power of commanders to assign officers to the duties for which they are most competent, some having greater merit in heavy, and others in light artillery. The system has worked exceedingly well, and I should greatly regret to see it changed or impaired by exceptions. If the organization by regiments be better, it ought to be adopted for the whole artillery service. If not, why should the exceptions to a good system be increased in number?

Where the organization is uniform throughout the service, the troops are better satisfied, and the administration of the Army is much more easy and efficient. Where there are exceptions, there is constant effort on the part of the men to change from one organization to another, discontent is engendered, and embarrassments arise in administration.

It rarely occurs that the service of artillery is required at one point to the number of ten or twelve companies. The exigencies of the service will require that these regiments (if organized as contemplated in the bill now returned to you) shall be broken into detachments, and the field officers, in such event, would be in command of fractions not proportional to their rank.

The First Regiment of South Carolina Artillery was organized by the State before the formation of the Confederacy, and, when it was transferred to this Government, it was necessarily accepted with the existing organization; but that organization was exceptional and objectionable for the reasons already stated. It has been retained in Fort Sumter, which is one of the points where such an organization is least detrimental to the service, but no satisfactory reason is perceived for augmenting the number of companies of which it is composed, or for the organization of another regiment.

The First Regiment of South Carolina Infantry, or a part of it, I am informed, has been assigned to duty and has received instruction in the artillery service, and can be so employed without the passage of the act in question, as long as the exigencies of the service may require. It still remains, however, infantry, and could, in case of necessity, be used as such in the field. If the act should become a law, this advantage would be lost, without any apparent compensating benefit.

2. The act seems to me objectionable as being special legislation.

It is well known that the artillery service is very generally preferred by our troops to infantry service. It is believed that there would be little difficulty now in raising a regiment of artillerists from citizens exempt from conscription, while such is not the case with infantry. If the example be once set of converting regiments into artillery, it needs little foresight to predict that Congress will be beset with applications for such change from regiments now serving as infantry, and claims will be sent forward for equal favors in each of the States. Wherever siege artillery is required, the delegations of the different States will naturally expect and apply for a grant of the same favor to some infantry regiment from their State, and this result would be far from conducive to the discipline of the Army and the good of the service.

There are now numbers of our citizens who, after having volunteered in the infantry, have been found too feeble in constitution to withstand the fatigue and exhaustion of the rapid movements on which the success of our military operations depends. Such soldiers would deem it a great favor to be transferred to the service of heavy artillery, for which they would be well fitted; and their claims for this favorite service appear to be better founded than those of the enlisted men of the infantry regiment designated in the act.

If the purpose of the act be, as it apparently is, to provide for twenty-four companies of artillerists to serve together, the command of these companies would be of sufficient importance to require the appointment of a brigadier general to command them, and it is feared that such special legislation, without apparent necessity for one State, would be made the precedent for similar demands from other States, thus leading to consequences which did not, perhaps, suggest themselves to Congress when the bill received its assent.

3. It is finally suggested, for the consideration of Congress whether some of the provisions of this bill are not equivalent to the exercise of the Executive functions by the legislative department of the Government, and therefore an infringement of the principles of the Constitution which so carefully separate the duties of these different Departments.

Congress has power to "make rules for the government and regulation of the land and naval forces" as well as to "raise armies."

Under these powers Congress could undoubtedly order the raising of regiments of artillery for seacoast defense, and by change of organization direct that a certain number of regiments of infantry be converted into artillery. But such is not the bill under discussion. Congress, in that bill, orders a specified regiment to be employed for seacoast defense.

If this be a legitimate exercise of legislative power, Congress can, of course, select other regiments and order them to the defense of the Indian country, and select again other regiments and order them to be sent to the Tennessee, the Virginia, or the Texan frontier.

Such orders seem to me purely Executive. They have hitherto been made through the Adjutant General of the Army, and it requires but little reflection to perceive that the exercise of such powers by Congress withdraws from the Executive the authority indispensable to the fulfillment of his functions as Commander in Chief.

These reasons have appeared to my mind decisive of the question, and I therefore respectfully return them to the Senate as those which have prevented my approval of the act, which is also herewith returned.   JEFFERSON DAVIS.

Richmond, Va., March 31, 1863.

To the Honorable House of Representatives, Confederate States of America.

I herewith return to the House the act to provide for holding elections for Representatives in the Congress of the Confederate States in the State of Tennessee, with a statement of the objections which have caused me to withhold my approval of the same.

The first clause of the fourth section of the first article of the Constitution authorizes Congress to legislate as to the time, place, and manner of holding elections for Representatives.

I have grave doubts whether this extends to the proposed change from the district to the general ticket system of representation, which seems to me to be rather to change the mode of representation than to alter the manner of holding elections.

The fifth section of the bill is, in my judgment, unconstitutional in this, that it assumes that a citizen may forfeit his right of citizenship by adhering to the enemy, and recognizes the right of a citizen to elect to be a citizen, not of his own State, but of the United States, a foreign nation. This directly repudiates State sovereignty and admits that a citizen's allegiance to his State may be renounced while resident therein.

This section is subject also to the objection that it exercises the power of prescribing the qualifications of voters, which belongs exclusively to the States. JEFFERSON DAVIS.

Richmond, Va., May 1st, 1863.

PROCLAMATIONS.

BY THE PRESIDENT OF THE CONFEDERATE STATES.

A PROCLAMATION.

It is meet that, as a people who acknowledge the supremacy of the living God, we should be ever mindful of our dependence on him; should remember that to him alone can we trust for our deliverance; that to him is due devout thankfulness for signal victories bestowed on us, and that by prayer alone can we hope to secure the continued manifestation of that protecting care which has hitherto shielded us in the midst of trials and danger. In obedience to his precepts, we have from time to time been gathered together with prayers and thanksgiving, and he has been graciously pleased to hear our supplications and to grant abundant exhibitions of his favor to our armies and our people; through many conflicts we have now attained a place among the nations which commands their respect, and to the enemy who encompass us around, and seek our destruction, the Lord of hosts has again taught the lesson of his inspired word, that "the battle is not to the strong, but to whomsoever he willeth to exalt." Again our enemy, with loud boasting of the power of their armed men and mailed ships, threaten us with subjugation and with evil machinations; seek even in our own homes and at our own firesides to pervert menservants and our maidservants into accomplices in their wicked designs. Under these circumstances, it is my privilege to invite you once more to meet together and to prostrate yourselves in humble supplications to Him who has been our constant and never-failing support in the past, and to whose protection and guidance we trust for the future. To this end, I, Jefferson Davis, President of the Confederate States of America, do issue this, my proclamation, setting apart Friday, the 27th day of March, as a day of fasting, humiliation, and prayer; and I do invite the people of the said States to repair, on that day, to their usual places of public worship, and to join in prayer to Almighty God that he will continue his merciful protection over our cause, that he will scatter our enemies, set at naught their evil designs, and that he will graciously restore to our beloved country the blessings of peace and security. In faith whereof, I have hereunto set my hand, at the city of Richmond, on the 27th day of February, in the year of our Lord 1863.   JEFFERSON DAVIS.

By the President:

J. P. BENJAMIN, *Secretary of State.*

BY THE PRESIDENT OF THE CONFEDERATE STATES.

A PROCLAMATION.

LETTERS PATENT REVOKING EXEQUATUR OF GEORGE MOORE, HER
BRITANNIC MAJESTY'S CONSUL AT RICHMOND

To All Whom It May Concern: Whereas, George Moore, Esq., Her Britannic Majesty's Consul for the port of Richmond and State of Virginia (duly recognized by the exequatur issued by a former Government, which was, at the time of the issue, the duly authorized agent for that purpose of the State of Virginia), did recently assume to act as consul for a place other than the city of Richmond, and a State other than the State of Virginia, and was, thereupon, on the twentieth day of February last, 1863, requested by the Secretary of State to submit to the Department of State his consular commission, as well as any other authority he may have received to act in behalf of the Government of Her Britannic Majesty, before further correspondence could be held with him as Her Majesty's Consul at the port of Richmond; and whereas, the said George Moore has lately, without acceding to said request, entered into correspondence, as Her Majesty's Consul, with the Secretary of War of these Confederate States, thereby disregarding the legitimate authority of this Government:

These, therefore, are to declare that I do no longer recognize the said George Moore as Her Britannic Majesty's Consul in any part of these Confederate States, nor permit him to exercise or enjoy any of the functions, powers, or privileges allowed to the consuls of Great Britain. And I do wholly revoke and annul any exequatur heretofore given to the said George Moore by the Government which was formerly authorized to grant such exequatur as agent of the State of Virginia, and do declare the said exequatur to be absolutely null and void from this day forward.

In testimony whereof, I have caused these letters to be made patent, and the seal of the Confederate States of America to be herewith affixed.

Given under my hand this fifth day of June, in the [SEAL.]   year of our Lord one thousand eight hundred and sixtythree.   JEFFERSON DAVIS.

By the President:

J. P. BENJAMIN, *Secretary of State.*

BY THE PRESIDENT OF THE CONFEDERATE STATES.

A PROCLAMATION.

Whereas, it is provided by an act of Congress entitled "An Act to further provide for the public defense," approved on the 16th day of April, 1862, and by another act of Congress approved on 27th of September, 1862, entitled "An Act to amend an act entitled 'An Act to provide further for the public defense,' approved

16th of April, 1862," that the President be authorized to call out and place in the military service of the Confederate States for three years, unless the war shall have been sooner ended, all white men who are residents of the Confederate States between the ages of eighteen and forty-five years at the time the call may be made, and who are not at such time legally exempted from military service, or such part thereof as in his judgment may be necessary to the public defense;

And whereas, in my judgment the necessities of the public defense require that every man capable of bearing arms between the ages aforesaid should now be called out to do his duty in the defense of his country, and in driving back the invaders now within the limits of the Confederacy:

Now, therefore, I, Jefferson Davis, President of the Confederate States of America, do, by virtue of the powers vested in me as aforesaid, call out and place in the military service of the Confederate States all white men residents of said States between the ages of eighteen and forty-five years, not legally exempted from military service, and I do hereby order and direct that all persons subject to this call and not now in the military service do, upon being enrolled, forthwith repair to the conscript camps established in the respective States of which they may be residents, under pain of being held and punished as deserters in the event of their failure to obey this call, as provided in said laws. And I do further order and direct that the enrolling officers of the several States proceed at once to enroll all persons embraced within the terms of this proclamation not heretofore enrolled. And I do further order that it shall be lawful for any person embraced within this call to volunteer for service before enrollment, and that persons so volunteering be allowed to select the arm of service and the company which they desire to join, provided such company be deficient in the full number of men allowed by law for its organization.

Given under my hand and the seal of the Confederate States of America, at the city of Richmond, this fifteenth [SEAL.] day of July, in the year of our Lord one thousand eight hundred and sixty-three.   JEFFERSON DAVIS.

By the President:

J. P. BENJAMIN, *Secretary of State.*

By the President of the Confederate States.

A PROCLAMATION.

Again do I call upon the people of the Confederacy—a people who believe that the Lord reigneth and that his overruling providence ordereth all things—to unite in prayer and humble submission under his chastening hand, and to beseech his favor on our suffering country.

It is meet that when trials and reverses befall us we should seek to take home to our hearts and consciences the lessons which they teach, and profit by the self-examination for which they prepare us. Had not our successes on land and sea made us self-confident and forgetful of our reliance on him; had not love of lucre eaten like a gangrene into the very heart of the land, converting too many among us into worshipers of gain and rendering them unmindful of their duty to their country, to their fellow-men, and to their God—who, then, will presume to complain that we have been chastened or to despair of our just cause and the protection of our Heavenly Father?

Let us rather receive in humble thankfulness the lesson which he has taught in our recent reverses, devoutly acknowledging that to him, and not to our own feeble arms, are due the honor and glory of victory; that from him, in his paternal providence, come the anguish and sufferings of defeat, and that, whether in victory or defeat, our humble supplications are due at his footstool.

Now, therefore, I, Jefferson Davis, President of these Confederate States, do issue this, my proclamation, setting apart Friday, the twenty-first day of August ensuing, as a day of fasting, humiliation, and prayer; and I do hereby invite the people of the Confederate States to repair on that day to their respective places of public worship, and to unite in supplication for the favor and protection of that God who has hitherto conducted us safely through all the dangers that environed us.

[SEAL.] In faith whereof, I have hereunto set my hand and the seal of the Confederate States, at Richmond, this twenty-fifth day of July, in the year of our Lord one thousand eight hundred and sixty-three.   JEFFERSON DAVIS.

By the President:

J. P. BENJAMIN, *Secretary of State.*

BY THE PRESIDENT OF THE CONFEDERATE STATES.

A PROCLAMATION.

The Soldiers of the Confederate States.

After more than two years of warfare scarcely equaled in the number, magnitude, and fearful carnage of .its battles, a warfare in which your courage and fortitude have illustrated your country and attracted not only gratitude at home, but admiration abroad, your enemies continue a struggle in which our final triumph must be inevitable. Unduly elated with their recent successes, they imagine that temporary reverses can quell your spirit or shake your determination, and they are now gathering heavy masses for a general invasion in the vain hope that by a desperate effort success may at length be reached.

You know too well, my countrymen, what they mean by success. Their malignant rage aims at nothing less than the extermination of yourselves, your wives, and children. They seek to destroy what they cannot plunder. They purpose as the spoils of victory that your homes shall be partitioned among the wretches whose atrocious cruelties have stamped infamy on their Government. They design to incite servile insurrection and light the fires of incendiarism wherever they can reach your homes, and they debauch the inferior race, hitherto docile and contented, by promising indulgence of the vilest passions as the price of treachery. Conscious of their inability to prevail by legitimate warfare, not daring to make peace lest they should be hurled from their seats of power, the men who now rule in Washington refuse even to confer on the subject of putting an end to outrages which disgrace our age, or to listen to a suggestion for conducting the war according to the usages of civilization.

Fellow-citizens, no alternative is left you but victory or subjugation, slavery, and the utter ruin of yourselves, your families, and your country. The victory is within your reach. You need but stretch forth your hands to grasp it. For this end all that is necessary is that those who are called to the field by every motive that can move the human heart should promptly repair to the post of duty, should stand by their comrades now in front of the foe, and thus so strengthen the armies of the Confederacy as to insure success. The men now absent from their posts would, if present in the field, suffice to create numerical equality between our force and that of the invaders; and when with any approach to such equality have we failed to be victorious? I believe that but few of those absent are actuated by unwillingness to serve their country, but that many have found it difficult to resist the temptation of a visit to their homes and the loved ones from whom they have been so long separated; that others have left for temporary attention to their affairs with the intention of returning, and then have shrunk from the consequence of the violation of duty; that others again have left their posts from mere restlessness and desire of change, each quieting the upbraidings of his conscience by persuading himself that his individual services could have no influence on the general result. These and other causes (although far less disgraceful than the desire to avoid danger or to escape from the sacrifices required by patriotism) are, nevertheless, grievous faults, and place the cause of our beloved country and of everything we hold dear in imminent peril.

I repeat that the men who now owe duty to their country, who have been called out and have not yet reported for duty, or who have absented themselves from their posts are sufficient in number to secure us victory in the struggle now impending. I call on you, then, my countrymen, to hasten to your camps in obedience to the dictates of honor and of duty, and I summon those who have absented themselves without leave, or who have remained absent beyond the period allowed by their furloughs, to repair without delay to their respective commands; and I do hereby declare that I grant a general pardon and amnesty to all officers and men within the Confederacy now absent without leave who shall with the least possible delay return to their proper posts of duty; but no excuse will be received for any delay beyond twenty days after the first publication of this proclamation in the State in which the absentee may be at the date of publication. This amnesty and pardon shall extend to all who have been accused, or who have been convicted and are undergoing sentence for absence without leave or desertion, excepting only those who have been twice convicted of desertion.

Finally, I conjure my countrywomen, the wives, mothers, sisters, and daughters of the Confederacy, to use their all-powerful influence in aid of this call, to add one crowning sacrifice to those which their patriotism has so freely and constantly offered on their country's altar, and to take care that none who owe service in the field shall be sheltered at home from the disgrace of having deserted their duty to their families, to their country, and to their God.

Given under my hand and the seal of the Confederate [SEAL.] States, at Richmond, this first day of August, in the year of our Lord one thousand eight hundred and sixty-three.

JEFFERSON DAVIS.

By the President:

J. P. BENJAMIN, *Secretary of State.*

ADDRESSES.

ADDRESS.

To the People of the Confederate States.

In compliance with the request of Congress, contained in resolutions passed on the 4th day of the current month, I invoke your attention to the present condition and future prospects of our country and to the duties which patriotism imposes on us all during this great struggle for our homes and our liberties. These resolutions are in the following language:

Whereas a strong impression prevails through the country that the war now being waged against the people of the Confederate States may terminate during the present year; and whereas, this impression is leading many patriotic citizens to engage largely in the production of cotton and tobacco, which they would not otherwise do; and whereas, in the opinion of Congress, it is of the utmost importance, not only with a view to the proper subsistence of our armies, but the interest and welfare of all the people, that the agricultural labor of the country should be employed chiefly in the production of a supply of food to meet every contingency: Therefore,

Resolved by the Congress of the Confederate States of America, That it is the deliberate judgment of Congress that the people of these States, while hoping for peace, should look to prolonged war as the only condition proffered by the enemy short of subjugation; that every preparation necessary to encounter such a war should be persisted in; and that the amplest supply of provisions for armies and people should be the first object of all agriculturists; wherefore, it is earnestly recommended that the people, instead of planting cotton and tobacco, shall direct their agricultural labor mainly to the production of such crops as will insure a sufficiency of food for all classes and for every emergency, thereby with true patriotism subordinating the hope of gain to the certain good of the country.

SEC. 2. That the President is hereby requested to issue a proclamation to the people of these States urging upon them the necessity of guarding against the great perils of a short crop of provisions and setting forth such reasons therefor as his judgment may dictate.

Fully concurring in the views thus expressed by the Congress, I confidently appeal to your love of country for aid in carrying into effect the recommendations of your Senators and Representatives. We have reached the close of the second year of the war, and may point with just pride to the history of our young Confederacy. Alone, unaided, we have met and overthrown the most formidable combination of naval and military armaments that the lust of conquest ever gathered together for the subjugation of a free people. We began this struggle without a single gun afloat, while the resources of our enemy enabled them to gather fleets which, according to their official list published in August last, consisted of 427 vessels, measuring 340,036 tons and carrying 3,268 guns. Yet we have captured, sunk, or destroyed a number of these vessels, including two large frigates and one steam sloop of war, while four of their captured steam gunboats are now in our possession, adding to the strength of our little Navy, which is rapidly gaining in numbers and efficiency. To oppose invading forces composed of levies which have already exceeded 1,300,000 men, we had no resources but the unconquerable valor of a people determined to be free, and we were so destitute of military supplies that tens of thousands of our citizens were reluctantly refused admission into the service from our inability to provide them with arms, while for many months some of our important strongholds owed their safety chiefly to a careful concealment of the fact that we were without a supply of powder for our cannon. Your devotion and patriotism have triumphed over all these obstacles and called into existence the munitions of war, the clothing, and the subsistence which have enabled our soldiers to illustrate their valor on numerous battlefields, and to inflict crushing defeats on successive armies, each of which an arrogant foe fondly imagined to be invincible.

The contrast between our past and present condition is well calculated to inspire full confidence in the triumph of our arms. At no previous period of the war have our forces been so numerous, so well organized, and so thoroughly disciplined, armed, and equipped as at present. The season of high water, on which our enemies relied to enable their fleets of gunboats to penetrate into our country and devastate our homes, is fast passing away; yet our strongholds on the Mississippi still bid defiance to the foe, and months of costly preparations for their reduction have been spent in vain. Disaster has been the result of their every effort to turn or to storm Vicksburg and Port Hudson, as well as of every attack on our batteries on the Red River, the Tallahatchie, and other navigable streams. Within a few weeks the falling waters and the increasing heat of summer will complete their discomfiture and compel their baffled and defeated forces to the abandonment of expeditions on which was based their chief hope of success in effecting our subjugation. We must not forget, however, that the war is not yet ended, and that we are still confronted by powerful armies and threatened by numerous fleets; and that the Government which controls these fleets and armies is driven to the most desperate efforts to effect the unholy purposes in which it has thus far been defeated. It will use its utmost energy to arrest the impending doom, so fully merited by the atrocities it has committed, the savage barbarities which it has encouraged, and the crowning infamy of its attempt to excite a servile population to the massacre of our wives, our daughters, and our helpless children. With such a contest before us there is but one danger which the Government of your choice regards with apprehension, and to avert this danger it appeals to the never-failing patriotism and spirit of self-sacrifice which you have exhibited since the beginning of the war. The very unfavorable season, the protracted droughts of last year, reduced the harvests on which we depended far below an average yield, and the deficiency was unfortunately still more marked in the northern portion of the Confederacy, where supplies were specially needed for the Army. If through a confidence in early peace, which may prove delusive, our fields should be now devoted to the production of cotton and tobacco instead of grain and live stock, and other articles necessary for the subsistence of the people and the Army, the consequences may prove serious, if not disastrous, especially should the **present** season prove as unfavorable as the last.

Your country, therefore, appeals to you to lay aside all thought of gain, and to devote yourselves to securing your liberties, without which those gains would be valueless. It is true that the wheat harvest in the more southern States, which will be gathered next month, promises an abundant yield; but even if this promise be fulfilled, the difficulty of transportation, enhanced as it has been by an unusually rainy winter, will cause embarrassments in military operations and suffering among the people, should the crops in the middle and northern portions of the Confederacy prove deficient. But no uneasiness need be felt in regard to a mere supply of bread for man. It is for the large amount of corn and forage required for the raising of live stock and for the supply of the animals used in military operations that your aid is specially required. These articles are too bulky for distant transportation, and in them the deficiency in the last harvest was most felt. Let fields be devoted exclusively to the production of corn, oats, beans, peas, potatoes, and other food for man and beast; let corn be sown broadcast for fodder in immediate proximity to railroads, rivers, and canals, and let all your efforts be directed to the prompt supply of these articles in the districts where our armies are operating. You will thus add greatly to their efficiency and furnish the means without which it is impracticable to make those prompt and active movements which have hitherto stricken terror into our enemies and secured our most brilliant triumphs.

Having thus placed before you, my countrymen, the reasons for the call made on you for aid in supplying the wants of the coming year, I add a few words of appeal in behalf of the brave soldiers now confronting your enemies, and to whom your Government is unable to furnish all the comforts they so richly merit. The supply of meat for the Army is deficient. This deficiency is only temporary, for measures have been adopted which will, it is believed, soon enable us to restore the full ration. But that ration is now reduced at times to one-half the usual quantity in some of our armies. It is known that the supply of meat throughout the country is sufficient for the support of all, but the distances are so great, the condition of the roads has been so bad during the five months of winter weather through which we have just passed, and the attempt of groveling speculators to forestall the market and make money out of the lifeblood of our defenders have so much influenced the withdrawal from sale of the surplus in the hands of the producers that the Government has been unable to gather full supplies.

The Secretary of War has prepared a plan, which is appended to this address, by the aid of which, or some similar means to be adopted by yourselves, you can assist the officers of the Government in the purchase of the bacon, the pork, and the beef known to exist in large quantities in different parts of the country.

Even if the surplus be less than is believed, is it not a bitter and humiliating reflection that those who remain at home, secure from hardship and protected from danger, should be in the enjoyment of abundance, and that their slaves also should have a full supply of food, while their sons, brothers, husbands, and fathers are stinted in the rations on which their health and efficiency depend?

Entertaining no fear that you will either misconstrue the motives of this address or fail to respond to the call of patriotism, I have placed the facts fully and frankly before you. Let us all unite in the performance of our duty, each in his sphere, and with concerted, persistent, and well-directed effort there seems little reason to doubt that under the blessing of Him to whom we look for guidance, and who has been to us our shield and our strength, we shall maintain the sovereignty and independence of these Confederate States, and transmit to our posterity the heritage bequeathed to us by our fathers.   JEFFERSON DAVIS.

Executive Office, Richmond, April 10, 1863.

ADDRESS.

HEADQUARTERS ARMY OF TENNESSEE,
October 14, 1863.

Soldiers: A grateful country has recognized your arduous service, and rejoiced over your glorious victory on the field of Chickamauga. When your countrymen shall more fully learn the adverse circumstances under which you attacked the enemy—though they cannot be more thankful—they may admire more the gallantry and patriotic devotion which secured your success. Representatives of every State of the Confederacy, your steps have been followed with affectionate solicitude by friends in every portion of the country. Defenders of the heart of our territory, your movements have been the object of intensest anxiety. The hopes of our cause greatly depend upon you, and happy it is that all can securely rely upon your achieving whatever, under the blessing of Providence, human power can effect.

Though you have done much, very much yet remains to be done. Behind you is a people providing for your support and depending on you for protection. Before you is a country devastated by your ruthless invader, where gentle women, feeble age, and helpless infancy have been subjected to outrages without parallel in the warfare of civilized nations. With eager eyes they watch for your coming to their deliverance, and the homeless refugee pines for the hour when your victorious arms shall restore his family to the shelter from which they have been driven. Forced to take up arms to vindicate the political rights, the freedom, equality, and State sovereignty which were the heritage purchased by the blood of your revolutionary sires, you have but the alternative of slavish submission to despotic usurpation, or the independence which vigorous, united, persistent effort will secure. All which fires the manly breast, nerves the patriot, and exalts the hero, is present to stimulate and sustain you.

Nobly have you redeemed the pledges given in the name of freedom to the memory of your ancestors and the rights of your posterity. That you may complete the mission to which you are devoted, will require of you such exertion in the future as you have made in the past—continuance in the patient endurance of toil and danger, and that self-denial which rejects every consideration at variance with the public service as unworthy of the holy cause in which you are engaged.

When the war shall have ended, the highest meed of praise will be due, and probably given, to him who has claimed least for himself in proportion to the service he has rendered, and the bitterest self-reproach which may hereafter haunt the memory of any one will be to him who has allowed selfish aspiration to prevail over a desire for the public good. United as you are in a common destiny, obedience and cordial coöperation are essentially necessary, and there is no higher duty than that which requires each to render to all what is due to their station. He who sows the seeds of discontent and distrust prepares for the harvest of slaughter and defeat. To zeal you have added gallantry; to gallantry, energy; to energy, fortitude. Crown these with harmony, due subordination, and cheerful support of lawful authority, that the measure of your duty may be full.

I fervently hope that the ferocious war, so unjustly waged against our country, may be soon ended, that, with the blessing of peace, you may be restored to your homes and the useful pursuits; and I pray that our Heavenly Father may cover you with the shield of his protection in the hours of battle, and endow you with the virtues which will close your trials in victory complete.

JEFFERSON DAVIS.

RESOLUTIONS OF THANKS.

1. *Resolved by the Congress of the Confederate States of America,* That the bold, intrepid, and gallant conduct of Major General J. Bankhead Magruder, Colonel Thomas Green, Major Leon Smith, and other officers, and of the Texan Rangers and soldiers engaged in the attack on, and victory achieved over, the land and naval forces of the enemy at Galveston, on the first of January, 1863, eminently entitle them to the thanks of Congress and the country.

2. *Resolved,* That this brilliant achievement, resulting, under the providence of God, in the capture of the war steamer "Harriet Lane" and the defeat and ignominious flight of the hostile fleet from the harbor, the recapture of the city, and the raising of the blockade of the port of Galveston, signally evinces that superior force may be overcome by skillful conception and daring courage.

3. *Resolved,* That the foregoing resolutions be communicated by the Secretary of War to Major General Magruder, and by him to his command.

Approved February 25, 1863.

Resolved by the Congress of the Confederate States of America, That the thanks of Congress are eminently due, and are hereby cordially given, to Brigadier General N. B. Forrest, and the officers and men under his command, for gallantry and successful enterprise during the present war, and especially for the daring and skill exhibited in the capture of Murfreesboro, on the 13th of July last, and in subsequent brilliant achievements.

Approved May 1, 1863.

Resolved by the Congress of the Confederate States of America, That the thanks of Congress are due, and are hereby tendered, to General John H. Morgan, and the officers and men of his command, for their varied, heroic, and invaluable services in Tennessee and Kentucky immediately preceding the battles before Murfreesboro, services which have conferred upon their officers fame as enduring as the records of the struggle which they have so brilliantly illustrated.

Approved May 1, 1863.

Resolved by the Congress of the Confederate States of America, That the thanks of Congress are eminently due, and are hereby most cordially tendered, to General G. T. Beauregard, and the officers and men of his command, engaged in the affair, for their brilliant and signal defeat of the ironclad fleet of the enemy, in the harbor of Charleston, on the seventh of April, one thousand eight hundred and sixty-three.

Resolved, That the President be requested to communicate this resolution to General Beauregard and his command.

Approved May 1, 1863.

Resolved by the Congress of the Confederate States of America, That the thanks of Congress are due, and are hereby tendered, to Major Oscar M. Watkins, and the officers and men under his command, for the signal victory achieved over the naval forces of the United States at Sabine Pass, on the twenty-first of January, eighteen hundred and sixty-three, resulting in the dispersion of the blockading squadron of the enemy, and the capture of two of his gunboats.

Approved May 1, 1863.

Resolved, That the thanks of Congress are due, and are hereby tendered, to Brigadier General Wheeler, and the officers and men of his command, for their daring and successful attacks upon the enemy's gunboats and transports in the Cumberland River.

Approved May 1, 1863.

The Congress of the Confederate States of America do resolve, That the thanks of Congress are due, and are hereby tendered, to the officers and soldiers engaged in the defense of Fort McAllister, Georgia, on the first of February and third of March last, for the gallantry and endurance with which they successfully resisted the attacks of the ironclad vessels of the enemy.

Resolved further, That the foregoing resolution be communicated by the Secretary of War to the General commanding the Department of South Carolina, Georgia, and Florida, and by him to be made known in appropriate general orders to the officers and troops to whom it is addressed.

Approved May 1, 1863.

APPOINTMENT OF VICE PRESIDENT STEPHENS AS MILITARY COMMISSIONER TO UNITED STATES.

TENDER OF SERVICES BY MR. STEPHENS TO MR. DAVIS.

LIBERTY HALL, GA., June 12, 1863.

Hon. Jefferson Davis, Richmond, Va.

Dear Sir: I have just seen what purports to be a letter addressed to you by Major General D. Hunter, commanding the Federal forces at Port Royal, S. C., bearing date the 23d of April last. Of the extraordinary character of this paper, its tone, temper, and import, whether genuine or not, it is not my purpose to speak. It may be a forgery.* All I know of it is from its publication, as we have it in our newspapers. But it has occurred to me if it be genuine, this, together with other matters of controversy I see likewise in the papers, in relation to the future exchange of certain classes of prisoners of war, may necessarily lead to a further conference with the authorities at Washington upon the whole subject. In that event I wish to say to you briefly, that if you think my services in such a mission would be of any avail in effecting a correct understanding and agreement between the two Governments upon those questions involving such serious consequences, they are at your command.

---

*Mr. Stephens states that "it was genuine, and of a character not much short of savage."

You will remember while we were at Montgomery, when the first commissioners were sent to Washington with a view to settle and adjust all matters of difference between us and the United States, without a resort to arms, you desired me to be one of those clothed with this high and responsible trust. I then declined, because I saw no prospect of success—did not think, upon a survey of the whole field, that I could effect anything good or useful in any effort I could *then* make on that line. You will allow me now to say that at *this time* I think *possibly* I might be able to do some good not only on the *immediate* subject in hand, but were I in conference with the authorities at Washington on *any point* in relation to the *conduct* of the war, I am not without hopes that *indirectly* I could now turn attention to a general adjustment upon such basis as might ultimately be acceptable to both parties and stop the further effusion of blood in a contest so irrational, unchristian, and so inconsistent with all recognized American principles.

The undertaking, I know, would be a great one. Its magnitude and responsibility I fully realize. I might signally fail. This I also fully comprehend; but still, be assured, I am not without *some* hopes of success, and whenever or wherever I see any prospect of the *possibility* of being useful or of doing good I am prepared for any risk, any hazards, and all responsibilities commensurate with the object. Of course, I entertain but one idea of the basis of final settlement or adjustment; that is, the recognition of the sovereignty of the States and the right of each in its sovereign capacity to determine its own destiny. This principle lies at the foundation of the American system. It was what was achieved in the first war of Independence, and must be vindicated in the second. The full recognition of this principle covers all that is really involved in the present issue. That the Federal Government is yet *ripe* for such acknowledgment I, by no means, believe, but that *the time has come* for a proper presentation of the question to the authorities at Washington I do believe—such presentation as can be made only in a diplomatic way. While, therefore, a mission might be dispatched on a *minor* point, the greater one could possibly, with prudence, discretion, and skill, be opened to view and brought in discussion in a way that would *lead eventually* to successful results. This would depend upon many circumstances, but no little upon the character and efficiency of the agent. It so occurs to me, and so feeling I have been prompted to address you these lines. My object is, solely, to inform you that I am ready and willing to undertake such a mission with a view to such ulterior ends, if any fit opportunity offers in the present state of our affairs in relation to the exchange of prisoners, or any other matter of controversy growing out of the *conduct* of the war, and if also you should be of opinion that I could be useful in such position. I am at your service, heart and soul, at any post you may assign me where I see any prospect of aiding, assisting, or advancing the great cause we are engaged in and of securing with its success the blessings of permanent peace, prosperity, and constitutional liberty.

Should the *present* position of affairs in your opinion be suitable, of which I am not so well informed as you are, and this suggestion so far meet your approval as to cause you to wish to advise further with me on the subject, you have but to let me know; otherwise no reply is necessary, and none will be expected.

With best wishes for you personally and our common country in this day of her trial, I remain yours, etc.,

ALEXANDER H. STEPHENS.

REPLY OF MR. DAVIS.

RICHMOND, July 2, 1863.

Hon. Alexander H. Stephens, Richmond, Va.

Sir: Having accepted your patriotic offer to proceed as a military commissioner under flag of truce to Washington, you will receive herewith your letter of authority to the Commander in Chief of the Army and Navy of the United States. The letter is signed by me, as Commander in Chief of the Confederate land and naval forces.

You will perceive from the terms of the letter that it is so worded as to avoid any political difficulties in its reception. Intended exclusively as one of those communications between belligerents which public law recognizes as necessary and proper between hostile forces, care has been taken to give no pretext for refusing to receive it on the ground that it would involve a tacit recognition of the independence of the Confederacy. Your mission is simply one of humanity, and has no political aspect.

If objection is made to receiving your letter on the ground that it is not addressed to Abraham Lincoln as *President,* instead of Commander in Chief, etc., then you will present the duplicate letter which is addressed to him as President and signed by me as President. To this letter objection may.be made on the ground that I am not recognized to be President of the Confederacy. In this event you will decline any further attempt to confer on the subject of your mission, as such conference is admissible only on the footing of perfect equality.

My recent interviews with you have put you so fully in possession of my views that it is scarcely necessary to give you any detailed instructions, even were I at this moment well enough to attempt it. My whole purpose is in one word to place this war on the footing of such as are waged by civilized people in modern times, and to divest it of the savage character which.has been impressed on it by our enemies, in spite of all our efforts and protests. War is full enough of unavoidable horrors under all its aspects to justify and even to demand of any Christian rulers who may be unhappily engaged in carrying it on to seek to restrict its calamities and to divest it of all unnecessary severities. You will endeavor to establish the cartel for the exchange of prisoners on such a basis as to avoid the constant difficulties and complaints which arise, and to prevent for the future what we deem the unfair conduct of our enemies in evading the delivery of the prisoners who fall into their hands; in retarding it by sending them on circuitous routes, and by detaining them sometimes for months in camps and prisons; and in persisting in taking captive noncombatants.

Your attention is called also to the unheard-of conduct of Federal officers in driving from their homes entire communities of women and children, as well as of men, whom they find in districts occupied by their troops, for no other reason than because these unfortunates are faithful to the allegiance due to their States, and refuse to take an oath of fidelity to their enemies.

The putting to death of unarmed prisoners has been a ground of just complaint in more than one instance; and the recent execution of officers of our army in Kentucky, for the sole cause that they were engaged in recruiting service in a State which is claimed as still one of the United States, but is also claimed by us as one of the Confederate States, must be repressed by retaliation if not unconditionally abandoned, because it would justify the like execution in every other State of the Confederacy; and the practice is barbarous, uselessly cruel, and can only lead to the slaughter of prisoners on both sides—a result too horrible to be contemplated without making every effort to avoid it.

On these and all kindred subjects you will consider your authority full and ample to make such arrangements as will temper the present cruel character of the contest, and full confidence is placed in your judgment, patriotism, and discretion that, while carrying out the objects of your mission, you will take care that the equal rights of the Confederacy be always preserved.

Very respectfully, JEFFERSON DAVIS.

LETTER OF PRESIDENT DAVIS TO PRESIDENT LINCOLN.

HEADQUARTERS, RICHMOND, July 2, 1863.

Sir: As Commander in Chief of the land and naval forces now waging war against the United States, I have the honor to address this communication to you, as Commander in Chief of their land and naval forces.

Numerous difficulties and disputes have arisen in relation to the execution of the cartel of exchange heretofore agreed on by the belligerents, and the commissioners for the exchange of prisoners have been unable to adjust their differences. Their action on the subject of these differences is delayed and embarrassed by the necessity of referring each subject as it arises to superior authority for decision. I believe that I have just grounds of complaint against the officers and forces under your command for breach of the terms of the cartel, and, being myself ready to execute it at all times in good faith, I am not justified in doubting the existence of the same disposition on your part.

In addition to this matter, I have to complain of the conduct of your officers and troops in many parts of the country, who violate all the rules of war by carrying on hostilities not only against armed foes but against noncombatants, aged men, women, and children; while others not only seize such property as is required for the use of your forces, but destroy all private property within their reach, even agricultural implements; and openly avow the purpose of seeking to subdue the population of the districts where they are operating by the starvation that must result from the destruction of standing crops and agricultural tools.

Still, again, others of your officers in different districts have recently taken the lives of prisoners who fell into their power, and justify their act by asserting a right to treat as spies the military officers and enlisted men under my command, who may penetrate for hostile purposes into States claimed by me to be engaged in the warfare now waged against the United States, and claimed by the latter as having refused to engage in such warfare.

I have heretofore, on different occasions, been forced to make complaint of these outrages, and to ask from you that you should either avow or disclaim having authorized them, and have failed to obtain such answer as the usages of civilized warfare require to be given in such cases.

These usages justify, and indeed require, redress by retaliation as the proper means of repressing such cruelties as are not permitted in warfare between Christian peoples. I have, notwithstanding, refrained from the exercise of such retaliation, because of its obvious tendency to lead to a war of indiscriminate massacre on both sides, which would be a spectacle so shocking to humanity and so disgraceful to the age in which we live and the religion we profess that I cannot contemplate it without a feeling of horror that I am disinclined to doubt you would share.

With the view, then, of making one last solemn attempt to avert such calamities, and to attest my earnest desire to prevent them, if it be possible, I have selected the bearer of this letter, the Hon. Alexander H. Stephens, as a military commissioner to proceed to your headquarters under flag of truce, there to confer and agree on the subjects above mentioned; and I do hereby authorize the said Alexander H. Stephens to arrange and settle all differences and disputes which may have arisen or may arise in the execution of the cartel for exchange of prisoners of war, heretofore agreed on between our respective land and naval forces; also to agree to any just modification that may be found necessary to prevent further misunderstandings as to the terms of said cartel; and finally to enter into such arrangement or understanding about the mode of carrying on hostilities between the belligerents as shall confine the severities of the war within such limits as are rightfully imposed not only by modern civilization but by our common Christianity.

I am, very respectfully, your obedient servant,

JEFFERSON DAVIS,
Commander in Chief of the land and naval
forces of the Confederate States.

To ABRAHAM LINCOLN,
Commander in Chief of the land and naval forces of the United States.

REPLY OF THE UNITED STATES GOVERNMENT.

The request is inadmissible. The customary agents and channels are adequate for all needful military communications and conference between the United States forces and the insurgents.

MET AT RICHMOND, VA., DECEMBER 7, 1863. ADJOURNED FEBRUARY 17, 1864.

MESSAGES.

RICHMOND, VA., December 7, 1863.

To the Senate and House of Representatives of the Confederate States.

The necessity for legislative action arising out of the important events that have marked the interval since your adjournment, and my desire to have the aid of your counsel on other matters of grave public interest, render your presence at this time more than ordinarily welcome. Indeed, but for serious obstacles for convoking you in extraordinary session and the necessity for my own temporary absence from the seat of government, I would have invited you to an earlier meeting than that fixed at the date of your adjournment.

Grave reverses befell our arms soon after your departure from Richmond. Early in June [July] our strongholds at Vicksburg and Port Hudson, together with their entire garrisons, capitulated to the combined land and naval forces of the enemy. The important interior position of Jackson next fell into their temporary possession. Our unsuccessful assault upon the post at Helena was followed at a later period by the invasion of Arkansas, and the retreat of our army from Little Rock gave to the enemy the control of the important valley in which it is situated.

The resolute spirit of the people soon rose superior to the temporary despondency naturally resulting from these reverses. The gallant troops, so ably commanded in the States beyond the Mississippi, inflicted repeated defeats on the invading armies in Louisiana and on the coast of Texas. Detachments of troops and active bodies of partisans kept up so effective a war on the Mississippi River as practically to destroy its value as an avenue of commerce.

The determined and successful defense of Charleston against the joint land and naval operations of the enemy afforded an inspiring example of our ability to repel the attacks even of the ironclad fleet on which they chiefly rely, while on the northern frontier our success was still more marked.

The able commander* who conducted the campaign in Virginia determined to meet the threatened advance on Richmond, for which the enemy had made long and costly preparations, by forcing their armies to cross the Potomac and fight in defense of their own capital and homes.   Transferring the battlefield to their own soil, he succeeded in compelling their rapid retreat from Virginia, and in the hard-fought battle of Gettysburg inflicted such severity of punishment as•disabled them from early renewal of the campaign as originally projected.   Unfortunately the communications on which our general relied for receiving his supplies of munitions were interrupted by extraordinary floods, which so swelled the Potomac as to render impassable the fords by which his advance had been made, and he was thus forced to a withdrawal, which was conducted with deliberation after securing large trains of captured supplies, and with a constant and unaccepted tender of battle.   On more than one occasion the enemy has since made demonstrations of a purpose to advance, invariably followed by a precipitate retreat to intrenched lines on the approach of our forces.

The effective check thus offered to the advance of the invaders at all points was such as to afford hope of their early expulsion from portions of the territory previously occupied by them, when the country was painfully surprised by the intelligence that the officer† in command of Cumberland Gap had surrendered that important and easily defensible pass without firing a shot, upon the summons of a force still believed to have been inadequate to its reduction, and when reënforcements were in supporting distance and had been ordered to his aid.   The entire garrison, including the commander, being still held prisoners by the enemy, I am unable to suggest any explanation of this disaster, which laid open Eastern Tennessee and Southwestern Virginia to hostile operations and broke the line of communication between the seat of government and Middle Tennessee.   This easy success of the enemy was followed by an advance of General Rosecrans into Georgia; and our army evacuated Chattanooga and availed itself of the opportunity thus afforded of winning, on the field of Chickamauga, one of the most brilliant and decisive victories of

---

*Robert E. Lee.   †John W. Frazer.

the war. This signal defeat of General Rosecrans was followed by his retreat into Chattanooga, where his imperiled position had the immediate effect of relieving the pressure of the invasion at other points, forcing the concentration for his relief of large bodies of troops withdrawn from the armies in the Mississippi Valley and in Northern Virginia. The combined forces thus accumulated against us in Tennessee so greatly outnumbered our army as to encourage the enemy to attack. After a long and severe battle, in which great carnage was inflicted on him, some of our troops inexplicably abandoned a position of great strength, and by a disorderly retreat compelled the commander* to withdraw the forces elsewhere successful, and finally to retreat with his whole army to a position some twenty or thirty miles to the rear. It is believed that if the troops who yielded to the assault had fought with the valor which they had displayed on previous occasions, and which was manifested in this battle on the other parts of the line, the enemy would have been repulsed with very great slaughter, and our country would have escaped the misfortune and the Army the mortification of the first defeat that has resulted from misconduct by the troops. In the meantime the army of General Burnside was driven from all its field positions in Eastern Tennessee and forced to retreat into its intrenchments at Knoxville, where for some weeks it was threatened with capture by the forces under General Longstreet. No information has reached me of the final result of the operations of our commander, though intelligence has arrived of his withdrawal from that place.

While, therefore, our success in driving the enemy from our soil has not equaled the expectations confidently entertained at the commencement of the campaign, his progress has been checked. If we are forced to regret losses in Tennessee and Arkansas, we are not without ground for congratulation on successes in Louisiana and Texas. On the seacoast he is exhausted by vain efforts to capture our ports, while on the northern frontier he has in turn felt the pressure and dreads the renewal of invasion. The indomitable courage and perseverance of the people in the defense of their homes have been nobly attested by the unanimity with which the Legislatures of Virginia, North Caro-

---

*Braxton Bragg.

lina, and Georgia have recently given expression to the popular
sentiment, and like manifestations may be anticipated from all the
States. Whatever obstinacy may be displayed by the enemy in
his desperate sacrifices of money, life, and liberty in the hope of
enslaving us, the experience of mankind has too conclusively
shown the superior endurance of those who fight for home,
liberty, and independence to permit any doubt of the result.

FOREIGN RELATIONS.

I regret to inform you that there has been no improvement in
the state of our relations with foreign countries since my message* in January last. On the contrary, there has been a still
greater divergence in the conduct of European nations from that
practical impartiality which alone deserves the name of neutrality,
and their action in some cases has assumed a character positively
unfriendly.

You have heretofore been informed that by common understanding the initiative in all action touching the contest on this
continent had been left by foreign powers to the two great maritime nations of Western Europe, and that the Governments of
these two nations had agreed to take no measures without previous
concert. The result of these arrangements has, therefore, placed
it in the power of either France or England to obstruct at pleasure
the recognition to which the Confederacy is justly entitled, or
even to prolong the continuance of hostilities on this side of the
Atlantic, if the policy of either could be promoted by the postponement of peace. Each, too, thus became possessed of great
influence in so shaping the general exercise of neutral rights in
Europe as to render them subservient to the purpose of aiding
one of the belligerents to the detriment of the other. I referred
at your last session to some of the leading points in the course
pursued by professed neutrals which betrayed a partisan leaning
to the side of our enemies, but events have since occurred which
induce me to renew the subject in greater detail than was then
deemed necessary. In calling to your attention the action of those
Governments, I shall refer to the documents appended to President Lincoln's messages, and to their own correspondence, as

---

*Page 276.

disclosing the true nature of their policy and the motives which guided it. To this course no exception can be taken, inasmuch as our attention has been invited to those sources of information by their official publication.

In May, 1861, the Government of Her Britannic Majesty informed our enemies that it had not "allowed any other than an intermediate position on the part of the Southern States," and assured them "that the sympathies of this country [Great Britain] were rather with the North than with the South."

On the 1st day of June, 1861, the British Government interdicted the use of its ports "to armed ships and privateers, both of the United States and the so-called Confederate States," with their prizes. The Secretary of State of the United States fully appreciated the character and motive of this interdiction when he observed to Lord Lyons, who communicated it, "that this measure and that of the same character which had been adopted by France would probably prove a deathblow to Southern privateering."

On the 12th of June, 1861, the United States Minister in London informed Her Majesty's Secretary for Foreign Affairs that the fact of his having held interviews with the Commissioners of this Government had given "great dissatisfaction," and that a protraction of this relation would be viewed by the United States "as hostile in spirit, and to require some corresponding action accordingly." In response to this intimation Her Majesty's Secretary assured the Minister that "he had no expectation of seeing them any more."

By proclamation issued on the 19th and 27th of April, 1861, President Lincoln proclaimed the blockade of the entire coast of the Confederacy, extending from the Potomac to the Rio Grande, embracing, according to the returns of the United States Coast Survey, a coast line of 3,549 statute miles, on which the number of rivers, bays, harbors, inlets, sounds, and passes is 189. The navy possessed by the United States for enforcing this blockade was stated in the reports communicated by President Lincoln to the Congress of the United States to consist of twenty-four vessels of all classes in commission, of which half were in distant seas. The absurdity of the pretension of such a blockade in face of the authoritative declaration of the maritime rights of neutrals made at Paris in 1856 was so glaring that the attempt was regarded as an experiment on the forbearance of neutral powers which they would promptly resist.   This conclusion was justified by the facts that the Governments of France and Great Britain determined that it was necessary for their interests to obtain from both belligerents "securities concerning the proper treatment of neutrals."   In the instructions which "confided the negotiations on this matter" to the British Consul in Charleston, he was informed that "the most perfect accord on this question exists between Her Majesty's Government and the Government of the Emperor of the French," and these instructions were accompanied by a copy of the dispatch of the British Foreign Office of the 18th May, 1861, stating that there was no difference of opinion between Great Britain and the United States as to the validity of the principles enunciated in the fourth article of the declaration of Paris in reference to blockades.   Your predecessors of the Provisional Congress had, therefore, no difficulty in proclaiming, nor I in approving, the resolutions which abandoned in favor of Great Britain and France our right to capture enemy's property when covered by the flags of those powers.   The "securities" desired by these Governments were understood by us to be required from both belligerents.   Neutrals were exposed on our part to the exercise of the belligerent right of capturing their vessels when conveying the property of our enemies.   They were exposed on the part of the United States to interruption in their unquestioned right of trading with us by the declaration of the paper blockade above referred to.   We had no reason to doubt the good faith of the proposal made to us, nor to suspect that we were to be the only parties bound by its acceptance.   It is true that the instructions of the neutral powers informed their agents that it was "essential under present circumstances that they should act with great caution in order to avoid raising the question of the recognition of the new Confederation," and that the understanding on the subject did not assume, for that reason, the shape of a formal convention.   But it was not deemed just by us to decline the arrangement on this ground, as little more than ninety days had then elapsed since the arrival of our Commissioners in Europe, and neutral nations were fairly entitled to a reasonable delay in acting on a subject of so much importance, and which from their point of view presented difficulties that we, perhaps, did not fully appreciate. Certain it is that the action of this Government on the occasion and its faithful performance of its own engagements have been such as to entitle it to expect on the part of those who sought in their own interests a mutual understanding the most scrupulous adherence to their own promises. I feel constrained to inform you that in this expectation we have been disappointed, and that not only have the governments which entered into these arrangements yielded to the prohibition against commerce with us which has been dictated by the United States in defiance of the law of nations, but that this concession of their neutral rights to our detriment has on more than one occasion been claimed in intercourse with our enemies as an evidence of friendly feeling toward them. A few extracts from the correspondence of Her Majesty's Chief Secretary of State for Foreign Affairs will suffice to show marked encouragement to the United States to persevere in its paper blockade, and unmistakable intimations that Her Majesty's Government would not contest its validity.

On the 21st of May, 1861, Earl Russell pointed out to the United States Minister in London that "the blockade might no doubt be made effective, considering the small number of harbors on the Southern coast, even though the extent of 3,000 miles were comprehended in terms of that blockade." On the 14th of January, 1862, Her Majesty's Minister in Washington communicated to his Government that, in extenuation of the barbarous attempt to destroy the port of Charleston by sinking a stone fleet in the harbor, Mr. Seward had explained "that the Government of the United States had last spring, with a navy very little prepared for so extensive an operation, undertaken to blockade upward of 3,000 miles of coast. The Secretary of the Navy had reported that he could stop up the 'large holes' by means of his ships, but that he could not stop up the 'small ones.' It had been found necessary, therefore, to close some of the numerous small inlets by sinking vessels in the channel."

On the 6th of May, 1862, so far from claiming the rights of British subjects as neutrals to trade with us as belligerents, and to disregard the blockade on the ground of this explicit confession by our enemy of his inability to render it effective, Her Majesty's Secretary of State for Foreign Affairs claimed credit with the

United States for friendly action in respecting it. His Lordship stated that "the United States Government, on the allegation of a rebellion pervading from nine to eleven States of the Union, have now for more than twelve months endeavored to maintain a blockade of 3,000 miles of coast. This blockade, kept up irregularly, but when enforced, enforced severely, has seriously injured the trade and manufactures of the United Kingdom. Thousands are now obliged to resort to the poor rates for subsistence, owing to this blockade. Yet Her Majesty's Government have never sought to take advantage of the obvious imperfections of this blockade in order to declare it ineffective. They have, to the loss and detriment of the British nation, scrupulously observed the duties of Great Britain toward a friendly State."

Again, on the 22d of September, 1862, the same noble earl asserted that the United States were "very far indeed" from being in "a condition to ask other nations to assume that every port of the coasts of the so-styled Confederate States is effectively blockaded."

When, in view of these facts, of the obligation of the British nation to adhere to the pledge made by their Government at Paris in 1856, and renewed to this Confederacy in 1861, and of these repeated and explicit avowals of the imperfection, irregularity, and inefficiency of the pretended blockade of our coast, I directed our commissioner at London to call upon the British Government to redeem its promise and to withhold its moral aid and sanction from the flagrant violation of public law committed by our enemies, we were informed that Her Majesty's Government could not regard the blockade of the Southern ports as having been otherwise than "practically effective" in February, 1862, and that "the manner in which it has since been enforced gives to neutral governments no excuse for asserting that the blockade has not been efficiently maintained." We were further informed, when we insisted that by the terms of our agreement no blockade was to be considered effective unless "sufficient really to prevent access to our coast," "that the declaration of Paris was, in truth, directed against the blockades not sustained by any actual force, or sustained by a notoriously inadequate force, such as the occasional appearance of a man-of-war in the offing, or the like."

It was impossible that this mode of construing an agreement

so as to make its terms mean almost the reverse of what they plainly conveyed could be considered otherwise than as a notification of the refusal of the British Government to remain bound by its agreement or longer to respect those articles of the declaration of Paris which had been repeatedly denounced by British statesmen and had been characterized by Earl Russell as "very imprudent" and "most unsatisfactory."

If any doubt remained of the motives by which the British ministry have been actuated in their conduct, it would be completely dissipated by the distinct avowals and explanations contained in the published speech recently made by Her Majesty's Secretary for Foreign Affairs. In commenting on the remonstrances of this Government against the countenance given to an ineffective blockade, the following language is used:

It is said we have, contrary to the declaration of Paris, contrary to international law, permitted the blockade of 3,000 miles of American coast. It is quite true we did so, and the presumable cause of complaint is quite true, that although the blockade is kept up by a sufficient number of ships, yet these ships were sent into the U. S. Navy in a hurry, and are ill-fitted for the purpose, and did not keep up so completely and effectively as was required, an effective blockade.

This unequivocal confession of violation, both of agreement with us and of international law, is defended on grounds the validity of which we submit with confidence to the candid judgment of mankind.

These grounds are thus stated:

Still, looking at the law of nations, it was a blockade we, as a great belligerent power in former times, should have acknowledged. We ourselves had a blockade of upward of 2,000 miles, and it did seem to me that we were bound in justice to the Federal States of America to acknowledge that blockade. But there was another reason which weighed with me. Our people were suffering severely for the want of that material which was the main staff of their industry, and it was a question of self-interest whether we should not break the blockade. But in my opinion the men of England would have been forever infamous if, for the sake of their own interest, they had violated the law of nations and made war, in conjunction with these slaveholding States of America, against the Federal States.

In the second of these reasons our rights are not involved, although it may be permitted to observe that the conduct of governments has not heretofore to my knowledge been guided by the principle that it is infamous to assert their rights whenever the invasion of those rights creates severe suffering among their people and injuriously affects great interests. But the intimation that relations with these States would be discreditable because they are slaveholding would probably have been omitted if the official personage who has published it to the world had remembered that these States were, when colonies, made slaveholding by the direct exercise of the power of Great Britain, whose dependencies they were, and whose interests in the slave trade were then supposed to require that her colonies should be made slaveholding.

But the other ground stated is of a very grave character. It asserts that a violation of the law of nations by Great Britain in 1807, when that Government declared a paper blockade of 2,000 miles of coast (a violation then defended by her courts and jurists on the sole ground that her action was retaliatory), affords a justification for a similar outrage on neutral rights by the United States in 1861, for which no palliation can be suggested; and that Great Britain "is bound, in justice to the Federal States," to make return for the war waged against her by the United States in resistance of her illegal blockade of 1807, by an acquiescence in the Federal illegal blockade of 1861. The most alarming feature in this statement is its admission of a just claim on the part of the United States to require of Great Britain during this war a disregard of the recognized principles of modern public law and of her own compacts, whenever any questionable conduct of Great Britain, "in former times," can be cited as a precedent. It is not inconsistent with respect and admiration for the great people whose Government have given us this warning, to suggest that their history, like that of mankind in general, offers exceptional instances of indefensible conduct "in former times," and we may well deny the morality of violating recent engagements through deference to the evil precedents of the past.

After defending, in the manner just stated, the course of the British Government on the subject of the blockade, Her Majesty's Foreign Secretary takes care to leave no doubt of the further purpose of the British Government to prevent our purchase of vessels in Great Britain, while supplying our enemies with rifles and other munitions of war, and states the intention to apply to Parliament for the furtherance of this design. He gives to the United States the assurance that he will do in their favor not only "everything that the law of nations requires, everything that the present foreign enlistment act requires," but that he will ask the sanction of Parliament "to further measures that Her Majesty's ministers may still add." This language is so unmistakably an official exposition of the policy adopted by the British Government in relation to our affairs that the duty imposed on me by the Constitution of giving you, from time to time, "information of the state of the Confederacy," would not have been performed if I had failed to place it distinctly before you.

I refer you for fuller details on this whole subject to the correspondence of the State Department which accompanies this message. The facts which I have briefly narrated are, I trust, sufficient to enable you to appreciate the true nature of the neutrality professed in this war. It is not in my power to apprise you to what extent the Government of France shares the views so unreservedly avowed by that of Great Britain, no published correspondence of the French Government on the subject having been received. No public protest nor opposition, however, has been made by His Imperial Majesty against the prohibition to trade with us imposed on French citizens by the paper blockade of the United States, although I have reason to believe that an unsuccessful attempt was made on his part to secure the assent of the British Government to a course of action more consonant with the dictates of public law and with the demands of justice toward us.

The partiality of Her Majesty's Government in favor of our enemies has been further evinced in the marked difference of its conduct on the subject of the purchase of supplies by the two belligerents. This difference has been conspicuous since the very commencement of the war. As early as the 1st of May, 1861, the British Minister in Washington was informed by the Secretary of State of the United States that he had sent agents to England, and that others would go to France to purchase arms; and this fact was communicated to the British Foreign Office, which interposed no objection. Yet in October of the same year Earl Russell entertained the complaint of the United States Minister in London that the Confederate States were importing contraband of war from the island of Nassau, directed inquiry into the matter, and obtained a report from the authorities of the island denying the allegations, which report was inclosed to Mr. Adams and received by him as satisfactory evidence to dissipate "the suspicion naturally thrown upon the authorities of Nassau by that únwarrantable act." So, too, when the Confederate Government purchased in Great Britain, as a neutral country (and with strict observance both of the law of nations and the municipal law of Great Britain), vessels which were subsequently armed and commissioned as vessels of war, after they had been far removed from English waters, the British Government, in violation of its own laws and in deference to the importunate demands of the United States, made an ineffectual attempt to seize one vessel, and did actually seize and detain another which touched at the island of Nassau on her way to a Confederate port, and subjected her to an unfounded prosecution at the very time when cargoes of munitions of war were being openly shipped from British ports to New York, to be used in warfare against us. Even now the public journals bring intelligence that the British Government has ordered the seizure in a British port of two vessels, on the suspicion that they may have been sold to this Government and may be hereafter armed and equipped in our service, while British subjects are engaged in Ireland by tens of thousands to proceed to the United States for warfare against the Confederacy, in defiance both of the law of nations and of the express terms of the British statutes, and are transported in British ships, without an effort at concealment, to the ports of the United States, there to be armed with rifles imported from Great Britain and to be employed against our people in a war for conquest. No royal prerogative is invoked, no executive interference is interposed against this flagrant breach of municipal and international law on the part of our enemies, while strained constructions are placed on existing statutes, new enactments proposed, and questionable expedients devised for precluding the possibility of purchase by this Government of vessels that are useless for belligerent purposes, unless hereafter armed and equipped outside of the neutral jurisdiction of Great Britain.

For nearly three years this Government has exercised unquestioned jurisdiction over many millions of willing and united people. It has met and defeated vast armies of invaders, who have in vain sought its subversion. Supported by the confidence and affection of its citizens, the Confederacy has lacked no element which distinguishes an independent nation according to the principles of public law. Its legislative, executive, and judicial Departments, each in its sphere, have performed their appropriate functions with a regularity as undisturbed as in a time of profound peace, and the whole energies of the people have been developed in the organization of vast armies, while their rights and liberties have rested secure under the protection of courts of justice. This Confederacy is either independent or it is a dependency of the United States; for no other earthly power claims the right to govern it. Without one historic fact on which the pretension can rest, without one line or word of treaty or covenant which can give color to title, the United States have asserted, and the British Government has chosen to concede, that these sovereign States are dependencies of the Government which is administered at Washington. Great Britain has accordingly entertained with that Government the closest and most intimate relations, while refusing, on its demands, ordinary amicable intercourse with us, and has, under arrangements made with the other nations of Europe, not only denied our just claim of admission into the family of nations, but interposed a passive though effectual bar to the knowledge of our rights by other powers. So soon as it had become apparent by the declarations of the British Ministers in the debates of the British Parliament in July last that Her Majesty's Government was determined to persist indefinitely in a course of policy which under professions of neutrality had become subservient to the designs of our enemy, I felt it my duty to recall the Commissioner formerly accredited to that Court, and the correspondence on the subject is submitted to you.

It is due to you and to our country that this full statement should be made of the just grounds which exist for dissatisfaction with the conduct of the British Government. I am well aware that we are unfortunately without adequate remedy for the injustice under which we have suffered at the hands of a powerful nation, at a juncture when our entire resources are absorbed in the defense of our lives, liberties, and independence, against an enemy possessed of greatly superior numbers and material resources. Claiming no favor, desiring no aid, conscious of our own ability to defend our own rights against the utmost efforts of an infuriate foe, we had thought it not extravagant to expect that assistance would be withheld from our enemies, and that the conduct of foreign nations would be marked by a genuine impartiality between the belligerents. It was not supposed that a professed neutrality would be so conducted as to justify the Foreign Secretary of the British nation in explaining, in correspondence with our enemies, how "the impartial observance of neutral obligations by Her Majesty's Government has thus been exceedingly advantageous to the cause of the more powerful of the two contending parties." The British Government may deem this war a favorable occasion for establishing, by the temporary sacrifice of their neutral rights, a precedent which will justify the future exercise of those extreme belligerent pretensions that their naval power renders so formidable. The opportunity for obtaining the tacit assent of European governments to a line of conduct which ignores the obligations of the declaration of Paris, and treats that instrument rather as a theoretical exposition of principle than a binding agreement, may be considered by the British ministry as justifying them in seeking a great advantage for their own country at the expense of ours. But we cannot permit, without protest, the assertion that international law or morals regard as "impartial neutrality" the conduct avowed to be "exceedingly advantageous" to one of the belligerents.

I have stated that we are without adequate remedy against the injustice under which we suffer. There are but two measures that seem applicable to the present condition of our relations with neutral powers. One is to imitate the wrong of which we complain, to retaliate by the declaration of a paper blockade of the coast of the United States, and to capture all neutral vessels trading with their ports that our cruisers can intercept on the high seas. This measure I cannot recommend. It is true that in so doing we should but follow the precedents set by Great Britain and France in the Berlin and Milan decrees, and the British orders in council at the beginning of the present century. But it must be remembered that we ourselves protested against those very measures as signal violations of the law of nations, and declared the attempts to excuse them on the ground of their being retaliatory utterly insufficient. Those blockades are now quoted by writers on public law as a standing reproach on the good name of the nations who were betrayed by temporary exasperation into wrongdoing, and ought to be regarded rather as errors to be avoided than as examples to be followed.

The other measure is not open to this objection. The second article of the declaration of Paris, which provides "that the neutral flag covers enemy's goods, with the exception of contraband of war," was a new concession by belligerents in favor of neutrals, and not simply the enunciation of an acknowledged preëxisting rule like the fourth article, which referred to blockades. To this concession we bound ourselves by the convention with Great Britain and France, which took the shape of the resolutions adopted by your predecessors on the 13th of August, 1861. The consideration tendered us for that concession has been withheld. We have therefore the undeniable right to refuse longer to remain bound by a compact which the other party refuses to fulfill. But we should not forget that war is but temporary, and that we desire that peace shall be permanent. The future policy of the Confederacy must ever be to uphold neutral rights to their full extent. The principles of the declaration of Paris commend themselves to our judgment as more just, more humane, and more consonant with modern civilization than those belligerent pretensions which great naval powers have heretofore sought to introduce into the maritime code. To forego our undeniable right to the exercise of those pretensions is a policy higher, worthier of us and our cause, than to revoke our adherence to principles that we approve. Let our hope for redress rest rather on a returning sense of justice which cannot fail to awaken a great people to the consciousness that the war in which we are engaged ought rather to be made a reason for forbearance of advantage than an occasion for the unfriendly conduct of which we make just complaint.

The events of the last year have produced important changes in the condition of our Southern neighbor. The occupation of the capital of Mexico by the French army, and the establishment of a provisional government, followed by a radical change in the constitution of the country, have excited lively interest. Although preferring our own Government and institutions to those of other countries, we can have no disposition to contest the exercise by them of the same right of self-government which we assert for ourselves. If the Mexican people prefer a monarchy to a republic, it is our plain duty cheerfully to acquiesce in their decision and to evince a sincere and friendly interest in their prosperity. If, however, the Mexicans prefer maintaining their former institutions, we have no reason to apprehend any obstacle to the free exercise of their choice. The Emperor of the French has solemnly disclaimed any purpose to impose on Mexico a form of government not acceptable to the nation; and the eminent personage to whom the throne has been tendered declines its acceptance unless the offer be sanctioned by the suffrages of the people. In either event, therefore, we may confidently expect the continuance of those peaceful relations which have been maintained on the frontier, and even a large development of the commerce already existing to the mutual advantage of the two countries.

It has been found necessary since your adjournment to take action on the subject of certain foreign Consuls within the Confederacy. The nature of this action and the reasons on which it was based are so fully exhibited in the correspondence of the State Department, which is transmitted to you, that no additional comment is required.

In connection with this subject of our relations with foreign countries, it is deemed opportune to communicate my views in reference to the treaties made by the Government of the United States at a date anterior to our separation, and which were consequently binding on us as well as on foreign powers when the separation took effect. It was partly with a view to entering into such arrangements as the change in our Government had made necessary that we felt it our duty to send commissioners abroad for the purpose of entering into the negotiations proper to fix the relative rights and obligations of the parties to those treaties. As this tender on our part has been declined, as foreign nations have refused us the benefit of the treaties to which we were parties, they certainly have ceased to be binding on us, and in my opinion our relations with European nations are therefore now controlled exclusively by the general rules of the law of nations. It is proper to add that these remarks are intended to apply solely to treaty obligations toward foreign governments, and have no reference to rights of individuals.

FINANCES.

The state of the public finances is such as to demand your earliest and most earnest attention. I need hardly say that a prompt and efficacious remedy for the present condition of the currency is necessary for the successful performance of the functions of government. Fortunately the resources of our country are so ample and the spirit of our people so devoted to its cause that they are ready to make any necessary contribution. Relief is thus entirely within our reach if we have the wisdom to legislate in such manner as to render available the means at our disposal.

At the commencement of the war we were far from anticipating the magnitude and duration of the struggle in which we were engaged. The most sagacious foresight could not have predicted that the passions of the Northern people would lead them blindly to the sacrifice of life, treasure, and liberty in so vain a hope as that of subjugating thirteen independent States inhabited by many millions of people whose birthright of freedom is dearer to them than life. A long exemption from direct taxation by the General Government had created an aversion to its raising revenue by any other means than by duties on imports, and it was supposed that these duties would be ample for current peace expenditure, while the means for conducting the war could be raised almost exclusively by the use of the public credit.

The first action of the Provisional Congress was therefore confined to passing a tariff law, and to raising a sum of $15,000,000 by loan, with a pledge of a small export duty on cotton to provide for the redemption of the debt. At its second session war was declared to exist between the Confederacy and the United States, and provision was made for the issue of $20,000,000 in Treasury notes, and for borrowing $30,000,000 on bonds. The tariff was revised and preparatory measures taken to enable Congress to levy internal taxation at its succeeding session. These laws were passed in May, and the States of Virginia, North Carolina, Tennessee, and Arkansas having joined the Confederacy, the Congress adjourned to meet in the city of Richmond in the following month of July.

Prior to the assembling of your predecessors in Richmond at their third session, near the end of July, 1861, the President of the

United States had developed in his message the purpose "to make the contest a short and a decisive one," and had called on Congress for 400,000 men and $400,000,000. The Congress had exceeded the Executive recommendation, and had authorized the levy of half a million of volunteers, besides largely increasing the regular land and naval forces of the United States. The necessity thus first became urgent that a financial scheme should be devised on a basis sufficiently large for the vast proportions of the contest with which we were threatened. Knowing that the struggle, instead of being "short and decisive," would be indefinite in duration, and could end only when the United States should awaken from their delusion of conquest, a permanent system was required fully adapted to the great exigencies before us.

The plan devised by Congress at that time was based on the theory of issuing Treasury notes convertible at the pleasure of the holder into 8 per cent bonds, the interest of which was to be payable in coin, and it was correctly assumed that any tendency to depreciation that might arise from overissue of the currency would be checked by the constant exercise of the holder's right to fund the notes at a liberal interest, payable in specie. This system depended for success on the continued ability of the Government to pay the interest in specie, and means were therefore provided for that purpose in the law authorizing the issues. An internal tax, termed a war tax, was levied, the proceeds of which, together with the revenue from imports, were deemed sufficient for the object designed. This scheme required for its operation that our commerce with foreign nations should not be suspended. It was not to be anticipated that such suspension would be permitted otherwise than by an effective blockade; and it was absurd to suppose that a blockade "sufficient really to prevent access" to our entire coast could be maintained.

We had the means, therefore (if neutral nations had not combined to aid our enemies by the sanction of an illegal prohibition on their commerce), to secure the receipt into the Treasury of coin sufficient to pay the interest on the bonds, and thus maintain the Treasury notes at rates nearly equal to par in specie. So long as the interest continued to be thus paid with the reserve of coin preexisting in our country, experience sustained the expectations of those who devised the system. Thus, on the 1st of the following

December coin had reached a premium of only about 20 per cent, although it had already become apparent that the commerce of the country was threatened with permanent suspension by reason of the conduct of neutral nations, and that the necessary result must be the exhaustion of our specie reserve. Wheat, in the beginning of the year 1862, was selling at $1.30 per bushel, not exceeding, therefore, its average price in time of peace. The other agricultural products of the country were at similar moderate rates, thus indicating that there was no excess of circulation, and that the rate of premium on specie was heightened by the exceptional causes which tended to its exhaustion without the possibility of renewing the supply.

This review of the policy of your predecessors is given in justice to them, and it exhibits the condition of the finances at the date when the permanent Government was organized.

In the meantime the popular aversion to internal taxation by the General Government had influenced the legislation of the several States, and in only three of them, South Carolina, Mississippi, and Texas, were the taxes actually collected from the people. The quotas devolving upon the remaining States had been raised by the issue of bonds and State Treasury notes, and the public debt of the country was thus actually increased instead of being diminished by the taxation imposed by Congress.

Neither at the first nor second session of the present Congress were means provided by taxation for maintaining the Government, the legislation being confined to authorizing further sales of bonds and issues of Treasury notes. Although repeated efforts were made to frame a proper system of taxation, you were confronted with an obstacle which did not exist for your predecessors, and which created grave embarrassment in devising any scheme of taxation. About two-thirds of the entire taxable property of the Confederate States consists of lands and slaves. The general power of taxation vested in Congress by the Provisional Constitution (which was to be only temporary in its operation) was not restricted by any other condition than that "all duties, imposts, and excises should be uniform throughout the States of the Confederacy." But the permanent Constitution, sanctioning the principle that taxation and representation ought to rest on the same basis, specially provides that "representatives and direct taxes shall be apportioned among the several States according to their respective numbers, which shall be determined by adding to the whole number of free persons, including those bound to service for a term of years, and excluding Indians not taxed, three-fifths of all slaves."

It was further ordered that a census should be made within three years after the first meeting of Congress, and that "no capitation or other direct tax shall be laid unless in proportion to the census or enumeration hereinbefore directed to be taken."

It is plain that under these provisions capitation and direct taxes must be levied in proportion to the census when made. It is also plain that the duty is imposed on Congress to provide for making a census prior to the 22d of February, 1865. It may further be stated that according to the received construction of the Constitution of the United States (a construction acquiesced in for upward of sixty years) taxes on lands and slaves are direct taxes, and the conclusion seems necessarily to be that, in repeating without modification in our Constitution this language of the Constitution of 1787, our convention intended to attach to it the meaning which had been sanctioned by long and uninterrupted acquiescence.

So long as there seemed to be a probability of being able to carry out these provisions of the Constitution in their entirety and in conformity with the intentions of its authors there was an obvious difficulty in framing any system of taxation. A law which should exempt from the burden two-thirds of the property of the country would be as unfair to the owners of the remaining third as it would be inadequate to meet the requirements of the public service.

The urgency of the need was such, however, that after very great embarrassment and more than three months of assiduous labor you succeeded in framing the law of the 24th April, 1863, by which you sought to reach, so far as was practicable, every resource of the country except the capital invested in real estate and slaves, and by means of an income tax and a tax in kind on the produce of the soil, as well as by licenses on business occupations and professions, to command resources sufficient for the wants of the country. But a very large proportion of these resources could be made available only at the close of the present and the commencement of the ensuing year, while the intervening exigencies permitted no delay. In this state of affairs, superinduced almost unavoidably by the fortunes of the war in which we are engaged, the issues of Treasury notes have been increased until the currency in circulation amounts to more than $600,000,000, or more than threefold the amount required by the business of the country.

I need not enlarge upon the evil effects of this condition of things. They are unfortunately but too apparent. In addition to the difficulty presented to the necessary operations of the Government and the efficient conduct of the war, the most deplorable of all its results is undoubtedly its corrupting influence on the morals of the people. The possession of large amounts of Treasury notes has naturally led to a desire for investment, and with a constantly increasing volume of currency there has been an equally constant increase of price in all objects of investment. This effect has stimulated purchase by the apparent certainty of profit, and a spirit of speculation has thus been fostered which has so debasing an influence and such ruinous consequences that it is our highest duty to remove the cause, and no measures directed to that end can be too prompt or too stringent.

Reverting to the constitutional provisions already cited, the question recurs whether it be possible to execute the duty of apportioning taxation in accordance with the census ordered to be made as a basis. So long as this appeared to be practicable, none can deny the propriety of your course in abstaining from the imposition of direct taxes till you could exercise the power in the precise mode pointed out by the terms of the fundamental law. But it is obvious that there are many duties imposed by the Constitution which depend for their fulfillment on the undisturbed possession of the territory within which they are to be performed. The same instrument which orders a census to be made in all the States imposes the duty on the Confederacy "to guarantee to every State a republican form of government." It enjoins on us "to protect each State from invasion;" and while declaring that its great objects and purposes are "to establish justice, insure domestic tranquillity, and secure the blessings of liberty to ourselves and our posterity," it confers the means and thereby imposes on us the paramount duty of effecting its intent by "laying and collecting taxes, imposts, and excises necessary to pay the debts, provide for the common defense, and carry on the Government of the Confederate States."

None would pretend that the Constitution is violated because, by reason of the presence of hostile armies, we are unable to guarantee a republican form of government to these States or portions of States now temporarily held by the enemy, and as little justice would there be in imputing blame for the failure to make the census when that failure is attributable to causes not foreseen by the authors of the Constitution and beyond our control. The general intent of our constitutional charter is unquestionably that the property of the country is to be taxed in order to raise revenue for the common defense, and the special mode provided for levying this tax is impracticable from unforeseen causes. It is in my judgment our primary duty to execute the general intent expressed by the terms of the instrument which we have sworn to obey, and we cannot excuse ourselves for the failure to fulfill this obligation on the ground that we are unable to perform it in the precise mode pointed out. Whenever it shall be possible to execute our duty in all its parts we must do so in exact compliance with the whole letter and spirit of the Constitution. Until that period shall arrive we must execute so much of it as our condition renders practicable. Whenever the withdrawal of the enemy shall place it in our power to make a census and apportionment of direct taxes, any other mode of levying them will be contrary to the will of the lawgiver, and incompatible with our obligation to obey that will; until that period, the alternative left is to obey the paramount precept and to execute it according to the only other rule provided, which is to "make the tax uniform throughout the Confederate States."

The considerations just presented are greatly enforced by the reflection that any attempt to apportion taxes amongst States, some of which are wholly or partially in the occupation of hostile forces, would subvert the whole intention of the framers of the Constitution, and be productive of the most revolting injustice instead of that just correlation between taxation and representation which it was their purpose to secure. With large portions of some of the States occupied by the enemy, what justice would there be in imposing on the remainder the whole amount of the taxation of the entire State in proportion to its representation?

What else would this be in effect than to increase the burthen of those who are the heaviest sufferers by the war, and to make our own inability to protect them from invasion, as we are required to do by the Constitution, the ground for adding to their losses by an attempted adherence to the letter, in violation of the spirit of that instrument? No such purpose could have been entertained and no such result contemplated by the framers of the Constitution. It may add weight to these considerations if we reflect that, although the Constitution provided that it should go into operation with a representation temporarily distributed among the States, it expressly ordains, after providing for a census within three years, that this temporary distribution of representative power is to endure "until *such* enumeration shall be made." Would any one argue that because the census cannot be made within the fixed period the Government must at the expiration of that period perish for want of a representative body? In any aspect in which the subject can be viewed I am led to the conclusion already announced, and which is understood to be in accordance with a vote taken in one or both Houses at your last session. I shall, therefore, until we are able to pursue the precise mode required by the Constitution, deem it my duty to approve any law levying the taxation which you are bound to impose for the defense of the country in any other practicable mode which shall distribute the burthen uniformly and impartially on the whole property of the people.

In your former legislation you have sought to avoid the increase in the volume of notes in circulation by offering inducements to voluntary funding. The measures adopted for that purpose have been but partially successful, and the evil has now reached such a magnitude as to permit no other remedy than the compulsory reduction of the currency to the amount required by the business of the country. This reduction should be accompanied by a pledge that under no stress of circumstances will that amount be exceeded. No possible mode of using the credit of the Government can be so disastrous as one which disturbs the basis of all exchanges, renders impossible all calculations of future values, augments, in constantly increasing proportions, the price of all commodities, and so depreciates all fixed wages, salaries, and incomes as to render them inadequate to bare subsistence. If to these be added the still more fatal influence on the morals and character öf the people, to which I have already adverted, I am persuaded you will concur in the conclusion that an inflexible adherence to a limitation of the currency at a fixed sum is an indispensable element of any system of finance now to be adopted.

The holders of the currency now outstanding can be protected in the recovery of their just claims only by substituting for their notes some other security. If the currency is not greatly and promptly reduced, the present scale of inflated prices will not only continue to exist, but by the very fact of the large amounts thus made requisite in the conduct of the war those prices will reach rates still more extravagant, and the whole system will fall under its own weight, thus rendering the redemption of the debt impossible, and destroying its whole value in the hands of the holder. If, on the contrary, a funded debt, with interest secured by adequate taxation, can be substituted for the outstanding currency, its entire amount will be made available to the holder, and the Government will be in a condition enabling it, beyond the reach of any probable contingency, to prosecute the war to a successful issue. It is therefore demanded, as well by the interest of the creditor as of the country at large, that the evidences of the public debt now outstanding in the shape of Treasury notes be converted into bonds bearing adequate interest, with a provision for taxation sufficient to insure punctual payment and final redemption of the whole debt.

The report of the Secretary of the Treasury presents the outlines of a system which, in conjunction with existing legislation, is intended to secure the several objects of a reduction of the circulation within fixed, reasonable limits; of providing for the future wants of the Government; of furnishing security for the punctual payment of interest and final extinction of the principal of the public debt, and of placing the whole business of the country on a basis as near a specie standard as is possible during the continuance of the war. I earnestly recommend it to your consideration, and that no delay be permitted to intervene before your action on this vital subject. I trust that it will be suffered to engross your attention until you shall have disposed of it in the manner best adapted to attain the important results which your country anticipates from your legislation.

It may be added that in considering this subject the people ought steadily to keep in view that the Government in contracting debt is but their agent; that its debt is their debt. As the currency is held exclusively by ourselves, it is obvious that, if each person held Treasury notes in exact proportion to the value of his means, each would in fact owe himself the amount of the notes held by him; and were it possible to distribute the currency among the people in this exact proportion, a tax levied on the currency alone to the amount sufficient to reduce it to proper limits would afford the best of all remedies. Under such circumstances the notes remaining in the hands of each holder after the payment of his tax would be worth quite as much as the whole sum previously held, for it would purchase at least an equal amount of commodities. This result cannot be perfectly attained by any device of legislation, but it can be approximated by taxation. A tax on all values has for its effect not only to impose a due share of the burden on the note holder, but to force those who have few or none of the notes to part with a share of their possessions to those who hold the notes in excess in order to obtain the means of satisfying the demands of the taxgatherer. This is the only mode by which it is practicable to make all contribute as equally as possible in the burden which all are bound to share, and it is for this reason that taxation adequate to the public exigencies, under our present circumstances, must be the basis of any funding system or other remedy for restoring stability to our finances.

THE ARMY.

To the report of the Secretary of War you are referred for details relative to the condition of the Army and the measures of legislation required for maintaining its efficiency, recruiting its numbers, and furnishing the supplies necessary for its support.

Though we have lost many of the best of our soldiers and most patriotic of our citizens (the sad but unavoidable result of the battles and toils of such a campaign as that which will render the year 1863 ever memorable in our annals), the Army is believed to be in all respects in better condition than at any previous period of the war. Our gallant defenders, now veterans, familiar with danger, hardened by exposure, and confident in themselves and their officers, endure privations with cheerful fortitude and welcome battle with alacrity. The officers, by experience in field service and the action of examining boards in relieving the incompetent, are now greatly more efficient than at the commencement of the war. The assertion is believed to be fully justified that, regarded as a whole, for character, valor, efficiency, and patriotic devotion, our Army has not been equaled by any like number of troops in the history of war.

In view of the large conscription recently ordered by the enemy and their subsequent call for volunteers, to be followed if ineffectual by a still further draft, we are admonished that no effort must be spared to add largely to our effective force as promptly as possible. The sources of supply are to be found by restoring to the Army all who are improperly absent, putting an end to substitution, modifying the exemption law, restricting details, and placing in the ranks such of the able-bodied men now employed as wagoners, nurses, cooks, and other employees as are doing service for which the negroes may be found competent.

The act of 16th of April, 1862, provides "that persons not liable for duty may be received as substitutes for those who are, under such regulations as may be prescribed by the Secretary of War." The policy of granting this privilege has not been sustained by experience. Not only has the numerical strength of the Army been seriously impaired by the frequent desertions for which substitutes have become notorious, but dissatisfaction has been excited among those who have been unable or unwilling to avail themselves of the opportunity thus afforded of avoiding the military service of their country.

I fully concur in the opinion expressed by the Secretary that there is no ground for the objection that a new provision to include those who furnished substitutes under the former call would be a breach of contract. To accept a substitute was to confer a privilege, not to enter into a contract, and whenever the substitute is rendered liable to conscription, it would seem to follow that the principal, whose place he had taken, should respond for him, as the Government had received no consideration for his exemption. Where, however, the new provision of law would fail to embrace a substitute now in the ranks, there appears, if the principal should again be conscribed, to be an equitable ground for compensation to the conscript, who then would have added to the service a soldier not otherwise liable to enrollment.

On the subject of exemptions, it is believed that abuses cannot be checked unless the system is placed on a basis entirely different from that now provided by law. The object of your legislation has been not to confer privileges on classes, but to exonerate from military duty such number of persons skilled in the various trades, professions, and mechanical pursuits as could render more valuable service to their country by laboring in their present occupation than by going into the ranks of the Army. The policy is unquestionable, but the result would, it is thought, be better obtained by enrolling all such persons and allowing details to be made of the number necessary to meet the wants of the country. Considerable numbers are believed to be now exempted from the military service who are not needful to the public in their civil vocation.

Certain duties are now performed throughout the country by details from the Army which could be as well executed by persons above the present conscript age. An extension of the limit so as to embrace persons over forty-five years and physically fit for service in guarding posts, railroads, and bridges, in apprehending deserters, and, where practicable, assuming the place of younger men detailed for duty with the Niter, Ordnance, Commissary, and Quartermaster's Bureaus of the War Department, would, it is hoped, add largely to the effective force in the field without an undue burden on the population.

If to the above measures be added a law to enlarge the policy of the act of the 21st of April, 1862, so as to enable the Department to replace not only enlisted cooks, but wagoners and other employees in the Army, by negroes, it is hoped that the ranks of the Army will be so strengthened for the ensuing campaign as to put to defiance the utmost efforts of the enemy.

In order to maintain unimpaired the existing organization of the Army until the close of the war, your legislation contemplated a frequent supply of recruits, and it was expected that before the expiration of the three years for which the men were enrolled under act of 16th of April, 1862, the majority of men in each company would consist of those who joined it at different dates subsequent to the original muster of the company into service, and that the discharge of those who had completed their term would at no time be sufficient to leave the company with a less number than is required to enable it to retain its organization. The difficulty of obtaining recruits from certain localities and the large number of exemptions from military service granted by different laws have prevented sufficient accessions in many of the companies to preserve their organizations after the discharge of the original members. The advantage of retaining tried and well-approved officers and of mingling recruits with experienced soldiers is so obvious and the policy of such a course is so clearly indicated that it is not deemed necessary to point out the evil consequences which would result from the destruction of the old organizations, or to dwell upon the benefits to be secured from filling up the veteran companies as long before the discharge of the earlier members as may be possible. In the cases where it may be found impracticable to maintain regiments in sufficient strength as to justify the retention of the present organization, economy and efficiency would be promoted by consolidation and reorganization. This would involve the necessity of disbanding a part of the officers and making regulations for securing the most judicious selection of those who are retained, while least wounding the feelings of those who are discharged.

Experience has shown the necessity for further legislation in relation to the horses of the cavalry. Many men lose their horses by casualties of service which are not included in the provisions made to compensate the owner for the loss, and it may thus not unfrequently happen that the most efficient troopers, without fault of their own—indeed, it may be because of their zeal and activity—are lost to the cavalry service.

It would also seem proper that the Government should have complete control over every horse mustered into service, with the limitation that the owner should not be deprived of his horse except upon due compensation being made therefor. Otherwise mounted men may not keep horses fit for the service, and the question whether they should serve mounted or on foot would depend not upon the qualifications of the men, but upon the fact of their having horses.

Some provision is deemed requisite to correct the evils arising from the long-continued absence of commissioned officers. Where it is without sufficient cause, it would seem but just that the commission should be thereby vacated. Where it results from capture by the enemy, which under their barbarous refusal to exchange prisoners of war may be regarded as absence for an indefinite time, there is a necessity to supply their places in their respective commands. This might be done by temporary appointments to endure only until the return of the officers regularly commissioned. Where it results from permanent disability incurred in the line of their duty, it would be proper to retire them and fill the vacancies according to established mode. I would also suggest the organization of an invalid corps, and that the retired officers be transferred to it. Such a corps, it is thought, could be made useful in various employments for which efficient officers and troops are now detached.

An organization of the general staff of the Army would be highly conducive to the efficiency of that most important branch of the service. The plan adopted for the military establishment furnishes a model for the staff of the Provisional Army, if it be deemed advisable to retain the distinction; but I recommend to your consideration the propriety of abolishing it and providing for the organization of the several staff corps in such number and with such rank as will meet all the wants of the service. To secure the requisite ability for the more important positions, it will be necessary to provide for officers of higher rank than is now authorized for these corps. To give to officers the proper relation and cointelligence in their respective corps, and to preserve in the chief of each the influence and control over his subordinates, there should be no gradation on the basis of the rank of the general with whom they might be serving by appointment. To the personal staff of a general it would seem proper to give a grade corresponding with his rank, and the number might be fixed to correspond with his command. To avoid the consequence of discharge upon a change of duty the variable portion of the personal staff might be taken from the line of the Army and allowed to retain their line commissions.

The disordered condition of the currency, to which I have already alluded, has imposed on the Government a system of supplying the wants of the Army which is so unequal in its operation, vexatious to the producer, injurious to the industrial interest, and productive of such discontent among the people as only to be justified by the existence of an absolute necessity. The report of the Secretary on this point establishes conclusively that the necessity which has forced the bureaus of supply to provide for the Army by impressment has resulted from the impossibility of purchase by contract or in the open market, except at such rapidly increased rates as would have rendered the appropriations inadequate to the wants of the Army. Indeed, it is believed that the temptation to hoard supplies for the higher prices which could be anticipated with certainty has been checked mainly by fear of the operation of the impressment law, and that commodities have been offered in the markets principally to escape impressment and obtain higher rates than those fixed by appraisement. The complaints against this vicious system have been well founded, but the true cause of the evil has been misapprehended. The remedy is to be found not in a change of the impressment law, but in the restoration of the currency to such a basis as will enable the Department to purchase necessary supplies in the open market, and thus render impressment a rare and exceptionable process.

The same remedy will effect the result, universally desired, of an augmentation of the pay of the Army. The proposals made at your previous sessions to increase the pay of the soldier by an additional amount of Treasury notes would have conferred little benefit on him, but a radical reform of the currency will restore the pay to a value approximating that which it originally had, and materially improve his condition.

The reports from the Ordnance and Mining Bureaus are very gratifying, and the extension of our means of supply of arms and munitions of war from our home resources has been such as to insure our ability soon to become mainly, if not entirely, independent of supplies from foreign countries. The establishments for the casting of guns and projectiles, for the manufacture of small arms and of gunpowder, for the supply of niter from artificial niter beds, and mining operations generally, have been so distributed through the country as to place our resources beyond the reach of partial disasters.

The recommendations of the Secretary of War on other points are minutely detailed in his report, which is submitted to you, and, extending as they do to almost every branch of the service, merit careful consideration.

EXCHANGE OF PRISONERS.

I regret to inform you that the enemy has returned to the barbarous policy with which they inaugurated the war, and that the exchange of prisoners has been for some time suspended.* The correspondence of the commissioners of exchange is submitted to you by the Secretary of War, and it has already been published for the information of all now suffering useless imprisonment. The conduct of the authorities of the United States has been consistently perfidious on this subject. An agreement for exchange in the incipiency of the war had just been concluded when the fall of Fort Donelson reversed the previous state of things and gave them an excess of prisoners. This agreement was immediately repudiated by them, and so remained until the fortune of war again placed us in possession of the larger number. A new cartel was then made; and under it, for many months, we restored to them many thousands of prisoners in excess of those whom they held for exchange, and encampments of the surplus paroled prisoners delivered up by us were established in the United States, where the men were able to receive the comforts and solace of constant communication with their homes and families. In July last the fortune of war again favored the enemy, and they were enabled to exchange for duty the men previously delivered to them against those captured and paroled at Vicksburg and Port Hudson. The prisoners taken at Gettysburg, however, remained in their hands, and should have been at once returned to our lines on parole, to await exchange. Instead of executing a duty imposed by the plainest dictates of justice and good faith, pretexts were instantly sought for holding them in permanent captivity. General orders rapidly succeeded each other from the bureaus at Washington, placing new constructions on an agreement which had given rise to no dispute while we retained the advantage in the number of prisoners. With a disregard of honorable obligations almost unexampled, the enemy did not hesitate, in addition to retaining the prisoners captured by them, to de-

---

*See page 339 for correspondence which resulted in the appointment of Vice President Stephens as military commissioner to United States for purpose of settling differences arising in the execution of the cartel for exchange of prisoners of war.

clare null the paroles given by the prisoners captured by us in the same series of engagements and liberated on condition of not again serving until exchanged. They have since openly insisted on treating the paroles given by their own soldiers as invalid, and those of our soldiers, given under precisely similar circumstances, as binding. A succession of similar unjust pretensions has been set up in a correspondence tediously prolonged, and every device employed to cover the disregard of an obligation which, between belligerent nations, is to be enforced only by a sense of honor.

No further comment is needed on this subject, but it may be permitted to direct your special attention to the close of the correspondence submitted to you, from which you will perceive that the final proposal made by the enemy, in settlement of all disputes under the cartel, is that we should liberate all prisoners held by us without the offer to release from captivity any of those held by them.

In the meantime a systematic and concerted effort has been made to quiet the complaints in the United States of those relatives and friends of the prisoners in our hands, who are unable to understand why the cartel is not executed in their favor, by the groundless assertion that we are the parties who refuse compliance. Attempts are also made to shield themselves from the execration excited by their own odious treatment of our officers and soldiers, now captive in their hands, by misstatements, such as that the prisoners held by us are deprived of food. To this last accusation the conclusive answer has been made that, in accordance with our law and the general orders of the Department, the rations of the prisoners are precisely the same, in quantity and quality, as those served out to our own gallant soldiers in the field, and which have been found sufficient to support them in their arduous campaigns, while it is not pretended by the enemy that they treat prisoners by the same generous rule. By an indulgence, perhaps unprecedented, we have even allowed the prisoners in our hands to be supplied by their friends at home with comforts not enjoyed by the men who captured them in battle. In contrast to this treatment the most revolting inhumanity has characterized the conduct of the United States toward prisoners held by them. One prominent fact, which admits no denial or palliation, must suffice as a test. The officers of our Army, natives of southern and semitropical climates, and unprepared for the cold of a northern winter, have been conveyed for imprisonment during the rigors of the present season to the most northern and exposed situation that could be selected by the enemy. There, beyond the reach of comforts, and often even of news from home and family, exposed to the piercing cold of the northern lakes, they are held by men who cannot be ignorant of, even if they do not design, the probable result. How many of our unfortunate friends and comrades, who have passed unscathed through numerous battles, will perish on Johnson's Island, under the cruel trial to which they are subjected, none but the Omniscient can foretell. That they will endure this barbarous treatment with the same stern fortitude that they have ever evinced in their country's service, we cannot doubt. But who can be found to believe the assertion that it is our refusal to execute the cartel, and not the malignity of the foe, which has caused the infliction of such intolerable cruelty on our loved and honored defenders?

TRANS-MISSISSIPPI DEPARTMENT.

Regular and punctual communication with the Trans-Mississippi is so obstructed as to render difficult a compliance with much of the legislation vesting authority in the Executive branch of the Government. To supply vacancies in office; to exercise discretion on certain matters connected with the military organizations; to control the distribution of the funds collected from taxation or remitted from the Treasury; to carry on the operations of the Post Office Department, and other like duties, require, under the Constitution and existing laws, the action of the President and Heads of Departments. The necessities of the military service frequently forbid delay, and some legislation is required providing for the exercise of temporary authority until regular action can be had at the seat of government. I would suggest, especially in the Post Office Department, that an assistant be provided for the States beyond the Mississippi, with authority in the Head of that Department to vest in this assistant all such powers now exercised by the Postmaster General as may be requisite for provisional control of the funds of the Department in those States and their application to the payment of mail contractors; for superintendents of the local post offices and the contracts for carrying the mail; for the temporary employment of proper persons to fulfill the duties of postmasters and contractors in urgent cases, until appointments can be made, and for other like purposes. Without some legislative provision on the subject, there is serious risk of the destruction of the mail service by reason of the delays and hardships suffered by contractors under the present system, which requires constant reference to Richmond of their accounts, as well as of the returns of the local postmasters, before they can receive payment for services rendered. Like provision is also necessary in the Treasury Department, while for military affairs it would seem to be sufficient to authorize the President and Secretary of War to delegate to the commanding general so much of the discretionary powers vested in them by law as the exigencies of the service shall require.

NAVY.

The report of the Secretary of the Navy gives in detail the operations of that Department since January last, embracing information of the disposition and employment of the vessels, officers, and men, and the construction of vessels at Richmond, Wilmington, Charleston, Savannah, Mobile, Selma, and on the rivers Roanoke, Neuse, Pedee, Chattahoochee, and Tombigbee; the accumulation of ship timber and supplies, and the manufacture of ordnance, ordnance stores, and equipments. The foundries and workshops have been greatly improved, and their capacity to supply all demands for heavy ordnance for coast and harbor defenses is limited only by our deficiency in the requisite skilled labor. The want of such labor and of seamen seriously affects the operations of the Department.

The skill, courage, and activity of our cruisers at sea cannot be too highly commended. They have inflicted heavy losses on the enemy without suffering a single disaster, and have seriously damaged the shipping interests of the United States by compelling their foreign commerce to seek the protection of neutral flags.

Your attention is invited to the suggestions of the report on the subject of supplying seamen for the service, and of the provisions of the law in relation to the Volunteer Navy.

POST OFFICE.

The Postmaster General reports the receipts of that Department for the fiscal year ending the 30th of June last to have been $3,-337,853.01, and the expenditures for the same period $2,662,804.-67. The statement thus exhibits an excess of receipts amounting to $675,048.34, instead of a deficiency of more than $1,000,000, as was the case in the preceding fiscal year. It is gratifying to perceive that the Department has thus been made self-sustaining in accordance with sound principle, and with the express requirement of the Constitution that its expenses should be paid out of its own revenues after the 1st of March, 1863.

The report gives a full and satisfactory account of the operations of the Post Office Department for the last year, and explains the measures adopted for giving more certainty and regularity to the service in the States beyond the Mississippi, and on which reliance is placed for obviating the difficulties heretofore encountered in that service.

The settlement of the accounts of the Department is greatly delayed by reason of the inability of the First Auditor to perform all the duties now imposed on him by law. The accounts of the Department of State, of the Treasury, of the Navy, and of Justice, are all supervised by that officer, and more than suffice to occupy his whole time. The necessity for a third auditor to examine and settle the accounts of a Department so extensive as that of the Post Office appears urgent, and his recommendation on that subject meets my concurrence.

CONDUCT OF ENEMY.

I cannot close this message without again adverting to the savage ferocity which still marks the conduct of the enemy in the prosecution of the war. After their repulse from the defenses before Charleston they first sought revenge by an abortive attempt to destroy the city with an incendiary composition thrown by improved artillery from a distance of four miles. Failing in this, they changed their missiles, but fortunately have thus far succeeded in killing only two women in the city. Their commanders, Butler, McNeil, and Turchin, whose terrible barbarities have made their names widely notorious and everywhere execrable, are still honored and cherished by the authorities at Washington. The first-named, after having been withdrawn from the scenes of his cruelties against women and prisoners of war, in reluctant concession to the demands of outraged humanity in Europe, has just been put in a new command at Norfolk, where helpless women and children are again placed at his mercy.

Nor has less unrelenting warfare been waged by these pretended friends of human rights and liberties against the unfortunate negroes. Wherever the enemy have been able to gain access they have forced into the ranks of their army every able-bodied man that they could seize, and have either left the aged, the women, and the children to perish by starvation, or have gathered them into camps where they have been wasted by a frightful mortality. Without clothing or shelter, often without food, incapable without supervision of taking the most ordinary precautions against disease, these helpless dependents, accustomed to have their wants supplied by the foresight of their masters, are being rapidly exterminated wherever brought in contact with the invaders. By the Northern man, on whose deep-rooted prejudices no kindly restraining influence is exercised, they are treated with aversion and neglect. There is little hazard in predicting that in all localities where the enemy have gained a temporary foothold the negroes, who under our care increased sixfold in number since their importation into the colonies by Great Britain, will have been reduced by mortality during the war to no more than one-half their previous number.

Information on this subject is derived not only from our own observation and from the reports of the negroes who succeed in escaping from the enemy, but full confirmation is afforded by statements published in the Northern journals by humane persons engaged in making appeals to the charitable for aid in preventing the ravages of disease, exposure, and starvation among the negro women and children who are crowded into encampments.

The frontier of our country bears witness to the alacrity and efficiency with which the general orders of the enemy have been executed in the devastation of farms, the destruction of the agricultural implements, the burning of the houses, and the plunder of everything movable. Its whole aspect is a comment on the ethics of the general order issued by the United States on the 24th of April, 1863, comprising "Instructions for the Government of Armies of the United States in the Field," and of which the following is an example:

Military necessity admits of all direct destruction of life or limb of *armed* enemies, and of other persons whose destruction is incidentally *unavoidable* in the armed contests of the war; it allows of the capturing of every armed enemy, and every enemy of importance to the hostile Government, or of peculiar danger to the captor; it allows of all destruction of property, and obstructions of the ways and channels of traffic, travel, or communication, and of all withholding of sustenance of means of life from the enemy; of the appropriation of whatever an enemy's country affords necessary for the subsistence and safety of the Army, and of such deception as does not involve the breaking of good faith, either positively pledged regarding agreements entered into during the war or supposed by the modern law of war to exist. Men who take up arms against one another in public war do not cease on this account to be moral beings, responsible to one another and to God.

The striking contrast to these teachings and practices presented by our army when invading Pennsylvania illustrates the moral character of our people. Though their forbearance may have been unmerited and unappreciated by the enemy, it was imposed by their own self-respect which forbade their degenerating from Christian warriors into plundering ruffians, assailing the property, lives, and honor of helpless noncombatants. If their conduct, when thus contrasted with the inhuman practices of our foe, fail to command the respect and sympathy of civilized nations in our day, it cannot fail to be recognized by their less deceived posterity.

The hope last year entertained of an early termination of the war has not been realized. Could carnage have satisfied the appetite of our enemy for the destruction of human life, or grief have appeased their wanton desire to inflict human suffering, there has been bloodshed enough on both sides, and two lands have been sufficiently darkened by the weeds of mourning to induce a disposition for peace.

If unanimity in a people could dispel delusion, it has been displayed too unmistakably not to have silenced the pretense that the Southern States were merely disturbed by a factious insurrection, and it must long since have been admitted that they were but exercising their reserved right to modify their own Government in such manner as would best secure their own happiness. But these considerations have been powerless to allay the unchristian hate of those who, long accustomed to draw large profits from a union with us, cannot control the rage excited by the conviction that they have by their own folly destroyed the richest sources of their prosperity. They refuse even to listen to proposals for the only peace possible between us—a peace which, recognizing the impassable gulf which divides us, may leave the two peoples separately to recover from the injuries inflicted on both by the causeless war now waged against us. Having begun the war in direct violation of their Constitution, which forbade the attempt to coerce a State, they have been hardened by crime until they no longer attempt to veil their purpose to destroy the institutions and subvert the sovereignty and independence of these States. We now know that the only reliable hope for peace is in the vigor of our resistance, while the cessation of their hostility is only to be expected from the pressure of their necessities.

The patriotism of the people has proved equal to every sacrifice demanded by their country's need. We have been united as a people never were united under like circumstances before. God has blessed us with success disproportionate to our means, and under his divine favor our labors must at last be crowned with the reward due to men who have given all they possessed to the righteous defense of their inalienable rights, their homes, and their altars.

JEFFERSON DAVIS.

RICHMOND, VA., December 9th, 1863.

To the Senate and House of Representatives.

I herewith transmit a communication from the Secretary of State, covering copies of his correspondence referred to in my message delivered yesterday; and I invite your attention to the reason he gives for withholding them until to-day.

JEFFERSON DAVIS.

RICHMOND, VA., Dec. 11, 1863.

To the Senate and House of Representatives.

I herewith transmit for your consideration a communication from the Secretary of the Treasury, covering estimates of sums needed for the public service among the Indian tribes.

I recommend an appropriation of the amount specified for the purpose indicated.

JEFFERSON DAVIS.

RICHMOND, VA., Dec. 15, 1863.

To the Senate of the Confederate States.

In response to your resolution of the 10th inst., asking to be furnished with "copies of the several reports of Major General

Whiting in relation to running the blockade of Wilmington, North Carolina," I herewith transmit a communication from the Secretary of War, covering copies of the reports referred to.

JEFFERSON DAVIS.

RICHMOND, VA., Dec. 16, 1863.

To the House of Representatives.

In response to your resolution of the 10th instant, I herewith transmit for your information a communication from the Secretary of War relative to the exemption of mail contractors "under the act of April 14, 1863," and to the action of the Department upon the subject.

JEFFERSON DAVIS.

RICHMOND, VA., Dec. 16, 1863.

To the Senate and House of Representatives.

I herewith transmit for your consideration a communication from the Attorney General *ad interim,* submitting additional estimates for the expenditures of the Department of Justice.

I recommend an appropriation of the amount specified for the purpose designated.

JEFFERSON DAVIS.

RICHMOND, VA., Dec. 16, 1863.

To the Senate and House of Representatives.*

I herewith transmit for your consideration, in secret session, a communication from the Secretary of the Treasury, covering a report in relation to foreign cotton loans.

I recommend the ratification by Congress of the accompanying contract† for a second foreign loan, and of the issue of the cotton certificates made for the use of the Navy Department.

JEFFERSON DAVIS.

RICHMOND, VA., Dec. 17, 1863.

To the House of Representatives.

In partial response to your resolution of the 11th instant, I herewith transmit a communication from the Secretary of War, cov-

---

*A duplicate of this message was transmitted to Congress later in the day, inclosing additional papers.

†With Emile Erlanger & Co., Paris.

ering a list of exempts in the States of Virginia, North Carolina, South Carolina, and Georgia.

Further information on this subject will be communicated when received.   JEFFERSON DAVIS.

RICHMOND, VA., Dec. 19, 1863.

To the Senate of the Confederate States.

I herewith transmit for your information a communication from the Secretary of War, covering copies of several reports of military operations.   JEFFERSON DAVIS.

[The same message was sent to the House of Representatives.]

RICHMOND, VA., Dec. 21, 1863.

To the Senate of the Confederate States.

In response to your resolution of the 10th instant, I herewith transmit for your information a communication from the Secretary of War relative to the Quartermaster General.

JEFFERSON DAVIS.

RICHMOND, VA., Dec. 22, 1863.

To the House of Representatives.

In response to your resolution of the 10th inst., I herewith transmit for your information a communication from the Secretary of War, covering "a list of the officers of artillery in the Provisional Army, for the performance of ordnance duty, appointed since the 16th day of September, 1862," and the "roll of merit" reported by the Board of Examiners.   JEFFERSON DAVIS.

RICHMOND, VA., Dec. 23, 1863.

To the Senate and House of Representatives.

I herewith transmit for your information a communication from the Secretary of War, covering "General Lee's report of the operations of the Army of Northern Virginia, from the date of his assumption of command to and including the battle of Fredericksburg, December 13, 1863," and the subordinate reports appertaining thereto.   JEFFERSON DAVIS.

RICHMOND, VA., December 28, 1863.

To the Senate of the Confederate States.

I herewith transmit a communication from the Secretary of State, covering a copy of that portion of his correspondence referred to in my message of the 7th instant, which has not been previously submitted. JEFFERSON DAVIS.

[The same message was sent to the House of Representatives.]

RICHMOND, VA., December 28, 1863.

To the Senate and House of Representatives.

I herewith transmit a communication from the Secretary of War, covering copies of additional reports of military operations of the year 1862 which should have accompanied the report of Gen. R. E. Lee, submitted for your information on the 24th [23d] instant. JEFFERSON DAVIS.

RICHMOND, VA., December 29, 1863.

To the House of Representatives.

In response to your resolution of the 11th inst., I herewith transmit for your information a communication from the Secretary of War, covering a copy of the report of Gen. J. E. Johnston of his operations in Mississippi during the months of May, June, and July, 1863, together with a copy of the report of Lieut. Gen. J. C. Pemberton of his operations during the same time.

JEFFERSON DAVIS.

RICHMOND, VA., December 31, 1863.

To the Senate of the Confederate States.

I herewith transmit for your information a communication from the Secretary of War, covering copies of several reports of military operations. JEFFERSON DAVIS.

[The same message was sent to the House of Representatives.]

RICHMOND, VA., Dec. 31st, 1863.

To the House of Representatives.

In response to your resolution of the 18th inst., I herewith transmit a communication from the Secretary of War, covering a copy of the report of Brig. Gen. Echols, relative to the battle of Droop Mountain. JEFFERSON DAVIS.

RICHMOND, VA., December 31, 1863.

To the House of Representatives.

In further response to your resolution of the 11th inst., I herewith transmit for your information a communication from the Secretary of War, covering copies of several reports of military operations. JEFFERSON DAVIS.

RICHMOND, VA., Jan. 7, 1864.

To the Senate and House of Representatives.

I herewith transmit for your consideration a communication from the Secretary of the Treasury, submitting an estimate of the amount "necessary for the payment of interest on the Removal and Subsistence Fund due the Cherokee Indians in North Carolina."

I recommend an appropriation of the sum specified for the purpose indicated. JEFFERSON DAVIS.

RICHMOND, VA., January 7, 1864.

To the Senate and House of Representatives.

I herewith transmit for your information a communication from the Secretary of War, covering copies of several additional reports of military operations. JEFFERSON DAVIS.

RICHMOND, VA., January 7, 1864.

To the Senate and House of Representatives.

I herewith transmit for your information a communication from the Secretary of War, covering a copy of the report of Brig. Gen. R. S. Ripley of operations from August 21 to September 10, 1863. JEFFERSON DAVIS.

RICHMOND, VA., January 8, 1864.

To the Senate of the Confederate States.

I herewith transmit for your information a communication from the Secretary of War, covering copies of the "report of Gen. J. E.

Johnston of his operations in the Department of Mississippi and East Louisiana," and of the report of Lieut. Gen. J. C. Pemberton of the battles of Port Gibson, Baker's Creek, and the siege of Vicksburg, to which is appended a copy of the correspondence of the Department with him relative to some points of the report which were thought to require explanation.

JEFFERSON DAVIS.

RICHMOND, VA., Jan. 11, 1864.

To the Senate and House of Representatives.

I herewith submit for your consideration a communication from the Attorney General, containing an estimate of an additional sum required by the Department of Justice.

I recommend that an appropriation be made of the amount specified for the purpose indicated.   JEFFERSON DAVIS.

RICHMOND, VA., January 11, 1864.

To the House of Representatives.

In partial response to your resolution of the 11th ult., I herewith transmit for your information a communication from the Secretary of War, showing "the number of officers and men, including the police and mounted guard, employed in executing the conscript law" in the States of Virginia, North Carolina, South Carolina, and Georgia. Further information on the subject will be furnished when received.   JEFFERSON DAVIS.

RICHMOND, VA., January 12, 1864.

To the Senate and House of Representatives.

I herewith transmit for your consideration a communication from the Secretary of the Treasury, submitting "the condensed estimates of appropriations required for the support of the Government for the period from January 1 to June 30, 1864, inclusive."

It was intended that these estimates should accompany my message* of the 7th ultimo, but they seem to have failed to reach the committees.

I recommend that appropriations be made of the sums specified for the purposes indicated.   JEFFERSON DAVIS.

---

*Page 345.

RICHMOND, VA., Jan. 13, 1864.

To the House of Representatives.

In response to your resolution of the 12th ultimo, I herewith transmit for your information a communication from the Secretary of War, covering a list of those persons who have been specially noticed and promoted from the ranks for gallantry in the field. JEFFERSON DAVIS.

RICHMOND, VA., Jan. 13, 1864.

To the House of Representatives.

In response to your resolution of the 17th ult., I herewith transmit for your information a communication from the Secretary of War, relative to the steps taken in reference to "An Act to prevent the absence of officers and soldiers without leave," approved the 16th of April, 1863. JEFFERSON DAVIS.

RICHMOND, January 13, 1864.

To the Senate and House of Representatives.

I herewith transmit for your information a communication from the Secretary of War, covering a copy of Maj. Gen. Hindman's report of his operations while in command of the Trans-Mississippi District. JEFFERSON DAVIS.

RICHMOND, VA., January 15, 1864.

To the Senate of the Confederate States of America.

I have received from your honorable body, through the hands of your secretary, a copy of the report and resolution adopted by you in executive session on the 9th instant.

The resolution is in the following words:

Resolved, That the Senate do advise and consent to the appointment of the military officers nominated in the four several messages of the President dated on the 8th instant, all of whom are from States west of the Mississippi River, for the reasons stated in the foregoing report; and that the action of the Senate herein is not to be construed as sanctioning or recognizing the right of the Executive, in nominating officers to the Senate, to fix the time at which they shall take rank anterior to the preceding session of Congress, or at any time during such session.

By the first four lines of the resolution I am informed that the Senate acknowledge the legality and concur in the propriety of my action in regard to these nominations, by their advising and consenting to the appointments as proposed. This is the whole action usually taken on nominations, and seems to exhaust the authority over appointments vested in the Senate by the Constitution.

The reservation, however, in the present instance, that the Senate is not to be considered as sanctioning or recognizing the right of the Executive to do in the future what the Senate have approved of his doing in the cases before them, as explained in the report to which the resolution refers, imposes on me the necessity of this communication.

On referring to that report I confess to my surprise at finding myself apparently charged with a violation of the Constitution, although no foundation exists for the implication conveyed in the report. I feel sure, therefore, that neither the committee nor the Senate could have intended or sanctioned such a charge; but I could not in justice to myself fail to call your attention to the language employed. It is as follows:

. . . The only difficulty presented to the committee is, that the date at which the officers nominated are to take rank is anterior to the last session of Congress.

The committee are of opinion that the Constitution contemplates that all officers appointed in the recess of Congress shall hold under such appointment only to the close of the next session of Congress, and that they should be renominated, if it is intended to retain them in their offices, to the Senate at its first session after their appointment. This has not been done in this case.

The Senate cannot but agree with me that the plain inference from these passages is that the Constitution has been violated by my having appointed these officers during the recess and retained them in office without nominating them to the Senate at its next session. It has thus become incumbent on me (while satisfied that neither the committee nor the Senate could have intended to make such an accusation) to repel any inference that might hereafter be drawn from my silence on the subject, by stating that not only had no appointments of these officers been made prior to the nominations on which the Senate has just acted, but that the fact of the necessity for the appointments reached the Executive only since the commencement of your present session, by communication received last month from the Trans-Mississippi Department.

Upon the point suggested in the close of the resolution, that the

Executive is without the right to make a nomination to a military grade, coupled with rank from a date prior to a former session of the Senate, it is not deemed proper to anticipate any future disagreement with the Senate by presenting the reasons for the opposite conclusion as being the only one consistent with the laws for the regulation of the Army, as well as with long-settled usage and the necessities of the service.

When the occasion shall arise I cannot doubt that the Senate will, notwithstanding this resolution, refuse to abandon its own constitutional power to act on nominations at its pleasure, according to the merits of each case and the good of the service. I am confirmed in this conclusion by observing that the resolution was passed without a call for the yeas and nays, and therefore with probably less than the usual consideration, as well as by the further reflection that as Executive nominations which meet the disapproval of the Senate on any ground are always subject to rejection without assignment of reasons, experience will show that no advantage can arise from the Senate's curtailing its own discretion in future cases by binding its own judgment in advance.

JEFFERSON DAVIS.

CONFEDERATE STATES OF AMERICA, EXECUTIVE DEPARTMENT,
RICHMOND, VA., Jan. 15, 1864.

Hon. E. S. Dargan, M. C. from Alabama.

Sir: In further response to your letter to the President of the 22d ult., and by his direction, I have the honor to inclose to you the reports* of the Secretary of the Navy and of the Secretary of War upon the subject to which it relates. Very respectfully,

Yr. obt. Sert. BURTON N. HARRISON, *Private Secretary.*

RICHMOND, VA., Jan. 18, 1864.

To the House of Representatives.

In response to your resolution of the 30th ultimo, I herewith transmit for your information a communication from the Secretary of War, covering copies of regulations and orders relative to the payment of assessments of damages made by commanding of-

---

*Relative to the Erlanger loan, and cotton accumulated by the Treasury Department.

ficers in the field, "without intervention of courts-martial or boards of survey." JEFFERSON DAVIS.

RICHMOND, VA., Jan. 19, 1864.

To the House of Representatives.

In response to your resolution of the 11th instant, I herewith transmit for your information a communication from the Secretary of War, relative to "the collection and distribution of the 'tax in kind,' under the act approved April 24, 1863."

JEFFERSON DAVIS.

RICHMOND, VA., January 19, 1864.

To the Senate and House of Representatives.

I herewith transmit for your information a communication from the Secretary of War, covering copies of several additional reports of military operations during the last year.

JEFFERSON DAVIS.

RICHMOND, VA., Jan. 25, 1864.

To the House of Representatives.

In response to your resolution of the 11th ult., I herewith transmit a communication from the Secretary of War, showing, as far as the records of the Department enable him to do, the number of men liable to conscription who have been removed from the Commissary and Quartermaster's Departments, to give place to disabled soldiers, as directed by law. JEFFERSON DAVIS.

RICHMOND, VA., January 26, 1864.

To the Senate and House of Representatives.

I herewith transmit for your information a communication from the Secretary of War, covering a copy of an additional report of military operations during the last year.

JEFFERSON DAVIS.

RICHMOND, VA., January 26, 1864.

To the Senate of the Confederate States.

In response to your resolution of the 16th instant, I herewith transmit a communication from the Secretary of War, covering information relative to the officers appointed under the act to raise troops, approved October 11, 1862.   JEFFERSON DAVIS.

RICHMOND, January 27, 1864.

To the Senate.

I submit to the Senate herewith the nomination of A. R. Lawton, of Georgia, to be Quartermaster General, with the rank of brigadier general, to take rank from the 13th day of April, 1861, and deem it proper to communicate the reasons which induce this course.

On the passage of the act of the 20th of March last, entitled "An Act to amend an act for the establishment and organization of the general staff for the Army of the Confederate States of America," inquiry was made to aid in the selection of the most competent person then made eligible, and the office of Quartermaster General was tendered to General Lawton, who was averse to accepting it if it involved a nomination and new appointment, for the reasons that it withdrew him from service in the field, interfered with his chances for promotion, and that, as he was then the oldest brigadier in the service, he would, by acceptance of a new commission, be deprived of his relative rank as compared with other brigadiers. There were two other officers recommended to me as specially fitted to discharge the duties of Quartermaster General, who could be spared from service in the field, and they were both major generals and could not therefore be expected to accept a lower grade in the staff than that which they held in the line.

The name of the officer then performing the duties of Quartermaster General was also presented to me with recommendations entitled to carry great respect, but my own observation of the manner in which those duties had been discharged had previously satisfied me that the public interests required an officer of greater ability and one better qualified to meet the pressing emergencies of the service during the war.

On examination of the law above referred to, its language, although not free from doubt, was held, after consultation and advice, to justify the conclusion that the intention of Congress would be fulfilled by assigning to the performance of the duties of Quartermaster General an officer already confirmed as brigadier general in the Provisional Army, without again submitting his nomination to the Senate. The grounds for this conclusion were that the eighth section of the act of 6th of March, 1861, organizing the Regular Army, expressly authorized the Executive to assign the brigadier generals to any duties he might specially direct, and when the five brigadier generals were raised to the rank of generals by the act of 16th of May, 1861, the President was again empowered to assign them to such commands and "duties" as he might specially direct. As it had, therefore, been permitted by Congress that any one of the generals of the Regular Army might be assigned to staff or any other duty at Executive discretion, it seemed a fair inference that when by the law of last session provision was made that the rank, pay, and allowances of Quartermaster General should be those of a brigadier in the Provisional Army the will of the Legislature was as well fulfilled by assigning to the duties of that office one who was already a brigadier general of the Provisional Army as by nominating a new officer.

This view of the question was fortified by the fact that the law last referred to did not create an office, but only provided that during the war the officer discharging the duties of Quartermaster General should have the rank of brigadier general, and by the further fact that the original act of 26th of February, 1861, for the establishment and organization of the general staff, contained a provision still in force, that officers of the Quartermaster General and other staff departments might by order of the President be assigned to the command of troops, according to their rank in the Army, thus indicating that positions in the quartermaster's and other staff departments were not distinct offices, but were posts of duty to which officers of the Army were appointed, and from which they might be withdrawn and assigned to other duties at Executive discretion. This is a provision of our law that did not exist in the former service of the United States, in which when an officer of the Army entered the Quartermaster's Department he surrendered his commission in the line and his right to command troops.

I am advised, however, that such is not the construction given to the law by many Senators, and I so far conform to their views as to give the Senate an opportunity to advise the Executive in relation to the appointment of this officer.

This statement was also necessary in explanation of the proposal that General Lawton's rank should date from the 13th of April, 1861, that being the date of his present commission of brigadier general in the Provisional Army.

Since the foregoing message was written I observe by the published proceedings of the Senate that it has adopted the following resolutions:

Resolved, That, in the opinion of the Senate, A. C. Myers is now Quartermaster General of the C. S. Army, and is by law authorized and required to discharge the duties thereof.

Resolved, That A. R. Lawton is not authorized by law to discharge the duties of said office.

Refraining from any further remark on these resolutions than the expression of my conviction that they are not sustained by the Constitution or the law, their passage enforces the propriety of submitting to you the nomination which accompanies this message.

JEFFERSON DAVIS.

RICHMOND, VA., Jan. 27, 1864.

To the Senate of the Confederate States.

In response to your resolution of the 20th inst., I herewith transmit a communication from the Secretary of the Treasury, conveying information relative to the Chief Collector of Taxes for the State of Louisiana.   JEFFERSON DAVIS.

RICHMOND, VA., January 29, 1864.

To the House of Representatives.

In response to your resolution of the 11th ultimo, I herewith transmit for your information a copy of my correspondence, together with that of the Secretary of War and of the Adjutant and Inspector General, with General Joseph E. Johnston during the months of May, June, and July, 1863, concerning his command and the operations in his department.

As the resolution fixes definitely the dates within which the cor-

respondence is desired, I have not deemed it proper to add anything which was prior or subsequent to those dates.

JEFFERSON DAVIS.

RICHMOND, VA., January 29, 1864.

To the Senate and House of Representatives.

I herewith transmit for your consideration, in secret session, a
communication from the Secretary of the Treasury, to which I
invite your special attention.

I recommend an appropriation of the sum specified for the purpose indicated. JEFFERSON DAVIS.

RICHMOND, VA., January 30, 1864.

To the House of Representatives.

In response to your resolution of the 21st inst., I herewith transmit a communication from the Secretary of War, showing the
present state of the question pending between the two Governments, of the Confederate States and the United States, relative
to the exchange of prisoners. JEFFERSON DAVIS.

RICHMOND, VA., Jan. 30, 1864.

To the Senate and House of Representatives.

I herewith transmit for your consideration a communication
from the Secretary of War, covering an estimate* of an additional
sum needed by the Engineer Bureau.

I recommend an appropriation of the amount specified for the
purpose indicated. JEFFERSON DAVIS.

February 3, 1864.

The Senate and House of Representatives of the Confederate States.

The present state of the Confederacy, in my judgment, requires
that I should call your attention to a condition of things existing
in the country which has already been productive of serious evil,
and which threatens still graver consequences unless an adequate

---

*Of amount required to pay claims for the loss of slaves by impress-
ment, etc.

remedy shall be speedily applied by the legislation of Congress. It has been our cherished hope—and hitherto justified by the generous self-devotion of our citizens—that when the great struggle in which we are engaged was passed we might exhibit to the world the proud spectacle of a people unanimous in the assertion and defense of their rights and achieving their liberty and independence after the bloodiest war of modern times without the necessity of a single sacrifice of civil right to military necessity. But it can no longer be doubted that the zeal with which the people sprang to arms at the beginning of the contest has, in some parts of the Confederacy, been impaired by the long continuance and magnitude of the struggle.

While brigade after brigade of our brave soldiers who have endured the trials of the camp and battlefield are testifying their spirit and patriotism by voluntary reënlistment for the war, discontent, disaffection, and disloyalty are manifested among those who, through the sacrifices of others, have enjoyed quiet and safety at home. Public meetings have been held, in some of which a treasonable design is masked by a pretense of devotion to State sovereignty, and in others is openly avowed. Conventions are advocated with the pretended object of redressing grievances, which, if they existed, could as well be remedied by ordinary legislative action, but with the real design of accomplishing treason under the form of law. To this end a strong suspicion is entertained that secret leagues and associations are being formed. In certain localities men of no mean position do not hesitate to avow their disloyalty and hostility to our cause, and their advocacy of peace on the terms of submission and the abolition of slavery. In districts overrun by the enemy or liable to their encroachments, citizens of well-known disloyalty are holding frequent communication with them, and furnishing valuable information to our injury, even to the frustration of important military movements. And yet must they, through too strict regard to the technicalities of the law, be permitted to go at large till they have perfected their treason by the commission of an overt act? After the commission of the act the evidence is often unattainable, because within the enemy's lines. Again and again such persons have been arrested, and as often they have been discharged by the civil authorities, because the Government could not procure the testimony from within the lines of the enemy. On one occasion, when a party of officers were laying a torpedo in James River, persons on shore were detected communicating with the enemy, and were known to pilot them to a convenient point for observing the nature of the service in which the party were engaged. They were arrested and were discharged on *habeas corpus,* because, although there was moral certainty of their guilt, it could not be proved by competent testimony. Twice the Government has received secret and confidential information of plots to release the prisoners confined in Richmond. This information was sufficiently definite to enable preventive measures to be adopted with success; but as it pointed out the guilty conspirators by strong suspicion only, and not by competent testimony, they could not be arrested, and are still at large, ready to plot again. A citizen possessing the means and opportunity of doing much injury to the service was arrested for disloyalty. He was twice tried before different commissioners. Upon each examination he avowed his hostility to our cause and his desire to join the enemy. Both commissioners decided that it would be dangerous to suffer him to go at large. Yet, upon the demand of the civil authorities, he had to be released for want of competent legal testimony.

The Capital of the Government is the object of peculiar attention to the enemy. I have satisfactory reasons for believing that spies are continually coming and going in our midst. Information has been repeatedly received from friendly parties at the North that particular individuals then in Richmond were sent as spies by the enemy. Yet, however accurate and reliable such information might be, it was not competent testimony; and it was idle to arrest them only to be discharged by the civil authorities. Important information of secret movements among the negroes fomented by base white men has been received from faithful servants, but no arrests of instigators could be made because there was no competent testimony. Apprehensions have more than once been entertained of a servile insurrection in Richmond. The Northern papers inform us that Butler is perfecting some deep-laid scheme to punish us for our refusal to hold intercourse with him. If, as is not improbable, his designs should point to servile insurrection in Richmond, incendiarism, and the destruction of public works so necessary to our defense, and so impossible to be replaced, how can we hope to fathom it and reach the guilty emissaries and contrivers but by incompetent negro testimony? In some of the States civil process has been brought to bear with disastrous efficiency upon the Army. Every judge has the power to issue the writ of *habeas corpus,* and if one manifests more facility in discharging petitioners than his associates the application is made to him, however remote he may be. In one instance a general on the eve of an important movement, when every man was needed, was embarrassed by the command of a judge—more than two hundred miles distant—to bring if in his custody, or send if in custody of another, before him, on *habeas corpus,* some deserters who had been arrested and returned to his command. In another, the commandant of a camp of conscripts, who had a conscript in camp, was commanded to bring him before a judge more than a hundred miles distant, although there was a judge competent to hear and determine the cause resident in the place where the writ was executed. He consulted eminent counsel, and was advised that, from the known opinions of the judge selected, the conscript would undoubtedly be released, and the officer was therefore advised to discharge him at once, and return the facts informally; that such a return was not technically sufficient, but would be accepted as accomplishing the purpose of the writ. He acted on the advice of his counsel, and was immediately summoned by the judge to show cause why he should not be attached for a contempt in making an insufficient return, and was compelled to leave his command at a time when his services were pressingly needed by the Government and travel over a hundred miles and a considerable distance away from any railroad, to purge himself of the technical contempt. These particular instances may serve to show the nature of the delays, difficulties, and embarrassments which are constantly occurring. And injurious as they are, they are but light and trivial in comparison with evils which are reasonably to be anticipated.

It is understood that questions are to be multiplied as to the constitutionality of the late act of Congress placing in the military service those who had furnished substitutes. If a single judge, in any State, should hold the act to be unconstitutional, it is easy to foresee that that State will either furnish no soldiers from this class, or furnish them only when too late for the pressing need of the country. Every application will be made to that particular judge, and he will discharge the petitioners in each. And although the officer may have the right of appeal, yet the delay will be tantamount in its consequences to a discharge. Indeed, this result is likely to ensue, though every judge in the Confederacy should hold the law to be perfectly constitutional and valid.

A petition for a *habeas corpus* need not and ordinarily does not disclose the particular grounds upon which the petitioner claims his discharge. A general statement on oath that he is illegally restrained of his liberty is sufficient to induce and even to require the judge to issue the writ. In every case the enrollment will be followed by the writ, and every enrolling officer will be kept in continual motion to and from the judge, until the embarrassment and delay will amount to the practical repeal of the law. Its provisions will add no more soldiers to the Army. But this is not all. We shall not be able to retain those already in the service. Nothing has done so much to inspirit our brave soldiers as the determination evinced by Congress to send to their aid those who have thus far lived in ease at home while they have endured dangers, toils, and privations. When the hope of equal justice and of speedy reënforcement shall thus have failed, disappointment and despondency will displace the buoyant fortitude which animates them now. Desertion, already a frightful evil, will become the order of the day. And who will arrest the deserter, when most of those at home are engaged with him in the common cause of setting the Government at defiance? Organized bands of deserters will patrol the country, burning, plundering, and robbing indiscriminately, and our armies, already too weak, must be still further depleted at the most imminent crisis of our cause, to keep the peace and protect the lives and property of our citizens at home. Must these evils be endured? Must the independence for which we are contending, the safety of the defenseless families of the men who have fallen in battle and of those who still confront the invader, be put in peril for the sake of conformity to the technicalities of the law of treason?

Having thus presented some of the threatening evils which exist, it remains to suggest the remedy. And in my judgment that is to be found only in the suspension of the privilege of the writ of *habeas corpus.* It is a sharp remedy, but a necessary one. It is a remedy plainly contemplated by the Constitution. All the powers of the Government, extraordinary as well as ordinary, are a sacred trust, to be faithfully executed whenever the public exigency may require. Recognizing the general obligation, we cannot escape from the duty in one case more than in another. And a suspension of the writ when demanded by the public safety is as much a duty as to levy taxes for the support of the Government. If the state of invasion declared by the Constitution to be a proper case for the exercise of this power does not exist in our country now, when can it ever be expected to arise? It is idle to appeal against it to the history of the old Union. That history contains no parallel case. England, whose reverence for the great bill of right is at least as strong as our own, and the stability of whose institutions is the admiration of the world, has repeatedly within the last hundred years resorted to this remedy when only threatened with invasion. It may occasion some clamor, but this will proceed chiefly from the men who have already been too long the active agents of evil. Loyal citizens will not feel danger, and the disloyal must be made to fear it. The very existence of extraordinary powers often renders their exercise unnecessary. To temporize with disloyalty in the midst of war is but to quicken it to the growth of treason. I therefore respectfully recommend that the privilege of the writ of *habeas corpus* be suspended.

JEFFERSON DAVIS.

RICHMOND, VA., Feb. 3, 1864.

To the Senate of the Confederate States.

In response to your resolution of the 15th ult., I herewith transmit for your information in executive session a communication from the Secretary of War, relative to the general officers appointed under the act approved October 13, 1862.

JEFFERSON DAVIS.

RICHMOND, VA., Feb. 5, 1864.

To the House of Representatives.

In response to your resolution of the 25th ultimo, I herewith transmit for your information a communication from the Secretary of War, relative to the steps taken to carry out the provisions of the act of Congress "in relation to the arrest and disposition of slaves who have been recaptured from the enemy."

JEFFERSON DAVIS.

RICHMOND, February 5, 1864.

To the House of Representatives.

I herewith transmit communications from the Secretaries of the Treasury and of War, which convey the information asked for in your resolution of the 13th ultimo, relative to the amount of money forwarded to the Trans-Mississippi Department since the adjournment of Congress, and to the adjustment of claims against the Government for articles illegally impressed and not paid for at the time.

JEFFERSON DAVIS.

RICHMOND, VA., Feb. 8, 1864.

To the House of Representatives.

I herewith transmit a communication from the Secretary of War, in response to your resolution of the 15th ult., requesting to be informed "by what authority Gens. Sam Jones and Imboden have prohibited the transportation of food from the military districts in which they are located to the city of Richmond for private use and consumption."

JEFFERSON DAVIS.

RICHMOND, VA., Feb. 8, 1864.

To the House of Representatives.

In response to your resolution of the 12th ultimo, I herewith transmit for your information a communication from the Secretary of War, relative to the "domestic passport system" now enforced upon citizens traveling in some parts of the Confederate States outside of the lines of the armies.

JEFFERSON DAVIS.

RICHMOND, VA., February 8, 1864.

To the House of Representatives.

In response to your resolution of the 12th ultimo, I herewith transmit for your information a communication from the Secretary of War, stating that the records of the War Office "do not show any authority granted to raise troops of conscript age, except in localities where the operation of the conscript law has been suspended, or from the control of the enemy it cannot be enforced."

JEFFERSON DAVIS.

RICHMOND, VA., Feb. 8, 1864.

To the Senate and House of Representatives.

I herewith transmit for your information a communication from the Secretary of War, covering a copy of the report by Gen. Jno. S. Williams of the operations of the forces under his command at Blue Springs, Henderson, and Rheatown, Tenn.

JEFFERSON DAVIS.

RICHMOND, VA., Feb. 11, 1864.

To the Senate and House of Representatives.

I herewith transmit for your consideration a communication from the Secretary of War, submitting an estimate of the sum needed for the conscription service.

I recommend an appropriation of the amount specified for the purpose indicated. JEFFERSON DAVIS.

RICHMOND, VA., Feb. 11, 1864.

To the House of Representatives.

In response to your resolution of the 31st December, 1863, I herewith transmit for your information a communication from the Secretary of War, concerning the "correspondence with Gen. Whiting relative to the defense of Wilmington, North Carolina," and the aid which "can be given by further legislation to the complete defense of that important post." JEFFERSON DAVIS.

RICHMOND, VA., Feb. 11, 1864.

To the Senate and House of Representatives.

I herewith transmit for your consideration a communication from the Secretary of the Treasury, submitting estimates of additional sums needed for the support of the Government.

I recommend an appropriation of the amount specified for the purposes indicated. JEFFERSON DAVIS.

RICHMOND, VA., Feb. 11, 1864.

To the Senate and House of Representatives.

I herewith transmit, and recommend to your favorable consideration in secret session, a communication from the Secretary of the Navy, asking for authority to transfer the amount appropriated under secret act No. 6, approved September 19, 1862, to the appropriation under secret act No. 31, approved October 6, 1862.

JEFFERSON DAVIS.

RICHMOND, VA., February 12, 1864.

To the House of Representatives.

In response to your resolution of the 21st ultimo, I herewith transmit for your information a communication from the Secretary of War, relative to the delivery of the "tax in kind" at the Government depots by the producers.   JEFFERSON DAVIS.

RICHMOND, VA., Feb. 12, 1864.

To the House of Representatives.

In response to your resolution of the 29th ultimo, I herewith transmit for your information a communication from the Secretary of War, submitting copies of papers relating "to the trial and conviction of W. E. Coffman by a military court," and to "a writ of *habeas corpus* issued from the circuit court of Rockingham County, Va., to prevent the execution of said Coffman."

JEFFERSON DAVIS.

RICHMOND, VA., Feb. 12, 1864.

To the Senate and House of Representatives.

I herewith transmit for your information a communication from the Secretary of War, covering copies of several additional reports of General Beauregard, connected with the defense of Charleston.   JEFFERSON DAVIS.

RICHMOND, VA., Feb. 12, 1864.

To the Senate of the Confederate States.

In response to your resolution of the 2d ult., I herewith transmit for your information a communication from the Secretary of the Treasury, relative to the assessment and collection of taxes under the act approved May 1, 1863.   JEFFERSON DAVIS.

RICHMOND, VA., Feby. 12, 1864.

To the Senate and House of Representatives.

I herewith transmit for your consideration a communication from the Secretary of the Treasury, submitting an estimate of additional sums needed for the support of the Government.

I recommend an appropriation of the amount specified for the purposes indicated.   JEFFERSON DAVIS.

RICHMOND, VA., February 13, 1864.

To the Senate and House of Representatives of the Confederate States.

I feel impelled by the condition of the country earnestly to recommend to your adoption the extension of the conscription already recommended* in my annual message of the 7th of December last, and to inform you that the preparations made by the enemy for the campaign of the present year warn us that our armies in the field must be reënforced to the utmost possible extent.

The agricultural interests of the country must be protected and fostered, or we shall be unable to raise the supplies necessary for the subsistence of the Army as well as of the people at home. How is this to be done?

There is no possibility of affording adequate local protection by our armies in the field, which must of necessity be kept concentrated to resist the main columns of the invading forces of the enemy. Our farms and depots can be protected from destructive raids only by men who remain at home engaged in manufactural, agricultural, and other pursuits. There are but two modes of rendering these classes available for such purposes. One is by calling them out as militia; the other by enrolling them under Confederate authority. I propose in a few words to contrast these modes.

If those left at home are available only as militia, it will become necessary to make requisitions for them on the States in advance of any pressing necessity for their services, because of the delays

---

*See page 370.

which are always involved in obtaining forces under such calls. When called out it will naturally result that the men will be retained for long periods in the field or in camp, to be ready for emergencies, as they could not, if discharged, be promptly recalled when required. This method of using the reserves will tell with disastrous effect on our agriculture.

On the other hand, troops for local defense and special service, as organized under the act of 21st of August, 1861, would afford the Commander in Chief the means of calling out the men embraced in such organizations at a moment's warning, and enable him, without imprudence, to dismiss them the moment the danger had disappeared. They would probably not be absent from the fields and workshops more than two or three weeks at a time, and there would thus be no serious interruption to the productive industry of the country. If the spirit which rendered the volunteering so general among all classes of citizens at the beginning of the war were still prevalent, there would be no necessity for the proposed legislation, as the citizens would readily join the organizations provided in the law above mentioned. But as this is not the case, it is necessary that conscription for local defense should replace volunteering.

If Congress should decline to adopt this measure, which my sense of what is needed for the public defense forces me again to urge upon its attention, I am unable to perceive from what source we are to obtain the men necessary not only to repel raids but to relieve the large number of able-bodied soldiers now detailed from the Army for local service in the States.

I trust that my conviction of the pressing necessity for this legislation in aid of the public defense will be received by Congress as a sufficient justification for this renewal of the recommendation contained in the message addressed to you at the commencement of the present session.   JEFFERSON DAVIS.

RICHMOND, VA., February 15, 1864.

To the Senate of the Confederate States.

In response to your resolution of the 12th inst., I herewith transmit a communication from the Secretary of War, conveying the information asked for relative to Gen. A. R. Lawton and Gen. J. B. Gordon.

The terms of the inquiry to which this reply is made suggest the propriety of informing the Senate that other general officers, who have been wounded in battle and separated from their commands, have been regarded as having a continuing right to receive the prescribed pay and allowances of their grade, notwithstanding the appointment of others to supply the want created by their indefinite absence. For example, the recent nominations of brigadier generals, who had been selected to command the brigades of Gen. W. H. F. Lee, of Virginia, and of Gen. D. W. Adams, of Louisiana, were not intended to vacate the commissions or to suspend the pay of those gallant officers, but to use the authority to appoint supernumerary generals for one of the purposes for which it was understood to have been given. JEFFERSON DAVIS.

RICHMOND, VA., Feb. 15, 1864.

To the Senate and House of Representatives.

I herewith submit for your consideration a communication from the Secretary of War, covering an estimate of an additional appropriation required by the War Department.

JEFFERSON DAVIS.

RICHMOND, VA., Feb. 15, 1864.

To the Senate and House of Representatives.

I herewith transmit for your information communications from the Secretary of War, covering copies of several additional reports of military operations. JEFFERSON DAVIS.

RICHMOND, VA., February 15, 1864.

To the Senate of the Confederate States.

In response to your resolution of December 24, 1863, I herewith transmit for your information a communication from the Secretary of War, submitting copies of the charges and specifications, and of the accompanying papers, in the case of Major H. C. Guerin, C. S. JEFFERSON DAVIS.

RICHMOND, VA., February 16, 1864.

To the House of Representatives.

In response to your resolution of the 5th instant, I herewith transmit a communication from the Secretary of War, conveying the information asked for relative to the hospitals in and near the city of Richmond, and to the surgeons and assistant surgeons attached to them.   JEFFERSON DAVIS.

RICHMOND, VA., February 16th, 1864.

To the House of Representatives.

In partial response to your resolution of the 11th December, 1863, I herewith transmit a communication from the Secretary of War, conveying the information asked for relative to the officers of the Commissary Department who have failed to render their accounts, and stating the cause of his inability at present to furnish the desired information concerning such officers of the Quartermaster's Department.   JEFFERSON DAVIS.

RICHMOND, VA., Feb. 17, 1864.

To the Senate and House of Representatives.

I herewith transmit for your consideration a communication from the Secretary of the Navy, covering an estimate for an additional appropriation required under an act* approved on the 16th inst.   JEFFERSON DAVIS.

RICHMOND, VA., Feb. 17, 1864.

To the Senate and House of Representatives.

I herewith submit for your consideration a communication from the Secretary of War, covering an estimate for an additional appropriation required by the Bureau of Indian Affairs.

JEFFERSON DAVIS.

RICHMOND, VA., February 17, 1864.

To the Senate of the Confederate States.

In response to your resolution of the 12th ult., I herewith transmit a communication from the Secretary of War, conveying the

---

*To pay allowances authorized to officers of the Navy.

information asked for relative to the returns of the company commanders of the Army for the clothing transferred to them for issue and distribution.   JEFFERSON DAVIS.

RICHMOND, VA., Feb. 17, 1864.

To the Senate and House of Representatives.

I herewith submit for your consideration a communication from the Secretary of the Navy, covering an estimate for an additional appropriation required under an act approved on the 16th instant.

JEFFERSON DAVIS.

VETO MESSAGES.

RICHMOND, VA., December 31, 1863.

To the Senate of the Confederate States of America.

The act entitled "An Act to amend an act entitled 'An Act to aid the State of Kentucky, and for other purposes,'" approved 29th of January, 1862, has been duly considered, and I find myself constrained, though very reluctantly, because of the purpose in view, to return the same to the House in which it originated with a statement of the objections which cause me to withhold my approval.

The act to which this is amendatory was for the declared object of aiding the Governor and Council of Kentucky to raise and organize troops in that State for the Confederate service, and to supply them with clothing, subsistence, transportation, arms, and ammunition. The second section of that act carefully provided the manner of making requisitions on the appropriation, so as to secure its application to the object for which it was designed—viz., to provide for troops raised for the Confederate service anterior to their being mustered into the same, and therefore before they could be supplied by the officers of the Confederate Army

The act now before me devotes one-half of that appropriation to a purpose entirely different from that originally contemplated, and authorizes the Governor and Council to draw from the Treasury a million of dollars, to be expended in purchasing clothing for the use and benefit of the Kentucky troops now in the service. These already receive the same allowance of clothing as all other troops. The act under consideration makes an appropriation for an object for which other money is appropriated, and directs its expenditure by agents other than the bonded officers charged with supplying clothing to the whole Army. If it be designed, as equity would seem to require, to make a proportionate provision for all the other troops, the Senate will not fail to observe the very large expenditure which it would involve, and that the method is objectionable, because it would be to employ two sets of agents to perform the same duty, who, buying in the same market, would necessarily be bidders against each other.

If the allowance of clothing be not sufficient, a better remedy would seem to be an increase of the appropriation for the clothing for the whole Army, that the grateful duty might in that case be performed by the Confederate authorities of issuing to the soldier whatever additional allowance the Government may be able to procure and his wants may require.

It will be further perceived that to recognize as well founded the implication contained in this bill that extra supplies of clothing furnished to the soldiers ought to be paid for by the Confederacy would lay the foundation for large claims to be made hereafter by the States for reimbursement on account of clothing supplied by them to their soldiers.

If the discrimination made by this act in favor of the gallant soldiers of our sister State of Kentucky originates from the natural sympathy excited by their separation from such comforts as they might expect to receive if able to communicate with their homes, Congress will not fail to perceive that there are many other troops in the service in like condition, and whose claims to consideration stand on precisely the same footing.

JEFFERSON DAVIS.

RICHMOND, VA., February 11, 1864.

The House of Representatives of the Confederate States of America.

Having carefully considered the act entitled "An Act to provide for wounded and disabled officers, soldiers, and seamen an asylum to be called the 'Veteran Soldiers' Home,'" I feel constrained to

return it with my objections to the House of Representatives, in
which it originated. The object of the act appeals most strongly
to the sympathies of all; but in providing the means for effectu-
ating that object, it enacts provisions which, in my judgment, are
unwarranted by the Constitution. Without affirming that the act
creates a perfect corporation, there can be no doubt that it confers
upon the board of managers of the institution which it is intended
to found corporate powers and franchises of a well-defined character, which constitute them what is known as a quasi corporation. They are to organize themselves into a board, by the
election of a president, treasurer, and their necessary officers;
are to continue in office until their successors are appointed, thus
providing for a continual succession; and they are to be subject
to the general approval and direction of the Secretary of War,
thus constituting the Secretary a visitor, a usual incident of
eleemosynary corporations. They have powers to make by-
laws, or, as the act expresses it, the "power to make all requisite
rules and regulations" for the government of the institution; and
they are authorized to receive endowments from individuals and
from the States. These are all ordinary and well-known corporate franchises. But if any doubt could exist as to whether
they are granted to the board as a corporation, or quasi corporation, or only intrusted to them as individual trustees, that doubt
is removed by the second section of the act. That section provides that the treasurer shall give bond with security for the
faithful discharge of his duties, which bond shall be payable to
the said board of managers and their successors in office, and
may by them be put in suit in any State or Confederate court
having jurisdiction. It cannot be understood that this bond is to
be taken to and sued upon by the board of managers in their individual capacities as natural persons. This is evident from two
considerations:

First. Such a power would be supererogatory and useless,
since as natural persons they already had by the common law
ample right to make any contract and take any bond or other
security not contravening the policy of the law.

Second. The right of action on a bond payable to the managers as individuals would, in the courts of law, remain in and
be under the control of the managers after they had gone out of

office; and in case of the death of all of them would belong to the personal representative of the last survivor; and to prevent these inconveniences it is expressly provided that the bond should be payable to and be sued on by "the board of managers and their successors in office," which could be accomplished only by constituting them to that extent a corporation.

From these considerations it is apparent that the intent of the act is to confer corporate powers upon the board of managers; and that intent is, in my judgment, beyond the powers intrusted to Congress by the Constitution. However enlightened opinions may have differed under the old Government, the whole history and theory of the contest in which we are engaged and the express recognition in our Constitution of the sovereignty of the States preclude all idea of so widely extending by construction the field of implied powers. That there is no such power expressly granted need scarcely be remarked.

But if this view of the intent and operation of the act be discarded as incorrect, then it can be susceptible of but one other interpretation. It provides for the support and comfort of soldiers and seamen disabled in the public service—a class in all countries regarded as the peculiar objects of governmental benevolence. The institution which it founds is endowed, in part at least, from the funds of the Government. The real estate necessary for the purpose of this act is to be leased or purchased by the Secretary of War, under the approval of the President, as the property of the Government. Officers in the service and pay of the Government are to be assigned for duty at the asylum. Its whole management is to be subject to the general direction and control of a high officer of the Government—the Secretary of War; and the board of managers are required to report to the Secretary, to be communicated to Congress at every regular session, a statement of the condition of the institution. It is then a Government institution, and its officers are officers of the Confederate States; but they are not to be appointed in any of the ways by which alone such appointments can be constitutionally made—neither by the President, with the advice and consent of the Senate, nor by the President alone, nor by the courts of law, nor by the Head of a Department. The managers are to be appointed by the Governors of the several States, and they in turn are to appoint their president and treasurer and fix their salaries.

These two are, in my judgment, the only interpretations of which the act is susceptible; and under either view its provisions are violative of the Constitution.   JEFFERSON DAVIS.

PROCLAMATION.

BY THE PRESIDENT OF THE CONFEDERATE STATES.

A PROCLAMATION.

The Senate and House of Representatives of the Confederate States of America have signified their desire that a day may be recommended to the people, to be set apart and observed as a day of humiliation, fasting, and prayer, in the language following, to wit:

"Reverently recognizing the providence of God in the affairs of man, and gratefully remembering the guidance, support, and deliverance granted to our patriotic fathers in the memorable war which resulted in the independence of the American colonies, and now reposing in him our supreme confidence and hope in the present struggle for civil and religious freedom, and for the right to live under a government of our own choice, and deeply impressed with the conviction that without him nothing is strong, nothing wise, and nothing enduring; in order that the people of this Confederacy may have the opportunity at the same time of offering their adoration of the great Sovereign of the universe, of penitently confessing their sins, and strengthening their vows and purposes of amendment in humble reliance upon his gracious and almighty power:

"*The Congress of the Confederate States of America do resolve,* That it be recommended to the people of these States that Friday, the eighth day of April next, be set apart and observed as a day of humiliation, fasting, and prayer, that Almighty God would so preside over our public councils and authorities, that he would so inspire our armies and their leaders with wisdom, courage, and perseverance, and so manifest himself in the greatness of his goodness and majesty of his power, that we may be safely and successfully led, through the chastenings to which we are being subjected, to the attainment of an honorable peace; so that while we enjoy the blessings of a free and happy government we may ascribe to him the honor and the glory of our independence and prosperity."

A recommendation so congenial to the feelings of the people will receive their hearty concurrence; and it is a grateful duty to the Executive to unite with their representatives in inviting them to meet in the courts of the Most High. Recent events awaken fresh gratitude to the Supreme Ruler of nations. Our enemies have suffered repeated defeats, and a nefarious scheme to burn and plunder our capital, and to destroy our civil government by putting to death the chosen servants of the people, has been baffled and set at naught. Our armies have been strengthened, our finances promise rapid progress to a satisfactory condition, and our whole country is animated with a hopeful spirit and a fixed determination to achieve independence.

In these circumstances it becomes us, with thankful hearts, to bow ourselves before the throne of the Most High, and, while gratefully acknowledging so many mercies, confess that our sins as a people have justly exposed us to his chastisement. Let us recognize the sufferings which we have been called upon to endure, as administered by a Fatherly hand for our improvement, and with resolute courage and patient endurance let us wait on him for our deliverance.

In furtherance of these objects, now, therefore, I, Jefferson Davis, President of the Confederate States of America, do issue this, my proclamation, calling upon the people of the said States, in conformity with the desire expressed by their representatives, to set apart Friday, the eighth day of April, as a day of humiliation, fasting, and prayer; and I do hereby invite them on that day to repair to their several places of public worship and beseech Almighty God "to preside over our public councils, and so inspire our armies and leaders with wisdom, courage, and perseverance, and so manifest himself in the greatness of his goodness and in the majesty of his power, that we may secure the blessings of an honorable peace and of free government, and that we, as a people, may ascribe to him all the honor and glory of his name."

Given under my hand and the seal of the Confederate
States of America, at the city of Richmond, on this twelfth
day of March, in the year of our Lord one thousand eight
hundred and sixty-four.   JEFFERSON DAVIS.

[L. S.]

By the President:

J. P. BENJAMIN, *Secretary of State.*

ADDRESS.

General Orders No. 19.

ADJT. AND INSP. GENERAL'S OFFICE,
RICHMOND, February 10, 1864.

The following address of the President is published for the
information of the Army:

Soldiers of the Armies of the Confederate States.

In the long and bloody war in which your country is engaged
you have achieved many noble triumphs. You have won glorious
victories over vastly more numerous hosts. You have cheerfully
borne privations and toil to which you were unused. You have
readily submitted to restraints upon your individual will that the
citizen might better perform his duty to the State as a soldier.
To all these you have lately added another triumph—the noblest
of human conquests—a victory over yourselves.

As the time drew near when you who first entered the service
might well have been expected to claim relief from your arduous
labors and restoration to the endearments of home you have
heeded only the call of your suffering country. Again you come
to tender your service for the public defense—a free offering,
which only such patriotism as yours could make—a triumph
worthy of you and of the cause to which you are devoted.

I would in vain attempt adequately to express the emotions
with which I received the testimonials of confidence and regard
which you have recently addressed to me. To some of those
first received separate acknowledgments were returned. But it is
now apparent that a like generous enthusiasm pervades the whole

Army, and that the only exception to such magnanimous tender
will be of those who, having originally entered for the war,
cannot display anew their zeal in the public service. It is, therefore, deemed appropriate, and it is hoped will be equally acceptable, to make a general acknowledgment, instead of successive special responses. Would that it were possible to render
my thanks to you in person, and in the name of our common
country as well as in my own, while pressing the hand of each
war-worn veteran, to recognize his title to our love, gratitude, and
admiration!

Soldiers! By your will (for you and the people are but one) I
have been placed in a position which debars me from sharing your
dangers, your sufferings, and your privations in the field. With
pride and affection my heart has accompanied you in every march;
with solicitude it has sought to minister to your every want; with
exultation it has marked your every heroic achievement. Yet
never, in the toilsome march, nor in the weary watch, nor in the
desperate assault, have you rendered a service so decisive in results as in this last display of the highest qualities of devotion and
self-sacrifice which can adorn the character of the warrior patriot.

Already the pulse of the whole people beats in unison with
yours. Already they compare your spontaneous and unanimous
offer of your lives for the defense of your country with the halting and reluctant service of the mercenaries who are purchased
by the enemy at the price of higher bounties than have hitherto
been known in war. Animated by this contrast, they exhibit
cheerful confidence and more resolute bearing. Even the mur-
murs of the weak and timid, who shrink from the trials which
make stronger and firmer your noble natures, are shamed into
silence by the spectacle which you present. Your brave battle
cry will ring loud and clear through the land of the enemy as well
as our own, will silence the vainglorious boastings of their cor-
rupt partisans and their pensioned press, and will do justice to
the calumny by which they seek to persuade a deluded people
that you are ready to purchase dishonorable safety by degrading
submission.

Soldiers! The coming spring campaign will open under auspices well calculated to sustain your hopes. Your resolution
needed nothing to fortify it. With ranks replenished under the

influence of your example and by the aid of your representatives, who give earnest of their purpose to add, by legislation, largely to your strength, you may welcome the invader with a confidence justified by the memory of past victories. On the other hand, debt, taxation, repetition of heavy drafts, dissensions, occasioned by the strife for power, by the pursuit of the spoils of office, by the thirst for the plunder of the public Treasury, and, above all, the consciousness of a bad cause, must tell with fearful force upon the overstrained energies of the enemy. His campaign in 1864 must, from the exhaustion of his resources both in men and money, be far less formidable than those of the last two years, when unimpaired means were used with boundless prodigality and with results which are suggested by the mention of the glorious names of Shiloh and Perryville, and Murfreesboro and Chickamauga, and the Chickahominy and Manassas, and Fredericksburg and Chancellorsville.

Soldiers! Assured success awaits us in our holy struggle for liberty and independence, and for the preservation of all that renders life desirable to honorable men. When that success shall be reached, to you—your country's hope and pride—under Divine Providence, will it be due. The fruits of that success will not be reaped by you alone, but your children and your children's children, in long generations to come, will enjoy blessings derived from you that will preserve your memory ever living in their hearts.

Citizen-defenders of the homes, the liberties, and the altars of the Confederacy! That the God whom we all humbly worship may shield you with his Fatherly care, and preserve you for safe return to the peaceful enjoyment of your friends and the association of those you most love, is the earnest prayer of your Commander in Chief. JEFFERSON DAVIS.

Richmond, February 9, 1864.

By order:

S. COOPER, *Adjutant and Inspector General.*

OFFICIAL REGULATIONS TO CARRY INTO EFFECT THE ACT "TO IMPOSE REGULATIONS UPON THE FOREIGN COMMERCE OF THE CONFEDERATE STATES TO PROVIDE FOR THE PUBLIC DEFENSE."

I.—AS TO THE SEA.

1. The owners of any vessel intending to sail from a Confederate port with a cargo consisting in whole or in part of cotton, tobacco, military and naval stores, sugar, molasses, or rice, shall, before lading on board of any such articles, file with the collector of the port from which the vessel is to sail a copy of her register with a declaration of the names of the owners and officers thereof, the place of their birth and of their residence for the preceding year, together with the port or place to which the said vessel proposes to sail. The said declaration shall also set forth the quantity and value, in Confederate currency, of the cargo proposed to be taken out, as also the consent of the said owners that one-half of the tonnage of the said vessel may be employed by the Confederate Government for its own use, both on the outward and homeward voyage, at the rate of freight hereinafter mentioned. The collector shall submit a statement as to the owners and officers to the military commandant of the port, and if he shall not object to their loyalty or to the sailing of the vessel for reasons of military necessity the collector shall grant a permit for the lading of the said vessel, one-half for account of the owners and one-half for account of the Confederate States.

2. Before the said lading shall be completed the owners of the vessel shall execute to the Confederate States a bond in double the value of the vessel, with security deemed adequate by the collector, conditioned that she will pursue the voyage designated, and that she will return with reasonable dispatch to a Confederate port after her outward cargo shall be discharged, with a cargo consisting one-half of articles not prohibited by the laws of the Confederate Government and the other half of such articles as the Government shall offer for shipment from such port, at the rate of freight hereinafter mentioned.

3. Each shipper of any portion of the cargo proposed to be laden on board the said vessel shall, before the lading thereof,

make application to the collector for a permit to lade the same, which application shall declare the articles to be shipped and the quantity and value thereof in Confederate currency, the port of destination, and the name of the consignee. A permit shall be granted by the collector if the application is deemed satisfactory. The lading shall be had under the inspection of a revenue officer, who shall be charged with the duty of seeing that the goods laden conform to the permit.

4. Before the completion of the lading on board or the granting a clearance each shipper of any portion of the cargo shall execute and deliver to the collector a bond to the Confederate States in double the value of his shipment in Confederate money, with security deemed adequate by the collector, with condition that at least one-half the net proceeds of said shipment shall be invested in goods or articles not prohibited by law, and that the said goods or articles shall be shipped by the same or some other vessel to the Confederate States within sixty days from the unlading of said cargo; or that the said half of the net proceeds shall be paid in coin or sterling exchange to the proper agent of the Confederate States, to be reimbursed to the shipper by the delivery to him of cotton at the port of departure in the Confederate States at the rate of 10 pence sterling per pound for middling uplands.

5. The freight to be paid by the Confederate States on all cotton and tobacco shipped from a Confederate port shall be 5 pence sterling per pound, payable on delivery at the port of destination in coin or sterling exchange. Return freight shall be at the rate of £25 per ton, payable on its delivery in the Confederate port, in cotton at 10 pence sterling per pound for middling uplands, and at a proportionate price for cotton of other qualities. In calculating the ton of freight by weight, 2,240 pounds shall be allowed; by measure, 40 cubic feet shall be allowed.

6. If the outward-bound vessel shall consent, at the request of the Government, to take two-thirds of her cargo for account of the Confederate States, the outward freight shall be 6 pence sterling per pound; and whenever the Government is not prepared to fill up any portion of the tonnage reserved for its use at the time at which any vessel may be made ready to sail, the owners may fill up the same on their own account; but no vessel shall, without consent of the Government, sail on her outward voyage

until one-third of her cargo shall be laden for the use of the Government.

7. The rate of freight for articles other than cotton and tobacco shall be adjusted at the same relative rate and be payable in the same way.

8. The Government reserves the right to limit or prohibit the shipment of resin, turpentine, or any manufacture thereof, whenever deemed dangerous to its own shipment.

9. Upon the completion of the lading of the vessel, and before receiving her clearance, there shall be delivered to the collector, in addition to the usual manifest, another, setting forth the names, ages, and description of her officers and crew and of every passenger intending to sail in her. The said last-mentioned manifest shall be delivered to the commandant of the port, who shall thereupon cause the entire vessel to be searched, and if satisfied that the parties on board are persons who may safely be permitted to leave the Confederacy, and the passengers have the proper passports, he shall certify the same on the manifest and return the same to the collector, whereupon, and not before, a clearance shall be granted to the vessel, and she shall be permitted to sail.

10. The owners of each vessel and of each portion of a cargo sailing from a Confederate port shall be allowed to take up their respective bonds by producing to the collector the certificate of the proper agent of the Confederate Government at the port of delivery, setting forth the particulars showing that the said party has complied with the obligation of the said bond so far as the same was practicable ; and the collector, upon being duly satisfied, shall be authorized to surrender the said bonds.

11. Nothing in these regulations shall be so construed as to conflict with the proviso of the law which declares "that nothing in this act shall be construed to prohibit the Confederate States, or any of them, from exporting any of the articles herein enumerated on their own account ;" nor shall a bond be required of a State in any case.

12. The penalties of all bonds executed in conformity with these regulations shall be recovered in full on proof of breach of the conditions of the bond, and without proof of any damage suffered by the Confederate States in consequence of such breach, and all

bonds shall be executed in such force as to give effect to this regulation.

13. Vessels sent into the Confederacy for the purpose of exporting cotton received in payment of any Confederate bond or obligation shall be subject to these regulations only as far as relates to such portion of the tonnage, if any, as may remain vacant after the lading of the cotton received in payment as aforesaid.

14. The regulations for overland commerce with neutral countries will be issued separately within a few days.

Approved.

C. G. MEMMINGER, *Secretary of the Treasury.*
JAMES A. SEDDON, *Secretary of War.*
Approved March 5, 1864.

JEFF'N DAVIS.

RESOLUTIONS OF THANKS.

Whereas, the campaigns of the brave and gallant armies covering the capital of the Confederate States during the two successive years of eighteen hundred and sixty-two and eighteen hundred and sixty-three, under the leadership and command of General Robert E. Lee, have been crowned with glorious results, defeating greatly superior forces massed by the enemy for the conquest of these States, repelling the invaders with immense losses, and twice transferring the battlefield from our own country to that of the enemy; And whereas, the masterly and glorious achievements, rendering forever memorable the fields of the "Seven Days of Great Battles," which raised the siege of Richmond, as well as those of Cedar Run, Second Manassas, Harper's Ferry, Boonsboro, Sharpsburg, Shepherdstown, Fredericksburg, Winchester, Gettysburg, and Chancellorsville, command the admiration and gratitude of our country; And whereas, these and other illustrious services rendered by this able commander since the commencement of our war of independence have especially endeared him to the hearts of his countrymen, and have imposed on Congress the grateful duty of giving expression to their feelings: Therefore,

Resolved by the Congress of the Confederate States of America,

That the thanks of Congress are due, and are tendered, to General Robert E. Lee and to the officers and soldiers of the Confederate armies under his command, for the great and signal victories they have won over the vast hosts of the enemy, and for the inestimable services they have rendered in defense of the liberty and independence of our country.

Resolved, That the President be requested to communicate these resolutions to General Robert E. Lee, and to the officers and soldiers herein designated.

Approved January 8, 1864.

Whereas, Major Heros von Borcke, of Prussia, Adjutant and Inspector General of the cavalry corps of the Army of Northern Virginia, having left his own country to assist in securing the independence of ours, and by his personal gallantry in the field having won the admiration of his comrades as well as that of his commanding general, all of whom deeply sympathize with him in his present sufferings from the wounds received in battle: Therefore,

Resolved by the Congress of the Confederate States of America, That the thanks of Congress are due, and the same are hereby tendered, to Major von Borcke for his self-sacrificing devotion to our Confederacy, and for his distinguished services in support of its cause.

Resolved, That a copy of the foregoing resolution be transmitted to Major von Borcke by the President of the Confederate States.

Approved January 30, 1864.

Whereas, the Congress of the Confederate States have received, with the liveliest emotions, the cheering intelligence that a large portion of the Tennessee troops composing the Army of Tennessee, under the command of General Joseph E. Johnston, have tendered their services to the country during the war; it is, therefore,

Resolved by the Congress of the Confederate States of America, That the thanks of Congress are hereby cordially given to the gallant soldiers of Tennessee, who have, in advance of the legislation of Congress, and before their three years' term of service had expired, voluntarily tendered their services to the country during the war, with the heroic determination never to abandon the field till the last vandal invader is driven from our soil and our freedom won.

Resolved, That, in view of the magnitude of the struggle in which we are engaged, and the great stake at issue—the freedom of our country—the Congress indulges the confident hope that the example so heroically set by their brothers in arms will be followed by our whole Army, thus giving to the world, after nearly three years of arduous struggle, an earnest of their determination to die or be free.

Resolved, That the President be requested to have the foregoing preamble and resolution sent to the commanders of the Army, with the request that they communicate them to the officers and soldiers, as an evidence of the high appreciation in which they are gratefully held by the Congress of the Confederate States of America for their heroic valor displayed on so many memorable occasions, and for their fortitude and perseverance under so many trials.

Approved February 3, 1864.

The Congress of the Confederate States having learned through the public press of the reënlistment for the war of the North Carolina brigade in the Army of Northern Virginia serving under General Robert D. Johnston: Therefore,

Resolved by the Congress of the Confederate States of America, That the patriotism and spirit of the North Carolina troops, evinced by their prompt and voluntary devotion of themselves afresh to the service of the country, are beyond all praise, and deserve the unbounded gratitude of the country.

Approved February 6, 1864.

Resolved by the Congress of the Confederate States of America, That the thanks of Congress are tendered to the gallant troops from the State of Louisiana in the Army of Tennessee, who have, with signal unanimity, volunteered their services for the war.

Sec. 2. *Resolved,* That the lofty and self-sacrificing spirit exhibited by this noble act deserves, and will receive, the commendation and gratitude of every true patriot.

Sec. 3. *Resolved,* That the thanks of Congress are equally due, and are tendered, to the patriotic and self-sacrificing troops who, at the commencement of the war, placed their services at the disposal of their country without condition or limit as to time.

Approved February 6, 1864.

Resolved, That the thanks of Congress are due, and are hereby tendered, to the officers and men of the Second Florida Regiment, who, after a service of distinguished gallantry and heroic suffering for nearly three years, did, on the twenty-eighth ultimo, at a meeting held near Rapidan Station, Virginia, resolve to reënlist for the war at the expiration of their present term of service.

Approved February 6, 1864.

Whereas, the Alabama troops composing the brigade commanded by Brigadier General Cullen A. Battle, in the Army of Northern Virginia, volunteered in the service of the Confederate States, in the early part of the year eighteen hundred and sixty-one, upon the first call for troops for the defense of Virginia, have participated in every battle fought by that army, from the battle of Seven Pines to that of Gettysburg, always winning by their gallantry and devotion deserved praise and honor, and now, after enduring for nearly three years the hardships and dangers of active military service, have reënlisted for the war: Therefore,

Resolved by the Congress of the Confederate States of America, That the thanks of Congress are due, and are hereby cordially tendered, to the Alabama troops, who, by their renewing the offer of their services to the country for the war in advance of any legislative action, have shown a spirit undaunted, a heroic determination to battle ever until the independence of their country is established, and a consecration to the cause of liberty worthy of imitation by their comrades.

Resolved, That the President be requested to communicate a copy of the foregoing preamble and resolution to the commander and troops of said brigade as an evidence of the grateful appreciation by Congress of their fortitude and heroism during the trials and dangers of past services, and of their late act of patriotism, confirming the faith and reassuring the hope of the patriot.

Approved February 6, 1864.

The Congress of the Confederate States of America, having learned that the division of troops commanded by Major General Rodes have reënlisted for the war, do—

Resolve, That the thanks of Congress are due, and are hereby tendered, to the officers and troops commanded by Major General Rodes for the patriotism exhibited by them in reënlisting for the war as well as for the gallantry they have always displayed upon the field of battle; and they are assured that their country will always bear in grateful remembrance the noble manner in which they have come to her assistance in the hour of her need.

Resolved, further, That the President be requested to communicate this resolution to General Rodes and the officers and troops under his command.

Approved February 6, 1864.

Resolved by the Congress of the Confederate States of America, That the thanks of Congress are due, and hereby cordially tendered, to the gallant brigade of North Carolina troops commanded by Brigadier General S. D. Ramseur, in the Army of Northern Virginia, for their devoted patriotism in unanimously offering their valuable services to the Confederacy for the war, after having already signalized their patriotic zeal, fortitude, and valor on many fields of battle and in many scenes of trial.

Approved February 6, 1864.

Resolved by the Congress of the Confederate States of America, That the thanks of Congress are due, and are hereby tendered, to Colonel Thomas G. Lamar and the officers and men engaged in the gallant and successful defense of Secessionville against the greatly superior numbers of the enemy on the sixteenth day òf June, eighteen hundred and sixty-two.

Approved February 8, 1864.

Resolved, That the thanks of Congress are eminently due, and are hereby cordially given, to Captain Odlum, Lieutenant Richard Dowling, and the forty-one men composing the Davis Guards, under their command, for their daring, gallant, and successful defense of Sabine Pass, Texas, against the attack made by the enemy on the eighth of September last, with a fleet of five gunboats and twenty-two steam transports, carrying a land force of fifteen thousand men.

Resolved, That this defense, resulting, under the providence of God, in the defeat of the enemy, the capture of two gunboats, with more than three hundred prisoners, including the commander of the fleet, the crippling of a third gunboat, the dispersion of the transports, and preventing the invasion of Texas, constitutes, in the opinion of Congress, one of the most brilliant and heroic achievements in the history of this war, and entitles the Davis Guards to the gratitude and admiration of their country.

Resolved, That the President be requested to communicate the foregoing resolutions to Captain Odlum, Lieutenant Dowling, and the men under their command.

Approved February 8, 1864.

Resolved by the Congress of the Confederate States of America, That the thanks of Congress are eminently due, and are hereby cordially tendered, to General G. T. Beauregard and the officers and men of his command for their gallant and successful defense of the city of Charleston, South Carolina—a defense which for the skill, heroism, and tenacity displayed by the defenders during an attack scarcely paralleled in warfare—whether we consider the persistent efforts of the enemy or his almost boundless resources in the most improved and formidable artillery and the most powerful engines of war hitherto known—is justly entitled to be pronounced glorious by impartial history and an admiring country.

Resolved, That the President be requested to communicate the foregoing resolution to General Beauregard and the officers and men of his command.

Approved February 8, 1864.

Resolved, That the thanks of Congress are due, and are hereby tendered, to Major General Patrick R. Cleburne and the officers and men under his command for the victory obtained by them over superior forces of the enemy at Ringgold Gap, in the State of Georgia, on the twenty-seventh day of November, eighteen hundred and sixty-three, by which the advance of the enemy was impeded, our wagon train and most of our artillery saved, and a large number of the enemy killed and wounded.

Resolved, That the President be requested to communicate the foregoing resolution to Major General Cleburne and his command.

Approved February 9, 1864.

Resolved by the Congress of the Confederate States of America, That the thanks of Congress and of the country are due, and are hereby tendered, to the members of McClung's battery for the chivalrous and patriotic manner in which they have revolunteered and tendered their services for the war, and that a copy of this resolution be transmitted to them without delay.

Approved February 13, 1864.

Resolved by the Congress of the Confederate States of America, That the thanks of Congress are eminently due, and are hereby tendered, to the officers and men of the Tenth Mississippi Regiment for having patriotically and in a spirit of self-sacrificing devotion reënlisted for the war.

Resolved, That a record of these proceedings be forthwith furnished to the troops comprising the Tenth Mississippi Regiment.

Approved February 13, 1864.

Resolved by the Congress of the Confederate States of America, That the communication of Major Francis W. Smith, commanding a battalion of Virginia artillery, stationed at Drewry's Bluff, composed of "United artillery," Captain Thomas Kevill; "Johnston artillery," Captain B. J. Epes; "Neblett's artillery," Captain W. G. Coleman; and "Southside artillery," Captain J. W. Drewry, announcing their voluntary reënlistment for the war, is hailed with pleasure by Congress as an evidence of unfaltering devotion to the cause of liberty and independence and of stern determination to resist to the utmost the wicked purposes of a relentless and merciless foe.

Resolved, That the thanks of Congress are due, and are hereby tendered, to the officers and men of this command for their gallant and patriotic conduct "in unanimously reënlisting for the war under such regulations as Congress may prescribe."

Approved February 15, 1864.

Resolved by the Congress of the Confederate States of America,
That the thanks of Congress and of the country are due, and are
hereby tendered, to the officers and men of the Twenty-Eighth and
Thirteenth Regiments of North Carolina troops, who have so
gallantly revolunteered for the war, and have pledged themselves,
their lives, and fortunes never to lay down their arms until our
soil is freed from the invading foe and our independence obtained.

Approved February 15, 1864.

Resolved by the Congress of the Confederate States of America,
That the thanks of Congress are due, and are hereby, through
its representatives in Congress, tendered, to the officers and men
of the Third Georgia Regiment, who were the first to leave their
State to battle on the soil of Virginia, whose gallant dead have
been left on many of her historic battlefields, and which entire
regiment, to a man, have cheerfully and unanimously reënlisted
for the war, heroically resolving that, as they were among the first
to take up arms in the cause of liberty and independence, they will
be the last to lay them down.

Approved February 15, 1864.

Resolved by the Congress of the Confederate States of America,
That the thanks of Congress are due, and are hereby gratefully
tendered, to the officers and men of the gallant Twenty-Second
Regiment of Virginia Infantry for their noble zeal and patriotism
in reënlisting for the war.

Approved February 15, 1864.

Resolved by the Congress of the Confederate States of America,
That the thanks of Congress are hereby tendered to Hart's battery, Hampton's legion, South Carolina volunteers, for their gallant and patriotic resolution, recently adopted, to reënlist for the
war.

Approved February 15, 1864.

Resolved by the Congress of the Confederate States of America,
That the thanks of Congress are due to the officers and men of the
Forty-Sixth and Fifty-Fifth Regiments of Tennessee volunteers

for the promptness and patriotism they have displayed in unanimously reënlisting for the war "under such regulations as Congress may prescribe."

Approved February 15, 1864.

Resolved by the Congress of the Confederate States of America, That the thanks of Congress are hereby tendered to the officers and men of the Sixteenth Regiment of Mississippi troops, Colonel Samuel E. Baker commanding, for their patriotic resolution, recently adopted, to reënlist for the war.

Approved February 15, 1864.

Whereas, in addition to the various brigades and regiments of veteran troops from the State of Alabama to whom Congress has heretofore given evidence of grateful appreciation by vote of thanks for reënlisting for the war, other brigades and regiments are nobly coming to the rescue of their imperiled country by such reënlistment, thus furnishing evidence that the citizen soldiery from that State have determined never to abandon the struggle in which we are engaged until our independence shall have been achieved: Therefore—

Resolved by the Congress of the Confederate States of America, That the thanks of Congress are due, and are hereby tendered, alike to the gallant soldiery from the State of Alabama who, in the first instance, enlisted for the war, and to those who, notwithstanding the toils and hardships of many a weary march and perils of many a hard-fought battle, have voluntarily come forward and offered their labors and lives.

Resolved, That such noble examples of heroism and self-sacrifice will ever be remembered by a grateful country, and should stimulate all those who remain at home to redouble their exertions to provide, not only for the comfort and efficiency of those patriotic warriors, but for their families and loved ones whom they have left behind.

Approved February 15, 1864.

Resolved by the Congress of the Confederate States of America, That the thanks of Congress are due, and are hereby heartily tendered, to the Seventh and Twelfth Regiments Virginia Cavalry, for the patriotic and indomitable spirit they have displayed in so promptly reënlisting for the war, and that they have entitled themselves to the lasting gratitude of their country in thus renewing their vows of consecration to the sacred cause of Southern independence.

Approved February 15, 1864.

Resolved by the Congress of the Confederate States of America, That the thanks of the Congress are due, and are hereby cordially tendered, to the gallant troops of Lomax's cavalry brigade, for their patriotic example in reënlisting for the war, and that the lofty and determined spirit they have displayed in thus dedicating themselves afresh to the cause of independence will entitle them to the lasting gratitude of their country.

Approved February 15, 1864.

Resolved by the Congress of the Confederate States of America, That the thanks of the Congress are due, and are hereby tendered, to the troops in the Provisional Army of the Confederate States from the State of Georgia, who have so promptly and so gallantly reënlisted for the war.

Sec. 2. That the action of those who, from the beginning, have stood in front of danger and endured every hardship, in thus so cheerfully resolving to remain the voluntary bulwark of our country's defense, is commended by the Congress to all the people of the Confederate States as an example worthy of patriotic emulation, and should be accepted by every one as the signal for renewed devotion to the cause and for increased and universal energy in the prosecution of a struggle on the issue of which depends not only Confederate and State independence, but the very existence of constitutional government in America.

Approved February 15, 1864.

Resolved by the Congress of the Confederate States of America, That the thanks of Congress are due, and are hereby tendered, to the officers and men of the Sixty-First Virginia Regiment of Infantry and the Fifth Virginia Regiment of Cavalry, for having patriotically, and in a spirit of self-sacrificing devotion, reënlisted for the war.

Sec. 2. *Resolved,* That a record of these proceedings be forthwith furnished to the troops composing the above-named regiments.

Approved February 15, 1864.

Resolved by the Congress of the Confederate States of America, That the thanks of the Congress of the Confederate States are due, and are hereby tendered, to Commander John Taylor Wood, Confederate States Navy, and to the officers and men under his command, for the daring and brilliantly executed plans which resulted in the capture of the United States transport schooner "Elmore," on the Potomac River; of the ship "Allegheny," and the United States gunboats "Satellite" and "Reliance;" and the United States transport schooners "Golden Rod," "Coquette," and "Two Brothers," on the Chesapeake; and, more recently, in the capture from under the guns of the enemy's works of the United States gunboat "Underwriter," on the Neuse River, near Newbern, North Carolina, with the officers and crews of the several vessels brought off as prisoners.

Approved February 15, 1864.

Resolved by the Congress of the Confederate States of America, That the thanks of Congress are tendered to the Fifteenth, Twenty-Seventh, and Thirtieth Regiments of North Carolina troops for their patriotic devotion to our cause in reënlisting for the war.

Approved February 15, 1864.

Resolved by the Congress of the Confederate States of America, That the thanks of Congress are eminently due, and are hereby tendered, to the enlisted men of Douglas's (Texas) battery for the patriotic resolutions adopted by them on the eighteenth day of January last, and by which they reënlisted in the military service of the country for the war.

Approved February 16, 1864.

Resolved by the Congress of the Confederate States of America, That the reënlistment of the Fifteenth and Twenty-Seventh Regiments of North Carolina troops, Cooke's brigade, is a grateful

testimony of devotion to the great cause of Southern independence, and entitles them to the thanks of Congress and the country.

Resolved, That the thanks of Congress are hereby tendered to
the officers and men of said regiments for their noble and patriotic conduct in reënlisting for the war.

Approved February 16, 1864.

Resolved by the Congress of the Confederate States of America,
That Congress hails with delight the manifestations evinced by
the brave and gallant officers and privates of the Ninth Regiment,
Alabama Volunteers, who have stood under the fire of the enemy
for near three years, never to yield to Northern oppression; and
for this act of patriotism and exalted self-sacrifice in reënlisting
for the war the thanks of Congress and the country are eminently
due them. That the example of those brave men who have endured the dangers and perils of the war since its commencement
is a happy omen for the future, and should encourage Congress
and the country to rest with an abiding hope and confidence in the
success of our arms and the final triumph of liberty, under the
lead of those brave and unconquerable spirits.

Approved February 16, 1864.

Resolved by the Congress of the Confederate States of America,
That the thanks of Congress are due, and are hereby tendered, to
General E. Kirby Smith for the signal victory achieved by him in
the battle of Richmond, Kentucky, on the thirtieth of August,
eighteen hundred and sixty-one [1862], and to all the officers and
soldiers of his command engaged in that battle; and especially to
General Churchill, General Cleburne, and Colonel Preston Smith,
of whom he says: "I almost fear to particularize, lest I do not full
justice to all. But I cannot close without expressing my admiration at the promptness and intelligence with which Generals
Churchill, Cleburne, and Colonel Preston Smith executed the
orders given to them."

Sec. 2. *Resolved,* That special acknowledgments and commendation are declared for that highest order of generalship with
which this victory was followed up, utterly annihilating with five
thousand an army of ten thousand, of whom full five thousand
were actually captured, besides the slain in battle; and for the

brilliant campaign, in which the speed, vigor, and constancy of a rapid advance resulted in planting the Confederate flag upon the capitol of Kentucky, and upon the shores of the Ohio River, in front of the great city of Cincinnati.

Sec. 3. *Resolved,* That the superior generalship displayed in rapidly gathering the immediate fruits of a victory, and in following it promptly with a campaign of activity, enterprise, and unwearied constancy, renders it worthy of the applause of the Government and the emulation of the Army.

Sec. 4. *Resolved,* That the President is requested, in appropriate general orders, to make public the sense of Congress in the premises, and to cause the same to be communicated to General E. Kirby Smith and the officers named, and to be read at the head of each regiment engaged in that battle.

Approved February 17, 1864.

Whereas, Poague's artillery battalion, Third Army Corps, Northern Virginia, has patriotically reënlisted to serve during the war: Therefore—

Resolved by the Congress of the Confederate States of America, That the thanks of Congress and of the country are due, and are hereby tendered, to the officers and men of said battalion for this act of noble and patriotic devotion to the cause in which we are engaged.

Approved February 17, 1864.

Resolved by the Congress of the Confederate States of America, That the thanks of Congress are eminently due, and are hereby tendered, to the officers and men of the Thirty-Ninth [Seventh] Mississippi Regiment for their patriotic determination to continue in the service until the independence of these States shall have been firmly established.

Resolved, That the President be requested to transmit a copy of this resolution to the regiment whose patriotic devotion to their country's cause it is designed to acknowledge.

Approved February 17, 1864.

Resolved by the Congress of the Confederate States of America, That the thanks of Congress and the country are due, and are hereby tendered, to the officers and men of the Thirty-Seventh Regiment of North Carolina troops for their gallant conduct in re-volunteering for the war.

Approved February 17, 1864.

The Congress of the Confederate States of America do resolve, That the thanks of Congress are due, and are hereby tendered, to the enlisted men of the Surry Light Artillery, Captain J. D. Hark-ins, for their patriotic resolutions adopted on the ninth day of February, eighteen hundred and sixty-four, and for their man-ifestation of zeal in our struggle and devotion to their country's cause by reënlisting for the war.

Approved February 17, 1864.

Whereas, the Pee Dee Artillery of South Carolina Volunteers, early in the present struggle for Southern independence, tendered their services to the Government for the period of the war, and have recently renewed their pledge to serve their country until the last invader is driven from our soil: Therefore—

Resolved by the Congress of the Confederate States of America, That the thanks of Congress are due, and are cordially tendered, Pee Dee Artillery of South Carolina Volunteers, for their patri-otic reënlistment for the war.

Approved February 17, 1864.

Resolved by the Congress of the Confederate States, That the thanks of Congress are due, and are hereby tendered, to Orr's Rifles, the First, Twelfth, Thirteenth, and Fourteenth Regiments, South Carolina Volunteers, composing McGowan's Brigade, for their patriotic devotion to the cause of Southern independence, as manifested by their recent action, unanimously reiterating their determination to serve during the war; in thus renewing their pledges, after nearly three years of arduous and gallant service, they have met the expectation of their country, and are entitled to its approbation.

Approved February 17, 1864.

Resolved by the Congress of the Confederate States of America, That the thanks of Congress are again due, and are hereby tendered, to General N. B. Forrest and the officers and men of his command for meritorious service in the field, and especially for the daring, skill, and perseverance exhibited in the pursuit and capture of the largely superior forces of the enemy near Rome, Georgia, in May last; for gallant conduct at Chickamauga, and for his recent brilliant services in West Tennessee.

Approved February 17, 1864.

Resolved by the Congress of the Confederate States of America, That the thanks of Congress are due, and hereby cordially tendered, to Lieutenant General James Longstreet and the officers and men of his command for their patriotic services and brilliant achievements in the present war, sharing, as they have, the arduous fatigues and privations of many campaigns in Virginia, Maryland, Pennsylvania, Georgia, and Tennessee, and participating in nearly every great battle fought in those States; the commanding General ever displaying great ability, skill, and prudence in command, and the officers and men the most heroic bravery, fortitude, and energy, in every duty they may have been called upon to perform.

Resolved, That the President be requested to transmit a copy of the foregoing resolution to Lieutenant General Longstreet for publication to his command.

Approved February 17, 1864.

Resolved by the Congress of the Confederate States of America, That the thanks of Congress are due, and are hereby cordially tendered, to Major General J. E. B. Stuart and to the officers and men under his command for their distinguished gallantry and skill during the present war, especially as displayed in the summer of eighteen hundred and sixty-two, in the raid around the army of McClellan across the Chickahominy, the expedition into Pennsylvania, and to Catlett's Station, and in the battles of Fleetwood, Chancellorsville, and other places.

That the President be requested to communicate this resolution to General Stuart and the officers and men under his command.

Approved February 17, 1864.

Robert E. Lee.

ROBERT EDWARD LEE was born in Stratford, Westmoreland County, Virginia, January 19, 1807. His father was General Henry Lee, the "Light-Horse Harry" of the Revolutionary War. He attended school at Alexandria, Va., until 1825, when he entered the Military Academy at West Point, from which he graduated in 1829 without a demerit, second in a class of forty-six; was appointed second lieutenant of engineers and assigned to duty at Old Point and on the coasts; was assistant to the Chief of Engineers at Washington in 1834, and the next year was on the commission to mark the boundary line between Ohio and Michigan; was promoted first lieutenant in 1836 and captain of engineers in 1838. In 1837 was ordered to the Mississippi River to make special plans and surveys for its improved navigation; in 1840 was a military engineer; in 1842 was stationed at Fort Hamilton, N. Y., and in 1844 one of the Board of Visitors at West Point. At the beginning of the Mexican War, he was assigned to duty as Chief Engineer of the Army under General Wool, with the rank of captain, and at the request of General Scott was assigned to his personal staff. He rendered conspicuous service throughout that war, particularly at Vera Cruz, Cerro Gordo, Cherubusco, Molino del Rey, and Chapultepec. He was three times brevetted for gallant conduct during the war, the last being colonel of engineers. General Scott, in his official report, said of him, "I am compelled to make special mention of Captain R. E. Lee;" again, of one of his acts, he said it was "the greatest feat of physical and moral courage performed by any individual in my knowledge pending the campaign;" and again referred to him as being "as distinguished for execution as for science and daring," adding that his "success in Mexico was largely due to the skill, valor, and undaunted energy of Robert E. Lee;" and with emphasis he pronounced him "the greatest military genius in America." After the Mexican War, up to 1852, he was with the engineers' corps, headquarters at Baltimore; then Superintendent of the Mil-

437

itary Academy at West Point until 1855, when he was promoted and assigned to the Second Cavalry, under Col. Albert Sidney Johnston. He was engaged with this regiment fighting the Indians on the frontier of Texas and Mexico from 1856 to 1861, except that in October, 1859, he was temporarily at Washington during the John Brown raid at Harpers Ferry, and was sent by the President to suppress that movement, a duty promptly discharged by him. He was in command of the Department of Texas in 1860-61, when the Southern States began to secede from the Union, and was called to Washington about the date of the inauguration of President Lincoln. When it became known that war was to follow, he was offered high position in the United States Army, and was the choice of General Scott for the chief command. When told by a prominent gentleman, who was speaking for the President, that he could have the command of the Army, he replied that, "though opposed to secession and deprecating war, he would take no part in the invasion of the Southern States." Promptly— that is, within three days—after his State, Virginia, passed her ordinance of secession, he resigned his commission in the Army, as he said he felt conscientiously bound by the act of his State. In a letter to his sister, written then, he said: "We are now in a state of war which will yield to nothing. The whole South is in a state of revolution into which Virginia, after a long struggle, has been drawn; and though I recognize no necessity for this state of things, and would have forborne and pleaded to the end for the redress of grievances, real or supposed, yet in my own person I had to meet the question whether I should take part against my native State. With all my devotion to the Union, and the feeling of loyalty and duty of an American citizen, I have not been able to make up my mind to raise my hand against my relatives, my children, my home. I have, therefore, resigned my commission in the Army, and, save in defense of my native State—with the sincere hope that my poor services may never be needed—I hope I may never be called upon to draw my sword."

April 23, 1861, he was made commander in chief of the Virginia State forces, and began the work of organization for the State's defense. On April 25 he said: "No earthly power would give me as much pleasure as to restore peace to my country, but I fear it is now out of the power of man, and in God alone must be our

trust. I think our policy should be purely on the defensive, to resist aggression, and allow time to allay the passions, and permit
reason to resume her sway."

May 14, 1861, he was appointed brigadier general in the Confederate States Army, and on June 14, 1861, a full general; August
3rd, 1861, was given command of operations in the Trans-Alle-
ghany region of Virginia; November 5, 1861, was placed in
charge of the defenses on the coast of South Carolina, Georgia,
and Florida; March 13, 1862, assigned to duty at Richmond, and
charged with the conduct of all military operations of the Confederate States Army, under the direction of the President; June
1st, 1862, was placed in command of the Army of Northern Virginia, which position he held until the surrender of his army at
Appomattox, April 9, 1865; January 31, 1865, was made general
in chief, and on February 6, 1865, was assigned to the command
of all of the armies of the Confederate States.

Not long subsequent to the closing of the war, he said, "All
that the South has ever desired was that the Union as established
by our fathers should be preserved, and that the Government as
originally organized should be administered in purity and truth;"
and later he said, "I had no other guide, nor had I any other object
than the defense of those principles of American liberty upon
which the constitutions of the several States were originally
founded, and unless they are strictly observed, I fear there will
be an end of Republican government in this country." He devoted his few years after the war to efforts to restore harmony to
the people of the whole country, and to the education of young
men. He became President of Washington and Lee University,
and gave his entire time and talents to that institution. He died
at his home, in Lexington, October 12, 1870. When he died, it
was said of him: "The grave of this noble hero is bedewed with
the most tender and sacred tears ever shed upon a human tomb.
A whole nation has risen up in the spontaneity of its grief to
render the tribute of its love." Benjamin H. Hill, of Georgia,
said of him: "When the future historian shall come to survey the
character of Lee, he will find it rising like a huge mountain above
the undulating plain of humanity, and he must lift his eyes high
toward Heaven to catch its summit. He possessed every virtue
of other great commanders without their vices. He was a foe

without hate, a friend without treachery, a soldier without cruelty, a victor without oppression, and a victim without murmuring. He was a public officer without vices, a private citizen without wrong, a neighbor without reproach, a Christian without hypocrisy, and a man without guile.   He was a Cæsar without his ambition, Frederick without his tyranny, Napoleon without his selfishness, and Washington without his reward.   He was obedient to authority as a servant, and royal in authority as a true king. He was as gentle as a woman in life, modest and pure as a virgin in thought, watchful as a Roman vestal in duty, submissive to law as Socrates, and grand in battle as Achilles."

Second Congress.

FIRST SESSION.

MET AT RICHMOND, VA., MAY 2, 1864.   ADJOURNED JUNE 14, 1864.

MESSAGES.

RICHMOND, May 2, 1864.

To the Senate and House of Representatives of the Confederate States of America.

You are assembled under circumstances of deep interest to your country, and it is fortunate that, coming as you do newly elected by the people and familiar with the condition of the various localities, you will be the better able to devise measures adapted to meet the wants of the public service without imposing unnecessary burdens on the citizen. The brief period which has elapsed since the last adjournment of Congress has not afforded sufficient opportunity to test the efficacy of the most important laws then enacted, nor have the events occurring in the interval been such as materially to change the state of the country.

The unjust war commenced against us in violation of the rights of the States, and in usurpation of power not delegated to the Government of the United States, is still characterized by the barbarism with which it has heretofore been conducted by the enemy. Aged men, helpless women, and children appeal in vain to the humanity which should be inspired by their condition for immunity from arrest, incarceration, or banishment from their homes. Plunder and devastation of the property of noncombatants, destruction of private dwellings, and even of edifices devoted to the worship of God; expeditions organized for the sole purpose of sacking cities, consigning them to the flames, killing the unarmed inhabitants, and inflicting horrible outrages on women and children, are some of the constantly recurring atrocities of the invader. It cannot reasonably be pretended that such acts conduce to any end which their authors dare avow before the civilized world, and sooner or later Christendom must mete out to them

443

the condemnation which such brutality deserves. The suffering thus ruthlessly inflicted upon the people of the invaded districts has served but to illustrate their patriotism. Entire unanimity and zeal for their country's cause have been preëminently conspicuous among those whose sacrifices have been the greatest. So the Army, which has borne the trials and dangers of the war, which has been subjected to privations and disappointments (tests of manly fortitude far more severe than the brief fatigues and perils of actual combat), has been the center of cheerfulness and hope. From the camp comes the voice of the soldier patriots invoking each who is at home, in the sphere he best may fill, to devote his whole energies to the support of a cause in the success of which their confidence has never faltered. They—the veterans of many a hard-fought field—tender to their country, without limit of time, a service of priceless value to us, one which posterity will hold in grateful remembrance.

In considering the state of the country the reflection is naturally suggested that this is the Third Congress of the Confederate States of America. The Provisional Government was formed, its Congress held four sessions, lived its appointed term, and passed away. The permanent Government was then organized, its different departments established, a Congress elected, which also held four sessions, served its full constitutional term, and expired. You, the Second Congress under the permanent Government, are now assembled at the time and place appointed by law for commencing your session. All these events have passed into history, notwithstanding the threat of our prompt subjugation made three years ago by a people that presume to assert a title to govern States whose separate and independent sovereignty was recognized by treaty with France and Great Britain in the last century, and remained unquestioned for nearly three generations. Yet these very Governments, in disregard of duty and treaty obligations which bind them to recognize as independent Virginia and other Confederate States, persist in countenancing by moral influence, if not in aiding by unfair and partial action, the claim set up by the Executive of a foreign Government to exercise despotic sway over the States thus recognized, and treat the invasion of them by their former limited and special agent as though it were the attempt of a sovereign to suppress a rebellion against lawful authority. Ungenerous advantage has been taken of our present condition, and our rights have been violated, our vessels of war detained in ports to which they had been invited by proclamations of neutrality, and in one instance our flag also insulted where the sacred right of asylum was supposed to be secure; while one of these Governments has contented itself with simply deprecating, by deferential representations, the conduct of our enemy in the constantly recurring instances of his contemptuous disregard of neutral rights and flagrant violations of public law. It may be that foreign governments, like our enemies, have mistaken our desire for peace, unreservedly expressed, for evidence of exhaustion, and have thence inferred the probability of success in the effort to subjugate or exterminate the millions of human beings who, in these States, prefer any fate to submission to their savage assailants. I see no prospect of an early change in the course heretofore pursued by these Governments; but when this delusion shall have been dispelled and when our independence by the valor and fortitude of our people shall have been won against all the hostile influences combined against us, and can no longer be ignored by open foes or professed neutrals, this war will have left with its proud memories a record of many wrongs which it may not misbecome us to forgive, some for which we may not properly forbear from demanding redress. In the meantime it is enough for us to know that every avenue of negotiation is closed against us; that our enemy is making renewed and strenuous efforts for our destruction, and that the sole resource for us, as a people secure in the justice of our cause and holding our liberties to be more precious than all other earthly possessions, is to combine and apply every available element of power for their defense and preservation.

On the subject of the exchange of prisoners I greatly regret to be unable to give you satisfactory information. The Government of the United States, while persisting in failure to execute the terms of the cartel, make occasional deliveries of prisoners, and then suspend action without apparent cause. I confess my inability to comprehend their policy or purpose. The prisoners held by us, in spite of humane care, are perishing from the inevitable effects of imprisonment and the homesickness produced by the hopelessness of release from confinement. The spectacle of their suffering augments our longing desire to relieve from similar trials our own brave men who have spent so many weary months in a cruel and useless imprisonment, endured with heroic constancy. The delivery, after a suspension of some weeks, has just been resumed by the enemy; but as they give no assurance of intent to carry out the cartel, an interruption of the exchange may recur at any moment.

The reports of the Departments, herewith submitted, are referred to for full information in relation to the matters appertaining to each. There are two of them on which I deem it necessary to make special remark. The report of the Secretary of the Treasury states facts justifying the conclusion that the law passed at the last session for the purpose of withdrawing from circulation the large excess of Treasury notes heretofore issued has had the desired effect, and that by the 1st of July the amount in circulation will have been reduced to a sum not exceeding $230,000,000. It is believed to be of primary importance that no further issue of notes should take place, and that the use of the credit of the Government should be restricted to the two other modes provided by Congress—viz., the sale of bonds and the issue of certificates bearing interest for the price of supplies purchased within our limits. The law as it now stands authorizes the issue by the Treasury of new notes to the extent of two-thirds of the amount received under its provisions. The estimate of the amount funded under the law is shown to be $300,000,000, and if two-thirds of this sum be reissued we shall have an addition of $200,000,000 to our circulation, believed to be already ample for the business of the country. The addition of this large sum to the volume of the currency would be attended by disastrous effects and would produce the speedy recurrence of the evils from which the funding law has rescued the country. If our arms are crowned with the success which we have so much reason to hope, we may well expect that this war cannot be prolonged beyond the current year, and nothing would so much retard the beneficent influence of peace on all the interests of our country as the existence of a great mass of currency not redeemable in coin. With our vast resources the circulation, if restricted to its present volume, would be easily manageable, and by gradual absorption in payment of public dues would give place to the precious metals, the only basis of a currency adapted to commerce with foreign countries. In our present circumstances

I know of no mode of providing for the public wants which would entail sacrifices so great as a fresh issue of Treasury notes, and I trust that you will concur in the propriety of absolutely forbidding any increase of those now in circulation.

Officers have been appointed and dispatched to the trans-Mississippi States and the necessary measures taken for the execution of the laws enacted to obviate delays in administering the Treasury and other Executive Departments in those States, but sufficient time has not elapsed to ascertain the results.

In relation to the most important of all subjects at the present time, the efficiency of our armies in the field, it is gratifying to assure you that the discipline and instruction of the troops have kept pace with the improvement in material and equipment. We have reason to congratulate ourselves on the results of the legislation on this subject, and on the increased administrative energy in the different bureaus of the War Department, and may not unreasonably indulge anticipations of commensurate success in the ensuing campaign.

The organization of reserves is in progress, and it is hoped they will be valuable in affording local protection without requiring details and detachments from active force.

Among the recommendations contained in the report of the Secretary of War, your attention is specially invited to those in which legislation is suggested on the following subjects—viz.:

The tenure of office of the general officers in the Provisional Army, and a proper discrimination in the compensation of the different grades.

The provision required in aid of invalid officers who have resigned in consequence of wounds or sickness contracted while in service.

The amendment of the law which deprives officers in the field of the privilege of purchasing rations, and thus adds to their embarrassment, instead of conferring the benefit intended.

The organization of the general staff of the Army, in relation to which a special message will shortly be addressed to you, containing the reasons which compel me to withhold my approval of a bill passed by your predecessors at too late a period of the session to allow time for returning it for their reconsideration.

The necessity for an increase in the allowance now made for the transportation of officers traveling under orders.

The mode of providing officers for the execution of the conscript laws.

The means of securing greater dispatch and more regular administration of justice in examining and disposing of the records of cases reported from the courts-martial and military courts in the Army.

The recent events of the war are highly creditable to our troops, exhibiting energy and vigilance combined with the habitual gallantry which they have taught us to expect on all occasions. We have been cheered by important and valuable successes in Florida, northern Mississippi, western Tennessee and Kentucky, western Louisiana, and eastern North Carolina, reflecting the highest honor on the skill and conduct of our commanders and on the incomparable soldiers whom it is their privilege to lead. A naval attack on Mobile was so successfully repulsed at the outer works that the attempt was abandoned, and the nine months' siege of Charleston has been practically suspended, leaving that noble city and its fortresses imperishable monuments to the skill and fortitude of its defenders. The armies in northern Georgia and in northern Virginia still oppose with unshaken front a formidable barrier to the progress of the invader, and our generals, armies, and people are animated by cheerful confidence.

Let us, then, while resolute in devoting all our energies to securing the realization of the bright auspices which encourage us, not forget that our humble and most grateful thanks are due to Him without whose guidance and protecting care all human efforts are of no avail, and to whose interposition are due the manifold successes with which we have been cheered.

JEFFERSON DAVIS.

To the Senate of the Confederate States.

The action of the Senate on the nominations for field officers of the Eleventh Mississippi Regiment, which occurred on the eve of your adjournment at the last session, was not communicated to me till after the adjournment. I was then unable to return the nomination of Colonel Green for your reconsideration (his rejection appearing to have been based on an error), and have kept the whole subject open for further action at the present session, when you could be informed of the facts.

The resolution of the Senate is in the following words:

"Resolved, That the nomination of F. M. Green to be colonel of the Eleventh Mississippi Regiment be rejected for the reason that in the opinion of the Senate W. B. Lowry is the senior and ranking officer."

If the Senate had at the same time suspended its action on the other nominations, there could have been no difficulty in awaiting its present session for a settlement of the legal rights of the officers of this regiment, which cannot be affected by the action of the Executive, or the Senate, or of both combined, inasmuch as they are vested by act of Congress, which has the constitutional power to determine the rules of promotion in the service. But probably not perceiving, in the press of business at the close of the session, what would be the result of its action if carried into effect, the Senate confirmed the nominations of the lieutenant colonel and major, thus subordinating to two of his juniors the senior captain of the regiment, who had been in command of it to the entire satisfaction of his superior for more than nine months, and who had been adjudged to be the senior captain after an examination of the rights of the different claimants for seniority at the War Department.

I was compelled, in order to avoid this result, to decline commissioning either of the field officers confirmed by you, leaving each of the captains in his former rank of captain and leaving Captain Green in command of the regiment, till your attention had been called to the case and full information was placed within your reach.

The law and facts appear to me to admit of but one conclusion, and they are now presented as succinctly as possible.

1st. In this regiment, originally enlisted for twelve months, Captain Lowry was senior to Captain Green.

2d. Under act No. 306 of Provisional Congress (11th December, 1861) Captain Green's company reënlisted for the war, and he was reëlected captain under the provisions of the 4th section, and by the terms of act No. 397, of 15th February, 1862 (which may have been overlooked by the Senate), his commission under this reëlection took date from his former commission, so that he is a captain of the year 1861.

3d. On the 16th April, 1862, the conscript law was passed at the first session of the Permanent Congress, and by its first section all companies whose original term of service was for twelve months were allowed the privilege of reorganizing and electing officers, "who shall be commissioned by the President." But Congress did not extend to the officers thus reëlected the privilege of back date to their commissions, which had been accorded by the Provisional Congress to those who voluntarily reënlisted under the bounty and furlough laws.

Only two companies of the Eleventh Regiment volunteered reenlistment, of which Captain Green's was one, and Captain Franklin's the other. The remaining companies were reënlisted by conscription. Captain Franklin is no longer in the service. Under the laws as they stand on the Statute Book, Captain Green's commission is the only one in the regiment that bears date in 1861. The remaining commissions, being all under the conscript act of 1862, are necessarily subsequent to its passage.

It is due to candor to observe that the conclusion reached by the Senate in its resolution that Captain Lowry was the senior captain is in conformity with a general order issued by the War Department on the 9th July, 1862 (Gen. Orders No. 47, Par. 4), but many complaints having been made against the effects of this order, the whole subject was carefully investigated by me, and that order was modified on the 5th March, 1863, by Gen. Order No. 24, Par. 1. When, therefore, in the following May, the question of seniority between Captains Green and Lowry was presented to me for decision the question of law was no longer open, and nothing remained but to ascertain the facts, which were found to be in accordance with the foregoing narration.

I now respectfully send again to the Senate the nomination of Captain Green, to the office for which it has not been suggested he is incompetent, which he held for many months, and to which, according to my best judgment, he has rights vested in him by the laws. I am confident the Senate would never have consented to prejudice those rights if they had been in full possession of the facts.   JEFFERSON DAVIS.

Executive Department, Richmond, 4th May, 1864.

RICHMOND, VA., May 4, 1864.

To the Senate and House of Representatives.

I herewith transmit a communication* from the Secretary of the Navy, and invite your attention to his request for an early consideration of it.   JEFFERSON DAVIS.

RICHMOND, VA., May 5, 1864.

To the Senate and House of Representatives.

I herewith transmit for your consideration two communications from the Secretary of the Treasury, submitting estimates of additional appropriations required for the support of the Government.
                                        JEFFERSON DAVIS.

RICHMOND, VA., May 18, 1864.

To the Senate and House of Representatives.

I herewith transmit for your consideration a communication from the Secretary of the Treasury, submitting an estimate of an additional appropriation required for the support of the Government.   JEFFERSON DAVIS.

RICHMOND, VA., May 18, 1864.

To the Senate and House of Representatives.

I herewith transmit for your consideration a communication from the Attorney General, submitting estimates of additional appropriations required for the support of the Government.
                                        JEFFERSON DAVIS.

RICHMOND, VA., May 18, 1864.

To the Senate and House of Representatives.

Agreeably to the recommendation of the Secretary of State, I hereby nominate P. N. Lynch to be Special Commissioner of the Confederate States to the States of the Church.
                                        JEFFERSON DAVIS.

---

*Relative to a fund raised by ladies of South Carolina for the construction of an ironclad gunboat for the defense of that State.

RICHMOND, VA., May 19, 1864.

To the Senate and House of Representatives.

I herewith transmit for your information a communication from the Secretary of War, covering a copy of the reports of General Bragg and his subordinate commanders of the battle of Chickamauga.　　　　JEFFERSON DAVIS.

RICHMOND, VA., May 20, 1864.

To the House of Representatives.

In response to your resolution of the 10th inst., I herewith transmit for your information a communication from the Postmaster General relative to the steps taken to secure the transmission and delivery of the mails from the post office in this city during the past two weeks.　　　　JEFFERSON DAVIS.

RICHMOND, VA., May 20, 1864.

To the House of Representatives of the Confederate States of America.

The following resolution passed by the House on the 14th instant has been received:

Resolved, That the President be requested to inform the House, if not incompatible with the public interest, whether the reasons given in his special message for suspending the writ of *habeas corpus* still exist, and what additional reasons now exist to such extent that the public safety requires the continuance of the suspension thereof.

In my opinion the reasons given in the special message transmitted to Congress at its last session, recommending the suspension of the writ of *habeas corpus,* still exist in undiminished force and the present juncture especially requires the continuance of the suspension. The effects of the law for that purpose have been most salutary, and to that law in no inconsiderable degree are we indebted for the increased efficiency of the military preparations which have enabled our gallant armies, under the providence of God, to beat back the vast invading forces which still threaten us.

In my judgment it would be perilous, if not calamitous, to discontinue the suspension while the armies of the enemy are pressing on our brave defenders with persistent effort for their destruction and for the subjugation of our country.

It is a source of gratification to be able to inform you that the mere passage of the law suspending the writ was so effectual in restraining those who were engaged in treasonable practices and in dangerous complicity with our enemies that the instances are very few in which arrests were found necessary.

The effect of the law in preventing the abuse of the writ for the purpose of avoiding military service by men whose plain duty it is to defend their country can hardly be overestimated.

The sensitiveness exhibited in different parts of our country to the legislation on this subject is indicative of the love of freedom which is innate among the people, and which should ever be cherished as the sole guaranty for the preservation of their constitutional liberties. It is not doubted, however, that if those who have expressed dissatisfaction with the law had been in possession of the information which it was my duty to communicate to you, and which may not yet be revealed without injury to the public interest, they would fully have approved the exercise of the power of suspending the writ, which was intrusted to Congress by the Constitution. All trusts impose duties. The power was intrusted expressly with the intent that it should be used when necessary to the public safety in case of invasion. Congress, concurring with me that the exigency had arisen which required the exercise of the power, performed but a plain duty in passing the law, and such will, I doubt not, be the judgment of the people when the facts can be made known without detriment to their interests.

JEFFERSON DAVIS.

RICHMOND, VA., May 24th, 1864.

To the House of Representatives.

In further response to your resolution of the 10th inst., I herewith transmit for your information a communication from the Postmaster General relative to the steps taken to secure the transportation and delivery of the mails from the post office in this city during the past two weeks. JEFFERSON DAVIS.

RICHMOND, VA., May 28, 1864.

To the House of Representatives.

In response to a resolution of the House of Representatives of the 15th January last, I herewith transmit for your information a communication from the Secretary of War, covering a list of those who have been retired from the military service, "in accordance with the provisions of the act for ridding the Army of ignorant, disabled, and incompetent officers."   JEFFERSON DAVIS.

RICHMOND, VA., May 28, 1864.

To the Senate and House of Representatives.

I herewith transmit for your information a communication from the Secretary of War, covering copies of several reports of military operations, together with a copy of a letter from General R. E. Lee, in which he expresses his disapproval of the publication of such reports, and to which I invite your special attention.

JEFFERSON DAVIS.

RICHMOND, VA., May 30, 1864.

To the Senate of the Confederate States.

I invite your attention to the accompanying communication from the Secretary of the Navy, and, agreeably to his recommendation, hereby nominate the persons named upon the annexed list to the offices designated in the Provisional Navy. In addition to the annexed list, there are officers of the Navy now on shore duty who are deemed eminently qualified to command afloat, and it is not designed by these nominations to bar their future transfer to the Provisional Navy with their relative rank.

JEFFERSON DAVIS.

RICHMOND, VA., May 30, 1864.

To the Senate and House of Representatives.

I herewith transmit for your consideration communications from the proper officers, submitting estimates of the amounts required to carry out the provisions of the act, approved May 13, 1864, authorizing additional compensation to certain officers and employees in the civil and legislative departments of the Government.   JEFFERSON DAVIS.

RICHMOND, VA., May 30, 1864.

To the Senate and House of Representatives.

I herewith transmit for your consideration a communication from the Secretary of the Treasury, submitting an estimate of an additional sum required for the support of the Government.

JEFFERSON DAVIS.

RICHMOND, VA., June 1, 1864.

To the House of Representatives.

In response to your resolution of the 3d ultimo, I herewith transmit for your information a communication from the Secretary of War, stating that "no instructions have been issued to impressing officers and agents in addition to, or different from, those contained in General Order No. 30, bearing date March 4, 1864."

JEFFERSON DAVIS.

RICHMOND, VA., June 1, 1864.

To the House of Representatives.

In response to your resolution of the 25th ult., I herewith transmit for your information a communication from the Secretary of War, relative to the tobacco ration authorized to be furnished to the Army.

JEFFERSON DAVIS.

RICHMOND, VA., June 1, 1864.

To the Senate and House of Representatives.

I herewith transmit for your information a communication from the Secretary of War, covering copies of several additional reports of military operations. It is suggested that these reports should not be published or used otherwise than for the information of members and Senators of the Confederate States Congress.

JEFFERSON DAVIS.

RICHMOND, VA., June 1, 1864.

To the Senate and House of Representatives.

I herewith transmit for your information a communication from the Secretary of War, covering copies of additional reports of military operations in the year 1862.

JEFFERSON DAVIS.

RICHMOND, VA., June 1st, 1864.

To the House of Representatives.

In response to your resolution of the 5th ult., I herewith transmit for your information a communication from the Secretary of War, relative to the organization and disbanding of the Palmetto Battalion of Light Artillery.   JEFFERSON DAVIS.

RICHMOND, VA., June 2, 1864.

To the Senate and House of Representatives.

I herewith transmit for your information a communication from the Secretary of War, covering copies of additional reports of military operations during the year 1863.

JEFFERSON DAVIS.

RICHMOND, VA., June 4th, 1864.

To the House of Representatives.

In response to your resolution of the 5th ultimo, I herewith transmit a communication from the Secretary of War, conveying the information asked for relative to the organization and disbanding of Company K, of the 27th Regiment, South Carolina Volunteers.   JEFFERSON DAVIS.

RICHMOND, VA., June 4, 1864.

To the Senate and House of Representatives.

I herewith transmit for your consideration communications from the proper officers, submitting estimates of the amount required to be appropriated, for the period ending Dec. 31, 1864, under the act* approved June 2, 1864.   JEFFERSON DAVIS.

RICHMOND, VA., June 4th, 1864.

To the House of Representatives.

In response to your resolution of the 5th ult., I herewith transmit for your information a communication from the Secretary of War, relative to the "Holcomb Legion of South Carolina Volun-

---

*Increasing salary and mileage of Senators and members, and compensation of employees of the Senate and House of Representatives.

teers" and to "other legionary organizations" in the Provisional Army of the Confederate States.   JEFFERSON DAVIS.

RICHMOND, VA., June 8, 1864.
To the House of Representatives.

In response to a resolution of the House of Representatives, of January 15, 1864, I herewith transmit for your information a communication from the Secretary of War, covering a copy of the proceedings of the court of inquiry, relative to the capture of New Orleans.   JEFFERSON DAVIS.

RICHMOND, VA., June 8th, 1864.
To the Senate and House of Representatives.

I herewith transmit a communication from the Secretary of War, covering copies of additional reports of military operations during the year 1863.

It is suggested that these papers are intended to be used for the information of members of Congress, and that their publication at this time is considered unadvisable.   JEFFERSON DAVIS.

VETO MESSAGES.

RICHMOND, May 28, 1864.
To the Senate and House of Representatives.*

A bill "to provide and organize a general staff for armies in the field to serve during the war" was passed by your predecessors and submitted for my approval at the close of the last session.

I was unable to approve it, and now desire to state my objections to it, as well as my views on this important subject, in a hope that by a comparison of opinion some measure may be framed equally acceptable to the Legislative and Executive Departments of the Government.

I believe it to be established by the experience of Europe as well as our own that it is impracticable to organize and administer armies with efficiency without the aid of a general staff, permanent in its character, trained in its duties, aspiring to promotion in its

---

*Pocket veto.

own corps, and responsible to the head of the Department. Such a staff should be composed of a small body of officers, whose education, experience, activity, and special adaptation to their duties render them peculiarly competent to perform functions on which an army depends for its capacity to act with vigor. In Europe years of varied education in the schools, the cantonment, and the field fit the staff officer for his position, and a long experience in the lower grades is required before he is deemed competent to duty in a more important sphere. We are forced to make experimental appointments of officers unprepared by any previous training, and who can acquire only in actual service that experience which must serve in place of well-grounded instruction. It is scarcely possible to make this experience supply the defect of previous military education, otherwise than by the organization of the officers into one corps, responsible to one head, who can assign them to positions independent of the movements of general officers, and who, by judiciously varying the field or character of their duties, can give them larger opportunities for instruction and prevent their views being narrowed to the routine and usages of a single commander, himself, perhaps, without military education.

Hope of promotion, founded on their own merit and length of good service, is as necessary to the officers of the general staff as to those of the line, furnishing the best stimulus known to honorable exertion and zealous discharge of duty. This stimulus cannot exist unless the staff be organized into one corps, responsible to one chief, who, thus becoming intimately acquainted with the capacity and merits of each, is able properly to distribute the duties so as to secure the services of the right man in the right place, and to afford to each an opportunity for distinction. If, otherwise, each staff officer becomes dependent upon the particular commander with whom he is serving, no means of comparison exist between the relative merits of the officers. Each looks for promotion to the favor of his general, and rises in grade, not by his own relative merit, but by the patronage of his commander. A gallant and able commander, whose own promotion is exceptionally rapid by reason of his special merits, is thus enabled to lift to higher grades the officers of his staff to whom he has become attached by companionship in the field, although these officers may be far inferior in merit and length of service to others whose duties have connected them with generals less distinguished. Promotion thus becomes with the staff a matter of hazard, dependent not on the merit of the officer himself, but of the general with whom he serves, and heartburnings, jealousy, and discontent are the natural results of so false a system.

Again, if the general staff is not formed into corps, there will not be the "esprit" necessary in all military organizations, and there cannot be the cointelligence among the officers thereof which secures the certain and rapid communication of all information through the different parts of an army. There will also be embarrassment in their tenure of office and assignment to duty, as when a general officer dies or is relieved from his command there remain no duties to be performed by the staff which has been authorized for him especially. However valuable or meritorious the officers may be, they are displaced by the staff chosen by the successor of their commander. Nothing remains but to deprive them of their commissions, without fault of their own, or to keep them in service as supernumeraries, and thus to add to the number of officers already in excess of the wants of the Army.

Again, an organization of a general staff should possess flexibility, so that the proper number and class of staff officers can be sent where needed. If an inflexible rule of assignment be fixed by legislation, some commands will be cumbered with unnecessary officers, while others will be deficient in the number indispensable to perform the necessary duties. Legislation would surely be considered unwise if it allotted by inflexible rule the number of troops to be used in each military department; yet it would be scarcely more objectionable than the assignment of the same specified number of staff officers to each commander, according to his grade, thus applying a general rule to a series of cases each requiring special treatment.

The inspecting duties in an army ought not, in my judgment, to be separated from those of the adjutants. The erroneous impression prevails that an inspecting department, independent of the general staff, is established in most of the armies of Europe. The reverse is the fact, and the duties of inspection are so intimately connected with the other duties of the general staff that they can be properly performed by it alone. The objections to the separation are manifold. In the first place, officers having no other than inspecting duties must frequently be unemployed, even in war, while in peace their duties will occupy but very little time. Next, it is to be observed that where the adjutants and inspectors form one corps the duties of the adjutant make him familiar with the details of the service where reform and discipline are most needed, and thus render him more competent to effective inspection when assigned to that duty than he could be if exclusively employed as inspector. Lastly, the duties of an inspector are such as not to render the officer who performs them acceptable to his brother officers, if his duty be properly performed. It is not to be wondered at that an officer whose duties may not be inappropriately described as those of a detective should, if his duty be rigidly performed, incur somewhat of the odium of an informer; and when these duties constitute the sole service of an officer permanently attached to an army, he must become either so lax in their performance as to render him useless, or his professional pride and self-respect are wounded and his relations with his brother officers unfavorably affected by the distrust and dislike resulting from his official reports. When, however, an assistant adjutant and inspector general is from time to time assigned to the making of necessary inspections at various points, this temporary discharge of an unpleasant duty becomes but an incident in his professional career, and does not affect his relations with his brother officers.

Having stated these as the general principles which in my judgment should govern legislation on the subject, the objections to the bill passed at the last session can be more easily understood, and I proceed to state them briefly:

I. The first section of the bill authorizes a general commanding armies, or a separate army, to assign to duty one of the general officers under his command as chief of staff, one of the brigadier generals under his command as inspector general, and one other brigadier as chief quartermaster, one officer below the rank of brigadier as chief commissary, and one as chief of ordnance.

This power of assignment is given without reference to or consultation with the War Department or the Executive, and might be exercised in contravention of the views and judgment of both. Leaving out of view the question whether it is in accordance with the Constitution to make the commander of an army independent of the Commander in Chief in the discharge or any of the duties of his office, and looking only to the effect of such a system, it plainly creates in this branch of the service as many independent executives as there are generals commanding armies in the field, and thus destroys that unity of design and concert of action which are indispensable elements of success in war. The generals commanding armies would be by this section vested with the right to derange the organization of their commands as settled by the Commander in Chief by removing from their appropriate functions the commanders of corps, divisions, and brigades, whom the Executive had selected and the Senate had approved as specially fitted to lead the troops in battle.

That the general commanding the Army has, under the terms of this section, the right of assigning general officers under his command to the duties of the general staff without reference to the authority of the Executive is plain from the other sections, which declare that the President is to appoint, with the advice of the Senate, the staffs of all general officers other than those who command armies.

Nor does this section restrict the commanding general in relation to the branch of service or the grade of the officers whom he is permitted to assign to commissary and ordnance duties of the general staff. It is only necessary that they be below the rank of brigadier general. The commanding general would have the power, therefore, to assign a captain commissary to be chief of ordnance, or a lieutenant of infantry to be chief commissary, without check or control from the President or Senate, while the President would be without power to appoint subordinates to the officers thus selected by the general of the Army without submitting their nominations for the approval of the Senate. Not only, therefore, is all order of authority introverted by these provisions, but the officers assigned to duty by the commanding generals, not being permanent members of the general staff, would be independent of its chief, and inextricable confusion would necessarily result.

This section, so far from responding to the title of the bill by providing a general staff, in reality breaks up that which now exists, subdivides it into a number of small bodies, irresponsible to the head of the department, and destroys the possibility of any regular, consistent, and intelligent coöperation in the action of our forces, so essential to success. Its effect is to create a staff for generals, not a general staff.

If a contest should arise between the quartermasters general, the commissaries general, or the chiefs of ordnance of Generals A and B, in any district of country for supplies or means of transportation, who is to determine between these rivals, each equal in authority and each dependent on a separate chief? How are the chiefs of those bureaus in Richmond to apportion the supplies in store according to the wants of the different armies without authority to exact from them reports and returns? If it be said that these officers would become temporarily responsible to the heads of departments, how is this responsibility to be enforced if the orders of the general and those of the chief of the department should conflict? If ordnance depots are provided at different points for different commands, how is the officer in charge of these depots to act if ordered by the chief of ordnance of a general in the field to make a different disposal of the stores from that ordered by the head of the department in Richmond?

If such a bill should become a law, in vain would the War Department seek to exact rigid obedience to law or orders from the irresponsible staff created under its provisions. In vain would it seek for the information necessary for its guidance, or attempt to change the relative strength of armies to meet the varying movements of the enemy. The staff officers could be made the ready and safe means of thwarting the Government in its orders for the removal of troops from one command to reënforce threatened positions in another, and could be easily rendered subservient to the natural but dangerous propensity of most commanders to retain all the troops under their own control for the safety of their own commands, without reference to more urgent needs at other points.

It is scarcely necessary to add to these considerations more than a bare allusion to the tendency of such bodies of officers, when dependent for their own promotion on the favor of the special chiefs, to resort to agencies less commendable than the zealous discharge of their legitimate duties for the attainment of their desires.

II. Another very objectionable feature of the bill proposed is its effect on the officers of the general staff other than those who may be selected as the favorites of commanding generals.

Numbers of zealous, meritorious, and valuable officers have made the duties of the general staff objects of special study; have embraced the staff as a branch of the profession in which under existing laws they are entitled to promotion for merit and long service, just as the line officers have a right to promotion in their branch.

This bill deprives the staff officers of this the great incentive to the zealous discharge of duty. It debars them from promotion to the higher grades of their own branch of service, and bestows these prizes of honorable ambition on the officers of the line, who will thus monopolize the promotions to the higher grades, both in the line and staff, to the entire exclusion of the officers of the latter. Few will be willing to remain in the staff under such circumstances. Those who consent to continue will be those least ambitious of promotion, and the whole staff service will be impaired in tone and efficiency.

III. The assignment of general officers to staff duties as provided in the bill would leave many brigades, some divisions, and perhaps some corps without their appropriate commanders, and no provision is made to supply the vacancies thus created. Are their commands to be considered vacant and successors appointed? If so, what is to become of those assigned to staff duty, should the commanding general revoke the assignment? If the contrary, many brigades will be commanded by the officer next in rank to be assigned brigadier, however incompetent such officer may be to command a brigade, and the like would occur as to divisions and corps, in contravention of the policy, well considered and established, that general officers are appointed by selection for merit, and not promoted by seniority. If the commanding general is ordered to another command, is he to take his staff with him, or is he to leave it for service with his successor? In either case, is the whole general staff of each army to be changed at the caprice of the new commander? This must be the effect of the bill, for the power to assign necessarily implies the power to revoke, as it would otherwise be equivalent to a permanent appointment, that could be made only by the President, with the advice and consent of the Senate.

IV. The fourth objection to the bill is that it applies one rigid rule for the number of the general staff, based solely on the rank of the commander and having no reference to the necessities of a command. The staff allowed is excessive in number and rank in many instances and entirely inadequate in others. A law providing a general staff on such a basis as is assumed in this bill cannot, from its very nature, be executed according to its terms. The labor required of the staff connected with a brigade, division, or corps depends on the fact of its being part of an army or a separate command as well as on the number of men; the extent of the country over which operations are to be conducted; the abundance or scarcity of supplies in the district; the existence or absence of railroad, river, or other transportation; the concentration or dispersion of the troops, and the many other circumstances which control military movements in time of war. It is impossible to apply a rigid, unbending rule to such diverse cases. An organization into corps meets all these difficulties by providing for assignment of the proper number of officers to different commands according to the needs of each.

V. The number and rank of aids-de-camp allowed by the bill are believed to be greatly in excess of those allowed by other governments and quite unsuited to the nature of ours. They would rather impede than improve the service. They would encourage love of ostentation and feed a fondness for vain display, which should rather be discouraged than fostered. The experience of this war has demonstrated that the most efficient commanders, those who have most attracted the respect, gratitude, and admiration of their country, have avoided the large retinue of personal staff which this bill would seem to sanction as proper or desirable.

VI. The objection to the enormous increase in the number of officers and expenditure that would result from the passage of such a bill becomes a matter of serious concern when no corresponding increase of efficiency is secured; of still graver importance when the opposite result is to be feared.

According to the bill as passed the staff would embrace an addition of about 400 officers, involving an increased annual expenditure for pay, rations, forage, and allowance amounting to $1,138,-728 above the present staff as organized by general orders under existing legislation.

If generals are to be allowed to change the staff of each army to which they may be assigned at their pleasure, it is difficult to calculate the extent to which this abuse would grow, the number of men that would be drawn from useful service to cumber the staff, or the increase of expenditure involved.

Congress will perceive that with objections so radical it was impossible for me to approve the bill passed at the last session, and that the subject was too important to be treated in a hurried message within the last few hours of the close of a Congress. Concurring in the expediency of legislation for the organization of a general staff, I have thought a full exposition of my views on the subject would perhaps conduce to the framing of a measure which would carry into effect the views of the Legislative Department while excluding the provisions which have compelled me to decline approving that devised by your predecessors.

JEFFERSON DAVIS.

RICHMOND, June 6, 1864.

To the Senate of the Confederate States.

I regret that a sense of duty compels me to return to the Senate without my signature a joint resolution which originated in your honorable body entitled "Joint resolution in regard to the exemption of editors and employees of newspapers."

The terms of this resolution extend to editors of magazines and periodicals other than newspapers, together with their employees, the same exemption from military service as is now accorded in favor of newspapers.

I see no reason for exempting these citizens from the duty of defending their country which would not apply to all authors, publishers, booksellers, printers, and other persons connected with the publication of books, pamphlets, religious tracts, and other reading matter. At a moment when our lives, our liberty, and our independence are threatened by the utmost power of our enemies, when every citizen capable of bearing arms ought to be found in the ranks, I cannot but deem it impolitic to add to the list of exemptions without the most urgent necessity. Seeing no such necessity, and believing the precedent set by this resolution, if passed, to be productive of evil effect, I am constrained to return it without my approval.

JEFFERSON DAVIS.

RICHMOND, June 7, 1864.

To the Senate of the Confederate States of America.

A bill which originated in the Senate entitled "An Act to authorize the appointment of additional officers of artillery for ordnance duties" has been presented for my signature, but it contains a provision founded on an error of fact which compels me to return it without approval, that the error may be corrected.

The bill contains the following proviso: "*Provided,* That acting ordnance officers having been found duly qualified for appointment according to the regulations of the War Department, and being already on duty in the field under the orders of the Secretary of War, shall have preference of appointment under this act." There are no acting ordnance officers on duty in the field, and I learn on inquiry that the persons so designated are in reality merely employees of the Ordnance Bureau for the performance of ordnance duties in the field in the absence of legislation authorizing the appointment of officers. This proviso, therefore, has the effect, under an error of fact apparent in its terms, of restricting the Executive in the choice of persons to fill the offices created by the bill to a list of employees selected by a chief of bureau, which is plainly not in accordance with the expressed intention of Congress, nor with the terms of the Constitution.

JEFFERSON DAVIS.

RICHMOND, VA., June 10, 1864.

To the House of Representatives of the Confederate States of America.

I herewith return to your honorable body, with my objections, a bill which originated in the House entitled "An Act to amend an act entitled an act to impose regulations upon the foreign commerce of the Confederate States to provide for the public defense," approved February 6, 1864.

The principal provisions of the bill are unexceptionable, but one of its clauses requires to be guarded by some restriction or modification in order to prevent serious injury to the public service. For a proper understanding of the subject it is necessary to state certain facts, probably unknown to many members, and which have an important bearing on the policy of the Government.

Prior to the passage of the act of 6th of February, 1864, the

Government was without any means of making available the cotton and tobacco in its possession for the purchase abroad and importation of supplies essential to the conduct of the war and the efficiency of the Army, other than two or three steamers belonging to the departments, and such steamers belonging to private owners as could be obtained by contract. The prices charged to the Government were too excessive to be borne, while the profits of the private owners were so great as to enable them by the payment of extravagant wages and rewards to secure (against the possibility of competition on the part of the Government) the choice of the pilots, engineers, and other officers available for the service. The large majority of those engaged in the trade were foreigners who, by the aid of the fortifications and defenses established and maintained in our harbors at the Confederate expense, were thus enabled to accumulate rapid fortunes, while depreciating our currency and exhausting our country of the productions which form its most valuable resources for needful supplies during the war. In the beginning these vessels were by consent of the owners made partially available for public purposes, and a portion of their tonnage was reserved for public use, but always at very extravagant rates. Subsequently, however, even these profits were insufficient to satisfy the demands of some of the traders, and attempts were made to enhance gains by bringing State and Confederate officials into competition for the use of the vessels. The evil effects of the system were so apparent that the act of the 6th of February last was passed by your predecessors, and under its provisions regulations were adopted which were intended to guard the public interest, while still offering to private owners adequate profits to induce a continuance of the trade. For some weeks after the adoption of these regulations strenuous efforts were made by parties interested in the business to induce a relaxation of the regulations. Many of the vessels remained unemployed on the allegation of the owners that the terms imposed by the regulations were so onerous as to render impossible the continuance of the business. The regulations remained unchanged, for I was satisfied, from an examination of the subject, that this complaint was unfounded, and that the withdrawal of the vessels was an experiment by a combination among the owners on the firmness of the Government. The result proved the correctness of the view, for, after various attempts to obtain increased advantages, the vessels resumed their voyages. Their number has been largely increased, the ability to export produce and import supplies on Government account has been developed to a greater extent than had been anticipated, and the credit of the Government has been so improved in foreign markets that the quotations for its loan have rapidly advanced.

It is proper here to observe that among the efforts made to induce a change of the regulations, was a warning given to officers of the Government that the owners of vessels could make better bargains with Governors of States than with the Confederate Government, and that if the regulations were not relaxed in their favor, they would transfer their vessels to the Executives of the several States and thus withdraw them from the operations of the regulations.

Reverting to the terms of the act of 6th of February, 1864, it is to be observed that by the fifth section it was provided that nothing in the act "shall be construed to prohibit the Confederate States or any of them from exporting any of the articles herein enumerated on their own account." Holding in view this expression of the legislative will, the regulations authorized by the law were formed and are now in force, based substantially on the following policy:

First. That every vessel owned by private persons shall be considered on every voyage as chartered to the Confederate Government for one-half of her tonnage, outward and inward.

Second. That all private owners of cargo exported from the Confederacy shall bring in return supplies equal to one-half of the proceeds of their expected cargo.

Third. That the several States shall remain at liberty to charter the other half of each vessel, and shall be free to carry out or bring back cargo on that half without being subject to the regulations.

It will be perceived that the policy of these regulations places the several States on an equal footing with the Confederate Government so far as is possible, the only difference being that while the Confederacy imposes a forced charter for one-half of the tonnage in its favor, it has no authority to do more for the States

than to leave tne other half subject to their use by charter obtained
by consent of the owners.

When these regulations were accepted by the owners of vessels
they amounted in substance to an agreement on their part to charter half of their tonnage to the Confederacy on every voyage at
the rates stipulated in the regulations.

Now, the bill which I return to the House makes three provisions:

First. That cargo shipped by the States shall not be subject to
the regulations, and to this there can be no objection. It merely
reaffirms the law as it stands.

Second. That vessels owned by any State and employed for the
exclusive use of the State shall not be subject to the regulations;
and to this no objection is made, as it places vessels owned by any
State on the same footing as vessels owned by the Confederacy.

Third. That vessels chartered by any State for its exclusive
use shall not be subject to the regulations; and this is the provision to which objection is made, because it is liable to a construction which would authorize the States, instead of chartering
from the owners of vessels in the trade only that half which remains at their disposal under the regulations, and thus preserving
equality with the Confederate Government in this matter, to charter the entire tonnage of the vessels, thus depriving the Confederacy of a resource now at its disposal, and without which very
serious embarrassments to the public service would ensue. When
it is remembered that the number of private vessels in the service
is limited, that the profits of exporting produce are very large,
that the temptation to engage in the business will be great, it is
easy to perceive how grave might become the consequences of
sanctioning a system under which the several States and the
Confederate Government would be competitors for contracts with
the owners of the vessels engaged in this commerce, and how imminent the risk that the Confederacy would be deprived of this indispensable means of carrying on the war.

I trust, therefore, that the House will concur in the opinion that
the words "or chartered" should be stricken out of the closing
sentence of the bill, or that a clause should be added providing
"that nothing in this law shall be so construed as to affect the
rights of the Confederate States under existing regulations to the

use of one-half the tonnage of each vessel engaged in the trade, except such as are owned exclusively by a State."

JEFFERSON DAVIS.

To the House of Representatives of the Congress of the Confederate States.

I herewith return to you an act to amend an act entitled "An Act to reduce the currency and to authorize a new issue of notes and bonds," approved February 17, 1864, with the objections which induce me to withhold my approval thereof.

Under the provisions of the act of 17 February, 1864, all Treasury notes above the denomination of five dollars not bearing interest, which shall not have been funded east of the Mississippi on 1 April, 1864, and on 1 July west of the Mississippi, are made subject to a tax of 33 1-3 cents on the dollar. Notes of the denomination of one hundred dollars are made subject to a further tax of ten per cent per month until funded; and all these notes outstanding on 1 January, 1865, are then taxed 100 per cent.

The effect of these provisions east of the Mississippi is to reduce the nominal rate of all the notes one-third after the 1 April, to increase this reduction ten per cent per month on the one hundred dollar notes until 1 November, 1864, at which date they are extinguished, and on 1 January, 1865, to extinguish the other notes.

The amendatory act which it is now proposed to pass grants to certain persons the privilege of funding at par all these notes until 1st January, 1865; and thus in effect gives to them precisely the rights which are taken away from all other citizens by the original act.

The extent of this privilege may be measured by the fact that the one hundred dollar notes outstanding on 1 April were estimated by the Secretary of the Treasury to amount to one hundred and twenty-eight millions. In the hands of persons not embraced by the amendatory act, they have already lost one-third of their nominal value. They continue to lose 10 per cent per month, and finally, on 1 November, such as remain outstanding will cease to have any value. But in the hands of the persons described in the amendatory act they all stand good against the Government for their entire original value.

The persons to whom this privilege is granted are by the terms of the amendatory act disposed into two classes:

1. Loyal citizens or persons belonging to the Confederate States Army within the enemy's lines as prisoners of war.

2. Other loyal persons held as prisoners, who, by reason of the occupation by the enemy of the section of country in which they resided, and the interruption of the postal and telegraphic communication, or other unavoidable cause were prevented from obtaining timely information of the requirements of the said act, or who were so situated in consequence of movements of the enemy or the casualties of war as to be unable to comply with the provisions thereof.

The evidence which the act requires to establish the facts upon which the claim rests is the simple affidavit of the claimant; and it is only in case of his inability to make affidavit that suppletory proof is required. The persons described in this law comprehend the population remaining in several States of the Confederacy and large portions of other States. The only exception is of such as may be unwilling to make oath of loyalty. The law does not even restrict its benefits to loyal citizens, but expressly includes "other persons," and contains no indication of the meaning to be attached to the word "loyal" when applied to persons not citizens of the Confederate States.

It is known that very large amounts of Treasury notes have fallen into the hands of the enemy by the fortunes of war, and one of the results accomplished by your predecessors in affixing short delays for funding was to prevent these notes from becoming available to the plunderers who had robbed our citizens. It is too plain for doubt that our enemies, who have not hesitated in the attempt to defraud the Treasury and the people by means of counterfeited notes, would have little scruple or difficulty in devising means to bring themselves within the terms of the bill under consideration. It is but a moderate calculation to say that at the present moment taxes which have accrued to the Treasury, and on which this bill would take effect, amount to fifty millions of dollars, and this sum would probably be doubled at the end of the period fixed for claiming the benefit of its provisions.

The bill contains no adequate safeguard for the protection of the Treasury. No means are provided for testing the truth of the affidavits on which millions of dollars are to be paid out of the public purse. No commissioner, no court, no officer is directed or even authorized to investigate a claim. The oath of any man who is willing to swear to the requirements of the law is to be conclusive. The outstanding bills for one hundred dollars on the east of the Mississippi must amount to many millions of dollars, and cannot now be funded for more than forty-seven per cent of their nominal value, and such as are not funded by the 1st November next will be extinct. The bill leaves the Treasury at the mercy of dishonest men. for this whole amount with less protection than experience has shown to be necessary to guard it against an overcharge in the purchase of ordinary supplies.

It is not doubted that there are many exceptional cases in which the law of February last will operate harshly, and even unjustly. The desire to relieve prisoners of war, as evinced by the passage of this bill, is not only natural but commendable, and I would cheerfully coöperate with Congress in any measures necessary to attain that object, if so guarded as to protect the Treasury from fraudulent claims. In this bill there is an absence of necessary safeguards, and I am therefore unable to give it my approval.

JEFFERSON DAVIS.

June 11, 1864. Richmond, Va.

To the Senate of the Confederate States of America.

I return to the Senate, in which it originated, the joint resolution directing "the settlement of the claim of Zedekiah McDaniel and Francis M. Ewing for destroying the Federal gunboat 'Cairo' by means of a torpedo," with the objections which induce me to withhold my approval.

The character of this claim may be thus briefly stated. Z. McDaniel and F. M. Ewing were appointed Acting Masters in the Navy in August, 1862. Their letters of appointment stated that they were "appointed for special service on submarine batteries" and ordered them to report to Flag Officer William F. Lynch, at Jackson, Miss.

Submarine batteries were at that time the subject of device and experiment for river and harbor defenses, and these gentlemen were recommended as well qualified for such service, McDaniel as having been engaged a short time in preparing torpedoes, and Ewing as being enterprising and bold. In accepting their appointments it appears that they did not allege that they had invented or contrived a torpedo, nor were they appointed to use specially any one of the numerous devices, more or less ingenious, which had been suggested and brought to the notice of the Government.

They reported in obedience to orders and entered upon the duty of placing torpedoes in the Yazoo River under the immediate command of Commander Isaac N. Brown, and the gunboat "Cairo" was destroyed on the 14th December, 1862, by a torpedo placed by them in company with others.

In March, 1863, McDaniel and Ewing for the first time apprised the Department that they claimed a reward for their service on the ground that the torpedo which exploded under the "Cairo" was invented by them. The claim was based on the provisions of three acts of Congress: 1st. "An Act recognizing the existence of war between the United States and the Confederate States, and concerning letters of marque, prizes, and prize goods," No. 106, approved 6th May, 1861; 2d. An Act amendatory of the foregoing, No. 170, approved 21st May, 1861; 3d. An Act amendatory of this last-mentioned law, approved 21st April, 1862.

The second section of the act No. 170, above cited, secures to the inventor of "any new kind of armed vessel or floating battery or defense" certain rewards and privileges upon the condition that "he shall deposit a plan of the same, accompanied by suitable explanations or specifications, in the Navy Department, together with an affidavit setting forth that he is the inventor thereof." This deposit and affidavit are prerequisite to any exclusive rights in favor of the inventor, and a reservation is made specially in favor of the Government of the right of using such invention in all cases.

The very basis of the claim of these parties was the originality of their invention. The joint resolution under consideration recites that a board of naval officers have reported that the "Cairo" was destroyed "by means of a torpedo invented and used by them [McDaniel & Ewing] in the Yazoo River in 1862." This is an error, no board of officers of the Navy having even investigated or reported on this point. The description given of the torpedo by Commander Brown is on record, and does not justify the claim of original invention made by these parties. It represents the torpedo to have consisted of two demijohns connected together, filled with gunpowder, and exploded by means of the ordinary friction primer. The letter of Commander Brown further declares that other parties rendered "most material aid in the destruction of this vessel, and are justly entitled to much of the credit of the success."

Independently of this objection to the claim, the legislation above recited seemed to be conclusive against it. The policy of the law plainly provided that inventors should have the exclusive privilege of their inventions and should be entitled to the rewards promised them, only on condition that they should file in the Navy Department such a description of their invention as would enable the Government to render available the right of using the invention which it had reserved for itself. In the present case the Government was deprived of its right to use the alleged invention by the failure of the claimants to give the description or file the proper papers in the Department till May, 1863, or about five months after the destruction of the "Cairo." The high bounty of fifty per centum, the largest, it is believed, ever allowed for a similar service, was granted by Congress according to the act of 21st April, 1862, and it may be reasonably assumed that such extraordinary bounty was partly in consideration for this right expressly reserved to the country.

Upon these grounds and especially upon the important principles to which reference will be subsequently made, the Secretary of the Navy rejected the claim of McDaniel and Ewing, who appealed to the Executive from his decision. The views of the Head of the Navy Department were sustained, and application was then made to Congress, which afforded the claimants a fresh tribunal by directing the Secretary of the Treasury to adjust their claims. The joint resolution directing this reference was passed in February last, and the Secretary made a report to Congress at its present session stating the value of the vessel and armament destroyed, but also stating that no investigation had been made of the merits of the claim or of the originality of the invention. The

Naval Board called together at the request of the Secretary of the Treasury performed no other duty than estimating the value, but did not (nor could they under the joint resolution) act as a tribunal for the examination of the other questions involved in the claim.

My objections to the present joint resolution are:

1st. That there is error of fact in its recital that a board of naval officers had reported that the "Cairo" was destroyed "by means of a torpedo invented and used by the memorialists." Not only is it a mistake that such report was made, but it is believed to be very questionable whether the torpedo was an original invention of the memorialists.

2d. The claimants failed to give the Government the consideration which the law requires as a condition of the right to the reward—namely, such a description of the alleged invention as would enable the Government to enjoy freely its reserved rights of using the invention in its own service.

3d. The most serious objection is this, that the service on which this claim is founded was rendered by officers of the Navy specially appointed and paid for this service. They did not make known to the Department when they were appointed that they proposed to use a special torpedo of their own invention, for the use of which they expected a reward. So far as is known to the Government, all the means, the materials, the expenditures of the torpedo service in the Yazoo River, including the pay and allowances of these claimants, were at the charge of the Government, and the service was performed under the control of a Navy officer of superior rank; nor was the sanction of any officer of the Government asked or given that these claimants should conduct torpedo experiments at public expense, without risk of time, labor, or capital of their own, and with the right to large reward in the event of success.

No public officer charged with a special duty for which he is paid, and the means of performing which are also paid for by the Government, can be allowed to claim a reward for the performance of his duty without evils of the greatest character to the public service.

Large numbers of Army and Navy officers have been employed

in torpedo service and submarine defenses. Scarcely one has failed to suggest and essay new devices and combinations, many of which have proved successful. Numerous vessels have been destroyed, but the claim under consideration is the only one that has been presented to the attention of the Government. None of the other officers seem to have imagined that it was not their duty to devote all their mind, talent, and inventive faculties in performing the service to which they were assigned without any other pecuniary reward than the pay and allowances accorded by law to other officers of the same grade.

If the present joint resolution should give sanction to the opposite view of the duty of an officer, it is easy to perceive how injuriously it will affect the service. It is less easy to estimate the amount of the claims on the Treasury that would thus be sanctioned.

If these claimants are to be rewarded for the destruction of the "Cairo," why are they to receive the whole sum allowed by the law? There seems no ground for excluding the others who aided in the enterprise and who, in the language of Commander Brown, rendered most material aid, and are justly entitled to much of the credit of success.

My examination of the legislation leads me to a view of the policy of Congress quite different from that which would be implied by the passage of this joint resolution. The three acts above recited seem to me clearly to indicate a desire to encourage private enterprise and to stimulate the investment of private means in the effort to destroy the armed ships of the enemy by awarding a reward (originally of twenty per centum, afterwards increased to fifty per centum) to private armed vessels and to private individuals operating at their own expense with torpedoes or other devices for the public defense. They do not seem to me to have contemplated offering the same reward to the officers and seamen of the Navy, paid and maintained at public expense, for doing their duty in waging war on the vessels of the enemy on the high seas or in rivers and harbors.

I have deemed this full explanation of the facts and law of the case due to Congress as justifying the refusal to sign what is apparently an unimportant bill for the relief of private claimants, but is in reality the sanction of a principle deemed unsound and pernicious, involving in its consequences injury to the public service and heavy demands on the public Treasury.

JEFFERSON DAVIS.

Richmond, Va., June 11, 1864.

ADDRESS.

Circular.

HDQRS. DISTRICT OF INDIAN TERRITORY,
FORT TOWSON, C. N., May 14, 1864.

The following address of His Excellency, Jefferson Davis, President of the Confederate States, is hereby published for the information of the people of the Six Confederate Indian Nations.

S. B. MAXEY,
Brigadier General Commanding.

RICHMOND, February 22, 1864.

ISRAEL FOLSOM,
President of the Grand Council of the Six Confederate Indian Nations,

And Samuel Garland, Choctaw chief; John Jumper, Seminole chief; Samuel Chicote, Creek chief; George Washington, Caddo chief; Winchester Colbert, Governor Chickasaw Nation; Stand Watie, Cherokee chief:

I have received and read with much interest your communication of the 24th of November, 1863, which conveys to me for my information certain resolutions passed by the delegates of the Six Nations, and the executives of the same, in general council assembled.

The welfare of the citizens and soldiers you represent is identical with that of all the Confederate States in the great struggle in which we are now engaged for constitutional rights and independence, and you are regarded by this Government as peculiarly entitled to its fostering care.

I am, therefore, very much concerned to hear that you consider the Confederate Government has failed fully to redeem its pledges made to the Six Nations for supplies and protection. It is consolatory, however, to be assured by you that the attributed failure does not arise from any want of good faith on our part, but from other causes which you have mentioned. And you may rest assured that those officers and agents to whom you allude as having not only neglected their duty, but perverted their authority to the commission of wrong, this Government will hold to rigid responsibility, whenever the proper proof in each case is brought before it.

Your requests as well as your complaints have received my earnest consideration, and I take pleasure in saying that, while it will always gratify me to be able to grant the one, I will ever most respectfully give heed to the other. All treaty stipulations between us shall be sacredly observed and carried into effect to the full extent of my power as President of the Confederate States. The policy of constituting the territory of the Six Nations a separate military department, outside of the control of the commanding general of the department west of the Mississippi, has been thoroughly considered and discussed by the Executive Government here, with your delegates elect.

In pursuance of the result of that discussion I have caused the Indian Territory to be designated as a separate military district, and the Indian troops to be placed under the immediate command of General Cooper, the officer of your choice. It was thought manifestly better for the interest of all concerned that your Territory should be constituted a separate military district, rather than a department, so that the commanding general of the Trans-Mississippi Department may be responsible for the defense and protection of your district, as well as for all others under his charge, and will feel it his duty to aid and protect you with all the promptitude and efficiency that unity in the whole force will confer. This view has been presented to your delegates, and I hope, when fully explained, will meet with your approval.

You will learn from your delegates as well as through this channel that additional brigades in the Territory will be formed as rapidly as the number of regiments will warrant, and brigadiers appointed over them, in the selection of whom your recommendations will be specially regarded. As there are not yet a sufficient number of Indian troops to constitute a division, a major general cannot now be properly appointed; but as soon as there are at least three such brigades, I propose to appoint a major general to command them. In this view, but more especially in view of the public interest, I earnestly urge upon you the policy of making the requisite organization of Indian troops as rapidly as possible. As the law now stands, I have not the power to constitute such courts as you specify, but measures will be taken to secure justice to those claimants you describe, as fully and promptly as is practicable. Arrangements have been made with Major Le Flore to have a certain number of arms delivered on the west side of the Mississippi River for the Indians, and General Smith has been instructed to give every facility for their transportation.

Your last resolution, which instructs your delegates to assure the Confederate States of the unshaken loyalty of the Six Nations represented in the grand council to their treaties with this Government, is highly creditable to them, is what I expected from them, and claims my grateful recognition. The soldiers and people of the Six Nations in treaty and amity with us are regarded by this Government with the same tender care and solicitude as are the soldiers and people of all of the Confederate States.

Our cause is one, and our hearts must be united; we must all put forth our whole energy, cultivate harmony and confidence, practice fortitude, bring forth promptly every available man into the field, and resolve to do, and if need be to die, in defense of our birthright. And with the providence of God to guide and to shield us, victory will perch on our banners and bless us with peace, independence, and prosperity.

Accept my best wishes for health and happiness to yourselves and to the people of the Six Nations, and believe me, very truly, your friend,   JEFFERSON DAVIS.

RESOLUTIONS OF THANKS.

The Congress of the Confederate States of America do resolve, That the thanks of Congress are eminently due, and are hereby tendered, to the Thirty-Fourth and Thirty-Eighth Regiments of

North Carolina troops, for the promptness and unanimity with which they have reënlisted for the war.

Approved May 17, 1864.

The Congress of the Confederate States of America do resolve, That the thanks of Congress are due, and are hereby tendered, to the Texas brigade, composed of the First, Fourth, and Fifth Texas and Third Arkansas Regiments, for their eminently patriotic conduct in reënlisting for the war.

Approved May 17, 1864.

Resolved by the Congress of the Confederate States of America, That the thanks of Congress and the country are due, and are tendered, to Major General Robert F. Hoke and Commander James W. Cooke, and the officers and men under their command, for the brilliant victory over the enemy at Plymouth, North Carolina.

Approved May 17, 1864.

Resolved by the Congress of the Confederate States of America, That the thanks of Congress are due, and are hereby tendered, to Brigadier General Joseph Finegan, and the officers and men of his command, for the skill and gallantry displayed in achieving the signal victory of Ocean Pond, Florida, on the twentieth of February last.

Approved May 17, 1864.

Resolved by the Congress of the Confederate States of America, That the thanks of Congress are eminently due, and are hereby tendered, to Brigadier General F. M. Cockrell, and the officers and soldiers composing the First, Second, Third, Fourth, Fifth, and Sixth Regiments of Missouri infantry, First, Second, and Third Regiments of Missouri cavalry, the batteries of Bledsoe, Landis, Guibor, Walsh, Dawson, and Barrett, and Woodson's detached company, all in the service of the Confederacy east of the Mississippi River, for the prompt renewal of their pledges of fidelity to the cause of Southern independence for forty years, unless independence and peace, without curtailment of boundaries, shall be sooner secured.

Approved May 23, 1864.

Resolved by the Congress of the Confederate States of America, That the thanks of Congress are eminently due, and are hereby cordially tendered, to Major General N. B. Forrest, and the officers and men of his command, for their late brilliant and successful campaign in Mississippi, West Tennessee, and Kentucky—a campaign which has conferred upon its authors fame as enduring as the records of the struggle which they have so brilliantly illustrated.

Approved May 23, 1864.

The Congress of the Confederate States of America do resolve, That the thanks of Congress are eminently due, and are hereby cordially tendered, to the Ninth Regiment of Texas infantry, for their patriotic conduct in reënlisting for the war, and tendering their energies, lives, and honor to the service of the Confederate States till it is ended and our independence achieved.

Approved June 4, 1864.

Resolved by the Congress of the Confederate States of America, That the thanks of Congress are eminently due, and are hereby most cordially tendered, to Major General Richard Taylor, and the officers and men of his command, for the brilliant successes obtained by them over the enemy in Louisiana during the past year, and particularly for the victories at Mansfield and Pleasant Hill, on the eighth and ninth of April last, and their subsequent operations against the retreating army of the Federal General Banks, in the valley of the Red River.

Resolved, That the President communicate this resolution to Major General Taylor and the officers and men of his command.

Approved June 10, 1864.

SECOND SESSION.

MET AT RICHMOND, VA., NOVEMBER 7, 1864.   ADJOURNED
MARCH 18, 1865.

MESSAGES.

RICHMOND, VA., November 7, 1864.

To the Senate and House of Representatives of the Confederate States of America.

It is with satisfaction that I welcome your presence at an earlier day than that usual for your session, and with confidence that I invoke the aid of your counsels at a time of such public exigency.

The campaign which was commenced almost simultaneously with your session early in May last, and which was still in progress at your adjournment in the middle of June, has not yet reached its close. It has been prosecuted on a scale and with an energy heretofore unequaled. When we revert to the condition of our country at the inception of the operations of the present year, to the magnitude of the preparations made by the enemy, the number of his forces, the accumulation of his warlike supplies, and the prodigality with which his vast resources have been lavished in the attempt to render success assured; when we contrast the numbers and means at our disposal for resistance, and when we contemplate the results of a struggle apparently so unequal, we cannot fail, while rendering the full meed of deserved praise to our generals and soldiers, to perceive that a power higher than man has willed our deliverance, and gratefully to recognize the protection of a kind Providence in enabling us successfully to withstand the utmost efforts of the enemy for our subjugation.

At the beginning of the year the State of Texas was partially in possession of the enemy, and large portions of Louisiana and Arkansas lay apparently defenseless. Of the Federal soldiers who invaded Texas, none are known to remain except as prisoners of war. In northwestern Louisiana a large and well-appointed army, aided by a powerful fleet, was repeatedly defeated, and deemed itself fortunate in finally escaping with a loss of one-third of its numbers, a large part of its military trains, and many transports and gunboats. The enemy's occupation of that State is reduced to the narrow district commanded by the guns of his fleet. Arkansas has been recovered with the exception of a few fortified posts, while our forces have penetrated into central Missouri, affording to our oppressed brethren in that State an opportunity, of which many have availed themselves, of striking for liberation from the tyranny to which they have been subjected.

On the east of the Mississippi, in spite of some reverses, we have much cause for gratulation. The enemy hoped to effect during the present year, by concentration of forces, the conquest which he had previously failed to accomplish by more extended operations. Compelled therefore to withdraw or seriously to weaken the strength of the armies of occupation at different points, he has afforded us the opportunity of recovering possession of extensive districts of our territory. Nearly the whole of northern and western Mississippi, of northern Alabama, and of western Tennessee are again in our possession, and all attempts to penetrate from the coast line into the interior of the Atlantic and Gulf States have been baffled. On the entire ocean and gulf coast of the Confederacy the whole success of the enemy, with the enormous naval resources at his command, has been limited to the capture of the outer defenses of Mobile Bay.

If we now turn to the results accomplished by the two great armies, so confidently relied on by the invaders as sufficient to secure the subversion of our Government and the subjugation of our people to foreign domination, we have still greater cause for devout gratitude to Divine Power. In southwestern Virginia successive armies, which threatened the capture of Lynchburg and Saltville, have been routed and driven out of the country, and a portion of eastern Tennessee reconquered by our troops. In northern Virginia extensive districts formerly occupied by the enemy are now free from their presence. In the lower Valley their general, rendered desperate by his inability to maintain a hostile occupation, has resorted to the infamous expedient of converting a fruitful land into a desert by burning its mills, granaries, and homesteads, and destroying the food, standing crops, live stock, and agricultural implements of peaceful noncombatants. The main army, after a series of defeats in which its losses have been enormous, after attempts by raiding parties to break up our railroad communications, which have resulted in the destruction of a large part of the cavalry engaged in the work, after constant repulse of repeated assaults on our defensive lines, is, with the aid of heavy reënforcements, but with, it is hoped, waning prospect of further progress in the design, still engaged in an effort commenced more than four months ago to capture the town of Petersburg.

The army of General Sherman, although succeeding at the end of the summer in obtaining possession of Atlanta, has been unable to secure any ultimate advantage from this success. The same general, who in February last marched a large army from Vicksburg to Meridian with no other result than being forced to march back again, was able, by the aid of greatly increased numbers and after much delay, to force a passage from Chattanooga to Atlanta, only to be for the second time compelled to withdraw on the line of his advance without obtaining control of a single mile of territory beyond the narrow track of his march, and without gaining aught beyond the precarious possession of a few fortified points in which he is compelled to maintain heavy garrisons and which are menaced with recapture.

The lessons afforded by the history of this war are fraught with instruction and encouragement. Repeatedly during the war have formidable expeditions been directed by the enemy against points ignorantly supposed to be of vital importance to the Confederacy. Some of these expeditions have, at immense cost, been successful, but in no instance have the promised fruits been reaped. Again, in the present campaign was the delusion fondly cherished that the capture of Atlanta and Richmond would, if effected, end the war by the overthrow of our Government and the submission of our people. We can now judge by experience how unimportant is the influence of the former event upon our capacity for defense, upon the courage and spirit of the people, and the stability of the Government. We may in like manner judge that if the campaign against Richmond had resulted in success instead of failure; if the valor of the army, under the leadership of its accomplished commander, had resisted in vain the overwhelming masses which were, on the contrary, decisively repulsed; if we had been compelled to evacuate Richmond as well as Atlanta—the Confederacy would have remained as erect and defiant as ever. Nothing could have been changed in the purpose of its Government, in the indomitable valor of its troops, or in the unquenchable spirit of its people. The baffled and disappointed foe would in vain have scanned the reports of your proceedings, at some new legislative seat, for any indication that progress had been made in his gigantic task of conquering a free people. The truth so patent to us must ere long be forced upon the reluctant Northern mind. There are no vital points on the preservation of which the continued existence of the Confederacy depends. There is no military success of the enemy which can accomplish its destruction. Not the fall of Richmond, nor Wilmington, nor Charleston, nor Savannah, nor Mobile, nor of all combined, can save the enemy from the constant and exhaustive drain of blood and treasure which must continue until he shall discover that no peace is attainable unless based on the recognition of our indefeasible rights.

Before leaving this subject it is gratifying to assure you that the military supplies essentially requisite for public defense will be found, as heretofore, adequate to our needs, and that abundant crops have rewarded the labor of the farmer and rendered abortive the inhuman attempt of the enemy to produce by devastation famine among the people.

FOREIGN RELATIONS.

It is not in my power to announce any change in the conduct of foreign powers. No such action has been taken by the Christian nations of Europe as might justly have been expected from their history, from the duties imposed by international law, and from the claims of humanity. It is charitable to attribute their conduct to no worse motive than indifference to the consequences of a struggle which shakes only the republican portion of the American continent, and not to ascribe to design a course calculated to insure the prolongation of hostilities.

No instance in history is remembered by me in which a nation pretending to exercise dominion over another asserting its independence has been the first to concede the existence of such independence. No case can be recalled to my mind in which neutral powers have failed to set the example of recognizing the independence of a nation when satisfied of the inability of its enemy to subvert its Government, and this, too, in cases where the previous relation between the contending parties had been confessedly that of mother country and dependent colony; not, as in our case, that of coequal States united by Federal compact. It has ever been considered the proper function and duty of neutral powers to perform the office of judging whether in point of fact the nation asserting dominion is able to make good its pretensions by force of arms, and if not, by recognition of the resisting party, to discountenance the further continuance of the contest. And the reason why this duty is incumbent on neutral powers is plainly apparent when we reflect that the pride and passion which blind the judgment of the parties to the conflict cause the continuance of active warfare and consequent useless slaughter long after the inevitable result has become apparent to all not engaged in the struggle. So long, therefore, as neutral nations fail, by recognition of our independence, to announce that in their judgment the United States are unable to reduce the Confederacy to submission, their conduct will be accepted by our enemies as a tacit encouragement to continue their efforts, and as an implied assurance that belief is entertained by neutral nations in the success of their designs. A direct stimulus, whether intentional or not, is thus applied to securing a continuance of the carnage and devastation which desolate this continent and which they profess deeply to deplore.

The disregard of this just, humane, and Christian public duty by the nations of Europe is the more remarkable from the fact that authentic expression has long since been given by the Governments of both France and England to the conviction that the United States are unable to conquer the Confederacy. It is now more than two years since the Government of France announced officially to the Cabinets of London and Saint Petersburg its own conclusion that the United States were unable to achieve any decisive military success. In the answers sent by these powers no intimation of a contrary opinion was conveyed; and it is notorious that in speeches, both in and out of Parliament, the members of Her Britannic Majesty's Government have not hesitated to express this conviction in unqualified terms. The denial of our rights under these circumstances is so obviously unjust and discriminates so unfairly in favor of the United States that neutrals have sought to palliate the wrong of which they are conscious by professing to consider, in opposition to notorious truth and to the known belief of both belligerents, that the recognition of our independence would be valueless without their further intervention in the struggle, an intervention of which we disclaim the desire and mistrust the advantage. We seek no favor, we wish no intervention, we know ourselves fully competent to maintain our own rights and independence against the invaders of our country, and we feel justified in asserting that without the aid derived from recruiting their armies from foreign countries the invaders would ere this have been driven from our soil. When the recognition of the Confederacy was refused by Great Britain in the fall of 1862 the refusal was excused on the ground that any action by Her Majesty's Government would have the effect of inflaming the passions of the belligerents and of preventing the return of peace. It is assumed that this opinion was sincerely entertained; but the experience of two years of unequaled carnage shows that it was erroneous, and that the result was the reverse of what the British ministry humanely desired. A contrary policy, a policy just to us, a policy diverging from an unvarying course of concession to all the demands of our enemies, is still within the power of Her Majesty's Government, and would, it is fair to presume, be productive of consequences the opposite of those which have unfortunately followed its whole course of conduct from the commencement of the war until the present time. In a word, peace is impossible without independence, and it is not to be expected that the enemy will anticipate neutrals in the recognition of that independence.

When the history of the war shall be fully disclosed, the calm judgment of the impartial publicist will for these reasons be unable to absolve the neutral nations of Europe from a share in the moral responsibility for the myriads of human lives that have been unnecessarily sacrificed during its progress.

The renewed instances in which foreign powers have given us just cause for complaint need not here be detailed. The extracts from the correspondence of the State Department which accompany this message will afford such further information as can be given without detriment to the public interest, and we must reserve for the future such action as may then be deemed advisable to secure redress.

FINANCES.

Your especial attention is earnestly invited to the report of the Secretary of the Treasury, submitted in conformity with law.   The facts therein disclosed are far from discouraging, and demonstrate that with judicious legislation we shall be enabled to meet all the exigencies of the war from our abundant resources and avoid at the same time such an accumulation of debt as would render at all doubtful our capacity to redeem it.   The total receipts in the Treasury for the two quarters ending on the 30th of September, 1864, were $415,191,550, which sum, added to the balance of $308,-282,722 that remained in the Treasury on the 1st of April last, forms a total of $723,474,272.   Of this total, not far from half— that is to say, $342,560,327--has been applied to the extinction of the public debt, while the total expenditures have been $272,378,-505, leaving a balance in the Treasury on the 1st of October, 1864, of $108,535,440.

The total amount of the public debt, as exhibited on the books of the Register of the Treasury on the 1st of October, 1864, was $1,147,970,208, of which $539,340,090 was funded debt bearing interest, $283,880,150 was Treasury notes of the new issue, and the remainder consisted of the former issue of Treasury notes, which will be converted into other forms of debt, and will cease to exist as currency on the 31st of next month.

The report, however, explains that, in consequence of the absence of certain returns from distant officers, the true amount of the debt is less by about $21,500,000 than appears on the books of the Register, and that the total public debt on the 1st of last month may be fairly considered to have been $1,126,381,095.

The increase of the public debt during the six months from the 1st of April to the 1st of October was $97,650,780, being rather more than $16,000,000 per month, and it will be apparent, on a perusal of the report, that this augmentation would have been avoided and a positive reduction of the amount would have been effected but for certain defects in the legislation on the subject of finances, which are pointed out in the report and which seem to admit of easy remedy.

In the statements just made the foreign debt is omitted.   It consists only of the unpaid balance of the loan known as the cotton loan.   This balance is but £2,200,000 and is adequately provided for by about 250,000 bales of cotton owned by the Government, even if the cotton be rated as worth but 6 pence per pound.

There is one item of the public debt not included in the tables presented, to which your attention is required. The bounty bonds promised to our soldiers by the third section of the act of 17th of February, 1864, were deliverable on the 1st of October. The Secretary has been unable to issue them by reason of an omission in the law, no time being therein fixed for the payment of the bonds.

The aggregate appropriations called for by the different departments of the Government, according to the estimates submitted with the report, for the six months ending on the 30th of June, 1865, amount to $438,102,679, while the Secretary estimates that there will remain unexpended out of former appropriations, on the 1st of January, 1865, a balance of $467,416,504. It would therefore seem that former estimates have been largely in excess of actual expenditures, and that no additional appropriations are required for meeting the needs of the public service up to the 1st of July of next year. Indeed, if the estimates now presented should prove to be as much in excess of actual expenditures as has heretofore been the case, a considerable balance will still remain unexpended at the close of the first half of the ensuing year.

The chief difficulty to be apprehended in connection with our finances results from the depreciation of the Treasury notes, which seems justly to be attributed by the Secretary to two causes, redundancy in amount and want of confidence in ultimate redemption, for both of which remedies are suggested that will commend themselves to your consideration as being practical as well as efficient.

The main features of the plan presented are substantially these: First, that the faith of the Government be pledged that the notes shall ever remain exempt from taxation; second, that no issue shall be made beyond that which is already authorized by law; third, that a certain fixed portion of the annual receipts from taxation during the war shall be set apart especially for the gradual extinction of the outstanding amount until it shall have been reduced to $150,000,000; and fourth, the pledge and appropriation of such proportion of the tax in kind and for such number of years after the return of peace as shall be sufficient for the final redemption of the entire circulation.

The details of the plan, the calculations on which it is based, the efficiency of its operation, and the vast advantages which would result from its success are fully detailed in the report, and cannot be fairly presented in a form sufficiently condensed for this message. I doubt not it will receive from you that earnest and candid consideration which is merited by the importance of the subject.

The recommendations of the report for the repeal of certain provisions of the tax laws which produce inequality in the burden of taxation; for exempting all Government loans from taxation on capital, and from any adverse discrimination in taxation on income derived from them; for placing the taxation on banks on the same footing as the taxation of other corporate bodies; for securing the payment into the Treasury of that portion of the bank circulation which is liable to confiscation because held by alien enemies; for the conversion of the interest-bearing Treasury notes now outstanding into coupon bonds, and for the quarterly collection of taxation—all present practical questions for legislation, which, if wisely devised, will greatly improve the public credit and alleviate the burdens now imposed by the extreme and unnecessary depreciation in the value of the currency.

The returns of the Produce Loan Bureau are submitted with the report, and the information is conveyed that the Treasury agency in the Trans-Mississippi Department has been fully organized and is now in operation, with promise of efficiency and success.

The provision heretofore made to some extent for increasing the compensation of public officers, civil and military, is found to be in some places inadequate to their support, perhaps not more so anywhere tnan in Richmond, and inquiry with a view to appropriate remedy is suggested to your consideration. Your notice is also called to the condition of certain officers of the Treasury, who were omitted in the law heretofore passed for the relief of other public officers, as mentioned in the report of the Secretary of the Treasury.

DEPARTMENT OF WAR.

The condition of the various branches of the military service is stated in the accompanying report of the Secretary of War. Among the suggestions made for legislative action, with a view to add to the number and efficiency of the Army, all of which will receive your consideration, there are some prominent topics which merit special notice.

The exemption from military duty now accorded by law to all persons engaged in certain specified pursuits or professions is shown by experience to be unwise, nor is it believed to be defensible in theory. The defense of home, family, and country is universally recognized as the paramount political duty of every member of society, and in a form of government like ours, where each citizen enjoys an equality of rights and privileges, nothing can be more invidious than an unequal distribution of duties and obligations. No pursuit or position should relieve any one who is able to do active duty from enrollment in the Army, unless his functions or services are more useful to the defense of his country in another sphere. But it is manifest that this cannot be the case with entire classes. All telegraph operators, workmen in mines, professors, teachers, engineers, editors and employees of newspapers, journeymen printers, shoemakers, tanners, blacksmiths, millers, physicians, and the numerous other classes mentioned in the laws cannot in the nature of things be equally necessary in their several professions, nor distributed throughout the country in such proportions that only the exact numbers required are found in each locality; nor can it be everywhere impossible to replace those within the conscript age by men older and less capable of active field services. A discretion should be vested in the military authorities, so that a sufficient number of those essential to the public service might be detailed to continue the exercise of their pursuits or professions; but the exemption from service of the entire classes should be wholly abandoned. It affords great facility for abuses, offers the temptation as well as the ready means of escaping service by fraudulent devices, and is one of the principal obstructions to the efficient operation of the conscript laws.

A general militia law is needful in the interest of the public defense. The Constitution, by vesting the power in Congress, imposes on it the duty of providing "for organizing, arming, and disciplining the militia, and for governing such part of them as may be employed in the service of the Confederate States." The great diversity in the legislation of the several States on this subject, and the absence of any provision establishing an exact method for calling the militia into Confederate service, are sources of embarrassment which ought no longer to be suffered to impede defensive measures.

The legislation in relation to the cavalry demands change. The policy of requiring men to furnish their own horses has proven pernicious in many respects. It interferes with discipline, impairs efficiency, and is the cause of frequent and prolonged absence from appropriate duty. The subject is fully treated in the Secretary's report, with suggestions as to the proper measures for reforming that branch of the service.

The recommendation hitherto often made is again renewed, that some measure be adopted for the reorganization and consolidation of companies and regiments when so far reduced in numbers as seriously to impair their efficiency. It is the more necessary that this should be done, as the absence of legislation on the subject has forced generals in the field to resort to various expedients for approximating the desired end. It is surely an evil that a commanding officer should be placed in a position which forces upon him the choice of allowing the efficiency of his command to be seriously impaired or of attempting to supply by the exercise of doubtful authority the want of proper legal provision. The regard for the sensibility of officers who have heretofore served with credit, and which is believed to be the controlling motive that has hitherto obstructed legislation on this subject, however honorable and proper, may be carried to a point which seriously injures the public good; and if this be the case, it can scarcely be questioned which of the two considerations should be deemed paramount.

The Secretary's recommendations on the subject of facilitating the acquisition of the iron required for maintaining the efficiency of railroad communication on the important military lines are commended to your favor. The necessity for the operation in full vigor of such lines is too important to need comment.

The question in dispute between the two Governments relative to the exchange of prisoners of war has been frequently presented in former messages and reports, and is fully treated by the Secretary. The solicitude of the Government for the relief of our captive fellow-citizens has known no abatement, but has, on the contrary, been still more deeply evoked by the additional sufferings to which they have been wantonly subjected by deprivation of adequate food, clothing, and fuel, which they were not even permitted to purchase from the prison sutlers. Finding that the enemy attempted to excuse their barbarous treatment by the unfounded allegation that it was retaliatory for like conduct on our part, an offer was made by us with a view of ending all pretext for such recriminations or pretended retaliation.

The offer has been accepted, and each Government is hereafter to be allowed to provide necessary comforts to its own citizens held captive by the other. Active efforts are in progress for the immediate execution of this agreement, and it is hoped that but few days will elapse before we shall be relieved from the distressing thought that painful physical suffering is endured by so many of our fellow-citizens whose fortitude in captivity illustrates the national character as fully as did their valor in actual conflict.

EMPLOYMENT OF SLAVES.

The employment of slaves for service with the Army as teamsters or cooks, or in the way of work upon the fortifications, or in the Government workshops, or in hospitals and other similar duties, was authorized by the act of 17th of February last, and provision was made for their impressment to a number not exceeding 20,000, if it should be found impracticable to obtain them by contract with the owners. The law contemplated the hiring only of the labor of these slaves, and imposed on the Government the liability to pay for the value of such as might be lost to the owners from casualties resulting from their employment in the service.

This act has produced less result than was anticipated, and further provision is required to render it efficacious; but my present purpose is to invite your consideration to the propriety of a radical modification in the theory of the law.

Viewed merely as property, and therefore as the subject of impressment, the service or labor of the slave has been frequently claimed for short periods in the construction of defensive works. The slave, however, bears another relation to the State—that of a person. The law of last February contemplates only the relation of the slave to the master and limits the impressment to a certain term of service.

But for the purposes enumerated in the act, instruction in the manner of encamping, marching, and parking trains is needful; so that even in this limited employment length of service adds greatly to the value of the negro's labor. Hazard is also encountered in all the positions to which negroes can be assigned for service with the Army, and the duties required of them demand loyalty and zeal. In this respect the relation of person predominates so far as to render it doubtful whether the private right of property can consistently and beneficially be continued, and it would seem proper to acquire for the public service the entire property in the labor of the slave, and to pay therefor due compensation rather than to impress his labor for short terms; and this the more especially as the effect of the present law would vest this entire property in all cases where the slave might be recaptured after compensation for his loss had been paid to the private owner. Whenever the entire property in the service of a slave is thus acquired by the Government, the question is presented by what tenure he should be held. Should he be retained in servitude, or should his emancipation be held out to him as a reward for faithful service, or should it be granted at once on the promise of such service; and if emancipated, what action should be taken to secure for the freedman the permission of the State from which he was drawn to reside within its limits after the close of the public service? The permission would doubtless be more readily accorded as a reward for past faithful service, and a double motive for a zealous discharge of duty would thus be offered to those employed by the Government—their freedom and the gratification of the local attachment which is so marked a characteristic of the negro, and forms so powerful an incentive to his action. The policy of engaging to liberate the negro on his discharge after service faithfully rendered seems to me preferable to that of granting immediate manumission, or that of retaining him in servitude. If this policy should recommend itself to the judgment of Congress, it is suggested that, in addition to the duties heretofore performed by the slave, he might be advantageously employed as pioneer and engineer laborer, and in that event that the number should be augmented to 40,000.

Beyond these limits and these employments it does not seem to me desirable, under existing circumstances, to go. A broad moral distinction exists between the use of slaves as soldiers in defense of their homes and the incitement of the same persons to insurrection against their masters. The one is justifiable, if necessary, the other is iniquitous and unworthy of a civilized people; and such is the judgment of all writers on public law, as well as that expressed and insisted on by our enemies in all wars prior to that now waged against us. By none have the practices of which they are now guilty been denounced with greater severity than by themselves in the two wars with Great Britain, in the last and in the present century; and in the Declaration of Independence of 1776, when enumeration was made of the wrongs which justified the revolt from Great Britain, the climax of atrocity was deemed to be reached only when the English monarch was denounced as having "excited domestic insurrections amongst us."

The subject is to be viewed by us, therefore, solely in the light of policy and our social economy. When so regarded, I must dissent from those who advise a general levy and arming of the slaves for the duty of soldiers. Until our white population shall prove insufficient for the armies we require and can afford to keep in the field, to employ as a soldier the negro, who has merely been trained to labor, and as a laborer [under] the white man, accustomed from his youth to the use of firearms, would scarcely be deemed wise or advantageous by any; and this is the question now before us. But should the alternative ever be presented of subjugation or of the employment of the slave as a soldier, there seems no reason to doubt what should then be our decision. Whether our view embraces what would, in so extreme a case, be the sum of misery entailed by the dominion of the enemy, or be restricted solely to the effect upon the welfare and happiness of the negro population themselves, the result would be the same. The appalling demoralization, suffering, disease, and death which have been caused by partially substituting the invader's system of police for the kind relation previously subsisting between the master and slave have been a sufficient demonstration that external interference with our institution of domestic slavery is productive of evil only. If the subject involved no other consideration than the mere right of property, the sacrifices heretofore made by our people have been such as to permit no doubt of their readiness to surrender every possession in order to secure their independence. But the social and political question, which is exclusively under the control of the several States, has a far wider and more enduring importance than that of pecuniary interest. In its manifold phases it embraces the stability of our republican institutions, resting on the actual political equality of all its citizens, and includes the fulfillment of the task which has been so happily begun—that of Christianizing and improving the condition of the Africans who have, by the will of Providence, been placed in our charge. Comparing the results of our own experience with those of the experiments of others who have borne similar relation to the African race, the people of the several States of the Confederacy have abundant reason to be satisfied with the past, and will use the greatest circumspection in determining their course. These considerations, however, are rather applicable to the improbable contingency of our need of resorting to this element of resistance than to our present condition. If the recommendation above made, for the training of 40,000 negroes for the service indicated, shall meet your approval, it is certain that even this limited number, by their preparatory training in intermediate duties, would form a more valuable reserve force in case of urgency than threefold their number suddenly called from field labor, while a fresh levy could, to a certain extent, supply their places in the special service for which they are now employed.

OTHER DEPARTMENTS.

The regular annual reports of the Attorney General, the Secretary of the Navy, and the Postmaster General are appended, and give ample information relative to the condition of the respective Departments. They contain suggestions for legislative provisions required to remedy such defects in the existing laws as have been disclosed by experience, but none of so general or important a character as to require that I should do more than recommend them to your favorable consideration.

NEGOTIATIONS FOR PEACE.

The disposition of this Government for a peaceful solution of the issues which the enemy has referred to the arbitrament of arms has been too often manifested and is too well known to need new assurances. But while it is true that individuals and parties in the United States have indicated a desire to substitute reason for force, and by negotiations to stop the further sacrifice of human life, and to arrest the calamities which now afflict both countries, the authorities who control the Government of our enemies have too often and too clearly expressed their resolution to make no peace, except on terms of our unconditional submission and degradation, to leave us any hope of the cessation of hostilities until the delusion of their ability to conquer us is dispelled. Among those who are already disposed for peace many are actuated by principle and by disapproval and abhorrence of the iniquitous warfare that their Government is waging, while others are moved by the conviction that it is no longer to the interest of the United States to continue a struggle in which success is unattainable. Whenever this fast-growing conviction shall have taken firm root in the minds of a majority of the Northern people, there will be produced that willingness to negotiate for peace which is now confined to our side. Peace is manifestly impossible unless desired by both parties to this war, and the disposition for it among our enemies will be best and most certainly evoked by the demonstration on our part of ability and unshaken determination to defend our rights, and to hold no earthly price too dear for their purchase. Whenever there shall be on the part of our enemies a desire for peace, there will be no difficulty in finding means by which negotiation can be opened; but it is obvious that no agency can be called into action until this desire shall be mutual. When that contingency shall happen, the Government, to which is confided the treaty-making power, can be at no loss for means adapted to accomplish so desirable an end. In the hope that the day will soon be reached when under Divine favor these States may be allowed to enter on their former peaceful pursuits and to develop the abundant natural resources with which they are blessed, let us, then, resolutely continue to devote our united and unimpaired energies to the defense of our homes, our lives, and our liberties.

This is the true path to peace.   Let us tread it with confidence in the assured result.   JEFFERSON DAVIS.

RICHMOND, VA., November 9, 186.,
To the Senate and House of Representatives.

I herewith transmit for your consideration a communication from the Secretary of War, showing that a dangerous conspiracy exists in some of the counties of southwestern Virginia and in the neighboring portions of North Carolina and Tennessee, which it is found impracticable to suppress by the ordinary course of law. The facts are so fully exhibited by the report and accompanying papers, herewith submitted, that I consider it unnecessary to repeat them or to do more than invite your early attention to disclosures upon which I deem it my duty to recommend the suspension of the writ of *habeas corpus* in order that full efficacy may be given to the military power for the repression of the evil.

It may be proper here to add that after the expiration of the term for which the writ was suspended serious embarrassment was encountered, particularly at Mobile, Wilmington, and Richmond, on account of the inability of the military authorities to arrest and hold suspected persons against whom the testimony was sufficient to give full assurance that they were spies or holding treasonable communication with the enemy, though legal proof could not be adduced to secure their commitment and conviction by the courts, either because of the character of the evidence or of the necessity for concealing the sources of information, which were not infrequently within the enemy's lines.

JEFFERSON DAVIS.

RICHMOND, VA., Nov. 9, 1864.
To the Senate and House of Representatives.

I herewith transmit a communication from the Secretary of War, covering copies of several reports of military operations during the present year, and renew my suggestion that all such papers are submitted for the information of Congress, and that it is not considered advisable to publish them at this time.

JEFFERSON DAVIS.

RICHMOND, VA., November 11, 1864.

To the Senate and House of Representatives.

I herewith transmit for your information a communication from the Secretary of War, covering copies of the reports of Major General N. B. Forrest, relative to the battle of Tishomingo Creek, and of Captain B. L. Farinholt, relative to the engagement of the enemy with the reserve forces at Staunton River Bridge.

JEFFERSON DAVIS.

RICHMOND, VA., November 11, 1864.

To the House of Representatives.

In response to your resolution of the 14th June last, I herewith transmit communications from the Secretaries of the Treasury and of War, conveying the information desired, relative to the tax in kind and other taxes collected from the several States for the year 1863.　　　　　JEFFERSON DAVIS.

RICHMOND, VA., November 15, 1864.

To the Senate and House of Representatives.

I herewith transmit for your consideration a communication from the Secretary of War, submitting an estimate for an additional appropriation,* to be employed for the purpose which he indicates.　　　　　JEFFERSON DAVIS.

RICHMOND, VA., November 15, 1864.

To the Senate and House of Representatives.

I herewith transmit for your information a communication from the Secretary of War, covering a copy of the report by General G. T. Beauregard of operations on Morris Island during the months of July, August, and September, 1863.

JEFFERSON DAVIS.

RICHMOND, VA., Nov. 15, 1864.

To the Senate and House of Representatives.

I herewith transmit for your information, in secret session, a

---

*To compensate owners of the steamer "Phœnix," impressed by military authority, and sunk as an obstruction in Mobile harbor.

communication from the Secretary of State, submitting copies of the correspondence with our commissioners abroad, referred to in my message of the 7th inst.   JEFFERSON DAVIS.

RICHMOND, VA., November 21, 1864.

To the House of Representatives.

In response to your resolution of the 8th instant, I herewith transmit a communication from the Secretary of War, which conveys the information requested relative to the act of June 14, 1864, to "provide and organize a general staff."

The seventh section of the act invests the Executive with the discretion which has been exercised. The eighth section, by restricting appointments, indicates the course which has been pursued in the attempt to ascertain with accuracy the number of officers in the several staff corps, so as to distribute them in accordance with the order from the Adjutant General's office, a copy of which is annexed, as well as to ascertain whether there are not supernumerary staff officers now in commission who should be discharged.   JEFFERSON DAVIS

RICHMOND, VA., Nov. 21, 1864.

To the Senate of the Confederate States.

I response to your resolution of the 17th instant, I herewith transmit a communication* from the Secretary of State, which conveys the information requested.   JEFFERSON DAVIS.

RICHMOND, VA., November 21st, 1864.

To the House of Representatives.

In response to your resolution of the 9th inst., I herewith transmit communications from the Secretaries of the Treasury and of War, covering copies of all orders now in force which have been issued to the assessors and collectors of taxes.

JEFFERSON DAVIS.

---

*Stating that no intimation has been received by the Confederate Government of a willingness on the part of any State of the United States to go into convention with the States of the Confederacy for the purpose of negotiating a peace, or consulting on the best method of effecting a cessation of hostilities, or for any purpose whatever.

RICHMOND, VA., November 24, 1864.

To the House of Representatives.

In response to your resolution of the 8th instant, I herewith transmit a communication from the Secretary of War, relative to the special exchange of prisoners of war by the Commissioner of Exchange.   JEFFERSON DAVIS.

RICHMOND, VA., November 24th, 1864.

To the House of Representatives.

In response to your resolution of the 19th inst., I herewith transmit a communication from the Secretary of War, relative to the recent impressment of slaves by his order in the State of Virginia.
                     JEFFERSON DAVIS.

RICHMOND, VA., Nov. 24, 1864.

To the Senate of the Confederate States.

In response to your resolution of the 14th instant, adopted in secret session, I herewith transmit a communication from the Secretary of War, which conveys the information requested relative to the enlistment into our Army of prisoners of war who have taken the oath of allegiance to the Confederate States.
                     JEFFERSON DAVIS.

RICHMOND, November 26, 1864.

To the Senate of the Confederate States.

In response to your resolution of the 17th instant, I herewith transmit for your information a communication from the Secretary of War relative to the number of persons in "each State exempted from military service upon the certificate of the Governors, respectively, that they are officers necessary for the proper administration of the government of said States."   JEFF'N DAVIS.

RICHMOND, VA., November 26, 1864.

To the Senate of the Confederate States.

In response to your resolution of the 9th instant, I herewith transmit a communication from the Secretary of War, which conveys the information requested relative to the number of persons exempted or detailed for certain specified purposes, so far as the records of the Department enable him to furnish it.

JEFFERSON DAVIS.

RICHMOND, VA., Nov. 29, 1864.

To the Senate and House of Representatives.

I herewith transmit for your consideration a communication from the Secretary of the Treasury, covering estimates for additional appropriations required by the Navy Department.

JEFFERSON DAVIS.

RICHMOND, VA., Dec. 6, 1864.

To the Senate of the Confederate States.

In response to your resolution of the 14th ult., adopted in secret session, I herewith transmit a communication from the Secretary of War, which conveys the information desired relative to the rations furnished to prisoners of war.   JEFFERSON DAVIS.

RICHMOND, VA., Dec. 6, 1864.

To the House of Representatives.

In response to your resolution of the 23d ultimo, I herewith transmit a communication from the Secretary of War, which conveys the information requested relative to the arrangements which have been made "for the relief of our soldiers who are prisoners of war in the hands of the enemy."   JEFFERSON DAVIS.

RICHMOND, Dec. 6, 1864.

To the House of Representatives.

In response to your resolution of the 23d ultimo, I herewith transmit and invite your attention to a communication from the Secretary of War, relative to the "appointment under an act approved June 14, 1864, providing for the establishment and payment of claims for a certain description of property taken or informally impressed for the use of the Army."

JEFFERSON DAVIS.

RICHMOND, VA., Dec. 6, 1864.

To the House of Representatives.

In response to your resolution of the 23d ultimo, I herewith transmit communications from the Secretaries of the Treasury and of War, relative to the protection secured for the cotton under their control, belonging to the Confederate States, against exposure to the weather.   JEFFERSON DAVIS.

RICHMOND, VA., December 6, 1864.

To the Senate and House of Representatives.

I herewith transmit for your information a communication from the Secretary of War, covering copies of several additional reports of military operations.   JEFFERSON DAVIS.

RICHMOND, VA., Dec. 7, 1864.

To the Senate and House of Representatives.

I herewith transmit for your consideration a communication from the Secretary of War, covering an estimate "of funds required to meet our treaty obligations to the Indian Nations, for the period ending June 30th, 1865."   JEFFERSON DAVIS.

RICHMOND, VA., Dec. 7, 1864.

To the Senate and House of Representatives.*

I herewith transmit for your consideration a communication from the Secretary of War, covering [an estimate of funds] needed to meet [a deficiency in the appropriation to pay the officers and] employ[ees of the Department.]   JEFFERSON DAVIS.

RICHMOND, VA., Dec. 12, 1864.

To the Senate and House of Representatives.

I herewith transmit for your consideration a communication from the Secretary of the Treasury, showing the additional amount necessary to be appropriated to meet the estimated ex-

---

*This message was found badly mutilated, the words in brackets being supplied by the compiler.

penses of the Department of Justice, for the half year ending June 30, 1865.   JEFFERSON DAVIS.

RICHMOND, VA., Dec. 12, 1864.

To the House of Representatives.

In response to your resolution of the 19th ult., I herewith transmit a communication from the Secretary of War, which conveys the information requested, so far as the records of his Department enable him to furnish it, and states the reasons which make it impracticable for him to reply more definitely as to the amount of money expended in payment of the Army of the Trans-Mississippi since the assignment of Gen. E. K. Smith to the command of the Department.   JEFFERSON DAVIS.

RICHMOND, VA., Dec. 15, 1864.

To the Senate and House of Representatives.

I herewith transmit for your consideration a communication from the Secretary of War, relative to the increase of the amount to be appropriated for a purpose for which he has already submitted an estimate.   JEFFERSON DAVIS.

RICHMOND, VA., Dec. 15, 1864.

To the Senate and House of Representatives.

I herewith transmit for your consideration a communication from the Secretary of the Treasury, relative to certain transfers of appropriations required in connection with the service of his Department.   JEFFERSON DAVIS.

RICHMOND, VA., Dec. 15, 1864.

To the House of Representatives.

In response to your resolution of the 23d ult., I herewith transmit a communication from the Secretary of War, which conveys the information requested relative to the sale of cloth and clothing to officers of the armies in the field, under the act of February 17, 1864.   JEFFERSON DAVIS.

RICHMOND, VIRGINIA, December 15th, 1864.

To the Senate and House of Representatives.

I herewith transmit for your information a communication from the Secretary of State, covering further copies of his correspondence with our commissioners abroad, referred to in my message of the 7th inst. JEFFERSON DAVIS.

RICHMOND, December 19, 1864.

To the House of Representatives.

In response to your resolution of the 19th ult., I herewith transmit for your information a communication from the Secretary of War, relative to contracts for supplies to be paid for in cotton in the Trans-Mississippi Department. JEFFERSON DAVIS.

RICHMOND, VA., December 19, 1864.

To the Senate and House of Representatives.

I herewith transmit a communication from the Secretary of the Treasury, relative to a further foreign loan, and recommend his proposition to your favorable consideration in secret session. JEFFERSON DAVIS.

RICHMOND, VA., December 19, 1864.

To the Senate of the Confederate States.

In response to your resolution of the 25th ult., I herewith transmit a communication from the Secretary of War, which conveys the information desired relative to trials and convictions under the act to punish drunkenness in the Army. JEFFERSON DAVIS.

RICHMOND, VA., December 20, 1864.

To the House of Representatives.

I herewith transmit the reports made by the Heads of the Treasury and War Departments, in response to your resolution of the 6th instant, making various inquiries relative to the subject embraced in the act of February 6, 1864, entitled "A bill to impose regulations upon the foreign commerce of the Confederate States to provide for the public defense."

The importance of this subject induces me to present, at some length, my views upon the policy of the law, and upon its effects as developed by experience.

The first section of the law (which was passed at the fourth session of the First Congress and was the expression of its matured judgment) prohibits the exportation of the principal products of the Confederate States, except under uniform regulations, and the reason for this prohibition is expressed in the preamble to be this: "That the condition of the contest demands that the Confederate States should call into requisition whatever resources of men and money they have for the support of their cause."

The fifth section of the law indicates that the purpose of Congress in granting power to allow or refuse permission to export the products of our country was to enforce a return, in whole or in part, of the value of the produce exported "in military or other supplies for the public service."

But a full understanding of the policy of your predecessors can be attained only by taking into consideration another act passed on the same day, and entitled "An Act to prohibit the importation of luxuries or of articles not necessary or of common use.". This last-mentioned act actually prohibited during the pending war the importation of any articles not necessary for the defense and subsistence of the country; and among those excluded from importation were wines, spirits, jewelry, cigars, and all the finer fabrics of cotton, flax, wool, or silk, as well as all other merchandise serving only for the indulgence of luxurious habits.

In a word, the two acts were an exercise of the power to regulate commerce so as to make it subservient to the success of our struggle, by prohibiting the importation or exportation of merchandise or produce for any other purpose than national defense and necessary subsistence, until these vital objects should be placed beyond the reach of danger. The two laws form one common system, and they should be so regarded in considering the propriety of the repeal or modification of either.

When signing my approval of these acts I considered them as measures eminently wise and proper, and as well adapted to remedy existing evils. Complaints were rife throughout our country that its foreign commerce was almost exclusively in the hands of aliens; that our cotton, tobacco, and naval stores were being drained from the States, and that we were receiving in return cargoes of liquors, wines, and articles of luxury; that the imported goods, being held in few hands and in limited quantities, were sold at prices so exorbitant that the blockade runners, after purchasing fresh cargoes of cotton, still retained large sums of Confederate money, which they invested in gold for exportation and in foreign exchange, and that the whole course of the trade had a direct tendency to impoverish our country, demoralize our people, depreciate our currency, and enfeeble our defense. Congress believed these complaints well-founded, and in that belief I fully concurred. None doubted that a remedy was desirable, and your present inquiries seek information in relation to the efficiency of the remedy provided by the legislation then devised, as developed by actual experience.

My conviction is decided that the effect of the legislation has been salutary, that the evils existing prior to its adoption have been materially diminished, and that the repeal of the legislation or any modification impairing its efficiency would be calamitous. This opinion is shared by every Executive Department that has been intrusted with the execution of these laws and regulations, and thus enabled to form a judgment based on observation and experience.

The propriety and justice of a claim on the part of the Government that a share of all the vessels engaged in the blockade trade should be held subject to its use for the benefit of the whole people was so obvious that even before the legislation of Congress few owners refused to place at its disposal one-third of the tonnage, both outward and inward, for the importation of supplies and the exportation of the produce necessary to pay for them. On the passage of the laws it was deemed proper to increase the demand of the Government to one-half. This decision was based not only on the consideration that the Government was burdened with the entire expense of defending the ports of entry, but on the further reason that the enormous gains of the commerce were monopolized by foreigners, free to engage in commerce at their pleasure while our citizens were engrossed in the sacred duty of defending their homes and liberties, and therefore unable to compete for the trade. It was foreseen that this increase would be resisted, and in a message* on the subject, addressed by me to the House of Representatives on the 10th of June last, it was stated that—

For some weeks after the adoption of these regulations strenuous efforts were made by parties interested in the business to induce a relaxation of the regulations. Many of the vessels remained unemployed on the allegation of the owners that the terms imposed by the regulations were so onerous as to render impossible the continuance of the business. The regulations remained unchanged, for I was satisfied from an examination of the subject that this complaint was unfounded and that the withdrawal of the vessels was an experiment, by a combination among their owners, on the firmness of the Government. The result proved the correctness of this view, for after various attempts to obtain increased advantages the vessels resumed their voyages. Their number has been largely increased. The ability to export produce and import supplies on Government account has been developed to a greater extent than had been anticipated, and the credit of the Government has been so improved in foreign markets that the quotations for its loan have rapidly advanced.

In the same message it was also stated that—

Among the efforts made to induce a change of the regulations was a warning given to officers of the Government that the owners of vessels could make better bargains with the Governors of States than with the Confederate Government, and that if the regulations were not relaxed in their favor they would transfer their vessels to the Executives of the several States, and thus withdraw them from the operation of the regulations.

Reverting now to the precise inquiries contained in your resolution, I answer:

First. That no restriction whatever has been placed on the exercise of the right of any Confederate State to export on its own account any of the articles enumerated in the act entitled "An Act to impose regulations," &c., approved 6th of February, 1864.

Each State not only exports whatever it pleases, but the obligation imposed on private individuals to bring back into the country necessary supplies equal in value to one-half of the produce exported is not extended to the States. They are in these respects on a footing of absolute equality with the Confederate Government.

I am aware that complaints have been made of the effect of

---

*Page 466.

these regulations by the Governors of some of the States, but their objections are, in my judgment, without foundation.

It is not denied by any of them that when a State purchases a vessel it is left under the exclusive control of the State authorities, and that the Confederate Government claims no share of the outward or inward tonnage. It is also admitted that when the States purchase or charter any part of a vessel, not exceeding one-half, the Confederate States Government does not interfere with their enjoyment of the portion so purchased or chartered, and confines itself to exacting from the private owner the use of that half not conveyed to the State; but the complaint is that the Confederate Government will not further consent to yield, for the benefit of a single State, any part of that moiety of the tonnage of each vessel which it has secured under the regulations for the common use and benefit of all the States of which it is agent.

By the regulations, as now existing, half the tonnage of all the vessels engaged in the trade has been conveyed to the use of the Confederacy. Why should a single State be allowed to take for its separate use from the Confederacy any part of this half? Is it not enough that the remaining half is left open for purchase or charter by the State?

It is plain that a State and the owner of a vessel can have no motive for contracting in such manner as to diminish the tonnage claimed by the Confederacy, unless for a profit that is to be shared by both. Any concession, therefore, made on this point is in effect the loss of an interest which is the common property of all the States for the joint gain of a single State and of a private capitalist.

Again, the Army in the field is the Army of the Confederacy, which is charged with the duty of supplying it with clothing, subsistence, and munitions of war. The performance of this duty demands the most strenuous exertions and the command of all the resources that can be reached. Any diminution of our command of those resources by a modification of the existing legislation might lead to disastrous consequences. Under our present arrangements we are barely able to supply to our brave defenders a moderate share of those comforts which are indispensable to their efficiency. As long as privations are endured by all alike, there is a noble and patriotic emulation in the display of cheerful·

fortitude in enduring them. But if the common supply now distributed among all is diminished for the purpose of enabling any one State to add to the supplies furnished her own troops, the effect will be pernicious to an extent that can scarcely be appreciated in advance. I leave it to others to imagine the state of feeling which would ensue if the soldiers of the seaboard States were to be found amply supplied with all necessaries and comforts, standing side by side with the troops of interior States, who would be deprived of a part of what they now receive in consequence of a diminution of our present means of providing for all alike. If to this it should be answered that the interior States could enjoy the same advantages as the seaboard States by sending agents to the ports to represent them, thus placing all on an equal footing, the reply is obvious. The result would then be to bring all the States back to the same condition in which they now are—that is to say, each possessing its fair share of the advantages derived from the tonnage used by the Confederate Government.

It appears to me that any change in the present regulations so as to affect the rights of the Confederate Government must necessarily be either useless or mischievous—useless, if no advantage is to be gained by any one State over the others; mischievous in the extreme, if such an advantage is to be the effect of the change.

It has been suggested that there are many articles required by the people of the different States which can be obtained only through the aid of their governments, and that the efforts of the Confederate Government are confined exclusively to the supply of the needs of the Army. This is true; but one-half of all the tonnage of private owners remains open to employment by the States for the purpose suggested, though, perhaps, at somewhat greater cost than would be charged if they were permitted to use the portion reserved for the Confederacy. But I repeat that there is no justice apparent in the demand that all the States should sacrifice a common right for the profit of a single State, nor in diminishing the necessary comforts of the soldier for the benefit of those who remain at home. It is also competent for each State to purchase vessels for its own use or to purchase shares in common with one or more other States for the introduction of supplies necessary for the people without encroaching on the means used by the Confederacy for supplying the Army.

Second. Upon the second question, whether the regulations have caused any diminution in the number of vessels engaged in foreign commerce, the report of the Secretary of the Treasury gives such information as satisfactorily establishes the reverse to be the case.

In addition to the statements made by him, derived from official returns, the Secretary of War reports that many new steamers are understood to be on the way to engage in the trade, notwithstanding the impression which prevails that the stringency of the blockade is constantly increasing.

The number of vessels which arrived at two ports of the Confederacy between the 1st of November and 6th of December was forty-three, averaging more than one per day, and indicating no check in the trade. A further and conclusive proof that the profits of this commerce under present regulations are sufficiently tempting to secure its increase, is afforded by the fact that the shares of the companies engaged in it have greatly advanced in value. The shares of one company, originally of $1,000 each, were selling in July last for $20,000 each, and now command $30,-000. Those of another company have increased in the same period from $2,500 to $6,000; and all exhibit a large advance.

Third. Your third inquiry seeks information whether the legislation and regulations have been beneficial or otherwise in their effect on the success of our arms and the supply of means necessary to the public defense.

My opinion has already been indicated on this point, and the reports of the Secretaries are decided in the expression of their own convictions of the wisdom of the laws, and the beneficial effects produced by them, in connection with the regulations established for giving them effect.

These laws and regulations have enabled the Government not only to provide supplies to a much greater extent than formerly, and to furnish the means for meeting the installments on its foreign loan, but to put an end to a wasteful and ruinous contract system, by which supplies were obtained before Congress determined to exercise control over the imports and exports.

Instead of being compelled to give contractors a large profit on the cost of their supplies, and to make payment in cotton in our ports at 6 pence per pound, we now purchase supplies abroad by our agents at cost in the foreign market, and pay there in cotton, which sells at a net price of 24 pence per pound. When all the elements of calculation are taken into consideration, it is by no means an exaggeration to say that 100 bales of cotton exported by the Government will purchase abroad the same amount and value of supplies that 600 bales would purchase delivered to contractors in the Confederacy. A reference to the report of the Secretary of the Treasury shows that of 11,796 bales of cotton shipped since 1st of July last, but 1,272 were lost; not quite 11 per cent. If this be taken as a fair average, and it is believed to be so, out of 600 bales of cotton exported, 534 would arrive abroad and yield, at £40 per bale, £21,360, while the same 600 bales delivered on payment at a home port, at 6 pence per pound, would yield less than £6,000.

There are other advantages derived from buying abroad, rather than contracting with blockade runners, of no small magnitude, but the foregoing statement will show the enormous profits that were made by them when the Government was forced to contract instead of purchasing for itself, and will suggest a motive for the strenuous efforts they have not ceased to make to get rid of the regulations and procure a change in the policy of the Government. It is to the law and regulations that the Government owes its ability to command freight room, and then buy and sell for itself instead of being forced to make contracts so extravagant as those above described. It requires little sagacity to perceive that with temptation so great the owners of vessels would spare no pains to obtain contracts from the several States, if allowed to do so by law, with the view of again withdrawing from our use as far as possible the tonnage of their vessels, and thus compelling a return to the ruinous contract system.

The reports of the Secretaries will fully inform you of the quantity and nature of the supplies obtained by the Government under the present system, and their importance to the national defense will be perceived at a glance.

Fourth. To the fourth inquiry, whether experience has suggested the necessity of the repeal of said act, or any modification or amendment of its provisions, the foregoing remarks would seem to furnish a sufficient answer. But I conclude, by renewing the expression of my conviction that the result of any legislation checking or diminishing the control now exercised by the Government over our foreign commerce would be injurious to the public interest and would insure the renewal in aggravated form of the evils which it was the purpose of your predecessors to remedy by the laws now in force. JEFFERSON DAVIS.

[A similar message was communicated to the Senate under date of December 17, 1864, in response to its resolution of December 5, 1864.]

To the House of Representatives of the Confederate States of America.

When the act to regulate the pay and mileage of members and the compensation of officers of the Senate and House of Representatives was transmitted to me I found, upon examination of its provisions, some features inconsistent with the law for the organization of the Treasury Department, and the general policy of protecting the Treasury by checks and balances, so as to restrain officials by the records of the Department itself.

I did not, however, feel constrained to return the bill with objections, believing that every desirable end could be obtained by bringing the matter to your attention and recommending amendatory legislation. It was therefore signed on the 24th instant.

I invite you to a special examination of the clause by which the depositaries of the Treasury are directed to honor and pay drafts on the Treasury by members of Congress.

For a fuller exposition of the departure which that provision makes from the wise rules and regulations established by law for the protection of the Treasury, I refer you to the annexed letter of the Secretary of the Treasury. JEFFERSON DAVIS.

Richmond, Virginia, December 28, 1864.

RICHMOND, VA., Jan. 4, 1865.

To the Senate and House of Representatives.

I herewith transmit for your consideration a communication from the Secretary of War, covering an estimate for an additional appropriation* required by the Engineer Bureau.

JEFFERSON DAVIS.

*For the schooner "Isabel," seized by military authority and sunk as an obstruction in Dog River bar channel, Mobile Bay, May 5, 1862.

RICHMOND, VA., Jan. 4, 1865.

To the Senate of the Confederate States.

In response to your resolution of November 14th, 1864, I herewith transmit for your information a communication from the Secretary of War, covering a copy of the official report of General J. E. Johnston, relative to operations of the Army of Tennessee.

I invite your attention to the Secretary's remarks in reference to the delay which has occurred in responding to your resolution, and concur with him in suggesting that it is not advisable to publish this communication at present, or at a future time, without the correspondence which was contemporaneous, and which explains the events.   JEFFERSON DAVIS.

RICHMOND, VA., Jan. 4, 1865.

To the House of Representatives.

In response to your resolution of the 23d ult., I herewith transmit for your information a communication from the Secretary of the Navy, relative to "a flour and grist mill and bakery," established by the Department, at Albany, Georgia.

                                    JEFFERSON DAVIS.

RICHMOND, VA., January 5, 1865.

To the House of Representatives.

In response to your resolution of the 2d ultimo, relative to the impressment of slaves, I herewith transmit a communication from the Secretary of War, which conveys all the information I have on the subject.   JEFFERSON DAVIS.

RICHMOND, VA., Jan. 5, 1865.

To the House of Representatives.

In response to your resolution of the 25th November last, I herewith transmit communications, which furnish the information desired relative to the "commissioned officers attached to and employed in the different Departments and Bureaus in the city of Richmond."   JEFFERSON DAVIS.

RICHMOND, VA., Jan. 5, 1865.

To the House of Representatives.

In response to your resolution of the 30th ult., I herewith transmit a communication from the Secretary of the Navy, which conveys the information that "no coals were taken from the steamer 'Advance,' in October last, or at any other time, for the naval service."   JEFFERSON DAVIS.

RICHMOND, Jan. 5, 1865.

To the Senate and House of Representatives.

I herewith transmit for your consideration a communication from the Secretary of the Treasury, covering estimates of additional appropriations required for the service of the Agency of the Department west of the Mississippi River.

JEFFERSON DAVIS.

RICHMOND, Jan. 6, 1865.

To the Senate and House of Representatives.

I herewith transmit for your consideration a communication from the Secretary of War, covering an estimate for an additional appropriation required by the Bureau of Engineers.

JEFFERSON DAVIS.

RICHMOND, VA., Jan. 6, 1865.

To the House of Representatives.

In response to your resolution of the 19th November last, I herewith transmit a communication from the Secretary of War, which conveys the information desired, relative to the impressment of brandy, so far as the records of his office enable him to furnish it.   JEFFERSON DAVIS.

RICHMOND, VA., Jan. 6, 1865.

To the House of Representatives.

In response to your resolution of the 24th ult., relative to unpaid requisitions upon the Treasury, drawn by the Quartermaster General and the Commissary General, I herewith transmit a communication from the Secretary of the Treasury, which conveys the information desired.   JEFFERSON DAVIS.

EXECUTIVE DEPARTMENT, January 13, 1865.
To the House of Representatives, C. S. A.

I have just received the accompanying report from the Secretary of War stating that Henry S. Foote, a member of the House of Representatives from the State of Tennessee, has been arrested by a military officer in northern Virginia while endeavoring to pass our lines on his way to the enemy's country. As this arrest may involve a question of privilege, I submit the matter to you, in order that such disposal of the case may be made as to you shall seem proper.   JEFFERSON DAVIS.

RICHMOND, VA., January 14, 1865.
To the House of Representatives.

In response to your resolution of the 8th of November, 1864, I herewith transmit for your information a communication from Hon. Howell Cobb, who was President of the Provisional Congress, relative to the preparation of copies of the journals of that body, and of the proceedings of the Convention which framed the Provisional and Permanent Constitutions of the Confederate States. And I invite your attention to the suggestions he makes in reference to funds to be expended in the further prosecution of the work.   JEFFERSON DAVIS.

RICHMOND, VA., Jan. 14, 1865.
To the House of Representatives.

In response to your resolution of the 24 ultimo, I herewith transmit for your information a communication from the Secretary of War, relative to the passports which have been issued to certain youths to leave the Confederate States.   JEFFERSON DAVIS.

RICHMOND, VA., Jan. 20, 1865.
To the House of Representatives.

In response to your resolution of the 30th ult., I herewith transmit communications from the Secretaries of the Treasury and of

War, and from the Postmaster General, which convey the information called for in relation to the means employed to communicate with the Trans-Mississippi Department.

JEFFERSON DAVIS.

RICHMOND, VA., Jan. 20, 1865.

To the Senate and House of Representatives.

I herewith transmit for your consideration a communication from the Secretary of the Treasury, covering an estimate for an additional appropriation required for the public service.

JEFFERSON DAVIS.

EXECUTIVE OFFICE, RICHMOND, VA., January 24, 1865.

Gentlemen of the "Joint Committee on the State of the Country."

I have the honor to acknowledge the receipt of resolutions adopted by the General Assembly of Virginia in relation to certain restrictions said to have been placed on the transportation of supplies of food to the cities of Richmond and Petersburg.

Upon investigation I find that no orders have emanated from the War Department or the provost marshal of Richmond of the character supposed in the resolution. I, however, learn that there may be an order of the character spoken of emanating from the lieutenant general commanding the Confederate forces on the north side of the James River, which, if so, will be ascertained at once, he having been furnished with a copy of the resolution and called upon for information touching the same.

I am, gentlemen, very respectfully, your most obedient servant,

JEFFERSON DAVIS.

RICHMOND, VA., January 24, 1865.

To the House of Representatives.

In response to a resolution adopted by you on the 31st ult., I herewith transmit a communication from the Secretary of War, covering copies of his letters to Genl. E. Kirby Smith, relative to the general administration of the Trans-Mississippi Department.

JEFFERSON DAVIS.

RICHMOND, VA., February 3, 1865.

To the House of Representatives.

In response to your resolution of the 25th ultimo, I herewith transmit a communication from the Secretary of the Navy, covering copies of his correspondence with the Governor of North Carolina relative to "coals of the steamer 'Advance.'"

JEFFERSON DAVIS.

RICHMOND, VA., Feb. 3, 1865.

To the Senate of the Confederate States.

In response to your resolution of the 19th ultimo, I herewith transmit a communication from the Secretary of War, which conveys the information desired, relative to "the number of persons in each State exempted from military service by reason of being claimed as State officers," and to "the number of exemptions and details for express, telegraphic, and railroad companies, etc.," and explains the causes of delay in replying to previous resolutions on those subjects.   JEFFERSON DAVIS.

RICHMOND, VA., Feb. 3, 1865.

To the Senate and House of Representatives.

I herewith transmit for your consideration a communication from the Secretary of the Treasury, concerning an estimate for an additional appropriation required by the Navy Department.

JEFFERSON DAVIS.

RICHMOND, VA., Feb. 3, 1865.

To the Senate and House of Representatives.

I herewith transmit for your consideration a communication from the Secretary of the Treasury, covering an estimate for an additional appropriation required to meet the expenses of the Department of Justice during the six months ending June 30, 1865.

JEFFERSON DAVIS.

RICHMOND, VA., February 4th, 1865.

To the House of Representatives.

In response to your resolution of the 12th ult., I herewith transmit a communication from the Secretary of War, furnishing, as far as the records of his Department will enable him to do so, the information requested relative to the organization of the "Corps of Scouts" authorized to be created by the act of the last Congress to facilitate communication with the Trans-Mississippi Department.   JEFFERSON DAVIS.

RICHMOND, VA., February 4, 1865.

To the Senate of the Confederate States.

In response to your resolution of November 28, 1864, I herewith transmit a communication from the Secretary of War, relative to the removal of the sick and wounded officers of the Army from the almshouse in this city, which was used as a hospital, and to the accommodations which have been provided for the patients elsewhere.   JEFFERSON DAVIS.

EXECUTIVE OFFICE, RICHMOND, February 6, 1865.

To the Senate and House of Representatives of the Confederate States of America.

Having recently received a written notification, which satisfied me that the President of the United States was disposed to confer informally with unofficial agents which might be sent by me with a view to the restoration of peace, I requested the Hon. Alexander H. Stephens, the Hon. R. M. T. Hunter, and the Hon. John A. Campbell to proceed through our lines, and to hold conference with Mr. Lincoln, or with any one he might depute to represent him.

I herewith transmit for the information of Congress the report of the eminent citizens above named, showing that the enemy refused to enter into negotiations with the Confederate States, or with any one of them separately, or to give to our people any other terms or guaranties than those which the conqueror may grant, or to permit us to have peace on any other basis than our unconditional submission to their rule, coupled with the acceptance of their recent legislation on the subject of the relations between the white and black populations of each State.   Such is, as I understand it, the effect of the amendment to the Constitution which has been adopted by the Congress of the United States.

                    JEFFERSON DAVIS.

RICHMOND, VA., February 5, 1865.

To the President of the Confederate States.

Sir: Under your letter of appointment of the 28th ult., we proceeded to seek an "informal conference" with Abraham Lincoln, President of the United States, upon the subject mentioned in the letter. The conference was granted, and took place on the 30th inst., on board of a steamer in Hampton Roads, where we met President Lincoln and the Hon. Mr. Seward, Secretary of State of the United States. It continued for several hours, and was both full and explicit.

We learned from them that the message of President Lincoln to the Congress of the United States, in December last, explains clearly and distinctly his sentiments as to the terms, conditions, and methods of proceeding, by which peace can be secured to the people, and we were not informed that they would be modified or altered to obtain that end. We understood from him that no terms or proposals of any treaty, or agreement, looking to an ultimate settlement, would be entertained or made by him with the Confederate States, because that would be a recognition of their existence as a separate power, which, under no circumstances, would be done; and for like reasons that no such terms would be entertained by him from the States separately; that no extended truce or armistice (as at present advised) would be granted, without a satisfactory assurance in advance of a complete restoration of the authority of the United States over all places within the States of the Confederacy.

That whatever consequence may follow from the reëstablishment of that authority must be accepted; but that individuals subject to pains and penalties under the laws of the United States might rely upon a very liberal use of the power confided to him to remit those pains and penalties if peace be restored.

During the conference, the proposed amendment to the Constitution of the United States, adopted by Congress on the 31st ult., was brought to our notice. This amendment declares that neither slavery nor involuntary servitude, except for crimes, should exist within the United States, or any place within their jurisdiction, and that Congress should have power to enforce this amendment by appropriate legislation. Of all the correspondence that preceded the conference herein mentioned, and leading to the same, you have heretofore been informed.

Very respectfully, your obedient servants,

ALEX. H. STEPHENS,
ROBERT M. T. HUNTER,
JOHN A. CAMPBELL.

MESSAGE OF PRESIDENT LINCOLN ON THE HAMPTON ROADS CONFERENCE, INCLUDING CORRESPONDENCE.

EXECUTIVE MANSION, Feb. 10, 1865.

To the Honorable House of Representatives.

In response to your resolution of the 8th inst., requesting information in relation to a conference held in Hampton Roads, I have the honor to state that on the date I gave Francis P. Blair, Senior, a card written as follows, to wit:

December 28, 1864.

Allow the bearer, F. P. Blair, Sr., to pass our lines, go South, and return.   A. LINCOLN.

That at the time I was informed that Mr. Blair sought the card as a means of getting to Richmond, Va., but he was given no authority to speak or act for the Government. Nor was I informed of anything he would say or do on his own account or otherwise.

Mr. Blair told me that he had been to Richmond and had seen Mr. Jefferson Davis, and he (Mr. Blair) at the same time left with me a manuscript letter as follows, to wit:

RICHMOND, VA., January 12, 1865.

F. P. Blair, Esq.

Sir: I have deemed it proper and probably desirable to you to give you in this form the substance of the remarks made by me to be repeated by you to President Lincoln, etc. I have no disposition to find obstacles in forms, and am willing now, as heretofore, to enter into negotiations for the restoration of peace. I am ready to send a Commission whenever I have reason to suppose it will be received, or to receive a Commission if the United States Government shall choose to send one. Notwithstanding the rejection of our former offers, I would, if you could promise that a Commission, Minister, or other agent would be received, appoint one immediately, and renew the effort to enter into a conference with a view to secure peace to the two countries.

Yours, etc.,   JEFFERSON DAVIS.

Afterwards, with a view that it should be shown to Mr. Davis, I wrote and delivered to Mr. Blair a letter, as follows, to wit:

WASHINGTON, January 18, 1865.

F. P. Blair, Esq.

Sir: You having shown me Mr. Davis's letter to you of the 12th inst., you may say to him that I have constantly been, am now, and shall continue ready to receive any agent whom he, or any other influential person now resisting the national authority, may informally send me, with a view of securing peace to the people of our common country.

Yours, etc.,   A. LINCOLN.

Afterwards Mr. Blair dictated for and authorized me to make an entry on the back of my retained copy of the letter just above recited which is as follows:

January 28, 1865.

To-day Mr. Blair tells me that on the 21st inst., he delivered to Mr. Davis the original, of which the within is a copy, and left it with him; that at the time of delivering Mr. Davis read it over twice in Mr. Blair's presence, at the close of which he (Mr. B.) remarked that the part about our common country related to the part of Mr. Davis's letter about the two countries, to which Mr. D. replied that he understood it.

A. Lincoln.

Afterwards the Secretary of War placed in my hands the following telegram, indorsed by him, as appears:

Office U. S. Military Telegraph, War Department.

(Cipher.) The following telegram was received at Washington January 29, 1865:

From Headquarters Army of the James,
6:30 p.m., January 29, 1865.

To Hon. E. M. Stanton, Secretary of War.

The following dispatch is just received from Major General Parke, who refers it to me for my action. I refer it to you in lieu of General Grant—absent. E. O. C. Ord, *Major General Comdg.*

Headquarters Army of the James.

The following dispatch is forwarded to you for your action. Since I have no knowledge of General Grant's having had any understanding of this kind, I refer this matter to you as the ranking officer present in the two armies. John G. Parke, *Major General Comdg.*

From Headquarters Ninth Army Corps,
January 29, 1865.

Major General John G. Parke, Headquarters Army of the Potomac.

Alexander H. Stephens, R. M. T. Hunter, and J. A. Campbell desire to cross my lines, in accordance with an understanding claimed to exist with Lieutenant General Grant, on their way to Washington as Peace Commissioners. Shall they be admitted? They desire an early answer, so as to come through immediately. They would like to reach City Point to-night if they can. If they cannot do this, they would like to come through to-morrow morning.

O. B. Willcox, *Major Commanding Ninth Corps.*

Respectfully referred to the President for such instructions as he may be pleased to give. Edwin M. Stanton, *Secretary of War.*

January 29, 1865, 8:30 p.m.

It appears that about the time of placing the foregoing telegram in my hands, the Secretary of War dispatched to General Ord as follows, to wit:

WAR DEPARTMENT, WASHINGTON CITY,
Jan. 29, 1865, 10 P.M.

Major General Ord.

This Department has no knowledge of any understanding by Gen. Grant to allow any person to come within his lines as Commissioners of any sort. You will therefore allow no one to come into your lines under such character or profession until you receive the President's instructions, to whom your telegrams will be submitted for his directions.

EDWIN M. STANTON, *Secretary of War.*

(Sent in cipher at 2 A.M.)

Afterwards, by my directions, the Secretary of War telegraphed Gen. Ord as follows, to wit:

WAR DEPARTMENT, WASHINGTON, D. C.,
Jan. 30, 1865, 10 A.M.

Major General E. O. C. Ord, Headquarters Army of the James.

By the direction of the President you are instructed to inform the three gentlemen, Messrs. Stephens, Hunter, and Campbell, that a message will be dispatched to them at or near where they now are without unnecessary delay.

EDWIN M. STANTON, *Secretary of War.*

Afterwards I prepared and put into the hands of Major Thomas T. Eckert the following instructions:

EXECUTIVE MANSION, WASHINGTON,
Jan. 30, 1865.

Major T. T. Eckert.

Sir: You will proceed with the documents placed in your hands, and on reaching General Ord will deliver him the letter addressed him by the Secretary of War. Then, by General Ord's assistance, procure an interview with Messrs. Stephens, Hunter, and Campbell, or any of them, deliver to him or them the paper on which your own letter is written. Note on the copy which you retain the time of delivery and to whom delivered. Receive their answer in writing, waiting a reasonable time for it, and which, if it contain their decision to come through without further conditions, will be your warrant to ask General Ord to pass them through as directed in the letter of the Secretary of War. If by their answer they decline to come, or propose other terms, do not have them pass through. And this being your whole duty return and report to me.

Yours truly, A. LINCOLN.

CITY POINT, Feb. 1, 1865.

Messrs. Alexander H. Stephens, J. A. Campbell, and R. M. T. Hunter.

Gentlemen: I am instructed by the President of the United States to place this paper in your hands with the information that if you pass through the United States military lines, it will be understood that you do so for the purpose of an informal conference on the basis of that letter, a copy of which is on the reverse side of this sheet; and that you choose to pass on such understanding, and so notify me in writing. I will procure the Commanding General to pass you through the lines and to Fortress Monroe under such military precautions as he may deem prudent, and at which place you will be met in due time by some person or persons for the purpose of such informal conference; and further, that you shall have protection, safe conduct, and safe return in all events.

THOMAS T. ECKERT, *Major and Aid-de-Camp.*

Afterwards, but before Major Eckert had departed, the following dispatch was received from General Grant:

OFFICE U. S. MILITARY TELEGRAPH, WAR DEPARTMENT.

(Cipher)

The following telegram was received at Washington, Jan. 31, 1865, from City Point, Va., 10:30 A.M., Jan. 31, 1865:

His Excellency Abraham Lincoln, President of the United States.

The following communication was received here last evening:

PETERSBURG, VA., Jan. 30, 1865.

Lieut. Gen. U. S. Grant, Commanding Armies of the United States.

Sir: We desire to pass your lines under safe conduct, and to proceed to Washington to hold a conference with President Lincoln upon the subject of the existing war, and with a view of ascertaining upon what terms it may be terminated, in pursuance of the course indicated by him in his letter to Mr. Blair of Jan. 18, 1865, of which we presume you have a copy, and if not, we wish to see you in person, if convenient, and to confer with you on the subject.

Very respectfully yours,   ALEXANDER H. STEPHENS,
J. A. CAMPBELL,
R. M. T. HUNTER.

I have sent directions to receive these gentlemen, and expect to have them at my quarters this evening awaiting your instructions.

U. S. GRANT, *Lieut. General,*
Commanding Armies of the United States.

This, it will be perceived, transferred General Ord's agency in the matter to General Grant. I resolved, however, to send Major Eckert forward with his message, and accordingly telegraphed General Grant as follows, to wit:

EXECUTIVE MANSION, WASHINGTON,
Jan. 31, 1865.

Lieut. Gen. Grant, City Point, Va.

A messenger is coming to you on the business contained in your dispatch. Detain the gentlemen in comfortable quarters until he arrives, and then act upon the message he brings as far as applicable, it having been made up to pass through Gen. Ord's hands, and when the gentlemen were supposed to be beyond our lines.

(Sent in cipher at 1:30 P.M.) A. LINCOLN.

When Major Eckert departed, he bore with him a letter of the Secretary of War to General Grant as follows, to wit:

WAR DEPARTMENT, WASHINGTON, D. C.,
Jan. 30, 1865.

Lieut. General Grant, Commanding, etc.

General: The President desires that you procure for the bearer, Major Thomas T. Eckert, an interview with Messrs. Stephens, Hunter, and Campbell, and if, on his return to you, he requests it, pass them through our lines to Fortress Monroe by such route and under such military precautions as you may deem prudent, giving them protection and comfortable quarters while there, and that you let none of this have any effect upon any of your movements or plans.

By order of the President.

EDWIN M. STANTON, *Secretary of War.*

Supposing the proper point to be then reached, I dispatched the Secretary of State with the following instructions, Major Eckert, however, going ahead of him:

EXECUTIVE MANSION, Jan. 31, 1865.

Hon. Wm. H. Seward, Secretary of State.

You will proceed to Fortress Monroe, Va., there to meet and informally confer with Messrs. Stephens, Hunter, and Campbell on the basis of my letter to F. P. Blair, Esq., of Jan. 18, 1865, a copy which you have. You will make known to them that three things are indispensable, to wit: 1st, the restoration of the national authority throughout all the States; 2d, no receding by the Executive of the United States on the slavery question from the position assumed thereon in the late annual message to Congress, and in the preceding documents; 3d, no cessation of hostilities short of an end of the war and the disbanding of all the forces hostile to the Government. You will inform them that all propositions of theirs not inconsistent with the above will be considered and passed upon in a spirit of sincere liberality. You will hear all they may choose to say and report it to me. You will not assume to definitely consummate anything.

Yours, etc., ABRAHAM LINCOLN.

On the day of its date the following telegram was sent to General Grant:

WAR DEPARTMENT, WASHINGTON,
Feb. 1, 1865.

Lieut. Gen. Grant, City Point, Va.

Let nothing which is transpiring change, hinder, or delay your military movements or plans.

(Sent in cipher at 9:30 A.M.)   A. LINCOLN.

Afterwards the following dispatch was received from General Grant:

OFFICE U. S. TELEGRAPH, WAR DEPARTMENT.

(In cipher.)

The following telegram was received at Washington at 2:30 P.M., Feb. 1, 1865, from City Point, Va., Feb. 1, 12:30 P.M., 1865:

His Excellency Abraham Lincoln, President of the United States.

Your dispatch is received. There will be no armistice in consequence of the presence of Mr. Stephens and others within our lines. The troops are kept in readiness to move at the shortest notice if occasion should justify it.   U. S. GRANT, *Lieut. Gen.*

To notify Major Eckert that the Secretary of State would be at Fortress Monroe and to put them in communication, the following dispatch was sent:

WAR DEPARTMENT, WASHINGTON,
Feb. 1, 1865.

T. T. Eckert, care Gen. Grant, City Point, Va.

Call at Fortress Monroe and put yourself under the direction of Mr. S., whom you will find there.   A. LINCOLN.

On the morning of the 2d inst. the following telegrams were received by me from the Secretary of State and Major Eckert:

FORTRESS MONROE, VA., 11:30 P.M.,
Feb. 1, 1865.

The President of the United States.

Arrived here this evening. Richmond party not here. I remain here.
WM. H. SEWARD.

CITY POINT, VA., 10 P.M.,
Feb. 1, 1865.

His Excellency A. Lincoln, President of the United States.

I have the honor to report the delivery of your communication and my letter at 4:15 this afternoon, to which I received a reply at 6 P.M., but not satisfactory. At 8 P.M. the following note, addressed to Gen. Grant, was received:

To Lieut. Gen. Grant.

Sir: We desire to go to Washington City to confer informally with the President personally, in reference to the matters mentioned in his letter to Mr. Blair of the 18th of January, ult., without any personal compromise on any question in the letter. We have the permission to do so from the authorities in Richmond.

Very respectfully yours,

Alexander H. Stephens,
R. M. T. Hunter,
J. A. Campbell.

At 9:30 P.M. I notified them that they could not proceed farther unless they complied with the terms expressed in my letter. The point of meeting designated in the above would not, in my opinion, be insisted upon. I think Fortress Monroe would be acceptable. Having complied with my instructions, will return to Washington to-morrow, unless otherwise ordered. Thomas T. Eckert, *Major, etc.*

On reading this dispatch of Major Eckert's, I was about to recall him and the Secretary of State, when the following telegram of General Grant to the Secretary of War was shown me:

Office U. S. Military Telegraph, War Department.

(In cipher.)

The following telegram was received at Washington at 4:35 A.M., Feb. 2, 1865, from City Point, Va., Feb. 1, 1865:

To Hon. E. M. Stanton, Secretary of War.

Now that the interview between Major Eckert, under his written instructions, and Mr. Stephens and party, has ended, I will state confidentially, but not officially, to become a matter of record, that I am convinced, upon conversation with Messrs. Stephens and Hunter, that their intentions are good and their desire sincere to restore peace and Union. I have not felt myself at liberty to express even views of my own, or to account for my reticence. This has placed me in an awkward position, which I could have avoided by not seeing them in the first instance. I fear now their going back without any expression from any one in authority will have a bad influence. At the same time I recognize the difficulties in the way of receiving these informal Commissioners at this time, and I do not know what to recommend. I am sorry, however, that Mr. Lincoln cannot have an interview with the two named in this dispatch, if not all three now within our lines. Their letter to me was all that the President's instructions contemplated to secure their safe conduct, if they had used the same language to Capt. Eckert.

U. S. Grant, *Lieut. General.*

This dispatch of General Grant changed my purpose, and accordingly I telegraphed him and the Secretary of War as follows:

WAR DEPARTMENT, WASHINGTON,
Feb. 2, 1865.

To Lieut. General Grant, City Point, Va.

Say to the gentlemen that I will meet them personally at Fortress Monroe as soon as I can get there.

(Sent in cipher at 9 A.M.)   A. LINCOLN.

WAR DEPARTMENT, WASHINGTON, D. C.,
Feb. 2, 1865.

To Hon. Wm. H. Seward, Fortress Monroe, Va.

Induced by a dispatch from General Grant, I join you at Fortress Monroe as soon as I can come.

(Sent in cipher at 9 A.M.)   A. LINCOLN.

Before starting, the following dispatch was shown me. I proceeded, nevertheless:

OFFICE U. S. MILITARY TELEGRAPH, WAR DEPARTMENT.

(In cipher.)

The following telegram was received at Washington, Feb. 2, 1865, from City Point, Va., 9 A.M., Feb. 2, 1865:

To Hon. W. H. Seward, Sec'y of State, Fortress Monroe.

[Copy to Hon. E. M. Stanton, Secretary of War.]

The gentlemen here have accepted the proposed terms and will leave for Fortress Monroe at 9:30 A.M.   U. S. GRANT, *Lieut. Gen.*

On the night of the 2d I reached Hampton Roads, and found the Secretary of State and Major Eckert in a steamer anchored off the shore, and learned of them that the Richmond gentlemen were in another steamer, also anchored off shore in the Roads, and that the Secretary of State had not yet seen or communicated with them. I ascertained that Major Eckert had literally complied with his instructions, and I saw for the first time the answer of the Richmond gentlemen to him, which, in his dispatch to me of the 1st, characterized as not satisfactory. That answer is as follows, to wit:

CITY POINT, VA., Feb. 1, 1865.

To Thos. T. Eckert, Major and Aid-de-Camp.

Major: Your note delivered by yourself this day has been considered. In reply, we have to say that we were furnished with a copy of the letter of President Lincoln to F. P. Blair, of the 18th of January, ult. Another copy of which is appended to your note. Our intentions are contained in the letter, of which the following is a copy:

RICHMOND, January 28, 1865.

In conformity with the letter of Mr. Lincoln, of which the foregoing is a copy, you are to proceed to Wishington City for an informal conference with him upon the issues involved in the existing war, and for the purpose of securing peace to the two countries.

With great respect, your obedient servant,   JEFFERSON DAVIS.

The substantial object to be attained by the informal conference is to ascertain upon what terms the existing war can be terminated honorably. Our instructions contemplate a personal interview between President Lincoln and ourselves at Washington; but, with this explanation, we are ready to meet any person or persons that President Lincoln may appoint, at such place as he may designate. Our earnest desire is that a just and honorable peace may be agreed upon, and we are prepared to receive or to submit propositions which may possibly lead to the attainment of that end.

Very respectfully yours,   ALEX. H. STEPHENS,
         ROBERT M. T. HUNTER,
         JOHN A. CAMPBELL.

A note of these gentlemen, subsequently addressed to General Grant, has already been given in Major Eckert's dispatch of the 1st inst. I also saw here for the first time the following note addressed by the Richmond gentlemen to Major Eckert:

         CITY POINT, VA., February 2, 1865.

Thomas T. Eckert, Major and A. D. C.

Major: In reply to your verbal statement that your instructions did not allow you to alter the conditions upon which a passport would be given to us, we say that we are willing to proceed to Fortress Monroe, and there to have an informal conference with any person or persons that President Lincoln may appoint, on the basis of his letter to Francis P. Blair of the 18th of January, ultimo, or upon any other terms or conditions that he may hereafter propose not inconsistent with the essential principles of self-government and popular rights, upon which our institutions are founded. It is our earnest wish to ascertain, after a free interchange of ideas and information, upon what principles and terms, if any, a just and honorable peace can be established without the further effusion of blood, and to contribute our utmost efforts to accomplish such a result. We think it better to add that in accepting your passport we are not to be understood as committing ourselves to anything, but to carry on this informal conference with the views and feelings above expressed.

Very respectfully yours, etc.,   ALEX. H. STEPHENS,
         R. M. T. HUNTER,
         J. A. CAMPRELL.

[*Note.* The above communication was delivered to me at Fortress Monroe at 4:30 P.M., Feb. 2, by Lieut. Col. Babcock, of Gen. Grant's Staff.

         THOS. T. ECKERT, *Major and A. D. C.*]

On the morning of the 3d the gentlemen, Messrs. Stephens, Hunter, and Campbell, came aboard of our steamer and had an interview with the Secretary of State and myself of several hours' duration. No question of preliminaries to the meeting was then and there made or mentioned. No other person was present. No papers were exchanged or produced, and it was in advance agreed that the conversation was to be informal and verbal merely. On my part the whole substance of the instructions to the Secretary of State, hereinbefore recited, was stated and insisted upon, and nothing was said inconsistent therewith, while, by the other party, it was not said that in any event or on any condition they ever would consent to reunion; and yet they equally omitted to declare that they would never so consent. They seemed to desire a postponement of that question and the adoption of some other course first, which, as some of them seemed to argue, might or might not lead to reunion, but which course we thought would amount to an indefinite postponement.

The conference ended without result.

The foregoing, containing, as is believed, all the information sought, is respectfully submitted.   ABRAHAM LINCOLN.

RICHMOND, VA., February 6th, 1865.

To the House of Representatives.

In response to your resolution of the 13th December last, I herewith transmit for your information a communication from the Secretary of War, relative to the "Cotton Bureau," established in the State of Texas, and covering copies of all documents on the subject on file in his office, and of his correspondence with the General commanding the Trans-Mississippi Department, in reference to the use of cotton as a means of procuring supplies for the Army.   JEFFERSON DAVIS.

RICHMOND, VA., Feb. 8, 1865.

To the House of Representatives.

In response to your resolution of the 25th ult., I herewith transmit a communication from the Secretary of War, covering a list of the quartermasters and assistant quartermasters now in the service and indicating the rank of each officer and the duty on which he is employed.   JEFFERSON DAVIS.

RICHMOND, VA., Feb. 8, 1865.

To the House of Representatives.

In response to your resolution of the 31st December last, I herewith transmit for your information a communication from the

Secretary of War, covering copies of "the reports of Generals Taylor, Price, and Magruder, with the report of General Smith appended, of their military operations in the Trans-Mississippi Department during the last eighteen months."

JEFFERSON DAVIS.

RICHMOND, VA., February 8th, 1865.

To the House of Representatives.

In response to your resolution of the 11th ult., I herewith transmit a communication from the Postmaster General, which conveys the information requested relative to the number of persons exempted as contractors to carry the mails on routes less than fifty miles in length, so far as the records of his office enable him to furnish it. JEFFERSON DAVIS.

RICHMOND, VA., Feb. 10, 1865.

To the Senate and House of Representatives.

I herewith transmit for your consideration a communication from the Secretary of the Treasury, covering an estimate for an additional appropriation required by the Navy Department.

JEFFERSON DAVIS.

RICHMOND, VA., Feb. 15, 1865.

To the Senate of the Confederate States.

In partial response to your resolution of the 24th ultimo, I herewith transmit communications from the Secretary of the Navy and the Postmaster General, relative to the number of white men between the ages of 18 and 45, and of negroes, whose services are necessary to their respective Departments.

The Secretary of War has been called on to furnish reports on this subject from the several bureaus specified in your resolution, which will be transmitted when received. JEFFERSON DAVIS.

RICHMOND, VA., Feb. 15, 1865.

To the House of Representatives.

In further response to your resolution of the 25th ultimo, I herewith transmit for your information a communication from the Secretary of the Navy, covering copies of the remainder of his correspondence with the Governor of North Carolina, relative to coal belonging to the steamer "Advance."

JEFFERSON DAVIS.

RICHMOND, VA., Feb. 15, 1865.

To the House of Representatives.

In response to your resolution of 24th December last, I herewith transmit a communication from the Secretary of War, which conveys the information requested, relative to the number of iron furnaces and forges worked by agents of the Government or by contractors during the year 1864, and to the cost per ton of the several kinds of iron furnished by them.   JEFFERSON DAVIS.

RICHMOND, VA., Feb. 15, 1865.

To the Senate and House of Representatives.

I herewith transmit for your consideration a communication from the Secretary of the Treasury, covering an estimate for an additional appropriation required by the Department of Justice.

JEFFERSON DAVIS.

RICHMOND, VA., February 20, 1865.

To the House of Representatives of the Confederate States of America.

I submit herewith to your honorable body a report from the Secretary of War, dated the 18th instant, exhibiting the condition to which the public service is now reduced by the want of means in the Treasury to furnish the supplies needful for the Army and for the public defense.   The urgency for the passage of some revenue bill has now become so pressing as to threaten the gravest consequences.   I am fully aware of the embarrassments which have retarded the action of the House in the performance of its exclusive constitutional function of originating a bill for raising revenue, and that the great diversity of opinion which must exist on so complex and difficult a subject has prevented the adoption of measures recommended by the Committee of Ways and Means of the House, as well as those recommended by the Secretary of the Treasury.   I would, however, respectfully suggest that our affairs are now in a position so critical that objections which under other circumstances would be regarded as insurmountable may well be waived in favor of any scheme of finance or taxation that will enable the Treasury promptly to meet our most pressing wants, and that immediate legislation, even if somewhat imperfect, is preferable to wiser measures if attended with delay.

In connection with this subject I would invoke your attention to the need of prompt action for adding to our strength in the field. Very few weeks now remain for preparation, and we are threatened by a concentration of forces around us which cannot be successfully resisted without the aid of large reënforcements to our armies.

It is with trust in your wisdom and patriotism that I obey the behest of the Constitution in placing before you this information of the state of the country, confident that you will need no further stimulus than the knowledge of these facts to induce such action as will avert the perils which now menace our country.

JEFFERSON DAVIS.

RICHMOND, VA., Feb. 20, 1865.

To the House of Representatives.

In response to your resolution of the 6th instant, I herewith transmit a communication from the Secretary of War, which conveys all the information in my possession relative to the non-destruction of the cotton in the city of Savannah, before its evacuation by our military forces. JEFFERSON DAVIS.

RICHMOND, VA., Feb. 20, 1865.

To the Senate and House of Representatives.

I herewith transmit for your consideration a communication from the Secretary of War, covering an estimate for an additional appropriation required by the Department. JEFFERSON DAVIS.

RICHMOND, VA., February 20, 1865.

To the Senate of the Confederate States.

In further response to your resolution of the 24th ult., I herewith transmit a communication from the Secretary of War, relative to the number of white men between the ages of 18 and 45, and of negroes, who, in addition to their own officers, are required to carry on the operations of the Bureau of his Department to which your inquiries refer, and of the railroad companies of the country; and indicating the railroads which he considers most necessary for military purposes and of which the repairs or construction should be affected by appropriations by the Government. In connection with the latter subject he makes a suggestion to which I invite your special attention.   JEFFERSON DAVIS.

RICHMOND, VA., February 21, 1865.

To the House of Representatives.

In response to your resolution of the 30th ultimo, I herewith transmit for your information a communication from the Secretary of War, relative to the accessions to the Army from each State since April 16, 1862; to the number of persons liable to conscription who have been exempted or detailed, and to the number of those between the ages of eighteen and forty-five, and not unfitted for active service in the field, who are employed in the several States in the manner indicated in your inquiry.

JEFFERSON DAVIS.

RICHMOND, VA., February 22, 1865.

To the House of Representatives.

In response to your resolution of the 25th ultimo, I herewith transmit for your information a communication from the Secretary of War, relative to the number of able-bodied men between the ages of eighteen and forty-five "claimed to be exempt from conscription by the Governor, laws, and resolutions of the State of Georgia."   JEFFERSON DAVIS.

RICHMOND, VA., February 24th, 1865.

To the House of Representatives.

I herewith transmit for your information copies of the correspondence requested in your resolution of the 24th ult., as follows —to wit:

"*Resolved,* That the President be requested to communicate to this House, if not incompatible with the public interest, all the correspondence between himself and General Joseph E. Johnston touching the command and movements of the Army of Tennessee, and all the correspondence between himself and Generals Beauregard and Hood touching the command and movements of the same army since the removal of General Johnston from the command of it, and up to the retreat of it to the south side of the Tennessee River."

The correspondence of the Secretary of War and of the Adjutant General will be found combined according to dates.

JEFFERSON DAVIS.

RICHMOND, VA., February 24th, 1865.

To the House of Representatives.

In response to your resolution of the 17th of May last, I herewith transmit for your information a copy of my own correspondence as well as that of the Secretary of War, and of the Adjutant and Inspector General, with Genl. Joseph E. Johnston, during the period indicated.

The resolution is in these words:

"*Resolved,* That the President be respectfully requested, in addition to the correspondence heretofore communicated to Congress between the President and Secretary of War and General Joseph E. Johnston in relation to the conduct of the war in the valley of the Mississippi, to communicate to Congress so much of said correspondence as has not as yet been called for by this House, commencing with a letter of November 24th, 1862, addressed by General Johnston to the Hon. Geo. W. Randolph, Secretary of War, and including General Johnston's reply to the letter of the President of July last, which closes the public correspondence."

To the copy of General Johnston's letters of August 8th and 20th, 1863, which is requested in the latter part of the resolution, has been added a copy of my reply, bearing date September 7th, 1863, and closing the correspondence to which it belongs; and, with a view to presenting the whole subject at once, I have included a copy of the printed correspondence heretofore communicated to Congress, which was published by order of the House and which has been submitted in response to the resolution of December 11th, 1863, as follows:

"*Resolved,* That the President be requested to communicate to the House, if not incompatible with the public interest, the orders given to and the correspondence had with General Jos. E. Johnston during the months of May, June, and July, 1863, concerning his command and the operations in his Department."

This communication would have been made at a much earlier date but for the fact that an important paper which had been handed to me by General Johnston in person at Chattanooga, and in which he objected to sending reënforcements from the Army of Tennessee to that in Mississippi, had been mislaid, and seemed necessary to the completeness of the correspondence. I have not yet been able to recover it, but [am] unwilling to delay my response to your resolution any longer on that account.

JEFFERSON DAVIS.

RICHMOND, VA., Feb. 25, 1865.

To the Senate and House of Representatives.

I herewith transmit for your consideration a communication from the Secretary of War, covering an estimate for an additional appropriation required by the War Department.

JEFFERSON DAVIS.

RICHMOND, VA., Feb. 27, 1865.

To the Senate and House of Representatives.

I herewith transmit for your consideration a communication from the Postmaster General, relative to "An Act fixing the salaries of certain civil officers in the Trans-Mississippi Department," and invite your special attention to his suggestions, with a view to further legislation on the subject if you deem it necessary.

JEFFERSON DAVIS.

RICHMOND, VA., Feb. 28, 1865.

To the Senate and House of Representatives.

I herewith transmit for your consideration a communication from the Secretary of War, relative to the construction and repair of railroads necessary for military purposes, and submitting an estimate of the amount required to be appropriated for these objects during the year 1865.

I invite your special attention to the subject.

JEFFERSON DAVIS.

RICHMOND, VA., February 28, 1865.

To the Senate and House of Representatives.

I herewith transmit for your information a communication from the Secretary of War, covering copies of several additional reports of military operations.   JEFFERSON DAVIS.

RICHMOND, VA., March 1, 1865.

To the Senate of the Confederate States.

I have received the following resolution adopted by you in secret session on the 12th January last:

"*Resolved,* That the President of the Confederate States be requested to communicate to the Senate, if in his opinion it be not incompatible with the public interests, the contemporaneous correspondence and documents mentioned in the letter of the Secretary of War of the 3d inst., communicating a copy of the report of Genl. Joseph E. Johnston, called for by a resolution of the Senate."

In response, I herewith transmit for your information copies of my own correspondence with Genl. J. E. Johnston during the time he commanded the Army of Tennessee in the field, as well as of the correspondence had with him by the Department.

The letter of the Secretary of War of this date, covering the papers forwarded by him, explains the delay in responding to your resolution.   JEFFERSON DAVIS.

RICHMOND, V.A., March 3, 1865.

To the Senate of the Confederate States.

I have this day received a copy of your resolution of the 1st inst., as follows:

"*Resolved,* That Major General Stephen D. Lee, having been appointed Lt. General under the act of Feb. 17, 1864, and having been relieved from the discharge of the duties in the command to which he was appointed, cannot be confirmed by the

Senate to the said command, but must now resume his former rank in the service."

In response, I have the honor to request the return of the nomination which was the occasion of the resolution, and to inform you that, before the action of the Senate in the premises was known, I had directed a new nomination of the officer referred to to be made, which should be free from the objection stated.

JEFFERSON DAVIS.

RICHMOND, VA., March 4, 1865.

To the Senate of the Confederate States.

In response to your resolution of the 21st ultimo, I herewith transmit for your information a communication from the Secretary of War, covering a copy of General John B. Hood's report of the operations of the Army of Tennessee while under his command.

JEFFERSON DAVIS.

RICHMOND, VA., March 6, 1865.

To the Senate of the Confederate States.

I have this day approved and signed an act which originated in the Senate entitled "An Act (S. 117) to authorize the commanders of reserves in each State to order general courts-martial and to revise the proceedings of courts-martial and military courts."

In the first section the general commanding reserves in each State is authorized to order general courts-martial for the trial of offenses committed against the military code by persons belonging to his command and to revise the proceedings.

In the second section military courts are authorized under certain circumstances to try offenses committed by members of the organization of reserves. But no provision is made by which the general commanding reserves is authorized to revise the proceedings of military courts in any case. From the title of the act it seems to have been the intention to confer this power, and I have thought it proper to invite your attention to what seems to be an oversight in not granting it. A copy of the act is inclosed.

JEFFERSON DAVIS.

RICHMOND, VA., March 6th, 1865.

To the House of Representatives.

In response to your resolution of the 23d ult., I herewith transmit for your information a communication from the Secretary of War, covering a copy of General John B. Hood's report of the operations of the Army of Tennessee while under his command.

JEFFERSON DAVIS.

To the Senate and House of Representatives of the Confederate States of America.

Having been this day informed that the two houses of Congress have concurred in fixing Saturday next as the day for the adjournment, I deem it proper and advisable to notify you that I expect at an early day to send a communication* which may require your deliberation and action, and therefore to request that you will prolong your session for a few days.

JEFFERSON DAVIS.

Richmond, March 9, 1865.

EXECUTIVE OFFICE, RICHMOND, VA., March 9th, 1865.

To the Senate and House of Representatives of the Confederate States.

I herewith transmit for your consideration a communication from the Secretary of the Treasury, covering estimates of appropriations required for the support of the Government during the year 1865.

JEFFERSON DAVIS.

RICHMOND, VA., March 9th, 1865.

To the House of Representatives.

I herewith transmit for your information a copy of the report of Lieut. Genl. S. D. Lee, of the operations of his corps of the Army of Tennessee during the recent campaign, under command of Genl. John B. Hood, whose report in response to your resolution of the 23d ult. was submitted on the 6th inst.

JEFFERSON DAVIS.

*See page 544.

RICHMOND, VA., March 11, 1865.

To the Senate of the Confederate States.

I have received a copy of your resolution of the 6th instant, as follows:

Resolved, That the President be respectfully requested to inform the Senate why he gives to aids-de-camp to general officers above the grade of brigadier general only the rank of first lieutenant in his nominations made to the Senate.

In response, I herewith transmit for your information a communication from the Secretary of War upon the same subject in response to the resolution of the House of Representatives of November 8, 1864, as follows:

Resolved, That the President be respectfully requested to inform this House whether any appointments have been made under the act entitled "An Act to provide and organize a general staff for the armies in the field to serve during the war," approved June 14, 1864; and if not, why such appointments have not been made in pursuance of said act.

The anticipation of amendatory legislation, as set forth in the annexed report, together with the discretionary power vested in the Executive by the seventh section of the act referred to, has caused me for the time being not to make appointments under said act.

In the case of aids-de-camp, it has been the practice, because of their personal and confidential relations to their chief, to appoint upon his nomination. To this practice there seems to be no paramount objection, while the rank of such officers is of the subaltern grade; but if they have high rank, for many and obvious considerations their selection cannot be controlled by the personal preferences of the general with whom they are to serve. But the suggested change in the mode of selection would impair the confidential relation which an aid should have to his chief, and be an unwelcome task to the appointing power.

The nominations of aids-de-camp have for the above reasons been continued as heretofore, though the legislative amendment expected had not been made.   JEFFERSON DAVIS.

EXECUTIVE OFFICE, Richmond, March 13, 1865.

To the Senate and House of Representatives of the Confederate States of America.

I have now under consideration the act entitled "An Act to

diminish the number of exemptions and details," which has passed both Houses, and was presented to me on Saturday, the 11th instant.

The act contains two provisions which would in practice so impair the efficiency of the service as to counterbalance, if not outweigh, the advantages that would result from the other clauses contained in it.

The third section exempts all skilled artisans and mechanics in the employment of the Government from all military service. A very important and indeed indispensable portion of our local defense troops consists of these mechanics and artisans. They amount to many thousands in the Confederacy; and while they are and should remain exempt from general service, no good cause is perceived why they should not, like all other citizens capable of bearing arms, be organized for local defense and be ready to defend the localities in which they are respectively employed against sudden raids and incursions. If exempt from this local service, it will be necessary to detach in many cases troops from the armies in the field to guard the towns and workshops where they are employed. It is believed that if this provision becomes a law the gain of strength resulting from the repeal of other exemptions enacted by the first section of the law would be more than counterbalanced by the loss of this local force.

The second provision to which I refer is that which revokes all details and exemptions heretofore granted by the President and Secretary of War, and prohibits the grant of such exemptions and details hereafter. There is little hazard in saying that such a provision could not be executed without so disorganizing the public service as to produce very injurious results. In every department of the Government, in every branch of the service throughout the country, there are duties to be performed which cannot be discharged except by men instructed and trained in their performance. Long experience makes them experts. Their services become in their peculiar sphere of duty worth to the country greatly more than any they could possibly render in the field. Some of these it would be impossible immediately to replace. The Treasury expert who detects a forged note at a glance; the accounting officer whose long experience makes him a living repository of the rules and precedents which guard the Treasury from frauds;

the superintendent of the manufacturing establishments of the Government which supply shoes, harness, wagons, ambulances, &c., for the Army; the employees who have been specially trained in the distribution and subdivision of mail matter among the various routes by which it is to reach its destination, are among the instances that are afforded by the daily experience of executive officers. To withdraw from the public service at once, and without any means of replacing them, the very limited number of experts, believed to be less than 100, who are affected by the bill, is to throw the whole machinery of Government into confusion and disorder, at a period when none who are not engaged in executive duties can have an adequate idea of the difficulties by which they are already embarrassed.

The desire of the Executive and the Secretary of War to obtain for the Army the services of every man available for the public defense can hardly be doubted, and Congress may be assured that nothing but imperative public necessity could induce the exercise of any discretion vested in them to retain men out of the Army. But no Government can be administered without vesting some discretion in executive officers in the application of general rules to classes of the population. Individual exceptions exist to all such rules, in the very nature of things, and these exceptions cannot be provided for by legislation in advance.

I earnestly hope that Congress will pass an amendment to the act now under consideration, in accordance with the foregoing recommendations, so that I may be able by signing both the act and amendment to secure unimpaired benefit from the proposed legislation.   JEFFERSON DAVIS.

EXECUTIVE OFFICE, RICHMOND, March 13, 1865.

To the Senate and House of Representatives of the Confederate States.

I have returned with my approval an act entitled "An Act to regulate the business of conscription." There is, however, one section of the act which seems to me to threaten injury to the service unless essentially modified.

The eighth section provides that there shall be in each Congressional district "a medical board composed of three surgeons, who, after due notice of the time and place of their meeting, shall visit each county of their district at least once in three months, and shall examine for discharge or recommendation for light duty all conscripts who have been furloughed under the provisions of the preceding section. Every discharge granted by said medical board shall be final and shall relieve the party from all military service in the future when the disability is permanent and the cause of it is set forth in the certificate."

It is greatly to be feared that under the terms of this section considerable numbers of men will be finally discharged from military service while competent to aid in the defense of their country. The terms of the law do not require that the disability shall be total, as well as permanent, in order to entitle the soldier to be discharged. The loss of a limb, or stiffness of a joint, or even the loss of the dexter forefinger, lameness, nearsightedness, partial deafness, are instances of disability, permanent but not total, and which may well exist without rendering the individual incompetent to perform valuable service in posts, garrisons, or even in active operations.

The number of surgeons required for the duty imposed by this section would be about 150 in addition to the local physicians. We have no medical officers to spare from attendance upon the troops and in hospitals, so that it would be necessary to appoint this number of new officers who would generally be drawn from men in active service in the field. After the first visit to the different counties these officers would have so little to do as to be practically supernumeraries supported by the Government at great cost, and with the loss of their services in the field. Of the three surgeons who are to compose the board, only two are to be public officers; so that any resident physician of a county, in connection with a single Army surgeon, would have power by action, from which there is no appeal, to discharge permanently from service any inhabitant of the county in which he practices his profession. When we consider the strong opposition manifested in many districts of the country to the system of conscription, and the many influences which are resorted to by those who seek to escape service, there is much cause to fear that the effect of these provisions will be to deplete our reduced forces to a serious extent, and I hope it will be the pleasure of Congress to repeal this section or materially to modify its provisions. JEFFERSON DAVIS.

RICHMOND, VA., March 13, 1865.

To the Senate and House of Representatives of the Confederate States of America.

When informed on Thursday last that it was the intention of Congress to adjourn *sine die* on the ensuing Saturday, I deemed it my duty to request a postponement of the adjournment* in order that I might submit for your consideration certain matters of public interest which are now laid before you. When that request was made, the most important measures that had occupied your attention during the session had not been so far advanced as to be submitted for Executive action, and the state of the country had been so materially affected by the events of the last four months as to evince the necessity of further and more energetic legislation than was contemplated in November last.

Our country is now environed with perils which it is our duty calmly to contemplate. Thus alone can the measures necessary to avert threatened calamities be wisely devised and efficiently enforced.

Recent military operations of the enemy have been successful in the capture of some of our seaports, in interrupting some of our lines of communication, and in devastating large districts of our country. These events have had the natural effect of encouraging our foes and dispiriting many of our people. The Capital of the Confederate States is now threatened, and is in greater danger than it has heretofore been during the war. The fact is stated without reserve or concealment, as due to the people whose servants we are, and in whose courage and constancy entire trust is reposed; as due to you, in whose wisdom and resolute spirit the people have confided for the adoption of the measures required to guard them from threatened perils.

While stating to you that our country is in danger, I desire also to state my deliberate conviction that it is within our power to avert the calamities which menace us, and to secure the triumph of the sacred cause for which so much sacrifice has been made, so much suffering endured, so many precious lives been lost. This result is to be obtained by fortitude, by courage, by constancy in enduring the sacrifices still needed; in a word, by the prompt and

---

*See page 539.

resolute devotion of the whole resources of men and money in the Confederacy to the achievement of our liberties and independence. The measures now required, to be successful, should be prompt. Long deliberation and protracted debate over important measures are not only natural, but laudable in representative assemblies under ordinary circumstances; but in moments of danger, when action becomes urgent, the delay thus caused is itself a new source of peril. Thus it has unfortunately happened that some of the measures passed by you in pursuance of the recommendations contained in my message* of November last have been so retarded as to lose much of their value, or have, for the same reason, been abandoned after being matured, because no longer applicable to our altered condition, and others have not been brought under examination. In making these remarks it is far from my intention to attribute the loss of time to any other cause than those inherent in deliberative assemblies, but only urgently to recommend prompt action upon the measures now submitted.

We need, for carrying on the war successfully, men and supplies for the Army. We have both within our country sufficient to obtain success. To obtain the supplies, it is necessary to protect productive districts and guard our lines of communication by an increase in the number of our forces; and hence it results that, with a large augmentation in the number of men in the Army, the facility of supplying the troops would be greater than with our present reduced strength. For the purchase of the supplies now required, especially for the armies in Virginia and North Carolina, the Treasury must be provided with means, and a modification in the impressment law is required. It has been ascertained by examination that we have within our reach a sufficiency of what is most needed for the Army, without having recourse to the ample provision existing in those parts of the Confederacy with which our communication has been partially interrupted by hostile operations. But in some districts from which supplies are to be drawn the inhabitants, being either within the enemy's lines or in very close proximity, are unable to make use of Confederate Treasury notes for the purchase of articles of prime necessity, and it is necessary that to some extent coin be paid in order to obtain

---

*Page 482.

supplies. It is therefore recommended that Congress devise the means for making available the coin within the Confederacy for the purpose of supplying the Army. The officers of the supply departments report that with $2,000,000 in coin the armies in Virginia and North Carolina can be amply supplied for the remainder of the year, and the knowledge of this fact should suffice to insure the adoption of the measures necessary to obtain this moderate sum.

The impressment law as it now exists prohibits the public officers from impressing supplies without making payment of the valuation at the time of impressment. The limit fixed for the issue of Treasury notes has been nearly reached, and the Treasury cannot always furnish the funds necessary for prompt payment; while the law for raising revenue, which would have afforded means for diminishing, if not removing, this difficulty, was unfortunately delayed for several months, and has just been signed. In this condition of things it is impossible to supply the Army, although ample stores may exist in the country, whenever the owners refuse to give credit to the public officer. It is necessary that this restriction on the power of impressment be removed. The power is admitted to be objectionable, liable to abuse, and unequal in its operations on individuals; yet all these objections must yield to absolute necessity. It is also suggested that the system of valuation now established ought to be radically changed. The legislation requires in such cases of impressment that the market price be paid; but there is really no market price in many cases, and the valuation is made arbitrarily and in a depreciated currency. The result is that the most extravagant prices are fixed, such as no one expects ever to be paid in coin. None believe that the Government can ever redeem in coin the obligation to pay $50 a bushel for corn, or $700 a barrel for flour. It would seem to be more just and appropriate to estimate the supplies impressed at their value in coin, to give the obligation of the Government for the payment of the price in coin with reasonable interest; or, at the option of the creditor, to return in kind the wheat or corn impressed, with a reasonable interest also payable in kind, and to make the obligations thus issued receivable for all payments due in coin to the Government. Whatever be the value attached by Congress to these suggestions, it is hoped that there will be no hesitation in so changing the law as to render it possible to supply the Army in case of necessity for the impressment of provisions for that purpose.

The measure adopted to raise revenue, though liberal in its provisions, being clearly inadequate to meet the arrear of debt and the current expenditure, some degree of embarrassment in the management of the finances must continue to be felt. It is to be regretted, I think, that the recommendation of the Secretary of the Treasury of a tax on agricultural income equal to the augmented tax on other incomes, payable in Treasury notes, was rejected by Congress. This tax would have contributed materially to facilitate the purchase of provisions and diminish the necessity that is now felt for a supply of coin.

The measures passed by Congress during the session for recruiting the Army and supplying the additional force needed for the public defense have been, in my judgment, insufficient; and I am impelled by a profound conviction of duty, and stimulated by a sense of the perils which surround our country, to urge upon you additional legislation on this subject.

The bill for employing negroes as soldiers has not reached me, though the printed journals of your proceedings inform me of its passage. Much benefit is anticipated from this measure, though far less than would have resulted from its adoption at an earlier date, so as to afford time for their organization and instruction during the winter months.

The bill for diminishing the number of exempts has just been made the subject of a special message,* and its provisions are such as would add no strength to the Army. The recommendation to abolish all class exemptions has not met your favor, although still deemed by me a valuable and important measure; and the number of men exempted by a new clause in the act just passed is believed to be quite equal to that of those whose exemption is revoked. A law of a few lines repealing all class exemptions would not only strengthen the forces in the field, but be still more beneficial by abating the natural discontent and jealousy created in the Army by the existence of classes privileged by law to remain in places of

---

*Page 540.

safety while their fellow-citizens are exposed in the trenches and the field.

The measure most needed, however, at the present time for affording an effective increase to our military strength is a general militia law, such as the Constitution authorizes Congress to pass, by granting to it power "to provide for organizing, arming, and disciplining the militia, and for governing such part of them as may be employed in the service of the Confederate States," and the further power "to provide for calling forth the militia to execute the laws of the Confederate States, suppress insurrections, and repel invasions." The necessity for the exercise of this power can never exist if not in the circumstances which now surround us.

The security of the States against any encroachment by the Confederate Government is amply provided by the Constitution by "reserving to the States, respectively, the appointment of the officers, and the authority of training the militia according to the discipline prescribed by Congress."

A law is needed to prescribe not only how and of what persons the militia are to be organized, but to provide the mode of calling them out. If instances be required to show the necessity for such general law, it is sufficient to mention that in one case I have been informed by the Governor of a State that the law does not permit him to call the militia from one county for service in another, so that a single brigade of the enemy could traverse the State and devastate each county in turn without any power on the part of the Executive to use the militia for effective defense; while in another State the Executive refused to allow the militia "to be employed in the service of the Confederate States" in the absence of a law for that purpose.

I have heretofore, in a confidential message* to the two Houses, stated the facts which induced me to consider it necessary that the privilege of the writ of *habeas corpus* should be suspended. The conviction of the necessity of this measure has become deeper as the events of the struggle have been developed. Congress has not concurred with me in this opinion. It is my duty to say that the time has arrived when the suspension of the writ is not simply advisable and expedient, but almost indispensable to the success-

---

*Page 395; see also page 498.

ful conduct of the war. On Congress must rest the responsibility of declining to exercise a power conferred by the Constitution as a means of public safety, to be used in periods of national peril resulting from foreign invasion. If our present circumstances are not such as were contemplated when this power was conferred, I confess myself at a loss to imagine any contingency in which this clause of the Constitution will not remain a dead letter.

With the prompt adoption of the measures above recommended and the united and hearty coöperation of Congress and the people in the execution of the laws and the defense of the country, we may enter upon the present campaign with cheerful confidence in the result. And who can doubt the continued existence of that spirit and fortitude in the people, and of that constancy under reverses, which alone are needed to render our triumph secure? What other resource remains available but the undying, unconquerable resolve to be free? It has become certain beyond all doubt or question that we must continue this struggle to a successful issue, or must make abject and unconditional submission to such terms as it shall please the conqueror to impose on us after our surrender. If a possible doubt could exist after the conference between our Commissioners and Mr. Lincoln, as recently reported* to you, it would be dispelled by a recent occurrence of which it is proper that you should be informed.

Congress will remember that in the conference above referred to our Commissioners were informed that the Government of the United States would not enter into any agreement or treaty whatever with the Confederate States, nor with any single State; that the only possible mode of obtaining peace was by laying down our arms, disbanding our forces, and yielding unconditional obedience to the laws of the United States, including those passed for the confiscation of our property, and the constitutional amendment for the abolition of slavery. It will be further remembered that Mr. Lincoln declared that the only terms on which hostilities could cease were those stated in his message of December last, in which we were informed that in the event of our penitent submission he would temper justice with mercy, and that the question whether we would be governed as dependent territories or per-

*Page 519.

mitted to have a representation in their Congress was one on which he could promise nothing, but which would be decided by their Congress after our submission had been accepted.

It has not, however, been hitherto stated to you that in the course of the conference at Fortress Monroe a suggestion was made by one of our Commissioners that the objection entertained by Mr. Lincoln to treating with the Government of the Confederacy, or with any separate State, might be avoided by substituting for the usual mode of negotiating through commissioners or other diplomatic agents the method sometimes employed of a military convention to be entered into by the commanding generals of the armies of the two belligerents. This he admitted was a power possessed by him, though it was not thought commensurate with all the questions involved. As he did not accept the suggestions when made, he was afterwards requested to reconsider his conclusion upon the subject of a suspension of hostilities, which he agreed to do, but said that he had maturely considered the plan and had determined that it could not be done. Subsequently, however, an interview with General Longstreet was asked for by General Ord, commanding the enemy's Army of the James, during which General Longstreet was informed by him that there was a possibility of arriving at a satisfactory adjustment of the present unhappy difficulties by means of a military convention, and that if General Lee desired an interview on the subject it would not be declined, provided General Lee had authority to act. This communication was supposed to be the consequence of the suggestion above referred to, and General Lee, according to instructions, wrote to General Grant on the 2d of this month proposing to meet him for conference on the subject, and stating that he was vested with the requisite authority. General Grant's reply stated that he had no authority to accede to the proposed conference; that his power extended only to making a convention on subjects purely of a military character, and that General Ord could only have meant that an interview would not be refused on any subject on which he (General Grant) had the right to act. It thus appears that neither with the Confederate authorities nor the authorities of any State, nor through the commanding generals, will the Government of the United States treat or make any terms or agreement whatever for the cessation of hostilities. There remains, then, for us no choice but to continue the contest to a final issue, for the people of the Confederacy can be but little known to him who supposes it possible that they would ever consent to purchase at the cost of degradation and slavery permission to live in a country garrisoned by their own negroes and governed by officers sent by the conqueror to rule over them.

Having thus fully placed before you the information requisite to enable you to judge of the state of the country, the dangers to which we are exposed, and the measures of legislation needed for averting them, it remains for me but to invoke your attention to the consideration of those means by which, above all others, we may hope to escape the calamities that would result from our failure. Prominent above all others is the necessity for earnest and cordial coöperation between all departments of government, State and Confederate, and all eminent citizens throughout the Confederacy. To you especially, as Senators and Representatives, do the people look for encouragement and counsel. To your action, not only in legislative halls but in your homes, will their eyes be turned for the example of what is befitting men who, by willing sacrifices on the altar of freedom, show that they are worthy to enjoy its blessings. I feel full confidence that you will concur with me in the conviction that your public duties will not be ended when you shall have closed the legislative labors of the session, but that your voice will be heard cheering and encouraging the people to that persistent fortitude which they have hitherto displayed, and animating them by the manifestation of that serene confidence which in moments of public danger is the distinctive characteristic of the patriot who derives courage from his devotion to his country's destiny and is thus enabled to inspire the like courage in others.

Thus united in a common and holy cause, rising above all selfish considerations, rendering all our means and faculties tributary to the country's welfare, let us bow submissively to the Divine will and reverently invoke the blessing of our Heavenly Father, that, as he protected and guided our sires when struggling in a similar cause, so he will enable us to guard safely our altars and our firesides and maintain inviolate the political rights which we inherited.   JEFFERSON DAVIS.

RICHMOND, VA., March 13, 1865.

To the House of Representatives.

Herewith I transmit a letter from the Secretary of War, covering several communications from officers of the Army in reference to the present condition of the country as connected with military defense, and especially with the matter of supplies for the Army. They will serve to elucidate the message* this day transmitted to you. The last in the order of time of those communications was received after my message was transmitted, and refers to a contingency which, if it should occur, must seriously affect the opinions which I then expressed. I invite your special attention to the papers submitted. JEFFERSON DAVIS.

RICHMOND, VA., March 13, 1865.

To the Senate and House of Representatives.

I herewith transmit for your information copies of the correspondence referred to in my message* of this date, in regard to the proposed conference to adjust terms of peace by means of a military convention. JEFFERSON DAVIS.

RICHMOND, VA., March 13th, 1865.

To the House of Representatives.

In response to your resolution of 23d November last, I herewith transmit for your information a communication from the Secretary of War, the Attorney General, and the Postmaster General, relative to the number, ages, etc., of the officers and employees in their respective Departments on duty in the city of Richmond.

The transmission of these papers has been delayed in order that the report of the Secretary of the Treasury relative to the number of employees in his Department, which was included in your call for information, might accompany them.

That report has not yet been received, but I have decided to withhold the present communications no longer on that account. JEFFERSON DAVIS.

---

*Page 544.

RICHMOND, VA., March 14, 1865.

To the Senate of the Confederate States.

I herewith transmit for your information a communication from the Postmaster General, relative to the removal of a postmaster from office. JEFFERSON DAVIS.

RICHMOND, VA., March 14, 1865.

To the House of Representatives.

In response to your resolution of the 2d inst., I herewith transmit for your information communications from the Secretary of the Navy and the commissioner for the exchange of prisoners, relative to the trial and execution of John Y. Beall, Acting Master in the C. S. Navy, by the authorities of the United States.

JEFFERSON DAVIS.

VETO MESSAGES.

To the Senate of the Confederate States of America.

I feel constrained to return to the Senate, without my approval, an act which originated in your honorable body, entitled, "An Act to increase the number of acting midshipmen in the Navy, and to provide the mode of appointment."

The act provides that the additional acting midshipmen "shall be appointed under the regulations prescribed by the Secretary of the Navy as follows: One from each Congressional district, upon the recommendation of the Representative in Congress; two at large from each State, upon the recommendation of the Senators thereof respectively; and ten at large by the President."

The Constitution, in the 2d article, 2d section, 2d clause, after giving to the President power to nominate, and by and with the advice and consent of the Senate to appoint all officers of the Confederate States whose appointments are not otherwise provided for, adds: "But the Congress may by law vest the appointment of such inferior officers as they think proper in the President alone, in the courts of law, or in the Heads of Departments."

The framers of the Constitution, in defining the powers of the several Departments of the Government, took care to designate the particular class of offices which the two Houses of Congress may fill, and thus excluded the idea of power to make selections for any others.

By the fifth clause of article 1st, section 2, the special power is given to the House of Representatives "to choose their Speaker and other officers," the word "their" being applicable not only to the Speaker, but to the "other officers."

By the act now before me, however, the two Houses empower their respective members to "choose" officers that are not "their officers," but officers of the Executive Department of the Government. The language is not susceptible of any other meaning. The acting midshipmen "shall be appointed upon the recommendation" of the Representatives or Senators, as the case may be.

But the Constitution, by granting to Congress no other power over officers created by law than that of vesting the appointment "in the President alone, in the courts of law, or in the Heads of Departments," thus withholds from that branch of the Government any participation in such appointments. But it may be remarked that this act gives the power of making the proposed appointments not to Congress as a body, but to the individual members of the two Houses, and that it is thus in conflict with the spirit and intent of the 1st clause of the 6th section of the 1st article of the Constitution, which enumerates the privileges accorded to Representatives and Senators individually. These privileges are carefully restricted to such as are necessary to enable them to discharge their duties as legislators. All other rights, powers, and privileges granted to Congress by the Constitution are conferred on the body collectively, or on one of the two Houses.

The power to make selections for appointment to office is nowhere accorded in that instrument to the Senators and Representatives individually; and it is believed to be an unquestioned principle of constitutional law that no legislation can add to the power vested by the Constitution in any member of any one of the three Departments of Government.

The power of Congress to vest by law the appointment of inferior officers in the President alone or in the Heads of Departments would seem to include a power to restrict, limit, or partially confer the authority, or to divide it between several Departments, provided they be those which may constitutionally exercise the function. But, if the view of the Constitution which has been presented be correct, it is clear that the Congress cannot vest in itself any right to a participation in the selection of officers of any class save those of the two Houses. The language of the act organizing the Navy is sometimes cited to support the opinion that acting midshipmen are not officers, but employees. In the first section of that act, the President is authorized to appoint certain commissioned officers, and to "employ as many masters, midshipmen, engineers, naval constructors, boatswains, gunners, carpenters, sailmakers, and other warrant and petty officers and seamen as he may deem necessary," &c.

If it were conceded that acting midshipmen are not officers, the bill would not on that account be the less liable, in my judgment, to the objections above set forth; for it is as little in accordance with the letter and the spirit of the Constitution for the members of Congress to participate in choosing employees as in choosing officers for the Executive or Judicial Departments. It is repugnant to the whole theory of our republican institutions, which are based on the fundamental idea of independent and distinct functions in each of the Departments of Government, the Legislative, Executive, and Judicial; and evil consequences must result from any departure from this principle.

But in no just sense can it be maintained that an acting midshipman is not an officer of the Navy. The very clause in the law just referred to implies that he is a "warrant officer;" but if there be doubt as to this, the question is decided by the 3rd section of the act of 21st April, 1862, which declares that "the warrant officers shall be as follows: Twenty passed midshipmen, one hundred and six acting midshipmen," &c., &c. The commissioned officer is appointed by and with the advice and consent of the Senate; the next grade, the warrant officer, belongs to that class of inferior officers which according to the Constitution may be established by law, and appointed by the President alone, or the Head of a Department.

The midshipman is of this class. His appointment is authorized by law, and his promotion provided for by regulations. He cannot be discharged or dismissed from service at the pleasure of his commander, nor without delinquency on his part, as a mere employee for temporary service. His name is placed in the Navy

Register, and the proper record kept of his entry into service, to determine his rank; and in all relations to officers and seamen he is entitled to be, and is, actually treated as an officer of the Navy.

The bill is returned in no spirit of unwillingness to receive the advice and recommendations of members of Congress, which are recognized to be entitled to special consideration, but from a sense of duty to constitutional obligations.   JEFFERSON DAVIS.

23d January, 1865.

RICHMOND, VA., January 25, 1865.

To the Senate of the Confederate States of America.

I return to your honorable body without my approval an act which originated in the Senate, entitled "An Act to authorize newspapers to be mailed to the soldiers free of postage."

The act provides "that all newspapers directed to any officer, musician, or private engaged in the actual service of the Confederate States may be transmitted through the mails free of postage."

The Constitution, article 1, section 8, clause 7, gives power to Congress "to establish post offices and post routes; but the expenses of the Post Office Department after the 1st day of March, in the year of our Lord 1863, shall be paid out of its own revenues."

This provision that the Post Office Department shall be self-sustaining was not contained in the Constitution of our former Government.   It is important that its spirit and object should be correctly determined now, because many members of the present Congress were also members of the Provisional Congress, which adopted this new clause, and legislation by them will be deemed hereafter to possess peculiar value as a precedent, and as a contemporaneous interpretation of the Constitution by those best acquainted with its meaning.

It was generally understood that the clause under consideration was intended by its framers to correct what were deemed to be two great vices that had been developed in the postal system of the United States.   The first was the injustice of taxing the whole people for the expense of the mail facilities afforded to individuals; and the remedy devised was to limit the Government to the furnishing of machinery for carrying the mails and compelling those who might use the facilities thus furnished to pay the expense thereof.

The second evil against which this clause was intended as a safeguard was the wasteful extravagance which grew out of the franking privilege, with its attendant abuses of large contracts for stationery, printing, binding, &c., and increased Government patronage with its train of corrupting influences.

With this knowledge of the purpose of the framers of the Constitution, and of the evils against which they intended to provide by the clause under consideration, I cannot escape the conclusion that to authorize the transmission of any mail matter free of postage is to violate the true intent and meaning of the Constitution.

If the act now before me should become a law, the Postmaster General would be bound to pay railroads and other carriers for conveying newspapers to the armies without reimbursement from any source whatever. He could not be repaid out of the general Treasury without a violation of the letter of the Constitution, nor out of the other revenues of his Department without in effect imposing on those who pay for carrying their own correspondence an additional charge to defray the cost of conveying newspapers for others.

If it be competent for Congress under the clause to order newspapers to be carried free of postage, the power exists to order free transmission of any other mail matter. But we must ever remember that Congress can exercise no implied powers—certainly none not necessary to carry into effect the powers expressly granted; and where shall we find in the Constitution any power in the Confederate Government, expressed or implied, for dividing either the people or the public servants into classes unequally burdened with postal charges?

In that part of the Constitution which specially treats of the burden of taxation, every precaution has been taken to secure uniformity and to guard against bounties or preferences of any kind; and although not directly applicable to the subject of postage, the spirit of the whole provision is so opposed to inequality in legislation that the passage may well serve for illustration. The first clause of article 1, section 8, gives to Congress power "to lay and collect táxes, duties, imposts, and excises for revenue necessary to pay the debts, provide for the common defense, and carry on the Government of the Confederate States; but no bounties shall be granted from the Treasury; nor shall any duties or taxes on importations from foreign nations be laid to promote or foster any branch of industry; and all duties, imposts, and excises shall be uniform throughout the Confederate States." It is true that the payment of postage is not properly a tax, but compensation for service rendered; yet it would scarcely be ingenuous to deny that so to regulate the rates of postage as to produce an excess of receipts over the expense of carrying mail matter for one class and to use this excess in order to carry free of cost the mail matter of another class would strongly conflict with the just equality of privileges and burdens which the above-cited clauses were designed to secure.

I regret to be compelled to object to a measure devised by Congress for the benefit or relief of the Army, but with my convictions on the subject it is not possible to approve the act now before me.

JEFFERSON DAVIS.

RICHMOND, VA., March 9, 1865.

To the Senate of the Confederate States.

I feel constrained to return the bill "To provide for the promotion of officers in certain cases" to the Senate, in which it originated, with a statement of the objections which have led me to withhold from it my signature.

The Constitution provides, in paragraph 2, section 2, article 2, that the President "shall have power, by and with the advice and consent of the Senate," to appoint officers of the Confederate States not otherwise provided for, "but the Congress may, by law, vest the appointment of such inferior officers, as they think proper, in the President alone, in the courts of law, or in the Heads of Departments."

In the bill under consideration it is declared that "it shall be competent to the commanding general in the field, or the Secretary of War, to order the promotions to be made of the officers next in grade," &c.

This seems to me to confer a power of appointment on commanding generals not warranted by the Constitution.

It may be further remarked that the power conferred upon the Secretary of War will be ineffectual except in the case where the officer next in rank is qualified to fill the temporary vacancy, a case in which the power would be least necessary in order to provide for the time being a competent commander.

JEFFERSON DAVIS.

RICHMOND, VA., March 11, 1865.

To the Senate of the Confederate States of America.

The act entitled "An Act to abolish the office of certain quartermasters and assistant quartermasters, commissaries and assistant commissaries, and to provide for the appointment of bonded agents in said departments," which originated in your honorable body, is herewith returned without my approval, and with a statement of the objections which have prevented my signing it.

The act abolishes the office of all quartermasters, assistant quartermasters, commissaries, and assistant commissaries at posts and depots, and of those engaged in purchasing and impressing supplies, except such as are above the age of forty-five years, or have been disabled in service or declared unfit for duty in the field. It requires those officers to be dropped from service (one-fourth in two months, one-fourth in four months, one-fourth in six months, and one-fourth within two years), and directs that their places be supplied by bonded agents, who are to be persons above the age of forty-five years or disabled in service, or unfit for duty in the field; and it revokes all details and repeals all authority to grant details of persons between the ages of eighteen and forty-five years for duty in the Quartermaster's and Commissary Departments, except skilled artisans and mechanics permanently employed, or persons disabled or unfit for duty in the field.

The object plainly intended by this act is one which meets my hearty concurrence and approval. Its obvious purpose is to strengthen the Army by placing in the ranks persons fit for active service, and whose places can be supplied by others unable to do duty in the field. On reference of the subject, however, to the Secretary of War, it has been found that this act could not be executed without seriously impairing our ability to supply the armies in the field during the approaching campaign, and that its

operation would be to drop officers who have been carefully selected by reason of their superior capacity and qualifications, while
retaining others of inferior merit and value.

The difficulty of furnishing supplies to the Army, owing to embarrassments in transportation, is greater now than it has been
at any previous period of the war.   This difficulty has prompted
the selection for that duty of the best and most active and competent officers in the Quartermaster's and Commissary Departments,
and such officers have within the last six months been in many
instances withdrawn from the armies where their services were
less important, and assigned to duty in purchasing, collecting, and
forwarding supplies.   This fact was, I feel confident, not known to
Congress when the act was passed; and it could not have been
intended to drop from service officers of special merit and retain
others of inferior value.   I am also satisfied, from the report made
to me by the Secretary of War, that the number of officers who
would be dropped under the provisions of this law is far less than
is supposed; that their value as soldiers in the ranks would in no
manner compensate for the loss of their services in their present
positions.   The total number of post and purchasing commissaries
in the States east of the Mississippi River is but 212, of whom
many are either over forty-five years of age, or otherwise exempt
from the operations of the proposed law.   The total number of
quartermasters collecting taxes in kind is 96, and on post duty
223, including officers in charge of manufactories of clothing,
shoes, harness, wagons, ambulances, &c.   A number of them are
over forty-five years of age, others would not be embraced by the
terms of the act, others still have special qualifications for the
superintendence of the important manufactures confided to their
care.

Taken altogether, it is doubted whether the officers who would
be dropped under the provisions of the bill would exceed 200 in
number, of whom 50 would go into the ranks in two months, 50 in
four months, and 50 more in six months.   This scarcely appre-
ciable addition to the force in the field would be dearly bought at
the sacrifice of efficiency in the two branches of service on which
the very·existence of the Army depends.   The terms of the act
exempt from its operation those now on duty in the field, so that
if it becomes a law it would not even be possible to avert the loss

of the best officers by returning them to duty in the field, and dropping others of inferior merit. The Secretary of War is left without discretion or choice in the matter.

The heads of the two branches of service affected by this act apprehend great embarrassment to their respective departments if it becomes a law. The machinery now organized would be impaired in its workings everywhere, and in some instances positively interrupted just at the opening of the most important campaign. Valuable and experienced officers would be withdrawn from service. Chief commissaries long accustomed to control operations in an entire State, quartermasters thoroughly informed as to the resources of their respective fields of duty, would at short intervals be dropped, and the heads of these bureaus would be embarrassed with the difficult duty in the midst of an active campaign of supplying the places with inexperienced and untried successors.

The representations made to me on the subjects embraced in this act by those under whose immediate superintendence its provisions would be executed, together with my own daily experience of the difficulties attendant on the efficient discharge of the duties of these two indispensable branches of the service, have created apprehensions of injurious effects from the passage of the act too serious to permit my approving it.   JEFFERSON DAVIS.

RICHMOND, VA., March 17, 1865.
To the House of Representatives of the Confederate States of America.

I return without my approval an act which originated in your honorable body, entitled "An Act to provide for the payment of arrears now due to the Army and Navy."

I have been led to believe that this act was passed in haste and without due consideration, and that some members who voted for it desire an opportunity for reconsidering their action.

The act provides for additional issue of Treasury notes to an amount not exceeding $80,000,000, to be used in payment of all arrears of pay and allowances due to persons in the military and naval service of the Confederate States; these notes "to be regarded in all respects as Treasury notes issued by virtue of the act to reduce the currency and authorize a new issue of notes and bonds, approved February 17, 1864."

The objections to this legislation are, in my judgment, manifold and grave.

First. The act of February 17, 1864, levied a tax on the Treasury notes then outstanding far exceeding that levied on any other species of property, and which could be justified only by the consideration that the additional contribution thus exacted from the holders of these public credits would be compensated in whole or in part by the increased value of the new currency which was issued for the old at the rate of $2 of the former for $3 of the latter. The act revoked all authority theretofore given to issue Treasury notes, and it was generally if not universally considered that the provisions of that law constituted an implied pledge of the faith of the Government that no further issues of notes should be made than those therein provided for. It would be scarcely consistent to take from the holder one-third of the nominal amount of the currency in hand for the purpose of reducing the currency as set forth in the title of the law; to unite with this exaction a previous authority to issue notes, and afterwards to provide for an expansion of the currency in opposition to the principles of the act of February 17, 1864, to the evident detriment of the holders of the currency under that act.

Second. Independently of the objection just stated, the effect of a new issue of Treasury notes would be disastrous. The passage of the law would be accepted as proof that there is no limit to the issue of Treasury notes except the pleasure of the Government, and the people will be persuaded that whenever an emergency arises it will be met by additional issues of paper money. Such a conviction, once rooted in the popular mind, could not be eradicated, and the depreciation of the notes in circulation would increase so rapidly as effectually to destroy the whole value of what is outstanding and leave the country without a circulation and the Government without credit.

Third. The bill, although intended by Congress for the benefit of the Army, to which we all acknowledge the most sacred obligations of justice and gratitude, would have an effect the reverse of that designed. It would despoil the soldier, instead of paying him. If money be raised by taxation for paying arrears due the Army, the demand thus created for the notes enhances the value and enables the public creditor who receives them to make them available for the purchase of what he needs. If, on the contrary, the soldier is to have his claim extinguished by the simple process of printing more paper money, and thus diminishing its value below even its present depreciation, his claims for his arrears of pay will have been practically repudiated instead of being paid. Justice to the soldier prompted Congress to pass this bill. The same motive induces me to withhold my approval of it; and if my objections shall appear to you well founded, when your attention is drawn to the supposed consequences that would result from this legislation, I am persuaded that you will concur in my opinion that it ought not to be adopted.

Fourth. There is a mechanical difficulty in the execution of the law of which Congress was not aware, and which under any circumstances would render the bill unavailing for its intended purpose of prompt payment of the arrears due the Army.

The removal of the Treasury Note Bureau from Columbia, the time required for reëstablishing it with its machinery at another locality and for preparing Treasury notes for the $50,000,000 or $60,000,000 remaining for issue under existing laws, together with other causes which it is unwise to relate, would prevent the issue of the notes provided for in this bill for at least three months to come.

It is gratifying to assure you of my belief that the receipts from the tax bill just passed, together with other resources within reach of the Treasury, will enable the Government to pay the arrears due to the Army and Navy sooner than the additional notes contemplated by the bill could be issued, and that the proposed increase of currency can thus be avoided without causing delay in satisfying the just claims of the defenders of our country.

JEFFERSON DAVIS.

PROCLAMATIONS.

General Orders No. 89.

HEADQUARTERS TRANS-MISSISSIPPI DEPARTMENT,
SHREVEPORT, LA., November 24, 1864.

The following proclamation of the President is republished for information in this Department:

A PROCLAMATION.

It is meet that the people of the Confederate States should, from time to time, assemble to acknowledge their dependence on Almighty God, to render devout thanks to his holy name, to bend in prayer at his footstool, and to accept, with fervent submission, the chastening of his all-wise and all-merciful providence.

Let us, then, in temples and in the field, unite our voices in recognizing, with adoring gratitude, the manifestations of his protecting care in the many signal victories with which our arms have been crowned; in the fruitfulness with which our land has been blessed, and in the unimpaired energy and fortitude with which he has inspired our hearts and strengthened our arms in resistance to the iniquitous designs of our enemies.

And let us not forget that, while graciously vouchsafing to us his protection, our sins have merited and received grievous chastisement; that many of our best and bravest have fallen in battle; that many others are still held in foreign prisons; that large districts of our country have been devastated with savage ferocity, the peaceful homes destroyed, and helpless women and children driven away in destitution; and that with fiendish malignity the passions of a servile race have been excited by our foes into the commission of atrocities from which death is a welcome escape.

Now, therefore, I, Jefferson Davis, President of the Confederate States of America, do issue this my proclamation, setting apart Wednesday, the 16th day of November next, as a day to be specially devoted to the worship of Almighty God; and I do invite and invoke all the people of these Confederate States to assemble on the day aforesaid, in their respective places of public worship, there to unite in prayer to our Heavenly Father that he bestow his favor upon us; that he extend over us the protection of his almighty arm; that he sanctify his chastisement to our improvement, so that we may turn away from evil paths and walk righteously in his sight; and that he may restore peace to our beloved country, healing its bleeding wounds, and securing to us the continued enjoyment of our own right to self-government and independence, and that he will graciously hearken to us while we ascribe to him the power and glory of our independence.

Given under my hand and the seal of the Confederate States at Richmond, this 26th day of October, in the year of our Lord 1864.

JEFFERSON DAVIS.

By the President:

J. P. BENJAMIN, *Secretary of State.*

The foregoing proclamation, owing to the irregularity of communication with the seat of Government, was not received until too late for the general observance of the day appointed. The commanding general therefore directs that the 16th day of December next be set apart for the object specified; that on that day all Government workshops be closed and labor suspended, and that, as far as practicable, all military duties cease. The troops are recommended to assemble at their respective places of worship, and the citizens of the Department invited to unite in the religious observance of the day.

By command of General E. Kirby Smith.

S. S. ANDERSON, *Assistant Adjutant General.*

By the President of the Confederate States.

A PROCLAMATION.

Whereas, It has been made known to me that Bennett G. Burley, an Acting Master in the Navy of the Confederate States, is now under arrest in one of the British North American Provinces on an application made by the Government of the United States for the delivery to that Government of the said Bennett G. Burley, under the treaty known as the Extradition Treaty, now in force between the United States and Great Britain;

And whereas, it has been represented to me that the said demand for the extradition of said Bennett G. Burley is based on the charge that the said Burley is a fugitive from justice, accused of having committed the crimes of robbery and piracy within the jurisdiction of the United States;

And whereas, it has further been made known to me that the accusations and charges made against the said Bennett G. Burley are based solely on the acts and conduct of said Burley in an enterprise or expedition made or attempted in the month of September last (1864) for the capture of the steamer "Michigan," an armed vessel of the United States, navigating the Lakes on the boundary line between the United States and the said British

North American Provinces, and for the release of numerous citizens of the Confederate States, held as prisoners of war by the United States, at a certain island called Johnson's Island;

And whereas, the said enterprise or expedition for the capture of said armed steamer "Michigan" and for the release of the said prisoners on Johnson's Island was a proper and legitimate belligerent operation, undertaken during the pending public war between the two Confederacies known respectively as the Confederate States of America and the United States of America; which operation was ordered, directed, and sustained by the authority of the Government of the Confederate States, and confided to its commissioned officers for execution, among which officers is the said Bennett G. Burley:

Now, therefore, I, Jefferson Davis, President of the Confederate States of America, do hereby declare and make known to all whom it may concern, that the expedition aforesaid, undertaken in the month of September last, for the capture of the armed steamer "Michigan," a vessel of war of the United States, and for the release of the prisoners of war, citizens of the Confederate States of America, held captive by the United States of America at Johnson's Island, was a belligerent expedition ordered and undertaken under the authority of the Confederate States of America, against the United States of America, and that the Government of the Confederate States of America assumes the responsibility of answering for the acts and conduct of any of its officers engaged in said expedition, and especially of the said Bennett G. Burley, an Acting Master in the Navy of the Confederate States.

And I do further make known to all whom it may concern that in the orders and instructions given to the officers engaged in said expedition, they were specially directed and enjoined to "abstain from violating any of the laws and regulations of the Canadian or British authorities in relation to neutrality," and that the combination necessary to effect the purpose of said expedition "must be made by Confederate soldiers and such assistance as they might (you may) draw from the enemy's country."

In testimony whereof I have signed this manifesto and directed the same to be sealed with the seal of the Department of State of the Confederate States of America, and to be made public.

Done at the city of Richmond on this 24th day of December, 1864.   JEFFERSON DAVIS.

By the President:

J. P. BENJAMIN, *Secretary of State.*

BY THE PRESIDENT OF THE CONFEDERATE STATES.

A PROCLAMATION.

The Congress of the Confederate States have, by a joint resolution, invited me to appoint a day of public fasting, humiliation, and prayer, with thanksgiving to Almighty God.

It is our solemn duty at all times, and more especially in a season of public trial and adversity, to acknowledge our dependence on his mercy, and to bow in humble submission before his footstool, confessing our manifold sins, supplicating his gracious pardon, imploring his divine help, and devoutly rendering thanks for the many and great blessings which he has vouchsafed to us.

Let the hearts of our people turn contritely and trustingly unto God; let us recognize in his chastening hand the correction of a Father, and submissively pray that the trials and sufferings which have so long borne heavily upon us may be turned away by his merciful love; that his sustaining grace be given to our people, and his divine wisdom imparted to our rulers; that the Lord of Hosts will be with our armies and fight for us against our enemies, and that he will graciously take our cause into his own hand and mercifully establish for us a lasting, just, and honorable peace and independence.

And let us not forget to render unto his holy name the thanks and praise which are so justly due for his great goodness and for the many mercies which he has extended to us amid the trials and suffering of protracted and bloody war.

Now, therefore, I, Jefferson Davis, President of the Confederate States of America, do issue this my proclamation, appointing Friday, the 10th day of March next, as a day of public fasting, humiliation, and prayer (with thanksgiving) for "invoking the favor and guidance of Almighty God," and I do earnestly invite all soldiers and citizens to observe the same in a spirit of reverence, penitence, and prayer.

Given under my hand and the seal of the Confederate States, at Richmond, this 25th day of January, in the year of our Lord one thousand eight hundred and sixty-five.   JEFFERSON DAVIS.

By the President:

J. P. BENJAMIN, *Secretary of State.*

ADDRESS. ·

DANVILLE, VA., April 4, 1865.

To the People of the Confederate States of America.

The General in Chief of our Army has found it necessary to make such movements of the troops as to uncover the capital and thus involve the withdrawal of the Government from the city of Richmond.

It would be unwise, even were it possible, to conceal the great moral as well as material injury to our cause that must result from the occupation of Richmond by the enemy.   It is equally unwise and unworthy of us, as patriots engaged in a most sacred cause, to allow our energies to falter, our spirits to grow faint, or our efforts to become relaxed under reverses, however calamitous.   While it has been to us a source of national pride that for four years of unequaled warfare we have been able, in close proximity to the center of the enemy's power, to maintain the seat of our chosen Government free from the pollution of his presence; while the memories of the heroic dead who have freely given their lives to its defense must ever remain enshrined in our hearts; while the preservation of the capital, which is usually regarded as the evidence to mankind of separate national existence, was an object very dear to us, it is also true, and should not be forgotten, that the loss which we have suffered is not without compensation.   For many months the largest and finest army of the Confederacy, under the command of a leader whose presence inspires equal confidence in the troops and the people, has been greatly trammeled by the necessity of keeping constant watch over the approaches to the capital, and has thus been forced to forego more than one opportunity for promising enterprise.   The hopes and confidence of the enemy have been constantly excited by the belief that their possession of Richmond would be the signal for our submission to their rule, and relieve them from the burden of war, as their failing resources admonish them it must be abandoned if not speedily brought to a successful close. It is for us, my countrymen, to show by our bearing under reverses how wretched has been the self-deception of those who have believed us less able to endure misfortune with fortitude than to encounter danger with courage. We have now entered upon a new phase of a struggle the memory of which is to endure for all ages and to shed an increasing luster upon our country.

Relieved from the necessity of guarding cities and particular points, important but not vital to our defense, with an army free to move from point to point and strike in detail the detachments and garrisons of the enemy, operating on the interior of our own country, where supplies are more accessible, and where the foe will be far removed from his own base and cut off from all succor in case of reverse, nothing is now needed to render our triumph certain but the exhibition of our own unquenchable resolve. Let us but will it, and we are free; and who, in the light of the past, dare doubt your purpose in the future?

Animated by the confidence in your spirit and fortitude, which never yet has failed me, I announce to you, fellow-countrymen, that it is my purpose to maintain your cause with my whole heart and soul; that I will never consent to abandon to the enemy one foot of the soil of any one of the States of the Confederacy; that Virginia, noble State, whose ancient renown has been eclipsed by her still more glorious recent history, whose bosom has been bared to receive the main shock of this war, whose sons and daughters have exhibited heroism so sublime as to render her illustrious in all times to come—that Virginia, with the help of her people, and by the blessing of Providence, shall be held and defended, and no peace ever be made with the infamous invaders of her homes by the sacrifice of any of her rights or territory. If by stress of numbers we should ever be compelled to a temporary withdrawal from her limits, or those of any other border State, again and again will we return, until the baffled and exhausted enemy shall abandon in despair his endless and impossible task of making slaves of a people resolved to be free.

Let us not, then, despond, my countrymen; but, relying on the never-failing mercies and protecting care of our God, let us meet the foe with fresh defiance, with unconquered and unconquerable hearts.   JEFF'N DAVIS.

General Orders No. 3.

Adjt. and Insp. General's Office, Richmond, Va., February 6, 1865.

I. The following act of Congress is published for the information of the Army:

AN ACT TO PROVIDE FOR THE APPOINTMENT OF A GENERAL IN CHIEF OF THE ARMIES OF THE CONFEDERATE STATES.

SECTION 1. The Congress of the Confederate States of America do enact that there shall be appointed by the President, by and with the advice and consent of the Senate, an officer, who shall be known and designated as General in Chief, who shall be ranking officer of the Army, and as such shall have command of the military forces of the Confederate States.

SEC. 2. That the act providing a staff for the general who may be assigned to duty at the seat of Government is hereby repealed, and that the General in Chief who may be appointed under the provisions of this act shall have a staff not less than that now allowed a general in the field, to be assigned by the President or to be appointed by him, by and with the advice and consent of the Senate.

Approved January 23, 1865.

II. General Robert E. Lee, having been duly appointed General in Chief of the Armies of the Confederate States, will assume the duties thereof, and will be obeyed and respected accordingly.

III. General Orders No. 23, of 1864, are hereby revoked.

By order: S. COOPER, *Adjutant and Inspector General.*

PRESIDENT'S OFFICE, RICHMOND, VA., March 20, 1865.

To the Secretary of the Senate.

Sir: I have the honor, by direction of the President, to request that you furnish him at the earliest practicable moment with a transcript of the journal of the Senate beginning with the morning of the 16th inst., and continuing to the adjournment on the 18th. He desires a transcript of the executive and secret sessions as well as of the open sessions.

Very respectfully, your obedient servant,

BURTON N. HARRISON, *Private Secretary.*

Index.

Index.

[The Index to the Diplomatic Correspondence is in Volume II.]

573

Cockrell, Francis M., resolution of thanks tendered command of, 480.

Coffman, W. E., trial and conviction of, referred to, 403.

Cold Harbor, Va., Battle of.

Two battles near Cold Harbor, Hanover County, Va., about 9 miles northeast of Richmond. The first, June 27, 1862, is also known as the battle of Gaines's Mill. The Federals, about 20,000, were a portion of McClellan's army, commanded by Gen. Porter; the Confederates, by Generals Lee and Jackson. The Federals were driven across the Chickahominy, with a loss of nearly 7,000; the Confederate loss was less.

The second was fought June 3, 1864. The Federals, about 150,000, were commanded by Gen. Grant; the Confederates, about 60,000, by Gen. Lee. The Federals were defeated with a loss from June 1 to June 12, of 14,931. Confederate loss less than 2,000.

Commerce, revocation of restrictions upon, across Rio Grande referred to, 317.

Commerce, Foreign:

Act amending act imposing regulations on, to provide for public defense vetoed, 466.

Bill imposing regulations upon, etc., discussed, 505.

Regulations on, 417.

Commissariat, inquiry in relation to, 125.

Commissariat, Chief of, report of, transmitted, 155.

Commissary Department:

Men liable to conscription removed from, referred to, 391.

Officers of, failing to render accounts referred to, 407.

Commissary General, report of, transmitted, 255.

Commissioners, Confederate States:

Appropriations for sending, recommended, 76.

Commissions of, explanation regarding, 311.

Correspondence with, transmitted, 155, 196, 313, 315, 499, 505.

Commissioners, Confederate States (Continued):

Discussed, 76, 279.

Mission of, discussed, 279.

Nomination of, 57, 128, 311.

Reasons for sending, to Russia transmitted, 315.

Recall of, from Great Britain, 357.

Seized by United States authorities, 141. (See also Trent Affair.)

Commissions for trials of offenses in Army recommended, 244.

Compromise of 1850.

The Compromise of 1850 comprises the passage through Congress of several measures of importance affecting more or less the slavery question. The chief provisions of these measures were for the admission into the Union of California, as a free State, the organization of the Territories of Utah and New Mexico, without restrictions as to slavery, the abolition of slave trade in the District of Columbia, and a fugitive slave law. These measures were passed largely through the influence of Henry Clay.

Confederate Army. (See Army, Confederate States.)

Confederate Commissioners. (See Commissioners, Confederate States.)

Confederate Congress. (See Congress, Confederate States.)

Confederate Constitution. (See Constitution, Confederate States.)

Confederate Flag. (See Flag, Confederate States.)

Confederate Navy. (See Navy, Confederate States.)

Confederate States of America.

A Confederacy of 11 States of the United States which seceded therefrom in 1860-1861, and formed an independent government. These States were Alabama, Arkansas, Florida, Georgia, Louisiana, Mississippi, North Carolina, South Carolina, Tennessee, Texas, and Virginia. The Executive power was vested in a President to be elected for 6 years and who was ineligible for reëlection. The legislative power was vested in a Senate and House of Representatives. The judicial power was vested in a Supreme

Court and such inferior tribunals as Congress might from time to time establish. The provisional Congress met at Montgomery, Ala., Feb. 4, 1861, and on Feb. 8 adopted a provisional Constitution. Jefferson Davis, of Miss., was chosen provisional President, and Alexander H. Stephens, of Ga., provisional Vice President, and they were inaugurated as such Feb. 18, 1861. A permanent Constitution was adopted Mch. 11, 1861, and Mr. Davis and Mr. Stephens were chosen as permanent President and permanent Vice President, respectively, Nov. 6, 1861, and were inaugurated Feb. 22, 1862. The permanent capital was fixed at Richmond, Va., July 20, 1861. The United States Government denied the right of any State to secede from the Union, and a bitter war ensued, which continued until Apr., 1865, when it was brought to a close by the surrender of the Confederate armies, and the States were restored to the Union.

Addresses of President to people of, 331, 568.

Admission into Confederacy of—

Kentucky, recommendations regarding application for, 145.

Missouri—

Consideration of Congress respecting, requested by President, 144.

Proclaimed, 166.

New States and Territories discussed, 117, 137.

North Carolina, 117.

Contemplated, 98.

Tennessee, 117.

Virginia, 77, 117.

Alien enemies in—

Banishment of, proclaimed, 131.

Regulations respecting, 132.

Sequestration of estates of, referred to, 308.

Appropriation for support of, recommended, 199, 313, 317, 387, 402, 404, 451, 454, 455, 517, 539.

Army of. (See Army, Confederate States.)

Attitude of United States toward, and beginning of war discussed, 32, 63, 117, 184, 277.

Confederate States of America (Continued):

Belligerency of, recognized by foreign powers referred to, 280.

Blockade of ports of—

Binding effect of, and attitude of foreign powers regarding, discussed, 142, 282, 349.

Proclamation announcing, discussed, 76.

Bonds of—

Act amending act to reduce currency and authorize new issue of notes and, vetoed, 470.

Act of South Carolina offering guaranty of, transmitted, 309.

Bounty, to soldiers referred to, 489.

Provision for borrowing on, discussed, 361.

British consul to, exequatur of, revoked, 325.

Referred to, 360.

Capital of, removed from Montgomery, Ala., to Richmond, Va., 117.

Resolution providing for, vetoed, 100.

Citizens of—

Addresses of President to, 331, 568.

Exchange or release of, transported from, referred to, 316.

Military arrests of, 243, 304.

List of prisoners at Salisbury, N. C., referred to, 308.

Commissioner of Kentucky on subject of banks sent to, 148.

Commissioner of North Carolina on subject of admission of State into Confederacy accredited to, 98.

Commissioners of. (See Commissioners, Confederate States.)

Commissioners of Kentucky on subject of admission of State into Confederacy sent to, 145.

Congress of. (See Congress, Confederate States.)

cavalry, was killed. The Federals captured 6,000 or 7,000 men, the Confederates continuing their retreat.

Farrand, Ebenezer, resolution of thanks tendered command of, 275.

Fasting and Prayer, day of, set apart by proclamation, 103, 135, 217, 227, 268, 324, 328, 412, 563, 567. Order regarding, 565.

Faulkner, Charles J., arrest and imprisonment of, by Federal authorities discussed, 142.

Fearn, Walker, secretary of commission to Russia, nomination of, 311.

Field Products:

Cotton—

Accumulated by Treasury Department referred to, 390.

Non-destruction of, in Savannah, Ga., referred to, 533.

Protection for, under control of Secretaries of Treasury and War referred to, 503.

Purchased for Government in Louisiana referred to, 311.

Sale of, in foreign markets under cover of certificates referred to, 317.

Sale or hypothecation of, or cotton certificates in Europe referred to, 319.

Use of, as means of procuring Army supplies, 530.

Vessels in Chesapeake Bay for exporting, referred to, 195.

Tobacco—

Rations of, for Army referred to, 455.

Vessels in Chesapeake Bay for exporting, referred to, 195.

Finances:

Act amending act to reduce currency and authorize new issue of notes and bonds vetoed, 470.

Discussed, and recommendations regarding, 77, 123, 139, 191, 235, 259, 293, 361, 446, 488, 532, 545.

Finances (Continued):

Effect of action of neutral nations upon, discussed, 362.

Loans—

Appropriation to carry out act authorizing foreign, recommended, 301.

Discussed and recommendations regarding, 77, 123, 361, 505.

Made by Branch Bank of Tennessee to Gen. Hindman referred to, 255.

Propriety of providing for payment of, by war tax discussed, 259.

Plan of—

Discussed, 489.

First devised discussed, 361.

Finegan, Joseph, resolution of thanks tendered command of, 480.

Fisher's Hill, Va., Battle of.

A battle near Winchester, Frederick County, Va., Sept. 22, 1864. The Federals, about 20,000, were commanded by Gen. Sheridan; the Confederates, a much smaller number, by Gen. Early. Federal loss, about 1,300; Confederate loss, about 1,000.

Fishing Creek, Ky., battle of, referred to, 200.

Five Forks, Va., Battle of.

A battle about 11 miles to the southwest of Petersburg, Va., Apr. 1, 1865. The Federals were commanded by Gen. Sheridan; the Confederates, being a portion of Lee's army, by Generals Johnston and Pickett. The Confederates were driven back to their main works, which were captured with many prisoners. Their loss in killed, wounded, and prisoners was over 5,000; Federal loss, about 1,000.

Flag, Confederate.

The flag of the Confederacy was sometimes called the "Stars and Bars." It was first provided that the flag should consist of a red field with a white space extending horizontally through the center, and equal in width to one-third the width of the flag. The union was a blue square extending across the upper red and the white stripe, in which stars representing the States were arranged in a circle, each star standing for a State,

Later a white flag with one blue star in the center was adopted. Battle flags were also adopted and used by some of the corps. In 1863, the Congress of the Confederate States passed the following act: "That the flag of the Confederate States shall be as follows: The field to be white, the length double the width of the flag, with the union (now used as the battle flag) to be of a square of two-thirds the width of the flag, having the ground red, thereon a broad saltier of blue, bordered with white, and emblazoned with mullets or five-pointed stars, corresponding in number to that of the Confederate States."

Flag, United States.

The flag of the United States was first provided for in a resolution of the Continental Congress, June 14, 1777. That resolution provided, "That the flag of the United States be 13 stripes, alternate red and white; that the union be 13 stars, white in a blue field, representing a new constellation." As a new State was admitted, a new star and stripe were added. The flag was thus increased in size by the addition of new stripes, which was objectionable, so that in 1818 it was reëstablished with 13 stripes, and one star was added to the original 13 for each State admitted into the Union. These stars are placed on the flag on the 4th of July succeeding the admission of the State.

Florida:

Florida, The.

A Confederate cruiser first called the *Oreto.* She was built in England, and left Liverpool Mch. 22, 1862, receiving her armament at the Bahamas Aug. 7. She was twice seized, but escaped, changed her name to the *Florida,* and inflicted much damage on the United States commerce. She was captured, Oct. 7, 1864, in the harbor of Bahia, Brazil, in violation of the rights of neutrals by a United States vessel, under the command of Capt. Collins, and was taken to Hampton Roads.

Foreign Powers (Continued):

Recognition of independence of Confederate States by—

Commissioners sent to request, 76.

Intervention not desired, 487.

Request for, discussed, 142.

Treaties with—

Discussed, 360.

Disregarded by, 444.

Not binding, 360.

Foreign Relations. (See Foreign Powers.)

Forrest, Nathan B.:

Report of, on—

Battle of Tishomingo Creek, Miss., transmitted, 499.

Evacuation and removal of public property from Nashville, Tenn., transmitted, 245.

Resolutions of thanks tendered command of, 337, 433, 481.

Forsyth, John, peace commissioner to United States:

Conduct of Federal Government in negotiations discussed, 70.

Correspondence between Secretary Seward, Judge Campbell, and commissioners, 84.

Transmitted, 82.

Nomination and appointment of, 55, 56.

Fort Donelson, Tenn., Battle of.

A battle at Fort Donelson, a Confederate fort on Cumberland River, near Dover, Stewart County, Tenn., about 60 miles northwest of Nashville. The Federals, 15,000, commanded by Gen. Grant, invested the fort Feb. 13, 14, 1862. The fort mounted 65 guns, and was held by Confederates, commanded by Gen. Floyd, 18,000 effective men. Commodore Foote, with 6 gunboats, joined with Gen. Grant in the attack. Gen. Wallace reënforced Gen. Grant with 13,000 men, increasing his forces to 27,000. On the 15th the Confederates advanced and attacked the Federals, but at night fell back within their works. The fort was surrendered by Gen. Buckner Feb. 16, his senior officers, Generals Floyd and Pillow, escaping by

the river. Federal loss in killed and wounded, 2,832; Confederate loss in killed, wounded, and prisoners, 14,600, with 65 guns and many small arms.

Referred to, 189, 196, 207, 245.

Fort Fisher, N. C., Battle of.

A battle at Fort Fisher, which is situated on a peninsula on the south coast of North Carolina, between the mouth of the Cape Fear River and the Atlantic Ocean, about 18 miles from Wilmington. It was occupied by the Confederates with a garrison of 2,300 men, and its works mounted with 75 guns. In Dec., 1864, the Federals sent an expedition against it commanded by Gen. Butler, of 73 vessels, carrying 655 guns, and also a land force of 6,500. The fort was bombarded Dec. 24, without effect. Gen. Butler was relieved of command and superseded by Gen. Terry, with reënforcements, 1,500 men. After desperate fighting on the 15th, in which the vessels as well as the land forces were engaged, the garrison surrendered. Federal loss, 110 killed and about 600 wounded; Confederate loss, including killed, wounded, and prisoners, about 2,000.

Fort Gaines, Ala., Reduction of. (See Mobile Bay, Battle of.)

Fort Henry, Tenn., Battle of.

A battle at Fort Henry, on the Tennessee River, in the northwestern portion of Tennessee, about 11 miles from Fort Donelson. This fort was held by the Confederates with a garrison of about 2,700 men, under Gen. Tilghman, the fort mounting 17 guns. The Federals, 15,000, commanded by Gen. Grant, with a fleet of 7 gunboats, commanded by Commodore Foote, attacked the fort Feb. 6, 1862. After a fight of a little over an hour, Gen. Tilghman surrendered himself and about 65 men, and probably the same number of invalids. The remainder of the garrison forces escaped to Fort Donelson. Federal loss, 48; Confederate loss in killed and wounded, 21.

Referred to, 207.

Fort McAlister, Ga., Battle of.

This fort was built by the Confederates during the war on the Ogeechee River, opposite Genesis Point, Ga., to guard the approach to Savannah. The fort mounted 23 guns and 1 mortar, and was garrisoned by about 300 Confederates. It was attacked by a portion of Gen. Sherman's forces, commanded by Gen. Hazen, Dec.

France (Continued):

Occupation of Mexican capital by army of, discussed, 359.

Treaties with—

Discussed, 360.

Disregarded by, 444.

Not binding, 360.

Franklin, Tenn., Battle of.

A battle near the town of Franklin, Williamson County, Tenn., about 18 miles to the southeast of Nashville, Nov. 30, 1864. The Federals, about 27,000, were commanded by Gen. Schofield; the Confederates, by Gen. Hood. The assaults were made by the Confederates, who were repulsed with heavy losses, including Gen. Patrick R. Cleburne, who was killed. The Federals during the night retreated to Nashville. Their loss in killed and wounded was about 2,300. Confederate loss, much heavier, estimated at about 6,000.

Frayser's Farm, Va., Battle of.

One of the Seven Days' Battles before Richmond, Va., about 12 miles to the southeast of that city, June 30, 1862. The Federals were commanded by Gen. McClellan, and the Confederates by Generals Longstreet and Hill.

Frazer, John W., surrender of Cumberland Gap, in command of, discussed, 346.

Fredericksburg, Va., Battle of.

A battle near the city of Fredericksburg, Spottsylvania County, Va., about 50 miles to the southwest of Washington City, Dec. 13, 1863. The Federals, 110,000, were commanded by Gen. Burnside; the Confederates, 80,000, by Gen. Lee. The Federals were repulsed, and retreated across the Rappahannock River. Federal loss, 1,284 killed, 9,600 wounded, and 1,769 prisoners; total, 12,653. Confederate loss, 608 killed, 4,116 wounded, and 653 prisoners; total, 5,377.

Referred to, 276, 384.

Fugitive Slave Laws.

These laws were acts passed by Congress, which provided in substance, that on the owner of a slave giving proof of such ownership before a magistrate of the locality where the fugitive slave was found, the magistrate should order the fugitive to be delivered to his owner without trial by jury, and penalties were fixed for the violation of the laws. These laws were passed by authority of the Constitution of the United States, as shown in article IV, section 3, of that instrument.

Funds sent abroad for military and naval purposes referred to, 242, 261.

Furloughs:

Act granting, vetoed, 162.

Medical Board of Examiners for granting, referred to, 240.

Furloughs and Discharges, act regulating, vetoed, 156.

G

Gaines Mills, Va., Battle of. (See Cold Harbor, Battle of.)

Galveston, Tex., recovery of, from United States forces, 276.

General, Confederate Army:

Act creating office of commanding, vetoed, 215.

Creation of grade of, recommended, 80.

General-in-Chief, Confederate Army, appointment of, 570.

General Staff, organization of, recommended, 373, 447.

Act providing for—

Reasons for applying pocket veto to, 457.

Referred to, 500.

Vetoed, 262.

Geneva Tribunal. (See also Alabama Claims.)

A tribunal organized to arbitrate the claims of the United States against Great Britain for injury to, and destruction of, commerce during the war. The claims were known as the Alabama claims. The tribunal was provided for by the treaty of Washington.

Georgia:

Advance of Gen. Rosecrans's army into, discussed, 346.

Conscript law, enforcement of, etc., in, referred to, 250, 387.

Exempts in, referred to, 383, 534.

Legislative action of, referred to, 347.

Gunpowder (Continued):

Appropriation for purchase of, recommended, 58.

Manufacture of, discussed, 199.

H

Habeas Corpus:

Judges threatened for maintaining, discussed, 140.

Suspension of writ of—
and orders regarding, 219, 220, 221, 222, 223, 224, 225, 226.

Continuance of, recommended, 452.

Copies of orders for, transmitted and discussed, 259.

Criminal jurisdiction of ordinary courts not interfered with by, 260.

Power of Executive regarding, discussed, 122.

Recommended, 395, 498, 548.

Habeas Corpus, Suspension of.

During the war the writ of *habeas corpus* was suspended in the United States many times by order of the President. Congress gave him this power by special acts. Many arrests were made of persons charged with disloyal practices and other offenses, and in some places great excitement was caused by these arrests. The Supreme Court of the United States in 1866 held that the privilege of this writ could not be suspended in the case of a civilian in districts where the action of the civil courts was not interrupted.

Halleck, Henry W., mentioned, 269, 270.

Halyburton, J. D., mentioned, 183.

Hampton Roads, Va., Battle of.

A famous naval battle in Hampton Roads, which is the channel connecting the estuary of James River with Chesapeake Bay, just south of and near to Fortress Monroe, Va., Mch. 8, 9, 1862. On Mch. 8, the Confederate ironclad, the *Merrimac*, commanded by Commodore Franklin Buchanan, came down the Elizabeth River, and attacked the vessels of the United States which were blockading the mouths of the James and Elizabeth Rivers. She destroyed the Union frigate, *Cumberland,* and burned the *Congress.*

On the next day, she was engaged for about 4 hours in a severe fight with the United States ironclad *Monitor.* When the *Cumberland* went down, over 100 lost their lives, and in the case of the *Congress,* only 218 survived in a crew of 434 men. Commodore Buchanan, becoming disabled, turned the command over to Lieut. Catesby Jones. In his report of the battle, Lieut. Jones, among other things, says: "We also engaged the *Monitor,* and sometimes at very close quarters. We once succeeded in running into her, and twice silenced her fire." In concluding his report, he says: "The pilots declaring that we could get no nearer the *Minnesota,* and believing her to be entirely disabled, and the *Monitor* having run into shoal water, which prevented our doing her any further injury, we ceased firing at 12 o'clock and proceeded to Norfolk. Our loss is 2 killed and 19 wounded."

Discussed, and reports of, transmitted, 197, 210.

Hampton Roads Conference. (See also Peace Negotiations.)

Discussed, 519, 549.

Message and correspondence of President Lincoln, 521.

Report of commissioners, 520.

Hanover Court House, Va., Battle of.

A battle near Hanover Court House, Hanover County, Va., about 17 miles to the north of Richmond, May 27, 1862. The Federals were commanded by Gen. Fitz-John Porter; the Confederates, by Gen. Branch. The latter were defeated with loss of 200 killed, and 700 prisoners. Federal loss, about 400.

Hardee, William J., report of, on battle of Shiloh, Tenn., transmitted, 309.

Hardy's Bluff, Va., defenses of, referred to, 202.

Harpers Ferry, Va., report regarding machinery removed from, transmitted, 125.

Harpers Ferry, Va., Battle of.

A battle at Harpers Ferry, Va. (now West Virginia), about 45 miles northwest of Washington City, Sept. 15, 1862. The Federals were commanded by Col. Dixon S. Miles; the Confederates, by Gen. T. J. Jackson. Col. Miles was mortally wounded, and surrendered 11,583 men, 73 guns, and many small arms. Federals killed and wounded, 217. The Confederates sustained no loss.

Harris, Wiley P., member of Vice Presidential notification committee, 30.

Harrison, Burton N.:

Secretary to President Davis, appointment of, referred to, 200.

Transcript of Senate journals requested by, for President, 570.

Hart's Battery, resolution of thanks tendered, 427.

Hatchers Run, Va., Battle of.

There were two engagements near Hatchers Run, to the south of Richmond. The first occurred Oct. 27, 1864, when the Confederates, under Gen. Lee, assaulted the Federals, under Gen. Hancock, and were repulsed after inflicting on the Federals a loss of about 1,900 men. On Feb. 5, 1865, the Federals, under Gen. Grant, assaulted the Confederate forces at or near the same place, and failed of success, sustaining a loss of about 2,000, the Confederate loss being about 1,100.

Hatteras Expedition.

An expedition sent from Fortress Monroe, Aug. 26, 1861, against the Confederate forts, Hatteras and Clark, in North Carolina. The expedition of 10 vessels, 150 guns, and 900 men was under the command of Commodore Stringham and Gen. Butler. The forts were garrisoned by the Confederates, about 650 men, under Capt. Barron. Fort Clark was easily reduced Aug. 27, and the next day, after heavy bombardment, Hatteras was captured. Capt. Barron and the entire garrison were made prisoners.

Hatteras Inlet, N. C., capture of, by Federal forces referred to, 129.

Hatteras, The, destruction of, by the *Alabama* referred to, 305.

Head, J. W., report of, on affair at Fort Donelson, Tenn., 245.

Helena, Ark., Battle of.

A battle at Helena, Phillips County, Ark., on the Mississippi River, about 100 miles below Memphis, July 4, 1863. The Federals were commanded by Gen. Prentiss; the Confederates, by Generals Holmes and Price. The latter made the attack and were repulsed, with loss in killed, wounded, and missing of about 1,600. Federal loss, less than 400.

Referred to, 345.

Henderson, Tenn., operations at, 402.

Hermitage, The.

The home of President Andrew Jackson, in Davidson County, Tenn., a few miles eastward from Nashville. Gen. Jackson lived there when he was elected President. He built the house after his own fashion, and it still remains as when he occupied it. He died at this place, and his remains are buried there. The State of Tennessee has erected a building on a portion of the farm owned by him which is used as a home for indigent ex-Confederate soldiers.

Heth, Henry, orders to, regarding martial law in counties of Virginia, 224.

Hindman, Thomas C.:

Appropriation to pay interest on money borrowed from banks in Tennessee by, recommended, 255.

Orders to, referred to, 242.

Report of, on operations of, in Trans-Mississippi District, 388.

Hoke, Robert F., resolution of thanks tendered command of, 480.

Holcomb Legion referred to, 456.

Hood, John B.:

Correspondence with, regarding Army of Tennessee transmitted, 534, 538, 539.

Mentioned, 539.

Hospitals, Military:

Appropriation for, recommended, 127.

In and near Richmond, Va., referred to, 407.

Referred to, 318.

House of Representatives, Confederate States:

Employees of, estimate for increased compensation of, transmitted, 456.

Act relative to, recommendations regarding, 513.

tacked and were repulsed with a loss of about 1,400 in killed and wounded. Federal loss, about 1,200.

Josselyn, Robert, resignation of, as secretary to President Davis referred to, 200.

Justice, Department of:

Appropriation for, recommended, 383, 387, 503, 518, 532.

Employees in, referred to, 552.

Report of, transmitted and discussed, 78, 192, 194, 496.

K

Kansas Aid Society.

An association formed in 1854 for the purpose of aiding and promoting free immigration into Kansas from Northern States, in order to prevent the establishment of slavery in that State.

Kansas-Nebraska Act.

An act passed by Congress in May, 1854, by the provisions of which Kansas and Nebraska were separated and organized into two distinct territories, the question of slavery being left to the people of the territories for settlement. The importance of the act consisted mainly in the fact that it virtually repealed the Missouri Compromise.

Kearsarge, The.

A United States man-of-war built at Portsmouth, N. H., in 1861. She was commanded by Capt. Winslow, and carried about 160 men and 7 guns. June 19, 1864, she attacked the Confederate warship, *Alabama*, off the harbor of Cherbourg, France. The *Alabama* was commanded by Capt. Semmes, with 60 men and 8 guns. The *Alabama* was disabled and sunk, her captain escaping.

Kenesaw Mountain, Ga., Battle of.

A battle at Kenesaw Mountain, Cobb County, Ga., about 25 miles northwest of Atlanta, June 27, 1864. The Federals were a portion of Sherman's army, commanded by Generals Thomas and McPherson. Two assaults were made on the Confederates by them, but they were repulsed. Federal loss, about 3,000; Confederate loss, 630.

Kennons Marshes, Va., defenses of, referred to, 202.

Kentucky:

Act amending act to aid, vetoed, 408.

Kentucky (Continued):

Admission of, into Confederacy, recommendations regarding application for, 145.

Appropriation for carrying into effect act to aid people of, recommended, 128.

Banks in, contributing money for subjugation of people of, discussed, 148.

Commissioner of, on subject of banks sent to Confederate States, 148.

Commissioners of, on subject of admission of, into Confederacy sent to Confederate States, 145.

Invasion of, by Federal forces and action of Confederate authorities discussed, 137.

Military operations in, 137, 448.

Neutrality of, not recognized by Federal authorities discussed, 137.

Kernstown, Va., Battle of. (See Winchester, Battles at.)

Knoxville, Tenn., Battle of.

A battle at Knoxville, Tenn., Nov. 17, 1863. The Federals, 12,000, commanded by Gen. Burnside, were assaulted by the Confederates, about 16,000, under Gen. Longstreet. This assault was repulsed, and again on Nov. 29 a second assault was made, without success. Reënforcements were sent the Federals from Chattanooga, whereupon the Confederates raised the siege and retired.

Ku-Klux Klan.

A secret organization in some of the Southern States during the reconstruction period, a few years subsequent to the war. It is believed that it was organized at Pulaski, Tenn., in 1866. It was claimed for the order or society that in the beginning its object was amusement, but it was charged against it that it meant to suppress the negro in politics. Its members appeared only at night, generally on horseback, carrying strange banners and devices, and dressed in startling and fantastic fashions. Congress passed an act in 1871 to suppress the order, and the President issued proclamations commanding them to disband, and they soon ceased to exist.

L.

of Cairo, Mch. 14, 1862. The Federals, 20,000, were commanded by Gen. Pope; the Confederates, a much smaller number, by Gen. McCown. The latter retired at night with small loss. Federal loss, 51.

New Orleans, La.:

Defenses of, referred to, 310.

Evacuation of, instructions to officers regarding, referred to, 240.

New Orleans, La., Capture of.

The city of New Orleans was attacked by the Federals, with a fleet under command of Admiral Farragut, in April, 1862. The forts protecting it were Fort Jackson and Fort St. Philip. It was defended also by an ironclad ram, *Manassas*, and a floating battery, the *Louisiana*, commanded by Commodore J. K. Mitchell. The Federal fleet consisted of 6 sloops of war, 16 gunboats, and 21 schooners. The bombardment was continued for several days. On May 1 the Federals occupied the city. Loss of life light on each side.

Proceedings of court of inquiry regarding, transmitted, 457.

Newbern, N. C., Capture of.

A battle at Newbern, Craven County, N. C., Mch. 14, 1862. The Federals were commanded by Gen. Burnside. They assaulted the Confederate works and captured the city, many of the Confederates retreating. Federal loss, about 100 killed and 470 wounded; Confederate loss, killed, wounded, and prisoners, about 2,500.

Referred to, 212.

Newspapers:

Act authorizing free mailage of, to soldiers vetoed, 556.

Joint resolution in regard to exemption of editors and employees of, vetoed, 465.

Nominations, Executive:

Communication correcting mistakes in, transmitted, 259.

Constitutional powers of Executive and Senate regarding, discussed, 388.

Reasons for making certain, transmitted, 392, 448.

Renomination of certain officers, advice of Senate regarding necessity of, requested, 246.

Nominations, Executive (Continued):

Return of, requested, 148, 241, 537.

Special session message regarding, 134.

Norfolk, Va.:

Evacuation of, instructions to officers regarding, referred to, 240.

Martial law in, proclaimed, and orders regarding, 219.

Norfolk, Va., Surrender of.

The Confederates were in occupation of Norfolk, Va., in 1861. May 10, 1862, an expedition was sent by the Federals, under Gen. Wool, from Fortress Monroe to attack the city. The Confederates withdrew, and the city was surrendered.

North Anna, Va., Battle of.

A battle at North Anna, Va., north of Richmond, May 23, 1864. The Federals were commanded by Gen. Grant; the Confederates, by Gen. Lee. After heavy fighting, the Federals were repulsed, with a loss of over 1,600 killed and wounded.

North Carolina:

Admission of, into Confederacy referred to, 117.

Contemplated, 98.

Appropriation to pay claims of, for supplies furnished troops recommended, 304.

Appropriation to refund excess of war tax paid by, recommended, 239.

Commissioner of, on subject of admission of, into Confederacy accredited to Confederate States, 98.

Confederate Constitution adopted by, 117.

Conscript law in, enforcement of, referred to, 387.

Exempts in, referred to, 383.

Conspiracy in, discussed, and recommendations regarding, 498.

Landing of Federal troops on coast of, referred to, 129.

Legislative action of, referred to, 347.

Military operations in, 298, 448.

Troops of, resolutions of thanks tendered, 422, 424, 427, 430, 432, 479,

Ky., Oct. 8, 1862. The Federals, 58,000, were commanded by Gen. Buell; the Confederates, 40,000, by Gen. Bragg. The battle lasted all day, and at night the Confederates retired toward the south and were not pursued. Federal loss, 916 killed, including Gen. Jas. S. Jackson and William T. Terrill, 3,000 wounded, and 500 missing; Confederate loss, killed, wounded, and missing, 3,300.

Personal Liberty Laws.

These were laws passed by many of the States of the North, prior to the war, through their Legislatures, impeding and hindering the operation of the provision of the Constitution of the United States which provided for the surrender of fugitive slaves. The Constitution of the United States, in section 2 of article 4, provided in substance that slaves escaping from one State into another should, on application of the owner thereof, be surrendered and delivered up to him. It was contended that these laws, known as personal liberty laws, were directly in contravention of the provision of the Constitution above cited.

Petersburg, Va.:

Flour impressed in, referred to, 304.

Martial law in, proclaimed, and orders regarding, 221.

Restrictions on transportation of food to, referred to, 517.

Petersburg, Va., Battle of.

A battle at Petersburg, Dinwiddie County, Va., 23 miles south of Richmond. The Federals were commanded by Gen. Grant, and besieged Petersburg, which was defended by the Confederates, under Gen. Lee. June 16, 1864, an attack was made by the Federals, Gen. Smith's corps. The assaults were continued without success for 4 days, with a Federal loss of about 7,800. July 4, another unsuccessful assault was made by the Federals, 50,000, commanded by Generals Burnside, Warren, and Ord, with loss of over 4,000. The city was held by the Confederates until Apr., 1865, when it was evacuated by them, and on the 3d was surrendered.

Phœnix, The, appropriation to owners of, recommended, 499.

Pickens, Francis W., mentioned, 92, 94, 95.

Pickett, J. T., mentioned, 88, 91.

Pike, Albert, treaties with Indians concluded by, 149.

Report submitted, 151.

Pillow, Gideon J.:

Relieved from command, 197.

Report of, on fall of Fort Donelson referred to, 207.

Resolution of thanks tendered command of, 168.

Pittsburg Landing, Tenn., Battle of. (See Shiloh, Battle of.)

Pleasant Hill, La., Battle of.

A battle at Pleasant Hill, La., about 20 miles to the south of Sabine Cross Roads, April 9, 1864. The Federals were commanded by Generals Banks and A. J. Smith; the Confederates, by Generals E. Kirby Smith and Dick Taylor. The Confederates made the attack, which was continued until night. Gen. Banks retreated toward Red River, having lost heavily in this campaign.

Poague's Artillery Battalion, resolution of thanks tendered, 432.

Pocket Veto, bill to provide and organize general staff for armies, 457.

Polk, Leonidas:

Report of, on Battle of Shiloh, Tenn., transmitted, 309.

Resolution of thanks tendered command of, 168.

Pope, John, mentioned, 276.

Popular Sovereignty.

Prior to the war, when the slavery issue was dividing the people, the question as to whether the Territories should be free or slave was prominent, and different methods were suggested and discussed as to how the issue should be determined. Many public men insisted that Congress should make the decision, while others contended that it should be kept out of the Congress, and "left to the people in their respective local governments." The term "Popular Sovereignty" was given to the latter doctrine.

Port Gibson, Miss., Battle of.

A battle in Mississippi, on the river below Vicksburg, May 1, 1863. The Federals, 25,000, commanded by Gen. Grant, were pursuing the Confederates, 12,000, commanded by Gen. Pemberton, who was moving toward Vicksburg. The Confederates assaulted were under the immediate command of Gen. Bowen. The attack was resisted successfully during the day, but at night the Confederates continued their march to Vicksburg. Federal loss, 131 killed, and about 800 wounded and missing; Confederate loss, about the same.

Referred to, 386.

Port Hudson, La., Surrender of.

Port Hudson was a fortified point on the Mississippi River, in La., about 20 miles above Baton Rouge. It was garrisoned and held by the Confederates under Gen. Gardner until July 9, 1863. It was assailed by the Federals, 12,000, under Gen. Banks, and a fleet under Admiral Farragut, Mch. 8, 1863. They were repulsed and the attack failed. May 23, same year, the attack was renewed by Generals Banks and Auger, 18,500 men, and Farragut's fleet, and again failed. The Federals then made siege of the place until after the surrender of Vicksburg, when, on July 9, it was surrendered with about 6,000 men and 50 guns.

Referred to, 345.

Port Republic, Va., Battle of.

A battle at Port Republic, Rockingham County, Va., about 90 miles northwest of Richmond, June 9, 1862. The Federals, commanded by Gen. Shields, attacked the Confederates, commanded by Gen. T. J. Jackson, and were defeated, with a loss of 500 men, with many small arms and considerable ammunition.

Port Royal, S. C., Expedition.

Port Royal is at the mouth of Broad River, southern coast of South Carolina, and was fortified and held by the Confederates, 1,700 South Carolina troops, commanded by Generals Drayton and Ripley, Nov., 1861. The Federals, 10,000, commanded by Gen. W. T. Sherman, assisted by a Federal fleet, under Commodore Dupont, made the attack. After severe fighting, the garrison retreated, with a loss of 40 guns.

Port Royal Ferry, S. C., engagement at, referred to, 200.

Portsmouth, Va., martial law in, proclaimed, 219.

Postage, rates of, recommendations regarding, 80.

Postal Contractors, exemption of—
Modification in law regarding, recommended, 312.
Referred to, 383, 531.

Postal Service:
Constitutional question of appropriating money for, referred to Congress, 252.
Discussed, 79, 138, 192, 237, 296, 377, 378.
Exemption law, modifications in, so as not to affect postmasters and postal contractors, recommended, 312.
Frauds perpetrated on revenues of, by Southern Express Co. referred to, 211.

Mails—
Carrying of, in certain sections prevented, referred to, 247.
Detention of Southwestern Mail referred to, 245.
Transmission of, in Richmond, Va., referred to, 452, 453.
Merging of telegraphic service in, discussed, 307.

Postmaster General, report of, transmitted and discussed, 79, 138, 192, 195, 237, 296, 304, 378, 496.

Postmasters:
Exemption law, modifications in, so as not to affect, recommended, 312.
Removal of certain, from office referred to, 318, 553.

Post Office Department:
Appropriation for, recommended, 99, 128, 306.
Auditor of Treasury for, recommended, 80.
Employees in, referred to, 552.
Frauds perpetrated on revenues of, by Southern Express Co. referred to, 211.
Legislation for, recommended, 80.
Number of men between 18 and 45 necessary in, 531.
Report of, transmitted and discussed, 79, 138, 192, 195, 237, 296, 304, 378, 496.

Trent Affair.

The *Trent* was a British merchant ship, on which James M. Mason and John Slidell, commissioners of the Confederate States, took passage at Havana, Cuba, for England, in the autumn of 1861. They had successfully run the blockade of the Confederate port, and landed in Cuba. On Nov. 8, the *Trent* was stopped in the old Bahama channel, while *en route* to England, by the United States ship, *San Jacinto*, commanded by Capt. Wilkes, and the commissioners, Mason and Slidell, were seized and carried as prisoners to Boston. This act was a breach of international law, and in violation of the rights of neutrals. The British Government promptly demanded the release of Mason and Slidell, and an apology by the United States. The demand was complied with, the act of Captain Wilkes disavowed, the commissioners restored to a British ship, and landed safely in England.

U

Uncle Sam.

A title given to the United States, sometimes represented by a person in national colors. An explanation of the origin of this title as applied to the Government is that the letters "U. S.," which appeared on large quantities of Government or army supplies during the war of 1812, were humorously declared to be the initials of one Samuel Wilson, an inspector of these supplies at Troy, N. Y., who was familiarly called " Uncle Sam." The letters " U. S." came to be used by him as a shipping mark.

United Confederate Veterans.

A federation of all the associations of Confederate veterans, soldiers and sailors. The federation has a written constitution which fully sets forth its objects and purposes. It endeavors to promote the cultivation of ties of friendship between ex-Confederates, and to aid and assist their widows and orphans, and also to assist in the collection of data in respect to the war, and the preservation of the records of the Confederacy. The organization is by camps, which are formed into brigades, divisions, and departments. There are 3 departments, called the Army of Virginia, Army of the Tennessee, and Army of the Trans-Mississippi.

United States Army. (See Army, United States.)

United States Constitution. (See Constitution, United States.)

United States Flag. (See Flag, United States.)

United States of America.

A Federal Republic occupying the central part of North America. It comprises (1905) 45 States, 4 Territories, and the District of Columbia; also Alaska, Hawaii, Porto Rico, the Philippine archipelago, and certain other small islands. The capital is Washington City, which is located in the District of Columbia. The name was adopted in 1776. In its government there are 3 great Departments, the Executive, Legislative, and Judicial. The Executive power is vested in a President, chosen every 4 years. He is assisted by a Cabinet, the members of which are appointed by him, by and with the consent of the Senate. The Legislative authority is vested in Congress, comprising a Senate and House of Representatives. The Senate consists of 2 members from each State, and the House at present of 386 members, chosen by the electors in the various States, in the proportion of one for about every 193,000 inhabitants. The Judicial authority is vested in a Supreme Court and such inferior tribunals as may be created from time to time, by Congress. The several States have each a republican form of government, administered by a Governor, and a Legislature composed of two houses, and

each State has extensive independent powers reserved to it under the Constitution of the United States. The Government is supreme in all powers delegated to it by the Constitution, while the several States are supreme in all reserved or nondelegated powers. Area of 45 States, 4 Territories, and District of Columbia, 3,025,601 square miles; including Alaska, 3,557,000 square miles. Population in 1900, of States, District of Columbia, and 4 Territories, 75,994,575.

Army of. (See Army, United States.)

Attitude of, toward Confederate States and beginning of war discussed, 32, 63, 117, 184, 277.

Constitution of. (See Constitution, United States.)

Constitutional rights of States discussed, 32, 63, 121, 184, 277.

Debt of, referred to, 186.

Declaration of war against Confederacy referred to, 63, 74.

Military preparations of, discussed, 71 (see also 60, 63, 82), 118, 277.

President of. (See Lincoln, Abraham.)

Rights and powers of, discussed, 32, 63, 121, 184, 277.

V

Vacancies in Public Office, recommendations regarding, 260.

Van Dorn, Earl:

Report of, on battle with Generals Sigel and Curtis in Arkansas transmitted, 214.

Resolution of thanks tendered command of, 232.

Vessels:

In Chesapeake Bay for exporting cotton or tobacco referred to, 195.

Restrictions upon, leaving ports of Confederate States referred to, 147.

Seized for public use referred to, 247, 308, 310, 311.

rison there under Maj. Anderson. After 4 years of the fiercest and bloodiest war in history, it ended in April, 1865, by the surrendering of the Confederate armies then in the field. During the conflict the United States enlisted 2,688,523 men, as shown in the message of President Grant to Congress Dec. 2, 1872. The Confederate States, as shown from statistics, enlisted between 650,000 and 700,000 men. A brief mention of the chief battles of the war will be found in this volume, under their appropriate names. The exact number of men enlisted by the Confederate States and their losses cannot be given here for want of the official records. The losses on the side of the United States for killed, wounds received in action, etc., were 9,584 officers and 349,944 men. Their public debt increased from about $90,000,000 in 1861 to over $2,600,000,000 in 1865. The results of the war were the abolition of slavery, the failure of the States in their efforts to secede, and their return to the Union.

Confederates, by Generals McCulloch and Price. The Federals made two attacks, both of which were repulsed, and they were defeated, with a loss in killed, wounded, and missing of 1,250. Gen. Lyon was killed. Confederate loss, about 1,100.

Winchester, Va., Battles at.

Winchester, in the Shenandoah Valley, Va., was the scene of several battles. The first, the Federals were commanded by Gen. Shields; the Confederates, by Gen. T. J. Jackson, Mch. 23, 1862. The latter retired to his main army. Federal loss, 600 in killed and wounded; Confederate loss, about 700. This engagement is called also the battle of Kernstown. In the second engagement, June 15, 1863, the Federals were commanded by Gen. Milroy; the Confederates, by Gen. Longstreet. The Federals were defeated, with a loss of over 4,000 men and many guns; Confederate loss, very small. The third engagement occurred here July 12, 1864, when Federals, under Gen. Averell, were attacked by Confederates, under Gen. Early. The Federals were defeated, with a loss of about 400. Another engagement took place here Sept. 19, 1864, when Federals, under Gen. Sheridan, attacked the Confederates, under Gen. Early. The latter retreated to and beyond Winchester, with a loss of 5,500; Federal loss, about 5,000. This is called also the battle of Opequan.

Winder, John H., orders to, regarding martial law in Richmond, Va., 220.

Wise, Henry A., report of, on fall of Roanoke Island referred to, 207.

Withers, Jones M., report of, on battle of Shiloh, Tenn., transmitted, 245.

Women of Confederacy, resolution of thanks tendered, 230.

Wood, John T., resolution of thanks tendered command of, 430.

Wyandotte Constitution. (See also Lecompton Constitution; Topeka Constitution.)

The final constitution adopted for the State of Kansas at Wyandotte, now a part of Kansas City, in that State. It was adopted in October, 1859; was ratified by a vote of 10,421 to 5,530, and made Kansas a free State.

Y

Yancey, William L., commissioner to Europe, nomination of, 57.

Yorktown, Va., Siege of.

Yorktown is situated on York River, 50 miles from Richmond. The Federals, commanded by Gen. McClellan, laid siege to Yorktown, which was garrisoned by Confederates, under Gen. Magruder, beginning Apr. 4, 1862. On that day, in an attack made by the Federals, they lost 35 killed and 120 wounded; Confederate loss, about 100. May 4, the Confederates evacuated the place, and retired up the Peninsula.